DATE DUE

Kate Chopin's Short Fiction

Kate Chopin's Short Fiction
A Critical Companion

Robert C. Evans
Compiler and General Editor

Edward Pate, Dianne Russell,
Jonathan Wright, and Carolyn Young
Editorial Team

LOCUST HILL PRESS
West Cornwall, CT

Library of Congress Cataloging-in-Publication Data

Kate Chopin's short fiction : a critical companion / Robert C. Evans,
compiler and general editor.
    p.   cm.
Includes bibliographical references.
ISBN 0-933951-98-1 (lib. bdg. : alk. paper)
    1. Chopin, Kate, 1851-1904--Criticism and interpretation.
2. Women and literature--United States--History--19th century.
3. Short story. I. Evans, Robert C.

PS1294.C63 Z75 2001
813'.4--dc21

                                                            2001029963

Printed on acid-free, 250-year-life paper
Manufactured in the United States of America

for

Robert F. Whitman

Robert Gale

David Brumble

and the other superb undergraduate teachers
who brought so many books and ideas to life
and were so kind in so many ways

Contents

Acknowledgments

I have had the good fortune to study with many superb men and women, three of whom are mentioned in the dedication of this book. To all my teachers I owe thanks that are increasingly clear to me as each year advances. I realize now, more than ever, that they are particularly bright links in a very long chain.

Many students—the latest links in that chain—are also represented in this book. I am grateful for their patience, their good humor, and their passion for learning. They, too, have been instructors in their own way, and this book will demonstrate how very much they have helped teach me. It has been my great pleasure to learn from them.

I am especially conscious, in finishing this volume, of how much I have also learned from the community of Chopin scholars, whose writings have been sources of genuine pleasure and illumination. I particularly wish to acknowledge the superb findings and insights of such writers as Per Seyersted, Bernard Koloski, Robert Arner, Barbara Ewell, Thomas Bonner, Patricia Lattin, and, above all, Joyce Coyne Dyer and Emily Toth. If this book serves no other purposes than calling the work of these scholars to the attention of a wider audience and making that work more easily accessible, it will have fulfilled a valuable function. My hope is that this study will encourage readers to seek out for themselves the books and articles from which I have learned so much.

A grant from the Andrew W. Mellon Foundation helped support not only this project but a number of others related to the ideal of "critical pluralism." For his guidance and support in supervising this grant, I am indebted to Alvin Kernan, who recently retired from the Foundation. On the homefront, the intricacies of the grant have always been unpuzzled by Fariba Deravi, my long-lost Iranian sister.

This book could not have been completed without the tireless support and endless patience of Tim Bailey and Carolyn Johnson of the AUM Library's Interlibrary Loan department. Nor could the book have been brought to fruition without (yet once more) the unfailing commitment and unflagging goodwill of Tom Bechtle, man of letters and publisher *extraordinaire*.

My colleagues, my friends, and my family all deserve deepest thanks, but this is especially true of

Ruth Dunham Evans

who consistently brings me far more friendship, love, and laughter than I could ever have hoped to enjoy or than anyone rightfully deserves. In her kindness, good humor, and encouragement she takes after her mother, Claramae, who turns eighty this year.

Preface

The critical reception of Kate Chopin (1851–1904) has been notoriously fickle. In her own day her early short stories—collected in *Bayou Folk* (1894) and *A Night in Acadie* (1897)—were widely read and widely praised, but the later publication of her novel *The Awakening* (1899) provoked equally widespread misgivings. Although many critics from her era recognized that the novel was well written, they were often troubled by its allegedly amoral or even immoral implications. Chopin's reputation and self-confidence were both apparently undermined by this negative response, and even though it is possible to over-state the injuries inflicted on her career by the novel's poor showing, there seems little doubt that damage was done. Her proposed third collection of stories—*A Vocation and a Voice*—was never printed in her lifetime (and indeed stayed unpublished for most of the twentieth century). She died in 1904, and for most of the next sixty years she was largely forgotten and ignored. A biography by Daniel Rankin *was* published in 1932, and it did reprint some of her tales. Her memory survived, however, mostly through the occasional republication of a few early stories, especially "Désirées's Baby."

By the late 1960s, though, the time was ripe for a resurgence of interest in Chopin's work. Feminist critics and readers of that period would prove much more receptive to *The Awakening* than Chopin's contemporaries had been, and the pioneering scholarship of Per Seyersted—a Norwegian male whose mother was a feminist—did much to make the author's writings more accessible in every way. Seyersted's biography of Chopin, along with his edition of her *Collected Works* (both published in 1969) inaugurated the current Chopin boom, which shows little sign of ending. Although the work of Seyersted and others (particularly Emily Toth) did much to revive interest in Chopin's life and also helped call attention to previously unpublished or neglected stories (most notably "The Story of an Hour" and "The Storm"), by far the most important critical attention was focused on her great novel, *The Awakening*, which is now recognized as one of the masterpieces of American fiction.

Throughout the 1970s and 1980s, studies of *The Awakening* proliferated. The novel was examined from almost every conceivable critical angle, and it was also devoured with genuine enthusiasm by readers at all levels and from diverse backgrounds. Various stories were also routinely read and studied (especially "The Story of an Hour" and the ever-dependable "Désirées's Baby"), but in general the critical situation of this period was almost exactly the reverse of what it had been in the final years of Chopin's life. In Chopin's own day, her collections of short stories were her most esteemed works, while her novel was viewed with some embarrassment; by the 1980s, however, *The Awakening* dominated the attention of most readers and critics, while the short stories (with a few exceptions) received far less attention. The stories were sometimes viewed as "minor," "local color" pieces—pieces written to appeal to a public that could not stomach stronger, more challenging work. Some of the stories were dismissed as superficial, sentimental, or conventional—and indeed some of them deserve that reputation. But Chopin composed more than a hundred pieces of short fiction, and it is increasingly being recognized that many of them are as powerful, challenging, moving, complex, and well-crafted as any short works in American literature.

The present book seeks both to reflect and to spur this renewed interest in Chopin's short fiction. It tries to offer the most complete account yet attempted of modern critical commentary on her stories. My desire is that this book, by reporting so thoroughly the best insights of recent students of the tales, will help set the stage for an even more productive round of further examination and appreciation. By showing in such detail what has already been done with the stories, I hope that this book will also help indicate how much there still is to do. Several features of the present volume will, I hope, make it useful both to beginning readers and to seasoned scholars. Among those features are the following:

 • *Widely comprehensive coverage.* The present book seeks to report *every* significant comment made about every one of Chopin's stories in each of the sources it cites. Thus, if an article focuses mainly on "Désirées's Baby" but also alludes, in passing, to ten other stories by Chopin, this book records not only the substantive discussion of the main story but also the off-hand or "minor" comments on the other works. The book attempts to collect and record *all* the meaningful comments made on *all* of Chopin's stories by *all* the critics mentioned in the bibliography, including comments made in book-length studies of Chopin when the indexes of those books have made it possible to trace such references.

• *Significantly detailed annotations.* Since most modern readers and students of Chopin have tended to be most interested in her major novel, most previous annotated bibliographies or bibliographical essays have naturally tended to focus on summarizing comments about *The Awakening.* Previous bibliographical studies *have* devoted attention to comments about the stories when those comments have been the main emphasis of an article or chapter, but often even the summaries of these commentaries have had to be rather brief, if only to save space. The present book, however, attempts to paraphrase comments about the stories in significant detail, so that no important suggestions are missed.

• *Chronological coverage, story by story.* Most previous bibliographical studies of Chopin's short fiction have tended, necessarily, to be synthetic: they have moved chronologically, year-by-year, and then alphabetically according to last name of the critic being summarized.[1] There are obvious advantages and conveniences to this kind of organization, but one major *disadvantage* is that comments on a particular story thus tend to be scattered widely throughout a book. A student or scholar searching for a sense of what has been said about a given story needs to flip constantly between the book itself and the book's index. In the present volume, however, each story is listed separately, in alphabetical order, and *all* the comments made by all the critics on that story are easily accessible in one place. Moreover, because those comments themselves are organized chronologically, a reader can easily follow the progress of a story's reception. A reader can also easily trace not only the critical debates the story has engendered but also whatever critical consensus may have developed. In addi-

---

[1] See, for instance, the two standard works: Marlene Springer, *Edith Wharton and Kate Chopin: A Reference Guide* (Boston: G.K. Hall, 1976), and Suzanne Disheroon Green and David J. Caudle, *Kate Chopin: An Annotated Bibliography of Critical Works* (Westport, CT: Greenwood Press, 1999). Both of these books have proven extremely helpful in enabling me to decide which critical works to include and annotate in the present volume.

tion, one can easily see how a particular critic's comments on a given story have evolved over time. Finally, this kind of organization also makes obvious which stories have so far received the most (and which the least) attention.

• *Significantly detailed plot summaries.* In order to help readers make sense of the many critical comments summarized here, the present book also includes significantly detailed summaries of the plots of all of Chopin's extant stories. These summaries (it is hoped) will allow readers to better comprehend particular critical comments on specific characters and plot developments. At the same time, I hope that these plot summaries are detailed enough to intrigue first-time readers of Chopin and make them want to seek out and read the original stories themselves. Finally, I hope that these unusually full summaries of plot will make it easier for such novice readers to comprehend and follow the original stories when they do read those works.

• *Coverage of works not usually included in annotated bibliographies.* Any student or teacher of literature knows that some of the most helpful material in print on any published writer consists of material published in reference volumes, such as the *Dictionary of Literary Biography.* In addition, dissertations often contain many useful facts and insights, especially in the case of a previously noncanonical author such as Chopin. However, standard annotated bibliographies or bibliographical essays usually either do not or cannot summarize the contents of major reference works or of important dissertations in any detail (if they mention them at all). The present book, on the other hand, *does* try to report the contents of major reference articles, and it also reports in detail the contents of a few especially significant dissertations. The later group includes, in particular, Robert Bush's 1957 study (one of the very earliest sustained examinations of Chopin's short fiction) and Peter James Peterson's unpublished 1972 dissertation (written in the early years of the Chopin "boom" and still one of the most detailed studies of the short fiction). It also includes the lengthy 1975 study by Robert Arner, which grew out of his earlier dissertation on Chopin but which was originally published in a journal not widely or easily available to most contemporary readers. Obviously not *all* dissertations on Chopin have been able to be included here, but I have tried to select several that seemed to me especially significant.

• *Coverage of comments made in specific editions of Chopin's works.* Among the works not usually included (or at least not very fully annotated) in standard bibliographical studies are the introductions, prefaces, and appendices of particular editions of Chopin's writings, especially editions of her short fiction. The present book tries to cover such sources in detail, not only because these sources tend to be authored by the most important students of Chopin's work but also because such works have tended to play a great role in reviving interest in her short fiction. For many years such introductions offered the fullest and most widely available discussions of her short stories. Even today, when the stories are much more widely accessible than they had been thirty years ago, new editions (such as the new Oxford edition of 2000, introduced by Pamela Knights) help provide important new perspectives on the fiction, either by printing different versions of the stories or by emphasizing new approaches to understanding them.

• *Detailed critical analysis of two representative stories.* Although the mere size of the present book will indicate how much work has already been done on Chopin's short stories, much more detailed investigation of many tales remains to be done. Comments on many of the stories have been made in passing by most critics; few works have received sustained individual readings. Even when certain works have been studied closely, they have usually been examined mainly from one particular point of view, or have been used as evidence to support a larger generalization about Chopin's career, or have been studied as expressions of a particular theme. For these reasons and others, it seemed useful to offer, in the final pages of this book, sustained, multi-dimensional study of two representative stories by Chopin in order to suggest just how rich her works can seem when they are examined in detail, especially with specific attention to their exact phrasing. One of the stories chosen, "Caline," is an effective but relatively little-known work; the other, "La Belle Zoraïde," is increasingly recognized as one of the most powerful tales Chopin composed. Even so, the latter story has still received relatively few "close readings." The appendices in the present book seek to remedy that lack. Moreover, by emphasizing the work of student-readers, the appendices also seek to illustrate that thoughtful, insightful perceptions of literary works need not be not entirely the monopoly of the kinds professional analysts so heavily represented in much of the rest of the book.

- *Further features.* In addition to providing the features just mentioned, the present book also offers a few other helpful traits. In the first place, it provides a convenient one-volume overview of the most significant modern work on Chopin's stories. In contrast, the two separate, previously-published annotated bibliographies by Marlene Springer and by Suzanne Disheroon Green and David J. Caudle cover, respectively, the periods from 1890 to 1975 and from 1976 to 1999. Secondly, the present book includes annotations of a few pre-1997 sources missed in the earlier bibliographies, even as it also includes some important sources omitted because they were published between 1997 and 2000. Finally, in some cases the present book includes discussions of particular stories even when those discussions were not indexed by the books in which they were previously published. For these reasons as well as for the others just mentioned, therefore, I hope that the present volume may be useful to all students of Chopin's short fiction.

In preparing the annotations of individual items, I have tried to be extremely thorough while, at the same time, giving readers every incentive to examine the original sources for themselves. For example, when an original source mentions a particular person by name, I have often identified that person in more general terms (as, say, a "friend" or "relative" or "acquaintance" of Chopin). Similarly, when an original source specifies other particulars (referring, say, to *The Atlantic Monthly*), I have often made my summary more general (by mentioning, for instance, "a major national magazine"). I have thus tried to give readers enough information to let them know what a particular scholar says, while also trying to encourage readers to return to the original sources for precise details. For the same reason, I have avoided direct quotations, preferring instead to paraphrase closely—even if this has sometimes meant that my paraphrases are more awkward and less direct than the original phrasing.

Descriptions of particular discussions of specific stories generally follow the order in which those discussions occur in the original sources. Although this method may sometimes lead to a certain "choppiness" in the annotations, it has also allowed me to be as faithful as possible to the sources on which I have drawn.

Even the present book, despite its length, inevitably omits *some* commentary on Chopin's short fiction, especially incidental references to stories mentioned in the hundreds of articles and chapters that focus primarily on *The Awakening*. I have tried, however, to deal with every published study in English that comments on the short stories at any length, and I hope that the present volume offers the fullest account yet prepared of the critical reception these stories have received.

I should stress, as I complete this project, how much I have enjoyed and learned from my reading of the works of Chopin's most devoted scholars, especially the writings of such persons as Per Seyersted, Emily Toth, Joyce Dyer, Bernard Koloski, and others. To a very great degree, their works and the works of the other scholars cited here have shown how criticism and scholarship at their best can help us better understand and more fully appreciate a great writer. I have learned from the facts they have uncovered, have benefitted from the hypotheses they have proposed, and have profited from the insights they have offered into some of the most compelling stories of one of our best American storytellers.—RCE

Works Cited

Aherne 1985. Aherne, John R. "Kate Chopin: An American de Maupassant." *Serendipity: Essays on Six Catholic Authors.* N.p.: Merrimack College Press, 1985. 80–87.

Anonymous 1894 [*The Critic*]. Anonymous. "Bayou Folk." *The Critic* 21 (5 May 1894): 299–300. Rpt in Petry 1996, 41.

Anonymous 1894 [*Review of Reviews*]. Anonymous. "The New Books." *Review of Reviews* 9 (May 1894): 625. Rpt in Petry 1996, 44.

Anonymous 1897 [*Post-Dispatch*]. Anonymous. "Among the New Books." *St. Louis Post-Dispatch* (11 December 1897): 4. Rpt in Petry 1996, 46–48.

Arms 1967. Arms, George. "Kate Chopin's *The Awakening* in the Perspective of Her Literary Career." *Essays on American Literature in Honor of J.B. Hubbell.* Ed. Clarence Gohdes. Durham, NC: Duke University Press, 1967. 215–28.

Arner 1970. Arner, Robert. "Kate Chopin's Realism: 'At the 'Cadian Ball' and 'The Storm.'" *Markham Review* 2 (1970): 1–4.

Arner 1971. Arner, Robert. "Characterization and the Colloquial Style in Kate Chopin's 'Vagabonds.'" *Markham Review* 2 (1971): 110–12.

Arner 1972. Arner, Robert. "Pride and Prejudice: Kate Chopin's 'Désirée's Baby.'" *Mississippi Quarterly* 25.2 (1972): 131–40. Rpt in Petry 1996, 139–46.

Arner 1975. Arner, Robert. Kate Chopin. Special issue of *Louisiana Studies* 14 (1975): 11–139.

Baker 1994. Baker, Christopher. "Chopin's 'The Storm.'" *Explicator* 52 (1994): 225–26.

Bauer 1996. Bauer, Margaret D. "Armand Aubigny: Still Passing After All These Years: The Narrative Voice and Historical Context of 'Désirée's Baby.'" Petry 1996, 161–83.

Baxter 1996. Baxter, Judith. "Introduction" and "Resource Notes." *The Awakening and Other Stories*, by Kate Chopin. Cambridge: Cambridge University Press, 1996. 6–8, 217–47.

Baym 1981. Baym, Nina. "Introduction." *The Awakening and Selected Stories*. New York: Modern Library, 1981. vii–xi.

Beale 1911. Beale, Robert Cecil. *The Development of the Short Story in the South*. Charlottesville, VA: Michie, 1911.

Beer 1997. Beer, Janet. *Kate Chopin, Edith Wharton and Charlotte Perkins Gilman: Studies in Short Fiction*. New York: St. Martin's Press, 1997.

Bell 1988. Bell, Pearl K. "Kate Chopin and Sarah Orne Jewett." *Partisan Review* 55 (1988): 238–53.

Bender 1974. Bender, Bert. "Kate Chopin's Lyrical Short Stories." *Studies in Short Fiction* 11 (1974): 257–66.

Bender 1996. Bender, Bert. "Kate Chopin's Quarrel with Darwin before *The Awakening*." Petry 1996, 99–116.

Benfey 1998. Benfey, Christopher. *Degas in New Orleans: Encounters in the Creole World of Kate Chopin and George Washington Cable*. New York: Knopf, 1998.

Berggren 1977. Berggren, Paula S. "'A Lost Soul': Work Without Hope in *The Awakening*." *Regionalism and the Female Imagination* 3.1 (1977): 1–7.

Berkove 1996. Berkove, Lawrence. "'Acting Like Fools': The Ill-Fated Romances of 'At the 'Cadian Ball' and 'The Storm.'" Petry 1996, 184–96.

Berthoff 1970. Berthoff, Warner. "Introduction." *Bayou Folk*, by Kate Chopin. New York: Garrett, 1970. v–xix.

Blythe 1992. Blythe, Anne M. "Kate Chopin's 'Charlie.'" Boren and Davis 1992, 207–15.

Bonner 1975. Bonner, Thomas. "Kate Chopin's European Consciousness." *American Literary Realism* 9 (1975): 281–84.

Bonner 1977. "Kate Chopin's *Bayou Folk* Revisited." *New Laurel Review* 7.2 (1977): 5–14.

Bonner 1982. Bonner, Thomas, Jr. "Christianity and Catholicism in the Fiction of Kate Chopin." *Southern Quarterly* 20 (1982): 118–25.

Bonner 1983. Bonner, Thomas, Jr. "Kate Chopin: Tradition and the Moment." *Southern Literature in Transition.* Ed. Philip Castille and William Osborne. Memphis: Memphis State University Press, 1983. 141–49.

Bonner 1988. Bonner, Thomas, Jr. "*The Awakening* in an American Literature Survey Course." Koloski 1988, 99–103.

Bonner and Bonner 1999. Bonner, Thomas, Jr., and Judith H. Bonner. "Kate Chopin's New Orleans: A Visual Essay." *Southern Quarterly* 37 (1999): 53–64.

Boren 1992. Boren, Lynda S. "Introduction." Boren and Davis 1992, 1–11.

Boren and Davis 1992. Boren, Lynda S., and Sara deSaussure Davis, eds. *Kate Chopin Reconsidered: Beyond the Bayou.* Ed. Lynda S. Boren and Sara deSaussure Davis. Baton Rouge: Louisiana State University Press, 1992.

Branscomb 1994. Branscomb, Jack. "Chopin's 'Ripe Figs.'" *Explicator* 52 (1994): 165–67.

Brown 1991. Brown, Pearl L. "Kate Chopin's Fiction: Order and Disorder in a Stratified Society." *University of Mississippi Studies in English* 9 (1991): 119–34.

Brown 1999. Brown, Pearl L. "Awakened Men in Kate Chopin's Creole Stories." *American Transcendental Quarterly* 13 (1999): 69–82.

Bryan 1993. Bryan, Violet Harrington. *The Myth of New Orleans in Literature: Dialogues of Race and Gender.* Knoxville: University of Tennessee Press, 1993.

Bryant 1999. Bryant, Jacqueline K. *The Foremother Figure in Early Black Women's Literature: Clothed in My Right Mind.* New York: Garland, 1999.

Burchard 1984. Burchard, Gina M. "Kate Chopin's Problematic Womanliness: The Frontier of American Feminism." *Journal of the American Studies Association of Texas* 15 (1984): 35–45.

Bush 1957. Bush, Robert. "Louisiana Prose Fiction, 1870–1900." Ph.D. Dissertation. State University of Iowa, 1957.

Camfield 1995. Camfield, Gregg. "Kate Chopin-hauer: Or, Can Metaphysics Be Feminized?" *Southern Literary Journal* 27.2 (1995): 3–22.

Carr 1996. Carr, Duane. *A Question of Class: The Redneck Stereotype in Southern Fiction.* Bowling Green, OH: Bowling Green State University Popular Press, 1996.

Castillo 1995. Castillo, Susan P. *Notes from the Periphery: Marginality in North American Literature and Culture.* New York: Peter Lang, 1995.

Cothern 1994. Cothern, Lynn. "Speech and Authorship in Kate Chopin's 'La Belle Zoraïde.'" *Louisiana Literature* 2.1 (1994): 118–25.

Cutter 1994. Cutter, Martha J. "Losing the Battle but Winning the War: Resistance to Patriarchal Discourse in Kate Chopin's Short Fiction." *Legacy* 11 (1994): 17–36. Reprinted in Cutter 1999.

Cutter 1999. Cutter, Martha J. *Unruly Tongue: Identity and Voice in American Women's Writing, 1850–1930.* Jackson: University of Mississippi Press, 1999.

Davis 1982. Davis, Sara deSaussure. "Kate Chopin." *American Realists and Naturalists.* Dictionary of Literary Biography, vol. 12. Ed. Donald Pizer and Earl N. Harbert. Detroit: Gale, 1982. 59–71.

Davis 1992a. Davis, Doris. "*The Awakening*: The Economics of Tension." Boren and Davis 1992, 143–53.

Davis 1992b. Davis, Sara deSaussure. "Chopin's Movement Toward Universal Myth." Boren and Davis 1992, 199–206.

Day 1994. Day, Karen. "The 'Elsewhere' of Female Sexuality and Desire in Kate Chopin's 'A Vocation and a Voice.'" *Louisiana Literature* 2.1 (1994): 108–17.

Dickey 1977. Dickey, Imogene. "Kate Chopin: Her Serious Literary Ambition." *Journal of the American Studies Association of Texas* 8 (1977): 18–22.

Dyer 1980–81. Dyer, Joyce Coyne. "Kate Chopin's Sleeping Bruties." *Markham Review* 10 (1980–81): 10–15.

Dyer 1981a. Dyer, Joyce Coyne. "Gouvernail, Kate Chopin's Sensitive Bachelor." *Southern Literary Journal* 14.1 (1981): 46–55.

Dyer 1981b. Dyer, Joyce Coyne. "Night Images in the Work of Kate Chopin." *American Literary Realism* 14 (1981): 216–30.

Dyer 1981c. Dyer, Joyce Coyne. "The Restive Brute: Symbolic Presentation of Repression and Sublimation in Kate Chopin's 'Fedora.'" *Studies in Short Fiction* 18 (1981): 261–65.

Dyer 1981d. Dyer, Joyce Coyne. "Symbolic Setting in Kate Chopin's 'A Shameful Affair.'" *Southern Studies* 20.4 (1981): 447–52.

Dyer 1983–84. Dyer, Joyce Coyne. "Epiphanies through Nature in the Stories of Kate Chopin." *University of Dayton Review* 16.3 (1983–84): 75–81.

Dyer 1984. Dyer, Joyce Coyne. "A Note on Kate Chopin's 'The White Eagle.'" *Arizona Quarterly* 40 (1984): 189–92.

Dyer 1985. Dyer, Joyce Coyne. "Techniques of Distancing in the Fiction of Kate Chopin." *Southern Studies* 24 (1985): 69–81.

Dyer 1993. Dyer, Joyce Coyne. *The Awakening: A Novel of Beginnings*. New York: Twayne, 1993.

Dyer 1994. Dyer, Joyce Coyne. "'Vagabonds': A Story Without a Home." *Louisiana Literature* 2.1 (1994): 74–82.

Elfenbein 1989. Elfenbein, Anna Shannon. *Women on the Color Line: Evolving Stereotypes and the Writings of George Washington Cable, Grace King, Kate Chopin*. Charlottesville: University Press of Virginia, 1989.

Ellis 1992. Ellis, Nancy S. "Insistent Refrains and Self-Discovery: Accompanied Awakenings in Three Stories by Kate Chopin." Boren and Davis 1992, 216–29.

Ellis 1994. Ellis, Nancy S. "Sonata No. 1 in Prose, the 'Von Stoltz': Musical Structure in an Early Work by Kate Chopin." *Louisiana Literature* 2.1 (1994): 145–56.

Erickson 1990. Erickson, Jon. "Fairytale Features in Kate Chopin's 'Désirée's Baby': A Case Study in Genre Cross-Reference." *Modes of Narrative: Approaches to Canadian, American and British Fiction*. Ed. Reingard M. Nischik and Barbara Korte. Würzburg: Königshausen & Neumann, 1990. 57–67.

Ewell 1986. Ewell, Barbara C. *Kate Chopin*. New York: Ungar, 1986.

Ewell 1992. Ewell, Barbara C. "Kate Chopin and the Dream of Female Selfhood." Boren and Davis 1992, 157–65.

Ewell 1994. Ewell, Barbara C. "Making Places: Kate Chopin and the Art of Fiction." *Louisiana Literature* 2.1 (1994): 157–71.

Ewell 1997. Ewell, Barbara C. "Regions of the Spirit: Nature vs. Dogma in Chopin's Religious Vision." *Performance for a Lifetime: A Festscrift Honoring Dorothy Harrell Brown: Essays on Women, Religion, and the Renaissance*. New Orleans: Loyola University, 1997. 102–15.

Ewell 1999. Ewell, Barbara C. "Unlinking Race and Gender: *The Awakening* as a Southern Novel." *Southern Quarterly* 37 (1999): 30–37.

Fetterley and Pryse 1995. Fetterley, Judith, and Marjorie Pryse, eds. *American Women Regionalists.* New York: Norton, 1995.

Fletcher 1966. Fletcher, Marie. "The Southern Woman in the Fiction of Kate Chopin." *Louisiana History* 7 (1966): 117–32.

Fluck 1982. Fluck, Winfried. "Tentative Transgressions: Kate Chopin's Fiction as a Mode of Symbolic Action." *Studies in American Fiction* 10 (1982): 151–71.

Foy 1991. Foy, Roslyn Reso. "Chopin's 'Désirée's Baby.'" *Explicator* 49 (1991): 222–23.

Fusco 1994. Fusco, Richard. *Maupassant and the American Short Story: The Influence of Form and the Turn of the Century.* University Park: Pennsylvania State University Press, 1994.

Gardiner 1982. Gardiner, Elaine. "'Ripe Figs': Kate Chopin in Miniature." *Modern Fiction Studies* 28 (1982): 379–82.

Garvey 1996. Garvey, Ellen Gruber. *The Adman in the Parlor: Magazines and the Gendering of Consumer Culture, 1880s to 1910s.* New York: Oxford University Press, 1996.

Gaudet 1986. Gaudet, Marcia. "Kate Chopin and the Lore of Cane River's Creoles of Color." *Xavier Review* 6.1 (1986): 45–52.

Gibbons 2000. Gibbons, Kaye. "Introduction." *The Awakening and Other Stories,* by Kate Chopin. Ed. Nina Baym. New York: Modern Library, 2000. i–lix.

Gilbert 1984. Gilbert, Sandra. "Introduction." *The Awakening and Selected Stories,* by Kate Chopin. New York: Penguin, 1984. 7–33.

Gilder 1898. Gilder, Jeannette L. ["J.L.G."] "Mrs. Chopin's 'Night in Acadie.'" *The Critic* 29 (16 April 1898): 266. Rpt in Petry 1996, 50.

Giorcelli 1988. Giorcelli, Cristina. "Edna's Wisdom: A Transitional and Numinous Merging." Martin 1988a, 109–48.

Goodwyn 1994. Goodwyn, Janet. "'dah you is, settin' down, lookin' jis' like w'ite folks!': Ethnicity Enacted in Kate Chopin's Short Fiction." *Yearbook of English Studies* 24 (1994): 1–11.

Green 1994. Green, Suzanne D. "Fear, Freedom, and the Perils of Ethnicity: Otherness in Kate Chopin's 'Beyond the Bayou' and Zora Neale Hurston's 'Sweat.'" *Southern Studies* 5 (1994): 105–24.

Green 1999. Green, Suzanne D. "Where Are We Going? Where Have We Been? Twenty Years of Chopin Criticism." Green and Caudle 1999, 13–30.

Green and Caudle 1999. Green, Suzanne D., and David J. Caudle. *Kate Chopin: An Annotated Bibliography of Critical Works*. Westport, CT: Greenwood Press, 1999.

Grover 1984. Grover, Dorys Crow. "Kate Chopin and the Bayou Country." *Journal of the American Studies Association of Texas* 15 (1984): 29–34.

Guidici 1991. Guidici, Cynthia. "Kate Chopin's 'Occasional' Women." *Conference of College Teachers of English Studies* 56 (1991): 25–34.

Gunning 1995. Gunning, Sandra. "Kate Chopin's Local Color Fiction and the Politics of White Supremacy." *Arizona Quarterly* 52.3 (1995): 61–86.

Hoder-Salmon 1992. Hoder-Salmon, Marilyn. *Kate Chopin's The Awakening: Screenplay as Interpretation*. Gainesville: University Press of Florida, 1992.

Howell 1979a. Howell, Elmo. "Kate Chopin and the Creole Country." *Louisiana History* 20 (1979): 209–19.

Howell 1979b. Howell, Elmo. "Kate Chopin and the Pull of Faith: A Note on 'Lilacs.'" *Southern Studies* 18 (1979): 103–9.

Inge 1989. Inge, Tonette Bond. "Kate Chopin." *American Short-Story Writers, 1800–1910*. Dictionary of Literary Biography, vol. 78. Ed. Bobby Ellen Kimbel and William E. Grant. Detroit: Gale, 1989. 90–110.

Johnson 1996. Johnson, Rose M. "A Ratio-nal Pedagogy for Kate Chopin's Passional Fiction: Using Burke's Scene-Act Ratio to Teach 'Story' and 'Storm.'" *Conference of College Teachers of English Studies* 60 (1996): 122–28.

Jones 1981. Jones, Anne Goodwyn. *Tomorrow Is Another Day: The Woman Writer in the South, 1859–1936*. Baton Rouge: Louisiana State University Press, 1981.

Juneja 1995. Juneja, Punim. "Suicide as Metaphor: Edna's Search for Identity." Kaul 1995, 113–25.

Kaul 1995. Kaul, Iqbal, ed. *Kate Chopin's The Awakening: Critical Essays*. New Delhi: Deep and Deep, 1995.

Klemans 1981. Klemans, Patricia A. "The Courageous Soul: Woman as Artist in American Literature." *CEA Critic* 43.4 (1981): 39–43.

Knights 2000. Knights, Pamela. "Introduction." *The Awakening and Other Stories*, by Kate Chopin. Oxford: Oxford University Press, 2000. ix–xlviii.

Koloski 1988a. Koloski, Bernard, ed. *Approaches to Teaching Kate Chopin's The Awakening.* New York: MLA, 1988.

Koloski 1988b. Koloski, Bernard. "Materials." Koloski 1988a, 3–18.

Koloski 1994. Koloski, Bernard. "The Anthologized Chopin: Kate Chopin's Short Stories in Yesterday's and Today's Anthologies." *Louisiana Literature* 2.1 (1994): 18–30.

Koloski 1996. Koloski, Bernard. *Kate Chopin: A Study of the Short Fiction.* New York: Twayne-Simon and Schuster, 1996.

Koloski 1999. Koloski, Bernard. "Introduction." *Bayou Folk and A Night in Acadie*, by Kate Chopin. New York: Penguin, 1999. vii–xxiv.

Ladenson 1976. Ladenson, Joyce Ruddel. "The Return of St. Louis' Prodigal Daughter: Kate Chopin After Seventy Years." *Midamerica* 2 (1976): 24–34.

Lanser 1981. Lanser, Susan Sniader. *The Narrative Act: Point of View in Prose Fiction.* Princeton: Princeton University Press, 1981.

Larsson 1993. Larsson, Donald F. (Revised by Thomas L. Erskine.) "Kate Chopin." *Critical Survey of Short Fiction.* Ed. Frank N. Magill. Rev. ed. 7 vols. Pasadena, CA: Salem, 1993. 2: 536–41.

Lattin 1978. Lattin, Patricia Hopkins. "Childbirth and Motherhood in Kate Chopin's Fiction." *Regionalism and the Female Imagination* 4.1 (1978): 8–12.

Lattin 1980. Lattin, Patricia Hopkins. "Kate Chopin's Repeating Characters." *Mississippi Quarterly* 33 (1980): 19–37.

Lattin 1982. Lattin, Patricia Hopkins. "The Search for Self in Kate Chopin's Fiction: Simple Versus Complex Vision." *Southern Studies* 21.2 (1982): 222–35.

Lattin 1988. Lattin, Patricia Hopkins. "Childbirth and Motherhood in *The Awakening* and 'Athénaïse.'" Koloski 1988a, 40–46.

Leary 1970a. Leary, Lewis. "Introduction." *The Awakening and Other Stories* by Kate Chopin. New York: Holt, Rinehart, 1970. iii–xx.

Leary 1970b. Leary, Lewis. "Kate Chopin, Liberationist?" *Southern Literary Journal* 3 (1970): 138–44.

Leary 1971. Leary, Lewis. *Southern Excursions: Essays on Mark Twain and Others.* Baton Rouge: Louisiana State University Press, 1971.

Llewellyn 1996. Llewellyn, Dara. "Reader Activation of Boundaries in Kate Chopin's 'Beyond the Bayou.'" *Studies in Short Fiction* 33 (1996): 255–62.

Lohafer 1983. Lohafer, Susan. *Coming to Terms with the Short Story.* Baton Rouge: Louisiana State University Press, 1983.

Lohafer 1989. Lohafer, Susan. "Preclosure and Story Processing." *Short Story Theory at a Crossroads.* Ed. Susan Lohafer and Jo Ellen Clarey. Baton Rouge: Louisiana State University Press, 1989. 249–75.

Lundie 1994. Lundie, Catherine. "Doubly Dispossessed: Kate Chopin's Women of Color." *Louisiana Literature* 2.1 (1994): 126–44.

Manders 1990. Manders, Eunice. "The Wretched Freeman." *Perspectives on Kate Chopin: Proceedings from the Kate Chopin International Conference: April 6, 7, 8 1989.* Natchitoches, LA: Northwestern Louisiana State University Press, 1990. 37–45.

Martin 1988a. Martin, Wendy, ed. *New Essays on The Awakening.* Cambridge: Cambridge University Press, 1988.

Martin 1988b. Martin, Wendy. "Introduction." Martin 1988a, 1–31.

McCullough 1999. McCullough, Kate. *Regions of Identity: The Construction of America in Women's Fiction, 1885–1914.* Stanford: Stanford University Press, 1999.

McMahan 1985. McMahan, Elizabeth. "'Nature's Decoy': Kate Chopin's Presentation of Women and Marriage in Her Short Fiction." *Turn of the Century Women* 2.2 (1985): 32–35.

Michaels 1990. Michaels, Walter Benn. "The Contracted Heart." *New Literary History* 21 (1990): 495–531.

Michaels 1998. Michaels, Walter Benn. "Local Colors." *Modern Language Notes* 113 (1998): 734–56.

Miner 1982. Miner, Madonne M. "Veiled Hints: An Affective Stylist's Reading of Kate Chopin's 'The Story of an Hour.'" *Markham Review* 11 (1982): 29–32.

Mitchell 1992. Mitchell, Angelyn. "Feminine Double Consciousness in Kate Chopin's 'The Story of an Hour.'" *CEA Magazine* 5.1 (1992): 59–64.

Moss 1993. Moss, Rose. "Barriers of Reticence and Reserve." *Still the Frame Holds: Essays on Women Poets and Writers.* Ed. Sheila Roberts and Yvonne Pacheco. San Bernardino: Borgo, 1993.

Newman 1986. Newman, Judie. "Kate Chopin: Short Fiction and the Arts of Subversion." *The Nineteenth-Century American Short Story.* Ed. A. Robert Lee. New York: Barnes and Noble, 1986. 150–63.

O'Brien 1976–77. O'Brien, Sharon. "Sentiment, Local Color, and the New Woman Writer: Kate Chopin and Willa Cather." *Kate Chopin Newsletter* 2.3 (1976–77): 16–24.

Padgett 1994. Padgett, Jacqueline Olson. "Kate Chopin and the Literature of the Annunciation, with a Reading of 'Lilacs.'" *Louisiana Literature* 2.1 (1994): 97–107.

Papke 1988. Papke, Mary E. "Chopin's Stories of Awakening." Koloski 1988, 73–79.

Papke 1990. Papke, Mary E. *Verging on the Abyss: The Social Fiction of Kate Chopin and Edith Wharton.* New York: Greenwood, 1990.

Pattee 1923. Pattee, Fred Lewis. *The Development of the American Short Story: An Historical Survey.* New York: Harper & Brothers, 1923.

Peel 1990. Peel, Ellen. "Semiotic Subversion in 'Désirée's Baby.'" *American Literature* 62 (1990): 223–37.

Peterson 1972. Petersen, Peter James. "The Fiction of Kate Chopin." Ph.D. Dissertation. University of New Mexico, 1972.

Petry 1979. Petry, Alice Hall. "Universal and Particular: The Local-Color Phenomenon Reconsidered." *American Literary Realism* 12 (1979): 111–26.

Petry 1996. Petry, Alice Hall, ed. *Critical Essays on Kate Chopin.* New York: G.K. Hall, 1996.

Potter 1971. "Negroes in the Fiction of Kate Chopin." *Louisiana History* 12 (1971): 41–58.

Rankin 1932. Rankin, Daniel. *Kate Chopin and Her Creole Stories*. Philadelphia: University of Pennsylvania Press, 1932.

Reilly 1937. Reilly, Joseph J. "Stories by Kate Chopin." *The Commonweal* 25 (26 March 1937): 606–7. Rpt in Petry 1996, 71–74.

Reilly 1942. Reilly, Joseph J. *Of Books and Men*. New York: Julian Messer, 1942.

Ringe 1975. Ringe, Donald A. "Cane River World: Kate Chopin's *At Fault* and Related Stories." *Studies in American Fiction* 3 (1975): 157–66.

Robinson 1992. Robinson, Roxana. "Introduction." *"A Matter of Prejudice" and Other Stories*, by Kate Chopin. New York: Bantam, 1992. vii–xxi.

Rocks 1972. Rocks, James E. "Kate Chopin's Ironic Vision." *Revue de Louisiane/Louisiana Review* 1.2 (1972): 110–20.

Rogers 1983. Rogers, Nancy E. "Echoes of George Sand in Kate Chopin." *Revue de Littérature Comparée* 57.1 (1983): 25–42.

Rosenblum 1986a. Rosenblum, Joseph. "Désirée's Baby." *Masterplots II: Short Story Series*. Ed. Frank N. Magill. 6 vols. Pasadena, CA: Salem, 1986. 2:572–74.

Rosenblum 1986b. Rosenblum, Joseph. "The Storm." *Masterplots II: Short Story Series*. Ed. Frank N. Magill. 6 vols. Pasadena, CA: Salem, 1986. 5:2235–37.

Rosenblum 1986c. Rosenblum, Joseph. "The Story of an Hour." *Masterplots II: Short Story Series*. Ed. Frank N. Magill. 6 vols. Pasadena, CA: Salem, 1986. 5:2241–43.

Rowe 1985. Rowe, Anne. "Kate Chopin." *The History of Southern Literature*. Ed. Louis D. Rubin, et al. Baton Rouge: Louisiana State University Press, 1985. 228–32.

Saar 1994. Saar, Doreen Alvarez. "The Failure and Triumph of 'The Maid of Saint Phillippe': Chopin Rewrites American Literature for American Women." *Louisiana Literature* 2.1 (1994): 59–73.

Seidel 1990. Seidel, Kathryn Lee. "Art as an Unnatural Act: Homoeroticism, Art, and Mademoiselle Reisz in *The Awakening*." *Perspectives on Kate Chopin: Proceedings of the Kate Chopin International Conference: April 6, 7, 8 1989*. Natchitoches, LA: Northwestern State University Press, 1990. 85–100.

Sempreora 1994. Sempreora, Margot. "Kate Chopin as Translator: A Paradoxical Liberation." *Louisiana Literature* 2.1 (1994): 83–98.

Seyersted 1969a. Seyersted, Per. *Kate Chopin: A Critical Biography.* Baton Rouge: Louisiana State University Press, 1969.

Seyersted 1969b. Seyersted, Per. "Introduction." *The Complete Works of Kate Chopin.* Ed. Per Seyersted. 2 vols. Baton Rouge: Louisiana State University Press, 1969. 1:21–33.

Seyersted 1974. Seyersted, Per. "Introduction." *The Storm and Other Stories,* by Kate Chopin. Old Westbury, NY: Feminist Press, 1974. 7–18.

Showalter 1988. Showalter, Elaine. "Tradition and the Female Talent: *The Awakening* as a Solitary Book." Martin 1988a, 33–57.

Showalter 1992. Showalter, Elaine. "Introduction." *The Awakening and Other Short Stories,* by Kate Chopin. Everyman's Library. New York: Knopf, 1992. v–xxvii. [A reprinting of Showalter 1988.]

Shurbutt 1993. Shurbutt, Sylvia Bailey. "The Cane River Characters and Revisionist Mythmaking in the Work of Kate Chopin." *Southern Literary Journal* 25.2 (1993): 14–23.

Simpson 1986. Simpson, Martin. "Chopin's 'A Shameful Affair.'" *Explicator* 45.1 (1986): 59–60.

Skaggs 1979. Skaggs, Peggy. "The Boy's Quest in Kate Chopin's 'A Vocation and a Voice.'" *American Literature* 51 (1979): 270–76.

Skaggs 1985. Skaggs, Peggy. *Kate Chopin.* Boston: Twayne, 1985.

Skredsvig 1993. Skredsvig, Keri Meyers. "Chopin's Choices and Challenges: Language and Limits in 'A Point at Issue.'" *Revista de Filologia y Linguistica de la Universidad de Costa Rica* 19.1 (1993): 77–85.

Solomon 1976. Solomon, Barbara H. "Introduction." *The Awakening and Selected Stories of Kate Chopin.* Edited by Barbara H. Solomon. New York: New American Library, 1976. vii–xxvii.

Steiling 1994. Steiling, David. "Multi-Cultural Aesthetic in Kate Chopin's 'A Gentleman of Bayou Têche.'" *Mississippi Quarterly* 47.2 (1994): 197–200.

Stein 1984. Stein, Allen F. *After the Vows Were Spoken: Marriage in American Literary Realism.* Columbus: Ohio State University Press, 1984.

Stepenoff 1987. "Freedom and Regret: The Dilemma of Kate Chopin." *Missouri Historical Review* 81.4 (1987): 447–66.

Taylor 1979. Taylor, Helen. "Introduction." *Portraits: Short Stories*, by Kate Chopin. London: Women's Press, 1979. vii–xix.

Taylor 1989. Taylor, Helen. *Gender, Race and Region in the Writings of Grace King, Ruth McEnery Stuart, and Kate Chopin*. Baton Rouge: Louisiana State University Press, 1989.

Taylor 1999. Taylor, Helen. "Walking through New Orleans: Kate Chopin and the Female *Flâneur*." *Southern Quarterly* 37 (1999): 21–29.

Thomas 1992. Thomas, Heather Kirk. "'What Are the Prospects for the Book?': Rewriting a Woman's Life." Boren and Davis 1992, 36–57.

Thomas 1995. Thomas, Heather Kirk. "Kate Chopin's Scribbling Women and the American Literary Marketplace." *Studies in American Fiction* 23.1 (1995): 19–34.

Thomas 1996. Thomas, Heather Kirk. "The 'House of Sylvie' in Kate Chopin's 'Athénaïse.'" Petry 1996, 207–17.

Tompkins 1976. Tompkins, Jane. "*The Awakening*: An Evaluation." *Feminist Studies* 3.3–4 (1976): 22–29.

Toth 1981. Toth, Emily. "Kate Chopin and Literary Convention: 'Désirée's Baby.'" *Southern Studies* 20.2 (1981): 201–8.

Toth 1984. Toth, Emily. "A Laughter of Their Own: Women's Humor in the United States." *Critical Essays on American Humor*. Ed. William Bedford Clark and W. Craig Turner. Boston: G.K. Hall, 1984. 199–215.

Toth 1988a. Toth, Emily. "Kate Chopin's New Orleans Years." *New Orleans Review* 15.1 (1988): 53–60.

Toth 1988b. Toth, Emily. "A New Biographical Approach." Koloski 1988a, 60–66.

Toth 1990a. Toth, Emily. *Kate Chopin: The Life of the Author of "The Awakening."* New York: William Morrow, 1990.

Toth 1990b. Toth, Emily. "The Shadow of the First Biographer: The Case of Kate Chopin." *Southern Review* 26 (1990): 285–92.

Toth 1991. Toth, Emily. "Introduction." *A Vocation and a Voice: Stories by Kate Chopin*. New York: Penguin, 1991. vii–xxvi.

Toth 1992. Toth, Emily. "Kate Chopin Thinks Back Through Her Mothers." Boren and Davis 1992, 15–25.

Toth 1994. Toth, Emily. "A New Generation Reads Kate Chopin." *Louisiana Literature* 2.1 (1994): 8–17.

Toth 1999a. Toth, Emily. "Kate Chopin's Life and Literary Career." Green and Caudle 1999, 1–12.

Toth 1999b. Toth, Emily. "Kate Chopin's Secret, Slippery Life Story." *Southern Quarterly* 37 (1999): 45–50.

Toth 1999c. Toth, Emily. *Unveiling Kate Chopin.* Jackson: University Press of Mississippi, 1999.

Toth and Seyersted 1998. Toth, Emily, and Per Seyersted, eds. Cheyenne Bonnell, assoc. ed. *Kate Chopin's Private Papers.* Bloomington: Indiana University Press, 1998.

Tuttleton 1996. Tuttleton, James W. *Vital Signs: Essays on American Literature and Criticism.* Chicago: Ivan R. Dee, 1996.

Valentine and Palmer 1987. Valentine, Kristin B., and Janet Larsen Palmer. "The Rhetoric of Nineteenth-Century Feminism in Kate Chopin's 'A Pair of Silk Stockings.'" *Weber Studies* 4.2 (1987): 59–67.

Vanlandingham 1990. Vanlandingham, Phyllis. "Kate Chopin and Editors, 'A Singular Class of Men.'" *Perspectives on Kate Chopin: Proceedings of the Kate Chopin International Conference: April 6, 7, 8 1989.* Natchitoches, LA: Northwestern State University Press, 1990. 159–67.

Wagner-Martin 1996. Wagner-Martin, Linda. "Kate Chopin's Fascination with Young Men." Petry 1996, 197–206.

Walker 1994. Walker, Nancy A. "Introduction." *The Awakening*, by Kate Chopin. New York: St. Martin's, 1994. 3–18.

Walker 1995. Walker, Nancy A. *The Disobedient Writer: Women and Narrative Tradition.* Austin: University of Texas Press, 1995.

Walker 1996. Walker, Nancy A. "Her Own Story: The Woman of Letters in Kate Chopin's Short Fiction." Petry 1996, 227–36.

Weatherford 1994. Weatherford, K.J. "Courageous Souls: Kate Chopin's Women Artists." *American Studies in Scandinavia* 26 (1994): 96–112.

Webb 1976. Webb, Bernice Larson. "The Circular Structure of Kate Chopin's Life and Writing." *New Laurel Review* 6.1 (1976): 5–14.

White 1984. White, Robert. "Inner and Outer Space in *The Awakening*." *Mosaic* 17 (1984): 97–109.

Winn 1992. Winn, Harbour. "Echoes of Literary Sisterhood: Louisa May Alcott and Kate Chopin." *Studies in American Fiction* 20 (1992): 205–8.

Wolff 1978. Wolff, Cynthia Griffin. "Kate Chopin and the Fiction of Limits: 'Désirée's Baby.'" *Southern Literary Journal* 10.2 (1978): 123–33.

Wolff 1979. Wolff, Cynthia Griffin. "Kate Chopin: 1851–1904." *American Writers: A Collection of Literary Biographies*. Supplement 1, Part 1. Ed. Leonard Unger. New York: Scribner's, 1979. 200–26.

Wolstenholme 1980. Wolstenholme, Susan. "Kate Chopin's Sources for 'Mrs. Mobry's Reason.'" *American Literature* 51 (1980): 540–43.

Zlotnick 1968. Zlotnick, Joan. "A Woman's Will: Kate Chopin on Selfhood, Wifehood, and Motherhood." *Markham Review* 3 (October 1968), n.p.

Kate Chopin's Short Fiction

SYNOPSES OF STORIES
AND
SUMMARIES OF CRITICISM

"After the Winter"

Written: 1891. First published: 1893. Included in *A Night in Acadie* (1897).

M'sieur Michel lives alone in a hovel high in the woods. People say that he has killed many men. When he was twenty-five he had a wife, a child, and a farm, for all of which he was thankful. He went away to war with his friend Joe Duplan and the other "Louisiana Tigers" and came back to find that some wives remain faithful and some do not. His did not. He felt that God had also abandoned him.

Now he hunts game and stays as far away from people as possible, only going into town to sell his game at the store.

On Easter Eve Trézinie asks Cami and LaFringante to go with her in the morning to pick flowers up on the hill to use in church on Easter. The three children climb up the hill and pick all the flowers up to Michel's cabin. When he comes home he is livid because someone has invaded his space. He storms into town, knowing that everyone will be in church. He plans to confront them all and tell them off, but when he enters the church a strange feeling envelops him. He sees the beautiful flowers, hears the organ, and listens to the voices joined in praise. He remembers all this from his childhood in that same church. His mind is in turmoil; there is no use trying to speak. He turns and runs for the safety of his hills and his solitude.

The next night he wanders down the hill in a different direction than the town. He smells the newly plowed earth and he wants to put his hands in it like he used to do twenty-five years ago. He sees a hedge between the two farms, just like the one he had planned to plant. He sees his old home and wonders who lives there now. A hand touches his shoulder; he turns and sees Joe Duplan. Joe tells Michel that he uses the house for extra guests and he uses the land to graze his cattle. He says that he has kept the farm up for Michel because he knows that one day Michel will return. He tells Michel to come back in the morning and says he will give him a horse and a plow, and then he disappears into the hedge.

Michel looks around and all the land looks lush, but as he looks beyond the land up the hills, they appear as a black shadow against the sky. **(DR)**

***

Reilly 1942: The ending is very fine (131). **Bush 1952:** The ending is a bit maudlin (an unusual trait in Chopin's fiction [242]). **Potter 1971:** The mulatto who commands the white man to take off his hat in church exemplifies the importance of religion to many of Chopin's black characters (56). **Peterson 1972:** Like "Beyond the Bayou," this is a story of transformation, but the imagery here is too obvious, the design is insufficiently strong, and the events are not especially credible. The children seem unintegrated into the main focus, and the transformation seems contrived (79–80). Here as elsewhere, Chopin uses children symbolically but also somewhat simplistically (103). **Rocks 1972:** Theme: the price one often pays for one's obsessions (117). **Arner 1975:** Partly resembling "A Matter of Prejudice," this tale shows how children help an older man overcome his mental and social alienation (partly caused by the Civil War) so that he becomes reconciled to reality. Natural imagery emphasizes his initial isolation, his later return to the fold, but also the difficulty of that transition (74). **Ringe 1975:** Topic: the range of social classes depicted in Chopin's fiction (159). **Lattin 1980:** As elsewhere, Chopin describes members of the Duplan family, her least intriguing and least dramatic group of repeating characters (21). Other repeating characters also appear here (25; 28). **Bonner 1982:** As elsewhere, Chopin emphasizes the specifics of Christian religious practice, which are linked here with seasonal imagery (123–24). **Davis 1982:** As elsewhere, Chopin uses imagery of springtime and religion to reinforce a theme of secular, personal rebirth (66). **Lattin 1982:** As elsewhere, Chopin features an alienated, stunted character who eventually and somewhat easily achieves integration (224–25). **Skaggs 1985:** As elsewhere, Chopin shows a real familiarity with children and their effects on others (27). **Ewell 1986:** Like "Beyond the Bayou," this tale juxtaposes the impact of children and war. Although sometimes implausible, the plot does skillfully oppose alienation and the communion available through both nature and worship. In both stories children help the main characters overcome present isolation and past traumas (95). As in "Ti Démon," the main character suffers from an intimidating reputation (175). **Papke 1990:** The story focuses on alienation but without explaining its origins in social strife. Chopin reunites the main character with society almost too simplistically, yet she does imply that such harmony is fragile (52–53). **Toth 1990a:** This was one of several stories from 1891 in which Chopin sought a friendly, interested readership (201). Perhaps a character in this story was based on a real young woman Chopin once knew. Although the tale was quickly accepted by a magazine for young readers, it never appeared in that magazine's pages—perhaps because of its incidental reference to feminine infidelity—the first time Chopin had mentioned this topic in her fiction (204–5). The story, which shows Chopin's turn toward a darker, more daring kind of realistic writing (206), later appeared in *A Night in Acadie*, in which all the stories are set in Louisiana (298). It accurately describes winter in the Cane River country (325). **Ellis 1992:** This is one of various stories in which, as in *The Awakening*, a character is transformed partly through his or her encounter with music. A passage in this story resembles one in Chopin's girlhood diary, and the rejuvenation here resembles the one in "Madame Martel's Christmas Eve" (216–20). **Koloski 1994:** The story is included in a soft-cover collection of Chopin's fiction published in 1992 (28). **Koloski 1996:** This story both resembles and differs from "Nég Créole," especially because of the race of the respective main characters. It also resembles "A Morning Walk." The story falls into three sections, opens with a social point of view, and is resolved mainly through the action of a single character (50–51). This is one of several of Chopin's children's tales that focuses on an unusual person who is transformed. It is one of a pair of children's stories set on a holiday and depicting the need to overcome alienation (71; 87). **Toth and Seyersted 1998:** The story is mentioned by Chopin in account books for 1892 (139), for 1896 (141), and for 1891 (148, 168). As elsewhere, she here describes a morose, angry male misfit (274). **Benfey 1999:** The story's somewhat sardonic tone may reflect Chopin's attitudes toward the Civil War. The embittered main character almost literally goes underground, but in the end he seems on the verge of a transformation both spiritually and in his attitudes toward race. The final sentence hints at mortality, and the story as a whole implies the difficulties of recapturing one's past life after war. It suggests the need for a change deeper than mere rebuilding (233–35). **Koloski 1999:** This is one of many stories by Chopin which either feature children or were written for them (xxii). Here as elsewhere she describes grown-ups who find connection with others (xxiii). **Toth 1999c:** The story had trouble reaching publication, perhaps because it alludes to adultery by women—the first such allusion in Chopin's fiction (132).

"Alexandre's Wonderful Experience"

Written: 1900. Included in *Private Papers* (1998).

Alexandre is a poor but industrious and imaginative 14-year-old who assists the old owner of an antiques shop. When a kind, well dressed, but apparently needy woman enters the shop to ask whether the owner might be interested in buying a chest of drawers from her, the old man pretends indifference so that she will eventually sell at a cheap price, even though both he and Alexandre know of a doctor who has been looking for just such a piece of furniture.

Alexandre, taking pity on the woman, goes to her house that night to tell her that the doctor is looking for a chest of drawers. He finds her home filled with antique furniture but realizes that the woman has begun to part with it, piece by piece, in order to afford treatments for her young daughter, who is obviously ill.

After leaving the house, Alexandre heads for the doctor's home to tell him about the valuable chest of drawers. Later, while returning from the doctor's, he is so tired that he decides to nap on the pavement. When he awakens he finds himself in the hospital, where he has been unconscious for some time. Leaving the hospital, he discovers that he has been fired from the antiques shop since the owner has discovered Alexandre's effort to put to doctor directly in touch with the kind woman.

Desperate, Alexandre finds a job selling clothes poles on the street and in the busy public market. Mocked because of his sickly appearance by the other street merchants, at first he barely notices one day when the kind woman calls to him from a passing carriage. Both she and the doctor—whom she did meet and has recently married—have been searching for him. She takes Alexandre back with her to live on their country estate, where her daughter is recuperating under the care of the woman's new husband. **(RCE)**

***

Seyersted 1969a: The businessman in this story may be a target of satire (214). **Ewell 1986:** This story, though skillful, is too predictable, especially in its conveniently happy ending. Nevertheless, the mockery of greed, the effectiveness of setting, and the descriptions of impassioned dreams are reminiscent of "Nég Créol." The protagonist's experiences may have seemed relevant to Chopin's own life at the time she was writing (176–77). **Toth 1990a:** For this tale, which resembles those of Horatio Alger, Chopin received fifty dollars, although the magazine which paid her never published the story (372–73). **Thomas 1992:** This is one of several works by Chopin written in 1900 that focus on sickness, death, or growing old (49–50). **Koloski 1996:** This is one of several children's stories by Chopin that depict the poor (71; 87). **Toth and Seyersted 1998:** An early draft was among a collection of Chopin manuscripts uncovered in the early 1990s (135). The tale is mentioned in various account books (142, 146, 151). It was published in 1979 (245), and the newly discovered manuscript resembles that version quite closely (246). It is reprinted here (261–68). This story was paid for (but never published) by a magazine for youth (275). A brief example of the slight variations between the two versions of the tale is offered here (283). **Toth 1999c:** An early version was discovered in 1992 (166). This story was paid for (but never published) by a magazine for youth. Perhaps changes in staffing accounted for the magazine's handling of the story (229).

"At Chênière Caminada"

Written: 1893. First Published: 1894. Included in *A Night in Acadie* (1897).

Tonie is a fisherman and lives with his mother on the Chênière Caminada. At church that Sunday, someone is playing the organ, which had not been played in several months. The music is beautiful and the congregation is entranced. Tonie looks to see who might be playing the instrument. He sees a pretty young girl with clear blue eyes and nut-brown hair. He sees her again after mass, standing in front of the church. She has ridden over from Grand Isle with two ladies he knows who keep a place on the island. Tonie is smitten with the girl.

Early the next morning Tonie gets Philibert to do his work and he heads for Grand Isle in his sailboat. He sees the girl again and watches her. He learns that her name is Claire Duvigné. Tonie tells her that he and his boat are available for her whenever she desires a ride. She always has two or three admirers around her, but one day she comes alone for a boat ride. As they sail they talk and, during the pleasant conversation and ride, Claire realizes that Tonie is in love with her. She suggests that they go back to shore and makes sure that she is never alone with him again.

In January Tonie runs into the two women from Grand Isle. He inquires about Claire and the ladies tell him that Claire died three weeks ago. At first Tonie is sad, but he cannot explain the changes that begin to happen to him. He begins to live again. When his mother questions him about Claire's death he explains, after much thought, that as long as she was alive he knew that he could never have her. He dreaded the day she would marry and bear another man's children. Tonie could not bear to think of her bringing her children to Grand Isle every summer and having to see her happily married to someone else. Now she will always belong to him. **(DR)**

***

Anonymous 1897 [*Post-Dispatch*]: This subtle story penetrates into the darker regions of the human psyche (48). **Rankin 1932:** The story was not accepted until a year after its composition, and some of its people and events show up again in *The Awakening*. One contemporary even claimed that the story, in its main concern and conclusion, reflects the life of a real woman from New Orleans (92). Through subtle implication, this tale illuminates a human spirit in a fashion unusual in contemporary short fiction (161–62). **Reilly 1937:** As elsewhere, Chopin deals subtly with the ambiguities of affection (73). **Reilly 1942:** As elsewhere, Chopin deals subtly with the ambiguities of affection. Her technique shows the subtlety of Maupassant, but her depiction of the hero's thinking is subtle in a different way. The resolution is similar to that in Browning's poem "Evelyn Hope" (134–35). **Bush 1957:** Like some of Chopin's other best stories, this one focuses on love—in this case on its transforming powers. As in other works, a lengthy period of potentially tragic ambiguity is suddenly resolved in a way that satisfies the protagonist (245–46). **Arms 1967:** Although this story is one of the five most successful works included in *A Night in Acadie*, it is somewhat damaged by maudlin superficiality. The plausible story is undercut by the sentimental ending, although it isn't clear whether Chopin herself endorsed this sentimentality or felt compelled to supply it (224–25). **Seyersted 1969a:** The story proved morally unobjectionable to its original editors because nothing results from the protagonist's sexual passions (55). Like *The Awakening*, this tale is also set at Grand Isle (219). **Berthoff 1970:** Chopin herself often visited the island mentioned here (viii). This is one of the more profound stories in *A Night in Acadie* and anticipates the concerns of *The Awakening* (xvii). **Peterson 1972:** In this tale the somewhat maudlin ending conflicts with the basic realism of the piece. Tonie's passion seems both adolescent and primitive, and the contrast between his perspective and the girl's creates one of Chopin's finest descriptions of alienation. The final scene between Tonie and his mother compromises the work's earlier dark tone, either because Chopin or her readers could not settle for a grimmer conclusion (128–30). **Dyer 1980–81:** Here as elsewhere Chopin reverses expectations by showing how a male can be fundamentally transformed by contact with a female (11). Tonie's initial response to Claire seems a bit maudlin and immature, although eventually his sexual desire becomes apparent. Even his appearance suggests his animal nature, and his later conduct is linked with the instinctive behavior of birds who seek shelter in oak trees (often associated in Chopin's works with females). Tonie's responses are less governed by social convention than those of 'Polyte in "Azélie." His desires are often extremely forceful, even brutish. Although the conclusion of the tale has struck some critics as implausible, Tonie's final feelings are consistent with his earlier obsessiveness (12–13). 'Polyte in "Azélie" is forced to confront pain of the sort Tonie is allowed to escape, while the boy in "A Vocation and a Voice" experiences many of the same conflicting feelings felt by both Tonie and by 'Polyte (13). Here as in "A Vocation and a Voice," Chopin symbolically associates external nature and internal desires (14). **Baym 1981:** The story exemplifies Chopin's depiction of Cajuns (xix). **Dyer 1981a:** Chopin's allusion in *The Awakening* to Tonie from this story complicates our response to the novel (47). **Dyer 1981d:** Here and in numerous other works, Chopin uses physical setting to imply what a character is feeling. Her frequent use of this technique is open to various explanations (451–52). **Bonner 1982:** This is one of several stories by Chopin in which Christianity is important (125). **Davis 1982:** As elsewhere, Chopin emphasizes the primal force of erotic desire (65). **Bonner 1983b:** Theme: prohibited desire (143–45). **Gilbert 1984:** Here as elsewhere Chopin presents a lower-class male who shows affection for an upper-class woman (16). **Skaggs 1985:** As elsewhere, Chopin explores romance, often of an odd variety. By linking erotic desire and death at sea, this work foreshadows *The Awakening* (34–35). **Ewell 1986:** In this story bodily desire is more successfully linked with affection than in "Azélie." After Claire's death, Tonie's passion for her becomes almost religious. Thus, here as in other stories, Chopin explores the relations of flesh and soul (97–98). **Martin 1988a:** This is one of various stories in which Chopin investigates conflicts between strong, often sexual feelings and the conventional ethics of society. The tale is frank in its treatment of desire and its results (4). **Toth 1988a:** This story, which reflects Chopin's personal familiarity with Grand Isle, anticipates *The Awakening* in setting, characters, imagery, and theme. Both the story and the novel reflect some of Chopin's nostalgia for her early years (59–60). **Taylor 1989:** This story, written in the aftermath of a powerful storm that devastated the island the work describes, both resembles and differs from works on the same topic by other writers. Chopin, however, more strongly emphasizes joyousness, eroticism, and quotidian details. The setting and tone of the story both seem idealized and relatively unproblematic (174–75). The story suggests the negative impact for women of reading romantic fiction (189). **Toth 1990a:** The story resembles a French poem Chopin had read as an adolescent (88). It laments the loss of a particular style of living (139) and is the first of her tales set on Grand Isle, also the setting of *The Awakening* (216). Composition of the story may have been prompted by the island's destruction in a hurricane (222). Although the tale was rejected by the prominent magazine that had asked

Chopin for a story (235), the narrative later appeared in *A Night in Acadie*, in which all the stories are set in Louisiana (298). **Ellis 1992:** This is one of various stories in which, as in *The Awakening*, a character is transformed partly through his or her encounter with music (216), in this case the sounds of an organ that are linked to Tonie's attraction to Claire. In characters, imagery, and themes, this story has many links with *The Awakening*, especially in the motif of death by drowning. The music here, unlike that in "After the Winter," carries a destructive potential, while Chopin's depiction of male psychology shows that she knew the minds of both men and women. Like the boy in "A Vocation and a Voice," Tonie in this story is torn between the promptings of his body and his soul (220–24). **Dyer 1993:** Tonie here is associated with animalistic passions—an aspect of his character not emphasized in *The Awakening*. Chopin does not clarify how our knowledge of him from the story should affect (if at all) our reading of the novel (64–65). **Fusco 1994:** This tale uses a structure often found in stories by Maupassant: movement from bad to good to bad fortune (167). **Koloski 1994:** The story is included in soft-cover collections of Chopin's fiction published in 1981 and 1984 (27). **Bender 1996:** As elsewhere, Chopin's basically Darwinian outlook leads her to examine the problems caused by an insufficiently assertive male (107). **Carr 1996:** This affecting tale exemplifies the importance of class divisions (56). **Koloski 1996:** This story resembles *The Awakening* in its places, people, and language. Chopin may have regarded Tonie as somewhat insane (48–49). As elsewhere, Chopin indicates her interest in opera (57). The title is the same as that of a story published earlier by Grace King (85). **Beer 1997:** Although Tonie is obsessive, his inability to express himself clearly keeps him from causing much overt disruption of standard conventions. On one level the tale is a fine instance of Chopin's local-color fiction, but the main character and his obsessions transcend the confines of that narrow genre. Chopin first describes him by telling us mainly how he differs from others, but then she emphasizes his own distinctive traits. The story describes local life in bluntly realistic detail, and it ends with an emphasis on a stunning sense of paradox. However, Tonie's relatively uncomplex personality and diction prevent his final feelings from seeming scandalous. We feel more genuine interest in him than we ever feel in the somewhat superficial Claire. By the end of the story, Tonie has come full circle in his outlook on life. Nancy Ellis emphasizes the impact sacred music has on Tonie; its influence contrasts with the effects of nature here. As a laborer, Tonie has an unromantic relationship with his surroundings. Although the very ending of the story might at first seem fairly generic, the ending contrasts with—and thus emphasizes—the depths revealed by the rest of the narrative. In a way, the story mimics the sudden descent of the very storm that had transformed the actual place the tale describes (52–54). **Toth and Seyersted 1998:** This story is mentioned in several of Chopin's account books (140, 149, 167). **Taylor 1999:** This is one of the few works by Chopin in which the physical dangers of living in New Orleans are mentioned

(25). **Toth 1999c:** Chopin transcribed passages from a French story into her diary. That story later helped inspire the present tale (50–51). Chopin composed her narrative shortly after a hurricane destroyed Grand Isle (79; 139). The story was rejected by a national magazine which had asked Chopin for a submission; the editor found the plot somewhat stale (159). As elsewhere in Chopin's work, a young man exhibits emotional immaturity (194). **Gibbons 2000:** This story marks an important stage in Chopin's development since it is not only successful as a work of art but also because it shows her skill at depicting the social and economic panorama of her time and place. Her depiction of Tonie is complex, and her presentation of the mockingbird symbol is subtle. By the end of the story, Tonie has shown endurance and achieved a kind of transcendence. Although the ending is overly maudlin and the tone is elsewhere too emotional, the depiction of the virtuous, confident hero is a success, especially in its emphasis on ideal human equality. The story is implicitly radical in its social philosophy and thus foreshadows the unconventionality of *The Awakening*. Yet Chopin's focus in this work is on her characters, not on teaching a lesson. Some contemporary readers may have been less sympathetic to Tonie than Chopin seems to have been. Her own positive attitude toward him was perhaps influenced by her reading of contemporary social philosophers (xxxiii–xxxv). Readers familiar with this story would have enjoyed meeting Tonie again when he reappears in *The Awakening* (xlvi). **Knights 2000:** This work, one of Chopin's most compelling, was produced during a particularly creative period—the fall and summer of 1893 (xv). As elsewhere, she juxtaposes contrasting cultures (xxxvi). One significant line was deleted when the story was republished (xlv).

"At the 'Cadian Ball"

Written: 1892. First published: 1892. Included in *Bayou Folk* (1894).

Bobinôt is in love with Calixta, a Spanish beauty. He does not want to go to the ball one night because doing so only makes his work harder and makes the wait for the next weekend seem longer. However, he is afraid that if he does not go he might lose Calixta to someone like Alcée Laballière, whom all the women find irresistible.

Madame Laballière's goddaughter, Clarisse, has come to live with her. She is beautiful and has many callers. Alcée works hard in the rice field all day and comes home sweaty and dirty. One day he comes in and embraces Clarisse, whispering words of love to her, but she rejects him. The next day a cyclone ruins his rice field. Clarisse's heart melts for his troubles and she offers her sympathy to Alcée, but he ignores her.

A few nights later, as Clarisse kneels by her window to say her prayers, she sees Alcée riding off with his saddlebags packed. She runs out onto the veranda and asks his servant where Alcée is going. After stammering around, the servant finally tells her that Alcée has gone to the 'Cadian ball to have some fun and that he might be gone several weeks.

At the ball, Alcée dances with Calixta. They sit on the veranda, talking softly and laughing. A Negro appears and tells Alcée that someone wants to see him under the tree. Alcée refuses to go. Then a voice calls his name, and he turns and sees Clarisse. Alcée leaves Calixta alone and goes home with Clarisse, fearing that something has happened at home that needs his attention.

Bobinôt comes out on the veranda and sits with Calixta. She asks him if he still wants to marry her. He is ecstatic and asks for a kiss, but she tells him he must wait.

When Alcée questions Clarisse's reasons for coming to get him, she confesses that she came after him because she loves him. **(DR)**

***

Rankin 1932: The tale was published on October 22, 1892 (133). **Reilly 1942:** The ending of this story is effectively dramatic (131). Here as elsewhere a woman merely pretends to toy with a man's affections; finally, though, Clarisse safeguards Alcée from the flirty Calixta (132). **Fletcher 1966:** The story typifies Chopin's frequent focus on youthful love, especially as experienced by virginal but assertive and not especially thoughtful young women who follow impulses that nonetheless eventually lead to good results (130). **Seyersted 1969a:** One of Chopin's stories for adults, this work was published in 1892 in *Two Tales*, an Eastern magazine (54). Only one Yankee appears in this story, which is set in an otherwise purely Latin Louisiana. The narrative illustrates the mixture of old French language and new American ideas, but the old French influence predominates. Lower-class Cajuns are distinguished from their Creole superiors, who regard the Cajuns with disdain (76). When Clarisse takes a kind of masculine initiative in pursuing Alcée, she is nonetheless careful to show conventionally feminine shyness (76–77). The story exemplifies Chopin's tales of youthful romance—an important segment of her writings set in Louisiana (77). Clarisse exemplifies the kind of female protagonist who attempts to control males through erratic behavior (110). "The Storm" is a sequel to this story (164). **Arner 1970:** This early story exemplifies some of the pitfalls of local color writing—the kind of fiction Chopin eventually outgrew. The plot, characters, and ethics of the work are highly conventional; Calixta is, in a sense, even punished for violating standard expectations about a woman's behavior. Alcée's choice of Clarisse is also highly conventional, especially as a reflection of American misgivings about women and sex. Chopin, however, never really explores Alcée's motives deeply, and the story as a whole is fairly sentimental and superficial (2). **Peterson 1972:** Here a social event merely mentioned in an earlier story assumes symbolic importance (98). The effectively open-ended nature of this story's conclusion made the later sequel possible. Chopin emphasizes the distinctions, rather than the similarities, among the four major characters. Chopin's use of natural imagery when describing Clarisse seems intentional but also somewhat clumsy. The two major settings are effectively contrasted (117–18). The final linkings are non-sensual, and although the ball ends, the narrative is left in cunning suspense. The story concludes with an emphasis on marriage, but in this case nothing is really resolved. This story is one of Chopin's finest (118–20). **Rocks 1972:** Here as elsewhere Chopin describes the passionate nature of courtship in Louisiana (118). **Seyersted 1974:** The independent-minded Clarisse in this story contrasts with the more compliant heroine of "A Visit to Avoyelles," written not long afterwards (13). **Arner 1975:** Here as elsewhere, the somewhat crude settings and characters contrast with an intriguing theme (56). Although "The Storm" is an explicit "sequel" to this work, Chopin probably did not plan such a sequel at the time she composed the first story (133–34). **Skaggs 1975:** Here Chopin presents the male impulse to dominate and seek to own women as a trait of both the lower as well as the upper classes. Although each main male character marries a woman who is not entirely happy to be his wife, each man is thrilled to have won a possession the other male coveted (279–81). **Solomon 1976:** The twin sets of couples might never have been formed if Clarisse had not shown such independent initiative. The same characters later appear in "The Storm" (xv). **Bonner 1977:** Here as elsewhere, *Bayou Folk* reveals Chopin's talent for creating rich characters and for presenting, rather than announcing, their traits (6). This is one of only three stories in *Bayou Folk* in which the author comments (7). The story shows the complications and results of love (10). The story illustrates the social and ethnic hierarchy of Louisiana (12). It is valuable in part because of its vibrant people and varied events (13). **Wolff 1978:** As elsewhere, Chopin deals with the instability of human experience (126). **Petry 1979:** Here as in other local color fiction, outsiders (in this case the railroad workers) often disrupt local customs (115). **Lattin 1980:** This story shares characters not only with "The Storm" (20) but also with "Loka," "Ozème's Holiday," and "In and Out of Old Nachitoches" (24–25). Its links to "The Storm" are often subtle and significant (26–28). **Dyer 1980–81:** This is one of many stories by Chopin in which a female is aroused by contact with a male (10–11). However, it is also one of various stories in which Chopin reveals a significant interest in the strong yearnings of males (15). **Dyer 1981a:** As elsewhere, Chopin uses repeating male professional characters, thus adding depth and continuity to her fiction (54). **Rogers 1983:** Like George Sand, Chopin focuses (in this tale) on a woman's complex sexuality (34). **Gilbert 1984:** This story reveals the importance of social status (16). **Grover 1984:** This story illustrates the tendency of many of Chopin's characters, whatever their ethnic background, to engage in joyous celebration (30). This story most effectively depicts the social distinctions that existed between Creoles and Cajuns (31). **Dyer 1985:** As elsewhere, Chopin relies on readers' stereotypes about unconventional characters in order to deal with topics she might not have been able to depict otherwise (80–81). **Skaggs 1985:** Like "Désireés's Baby," another of her most successful stories, this tale explores men's instinct to possess women. The story foreshadows both "The Storm" and *The Awakening*: Alcée here resembles Léonce in the novel. Each couple in the story seems both appropriately and inappropriately matched (22–25). **Ewell 1986:** This may be Chopin's most skillful blending of the topics of gender, power, and class. The evocative setting provides a suitable backdrop to the action, and even minor characters are effectively employed. Yet the story best depicts the impact of society on human minds and motives, leading to an intriguingly unstable resolution. The women seem particularly fettered by social pressures (even when they appear to exercise power over men), while a lower-class male such as Bobinôt must contend with social handicaps of his own. The final image of gunfire gives the story an ambiguous, foreboding conclusion (76–79). **Gaudet 1986:** The geographical setting of this story is quite precise and implies Cajun characters (50). **Elfenbein 1989:** Here as elsewhere Chopin shows how women suffer when they lack power, and she also depicts women of color who are relevant to her depiction of women in *The Awakening* (117–19). Calixta seems enticing because she seems racially exotic, but the fact that women such as Calixta must present themselves in certain ways in order to attract men suggests that Chopin may be criticizing the very racial stereotypes she is presenting (121). In stories such as this, which feature women of color, Chopin could deal more explicitly with topics she treated more cautiously when writing about white females. The women of color in these tales tend to be less simple characters than the white women, but they suffer more obvious mistreatment. Stories such as this one anticipate the racial dynamics depicted in *The Awakening* (126). Here as in "The Storm," Chopin associates feminine sexual passion with a woman already tainted by association with it, partly because of her behavior at the intriguingly-named place of Assumption. The fact that she is considered an outsider also makes her conduct seem less shocking, at least among the Cajun men (135). Although both male protagonists feel triumphant at the end of the story, their triumphs are illusory, as "The Storm" will show. The present story illustrates the force of sexual, racial, and class-based social influences, especially their ability to join men and women who have little else in common. Ironically, the two women share important traits, just as the two men do. Robert

Arner's reading of this work fails to perceive the story's possible satire of the social prejudices it describes (135–38). **Inge 1989:** This is one of the most successful examples of Chopin's skill at depicting a specific locale and its unique population, but the story's characters and ideas seem less complex than in some of her other works (108). **Papke 1990:** The main characters here reappear in "The Storm" (175). **Toth 1990a:** The story accurately reflects childhood life in Cloutierville (152) as well as the emphasis there on dancing (153). The seductive Alcée in this tale closely resembles a man from Cloutierville with whom the widowed Chopin became involved (169–70). The destructive storm in the story had a real-life precedent, and Chopin uses the tale to speculate imaginatively about the man with whom she was involved. Calixta, too, was closely modeled on a person from Cloutierville, and that woman's husband also resembled Bobinôt in the tale (211–13). This story was placed with four others on adult dilemmas at the end of *Bayou Folk* (224). Male characters in this story resemble some in the later tale "Ti Démon" (362). **Toth 1990b:** The efforts of an early scholar helped keep this story available during the first half of the twentieth century (291). **Brown 1991:** Like *The Awakening*, this story reflects the conflicts that could exist among Creoles and Cajuns, but by the end of the tale such tensions are resolved (130). **Robinson 1992:** This story is typical of Chopin's work in presenting Cajuns—especially Cajun females—as more free-spirited than their Creole counterparts. The story is one of Chopin's best presentations of the interaction of the two cultures. Here as elsewhere in her work, a key event occurs at midnight (xiii). Chopin tends to present Cajuns as industrious, generous, and less than brilliant, although Calixta is more lively and more socially prominent because of her partly Spanish ancestry (xiii–xiv). Clarisse, though, shows (even in the way she speaks) that she considers herself naturally superior to Calixta. The final gunshots bring a literal and figurative end to a period of carnivalesque freedom, and class customs reassert themselves. Clarisse is the least likeable of the major characters but enjoys the most authority, and her decision provides the momentum of the plot and keeps all three characters from making social missteps. Clarisse both chances the most and changes the most (xiv). Her victory, though, seems unmerited, and later (in "The Storm") it is Calixta who finally wins (xix). **Larsson 1993:** This tale is the precursor to a later story, "The Storm" (2: 539–40). **Shurbutt 1993:** This is one of various stories in which Chopin shows an unconventional female attempting to attain unconventional fulfillment (15; 21). **Cutter 1994:** Here as in other early stories, Chopin describes women whose efforts to express opposition are promptly silenced or suppressed (17). Even the strong women described here sometimes have trouble expressing themselves, especially about erotic matters (19–20). **Ewell 1994:** This is one of many stories by Chopin that show the dangers of ignoring the sexual or sensual aspects of human nature (168). **Koloski 1994:** A 1921 anthology of short fiction emphasized such matters as the story's sophisticated design, its straightforward presentation and balanced groupings of characters, its emphasis on local lan-

guage, its variety of emotions, its use of point of view, and its subtle ending (20). The story is included in soft-cover collections of Chopin's fiction
published in 1976, 1979, 1984, and 1992 (27). **Sempreora 1994:** The conventional role assigned to Calixta in this story is reversed in "The Storm" (88–
89). In the present tale Alcée is Calixta's superior, both sexually and economically (89), and in the end she seems undercut by his rejection of her
(90). **Toth 1994:** Alcée is based on a married man with whom Chopin had
an affair (10). **Baxter 1996:** The main characters are Acadians (7). Calixta
may resemble the woman who superseded Chopin in an affair with a married man (233). The story exemplifies Chopin's talent as a local color
writer (239) and lends itself to a creative writing exercise for students
(240). It was included in a collection that was well received by contemporary readers (241) and can be studied by evaluating the characters' social
status (247). **Bender 1996:** In this story, Chopin alters the usual Darwinian
emphasis on males as the dominant sex; she makes Clarisse the jealous,
dominant figure and shows how even Calixta takes the initiative in dealing with Bobinôt (107–8). **Berkove 1996:** The story shows the unfortunate
consequences of giving in to passion (185). All the main characters, except
Bobinôt, are passionate (185–86). Perhaps Alcée is just as imperceptive
about love as Bobinôt is (187–88). In this tale as in "The Storm," Chopin is
less sympathetic to passion than she seems; instead, she critiques
immorality from an ethical point of view. Thus the morality implied by
this story is more traditional than it seems at first (188). **Carr 1996:** Here as
elsewhere Chopin presents Cajun males in a condescending fashion (53–
54). **Koloski 1996:** The central characters of this story are among the most
vivid in the literature of Chopin's era (xiii). The story reflects a stoicism
prized by the Creoles (15) and is one of the best tales in *Bayou Folk*. Its
setting resembles that of "A Night in Acadie" and its plot resembles that
of "A No-Account Creole" and "Ma'ame Pélagie." Calixta's heritage is
partly Cuban (but not partly African-American). Ethnic background and
social status are tightly linked in this narrative, and in the end the
threatened social disturbance gives way to a renewed balance (20–22; 88).
This story establishes motifs important for subsequent narratives in *Bayou
Folk* (51) and reflects Chopin's interest in the human voice (55). It both
resembles and radically differs from its sequel, "The Storm," which ends
more uncertainly and stresses the power of nature more than the
pressures of society. The first tale reflects its era, but the sequel signals a
new outlook (75–77). Issues of class enrich rather than damage this story,
which was the first piece of Chopin's fiction included in an anthology (84).
A reading of this story is crucial to a proper understanding of "The Storm"
(88). **Beer 1997:** The apparent conclusion of this story is subverted by its
sequel, "The Storm." Such subversiveness is typical of Chopin's fiction.
Although the marriages that occur at the end of the present tale seem
economically fore-ordained, the resolution of this story leaves much
unresolved (59–60). **Toth and Seyersted 1998:** Alcée resembles a man
Chopin knew (126). This story is mentioned in several of Chopin's account

books (139, 149, 157). **Green 1999:** This is one of several stories by Chopin that have attracted great attention from critics (14). **Koloski 1999:** This is one of the best tales in *Bayou Folk*, although the follow-up tale ("The Storm") is even better. In the present story Chopin places marriage in a communal context, showing how social divisions influence individual lives. In the end, however, threatened social instability is suppressed (xiv). **McCullough 1999:** Clarisse responds with reserve when Alcée first shows his passion (318). **Toth 1999a:** Alcée in this tale resembles a man with whom Chopin herself was involved, but the latter figure may have been less important to Chopin's life than Toth had earlier assumed (4). **Toth 1999b:** As Bernard Koloski has demonstrated, this was one of eight stories by Chopin that were frequently republished in the twentieth century (46). **Toth 1999b:** This is one of the relatively few stories by Chopin that focus on sexuality or passion (49). **Toth 1999c:** This story alludes to child-care arrangements common in Cloutierville (89), and it also shows how romantic meetings were possible there (96). Alcée resembles a man with whom the widowed Chopin became involved (97), and in fact most of the major characters resemble persons from Cloutierville, including possibly Chopin herself (142–44). As in some of her other stories, men here indulge in passionate romance (151). **Knights 2000:** The story creatively relies on a particular academic's accounts of Acadian festivities (xxxv). Here as elsewhere Chopin depicts a diversity of cultures and languages while also showing how they mix and change (xxxvi). Her revisions of the first version of the tale make the work seem slightly less informal (xlvi).

"Athénaïse"

Written: 1895. First Published: 1896. Included in *A Night in Acadie* (1897).

An unnamed narrator tells the story of Athénaïse, the very young, strong-willed bride of Cazeau, who leaves their home one morning to visit her parents but does not return for three days. After receiving no word during all this time, Cazeau saddles his horse and rides to her parents' home some ten miles away. Upon arriving he discovers that Athénaïse has no intention of returning to him.

Athénaïse's brother asks her why she does not want to go home. She can think of not one reason, except that she does not like being married. Cazeau is a good man who loves her and treats her with kindness. Cazeau enters the room and simply asks her if she is ready to go home. She gathers her belongings, puts on her riding skirt, and goes home with Cazeau.

Feeling trapped, Athénaïse concocts with her brother a plan for her "escape." A few mornings later, Cazeau awakens and finds Athénaïse gone. He writes a letter telling her that he does not want her in his house again unless it is of her own free will.

Her destination is New Orleans. After a four-week stay in the city, where she meets and confides in a bachelor named Gouvernail who is obviously attracted to her, Athénaïse grows homesick. She misses her mother; she misses her home; and most of all, she misses her husband. When she discovers that she is pregnant with Cazeau's child, she happily writes him a letter and tells him that she is coming home. He walks out of the house to meet her, they embrace, and for the first time ever she returns his kiss. **(DR)**

***

Anonymous 1897 [*Post-Dispatch*]: This story illustrates Chopin's knowledge of female psychology (47–48). **Pattee 1923:** The story illustrates Chopin's talent for illuminating aspects of general human character and feelings; Athénaïse's emotions and reactions are ones we can imagine ourselves sharing (326). **Rankin 1932:** The story embodies Chopin's own sense of liberty and daring. Her presentation of Gouvernail is often intriguing, but while we puzzle over her comments about him the narrative proceeds to an ending that offers an impressive glimpse into the feisty heroine's innermost being (162–63). **Reilly 1937:** Here as elsewhere, motherhood is an important theme in Chopin's fiction. Emotion, artistry, and acute psychological perceptiveness combine with insightful character-depiction and a fitting, subtly moving conclusion to make this tale a small masterwork (73). **Reilly 1942:** The ending of this tale is skillfully affecting and touching and seems as genuine as the motherly feelings it describes (131). Here as in some of her other best works, Chopin focuses on the feelings natural to mothers. No other story by Chopin is narrated more attractively or with keener understanding than this work; it is surpassed only by "Désirée's Baby" (135). **Bush 1957:** In its focus on the psychology of a wife, this story foreshadows *The Awakening* (257). Gouvernail provides an urban substitute for Athénaïse's brother, but the older man is also wiser (258–59). Presumably Athénaïse was more deeply attached to Cazeau than she had known, and her pregnancy makes her affection clear to her. The story is lengthy and complex because the characters are richly drawn and undergo significant development. They are believable persons, and their tensions are persuasively drawn; Gouvernail is the one truly pathetic person. This work may be Chopin's finest piece of short fiction and is clearly superior to "Désirée's Baby" in skill and insight (259–60). **Fletcher 1966:** As in other tales, Chopin here emphasizes the powerful emotions aroused by motherhood (128). The candor with which this story deals with pregnancy was unusual for its day (130). **Arms 1967:** One of the five most successful tales included in *A Night in Acadie*, this work takes a more explicit approach to unusual attitudes toward sex than do the majority of tales from *Bayou Folk*. The tone of this story is non-moralistic, its view of truth is complex, and it shares certain themes with *The Awakening* (223–24). **Zlotnick 1968:** This is one of many stories in which Chopin implies ambivalent, unconventional responses to marriage (2). Here as elsewhere Chopin suggests that errors are a necessary price of freedom (4). **Seyersted 1969a:** Chopin took a deep interest in this tale, which deals with issues basic to feminine life, such as the impact of marriage and family and the possibility of freedom. Athénaïse typifies the kind of girl who follows tradition in marrying, then discovers that she prefers being single (112). Finally, however, she seems to overcome her focus on herself, at least in her new attitude toward children (113). Yet the story does imply (particularly through its symbolism) profound misgivings about the limits women face (113). Thus Cazeau's name seems to suggest the confinement of a house (or *casa*), while his dogs symbolize his patriarchal power. The heroine's name may suggest the goddess Athena, who patronized household tasks, and she is also likened to a slave. Gabe may suggest the Archangel Gabriel, who announced the Virgin Mary's pregnancy, while the oak-tree may imply the ancient feminine life-giving roles of being married and giving birth. The story is one of Chopin's most significant; it surpasses even "The Story of an Hour" in its thoughtful presentation of the existence of women (114). The story exemplifies the organic, artful artlessness of her Chopin's fiction; each detail counts, yet the characters reveal themselves gradually during the course of a coherent plot that moves with enough leisure to make the characters' minds seem convincingly realistic (130–31). The story opens and closes with similar settings and sounds, yet these resemblances underscore Cazeau's changed mood: both he and his wife have altered during the intervening narrative. Cazeau becomes increasingly humble while Athénaïse becomes increasingly mature. Chopin's presentation of the key scene of revelation is efficiently understated, while all the main characters are complexly and subtly described, often through small but significant details (131). Ultimately, Athénaïse seems better able to fit into her society than is Edna in *The Awakening* (149), and in that novel as in this story, Chopin uses spurs to symbolize patriarchal power (160). "Athénaïse" contains an implied anger towards men that is absent from a later story, "The Storm" (169). Spur imagery is used differently in this story than in the later "Charlie" (183). Daniel Rankin particularly valued the realism, liberty, innovation, and courage Chopin revealed in writing stories such as "Athénaïse" (188). This work is one of her most enduring achievements (199). Its shrimp imagery may carry sexual overtones (223). **Seyersted 1969b:** This story typifies the confident writing Chopin did following the success of *Bayou Folk*. Like many works from this period, it depicts a strong woman in the process of self-discovery. Although the work ends on a positive note, it nonetheless subtly satirizes the restraints women faced. Athénaïse becomes associated with the ever-branching tree of life (27). **Berthoff 1970:** This is one of the more profound stories in *A Night in Acadie* and anticipates the concerns of *The Awakening* (xvii). **Leary 1970a:** This is one of Chopin's best studies of feminine self-assertion. It scrutinizes marriage more carefully than any of her previous works had done. Although patriarchal conditions dictate the heroine's eventual surrender, the story does not judge the value of her quest for independence (x). **Leary 1970b:** This is one of Chopin's two best and most detailed tales (140). The story is less concerned with self-assertion than with self-realization (140). **Leary 1971:** This is clearly one of Chopin's best studies of the struggle of a youthful female to avoid being treated as a mere object. Chopin's exploration of matrimony here is fuller than any she had previously tried to offer. Although Athénaïse's rebellion is short-lived and not especially bold, her decision to go back to her husband is not an indictment of her yearning for freedom; instead, it is merely an indication of how difficult it is to escape the influence of patriarchal power (167). **Potter 1971:** This is one of five tales from *A Night in Acadie* in which slavery is a central focus. Here Cazeau is able to use his memory of the inhumanity of slavery as an impetus to give his wife her freedom (52). **Peterson 1972:** This very fine work was composed around the same time Chopin turned out less accomplished pieces (10). The treatment of the complexities of marriage is richer here than in some of Chopin's early writings (12). Aside from *The Awakening*, this story presents Chopin's best explorations of human psychology, which is less important to the work than the events the tale describes. Athénaïse rejects Cazeau less than she rejects marriage as an institution, just as Black Gabe rejected slavery rather than a cruel master. Her brother is a friendly male but poses no sexual threat; he makes no demands and does not intrude upon her sense of self. Marriage seems less a romantic attachment than an economic bond, and both lack of money and social prejudice prevent Athénaïse from achieving the independence she seeks. By embracing conventional maternity so wholly, Athénaïse trades one fantasy for another; in each case she responds to a deep-rooted human desire. The unusual tale ends on a fairly commonplace but objective note. Like other works by Chopin, this one emphasizes the tension between individual desire and an inflexible society or indifferent universe (155–62). Although Chopin herself never professed feminism, some of her works (such as this tale) are obviously relevant to feminist concerns (272). **Rocks 1972:** Here as elsewhere Chopin shows that people often freely choose not to alter their circumstances; they elect to renounce other options, but the choice is theirs and no decision is externally imposed (118). The story suggests the problems that result when marriage is not a free choice. As elsewhere, Chopin shows the complexities but also the rewards of marriage as well as its superiority to remaining single (118). **Bender 1974:** Subtle incestuous undercurrents seem present in the relation between Athénaïse and her brother. Cazeau's name, meanwhile, suggests his function as head of the household, and references to his spurs imply his dominance of his wife. Paradoxically, it is Athénaïse's taste of freedom and her exposure to a less ardent courtship that help make her realize her love for Cazeau, although her return is not Chopin's usual way of resolving the problems marriage often poses for women in her fiction (262–64). **Seyersted 1974:** Like other heroines Chopin created, Athénaïse retreats from unconventional self-assertion (14). **Arner 1975:** Here as in "Loka," a woman is reintegrated into society by her love of a child (55). The story foreshadows *The Awakening* in its depiction of a dissatisfied wife, its imagery of music, and its subtle characterization. Even critics who have praised the tale have failed to do it full justice. Both Cazeau and his wife eventually achieve more mature attitudes toward marriage (69–72). **Skaggs 1975:** Chopin here rather boldly equates the possessiveness of men to the possessiveness of slaveholders (282–83). **Ladenson 1976:** Athénaïse yearns for freedom but is somewhat hampered by her middle-class status. Her asexual friendship with Gouvernail fits a pattern found in other Chopin stories, since such friendships enhanced a woman's autonomy because of their flexibility. Athénaïse is aided by various persons to whom she has no sexual ties. Her final return may be ironic, since so much of the story has emphasized her struggle for freedom. Perhaps Chopin felt inhibited about making the heroine too independent (26–27). **Solomon 1976:** This is one of several tales by Chopin depicting women at different points of the life cycle (xvi). The title character's sojourn in the city helps her realize the limitations of urban life for a single woman (xvii). **Webb 1976:** This is one of various works by Chopin that center around movements into and away from New Orleans (6). The story moves from rural Louisiana, then to the city, and then back. In the city, Gouvernail functions much as Monteclin had earlier, and his perceptions help foreshadow the conclusion (10). Athénaïse's sudden transformation when she learns she is pregnant seems a bit improbable. In the same way that her brother had helped her to move to the city, Gouvernail helps her return home. Her encounter with her husband at the end of the story reverses the kinds of encounters they had experienced in the beginning. Similarities between the opening and closing scenes emphasize how much has changed in the interim. Both Athénaïse's somewhat improbable brother and her friend Gouvernail are disappointed. If the first seems too active, the second seems perhaps too passive. Latter-day readers may find the story unsatisfying and unbelievable, but in any case the work illustrates the typical cyclical structure of Chopin's fiction (11). **Lattin 1978:** Here as elsewhere, when Chopin presents pregnancy and/or motherhood as a positive experience, the experience is usually limited (1–2). The story shows how pregnancy could help a woman embrace her sexual nature (4). **Wolff 1978:** This is one of many stories by Chopin dealing with the instability of human experience (126). **Taylor 1979:** This was one of several tales Chopin had difficulty publishing (viii). It is one of several of her stories that subtly suggest the shortcomings of Catholicism (x) and is also one in which the experience of blacks plays an important thematic role (xiii–xiv). Moreover, it is one of several tales that emphasize the power of maternity (xvi). **Wolff 1979:** This story, possibly the best in Chopin's second collection, exemplifies Chopin's ethical neutrality as well as her skill at delineating complicated feelings and contexts. The oak tree is a complex symbol, and there are even slight hints of incestuous feelings in Athénaïse's relations with her brother. After becoming pregnant, however, she enters a new stage of sexual and emotional maturity (219–20). **Lattin 1980:** Our knowledge of Gouvernail in this story helps us understand his behavior in Chopin's other fiction—and vice versa (31–35). **Dyer 1980–81:** This is one of many stories by Chopin in which a female is aroused by contact with a male (10–11). However, readers who know only this work and a few other of Chopin's more famous writings may fail to realize her significant interest in *male* (not simply female) passions (15). **Baym 1981:** Here as in other stories, Chopin depicts rural Creoles who nonetheless possess considerable cultural and behavioral complexity (xx). In this tale as elsewhere, Chopin inserts a character from the city to emphasize (through contrast) the features of rural culture (xxi), and she adapts the objective narrative style of Maupassant to a society whose ethics are basically healthy even as she also manages to communicate her own regard for her characters (xxv). The title character is typical of other persons in Chopin's fiction who do not ponder or agonize over their sometimes paradoxical behavior (xxv–xxvi). **Dyer 1981a:** Readers who recall this story will more fully appreciate the appearance of Gouvernail in *The Awakening* (47; 49–51; 54). **Dyer 1981b:** Chopin's use of night imagery here is especially subtle and complex (222). Here as in "A Respectable Woman," Gouvernail plays a part in a story focusing on marital discord (223). Night imagery in this tale implies primal changes taking place in the title character, especially since the imagery is associated with earthiness and fecundity. The imagery is nearly archetypal and implies in the depths of the heroine's emotions, especially her sexual yearnings. The night imagery suggests meanings Chopin could not have conveyed effectively through open statement (223–24). Darkness symbolizes the title character's deepest desires (225). **Jones 1981:** This story clearly links the oppression of women and the oppression of slaves. Like Cazeau, even the somewhat androgynous Gouvernail feels possessive toward Athénaïse, but both men accept her desire for freedom. The pregnancy seems a contrived means of resolving the plot; important themes are not well integrated; and the conclusion may imply that Athénaïse will be imprisoned by motherhood (149–50). Here as in *The Awakening*, images of spurs (159) and of chained dogs (182) suggest male domination (159), and both works also link the oppression of women to slavery (173). **Davis 1982:** Like many of Chopin's stories, this one emphasizes the primal force of human emotions, which both separate and then reunite the married pair. Chopin's skill in delineating her characters makes the ending of this tale seem plausible (65). **Fluck 1982:** This was one of the various unconventional, innovative stories by Chopin that were often turned down for publication (163). **Lattin 1982:** As elsewhere, Chopin shows how change can simultaneously involve loss, maturation, and self-discovery (227). **Bonner 1983b:** The story explores prohibited desire (144). **Lohafer 1983:** Although this story has been highly praised, it has received few interpretations, and most readers are unfamiliar with it (103–4). One important theme is imperfect self-understanding and growing self-awareness. Athénaïse's mother is meek and protective, while the girl's brother is immature and possessive. Athénaïse herself is immature until she realizes she is pregnant; thereafter, her return to Cazeau is actually her achievement of womanhood (115–18). Early (male) critics emphasized Chopin's natural literary gifts rather than her craft, but her literary importance was recognized by the mid-twentieth century, and by the mid-fifties criticism of her work had begun to mature. In later decades some critics (but not all) began to appreciate her stories, especially this one, which they often praised for its complexity. Its meaning has always seemed clear, but its success has been debated. If one considers the work closely, it has much to suggest about the short story form (118–25). Through carefully subtle phrasing, the opening sentences help establish not only the tone of the story but also its central plot and psychological implications. Cazeau reveals his affection for Athénaïse despite his pretended indifference, and throughout the story both he and she mature (125–27). The story depicts a variety of geographical, psychological, and sociological changes for Athénaïse (127–29). Although the turning point in the story seems abrupt, it has been carefully foreshadowed. The story shows that womanhood develops according to a natural rhythm, not an arbitrary schedule or intellectual decision. The conclusion of the tale both resolves and echoes the opening (129–30). Like Athénaïse, Cazeau also matures as the work proceeds, and Chopin implies this process through subtle uses of language. The psychological development of the two main characters is complementary and balanced: by moving in opposite mental directions, they eventually converge. This story shows Chopin's mastery of the genre (130–32). Her lyric tale, like many other works of American fiction, juxtaposes social expectations with individual evolution (133). **Rogers 1983:** Here as elsewhere, Chopin, like George Sand, depicts the complexities of marriage (32). As this story illustrates, Chopin, more than George Sand, emphasizes maternity in her fiction (36–37). The traits and even the name of the heroine of this tale resemble those of a character created by Sand (41). **Burchard 1984:** Although at first the heroine of this story seems the opposite of the main character of "Regret," both women have ambivalent feelings about their proper roles. The husband here, like most of Chopin's male characters, is not a bad man. From start to finish (but especially at the end), Chopin seems unsympathetic to Athénaïse's allegedly selfish independence—an independence which is, in any case, less her own creation than the result of her brother's schemes (40–41). **Gilbert 1984:** Here as elsewhere Chopin interrogates marriage (16). **Stein 1984:** Here as elsewhere, Chopin presents a wife who ultimately is happy to submit to her husband (176). Because

Athénaïse seems so lacking at first in self-knowledge, it seems unlikely that Chopin is using this tale to protest against marriage itself (180). Athénaïse is emotionally and sexually naive, mercurial in her reactions, and inclined to avoid reality (180–81). Her escape to New Orleans seems unreasonable, juvenile, and somewhat tawdry, especially after she becomes involved with the amoral, sardonic Gouvernail. A relationship with him would handicap her life, but fortunately she achieves maturity and self-awareness through her pregnancy (181). By retracing her steps with her brother she symbolically renounces his influence. Luckily her husband displays an adult's wisdom and calm, and he greets her with gentle and genuine affection (182–83). Athénaïse's ill-defined pursuit of abstract liberty eventually gives way to a recognition that marriage (for her, at least) is the best means to happiness (183–84). **McMahan 1985:** Here as elsewhere Chopin depicts a woman who marries after not having given the matter much thought (32). Although Athénaïse's sudden change at the end of the story might at first seem incredible, it makes sense once we realize that the pregnancy allows her to come to terms with her sexuality, which she had earlier found distasteful because of her ignorance (32–33). **Newman 1986:** As in many of Chopin's tales, the view of marriage offered here seems to conflict with views implied by some of her other stories (152). Here as elsewhere, Chopin juxtaposes reality with simplistic fantasies of freedom. Athénaïse, her husband, and other characters may all be operating under (conflicting) romantic illusions, and Chopin seems to treat both them and their fantasies with healthy irony (159). **Rowe 1985:** The story may have bothered its first readers because Chopin did not express disapproval of her heroines (231). **Skaggs 1985:** This is one of several stories by Chopin that explore romance, often of an odd variety (32). Its heroine resembles Edna in *The Awakening*. Although Athénaïse eventually seems reconciled by motherhood to her role as a wife, she thereby sacrifices her freedom (36–38). **Ewell 1986:** This excellent tale foreshadows *The Awakening* in its subtlety of character and theme while also raising many troubling questions about marriage. The heroine's husband and suitor both offer her choices she is at first unprepared to make, and at first she seems naive about both marriage and freedom. Gouvernail is not as different from Cazeau as Athénaïse seems to think. Her pregnancy helps give her a maturer view of both her husband and herself, enhancing both her authority and her sensuality. In its setting, tone, ideas, and especially in its complex characterization, this is an effective story (108–12) that explores the links between sensuality (131; 183), motherhood (179), and selfhood. **Lattin 1988:** A reading of this story can be useful in teaching *The Awakening*, since the two works can be compared and contrasted in characters, events, and themes, particularly the theme of motherhood. Athénaïse's break with her husband is less radical than Edna's; Athénaïse needs company, whereas Edna is comfortable alone; Athénaïse welcomes pregnancy, while Edna feels partly trapped by her children (40–44). Gouvernail appears in both works, thus illustrating Chopin's wider fictional world, and his personality in the story is relevant to his conduct in the novel, particularly to his insight into Edna's character (44–46). **Martin 1988a:** This is one of various stories in which Chopin depicts a passionate woman without censuring or penalizing her in order to court the approval of readers (6). **Papke 1988:** This story offers a more affirmative view of motherhood than Chopin provides elsewhere (76). **Skaggs 1988:** In stories such as this, Chopin deals with some of the most profound and most widely shared issues of human life (80). **Toth 1988a:** Here as elsewhere, Chopin shows her awareness of the complex experience of motherhood (56). **Inge 1989:** This is one of Chopin's best stories, particularly in its vivid and efficient depiction of its heroine's thinking. Athénaïse seems sexually inexperienced, but she also seems to regard marriage and sex as violations of her personal identity. Gouvernail believes a real marriage requires reciprocal affection and consent—a realization Cazeau eventually shares when he learns not to treat Athénaïse as property. Because Cazeau is one of Chopin's most fully-rounded characters, readers can wish both him and Athénaïse well as each matures. Unlike other heroines Chopin depicted, Athénaïse eventually enjoys both erotic and social happiness, and she also develops ethically. In this superbly skillful story, Chopin suggests that a marriage grounded in mutual love and respect can help both parties enjoy freedom and growth (102). **Taylor 1989:** Although this work foreshadows *The Awakening*, it is less radical than the novel (179). Like the novel, this story explores the difficulties of marriage as a social form, just as it also concedes the significance of biology in affecting women's lives. Cazeau is one of Chopin's least appealing males and is often compared to a slave-owner. Although Athénaïse's brother seems to support her interest in freedom, he is also a representative of male control. Athénaïse regards herself as a commodity and is continually treated as one; she repeatedly lets men take the initiative. Even Gouvernail's name suggests the possibility that *he* might one day control her. Her freedom amounts to little more than limited resistance (180–82). The story, unlike *The Awakening*, ends happily, and other women are less important than in the novel (182–83). **Papke 1990:** Chopin here describes maternal fortitude and the transforming power of pregnancy, although she also deals with the sacrifices both entail (64–65). **Toth 1990a:** The title character carries the same name as one of Chopin's feminine ancestors (30; 274). The story reflects Chopin's disdain for parrots (48) as well as her complex attitudes toward being a mother (128). This was one of only several stories by Chopin published in the prominent magazine *The Atlantic* (235; 274). The tale had germinated for a number of years and took longer than usual to compose. Its plot partly resembles the life of Chopin's grandmother, especially in its emphasis on a frustrated marriage. The story was well received by the editors of *The Atlantic*, who added a subtitle that limited the critical resonance of the narrative. Gouvernail voices liberal ideas that circulated in Chopin's own circle (274–75). This tale later appeared in *A Night in Acadie*, in which all the stories are set in Louisiana. One reviewer had ambivalent reactions to the story but generally praised it, while a friend of Chopin offered an interpretation perhaps influenced by his own discussions with her (298–301). Another reviewer hailed the story's grasp of feminine psychology (303). One male reader particularly praised this tale (328). **Vanlandingham 1990:** This story was rejected by the editor of a major national journal (161). **Brown 1991:** As in other works, Chopin here depicts a woman stunted by the cultural expectations of her ethnic group (120–21). The conflict between husband and wife is partly a conflict of ethnic identities, and in some ways the story is even more provocative than *The Awakening*, especially in the way it associates pregnancy with sexual stimulation. Chopin shows, however, that Creole and Arcadian cultures, despite their other differences, share similarly confining views of married women (128–30). **Guidici 1991:** As elsewhere in Chopin, a change of place gives a woman new options and greater power, if only temporarily (27), and pregnancy gives a woman new power. In this case it provides a sense of autonomous creativity, so that Athénaïse is now an equal rather than wholly subservient (29). As in other stories by Chopin, disruption of a marriage enhances the wife's power (30). **Toth 1992:** This story took longer to compose than almost any other by Chopin, perhaps because it reflected details of the life of a female relative. Ironically, Athénaïse eventually is trapped (by motherhood) in a marriage she did not desire (18–19). Like other stories Chopin published in *The Atlantic*, this one shows an oppressed person submitting to oppression (19–20). The story perhaps shows how women are betrayed by their own bodies, as Chopin's relative had been (20–21). In this story as in others, the experiences of the main female may be relevant to the experiences of Chopin's married mother (21–22). Here as elsewhere Chopin shows a woman whose isolation makes freedom possible, if only temporarily (23). Here, unlike in some of her earlier fiction, Chopin seems less optimistic about the prospects for feminine independence (24). This is the final story she composed that seems to reflect the experiences of her forebears (25). **Bryan 1993:** Here as in other stories by Chopin, New Orleans is the setting for the most complicated phase of a character's development. Thus the city is associated with transformation, but Chopin's emphasis is usually on internal developments (55). Athénaïse's response to motherhood is precisely the opposite of Edna's in *The Awakening*, although neither character seems finally content with life in New Orleans (60–62). **Dyer 1993:** Gouvernail's personality in this story helps us appreciate the significance of his appearance in *The Awakening* (68–69). **Larsson 1993:** This story demonstrates that Chopin did see possibilities for growth and fulfillment in marriage if the relationship was rooted in mutuality. Tone and characterization are both delicately poised in this tale (2: 539). **Shurbutt 1993:** This is one of various stories in which Chopin explores the complex interactions of marriage and sexuality (17–19). **Cutter 1994:** Although Athénaïse at first resists male domination, her resistance is mocked or ignored, and eventually she submits. Nevertheless, the story ends on a note of literal and figurative disturbance (21–22). **Ewell 1994:** Here as elsewhere Chopin explores how women respond to social convention—an exploration partly prompted, it seems, by her own experiences as a middle-aged female (169). **Goodwyn 1994:** This story illustrates the ways Chopin often uses narrative structure to subvert the conventional values a tale seems to affirm (4). The interior story of black Gabe complicates and undercuts the apparently traditional values of the surrounding tale (6–7). This is one of various narratives in which Chopin shows the human tragedy involved in enforcing stereotypes (11). **Koloski 1994:** This story was included in an anthology of Southern fiction published in 1989 and in one devoted to Louisiana fiction published the following year. The second collection particularly praises this work as one of Chopin's best (25). The story is included in soft-cover collections of Chopin's fiction published in 1970, 1976, and 1981 (27). **Sempreora 1994:** The emphasis here on multiple perspectives may have been partly inspired by Chopin's recent translations of some short stories by Maupassant in which such an emphasis was lacking (87–88). **Walker 1994:** One early critic objected to the sensuality of this tale (12). **Juneja 1995:** Here as elsewhere, Chopin depicts a woman who deliberately challenges custom. Even her final decision is freely chosen (118). **Bender 1996:** Like other persons of color in Chopin's fiction, Sylvie here seems more attuned to natural wisdom than the more sophisticated whites. After learning that she is pregnant, Athénaïse behaves as Darwin would have predicted (102–3). Her acceptance of her sexuality fits the Darwinian pattern because it is linked with motherhood (110). **Berkove 1996:** In this story as elsewhere Chopin treats sexual relations from an ethical point of view (194). **Koloski 1996:** This is one of various stories by Chopin depicting assertive women. It presents one of the most vital females in the literature of Chopin's time (xii–xiii). One of several tales in which violent death seems a possibility (12), it presents a title character who is also mentioned in another of Chopin's narratives (19). "Athénaïse," however, is Chopin's best story and resembles some of her other finest work in its characters and topics. The opening contrasts strongly with the conclusion, and the tale falls into five parts infused with a mood of uncertainty. Although some critics have objected to the heroine's final choice, her decision is consistent with the values often found in Chopin's fiction and with the similar decisions of other characters in the tale. As in other works by Chopin, the characters here sometimes act on impulses that often reflect social customs, and these pressures affect even the males. Gouvernail is an unusually self-aware character—one capable of articulating (if sometimes only through allusion) Chopin's own view of life. The men in the tale adapt themselves to Athénaïse, but it is the baby who finally affects her most, and Gouvernail accepts this fact (36–40). Athénaïse resembles other characters by Chopin (52; 58; 71; 78). Voice is an important topic in this tale, which is one of Chopin's longer stories (88). **Thomas 1996:** Critics have overlooked the important role of the black character Sylvie, whose strong sense of selfhood contrasts with that of the title character (207), whose return to her husband may disappoint some readers (208). As elsewhere,

Chopin juxtaposes contrasting women characters (208). Although Sylvie is black, she is much more free than Athénaïse (208). She is thus unusual not only in Chopin's fiction but in other fiction of the time (209). Sylvie's business and personality are treated with respect, both by Chopin and by other characters (209–10). She commands and displays authority (210–11), and Athénaïse has the opportunity to learn from her stay at Sylvie's (211–12) as well as to witness Sylvie's greater economic security (212–13). This trait makes Sylvie an unusual character in American fiction of this period (213–14). The story reveals the limitations of conventional marriage (214), but Sylvie is Athénaïse's most helpful model in preparing for a mature married life (215). Composing the story helped prepare Chopin to write *The Awakening*, and the tale remains one of her most progressive and accomplished narratives (215–16). **Walker 1996:** Theme: the relations between women and writing (220). In many ways the title character of this tale foreshadows Edna in *The Awakening*. Athénaïse is associated with nature, while Gouvernail is linked to culture and the written word (221–22). He is associated with intellect while she is associated with the body, although at the end of the story she does engage in some writing in connection with her new maternal role (222). **Beer 1997:** This is one of various stories by Chopin that subvert the sort of predictable values and closure they superficially might seem to endorse (28). The tale undercuts easy expectations in a variety of ways, particularly in the ways it compares the situation of the title character to the circumstances of a slave. The story subverts absolutism and questions racist and sexist stereotypes, especially in its final depiction of Athénaïse's response to a child in need (31–32). Even if Athénaïse surrenders to cultural pressures, we are forced to ponder the price of that submission (37). This is one of various stories by Chopin that show how one character resists the ardor of another—a provocative topic when the ardor was that of a husband for his wife (42). Although the married couple are reunited by the end, the story nonetheless exposes the potential flaws and faults in marriage (42–43). The ending is in some ways the least significant section of the tale, and the story as a whole questions the values endorsed by the journal that originally published it—a journal that not only required Chopin to edit the piece but also tried, by adding a subtitle, to influence how the story was interpreted. More important than the relatively conventional ending is the transformation of Cazeau's thinking (43). Chopin implies the ways in which both Athénaïse and Cazeau have been misled by their cultural milieu; in some ways the changes Cazeau experiences are far more crucial than the ones experienced by Athénaïse (43–44). Like numerous other females depicted by Chopin, Athénaïse rejects the notion that marriage is the essence of her identity and the culmination of her evolution. Athénaïse refuses to be interpreted in this limited manner (43–45). **Bell 1998:** Chopin obviously respects the title character's independence (243). **Toth and Seyersted 1998:** This story is mentioned in several of Chopin's account books (141, 150, 160). **Bonner and Bonner 1999:** Here as elsewhere, Chopin uses a visit to New Orleans' Lake End for symbolic purposes (63). **Brown 1999:** In this story as elsewhere, Gouvernail is contrasted with more conservative or predictable men (71). Whereas Gouvernail provides the stimulus for another person's awakening in "A Respectable Woman," in this story he is the one who is awakened (75–78). **Ewell 1999:** Theme: maternity. **Koloski 1999:** This is one of Chopin's tales dealing with a moment of realization (viii). One of her best stories, it appears in one of the best, most convincing, and most charitable collections of short fiction published in her time and place (xvi). This is one of several tales in *A Night in Acadie* that focus on a transforming journey (xvi). The present work is perhaps the finest to be included in either of Chopin's two published anthologies. Its plot foreshadows the events of *The Awakening*; both works deal with a woman's growing realizations, but their endings differ radically. Both main characters evolve, and the reconciliation is voluntary, not forced. This is one of various stories by Chopin in which children inaugurate a transformation (xvi–xvii). **McCullough 1999:** Motherhood is important in this story as in others by Chopin. Here it is linked with an acceptance of sex and with an assumption of status. A happy ending is imposed here, as it is not in *The Awakening* (219–20). Athénaïse's growing self-knowledge parallels her absorption into the social hierarchy. At first she rejects marriage despite its social benefits. Chopin defuses some of her potentially radical emphasis on feminine sexual desire by tying it to maternity, by making Athénaïse seem a bit exotic, and by connecting her desire to economic improvement (220–24). **Toth 1999a:** The predictable conclusion of this work made it acceptable to male editors—men whom Chopin often did not please (9). **Toth 1999c:** This is one of various stories in which Chopin describes maternal emotions (70). The title character bears the same name as Chopin's grandmother, who was nearly ninety when the story was published. Her own marriage had been even less happy than the one the narrative describes (181–82). Gouvernail resembles a friend of Chopin, both physically and in temperament (186). The story is one of many of hers depicting vulnerable young women (194). Chopin's male friend, probably echoing Chopin's own views, suggested that the title character dislikes her husband less than she dislikes being married (196). One male reviewer enjoyed the insouciance with which Chopin described Gouvernail's attitudes toward marriage (197). **Gibbons 2000:** During the time when Chopin composed this complex and significant tale, she probably realized that such writing would not appeal to a broad readership (xxxvii). Chopin uses lucid, convincing diction to describe the complex fate of the decent, able husband. The story's language is clear, economical, and perfectly appropriate, while the depictions of Athénaïse and her brother are both highly credible. The story is extremely well crafted, and its conclusion is utterly satisfying. Chopin makes the ending seem both artistically convincing and ethically appealing (xxxviii–xxxix). **Knights 2000:** This tale was originally published alongside writings by Booker T. Washington, Henry James, and Sarah Orne Jewett (xv). Here as in other works, Chopin subverts romantic expectations (xxi) and creates an ambiguous story that has provoked divergent responses (xxiv). Here as in "Azélie," Chopin effectively uses symbolism of keys (xxxi). As in other works, Chopin here emphasizes sites of urban privacy (xxxiii). Her revisions of the first version of the tale make the work seem slightly less informal (xlvi). Here as elsewhere, either editors or Chopin herself added a subtitle to the first version of this work to tone down its impact (xlvi–xlvii).

"Aunt Lympy's Interference"

Written: 1896. First published: 1897. Included in *Complete Works* **(1969).**

Eighteen-year-old Melitte De Broussard is cleaning her room in her brother's house on a Saturday because Saturdays are her only free days now that she is teaching school. While at her chore, she looks out her southern window at the Annibelle house, seeing only a speck of the imposing white home. Almost every morning as she walks to school, she passes the Annibelle house where Victor Annibelle, now twenty-two, is always mending the fence. Melitte remarks on Victor's interminable efforts at repair, but he can never find his wits enough to reply until she is out of earshot. Though they were childhood playmates, now he is too tongue-tied to say anything to her, and on Saturdays, when Melitte does not go to school, he passes "frequently up and down the road" on his white horse.

One Saturday, her toddler nephew tells Melitte that she has a visitor. Thinking that Victor has stopped by on some pretext, Melitte removes the dust-cloth from her head and checks herself in the mirror. Melitte finds instead that her visitor is "proud and unbending" Aunt Lympy, the old family servant, who nursed Melitte as an infant. Aunt Lympy explains that the reason for her visit is that she heard something about Melitte in town that she needed to confirm. Wide-eyed, Melitte asks what it is. Aunt Lympy says she heard that Melitte "was turn school-titcher." Melitte confirms the truth of this, and the shame Aunt Lympy feels "crushed her into silence." Melitte is able to say nothing that assuages the old woman's feelings.

Less than a week after Aunt Lympy's visit, Melitte receives a "sad, self-condemnatory, reminiscent" letter from her mother's brother, Gervais Leplain, of New Orleans. He asks Melitte to come to New Orleans and be as one of his own daughters. He has enclosed money for her immediate needs and a promise that he and one of his daughters will come for her soon. Unknown to anyone but Leplain was the letter written by Aunt Lympy. Every line was either a "stinging rebuke" or an appeal to the memory of his dead sister, whose child was "tasting the bitter dregs of poverty."

Melitte's family, friends, and acquaintances rush to offer their congratulations on her good fortune. They point out the grand lifestyle of the Leplains: a house in la rue Esplanade with a cottage across the lake, summers in the north, clothing *en Parisienne*, and attendance at balls, dinners, and card parties. Being fond of the things around her, not realizing that they are "poor and pinched," Melitte is confused by the chorus of well-wishers. Melitte puts her uncle's money aside so that she may return it to him, and her failure to send a thank-you letter to Leplain earns her a sharp rebuke from her sister-in-law. Her sister-in-law's suggestion that Melitte close up the school is met with silence. Melitte wonders if everyone is telling her to go because no one cares about her. But then she ponders: why shouldn't she go and live in ease instead of staying in a place when no one has said that s/he cannot bear for Melitte to go?

On her way to school, the familiar brown and green road is a blur from the tears in her eyes, and she resolves to go live with Leplain. As she passes by Victor's house, he is not repairing the fence but leaning over it, waiting for her. Unseen by Melitte, Victor jumps over the fence and greets her when he catches up with her. In Melitte's mind, Victor echoes everyone else when he questions her about her departure. When she confirms that she will go, Victor says that he can't bear to have her depart. Melitte says nothing and hurries off to meet the group assembled by the school. For Melitte, however, Victor's words "possessed a power to warm and brighten greater than that of the sun and the moon."

After school, Victor returns to plead his case with Melitte. He interrupts her attempt to close up the school and expresses his desire for her to stay. Because he asks her not to go, Melitte decides to stay. As for Aunt Lympy, "she felt that her interference had not been wholly in vain." **(EP)**

***

Peterson 1972: The heroine is interesting, but the story (especially its conclusion) shows little originality (171). **Rocks 1972:** As elsewhere, Chopin suggests that each person must decide whether it is better to be content with one's present condition or attempt to alter one's future. The results of either choice cannot be predicted (115). **Lattin 1980:** This is one of various stories by Chopin featuring repeating characters (28). **Newman 1986:** Like many of Chopin's tales, this one suggests a view of marriage that seems to conflict with the views implied by some of her other stories. This work seems to affirm traditional ideas about the value of matrimony (152). **Skaggs 1985:** This is one of several tales featuring a black character concerned with social class (60). **Ewell 1986:** Although less penetrating than "Nég Créol," this story also examines the effects of financial need (a topic Chopin particularly stressed in early 1896). In addition, this is her last story concerning the fidelity of freed blacks. Yet humor, not pathos, is stressed in this tale, which ends with romantic fulfillment. The story shows, paradoxically, how a woman's effort to assert her freedom ultimately reinforces social expectations (123). **Lohafer 1989:** Nearly two hundred diverse readers were asked to respond to this effective, straightforward, but relatively unknown and fairly brief work. The story's sentences were numbered, and each respondent was asked to choose where (other than at its present ending) the story *might* have concluded (249–51). Only roughly half of the 169 total sentences were regarded by respondents as possible alternative endings. No single sentence was selected by more than roughly a quarter of the readers. Most of the possible endings the readers selected occur near the actual ending, but some possible ending-points occurred earlier (251–52). The story illustrates Chopin's typical insight into feminine psychology and into women's social options as she focuses on the heroine's conflicting feelings (252–54). Twelve percent of the respondents thought the story *could* end with the conclusion of Aunt Lympy's visit. More than twice that number thought the tale *could* conclude when Melitte seems to decide that she must accept her uncle's offer. Sixteen percent thought work *could* end when Victor confesses his desire to have Melitte remain. Most of the rest of the respondents thought the ending could have occurred among the final seven sentences of the tale (254–57). Although there was no obvious link between the grade level of the student respondents and their choices about possible concluding points, college-level readers tended to favor the points closest to the actual ending, especially points signaled by a repeated image or a significant word. High-school level students were significantly more likely to assume the story might end when Aunt Lympy leaves. These findings suggest that responses to art works are linked to level of training or experience (257–59). However, other findings seemed difficult to predict (259–61). The earlier possible closing points tended to come at the ends of paragraphs; tended to coincide with changes of locale; tended to be linked to the end of a disagreement; and tended to parallel a choice by the heroine (261–63). These and other findings from the survey have many implications for the ways stories are written, structured, analyzed, taught, read, and "processed," and the findings also have many implications for the art of narrative in general (263–75). **Goodwyn 1994:** This is one of various stories in which Chopin depicts the stereotype of the loyal black (10). **Koloski 1994:** The story is included in a soft-cover collection of Chopin's fiction published in 1979 (27). **Koloski 1996:** This is one of several children's stories by Chopin that depict the poor (11; 71; 86). **Thomas 1996:** This story is one of many works in which Chopin depicts aged black females, often in stereotypical terms (216–17). **Beer 1997:** This is one of various stories by Chopin that deal with the fidelity of blacks toward whites (35). **Toth and Seyersted 1998:** This story is mentioned in Chopin's account books (141, 150).

"Azélie"

Written: 1893. First published: 1894. Included in *A Night in Acadie* **(1897).**

Azélie lives with her father, her grandmother, and her little brother on the edge of Mr. Mathurin's plantation. They are from the Little River area, but they came here to try to make a living.

Azélie comes to the store to get supplies for her family, but she has no money. Mr. Mathurin has told the storekeeper, 'Polyte, to give her only the necessities on credit and nothing else. This time she asks for tobacco and whiskey for her father, but 'Polyte refuses. That night 'Polyte, asleep in the back room, hears someone in the store. He takes his gun and goes around to the outside, finding one of the shutters unlocked and open. The intruder is Azélie.

'Polyte confronts Azélie, calling her a thief. She denies the charge, saying that she broke in because 'Polyte would not give her the things her father required. She shows no remorse, nor does she even acknowledge that what she has done is wrong. 'Polyte orders her away and instructs her that when she needs something from the store she should tell him directly, but he warns her that she can never come into the store again.

From that time on 'Polyte is in love with Azélie. He cannot explain it. He gives her anything she wants and charges the items to his own account. He thinks about her constantly, waiting anxiously for any chance to see her.

When the time comes for Azélie's family to move back to the Little River, 'Polyte plans to ask her to marry him. He thinks that he can change her if her family is not around to influence her. He is disappointed, though, because Azélie refuses his proposal and leaves with her family. It becomes clear to 'Polyte that he is of little good at the store now. He tells Mr. Mathurin that he will be leaving to move to the Little River where Azélie is. **(DR)**

***

Rankin 1932: Mr. Mathurin resembles Chopin's husband, who owned and operated a country store (100). The story was published during a period when Chopin's work was receiving widespread encouragement from editors (136). **Reilly 1937:** This is one of various stories in which Chopin deals subtly with the ambiguities of affection (72). **Reilly 1942:** The ending of this story seems effectively inescapable (131). This story illustrates the tendency of Chopin's heroines to remain loyal once they have made a commitment (132–33). It also illustrates her typically deft and sometimes implicit handling of the complexities of love (133–34). **Seyersted 1969a:** The story exemplifies Chopin's tendency to be unusually frank in treating sexual desire (98). **Leary 1970a:** This is one of many works in which Chopin depicts the ambiguities and complexities of love (x). **Leary 1971:** Theme: reckless, potentially disastrous affection (166). **Peterson 1972:** This very fine realistic work was composed around the same time Chopin turned out less accomplished pieces (10). 'Polyte's name may suggest the Phaedra-Hippolytus legend, with its stress on passionate love. Azélie's motives and character are effectively unclear; more interesting to Chopin is 'Polyte's desire. He tries to whitewash his physical passion, but he is Chopin's first character to experience a devastating revelation. In this sense the present tale contrasts with such an earlier work as "After the Winter" (143–45). Here as elsewhere, Chopin offers an interesting study of the human mind (273). **Arner 1975:** As in "Caline," affection proves painfully disruptive here, fomenting a kind of demonic passion that profoundly unsettles not only 'Polyte but also Chopin's readers (66–67), perhaps because we recognize his affection as lust. Azélie's thievery seems to excite him, possibly since it seems to indicate her willingness to transgress in other ways, and Chopin's diction seems to imply a more shocking theme than it can openly state. In this story, erotic desire shows its darker aspects (66–68). **Dyer 1980–81:** Here as elsewhere Chopin reverses expectations by showing how a male can be fundamentally transformed by contact with a female (11). 'Polyte initially seems obsessed with control and protection, but this need is disrupted by his contacts with Azélie, who arouses impulses he will not be able to master. She is repeatedly linked with the mysterious moon, in whose light their most significant encounter also occurs (12). Although 'Polyte eventually tries to impose some respectable order on his passion by proposing marriage, Azélie rejects him. Moonstruck by the power of this woman, he can no longer live according to the rationality he once prized so highly. 'Polyte's responses are more governed by social convention than those of Tonie in "At Chênière Caminada." He is forced to confront pain of the sort Tonie is allowed to escape. The boy in "A Vocation and a Voice" experiences many of the same conflicting feelings felt by both 'Polyte and Tonie (13). Here as in "A Vocation and a Voice," Chopin symbolically associates external nature and internal desires (14). Like the boy in "A Vocation and a Voice," 'Polyte cannot suppress his instincts (15). **Dyer 1981d:** Here and in numerous other works, Chopin uses physical setting to imply what a character is feeling. Her frequent use of this technique is open to various explanations (451–52). **Davis 1982:** Like many of Chopin's stories, this one emphasizes the primal force of erotic desire, which makes other matters seem unimportant (65). **Skaggs 1985:** This is one of several stories by Chopin that explore romance, often of an odd variety (35). **Ewell 1986:** Like other stories written in 1893, this one focuses on fixated and often frustrated desire. Despite her loyalty to her father, Azélie lacks the strong ethical sense often found in Chopin's younger heroines, yet this lack (ironically) only inflames 'Polyte's almost humiliating preoccupation with her. Here a male makes an assumption usually attributed to women: that the object of love can be redeemed. Instead, 'Polyte loses both his ethical balance and his earlier sturdy sense of self by submitting to erotic infatuation (96–97). **Inge 1989:** Erotic passion eventually dominates 'Polyte's feelings toward Azélie, who personifies his own latent, suppressed amorality and deep-rooted desire for liberty. She embodies his own irrational impulses and illustrates the effects these can have on any person's conduct (100). **Papke 1990:** This is one of four pivotal stories in Chopin's career in which she momentarily overcomes gloomy views of women's possibilities and instead presents resolute and confident female protagonists (60). This tale also differs strikingly from other writings by Chopin because it offers a feminist (and very sophisticated) lesson in a rural setting. The title character almost seems to exist in a realm beyond good and evil and appears impervious to the thoughts and feelings of men. Her actions and attitudes disorient 'Polyte's conventional assumptions about women. He mistakenly assumes that she needs a male rescuer, but she needs nothing from him and seems content with her independence (although she also shows genuine commitment to her family). By depicting a character who seems at peace with her outcast status, Chopin perhaps criticizes standard views of ethics, but she offers no positive alternative to such views. Azélie is her own person, yet she has a beneficial effect on society despite her personal aloofness. She seems to live a charmed existence (60–62). **Toth 1990a:** Chopin's husband had run a general store like the one here (146), which is one of several places in which Chopin describes men and women meeting (168). A magazine paid fifty dollars for this tale (215)—one of a number in which highly emotional men are smitten with more pragmatic women (224). The story was first published almost without revision (245) and then later appeared in *A Night in Acadie*, in which all the stories are set in Louisiana (298). It was well received by one reviewer (299) and was reprinted, in digest form, by another journal (301). **Guidici 1991:** This is one of many stories by Chopin that center around rejected marriage proposals. These rejections give the women greater autonomy (28–29). Azélie's pride in herself as a provider for her family makes her resist and reject 'Polyte's well-intentioned efforts to usurp this role (30). **Shurbutt 1993:** Here as in other tales, Chopin offers an ironic perspective on the convention of the male as savior (20–21). **Ewell 1994:** This is one of many stories by Chopin that show the dangers of ignoring the sexual or sensual aspects of human nature (168). **Koloski 1994:** An anthology of short fiction in print between the early 1920s and late 1940s reprinted this story because of its absorbing characters. The anthology reported the availability of Chopin's fiction in major American libraries of its day (20). The story is also included in a 1970 soft-cover collection (27). **Carr 1996:** The titular character is typical of the passionate, scheming, amoral Acadian women Chopin typically describes (56). **Toth and Seyersted 1998:** This story is mentioned in Chopin's account books (140, 149, 160) as well as in a letter dated 1894 (206). **Brown 1999:** Before his encounter with Azélie, 'Polyte is a fairly conventional male in his outlook and behavior. His interactions with her help broaden his social and political views as well as his personal psychology (80–81). **Toth 1999b:** As Bernard Koloski has demonstrated, this was one of eight stories by Chopin that were frequently republished in the twentieth century (46). **Toth 1999c:** This story shows the kinds of romantic meetings possible in a place like Cloutierville (96). This was one of only four stories by Chopin published in the *Century* magazine, and most of them depict characters who become kind but also bland (136). Chopin claimed that this story, like others, was written quickly and required little revision (164). As in other examples of Chopin's short fiction, the young woman here seems vulnerable (194). **Knights 2000:** This work, one of Chopin's most compelling, was produced during a particularly creative period—the fall and summer of 1893 (xv). Even in this work for a fairly conventional magazine, Chopin shows a willingness to confront an unusual theme (xviii). Here as elsewhere she subverts romantic expectations (xxi) and implies the uncertainties of existence (xxvi). The story presents an unusually complex view of plantation life, especially by focusing on the store and the symbolic key (xxxi).

"Bambo Pellier"

Written: 1892. Destroyed or lost.

Ewell 1986: This is one of several non-extant stories mentioned in Chopin's records (190). **Toth 1990a:** Apparently Chopin destroyed this children's story, even though she had entered it (unsuccessfully) in a contest (207). **Toth and Seyersted 1998:** This story is mentioned in Chopin's account books (149, 158).

"La Belle Zoraïde"

Written: 1893. First published: 1894. Included in *Bayou Folk* **(1894).**

Manna-Loulou tells her mistress the story of La belle Zoraïde, who was a servant and goddaughter to a wealthy woman, Madame Delarivière. Madame has raised Zoraïde almost as if she is her own child. When it comes time for Zoraïde to marry, Madame picks out a mulatto who is the body servant of Dr. Langlé. Although the mulatto enjoys some social status and is therefore worthy of Zoraïde, she detests him.

Instead, Zoraïde is in love with Mézor, a dark black slave who works in the fields. When she tells Madame that she wants to marry Mézor rather than Ambroise, Madame is furious and forbids her from talking with Mézor. Nonetheless, Zoraïde and Mézor secretly see each other anyway. Madame finds out and has Dr. Langlé sell Mézor far away. Zoraïde is heartbroken, but she finds solace in knowing that she will have Mézor's baby to love.

When Zoraïde's baby is born, she is told that the baby died during delivery when in fact Madame had it sent out to her plantation to be raised.

Zoraïde loses her mind and begins caring for a bundle of rags shaped like a baby. Calling it her baby, she holds it and rocks it. Madame and the doctor decide to bring her real child back to her, but their action is too late, for Zoraïde is already mad.

Manna-Loulou's mistress expresses regret about the story she has heard. **(DR)**

***

Bush 1957: This is one of only two tragic tales published in *Bayou Folk* or *A Night in Acadie*; the rest are mainly optimistic. This is the only story by Chopin to focus on slavery. The work's narrative technique, particularly its setting in the past, makes it seem almost mythic (240–41). **Seyersted 1969a:** The story, one of only two about Louisiana before the Civil War, is more concerned with freedom for women than with attacking slavery (93–94). The tale exemplifies Chopin's interest in spontaneous passion (108–9).

Seyersted 1969b: Here as in her other stories about race, Chopin's focus is more on individual psychology than on social contexts. However, the story does seem to censure slavery (26). **Berthoff 1970:** This is one of the few explicitly dark tales in *Bayou Folk* (xvii). **Leary 1970a:** This is one of many works in which Chopin depicts the ambiguities and complexities of love (x). **Leary 1971:** Theme: meanness that frustrates affection (166). **Potter 1971:** Zoraïde is among the most tragic of Chopin's people, yet she suffers not because of the forces of nature but because of a perverse system (48–49). **Peterson 1972:** In this tale issues of race are explicit, while Chopin's own attitudes toward the topic are unclear (105). The story is less an attack on slavery than an attack on Madame Delarivière and her pride. She treats Zoraïde much like the play-thing that Zoraïde eventually embraces. The objective tone of the work contributes to its effectiveness and also to its ironic impact (133–35). This work is a little less risky than some of Chopin's later writing about feminine desire (142). **Rocks 1972:** Here and elsewhere Chopin describes the sufferings of blacks under slavery, but her concern is more with her characters as individual persons than as representative types (114). **Arner 1975:** Perhaps prompted by an event mentioned in *Uncle Tom's Cabin*, or perhaps derived from real life, the story is interesting especially for its emphasis on the restraints imposed on women. Although the tale is more maudlin than one might wish, Chopin redeems it by refusing to provide a complacent conclusion. She effectively and forthrightly explores the perverse idea that one person can own another—an idea buttressed, in this case, by a corrupt social system (50–51). **Solomon 1976:** This tale shows powerful compassion for its heroine, who is vulnerable both because she is female and because she is enslaved (xiv). The inner tale is bracketed by an outer narrative, giving the story a complexity resembling that found in Joseph Conrad's works (xiv–xv). The story seems even more ironic when we remember that Madame Delisle also appears in Chopin's story "A Lady of Bayou St. John." The strong compassion Madame Delisle shows for Zoraïde in the present tale is a feeling she herself deserves (xv). **Bonner 1977:** Here as elsewhere Chopin treats her black characters as individual persons rather than as stereotypes (6–7). The narrative perspective in this tale is particularly complex (7). Here and elsewhere in Chopin, mental illness is a major theme (10). The story shows love ruined (10). This is one of Chopin's more effective treatments in *Bayou Folk* of the human mind. The story implies the blurred boundaries between sanity and its opposite (12) and also illustrates the social and ethnic hierarchy of Louisiana (12). This is one of the best stories in *Bayou Folk* (13). **Lattin 1978:** This is one of various stories in which Chopin describes the genuine complications that can result from real (rather than merely imagined or potential) motherhood (2). Although this story shows the satisfactions motherhood could promise, in much of Chopin's writing actual motherhood leads to pain or a sacrifice of identity (5). **Wolff 1978:** This is one of many stories by Chopin dealing with the instability of human experience (126). Zoraïde's fate would not differ if she were purely black rather than only partly so (127). **Wolff 1979:** This is Chopin's most effective early tale and touches on many of the topics most commonly explored in her fiction (215–16). **Lattin 1980:** This is one of various stories by Chopin that seems richer because it uses characters who appear elsewhere (20; 29–31). **Dyer 1980–81:** This is one of many stories by Chopin in which a female is aroused by contact with a male (10–11). **Baym 1981:** The story exemplifies Chopin's interest in race relations (xix). **Dyer 1981d:** Here and in numerous other works, Chopin uses physical setting to imply what a character is feeling. Her frequent use of this technique is open to various explanations (451–52). **Jones 1981:** Here as elsewhere, Chopin uses the experiences of blacks in order to comment on oppression in general. Chopin attractively presents both the sensuality and the maternal instincts of Zoraïde. The whites are presented unfavorably, a fact exemplified by Madame Delisle's imperceptive final comment (151–52). **Davis 1982:** Theme: the power of erotic desire (64). **Gilbert 1984:** This story questions divisive racial discrimination (16). **Rogers 1983:** Like George Sand, Chopin focuses (in this tale) on a woman's complex sexuality (34). **Dyer 1985:** The events described in this tale must predate those described in "A Lady of Bayou St. John." Chopin uses white prejudices about the sexuality of blacks to deal with themes that would have been impermissible if all the story's characters were white, but she very subtly implies that Zoraïde and Madame Delisle are similarly sensual (74–79). **Newman 1986:** The story illustrates the tragedy of being locked into a stereotypical role. In the finale, however, Madame Delisle fails to perceive the tragedy (161). **Skaggs 1985:** This is one of several tales focusing on the interaction of affection and selfhood (17). The story exemplifies one of Chopin's most successful topics: the tragic consequences of the oppression of self and love (19–20). The ending resembles that of "A Lady of Bayou St. John": both title characters retreat into fantasy (20–21). **Ewell 1986:** This story presents Chopin's most appealing portrait of a stereotypical character in local-color writing: the suffering mulatto. Coming near the end of the *Bayou Folk* collection, the story sums up various topics touched on earlier, including insanity, complicated romances, and distinctions and discriminations based on race. Zoraïde takes greater initiative than the title character of "Désirée's Baby" (which the present story in some ways resembles), and she finally chooses total isolation over compliant submission. The frame narrative gives the work a reflexive complexity that is reinforced by different levels of self-awareness. Thus Madame Delisle is imperceptive in various ways that typify the subtlety of the story's themes and techniques—qualities that help make this one of Chopin's most successful works (72–73). **Toth 1988a:** Although this story reflects Chopin's personal familiarity with the customs of blacks in New Orleans, it also reveals her interest in timeless human suffering (58). The Creole dialect featured here may also have figured in Chopin's unfinished tale about Grand Isle (59). **Elfenbein 1989:** Here as elsewhere Chopin shows how women suffer when they lack power, and she also depicts women of color who are relevant to her depiction of women in *The Awakening* (117–18). In stories such as this, which feature women of color, Chopin could deal more explicitly with topics she treated more cautiously when writing about white females. The women of color in these tales tend to be less simple characters than the white women, but they suffer more obvious mistreatment. Stories such as this one anticipate the racial dynamics depicted in *The Awakening* (126). Here as in "Désirée's Baby," Chopin shows the disaster that can result from clinging to artificial distinctions. Madame Delisle and Zoraïde resemble each other partly because of the limits they face as women and partly because each feels a need to retreat into a kind of fantasy life (131). In this tale as in "A Lady of Bayou St. John," Madame Delisle seems content with passivity and routine; in a sense she lives off of the emotions of others (132). She and Zoraïde are each isolated, but in different ways. Manna-Loulou assumes that Madame Delisle will be able to understand and approve of Zoraïde's position and behavior, although Manna-Loulou may implicitly criticize (or even taunt) Madame Delisle's own passivity by describing Zoraïde's assertiveness—an assertiveness the mistress may wish she might also enjoy (132). Zoraïde's own mistress is assertive in a way that seems almost conventionally masculine; she is as much in love with authority as Zoraïde is with Mézor (132–33). Her egotism makes her incapable of perceiving fine distinctions or delicate feelings (133). This important story is the first by Chopin to describe explicitly a woman's erotic desires—a fact that helps explain the techniques of indirection she uses (such as the outer narrative and the focus on a non-white heroine). The story is also unconventional in describing a black person (Mézor) who is attractive not because of any white heritage but because of its absence; in contrast, Ambroise is unappealing not so much because he is of mixed race but because he has rejected his black heritage (134). The stark description of birth in this story anticipates the similar realism of *The Awakening*, while the tragic conclusion of the tale undercuts the romantic fictional convention that children could cause powerful and positive transformations (134). Ultimately, Madame Delisle is unable or unwilling to see the similarities between herself and Zoraïde; instead, she finds the story of another's tragedy personally reassuring. She will probably remain trapped in her thoughtless routine (134–35). **Inge 1989:** The conclusion of the tale emphasizes its social dimensions, particularly the ways racism and the suppression of liberty foster a legacy of corruption that taints even intended affection (98–99). **Taylor 1989:** This tale may have influenced a story by Ruth McEnery Stuart (124), although the focus of her tale is broader than that of Chopin's story (126). **Papke 1990:** This is one of Chopin's few stories in which social problems (rather than simply individual characters) seem a major focus (33). As in other works, Chopin here deals with conflicts between individual impulse and social obligations (60). **Toth 1990a:** The dancing here may resemble dances Chopin witnessed in New Orleans (126). The narrative shows her concern for black women despite her relative lack of interest in racial politics (136). She had heard French Creole dialect while at Grand

Isle (139) and also drew on her knowledge of New Orleans in writing the tale (216), which she composed on the same day its companion story, "A Lady of Bayou St. John," appeared in print. For the first time, Chopin here described birth for her readers. The story is progressive in its depiction of race (221–22) and is placed with four others about adult dilemmas at the end of *Bayou Folk* (224). It influenced other authors (248; 269; 325) and is one of several works by Chopin describing outlawed love (279). **Brown 1991:** Zoraïde's fate is ironically similar to that of Madame Delisle. The irony is greater since Madame Delisle probably learned of Zoraïde's withdrawal before her own retreat (131). **Guidici 1991:** Here as elsewhere a Chopin heroine fails to seize the opportunity for greater autonomy. Zoraïde should have demanded the right to choose her own husband (31). **Toth 1991:** Although this is one of Chopin's early narratives, it is dark and disturbing (xiii). **Bryan 1993:** This story and others by Chopin reflect the influence of George W. Cable (15). By making Manna-Loulou the narrator, Chopin gave herself the freedom not only to describe the handsomeness of Mézor but also to depict the lovers' desires with a certain objectivity. Madame Delisle sympathizes with the suffering slaves and their baby (55). This is one of the relatively few tales in which Chopin explicitly deals with matters of race and with other social concerns (62). **Larsson 1993:** This story implies Chopin's sympathy with basic human desires, although the ending (typically) refuses to moralize overtly (2: 537–38). **Shurbutt 1993:** Here as elsewhere, Chopin links marriage to slavery (18). **Cothern 1994:** Manna-Loulou's tale undercuts Madame Delisle's expectations about a proper story in the same way that Chopin and other local color writers undercut many of the conventions of narrative realism. Manna-Loulou, like Chopin and other local colorists, stands in between two cultures (118). Chopin's reliance on an internal narrator to tell the tale contributes to the dialogical complexity of the story, calls attention to the subjectivity of the narrative, and opens up the possibility of critical irony (119–20). Manna-Loulou stands in much the same relation to Madame Delisle as Chopin stood to her own contemporary audience of readers and editors (121). In Manna-Loulou's tale, truth and fiction become fluid categories and narrative becomes ambiguous (122). Mézor's exile from both his physical home and his native tongue suggests the degree to which language, in this story as in life, is linked to power, as Zoraïde's later descent into linguistic nonsense also shows (122–23). The pretense that the story is told in Creole rather than in English is both a challenge to the reader's authority and a stimulus to re-read the tale (123–24). This is one of various stories in which Chopin used an internal narrator, a device which allowed her greater authorial distance both from the tale and from the dominant culture she may have been implicitly critiquing (124). Chopin empowered a black woman by making her the narrator, and perhaps *The Awakening* would have seemed less threatening to Chopin's readers if it, too, had used the device of an internal narrator (124–25). **Goodwyn 1994:** This story reflects the cultural complexity of Chopin's writing, particularly its status as a kind of

post-colonial literature. In some respects the story subverts standard values (3–4). It is one of various narratives in which Chopin shows the human
tragedy involved in enforcing stereotypes (11). **Koloski 1994:** The story is
included in soft-cover collections of Chopin's fiction published in 1970,
1976, 1981, and 1984 (27). It also often appears in college textbooks (28–29).
Lundie 1994: Too often this story has been viewed as the tale of an oppressed woman rather than the tale of an oppressed woman of color (126).
Ironically, whereas contemporary readers responded positively to this tale
of black feminine sexuality, they were shocked when Chopin focused on
the desires of a white woman in *The Awakening* (127). Recent critics have
debated the degree to which Chopin perpetuated or challenged racist
stereotypes about black females in her fiction (128). In this tale, however,
Chopin's treatment of racial matters seems much more complicated than
either of these extreme positions would suggest (128). Madame Delarivière associates Zoraïde's love for Mézor with animalistic lust (135). Ambroise, meanwhile, behaves with the typical possessiveness Chopin often
attributes to male characters, while Zoraïde may exemplify racist stereotypes of the sensual woman of color (136). Significantly, Chopin
"purchased the ability to be a 'sexual realist' on the backs of black women
… long before she attempted it in *The Awakening*" (137). Nevertheless,
Chopin does complicate her depiction of Zoraïde and Manna-Loulou,
both of whom could easily have been presented as mere stereotypes (137–
38). Although Manna-Loulou never complains about being oppressed, she
is presented as a more sympathetic character than her mistress. The old
woman seems appealing and wise but is also passive, and her ambiguity
typifies the whole tone of this story, especially its ironic conclusion (139).
Gunning 1995: Although previous critics have compared the restricted
lives of Zoraïde and Madame Delisle, the contrasts between them are
more important. Both Manna-Loulou and Zoraïde are presented in ways
that suggest the dangers blacks can present to white supremacy. Zoraïde
allows white readers to fantasize about sex without suffering personal
punishment or changing their supremacist views. Mézor is an object of
both fear and fascination for a white (female) audience, including Madame
Delisle, for whom Zoraïde is a kind of alter-ego. Zoraïde's pregnancy
symbolizes the fear whites felt about the fertility of blacks, especially since
the two white women in the story are childless. The story alludes to white
supremacist notions of the mental instability of mullatoes, even as it
shows Madame Delisle failing to exercise the freedom she enjoys as a
white female (76–82). **Baxter 1996:** This work reveals Chopin's interest in
matters of race (219–20) and exemplifies her talent as a local color writer
(239). It lends itself to a creative writing exercise for students (240) and
was included in a collection that was well received by contemporary readers (241). The tale can be studied by evaluating the characters' social status
(247). **Koloski 1996:** This is one of the darker tales with which *Bayou Folk*
concludes. Its charming diction contrasts with its disturbing topic. Critics
have traditionally noted how this story challenges values, even if Madame

Delisle herself seems incapable of empathizing with Zoraïde (27–29). The setting of this story is mentioned in others by Chopin (43), and the story is one of several in which Chopin treats racial matters with thought and feeling (44; 47). One critic has linked this narrative thematically with "Désirée's Baby" and "The Storm" (88). **Walker 1996:** Madame Delisle in this story, like Edna in *The Awakening*, is passive in her approach to fiction (219). **Beer 1997:** Ann Goodwyn Jones sees Chopin using this story's focus on race to explore her own thoughts about subjugation (13). The story illustrates Chopin's multicultural emphases and postcolonial awarenesses. Typically, Zoraïde's fate can be diversely interpreted (26–28). Ironically, by the end of the story Zoraïde exemplifies the stereotypes she had earlier transcended (37). **Michaels 1998:** In this effective tale, Manna-Loulou claims to speak truly, but her story is filtered through the language of the English-speaking narrator. Chopin tries to emphasize the veracity of the tale by ending it in dialect. She thereby highlights the issue of the story's language. The fact that Manna-Loulou and Madame Delisle speak the same dialect helps to stress their regional similarities rather than their differences in class. Nonetheless, Chopin does emphasize racial distinctions. Chopin's final emphasis on the "real" language Manna-Loulou speaks contrasts with Zoraïde's choice of the fake baby and her mistress' preference for the bogus black man, M. Ambroise. The whole story calls the category of "mulatto" into question. The emphasis on true story-telling parallels the emphasis on racial purity. The racial distinctions between Manna-Loulou and her mistress are more important than their shared dialect. Anna Elfenbein's argument that Chopin questioned racism is less convincing than Helen Taylor's contention that Chopin accepted racist views (737–41). **Toth and Seyersted 1998:** As this story illustrates, in later life Chopin depicted maternal black women attractively (125). This story is mentioned in Chopin's account books (140, 149, 165). This work provides examples of the French spoken in New Orleans in Chopin's day (226). **Benfey 1999:** This story deals ironically with the theme of the return of the dead, explores the connections between birth and death, delves into the sociology of New Orleans, and shows the influence of writings by G.W. Cable. The bond between Zoraïde and Mézor is suggested by the syllable their names share, while the ambiguous personality of Madame Delarivière reflects the complexities of New Orleans itself, which almost becomes a character in this tale. The story epitomizes many traits of Chopin's most important recent writings (236–38). **Bonner and Bonner 1999:** This story shows Chopin's familiarity with Bayou St. John, which was on the outer edge of New Orleans (58). **Bryant 1999:** Here as elsewhere Chopin combines interests in ethnicity, gender, and economic status (31). Some critics, just like the passive Madame Delisle, fail to appreciate the larger meaning of Manna-Loulou's story. Even the narrator of the frame tale is impercipient or prejudiced—perhaps reflecting traits of Chopin herself (45–46). **Koloski 1999:** This tale, like some other stories near the end of *Bayou Folk*, is gloomy in atmosphere; the joy often expressed in the earlier tales has vanished. Instead, these later works show the malign influence of the past rather than focusing on a hopeful tomorrow (xv). The present tale is one of various works in which Chopin shows affection that exists across color lines, and in which she presents racial issues objectively (xx). **McCullough 1999:** In this story maternity cannot be understood apart from race and region. Motherhood is therefore revealed not as a universal category but as one that is socially constructed. Zoraïde's godmother acts more from political than maternal motives; her obsession with power becomes obvious when Zoraïde disobeys her. The godmother ignores Zoraïde's own maternal desires. Although the story flirts with racial stereotypes in describing Zoraïde's passion for Mézor, it escapes them (at least in part) by stressing her deliberate love for a black man. Ironically, Zoraïde's rejection of her own child is an attempt to retain personal control of her maternal feelings. In addition, the rag doll allows her to avoid marrying M. Ambroise. The doll also symbolizes the link between Zoraïde's erotic and maternal instincts since it represents her connection with Mézor. Motherhood also enters this story through the relation between the maternal Manna-Loulou and her childish owner. Manna-Loulou is, in one sense, the controlling figure, just as she is also in control of the story. On the other hand, Manna-Loulou herself is a character controlled by the white author, Chopin. Madame Delisle's misinterpretation of Manna-Loulou's tale conveniently side-steps issues of racial domination. However, by showing bogus concern for Zoraïde's baby, Madame Delisle actually resembles even more the white slave-owner in Manna-Loulou's story. The shift to French dialect at the end creates artistic, historical, and regional distance, but it also challenges Northern views of a monolithic South. The dialect helps emphasize the extent to which every aspect of life—including motherhood—is culturally contingent (209–19). Anna Elfenbein's reading of this story is especially effective (319). **Toth 1999a:** This is one of many tales whose themes early critics failed to connect to Chopin's own life and views (3). This story, like some of Chopin's other most currently popular works, first appeared in *Vogue* (9). **Toth 1999c:** In this tale Chopin attempts to adopt the perspective of an African-American female (12). The story reflects reminiscences she had heard about dancing by blacks in antebellum New Orleans (68), and one of Chopin's own children was probably tended to by a black woman (70). As in other tales, Chopin shows tenderness here toward African-American mothers (78). This story contains the first description of birth Chopin ever published. In this highly original tale, Chopin became the first white female writer of fiction in the United States to depict a dark-skinned African-American male as erotically attractive. The narrative was also one of the few of its time narrated from the perspective of a black woman. Such multiculturalism may have resulted from Chopin's own diverse ethnic and geographical backgrounds (138–39). The story illustrates the diverse characters and sometimes tragic tone of *Bayou Folk* (150–51), although it also exemplifies Chopin's frequent focus on admirable women

(154). Like many of her stories of illicit desire, this one was submitted to *Vogue*, which often published her most unconventional fiction (171–72). When visiting New Orleans, Chopin sometimes met with a local writer who had also composed a story similar to this one (207). **Gibbons 2000:** This story reveals not only Chopin's progress away from local color conventions but also her continuing allegiance to them. The figurative language is still often (but not always) hackneyed; the characters are often largely (but not entirely) stereotyped; and the tone is still greatly (but not completely) sentimental. This work, like several others, represents a potential turning point in Chopin's career (xxxii). **Knights 2000:** This work, one of Chopin's most compelling, was produced during a particularly creative period—the fall and summer of 1893 (xv). This is one of various works in which Chopin juxtaposes an individual life with a larger social context (xviii–xix). A revision of the original version of this extremely complex tale suggests that either Chopin or her editors felt that Mézor, not Zoraïde, should take the romantic initiative (xxiv–xxv). Here as elsewhere Chopin emphasizes endangered or suppressed languages and minorities. The dialect Manna-Loulou uses was a matter of controversy at the time Chopin wrote, but Chopin treats it with respect (xxxvi). As with other works, Chopin revised the original version in ways that slightly diminish the story's force (xlvi). Either editors or Chopin herself added a subtitle to the first version of this work to tone down its impact (xlvi–xlvii).

"The Bênitous' Slave"

Written: 1892. First published: 1892. Included in *Bayou Folk* (1894).

An unnamed narrator tells of old Uncle Oswald, a former slave who believes he belongs to the Bênitous family, even though it has been almost fifty years since they owned him. Monsieur had tried every way he knew to change Uncle Oswald's mind, but to no avail. In fact, there are no Bênitous left in the parish except one frail little woman who lives with her daughter in Natchitoches town.

Still, Uncle Oswald keeps running away from Monsieur, trying to find the Bênitous. Since he is so old and confused, he often gets hurt in these searches. Finally Monsieur, who is fond of Uncle Oswald, decides there is nothing to do but put him in a place where he can be safe and cared for. Reluctantly, he takes Uncle Oswald to Natchitoches to board the train for the institution. They arrive early, though, so Monsieur ties the horses at the hotel, settles Uncle Oswald on a shady bench, and goes inside. Uncle Oswald leans on his cane and watches the passers-by until he drowses off. A little girl passes just as Uncle Oswald nods off and drops his cane. When she picks it up and gives it back to him, he is pleased, and when she tells him that her name is Suzanne Bênitous, Uncle Oswald jumps up and follows her to Madame Bênitous' millinery shop. Monsieur finds him there after a frantic search. Both Madame Bênitous and her daughter are puzzled by the old servant who stands, hat in hand, patiently awaiting their instructions. Monsieur persuades Madame Bênitous to accept Uncle Oswald's gift of his services for the old man's peace of mind. So Uncle Oswald never runs away anymore. He chops wood, fetches water, carries packages, and even makes coffee, all happily and faithfully. **(CY)**

***

Rankin 1932: The story uses the Civil War merely as background rather than emphasizing it strongly (140). **Bush 1957:** Here as in other stories, Chopin depicts loyal slaves (243). **Seyersted 1969a:** This is one of several stories by Chopin illustrating the fidelity freed blacks often showed to whites (79). **Potter 1971:** This story shows how slavery has permanently corrupted Uncle Oswald's thinking, making him a sad figure who achieves happiness only by rejecting his freedom. He is not simply an Uncle Tom, nor is he truly devoted to his old white owners; instead, he is mentally disturbed, able to exist only by renouncing his liberty (48). **Peterson 1972:** This is one of several rather conventional tales about unusual personalities that Chopin composed for young readers (59–60). **Arner 1975:** This tale is comparable to "Old Aunt Peggy," which focuses on an elderly black female (62–63). **Bonner 1977:** This is one of only two stories in *Bayou Folk* that are narrated by a character in the tale. Such narration plays a key role here (7). This is one of several stories from *Bayou Folk* in which travel is a key device of plot (8). In this story and others, Chopin quickly describes a personality. Such brief and usually comic tales are often interspersed with longer, darker stories in *Bayou Folk* (9–10). **Dyer 1981a:** This is one of several stories by Chopin that use repeating male professional characters, thus adding depth and continuity to her fiction (54). **Jones 1981:** Although the story can be read as justifying slavery, it can also be read as exemplifying the title character's strong sense of selfhood and his determination to achieve his desires (150–51). **Toth 1981:** Here and in some other early tales, the black characters fit the stereotype of the happy slave (202). **Dyer 1985:** This is one of several tales by Chopin about extreme nostalgia (74). **Skaggs 1985:** This is one of several stories dealing with the selfhood of ex-slaves. Although disturbing, it is also psychologically realistic (16–17). It is also one of several tales featuring a black character concerned with social class (60). **Ewell 1986:** This somewhat disappointing tale is not much more than a conventional, maudlin depiction of a loyal freed black and his benevolent former owners (67). **Manders 1990:** Here as in several of her other stories featuring blacks, Chopin presents a variation of the conventional figure of the "wretched freeman"—the erstwhile slave who allegedly had benefited from subjection. However, her focus on former domestic slaves, rather than on the more abused fieldworkers, makes her depiction more credible (37–40). Both the elderly black and the young white in this work are depicted here as innocently childlike, but such pairing contributes to the complexity of the tale (40). **Toth 1990a:** The hotel depicted here had a real Louisiana counterpart (140). This somewhat conventional tale was one of three stories Chopin wrote in two days and was quickly purchased for publication (206–7). **Fusco 1994:** In this story as in others, the plot structure is extremely simple and resembles structures used in some earlier American fiction. Likewise, the tone is uncritical (146–47). **Goodwyn 1994:** This is one of various stories in which Chopin depicts the stereotype of the loyal black (10). **Bender 1996:** Chopin's Darwinian views help explain this tale of a slave who seems content with slavery (107). **Koloski 1996:** A detail in "A No-Account Creole" is clarified by a reference in this story (18), which depicts the striving for selfhood and safety (71–72). This was one of various narratives Chopin wrote for young people (66). **Tuttleton 1996:** Even the title of this tale implies its regional focus (182). **Beer 1997:** This is one of various stories by Chopin that deal with the fidelity of blacks toward whites (35). Ironically, Oswald's sense of himself as a slave outlasts the institution of slavery itself, thus showing the human impact of social systems. Oswald's fate illustrates the ways in which the South limited itself by practicing slavery (70–71). Ironically, the characters in this story achieve relief by buying even more deeply into the roles society has imposed on them (73). Chopin treats Oswald not as a stereotype but as an exemplary individual (76). The story seems more complex than Richard Fusco suggests (84). **Toth and Seyersted 1998:** This story is mentioned in Chopin's account books (139, 148, 166). **Koloski 1999:** This is one of many stories by Chopin which either feature children or were written for them (xxii). **McCullough 1999:** This is one of various stories by Chopin whose underlying attitudes seem implicitly racist (319). **Toth 1999c:** This was one of Chopin's early, conventional tales about the loyalty of blacks to whites (169).

"Beyond the Bayou"

Written: 1891. First published: 1893. Included in *Bayou Folk* **(1894).**

La Folle's cabin is on a point of land surrounded by a bayou. She never crosses the bayou because she was badly frightened by the sight of violence when she was a child and has not been "right" since then. She is called La Folle because of her obsessive fear.

Now she is middle-aged and lives alone on the other side of the bayou. The others on the plantation are used to La Folle's ways and pay no attention to her. P'tit Maître has several daughters and one son, whom La Folle loves as if he were her own. She calls him Chéri.

It is Saturday and La Folle has baked Chéri some croquignoles. He appears at her cabin with his pockets full of treats for her. He has his new rifle on his shoulder. He is ten years old and old enough for his own gun.

Chéri goes into the woods behind La Folle's cabin to hunt for squirrels. La Folle hears a gunshot followed by a cry of distress. She drops what she is doing and runs with fear in every step to find Chéri. She finds him lying on the ground with a gunshot in his leg. He has stumbled, and the gun has gone off. The boy thinks he is dying. La Folle picks him up and carries him to the edge of the bayou.

She cries and yells for help, but no one comes. The bayou is dry from lack of rain; La Folle closes her eyes and runs across the bayou. When she gets to the other side she opens her eyes and follows the footpath. By the time she gets to the house, she has attracted a following of people amazed that she has crossed the bayou. She is terrified. As soon as she hands Chéri over to his father she faints.

La Folle awakes in her own cabin with Tante Lizette caring for her. The doctor says she might die. She tells Tante Lizette to give her some herb tea to make her sleep. She sleeps soundly and wakes up early the next morning. She puts on her Sunday apron and walks straight to the main house. On her way she sees beautiful cotton fields and flowers; she smells the heavy fragrance of the magnolias; she is exultant. She knocks on the door and inquires about Chéri. His mother says that he is better but is sleeping.

La Folle sits down on the steps to wait for Chéri to wake up. She watches for the first time the sun rise on the world beyond the bayou. Her face holds a look of wonder and contentment. **(DR)**

***

Anonymous 1894 [*The Critic*]: The very simplicity and brevity of this tale contributes to its effectiveness (41). **Rankin 1932:** La Folle resembles one kind of person whom Chopin may well have met during her time in Cloutierville (103). The story uses the Civil War merely as background rather than emphasizing it strongly (140). **Bush 1957:** Like many stories by Chopin, this one focuses on an unconventional character whose chief impulse is affection. In this case, such affection is capable of healing a psychosis (243). Here as elsewhere, affection is shown to have a transforming power (244). **Arms 1967:** Despite being written for young readers, this story typifies Chopin's mature gifts as a local-color writer. Although the story risks seeming maudlin in its focus on an old black woman overcoming her anxiety to help a young white boy, the contrast between fear and affection seems intrinsic to the plot rather than mechanically imposed (222–23). **Seyersted 1969a:** La Folle is presented in psychologically complex ways that transcend conventional depictions (80). **Leary 1970a:** This is one of many works in which Chopin depicts the ambiguities and complexities of love (x). **Leary 1971:** Theme: the link between courage and affection (166). **Potter 1971:** The heroine here is a skillfully depicted individual who is distinctive even in appearance. Isolated and independent, she eventually overcomes her powerful anxiety thanks to the even greater force of her affection. The fact that she is black seems relatively minor (50). **Peterson 1972:** Chopin shows restraint in dealing with a potentially maudlin tale. She gives mythic themes a psychological dimension, and the crossing of the water has a baptismal quality, releasing La Folle into a sensuous experience she hasn't known before (64–66). Chopin's satisfaction with this tale prompted her to imitate it in "After the Winter" (78). Here as elsewhere, Chopin uses children symbolically but also somewhat simplistically (103). Typically, Chopin spotlights one character whose changed perspective ends the tale (114–15). Although written according to popular conventions, this story is one of Chopin's more original (271). **Rocks 1972:** This is one of many stories in which Chopin suggests that each person must decide whether it is better to be content with one's present condition or attempt to alter one's future. The results of either choice cannot be predicted. This is one of her most deeply suggestive tales. The story implies that pain sometimes provides the incentive for change (115–16). **Arner 1975:** This story illustrates Chopin's rapid development as a writer who became capable of treating thoughts and feelings in complex ways. The story is effective in its use of drama, diction, design, and depiction of character (23–24). This is one of Chopin's better stories showing the aftermath of the Civil War. Its language, characters, and setting are credible, and the syntax used at the very beginning helps emphasize important themes. La Folle's existence is framed by two jolting experiences, and mania is finally counterbalanced by affection (44–45). **Bonner 1977:** Here as elsewhere, *Bayou Folk* reveals Chopin's talent for creating rich characters and for presenting, rather than announcing, their traits (6). She treats her black characters as individual persons rather than as stereotypes (6–7). Here and elsewhere in Chopin, mental illness is a major theme (10). As in other *Bayou Folk* tales, the focus here on a threatened child helps resolve the plot (10). The story shows how intense affection leads to mental breakdown (11). This is one of Chopin's more effective treatments in *Bayou Folk* of the human mind. The story implies the blurred boundaries between sanity and its opposite (12). The story explores the topic of past vs. present (13). This is one of the best stories in *Bayou Folk* (13). **Wolff 1978:** This is one of many stories by Chopin dealing with the instability of human experience (126). **Wolff 1979:** Like many of Chopin's stories, this one touches on the topic on insanity, showing how madness breeds alienation which in turn breeds further madness (215). **Dyer 1981a:** This is one of several stories by Chopin that use repeating male professional characters, thus adding depth and continuity to her fiction (54). **Fluck 1982:** The story illustrates Chopin's concern with transgression and emancipation (162). **Lattin 1982:** This is one of several stories in which Chopin shows how change can simultaneously involve loss, maturation, and self-discovery (227–28; 230). **Aherne 1985:** This is one of Chopin's stories that emphasize children; it shows how affection can overwhelm dread (83). **Skaggs 1985:** This is one of several stories featuring characters whose lives and minds have been disrupted by the Civil War (15). **Ewell 1986:** This is one of several stories that skillfully employ contrasting locales (34–35). It explores a topic Chopin frequently examined: how love could triumph over the effects of hate. Chopin's rewriting of the original children's tale shows her growing craft, increasing thematic and psychological subtlety, and effective use of setting and design (particularly in the contrasts between La Folle's two late excursions). The child embodies the bonds that link humans across space and time, while the revised descriptions of setting help objectify La Folle's new mental state. Although the resolution here is less complex than is typical of Chopin's later endings, this story nonetheless shows her ability to treat familiar topics with skill and distinction (62–63). **Inge 1989:** Themes: the potential of affection to free and exult the human character; the archetypal movement toward self-knowledge by confronting the past; the transition from a state of almost animalistic existence to a more fully human life; and (as in Eudora Welty's later story "The Worn Path") the force of a woman's courage. In this tale Chopin gives landscape archetypal significance (94–95). **Papke 1990:** The story focuses on alienation but does not explain its origins in social strife. Chopin reunites the main character with society almost too simplistically, yet she does imply that such harmony is fragile (52–53). **Toth 1990a:** This tale describes a black woman scarred by the Civil War (70) and is one of several in which Chopin shows an interest in black females despite her relative lack of interest in racial politics (136). The protagonist, like others Chopin created, loves the beauty of her locale (155). Although published in a young persons' magazine, the story shows an interest in the serious topic of war. It was one of several stories from 1891 in which Chopin sought a friendly, interested readership (201–2), and it influenced her later work "Tante Cat'rinette" (235). **Boren 1992:** The idyllic setting contrasts with the dark circumstances of the main character. Chopin uses a particular place to reinforce a general theme presented through the lives of psychologically rich characters (3–5). **Goodwyn 1994:** This is one of various stories in which Chopin depicts the stereotype of the loyal black (10). **Green 1994:** The story both resembles and differs from Zora Neale Hurston's "Sweat" in its treatment of the ways society marginalizes certain groups (105–6). La Folle is enslaved both literally and psychologically (106), and even when she achieves a certain mental freedom at the end of the tale, that liberty is sharply limited (107). Unlike Hurston's Delia, however, La Folle is victimized mainly because of her race, rather than because of her race and gender combined (117). Her fear, which is rooted in a dread of alienation and is often described in imagery associated with bodily fluids, isolates her from other blacks as well as from the white youngster she dotes on (117–18). She has strong links with neither whites nor blacks. However, by acting as a substitute mother who is concerned for an injured child, she also begins to overcome her own marginality (119). Her full sense of freedom from fear occurs, significantly, on Sunday, and she then begins to reach out to others directly (120). Ironically, however, she is still treated with circumspection, although now she gently resists such treatment (121). In this sense she foreshadows the later, larger refusal of black Americans to continue to be subservient, and this implication is reinforced by Chopin's closing use of sun imagery (122). **Koloski 1994:** The story is included in soft-cover collections of Chopin's fiction published in 1970 and 1981 (27). This work also often appears in college textbooks (28–29). **Koloski 1996:** Crossing boundaries is an important topic in this story (40; 84), which movingly depicts the plight of an African-American (44; 47) and which has attracted more and more interest recently, even though it was originally written for a young audience (68–69). As in other works, Chopin here depicts an unusual person's powers of transformation, but this tale is one of her most effective (71–72). No proper names are mentioned in the story, which was one of Chopin's works for children (87). **Llewellyn 1996:** The sluggish bayou is an appropriate setting for La Folle's initially dormant existence, and it affects both her and the way we read the story. The bleak surrounding landscape also parallels her mental isolation and sense of danger. Her home is as far removed geographically from the master's house as she is removed in culture, race, and status. The other slave cabins are also distant in similar ways from the mansion. Chopin makes readers participate in La Folle's psychological experiences, partly by structuring the story around parallels of past and present. By crossing the bayou, La

Folle also transcends her past. The bayou symbolizes both her present isolation and her link to the past. The concluding sentence directly contrasts with the opening one, and the brevity of the story emphasizes the contrast. The story unfolds like a wave, rather than like a straight line, and the progress takes place not only on the page but also within the mind of the reader (255–62). **Wagner-Martin 1996:** This is one of many stories by Chopin featuring appealing black characters (203). **Beer 1997:** This is one of various stories by Chopin that deal with the fidelity of blacks toward whites (35). **Toth and Seyersted 1998:** As this story illustrates, in later life Chopin depicted maternal black women attractively (125). The work is mentioned in Chopin's account books (139, 148, 169). **Bryant 1999:** Here as elsewhere Chopin combines interests in ethnicity, gender, and economic status (31). Although La Folle finally asserts herself, she does so in a way that confirms her subordination. She fits various stereotypes and is juxtaposed with an equally stereotypical white heroine (48). **Green 1999:** This story calls into question Helen Taylor's notion that Chopin was a racist (23). **Koloski 1999:** Here as in other stories, Chopin depicts a character who reacts to a symbolic boundary (viii). This is one of many stories by Chopin which either feature children or were written for them, although its themes seem quite mature (xxii). **Toth 1999c:** This is one of Chopin's tales about the affection of African-American women toward white youngsters (12). It also depicts the lasting psychological damage caused by war (33) even while showing the strength of maternal feelings (78). The tale is one of the darker narratives included in *Bayou Folk* (151), but it is also one presenting an admirable woman (154). In its depiction of race relations, however, the story is highly conventional and probably did not present much of a challenge to Chopin (169). **Gibbons 2000:** This story reveals Chopin's growth beyond local color conventions, and the adventurousness of the heroine prefigures that of Edna in *The Awakening*. Although the style of the tale is conventional and emotional, the story foreshadows Chopin's later achievement in her great novel (xxxi–xxxii). **Knights 2000:** This was one of the numerous works Chopin composed in 1891 (xv). Even in this work for a fairly conventional magazine, Chopin shows a willingness to confront an unusual theme (xviii). One way to read the story is as a reassertion of a lost domination by whites, figured here in the final imagery of rebirth. However, the tale can also be interpreted in more complex terms, especially because of its empathy with its black protagonist. In the original version of the work, the story is especially accessible to young readers, perhaps in order to encourage new ways of thinking and behaving (xxx–xxxi). When originally published, this tale was printed with "local color" stories by other writers (xxxii). Here as elsewhere Chopin focuses on endangered minority languages (xxv). As with other works, Chopin revised the original version in ways that slightly diminish the story's force (xlvi).

"The Blind Man"

Written: 1896. First published: 1897. Included in *A Vocation and a Voice* **(1991).**

An unnamed narrator tells the story of a blind man in his faded, worn-out clothes selling pencils on the street and door to door. This is his first day out, because someone who had finally grown tired of his hanging around had given him the box of pencils and put him out to fend for himself. His stomach is gnawing with hunger and he is very hot.

He drifts to a side street where a group of children is playing. One of them tries to take his pencils away from him and, in defense, he shouts at the children, calling them names. A policeman sees the disturbance. Realizing that the man is blind, he simply sends him on his way. The blind man rambles on and comes to a street where there are loud electric cars with clanging bells. He starts to cross the street when something terrible happens.

A crowd quickly forms, with people running and women fainting. One of the wealthiest and most influential men in town has been killed by an electric car. He was rushing from his office to have dinner with his family before they left for their summer home on the coast and did not see the car.

The blind man does not know what all the commotion is about. He just crosses the street and stumbles along his way. **(DR)**

***

Peterson 1972: In this tale irony is especially strong, and although the ending is somewhat contrived, it effectively illustrates the idea that life can be as lacking in meaningful direction as the main character of this work (176–77). **Arner 1975:** This tale may reflect a mood of grimness in Chopin. Per Seyersted's contrast between the longstanding but largely overlooked pain of the blind man's life and the quick but notorious death of the rich man does not go far enough in explaining the resonance of the tale, which seems to suggest that all human lives are subject to inexplicable, enigmatic forces (99). **Skaggs 1985:** This is one of several tales that explore the unpredictability of persons and events (45–46). **Ewell 1986:** Perhaps this somewhat provocative and lively story was inspired by a similar work by Maupassant. Like other tales Chopin wrote at around the same time, this one seems to mock social inequities and injustice, although its tone is less bleak than the tone of Maupassant's work. The cleverly postponed ending implies that the on-lookers are as imperceptive in their own ways as the blind man they ignore, partly because they focus on wealth and status

(127). In its implied sarcasm, the story resembles "Miss McEnders" and "Elizabeth Stock's One Story" (167). **Stepenoff 1987:** This story reflects the urbanization occurring in Chopin's own hometown of St. Louis (455). It is one of the few stories in American fiction of the time to focus on urban life. Chopin shows little charitable feeling for the title character. The ending of the tale may reflect the sudden death of Chopin's own father. Unlike "A Pair of Silk Stockings," this work emphasizes the dangers of city life (458). **Toth 1990a:** This story mocking the wealthy was published in a magazine directed at up-scale readers (281). It is one of two stories about vision that Chopin wrote during the same year, perhaps because her own vision may have been weakening (286). The tale was intended for publication in *A Vocation and a Voice* (374). **Toth 1991:** This is one of many of Chopin's late works that were first printed in *Vogue* (xiii–xiv). It is one of various stories in *A Vocation and a Voice* that seem to satirize contemporary class relations (xxiv–xxv). **Fusco 1994:** Here as in other tales, Chopin initially misleads the reader (153). **Koloski 1994:** The story is included in a soft-cover collection of Chopin's fiction published in 1991 (29). **Toth and Seyersted 1998:** This story is mentioned in Chopin's account books (141, 150). It is one of several works in which she describes morose, angry male misfits (274). **Toth 1999c:** The subject of this tale—a physically handicapped man—was unusual for the women's magazine in which it was published (172). This was one of the various tales with dark themes that Chopin planned to publish in *A Vocation and a Voice* (208).

"Boulôt and Boulotte"

Written: 1891. First published: 1891. Included in: *Bayou Folk* (1894).

When the twins, Boulôt and Boulotte, become twelve years old, the family decides it is time for them to begin wearing shoes. The two are brown-skinned, black-eyed, plump children who live with their parents and a whole company of brothers and sisters halfway up a piney-wood hill. Now Boulôt and Boulotte can pay for the shoes themselves, because they have saved the money they have earned from selling wild fruit to the village ladies. In addition, they are to go to Natchitoches Parish and buy the shoes themselves. So the next Saturday afternoon, the whole group gathers to watch Boulôt and Boulotte set out together, with their savings tied in a nice handkerchief.

Before it is time for them to return, the same group gathers outside the cabin to watch for them. Soon they hear voices below, and then they see the twins coming, still hand-in-hand but still barefoot. Their sister screams in dismay and asks if they are crazy; they went to buy shoes but have come home barefoot. Boulôt is so embarrassed that he blushes and hangs his head. Then he lifts the fine new brogans that he is carrying. Boulotte, too, holds up her shoes for them to see: shiny high-heeled slippers with bright buttons. Looking down her nose at them, she retorts, "You think we go buy shoes fur ruin it in de dus'?" Then they all go inside feeling chastised, except for Boulotte (who had taken charge of the situation) and baby Seraphin (who did not care). **(CY)**

***

Rankin 1932: This brief but superb story, which is convincingly realistic and highly pleasing, inspired praise from William Dean Howells in a letter that is now lost (132). **Seyersted 1969a:** This children's tale inspired William Dean Howells to write to Chopin and encourage more such work—apparently their only correspondence and his only assessment of her writing (54). **Peterson 1972:** This is a well-wrought piece of fiction for (and about) youngsters. The tone is effective, although an earlier critic who praised the work for its depiction of poverty-stricken whites was probably too kind (58–59). **Arner 1975:** Although this story lacks a very strong plot, it is nonetheless one of the best examples available of the local color style in U.S. literature (43) and in one small respect it may foreshadow Faulkner's *Light in August* (61). **Bonner 1977:** In this story and others, Chopin quickly describes an event. Such brief and usually comic tales are often interspersed with longer, darker stories in *Bayou Folk* (9–10). **Skaggs 1985:** This is one of several tales depicting unusually independent girls (12–13). **Ewell 1986:** This extremely brief and very straightforward work exemplifies many of the most successful aspects of Chopin's craft, including her ability to pique our interest, her manipulation of perspective, her sharp and vivid focus, her ability to avoid a maudlin tone even when writing about the very young and the very poor, and especially her deft use of local color and regional speech. Such speech is emphasized only at the end, where it helps give the tale its comic touch (51–52). **Papke 1990:** Most of the stories Chopin wrote during this year seem fairly predictable, perhaps because she was focusing most of her activity on calling attention to her novels. This tale, though, is one of several from this period that present unusual female protagonists, most of whom defy social rules but do so for sensible purposes and therefore seem less defiant than they may first appear (52). **Toth 1990a:** William Dean Howells complimented this tale (192), which was one of several stories from 1891 in which Chopin sought a friendly, interested readership (201). It affectionately mocks the confusions of children (202). Chopin was paid five dollars for the story (204), which was later plagiarized (325). **Dyer 1993:** Although the story may emphasize dialect too much and be too simple in characterization, it is nonetheless important for the way it deals with twins, especially since twins also appear in *The Awakening*. In this tale Chopin shows how twins can differ in personality, and, significantly, she makes the female twin the more assertive of the two (38–39). **Koloski 1994:** The story is included in a soft-cover collection of Chopin's fiction published in 1979 (27). **Koloski 1996:** This is one of several children's stories by Chopin that depict the poor (71; 87). **Wagner-Martin 1996:** This is one of many stories by Chopin featuring appealing young boys (203). **Fusco 1997:** In this story as in others, the plot structure is extremely simple and resembles structures used in some earlier American fiction. Likewise, the tone is uncritical (146–47). **Beer 1997:** Previous readings of this story have tended to miss its serious implications. The twins resist wearing the shoes because doing so will divide and distinguish them, especially in terms of gender. The shoes symbolize the gender distinctions which will now separate them for the rest of their lives (82–83). Such differences are already hinted at when we first see the twins, but the distinctions become explicit near the end of the tale. Boulôt's shoes are practical, whereas Boulotte's shoes are pretty. Boulotte resists the restrictions the shoes symbolize. They represent an initiation into the world of adult distinctions, and Chopin's use of this symbolism gives this tale a seriousness it might otherwise seem to lack (83–84). **Toth and Seyersted 1998:** This story is mentioned in Chopin's account books (139, 148, 173). **Koloski 1999:** This is one of Chopin's tales that focuses on the young (viii; xxii). Here as elsewhere she describes children's responses to poverty (xxiii). **Toth 1999c:** William Dean Howells privately commended this tale (130). The story added to the varied tones of *Bayou Folk* (151).

"The Boy"

Unpublished fragment. Included in *Private Papers* (1998).

... a boy approaches a group of Catholic religious brothers and asks to see the Superior. An older man takes a kindly interest in him and offers to lead him to the Superior. Along the way, he asks what the boy wants. At first the boy says he would like to say confession; then he admits that he wants to live in the brotherhood. The older man promises to speak to the superior on the boy's behalf.... **(RCE)**

***

Toth and Seyersted 1998: This is an early version of "A Vocation and a Voice" (135). It was borrowed by Chopin's first biographer and was not rediscovered until the 1990s (245). It is reprinted here (269–71).

"Caline"

Written: 1892. First published: 1893. Included in *A Night in Acadie* (1897).

Caline lives with her parents in a small cabin in the woods. She is napping under a haystack one day when suddenly she is awakened by a strange sound, the sound of a train stopping abruptly. Her father also hears the train stop and is leaning on his plow. Something is wrong with the engine. The passengers come out of the cars to see what is wrong. Some of the ladies try to talk to Caline, but they cannot understand her dialect. One young man takes a sketch book out of his pocket and begins to draw Caline. Before he finishes his drawing, the train is repaired. All the passengers board the train and are gone.

Caline now can never watch the train pass again without wondering who the people on the train are, where they come from, and where they are going. She talks to the flagman, who tells her about the city. He lived there once and his sister lives there now. He tells Caline that his sister would not mind having someone to help around her house. He writes a note to his sister and gives it to Caline as she boards the train.

At first Caline loves the city, but after three weeks she is not so sure if she likes it or not. She cries because she now realizes that it was not the city or its crowds that she was looking for, but rather the young man who drew her picture. **(DR)**

***

Leary 1970a: This tale may have been influenced by Sarah Orne Jewett's "The White Heron" (viii).　**Leary 1971:** This story was probably influenced by Sarah Orne Jewett's "The White Heron" (165). **Rocks 1972:** This is one of many stories in which Chopin suggests that each person must decide whether it is better to be content with one's present condition or attempt to alter one's future. The results of either choice cannot be predicted (115). **Arner 1975:** Here as in *The Awakening* (since awakening is a significant theme of the story), Chopin shows how affection can produce illusions. The tale resembles John Greenleaf Whittier's "Maud Muller" (66). **Wolff 1978:** This is one of many stories by Chopin dealing with the instability of human experience (126). **Dyer 1980–81:** This is one of many stories by Chopin in which a female is aroused by contact with a male (10–11). **Dyer 1981d:** Here and in numerous other works, Chopin uses physical setting to imply what a character is feeling. Her frequent use of this technique is open to various explanations (451–52). **Skaggs 1985:** This is one of several stories by Chopin that explore romance (32). **Ewell 1986:** Highly praised by at least one contemporary, this delicate tale centers on a character who wakes up both literally and figuratively. Her final disenchantment—a topic also reflected in other stories Chopin wrote at around this time—is a kind of pain to which all humans can relate. Josephine Donovan in 1980 raised the possibility that the story may have been inspired by Jewett's "The White Heron" [however, see Leary 1970a and 1971] (100–101). **Inge 1989:** In this story, stirrings of sexuality are linked to final disappointment (100). **Toth 1990a:** The story, which resembles a work by a Norwegian writer (287), was reprinted in *A Night in Acadie* (298), and one male reader called it a small masterwork (328). **Koloski 1994:** The story is included in a soft-cover collection of Chopin's fiction published in 1970 (27). **Toth and Seyersted 1998:** This story is mentioned in Chopin's account books (140, 149, 155). The tone of this story resembles that of the "Doralise" fragment (272). **Toth 1999c:** This story, which Chopin originally published in *Vogue* (172), was one of only several in *A Night in Acadie* dealing with youthful females, most of whom suffer in some way (194). **Knights 2000:** This story, like others by Chopin, gains added interest when read in the context of the materials with which it was originally published (xix). Here as elsewhere Chopin depicts artists as strangers who unsettle local conditions (xxxiv). She also typically juxtaposes contrasting cultures (xxxvi).

"Cavanelle"

Written: 1894. First published: 1895. Included in *A Night in Acadie* (1897).

A customer at the dry goods store tells the story of Cavanelle, a clerk at the store who wears worn-out clothes and deprives himself of life's necessities in order to pay for voice lessons for his younger sister, Mathilde.

Cavanelle is totally devoted to his sister and her career in music. Every time the narrator goes into the store, Cavanelle talks to her about his sister. He says that her voice is the most beautiful he has ever heard and that with a little maturity and strength she will be the best opera singer in the world. The curiosity of the narrator grows so great that she finally requests to meet Mathilde and hear her sing. Cavanelle is excited and gives her directions to their home.

Upon arriving at the home of Cavanelle and his sister, the narrator finds herself sadly disappointed. Mathilde is a frail little girl with absolutely no stage presence, and her voice is horrible. All madame can say is that Cavanelle loves his sister and that love is blind.

It is now two years since madame last saw Cavanelle and Mathilde. Mathilde died about a year after her visit. Madame thinks that now Cavanelle surely can afford to buy himself a decent set of clothes and does not have to sacrifice the necessities of life. She is wrong. Cavanelle cares for his elderly, ailing aunt who lives with him now.

At first, the narrator is exasperated with Cavanelle, but after giving it a little more thought she realizes that Cavanelle is an angel. **(DR)**

***

Anonymous 1897 [*Post-Dispatch*]: This is one of various stories by Chopin that seems appealing because of its subtle depiction of altruism (47). **Rankin 1932:** The reference in the story to the varied colors of street cars reflects Chopin's own fascination with local transportation in New Orleans (92). The story is a superb, subtle, and polished depiction of its loyal, uncomplicated title character (169). Of the tales included in *A Night in Acadie*, only "Nég Créol" may excel this one in its skillful depiction of devotion (169). **Seyersted 1969a:** This story illustrates Chopin's frequent emphasis on generosity and beneficence (77). It is one of only four of her works based on a verifiably real incident (217). **Rocks 1972:** Here as elsewhere, Chopin demonstrates the complexities liberty can involve and shows that often true liberty entails a responsible concern for others (117). **Arner 1975:** This is one of Chopin's most puzzling tales, particularly in its final attitude toward the title character (74–75). **Berggren 1977:** Here and elsewhere Chopin shows that life often seems meaningless unless one has a vocation—a selfless dedication to a larger purpose. Stories such as this show the personal rewards of altruism. This story also shows that men, not only women, can feel enriched by helping others (1). **Dyer 1985:** As in "Juanita" and "Vagabonds," Chopin here draws on first-hand knowledge but presents the narrator ironically in order to achieve distance from the events she describes (78). **Skaggs 1985:** This is one of several tales by Chopin emphasizing altruistic self-denial (31). **Ewell 1986:** Chopin had some trouble finding a publisher for this story (88), in which she returned to Creole themes after having put them aside for nearly half a year. The tale was greatly rewritten, partly to make it less topical, although it was composed at a time when she was writing other topical works using a first-person point of view. The tone of the piece is highly reflective and desultory—facts that give added point to its circular structure. Paradoxically, Cavanelle serves himself by serving others (101–2). **Toth 1988a:** This story reflects Chopin's personal familiarity with public transportation in New Orleans (58). **Toth 1990a:** This tale was printed in a new magazine for Jewish women edited by a friend of Chopin. The story—for which Chopin was paid little—was composed slowly, rejected frequently, edited heavily, and printed along with a photo of the author. Both the magazine and the story won praise (246–48). The female singer resembled a later friend of Chopin (263). The tale later appeared in *A Night in Acadie*, in which all the stories are set in Louisiana (298). **Koloski 1994:** The females in this tale, which was included in a 1992 anthology of New Orleans fiction, struck its editors as still relevant (26). **Koloski 1996:** This is one of various stories that reflect Chopin's interest in opera (57). **Toth and Seyersted 1998:** This story is mentioned in Chopin's account books (140, 159, 166, 172–73) and appears in her diary for 1894 (190). Like other works by Chopin, this one features an attractive, needy female artist (272). **Bonner and Bonner 1999:** The streetcars mentioned in this story help establish the status of the streets on which they run (63). **Toth 1999c:** Chopin's story was the first work published by the first non-Jewish author in the first American journal intended for Jewish females (179).

"Charlie"

Written: 1900. Included in *Complete Works* (1969).

While the six other Laborde daughters—aged nineteen to five—are already assembled for their morning studies, their seventeen-year-old sister Charlotte (or "Charlie") is late once again. Dressed like a tom-boy, she has been out riding her horse and checking on the arrival of a new bicycle. When she finally enters the room, the governess is not amused. She banishes Charlie to another location and threatens to report the girl to her father. Charlie, meanwhile, using her talent for verse, composes a poetic plea for mercy, even as she comically taunts various black servants for allegedly interrupting her studies. Soon, though, she speeds off on her new bike to look for her father, to whom she is devoted. For him, Charlie is almost the son he never had.

Charlie is pained when she confesses to her father that she was late for her studies, and she is even more pained when she sees his own look of disappointment as he rides off without her. Soon, though, she invites herself to lunch at the modest home of some poor Cajun neighbors. She impresses them with imaginative tales and then heads off for the woods, ostensibly to hunt bears and tigers. Instead, while target-shooting, she accidentally hits the arm of a young man walking through the forest. Identifying himself as Firman Walton, he tells her that he had been headed to her home from New Orleans on a business trip. When he and Charlie finally arrive home, Charlie abruptly confesses the entire incident to her father.

Walton, invited to stay at the home until his wound heals, begins to take an interest in Julia, the eldest daughter. Charlie, though, apparently begins to take an interest in Walton, even dressing up for dinner the next evening. Later that night, however, her father informs her that he has made arrangements to send her to a well disciplined boarding school for young ladies in New Orleans. Far from being disappointed, Charlie secretly looks forward to the change. A young neighbor named Gus is disconcerted when he hears that Charlie will be leaving, since he has taken a quietly shy interest in her for some time.

In New Orleans, Charlie becomes obsessed with feminine fashions, although she eventually moderates these impulses when she enters the seminary. While there, she throws herself into learning music, art, dancing, and other lady-like accomplishments, although she especially shines as a poet. She makes friends with the other girls and enjoys the visits of her family, especially her father, who treats her with devoted affection. She now prides herself on her soft hands, her new learning, and her compliant temper. Then, one day, she is summoned home with the startling news that her father has been injured.

Although badly hurt, her father survives. Charlie takes charge of caring for him, but eventually she is stunned and angered when she learns that Julia has become engaged to Walton. Charlie abruptly changes back into her old tom-boy clothes and impulsively gallops off on her horse. She immediately regrets the outburst against Julia and achieves a new maturity as a result. She vows to become her father's new right hand (since the accident has cost him an arm). Gus offers to help her oversee the plantation, and, as she and Gus ride off together, Charlie abandons the hand cream she had so recently valued. After months go by, Gus raises the possibility of marriage. Charlie gives him reasons to hope, although she stresses her duties and devotion to her sisters and especially to her father. **(RCE)**

***

Seyersted 1969a: The loss of Charlie's father's arm may represent Chopin's subtle revenge on men who had criticized her, but the accident gives Charlie the chance to reassume an earlier man-like assertiveness, symbolized by her spurs. Freudian critics might relate Charlie's obsession with her father to Chopin's own early losses of various male members of her family (183). The story revolves around interaction between strength and weakness, male and female, and activity and passivity (183–84). **Peterson 1972:** The story has too many incidents and too many characters; it lacks dynamic tension and develops rather haphazardly. Charlie has some real appeal but is insufficiently interesting to justify so long a tale. The story makes interesting comments about gender roles, but its ending is safely romantic (260–62). The work is one of Chopin's better final pieces, most of which imply that her talent had begun to diminish (269). **Rocks 1972:** Here as elsewhere Chopin shows how people grow by being pulled in opposite directions (120). **Solomon 1976:** Composed (along with eight other works) after the controversy surrounding *The Awakening* but never printed while Chopin lived, this was one of her final tales. Charlie resembles Mark Twain's Huck Finn, especially in the negative reaction her independence provokes from society (xx). Chopin effectively uses humor as she describes Charlie's efforts to conform to expectations, and she complexly presents Charlie's interactions with her father (xx–xxi). There is even an odd touch of courtship in the father's attitude when he visits his daughter. When her father is injured, however, Charlie blossoms, since her practicality is now a trait on which the family—and her father—depend. Perhaps Chopin implies that a woman can achieve full independence only when she is freed from the influence of powerful men (xxi). Seyersted has suggested that this is the first tale in which Chopin presents a woman's struggle against males. Perhaps the story thus reflects on her recently published novel, *The Awakening* (xxv). **Webb 1976:** This is one of various works by Chopin that center around movements into and away from New Orleans (6). Charlie moves into the city because of one accident and returns home because of a second mishap (6–8). She is stunned both by her father's injury and her sister's engagement, and her return home is paralleled by a return to her earlier style of life (8). Chopin shows skillful restraint by merely implying a romantic ending, but she also makes clear that Charlie is now too independent ever to become subservient again (9). **Taylor 1979:** Here as elsewhere, Chopin depicts a female playing the conventionally masculine role of artist and ultimately enjoying some success both in romance and in art (xvii). **Dyer 1981a:** Gouvernail, a skeptical character present in some of Chopin's earlier work, would be inappropriate in this story (55). **Jones 1981:** This is perhaps the only accomplished story Chopin wrote following the failed reception of *The Awakening* (139). It de-emphasizes sexuality as an explicit theme, focusing instead on how society shapes the behavior of the sexes. Although it is unclear to what degree Chopin was aware of any incestuous overtones in the story, she deals obviously with androgyny, and the tale finally seems to suggest that a woman can achieve freedom only by sacrificing her sexuality (142–44). **Davis 1982:** Charlie's unusual views of marriage are symptoms of her unusual views of herself, and in this sense the story is typical of much of Chopin's fiction (62). This is one of Chopin's lengthiest and most effective narratives. Charlie sometimes resembles her creator, while the tale seems highly mature in its various kinds of complexity (70). **McMahan 1985:** The heroine here is unusual in Chopin's fiction because she does not rush (or is not rushed into) marriage (32). **Skaggs 1985:** This is one of Chopin's most maudlin tales (63–64). **Ewell 1986:** The title character must discover that independence cannot be unlimited. She functions at first almost as a son, while her sisters embody various feminine stereotypes. Eventually, though, she is literally and symbolically disarmed of her almost masculine power. She moves from one extreme of gender role-playing to another, but she partly enlarges her potential for fuller humanity as a result, achieving a kind of balance. Nevertheless, Charlie ultimately seems a more timid character than Edna in *The Awakening*—a fact that may reflect Chopin's own anxious reaction to the negative reception the novel faced (177–80). **Newman 1986:** This tale illustrates how Chopin's skills as a writer affected the topics she explored. The story traces its main character's development toward maturity, seeming to show her adaptation to social expectations. Even her nick-name makes Charlie seem almost male at first (153). As she grows older she initially seems to abandon her earlier independence, and her relationship with her father appears at times metaphorically incestuous. Despite this surface pattern of male dominance, however, the story is quite psychologically complicated, and ultimately Charlie undercuts male power and moves beyond the stereotyped patterns of behavior her culture offers (154). Two events are key, and both center on injuries to the arms of men, while hand imagery is generally important in this tale. Initially Charlie seems locked into a self-involved reality rooted merely in her own mind (154), a fact that makes her resemble Mark Twain's Tom Sawyer more than his Huck Finn: her fantasies injure both herself and others, and Chopin does not present Charlie as a genuinely creative writer (155). Her attempts to write imply her conceitedness and her lack of commitment to personal growth (155). She wants to preserve her static, dependent relationship with her father, although her imaginings prove hurtful to nearly everyone around her (155–56). Sent to New Orleans, she there merely adopts another (if seemingly contrasting) prescribed role—that of the model daughter. Her father's almost sexual possessiveness toward her, however, goes unrequited, since her attention is now focused on Walton (156). Her poems, both the ones about him and the ones on other topics, suggest both her social and literary limitations. Both before and after the accident involving Charlie's father, references to arms are significant (157), while imagery of flowers (especially their smells) becomes important after the girl returns home (157–58). This return marks the beginning of Charlie's true maturation and independence, a fact suggested by her destruction of her earlier verse, her abandonment of her mother's ring, and her attitudes toward Walton and Gus (attitudes which her sisters misinterpret). The two males contrast in their views of Charlie (158), who eventually escapes falling into either of the extreme traps her culture has set for women (159). By the conclusion of the story she seems a whole and potent individual who has side-stepped her own and others' limiting fantasies as well as her culture's common feminine stereotypes. She ultimately seems a woman of vigor who has moved beyond fantasy to confront the real world (159). **Martin 1988a:** This story implicitly conveys Chopin's resentment of the readers who had criticized her earlier heroines and who had rejected her third collection of short fiction. The accidental gun-shot in the story implies Chopin's wrath and her yearning for revenge against male reviewers of *The Awakening*. Although Charlie is temporarily penalized for violating stereotypes, she ultimately regains her earlier power, thus symbolizing Chopin's own rejection of oppression (10–11). **Inge 1989:** This long, episodic tale focuses on a character who often seems so odd that it appears hard for the narrator to take her completely seriously. The emphasis of the work, except near the end, seems mainly on people's interactions rather than on their thoughts or feelings. Ultimately, however, Chopin attains once more her accustomed level of skill and insight (108–9). **Toth 1990a:** This was Chopin's only optimistic story written in 1900. It may have been inspired by local news about a young woman masquerading as a man—a disguise Chopin associated with freedom. The story may comment directly on relations between Chopin's mother and aunt. Although the tale was relatively conservative, it was rejected for publication, and Chopin never tried to submit it again (375–77). **Guidici 1991:** Chopin would have appreciated the irony of a woman being sent to a "finishing" school. However, by later filling her mother's shoes Charlie actually achieves greater personal freedom (30–31). **Blythe 1992:** Although this is one of the lengthiest, best, and most affecting of Chopin's tales, the little analysis it has received has been largely misguided, beginning with Per Seyersted's claim that the story expresses anti-male aggression and may carry incestuous overtones (207). Instead, the relationship between Charlie and her father is perfectly normal and admirable, and Charlie herself is perhaps Chopin's best depiction of a young woman. The story traces her evolution from girl to woman and her fortunate union with a highly compatible mate (208). As a girl Charlie is high-spirited, sometimes headstrong, but deeply imaginative. The scenes with her father in the city are warm and affecting and carry no hint of unnatural attraction. After

Charlie frees herself of her misguided desire for Walton, she achieves the prospect of a balanced, purposeful life with a man who ideally suits her (208–14). Perhaps Chopin did not publish this story because of its length and because she wrote it mainly for herself. Hurt feelings about the negative reception of *The Awakening* probably did not influence her decision (215). **Hoder-Salmon 1992:** This was one of the few substantial pieces of fiction Chopin composed after the failure of *The Awakening*; it expresses an explicit hostility toward males (22). Here as elsewhere, Chopin uses imagery of trains to symbolize the conflict between civilization and nature (144). **Thomas 1992:** This is one of several works by Chopin written in 1900 that focus on sickness, death, or growing old (50–51). **Winn 1992:** In this story Chopin spells out with rare explicitness for her era some meanings only implied in Louisa May Alcott's *Little Women*, a book Chopin seems to have read and admired (205). Alcott's Jo and Chopin's Charlie both have boyish nicknames; both wear short hair; both have only female siblings (who are themselves similar); both have injured fathers; and in both cases the fathers' injuries permit their daughters to exert unusual authority (206). Both daughters nonetheless love and obey their fathers, and indeed Chopin's presentation of incestuous overtones is astonishingly obvious for her era. Moreover, like Jo, Charlie is eventually united with an older man (206–7). Both heroines are authors who destroy their writings; both use their writings for covert self-expression; and both stories feature indirect expressions of sexual energy. Chopin mocks the conventions of standard female behavior, but she also mocks Charlie's romantic verse while additionally implying the complexities of Charlie's links with her father (208). **Shurbutt 1993:** This is one of various stories in which Chopin shows an unconventional female attaining unconventional fulfillment (15; 21). **Cutter 1994:** Here as in some of her other late stories, Chopin creates a female voice that undercuts (often by mimicking) patriarchal language (17). Ironically, Charlie's professed loyalty to her father helps her keep the power she would lose by marrying. Her attempts to fit the image of the typical woman show the ludicrousness of that image. By the end of the story her forms of rebellion against male control have become more subtle but therefore more effective than they had been at the beginning (31–33). **Ewell 1994:** This is one of various late works in which Chopin pulls back from unconventionality, perhaps in reaction to the poor reception of *The Awakening* (169–70). **Fusco 1994:** Like Maupassant, Chopin here employs a complex set of structures built around a basic movement from bad to good to bad fortune. The first and third phases both emphasize mishaps involving males, although the latter is more serious. The first third of the story suggests an ambiguous downward spiral. The second third relies on contrast. Contrast is also emphasized in section three, the ending of which does have some positive aspects (169–72). **Koloski 1994:** The story is included in soft-cover collections of Chopin's fiction published in 1976 and 1979 (27). **Saar 1994:** Although this is one of Chopin's few stories depicting a female with "masculine" traits, those traits do not remain unchanged

(67). **Castillo 1995:** Although Charlie loves to ride her bicycle, she does not do so in the decorous way recommended in magazines of the day. The man Charlie eventually marries will give her the freedom she seeks. Charlie violates stereotypes of the Southern woman, just as she also undercuts plot conventions associated with fairy-tale romance. The man she originally desired would probably have been too restrictive (87–89). **Koloski 1996:** This is one of various stories that reflect Chopin's interest in opera (57). It also shows her frequent concern with the maturation of adolescent girls (71). This is the best of Chopin's late stories and is also her lengthiest tale. It resembles various earlier works in setting and topic, particularly the topic of the costs of self-fulfillment. The story is moving, sensitive, and somewhat sad. Critics who perceive anything odd about Charlie's relationship with her father are mistaken (77–79; 87–89). **Walker 1996:** Charlie's general vitality is reflected in her passion for writing—a passion that helps her succeed in various settings (219–20). **Toth and Seyersted 1998:** Early versions of the tale show, despite Chopin's assertions to the contrary, that she did revise her writings (131). "Jacques" was one title of a previous version of this tale (133). An early draft of the present story was among a collection of Chopin manuscripts uncovered in the early 1990s (135). The tale is mentioned in her account books (147, 151). The newly discovered version closely resembles the version already published (246). This is Chopin's longest holograph, but the handwriting is so difficult to read, and relations among the various versions of the tale are so complex, that attempting to produce a legible text with variant readings seemed unwise. Differences among the various versions are briefly discussed, but the originally published text seems the best available (284–85). **Koloski 1999:** This is one of Chopin's best final tales (xvi). **Toth 1999a:** An early version of this tale was rediscovered in 1992 (8). **Toth 1999b:** Until recently this was almost the only tale by Chopin that had been preserved in distinct manuscripts (49). **Toth 1999c:** An early version of this tale, discovered in 1992, shows Chopin's editorial decisions (166–68). The tone of the story is determinedly bright (232).

"The Christ Light"
See "The Going Away of Liza"

"Croque-Mitaine"

Written: 1892. Included in *Complete Works* (1969).

Mamzelle, a Parisian nanny, unsettles and attempts to control P'tit-Paul and his younger siblings with repeated reports that an ogre lives in the wood adjoining the children's playground. When P'tit Paul asks Uncle Juba if he has ever seen the dreaded figure of Croque-Mitaine, the old black man scoffs and reminds the boy that the wood is no more haunted than a vegetable patch, because the closest graveyard is four miles away. Mamzelle's decision to attend a ball at a nearby plantation gives the young boy his first opportunity to discover the truth about Croque-Mitaine for himself.

Ignoring Mamzelle's warning that Croque-Mitaine will devour the children in their beds if they do not lie still and sleep, P'tit Paul slips into the warm night on his nanny's heels and makes his way to the playground bench. In the first thirty minutes, only Uncle Juba passes by, chiding the boy for sitting in the full light of the moon as he goes. But in the second half-hour, a wild-eyed, horned beast carrying a pitchfork startles P'tit Paul from his drowsy vigil. The boy realizes that running from Croque-Mitaine is useless. Cowering from a corner of the bench, P'tit Paul watches, wide-eyed, as Croque-Mitaine draws closer, rests on his pitchfork, tears off his face and mops his head with a white cloth. From the next day on, the children only smile at each other whenever Mamzelle mentions the name of Croque-Mitaine, believing that the ogre of whom she speaks is none other than the sweaty Monsieur Alcée making his way to a masked ball. **(JW)**

***

Seyersted 1969a: This story about wealthy Creoles illustrates Chopin's insight into—and ability to create empathy with—the psyches of children (77). **Ewell 1986:** This children's tale is not especially successful and was not printed during Chopin's lifetime (100). **Toth 1990a:** This affectionately mocking tale was never accepted for publication (207). **Koloski 1996:** This tale, one of various stories by Chopin featuring members of the Laballière family (21), was originally written for young readers (87). **Beer 1997:** This is one of various stories in which Chopin explores the difference between the intention of a narrator and how the narration is actually interpreted. The governess's narration is subverted by P'tit Paul's investigation, and she is thus robbed of her authority. P'tit Paul, like the blacks he consults, asserts a measure of control over his own life by rejecting the superstition by which the governess seeks to control him, but his investigation generates a new story that is as subject to variable responses as any other. The present story suggests how fictions structure human experience, but it also implies how fragile such fictions can be (87–88). **Toth and Seyersted 1998:** This story is mentioned in Chopin's account books (149–62).

"Dead Men's Shoes"

Written: 1895. First published: 1897. Included in *A Night in Acadie* **(1897).**

Le Vieux Gamiche is dead, leaving Gilma alone in the world once again. He is now nineteen years old, but he has been with Gamiche since he was nine. Gilma is the only one who sheds tears at Gamiche's funeral.

Although Gamiche's relatives have come down from Caddo for the funeral, they choose to stay at the house during the service. There is Septime, the nephew, who is a cripple, and his widowed sister, Ma'me Brozé, with her two small girls.

When Gilma returns to the house after the funeral and walks into his room, he finds the room changed. All of his clothes and belongings have been removed and put in a pile on the back porch. All his blood rushes to his face, but he can think of nothing better to do than get on his horse and ride away. He packs a few things in his saddlebags and mounts Jupe. As Gilma passes Septime on the front porch, Septime yells out to him to leave the horse there since it does not belong to Gilma. Gamiche taught Gilma to respect the law, so he gets off the horse and returns him to the stable. He tells Septime that he will come back with a hundred affidavits saying that Jupe belongs to him and then heads down the road on foot.

He stops at Aunt Hally's to have her sign an affidavit. She signs and voices her concern that Septime might try to take her mule away from her. The next morning Gilma goes directly to Lawyer Paxton's office and explains Septime's attempt to keep Jupe. Paxton is not aware that Gamiche has died. As soon as he hears the news and learns who the young man in his office is, he goes to his safe and pulls out some papers. He scans the papers and announces to Gilma that Gamiche has left everything he owned to Gilma.

Gilma is stunned and elated. A hundred different emotions go through his head until he feels stifled in the small office. He thanks Paxton and leaves. Two days later he stops at Aunt Hally's. Still on foot, he has turned down the several offers of horses and wagons made to him. The news of his good fortune has preceded him. Aunt Hally is laughing and going on about how funny it will be to see Septime and his family loaded up and headed back to Caddo. Gilma has never been so uncomfortable in Aunt Hally's presence.

Gilma resents the sudden change in everyone's attitude towards him. He keeps remembering what the lawyer said about stepping into dead men's shoes. He does not feel that he has the right or the need to step into a dead man's shoes. Those kinds of situations are better suited for those who are not strong and young and independent.

Gilma goes back to Septime and tells him that he has the affidavits proving that Jupe belongs to him. Septime reminds him that everything belongs to him. Gilma says that as far as he is concerned, everything can stay with Gamiche's own flesh and blood; all he wants is his horse. He takes a picture of Gamiche, his walking stick, a gun, his dog, and his beloved horse, and then rides off. **(DR)**

***

Seyersted 1969a: Here as elsewhere, Chopin emphasizes decent, generous behavior (77). **Peterson 1972:** This is one of six stories Chopin composed between the summers of 1893 and 1895 in which she focuses on altruism. It is the only one in which she strays too close to sentimentality (125). **Lattin 1980:** This is one of various stories by Chopin featuring repeating characters (28). **Dyer 1981a:** Here as elsewhere Chopin uses repeating male professional characters, thus adding depth and continuity to her fiction (54). **Skaggs 1985:** This is one of several tales by Chopin emphasizing altruistic self-denial, but despite the fact that she complicates the hero's final motives, the conclusion still seems improbable and even a bit sentimental (31). **Ewell 1986:** Although the story's outcome seems a bit unconvincing, Chopin shows skill in juxtaposing diverse responses to generosity and self-concern (107–8). **Toth 1990a:** The title of the story is borrowed from a contemporary novel (237). The tale later appeared in *A Night in Acadie*, in which all the stories are set in Louisiana (298). **Fusco 1994:** This story resembles various tales by Maupassant in its emphasis on loss (159). **Koloski 1994:** The story is included in a soft-cover collection of Chopin's fiction published in 1992 (28). **Carr 1996 :** This is one of various stories in which a Creole adopts a Cajun, usually improving him in the process (55). **Koloski 1996:** The lawyer here appears in other tales by Chopin (26). **Thomas 1996:** As elsewhere, Chopin here depicts aged black females, often in stereotypical terms (216–17). **Toth and Seyersted 1998:** This story is mentioned in Chopin's account books (141, 150, 156). **Toth 1999c:** This is one of various tales by Chopin in which youthful men try to evade adult feelings (194).

"A December Day in Dixie"

Written in 1900. Included in *Complete Works* (1969).

Although the train was delayed in arriving, neither the narrator nor any of the other passengers who stepped off at the small junction seemed bothered, since they emerged into unusually cold and blustery weather. Fortunately, a nearby bar, owned by Emile Sautier, advertised hot coffee and appealing food. Emile's young, grimy wife complained openly that he had come home drunk the night before, but Emile silently stoked the fire at the stove as the passengers, indifferent to food, eagerly sought hot coffee. As they drank it, they could hear the cheerful sounds of the Sautiers' infant in the room next door. One passenger who knew the family explained that this was the same infant who had recently fallen into a nearby cistern. Fortunately his fall had been broken by some branches covering the opening, but he had lain there, crying for two hours before being discovered. His mother added that a snake had been staring at him the whole time, and although the narrator assumes that the baby must have been terrified, she remarks that infants probably find it hard to make clear distinctions between what is real and what they merely imagine.

Meanwhile, snow blanketed the landscape and draped the trees as the train to Natchitoches chugged through fields that were white both from the snow and from unpicked cotton. The narrator was overcome by the beauty of the scene, but a pragmatic fellow passenger merely complained about the cotton, still unpicked by the unmotivated blacks. The passenger wondered aloud whether cotton could continue to sustain the local economy and asked about the narrator's plans for her own plantation.

When the passengers arrived in Natchitoches, they discovered that the whole population—boys and girls, judges and lawyers, nuns and teachers and convent students—was obsessed with throwing snowballs, sparing nothing and no one, not even the passengers and their coach.

Within twenty-four hours, however, most of the snow had melted. Temperatures were climbing again, and flowers basked in the now-restored sun. The narrator took pleasure in the return of warmth as she walked toward an old female acquaintance. **(RCE)**

***

Rankin 1932: This vivid tale is based on Chopin's own return visit to Louisiana in December 1899. The wife it describes, along with her hapless mate, could have provided the makings of a very fine short story (191). Early in the ensuing year, Chopin revised the conclusion of the piece, changed its title, and submitted it to a journal. The editor paid ten dollars for the sketch but failed to publish it (193). **Peterson 1972:** This impressionistic piece lacks coherence, although its friendly tone gives it some appeal (259–60). **Dyer 1981a:** Gouvernail, a skeptical character present in some of Chopin's earlier work, would be inappropriate in this story (54–55). **Jones 1981:** In this strange story Chopin describes how the snow transforms the perceptions of the narrator and others (except for the unimaginative traveling companion, whose unvarying perspective is used for contrast). The story shows how southern existence is temporarily liberated but ultimately unchanged (151). **Ewell 1986:** The first version of this tale was fairly unfocused, while the rewritten and trimmed version ("One Day in Winter") suggests that Chopin's hopes for her fiction had narrowed. The transformative effects of the snow resemble those of a poetic sensibility: in each case surroundings are seen from a new perspective (176). **Toth 1990a:** Chopin spoke slightingly of this sketch, which was quickly accepted, and paid for, by a young persons' magazine that did not publish it (373). **Vanlandingham 1990:** Chopin seemed pessimistic about the chances of this piece being accepted for publication (165). **Thomas 1992:** This story resulted from a personal trip Chopin made in 1898 (41). This is one of several works she wrote in 1900 that focus on sickness, death, or growing old (49–50). **Toth 1994:** This is one of several stories by Chopin that mention the Normal school in Natchitoches (12). **Koloski 1996:** This story was originally written for young readers (87). **Toth and Seyersted 1998:** The story is mentioned in Chopin's correspondence (213). It was one of several tales accepted but never published (275). **Toth 1999c:** This was one of several stories by Chopin purchased for publication but never printed, apparently because the journal's staff had changed in the interim (229).

"Désirée's Baby"

Written: 1892. First published: 1893. Included in *Bayou Folk* (1897).

As Madame Valmondé drives over to L'Abri to see Désirée and her baby, she reminisces about how Désirée came into her life. One day, Monsieur found a little girl asleep at his estate entrance and took her home to Madame. Search as they might, they could not discover her name or where she belonged. Finally, the neighboring people decided she must have become separated from a group of travelers. Yet after a while Madame Valmondé decided that the girl she named Désirée had been sent by a loving God, since she had borne no child of her own. Désirée grew up beautiful and good, loving and true. It was only a matter of time before some young man would fall in love with her.

Armand Aubigny, the heir to a nearby plantation, happened to ride by one day and saw Désirée. Love struck his heart like a speeding bullet. Even though he had known Désirée since he was eight years old, it was if he had never seen her before. Monsieur Valmondé tried to be practical and to reason with Armand. After all, they knew nothing about Désirée's background, not even her name. Armand, however, dismissed this concern. Soon the two were wed.

Now Madame Valmondé was going to visit the baby she had not seen in four weeks. As she approached L'Abri she thought it did not look like "the shelter" its name implied. Armand's mother had been French, and after her marriage to his father she had refused to leave Paris. Only when she died had Armand's father brought the boy to Louisiana. Because the place had been without a mistress for many years until Désirée came, it looked cold and neglected, and it was reputed that young Aubigny's control was harsh and demanding, not easy-going like his father's had been.

Madame Valmondé found the young mother lying with the baby. She stooped to look at the infant, and exclaimed, "This is not the baby!" Désirée was delighted at her surprise, and told how he was growing, how loudly he cried, and how ecstatic Armand was over the child. In fact, Armand was so proud and pleased these days that he had not punished a single one of the Negroes since the baby's birth. And Désirée cried, "Oh mamma, I'm so happy; it frightens me."

Sure enough, when the baby is about three months old, Désirée realizes that something is threatening her serene world. Although she could not understand why, a peculiar and chilling change had occurred in her husband's manner. Désirée is miserable but mystified until one day she happens to be watching as a little quadroon boy stands beside the baby, fanning it. Her blood runs cold, and a great fear clutches her heart. When she runs to Armand and asks him to tell her what the baby's appearance means, Armand replies, "It means that the child is not white; it means that you are not white." Desperate, Désirée writes Madame Valmondé, who replies that she should come home with her baby. When Désirée asks Armand if she should go, he tells her to leave. In truth, Armand feels that God has been cruel and unfair to him, and he wants to punish God in return. Besides, he no longer loves Désirée because of this disgrace she has brought upon his proud name. Without changing her clothes, Désirée takes her child from his nurse and walks with him down among the grasses and trees on the banks of the bayou, and she never comes back.

A short time later, Armand causes a great bonfire to be lit, and he himself hands out the items to be burned. A small group of Negroes feed the flames with a cradle, a baby's layette, all the gowns and clothes from Désirée's wardrobe, and, last of all, a tiny packet of letters. Désirée had written these notes to Armand during their betrothal, and he had kept them in his drawer. Behind Désirée's notes in the very back of the drawer, Armand had found another letter, written by his mother to his father. He opens it and reads that she thanks God for her husband's love. But, above all, she wrote, "night and day, I thank the good God for having so arranged our lives that our dear Armand will never know that his mother, who adores him, belongs to the race that is cursed with the brand of slavery." **(CY)**

***

Anonymous 1894 [*The Critic*]: This story is even richer than some of the others with which it was first collected (41). **Beale 1911:** For composing this tale, Chopin deserves a lofty place in the history of American short fiction (63). **Pattee 1923:** The ending of the story typifies Chopin's talent for providing unusually strong conclusions. The impact of the last sentence lingers long after the book has been closed (326–27). **Rankin 1932:** Aspects of the landscape of Cloutierville, where Chopin once lived, suggest details of this narrative (100). The tale, one of her best works and possibly one of the greatest short stories ever written, was published in the very same issue of a magazine with another of Chopin's stories—one of only three occasions in her career of such simultaneous publication. Its superb final sentence is not a trick but an epiphany (133–34). The varied pathos of the tale is skillfully handled (140). **Reilly 1937:** Only this tale excels "Athénaïse" as an artistic success. Every word counts in this brief story, whose unexpected final twist evokes great emotion and insight. This is one of the best pieces of short fiction ever written. It displays all the virtues of Chopin's art, including subtlety, efficiency, assurance, psychological perceptiveness, and careful control of imagery and tone (73–74). **Reilly 1942:** This is Chopin's finest story. Every sentence, from the first to the powerful conclusion, contributes to the tragedy. The story shows Chopin's typical talents of straightforwardness, masterful phrasing, and subtle word-choice, and she quickly creates a sense of locale and mood and presents convincing personalities. Not even Maupassant wrote more efficiently than Chopin writes here, especially in her deft use of foreshadowing and in the way she makes small phrases resonate powerfully (135–36). **Bush 1957:** This is one of only two tragic tales published in *Bayou Folk* or *A Night in Acadie*; the rest are mainly optimistic (240–41). **Arms 1967:** Less thematically complex in its treatment of race and personhood than Twain's contemporary novel *Pudd'nhead Wilson*, this carefully structured and delicate story may not deserve its widespread acclaim (222). **Seyersted 1969a:** The story was so successful when initially published that its first editors enthusiastically published many more of Chopin's tales (54). It is one of two stories by Chopin set in pre-Civil War Louisiana (the other being "La Belle Zoraïde"). Her most famous story, it shows some frustration with the treatment of persons of mixed blood, but its economy and power make it resemble a story by Maupassant, and the unexpected, tragic ending, though a bit forced, equals anything the Frenchman could have written (94). This was Chopin's first major tale and shows her superbly in control of tone and implication (especially in the deathly imagery of the trees and ironic name of the house). The baby's racial identity is subtly suggested, and the story is rich in irony, its outcome as shocking to the reader as it is to Aubigny. The conclusion of the story is powerful yet somewhat handicapped by being a bit contrived (122). In 1906 a critic called this work one of the best short tales in English (186). In 1930 another critic said that the story, especially its touchingly understated conclusion, would be difficult to surpass (187). In 1936 still another critic praised the work as one of the best stories in English, especially in view of its brevity (188). **Seyersted 1969b:** Here as in her other stories about race, Chopin's focus is more on individual psychology than on social contexts (26). The concluding sentence of this work is powerfully biting but is also a bit contrived (31). **Leary 1970a:** Like many of Chopin's works, this one reveals how social customs affect private relationships. The story is told with feeling but also with restraint. It was probably influenced by the work of G.W. Cable, but it is more straightforward and less emotional than his writing. This story is easily comparable in power to Mark Twain's *Pudd'nhead Wilson*, which it preceded by a year (vii–viii). **Leary 1970b:** This is one of Chopin's best tales, although it can seem less impressive when re-read (140–41). **Leary 1971:** Theme: how social conventions affect human relations, particularly in matters of love. The story treats its sad topic without, in general, becoming maudlin. Its daring presentation of interracial sexuality may have been influenced by the writing of G.W. Cable, although Chopin's progressive presentation of the topic is more straightforward and objective than his (164). **Potter 1971:** Once more Chopin focuses on the tragedy a black woman suffers because of her race, yet Armand is also a self-destructive tragic figure who is full of self-contempt. This story is an unusually effective indictment of the effects of slavery and prejudice, not only on individuals but on everyone (49–50). **Arner 1972:** Critics who have complained that the story is insufficiently complex or that its ending is contrived have misread the work. The tale displays the complex unity typical of a great piece of writing. It shows the arbitrary nature of racial divisions; this, indeed, is the most shocking discovery Armand makes as the work concludes. Personal affection provides a potential antidote to racism, but Armand's attitude toward Désirée is never truly loving but is instead domineering. The social system in which he exists exacerbates his own flaws of character. Images of darkness are linked to Armand and images of whiteness to Désirée—a pattern that subtly foreshadows the conclusion. Yellow is also an important color, since all the "blacks" the story depicts are in fact yellow—another fact that suggests the crudeness of inflexible racial distinctions. Images of the divine (linked with Désirée) and of the satanic (linked with Armand) are also important and contribute to larger ironies. Armand's potent sexuality is expressed in his various relations with his slaves, whether erotic or sadistic. In the final analysis we are confident that Désirée will be compensated (in heaven) for her sufferings; she represents the Freudian superego, while Armand symbolizes the Freudian id. The story is one of the best by a very fine writer (139–46). **Peterson 1972:** In this tale issues of race are explicit, while Chopin's own attitudes toward the topic are unclear (105). In this and other stories for *Vogue*, constraints of space dictated a standard structure consisting of an introductory discussion followed by a quick dramatization (108). Because the story depends wholly on its final twist, it seems weaker each time it is read. The black-and-white imagery seems too pat and maudlin when the tale is re-read. Any social criticism seems muted, but the story is as effective as its genre allows it to be (109–12). **Rocks 1972:** This is one of Chopin's six best pieces of short fiction, and it is also unusual in focusing so much on plot developments. Elsewhere Chopin is more interested in conveying impressions than in describing events (113). **Seyersted 1974:** This work and others justify Chopin's reputation as a superb writer of local color fiction (11). **Arner 1975:** Although Chopin's intentions in describing society here are not reformist, discrimination is a central focus of this and other stories (47). Armand ultimately loses not only his wife and child but also his sense of personal identity as well as his sense of having acted justly. The story contrasts group prejudice with the true love that encourages appreciation of individuals. Armand, full of self-destructive and eventually Satanic pride (a fact emphasized by the closing bonfire), never loves Désirée as a full person (as her foster mother does). Even his ardor is described in destructive terms that foreshadow doom, and he is often linked with the color black. Providential imagery helps give the story a doubly ironic conclusion, while the use of imagery in general helps prepare for (and justify) what might otherwise seem a contrived concluding twist. Paradoxically, the contrasting black/white imagery reinforces on one level the very distinctions the story seems to mock. The story links racial oppression to oppression in marriage, and in fact the latter issue may be Chopin's true chief concern (51–55). **Skaggs 1975:** The common idea that men can own women lies beneath this story's more obvious concern with the mixing of races, and that idea may be even more detrimental to Désirée than racial discrimination itself. Although Désirée must suspect that it is Armand's bloodline (not hers) that is impure, she is still desperate to be his wife and the mother to his mixed-race child. She still longs to be possessed by him but realizes that, because he is a man, he controls her fate (278–79). **Ladenson 1976:** Armand remains in control thanks in large part to Désirée's final decision (31). **Solomon 1976:** This is perhaps Chopin's most famous tale. Characteristically, it features a female protagonist whose life is defined by her existence in a system rooted in the power of males (xiii). Her husband's self-centeredness and his sense that he owns his wife are reminiscent of traits of the Duke in Browning's poem "My Last Duchess" (xiii–xiv). Chopin efficiently depicts the change in mood after the baby is born; Désirée's privileged surroundings contrast ironically with her growing confusion and alienation. Although the ending of the story is a bit overdone, the story nonetheless effectively portrays not only a racism grounded in anxiety but also the destiny of women who are treated as flawed possessions (xiv). **Bonner 1977:** Here as elsewhere, *Bayou Folk* reveals Chopin's talent for creating rich characters and for presenting, rather than announcing, their traits (6). This story, often considered Chopin's finest, does not depend on dialect (8). Here as elsewhere in *Bayou Folk*, Chopin divides a story into distinct sections (8–9), uses a sudden twist to create irony (9), and uses time alterations as an important device (9). Moreover, here as elsewhere in *Bayou Folk*, a child destabilizes adults (10). The story shows affection ruined by arrogance (11). This is one of Chopin's more effective treatments in *Bayou Folk* of the human mind. The story implies the blurred boundaries between sanity and its opposite (12). Racial mixing is an important theme of the work (11–12). This is one of the best stories in *Bayou Folk* (13). **Lattin 1978:** This is one of various stories in which Chopin describes the genuine complications that can result from real (rather than merely imagined or potential) motherhood. Désirée is happy not only with her child but with the change its birth has produced in Armand (2). Although this story shows the satisfactions motherhood could promise, in much of Chopin's writing actual motherhood leads to pain or a sacrifice of identity (5). **Wolff 1978:** Although this story has long been admired, critics have tended to treat it merely as regional fiction or as an exemplar of a tale with a surprise ending. Neither perspective does full justice to the power of the work, which is the only tale by Chopin dealing with interracial sex. Here as in many stories, Chopin deals with instability and potential loss; thus the ending is not merely a convenient trick but a symptom of the nature of reality. By stripping the story of dialect and other potentially distracting features, Chopin clearly focuses on the importance of race, but she uses this topic to show that no human situation can ever be segmented into simple polarities. Many details of the story quickly imply a breakdown of clear racial distinctions, and Armand's potential for evil is one he shares with all human beings. Chopin effectively understates her presentation of the instability of existence. Here as in other works, she suggests the extent to which human experience is pervasively ambiguous and uncertain (123–33). **Taylor 1979:** Although this story involves female suffering, it also shows how males are handicapped by social conventions (xviii). **Wolff 1979:** Chopin's main concern is not with slavery or with improving society but with various kinds of distinctions, including those separating races, classes, emotions, and even different states of sanity. Like much of Chopin's writing, this story takes us to the thresholds of diverse emotional experiences (213–15). **Wolstenholme 1980:** The story is flawed because of its contrived conclusion (543). **Jones 1981:** Désirée despairs not so much because she thinks she and her child are black but because she assumes that Armand will no longer love her. Similarly, the ironic ending seems intended more to penalize Armand than to dehumanize blacks (152). **Toth 1981:** Here and in other stories Chopin uses the "tragic mulatto" stereotype in an original way, to show how anyone (even a man) can be victimized by racial prejudices that associate whites with reason and blacks with passion (203). This was one of Chopin's few stories to be reprinted and critically discussed throughout the twentieth century, although earlier commentators tended to overlook its political implications and its effective use of literary convention (204–5). The story shows how the culture of slavery warped both slaves *and* masters (205–6). Ironically, throughout the story Chopin links Désirée with imagery of whiteness and Armand with imagery of darkness (206). Both women *and* slaves were expected to be subservient, and Armand's father was unusual both in his choice of his mate and in his treatment of his slaves (207). Ironically, it is Armand, not Désirée, who finally fits the tragic mulatto stereotype, especially because of his uncontrolled emotions (207). The story demonstrates the paradoxically self-destructive effects of patriarchal domination and the tragedy of using stereotypes to make judgments (207–8). **Davis 1982:** This story, with its focus on the tragic results of interracial erotic desire, deserves its wide renown (64). **Fluck 1982:** Perhaps this story was so popular because it treated transgression in a distanced, melodramatic fashion. The story flirts with the possibility of extreme sexual transgression but then denies that possibility completely

(160). In this sense it is less daring than some of Chopin's other fiction, and perhaps this helps explain why the tale was so well received at the time (163). **Gilbert 1984:** This story questions divisive racial discrimination (16). **Stein 1984:** The marriage here had the potential to be one of the happier ones in Chopin's fiction, partly because Désirée seems so compliant (208). **Aherne 1985:** The irony here is superb (81–82). **McMahan 1985:** Chopin here shows how extreme affection can lead a woman to self-destruction. Armand resembles the husband in Robert Browning's poem "My Last Duchess," while Désirée resembles Ophelia in *Hamlet*. Désirée dies because she lacks independent self-respect (34). The title character is one of the many fascinating women Chopin depicted (although she did less well in characterizing men [84]). **Skaggs 1985:** See Skaggs 1975. **Ewell 1986:** This is the only story in which Chopin depicts a truly mean character, and even here the depiction is indirect (66). The tale is bracketed in *Bayou Folk* by two other stories about blacks. The ending turns the story upside-down but still seems perfectly appropriate, partly because the final irony has been so effectively but subtly prepared, even down to the ironic name of Armand's home. The larger-than-life characters seem more than mere individuals, and even the imagery of blackness implies ethical failings rather than suggesting race alone. Armand, like other tragic figures, reacts too much on impulse, and the closing image of the fire symbolizes the ardent compulsiveness that makes him proud, vengeful even toward God, and ultimately self-destructive. Paradoxes abound: Desirée's name literally means "desired"; Armand, seeking purity, defiles himself; and the villain of a story ostensibly sympathetic to blacks turns out to be half-black himself (69–72). **Gaudet 1986:** A marriage between a white and a black would have violated Louisiana law during the era in which this story is set. Perhaps Désirée herself is also part black; this would help explain the baby's dark appearance. Even Désirée's adoptive parents may assume she is a mulatto. Eye color is an important clue to racial identity in this tale. Ironically, if only Armand had discovered his own heritage earlier, he and Désirée might have lived happily. Perhaps Armand's mother was a Louisiana mulatto. In describing Armand, Chopin may be alluding to the common belief that mulattoes were very inflexible in dealing with their own slaves (49–50). **Rosenblum 1986a:** Although Chopin obviously rejects racial prejudice here, her main focus is the psychology of her characters. The story links racial and sexual oppression. Even though Désirée's mother is willing to take her back, Désirée realizes that her social status would still be undermined because of her supposedly mixed blood. Armand succumbs to social pressure, despite his assertions of autonomy. Ultimately he surrenders to convention. Chopin herself refuses to romanticize antebellum life in this tale. She uses the story to conduct a fictional experiment in which the baby is the catalyst. Neither Désirée nor Armand responds appropriately to this provocation; each simply considers the other at fault (2: 573–74). **Bonner 1988:** This story is often included in short fiction anthologies because of its regional focus (100). **Martin 1988a:** The article on Chopin in a classic reference work published in 1930 extolled this story highly (12). **Papke 1988:** Here as elsewhere Chopin scrutinizes conventional views of women by setting them in a complex social and historical context (73–74). **Elfenbein 1989:** As in other works, Chopin here shows how women suffer when they lack power, and she also depicts women of color who are relevant to her depiction of women in *The Awakening* (117–18). In stories such as this, which feature women of color, Chopin could deal more explicitly with topics she treated more cautiously when writing about white females. The women of color in these tales tend to be less simple characters than the white women, but they suffer more obvious mistreatment. Stories such as this one anticipate the racial dynamics depicted in *The Awakening* (126). The tale hinges on a sudden reversal and an atmosphere of malevolent fate. It counterpoints light and darkness, force and weakness, and erotic desire and emotional affection. Armand's tendency to see the world in rigid, black-and-white terms leads to his own downfall, whereas Désirée and her mother show the ability to love across racial lines. La Blanche's name, by conflicting with her ethnicity, suggests the practical limits of Armand's authority; moreover, both he and she transgress the very categories he considers so important. Armand is the only figure in the tale for whom race is so crucial a matter, perhaps because he distantly recalls his mother. Even if Désirée were not black, Armand would still have the authority to disown her if she simply committed adultery, even though he does the same thing with La Blanche. Even if Armand were discovered to be black, Désirée would still lose status for having been impregnated by a black male. Her dilemma is therefore irresolvable since she has no independent authority (126–27). As a woman, her status is contingent on being desired (hence the aptness of her name), yet she ends the story undesired. Her faith in both her biological father and her husband is abused; even when Armand desires her, his desire comes with strings attached. As a woman, Désirée is turned over by her step-father to her husband as if she were a material possession (127). Ironically, even when she is an adult, Désirée resembles an infant (128). Armand's delight in the birth of a son, along with the fact that the female Désirée was abandoned as a baby, suggests the sexism of their society. The fact that La Blanche lives away from the main house prefigures Désirée's own exile and may suggest that LaBlanche was once in the very same position as Désirée (128–29). Désirée's comments to her mother suggest how deeply she needs to cling to her self-delusions about Armand; her remarks imply that on one level she realizes how much she lacks independent authority. Désirée's mother remains silent after the birth just as she did before the marriage. Both Désirée and Armand do not truly know themselves; they find some stability only by enacting firmly prescribed roles (129). Ultimately Désirée is described in ways that are subtly religious and that resemble the terms used to describe persons who suffer for their faith, while Armand, in contrast, is described in almost hellish terms (129–30). Despite these glaring contrasts, however, the story is very subtly told; its strong effect is due in part to its efficiency, its seeming objectivity, its ironic reversal of expectation, and its pervasive mood of uncertainty (130). Désirée's failure to realize that her child is a mulatto shows how the genuine love associated with motherly affection transforms perception—a fact also evident in the response of her own mother (130). The story leaves us pondering numerous questions, but the one certainty it communicates is the extent of Armand's authority. Even God's power (or benevolence) is implicitly questioned, since the prayers of Désirée's mother have had no positive effects (131). **Inge 1989:** This is Chopin's most widely published story and one of the most well received. Even Armand's initial affection for Désirée seems reckless and egotistical, while the dilapidated condition of his ancestral home already creates an atmosphere of ill-fated melancholy. Unfortunately, Chopin's focus in this story on events makes the characters seem a bit thin; they are closer to being abstractions than complex personalities. Armand in particular seems a caricature. Nonetheless, the story shows great craft in its use of irony, images, subtle dialogue, and effective symbols, especially in the demonic attributes associated with Armand. Désirée shows little initiative and comes into open conflict with Armand only twice. In this tale Chopin skillfully likens the oppression of women to the oppression of slaves (97). **Taylor 1989:** Here as elsewhere Chopin refuses to provide a heroine with an improbable fortunate outcome (50). Ruth McEnery Stuart wrote no story comparable to this one in its focus on racial ambiguity (100). A modern French critic compared this work to the writing of Maupassant in its evocation of destiny, sympathy, and frustration (158). The story is atypical of Chopin's work in its tragic outcome and in its emphasis on an irreversible breakdown of social conventions. It is also one of Chopin's most effective works (166). **Erickson 1990:** The story uses fairy-tale motifs to explore the contrasts between the apparent and the real. The fairy-tale elements complicate and enrich the basically realistic mode of the tale, and *vice versa*. The optimism inherent in fairy-tale resolutions is undercut by Désirée's death, but the story gains in complexity because of its second conclusion (which focuses on Armand). The work draws on such fairy-tale motifs as the desired child and the discovered infant (57). Like many fairy-tale females, Désirée is basically passive (as when she is found asleep). The motif of the discovered infant usually leads one to expect a surprising revelation, often about the infant's parents (58). Like many fairy-tale females, Désirée is associated with imagery of light and gold and is courted by a romantic male who is stunned by her beauty (58–59). In fairy-tales, childbirth often leads to marital tensions, but these are usually resolved by the end of the tale. Chopin's story flirts with possible fairy-tale explanations of the child's uniqueness, but ultimately the story rejects these easy resolutions (60–61). Armand, moreover, is a darker figure than the typical fairy-tale prince, and this variation helps prepare for (and justify) the second ending (61–62). Ironically, if Désirée had continued to be patient and passive (rather than killing herself), the story might actually have had a conventional fairy-tale conclusion (63). By viewing the story in the light of fairy-tale conventions, the appropriateness of the second ending—with its punishment of the villain—seems clear (63–64). **Papke 1990:** Chopin here rejects an optimistic conclusion. She shows the oppressive aspects of conventional ideals of feminine behavior. This is one of Chopin's few stories in which social problems (rather than simply individual characters) seem a major focus (33). Whereas earlier tales by Chopin had closed by emphasizing harmony and happiness, this one does not. In presenting the two plantations, Chopin offers competing symbolic views of the South before the Civil War—one bright, one dark. Armand casts a shadow over his ancestral home and even literally blackens his new-born son, the single symbol of hope in this dreary place. Armand's father had guessed what might happen when his son married and had children, but both father and son denigrate Désirée rather than accepting any personal responsibility. Chopin thus shows how women are dominated by men, especially if they accept male values (as Désirée does). Any woman who fails to meet masculine expectations can be ruined, even if she has no power to meet them. Armand sees his wife as a physical object rather than as a person. Unfortunately, Désirée passively accepts her husband's view of her; her inability or refusal to reject his assessment finally destroys her. She cannot imagine existence without him. At least Armand's mother found, in exile, some relative freedom; similarly, Désirée's own mother is willing to take back her daughter, even if she cannot "prove" that the young woman is white. Both older women, then, suggest ways of circumventing racist dictates. Désirée, however, lacks her mother's strength. She is not responsible for her tragedy (society is), but her passivity contributes to her demise and contributes to the complexity of the tale (53–56; 4p). **Peel 1990:** This story shows how semiotics and politics can interact in great fiction: Désirée subverts sexual, racial, and economic categories, thereby undermining supposed certainties of all sorts. Désirée is initially attractive because she seems undefined; she even lacks a name. Other characters project their own yearnings onto her, so that her new name—which means "desired"— seems appropriate. In this respect and others she is like La Blanche, whose name is also ambiguous. Désirée does not cause, but rather reveals, the contradictions embedded in her culture, just as the baby is a threat to Armand not only because of its race but because it reveals a mother's power. By the end of the story, however, numerous seemingly clear-cut distinctions have collapsed, even though the structure of power has not significantly changed. Thus the story shows more sympathy for characters of mixed race than for blacks themselves, and Chopin's tendency to present Désirée as a mere acquiescent victim is also troubling. However, two possibilities—that Désirée is not white and that she does not kill herself—may make the story far more ambiguous and complex than is normally imagined (although Chopin refuses to provide any simplistically consoling view, either of the ending or of Désirée's character). Chopin suggests that semiotic subversion by itself may not lead to political change (223–37).

Toth 1990a: This story shows Chopin's realization of the ways black female slaves were abused sexually by their white male masters, and perhaps Chopin herself knew of instances of interracial sex (57–58). Her father-in-law resembled Armand by being an abusive husband (122), and
Chopin also knew people as romantically impulsive as Armand (150),
whose name may have been influenced by that of a man with whom she
became involved (215; 225). Other details may have been influenced by
real life (224). The story was strongly praised (247), was reprinted (266),
and inspired a dramatic adaptation (402). It was Chopin's only story to be
continually reprinted during the early twentieth century (404). **Foy 1991:**
Armand is more mentally complex than he seems at first, partly because of
his childhood memories of his mother. His racial prejudice is rooted in
personal psychological torment (222–23). **Guidici 1991:** Here as elsewhere
a Chopin heroine fails to seize the opportunity for greater autonomy (31).
Toth 1991: Although this is one of Chopin's early narratives, it is dark and
disturbing (xiii). This was almost the only work by Chopin to win wide
recognition for most of the twentieth century (xxi). **Ewell 1992:** Désirée is a
more passive, less complex figure than Mrs. Mallard in "The Story of an
Hour" (160). **Robinson 1992:** This story illustrates the degree of racial mixing which had taken place in American culture, and which had occurred
among some of Chopin's own ancestors (xvii). **Toth 1992:** Here as elsewhere Chopin creates characters whose names resemble those of real persons (16). **Bryan 1993:** This story and others by Chopin reflect the influence of George W. Cable (15). This is one of the relatively few tales in
which Chopin explicitly deals with matters of race and with other social
concerns (62). **Dyer 1993:** This and other stories by Chopin sometimes
eclipsed *The Awakening* in critical estimation (20). **Larrson 1993:** This is one
of Chopin's few stories to emphasize issues of race. The story explores
Chopin's favorite topic: the crime of forcing others to deny their individuality (2: 538). **Shurbutt 1993:** This is one of various stories in which Chopin
challenges a stereotype about women (22). **Fusco 1994:** This story is structured around an unexpected reversal, but Chopin uses this technique
sparingly in her early fiction (143). As in similar works by Maupassant, the
reversal does not abandon, but rather amplifies, a theme already emphasized. Chopin achieves a tone that is both distant and sympathetic toward
Désirée. The ending leaves open the possibility that Armand may already
have known of his mother's letter (150–52). As in other tales by Chopin,
the conclusion challenges our tendency to make premature assumptions
(154). **Goodwyn 1994:** As in other stories by Chopin, the social roles of
master and slave loom large in this tale (6). Désirée kills herself and her
child to keep the infant from being enslaved. Armand is not a simple villain but is himself complexly tragic, partly because he accepts a post-colonial system of values. Madame Valmondé symbolizes Chopin's critique of
that system (10–11). This is one of various narratives in which Chopin
shows the human tragedy involved in enforcing stereotypes (11). **Koloski
1994:** One anthologist of the early 1920s emphasized the interest created

by the story's events, while another editor from the same period called the tale one of the best ever written by an American (20). The work was available in many anthologies published between the 1920s and 1980s (21). The various editors gave many reasons for reprinting it, including such aspects as its emphasis on local color, its superb plotting, its indirection, its depiction of the South, and its ability to evoke terror (22–23). The story is included in softcover collections of Chopin's fiction published in 1970, 1976, 1979, 1981, and 1984 (27–28). This work also often appears in college textbooks (28–29). **Lundie 1994:** Too often this story has been viewed as the tale of an oppressed *woman* rather than as the tale of an oppressed woman *of color* (126). Recent critics have debated the degree to which Chopin perpetuated or challenged racist stereotypes about black females in her fiction (128). In this narrative, however, Chopin's treatment of racial matters seems much more complicated than either of these extreme positions would suggest (128). From the moment of publication this was always one of Chopin's most popular stories (129–30). Désirée's perception that she is not white robs her of any sense of selfhood (130), but the story is less about racism in general than about the particular sufferings of a black woman: Désirée would have suffered less from racism if she had been a man (130–31). Although Armand, for instance, knows by the end of the tale that he is black, his self-confidence remains unshaken, partly because he can pass as a white male (131). Ironically, the ending of the tale tempts us to feel glad or relieved when it is proven that Désirée is not black—as if being black were indeed negative (131–32). Similarly, we are encouraged to see Armand (the real black) as the villain of the piece: he is depicted as Satanic whereas Désirée is presented as saintly (132). Chopin's story reflects an awareness of contemporary attitudes toward race-mixing (132–33), but in the final analysis the true victim is a white female who is abused by a black male. The fact that she has had sex with him may lead her to feel tainted, or might have led her to be treated as such. The story thus may not be as sympathetic to African Americans, or as hostile to racist prohibitions against race-mixing, as it is sometimes depicted as being (134). The tale seems somewhat unsettling when examined closely (139–40). **Walker 1994:** Here as elsewhere, Chopin illustrates the disasters racism can cause (8). **Castillo 1995:** The heroine's name and the name of La Blanche are both ironic, as is often true in works by Chopin. The story is efficiently designed. Chopin shows boldness in suggesting the racial complexity of the ruling class. Désirée chooses suicide because she has few options, less because of her supposed race than because she is a woman (84–85). **Baxter 1996:** This work reveals Chopin's interest in matters of race (219–20) and exemplifies her talent as a local color writer (239). It was included in a collection that was well received by contemporary readers (241). It lends itself to a creative writing exercise for students (240) and can be studied by evaluating the characters' social status (247). **Bauer 1996:** Armand knew from the start about his mother's race and thus shows no surprise when he reads the letter (161). He has been self-consciously

"passing" as a white all along (162). He chooses Désirée as his wife precisely because no one knows her background. Because she can thus be
easily blamed if their child is too dark, she provides him an opportunity to
take the chance of having a baby (163). The narrator cannot be trusted
(163), especially when explaining why Armand's mother never visited
Louisiana (164). The narrator writes from the perspective of the local
community, which is partly responsible for the abuse Désirée suffers (164).
Armand abuses his slaves precisely because he knows that he himself is
half-black: he punishes them for his racial background while also seeking
to distance himself publicly from them (170). After all, his own child by La
Blanche is enslaved (171). As in other stories about "passing," Armand
ends the tale in isolation (172). The story shows Chopin's consciousness
that even Armand is in some sense a tragic figure (175). **Koloski 1996:** The
name of Armand's home is ironic in this story, which is one of only several antebellum narratives by Chopin. The house is prominently featured
and seems a perfect setting for the tragic events that occur within it. The
conclusion of the work is particularly effective. Apparently Armand's father accepted the black (*not* African-American) heritage of Armand's
mother, perhaps because of differences between racial attitudes in France
and those in the United States. The narrative was immediately well received and has long been highly acclaimed. It has frequently been
reprinted and is an especially effective anti-racist work. It anticipates some
of Chopin's other finest writings (24–27). It is one of various tales in which
she movingly depicts the plight of blacks in Southern society (44; 47), and
one critic has linked it with two other tales by Chopin about "dark
women" (88). **Tuttleton 1996:** Even the title of this tale implies its regional
focus (182). **Walker 1996:** This is one of many stories by Chopin in which
the reading of correspondence is very significant. Such correspondence often symbolizes the power of the general written word (220). **Beer 1997:**
This is one of the few stories by Chopin that critics have treated as a complex depiction of racial matters (12). Even a simplistic reading of this tale
suggests the centrality of race in the society Chopin describes (30). The title character is presented as she evolves into a conventional cliché, while
both she and Armand are destroyed by social conventions powerful
enough to obliterate affection. The identities of both characters are rooted
in race in a corrupt social system pervaded by ambiguities. Only Désirée's
mother seems to escape simplistic thinking (36–37). Armand resembles in
certain respects the husband in "Her Letters" (48). **Toth and Seyersted
1998:** Like Désirée, Chopin had a supportive mother (127). This story is
mentioned in Chopin's account books (139, 149, 153). **Benfey 1999:** Here as
elsewhere in Chopin's fiction, not only do the dead communicate through
uncovered correspondence (228) but birth and death are also linked (238).
Green 1999: This is one of several stories by Chopin that have attracted
great attention from critics (14). Cynthia Wolff's essay on this story emphasizes the tale's effectiveness (19). The tale calls into question Helen
Taylor's notion that Chopin was a racist (23). **Koloski 1999:** This is the

most tragic tale in *Bayou Folk* and is unusual for Chopin because its events take place prior to the Civil War. This is Chopin's starkest treatment of the failure to achieve equilibrium (xv). Armand's hostility toward Désirée implies his similar hostility toward his mother and father, who had apparently enjoyed a happy but racially mixed marriage. Although the story is often deliberately vague, its anti-racist message has always seem profoundly powerful. Other stories near the end of *Bayou Folk* are also gloomy in atmosphere; the joy often expressed in the earlier tales has vanished; they show the malign influence of the past rather than focusing on a hopeful tomorrow (xv). The present tale is one of various works in which Chopin shows affection that exists across color lines, and in which she presents racial issues objectively (xx). **McCullough 1999:** Racial ambiguity is important here as in "La Belle Zoraïde" (213), and in both stories race affects motherhood. In the present tale, however, race also affects economic status. By becoming a mother, Désirée is destroyed in several ways. However, while subverting traditional views of motherhood, Chopin does not really challenge standard stereotypes about race. Désirée's adoptive mother can treat Désirée so lovingly at the end partly because Désirée's fate does not call Madame Valmondé's race into question. The racial status quo is never really challenged here (217–19). Anna Elfenbein's reading of this story may be the best ever offered (319). The story's treatment of race is complex, as is its depiction of Désirée's adoptive mother (320). **Toth 1999a:** Armand's harshness resembles that of Chopin's father-in-law (5). This story, like some of Chopin's other most currently popular works, first appeared in *Vogue* (9). **Toth 1999b:** As Bernard Koloski has demonstrated, this was one of eight stories by Chopin that were frequently republished in the twentieth century (46). This is one of the relatively few stories by Chopin that focus on sexuality or passion (49). **Toth 1999c:** This tale, now considered a standard work of American literature (xx), may have been influenced by the cruelty of Chopin's father-in-law (64) and may also reflect the speed with which people in Louisiana sometimes became romantically entangled (86). Armand may share some traits with the man with whom the widowed Chopin became involved (108; 145), while a minor character bears the same name as a resident of Cloutierville (139). In this tale, Chopin set an unconventional, pro-female plot within a conventional narrative frame. Armand typifies an abusive husband. Meanwhile, Désirée's admirable mother resembles Chopin's own, while Armand has some resemblance to Chopin's father. The tale is similar in theme to works by Maupassant, Poe, and others, which often feature young women as victims. The story does, however, feature a powerful maternal figure (144–46). This tale added a frightening dimension to *Bayou Folk*, although no contemporary commentator observed how the narrative contributed to that collection's sardonic view of marriage (151–52). The story also contributes to the volume's emphasis on admirable women (154). Initially published in *Vogue* (171–72), the story may reflect Chopin's relations with her own mother (174). It was republished in a St. Louis newspaper (187).

Knights 2000: This is one of various works in which Chopin juxtaposes an individual life with a larger social context (xviii–xix). Here as elsewhere Chopin focuses on a moment of self-realization (xix). This story, like others by Chopin, gains added interest when read in the context of the materials with which it was originally published (xix). Many aspects of this story are intriguingly ambiguous, particularly Désirée herself but also the larger meaning of the tale. Even its title changed after its initial publication (xxv). Here as elsewhere Chopin focuses on endangered minority languages (xxv). Her revisions of the first version of the tale make the work seem slightly less informal (xlvi).

"Doctor Chevalier's Lie"

Written: 1891. First published: 1893. Included in *Complete Works* (1969).

Doctor Chevalier is looking over a book in his office sometime after midnight when he hears a gun shot, a familiar sound in that part of the city. The doctor does not hear the scream that usually accompanies a gun shot, but he still closes his book and waits for someone to summon him to the scene.

Arriving at the house where the shot was fired, Doctor Chevalier is struck by the familiarity of the scene. As in times past, groups of tawdry women are either scurrying about or leaning on the banisters. Some are hysterical or weeping, others are morbidly curious to see the dead girl lying on the floor. But, unlike before, when Doctor Chevalier examines the bullet hole in the girl's temple, he recognizes this girl.

The girl and her family had offered Doctor Chevalier and his friend shelter and hospitality during a hunting expedition in Arkansas less than a year ago. Her parents were extremely proud of their intelligent daughter and supported her plan to move to the city.

The doctor pronounces the girl dead and tells the women gathered around that he knows the girl and will see that she receives a proper burial. The following day, Doctor Chevalier, in order to advise the Arkansas couple of their loss and to protect them from shame, sends a lock of hair and a letter to the cabin, which tells of the girl's sickness, her tender last words, and death. In the city, word gets out that the doctor has cared for a woman of "doubtful repute." Some don't know what to think; others want to shun him. No one does, though, and the event is eventually forgotten. (JW)

***

Rankin 1932: The story was based on a real person and event (134–35). **Seyersted 1969a:** As elsewhere, Chopin here uses a character whose name is significant (in this case suggesting chivalry [114]). Daniel Rankin's claim that this tale was based on a real incident cannot be proven (217). **Rocks 1972:** Here as elsewhere Chopin shows how a transformation or new experience can be destructive (116–17). **Arner 1975:** This somewhat fatalistic tale, which emphasizes the influence of milieu on character, also contrasts opposed values while depicting the coldness of urban life (127). **Taylor 1979:** Although this story involves female suffering, it also shows how nearly all persons are handicapped by social conventions (xviii). **Skaggs 1985:** Chopin's attitude toward the girl seems more sympathetic than judgmental in this story that adumbrates some of her later work (58). **Ewell 1986:** Because it relies on symbolism, lacks conversation, and features an objective tone, the story has a quality of detachment despite being based on a real situation (82). **Toth 1988a:** The title character is based on a good-hearted doctor who had once attended Chopin herself (56). Chopin uses the story to defend this man. Only once before had she set a story in New Orleans (57). **Toth 1988b:** The appealing physician here was based on Chopin's own obstetrician (64). **Toth 1990a:** The title character partly resembles a doctor Chopin once knew (127). This early story already shows Chopin's willingness to treat serious subjects (202). The doctor here may have resembled a later friend of Chopin (260). **Fusco 1994:** The story was heavily influenced by the example of Maupassant (150). **Koloski 1994:** The story is included in a soft-cover collection of Chopin's fiction published in 1979 (27). **Walker 1996:** This is one of many stories by Chopin in which the reading of correspondence is very significant. Such correspondence often symbolizes the power of the general written word (220). **Beer 1997:** This efficient, effective tale exploits and then subverts social prejudices. It sets up a familiar situation but then focuses on the unusual and unexpected. Practically every aspect of the story has the potential to raise questions as both the doctor and the reader confront the unforeseen. The doctor provides an unexpected ending to a familiar tale, and his invention unsettles both his neighbors and Chopin's readers by allowing for the possibility that he may indeed deserve some blame. Our chief interest is in the doctor, not the corpse. The story illustrates the dishonesty of sexual attitudes during Chopin's era. Perhaps the doctor himself is a hypocrite who patronized the dead girl, or perhaps his motives are purely noble. Chopin leaves the matter ambiguous (74–77). **Toth and Seyersted 1998:** This story is mentioned in Chopin's account books (140, 174). **Toth 1999c:** The title character was based on a doctor Chopin knew who had been named a

Chevalier of the Legion of Honor (68–69). The story first appeared in *Vogue* (172). **Knights 2000:** This was one of the numerous works Chopin composed in 1891 (xv). Here as elsewhere, Chopin satirizes inadequate responses to life's complexities and creates an ambiguous story that has provoked divergent responses (xxiv).

"Doralise"

Fragment. Included in *Private Papers* (1998).

... Doralise is a young, blond Creole painter who hopes to sell her art work in French New Orleans, having been rejected by the merchants in Canal Street .... **(RCE)**

***

Toth and Seyersted 1998: This apparently distinct work (132) was among a collection of Chopin manuscripts uncovered in the early 1990s (135). It was apparently among the papers borrowed but not returned by her first biographer (245). The fragment bears slight resemblances to various stories by Chopin and, like some of her other writings, it features an attractive, needy female artist. Doralise also resembles a character in *The Awakening* (272). It is one of only two surviving works Chopin never finished (274). **Toth 1999b:** This fragment demonstrates Chopin's willingness to give up on work she found unsatisfying (49). **Toth 1999c:** Fragments survive of this abandoned story, which would have focused on a female painter in New Orleans (166–67).

"The Dream of an Hour"
See "The Story of an Hour"

"A Dresden Lady in Dixie"

Written: 1894. First published: 1895. Included in *A Night in Acadie* **(1897).**

Madame Valtour's cherished Dresden figurine is missing. Viny, the housemaid, says that only Pa-Jeff and Agapie have been in the sitting room while Madame was gone. Pa-Jeff has been a faithful servant to the family since his childhood, and he is an old man. Agapie is only twelve years old and often admires the figurine when she comes to play with the Valtour children. Madame hates to think of Agapie stealing; maybe she dropped the figurine while playing with it and is afraid to tell anyone.

Madame goes to Agapie's cabin and tells her mother what has happened. Her mother cries and vows that Agapie is not a thief. She carries Madame into Agape's room to prove that the figurine is not there, but there, among her playthings, is the figurine.

Agapie comes home about that time and sees her mother crying. She runs to comfort her. Madame tells her that she is not allowed in her house any longer, for Agapie will be a bad influence on her children.

Pa-Jeff is nearly one hundred years old and he becomes ill. Agapie cares for him by taking him soup and spending time with him. She has lost the color in her cheeks and is sad. Pa-Jeff reasons that he is old and she is still so young. He goes to the Valtours' house and confesses that he stole the figurine. He says that he began feeling guilty and hid it among Agapie's playthings.

Agapie grows up to regain the love and confidence of the Valtour family. She is even kinder to Pa-Jeff than ever. Pa-Jeff tells the story of his theft so many times that he begins to believe it himself. **(DR)**

***

Gilder 1898: This is a moving account of altruism (50). **Bush 1957:** Here as in other stories, Chopin depicts loyal slaves (243). **Seyersted 1969a:** The clever irony of the tale prevents its portrait of Pa-Jeff from seeming sentimental or melodramatic (79). **Potter 1971:** The story is effective partly because it depicts Pa Jeff not mainly as a former slave but as an affectionate human being; he achieves true selfhood only by rejecting his subservient past. He is willing to risk his own modest social standing to help someone else, thereby winning our deeper respect. Like Uncle Mortimer in "In Sabine," he is a black man who helps a white woman, although Uncle Mortimer saves a woman's body while Pa Jeff helps redeem a girl's soul

(53). His individuality is enhanced by his distinctive religious attitudes (56). **Peterson 1972:** This is one of six tales Chopin composed between the summers of 1893 and 1895 in which she focuses on altruism. In this work, Chopin nicely avoids the sentimental tone that could have handicapped the work (124). **Jones 1981:** Although Pa-Jeff can be seen as a stereotype, he can also be seen as one of a number of black characters by Chopin who are genuinely selfless, unlike some of the white people she depicts (151). **Bonner 1982:** This is one of various stories by Chopin that reflect the importance of selfless Christian love. The story's comic touches prevent it from seeming too maudlin (119–20). **Skaggs 1985:** This is one of several stories emphasizing altruistic self-denial. Although a bit maudlin, it seems psychologically credible (29). **Ewell 1986:** Although Pa-Jeff seems almost a caricature, his selflessness is a virtue emphasized in accompanying stories. Chopin keeps us interested by generating a minor mystery, and Pa-Jeff's speeches exhibit some verbal and ethical complexity (99–100). **Toth 1990a:** The story provoked a very good payment (246). Reprinted in *A Night in Acadie* (298), it was well received by reviewers who disliked some other tales in that collection (300). **Robinson 1992:** This is one of many stories by Chopin that depict harmony between the races—a harmony that was not entirely unknown or unrealistic following the Civil War (xix). **Goodwyn 1994:** This tale exemplifies post-colonial writing. The missing figurine carries both cultural and personal associations that symbolize white privilege. Paradoxically, Pa-Jeff asserts his real independent selfhood by seeming to affirm a racist stereotype. His morally heroic act appears to confirm white prejudices about his race, but for Agapie, at least, it also exposes the shallowness of such prejudice. Such subversion of simple perceptions is typical of Chopin's fiction (7–10). This is one of various narrative in which Chopin shows the human tragedy involved in enforcing stereotypes (11). **Koloski 1994:** The story is included in a soft-cover collection of Chopin's fiction published in 1992 (28). **Koloski 1996:** This is one of various stories by Chopin featuring black characters that have provoked diverse reactions from critics (45). **Beer 1997:** Although the story takes place after slavery has been abolished, it nonetheless shows a firm emphasis on hierarchy and class. The figurine symbolizes racial and economic status, and even though Pa-Jeff is admired, he is still not treated as fully or individually human. Nevertheless, he paradoxically asserts his own autonomy, creativity, and capacity for compassion by self-consciously (if falsely) affirming standard racial stereotypes. He sacrifices himself, partly to reward the girl who has treated him well, but he thereby makes her even more aware of the falsity of her society's values. Ironically, this awareness distances her from the old man who tried to help her and whose self-sacrificing lie made possible her own later success. Here as in other tales Chopin undercuts the clichés of conventional morality (32–37). This is one of various tales by Chopin in which undamaged property is a central narrative concern (72). **McCollough 1999:** Although this story shows some

cooperation between the races, its underlying implications still seem
basically racist (319).

"An Easter Day Conversion"
See "A Morning Walk"

**Written: 1897. First published: 1897. Included in *A Vocation and
a Voice* (1991).**

"An Egyptian Cigarette"

**Written: 1897. First published: 1900. Included in *A Vocation and
a Voice* (1991).**

An unnamed narrator is given a small box by her architect
friend, who has just returned from the Orient. The box contains six
hand-made cigarettes wrapped in pale yellow paper. After excus-
ing herself from the room (since some of the other ladies detest the
odor of cigarette smoke), the narrator goes into a smoking room,
lights one of the cigarettes, and takes a long drag.

She immediately feels sand blistering her cheek. She is chasing
her god, Bardja, but falls down and is now crawling in the sand.
Bardja turns his camel and rides away, saying that he will never
return. She feels the sand in her mouth, between her teeth. She
feels the cool water and then hears music in a temple and sees
flowers.

The smoke has left the room; there are five cigarettes left in the
box and one stub in the ashtray. She wonders what other visions
she might see if she smokes another cigarette. The architect comes
back into the room, asking if she feels well. She answers that she
has had a bad dream. **(DR)**

***

Seyersted 1969a: This story was completed shortly before Chopin began
work on *The Awakening* and may have helped inspire the latter work's

focus on passion and sensuality (132–33). **Peterson 1972:** This is the first of a number of adventuresome late stories. The meaning of the dream is ambiguous. The narrative stance is objective despite the subjective vision, although the wisdom of the heroine's final act seems open to question (178–80). Unlike some of the other late stories, this one does not mock romance (198). **Rocks 1972:** Here as elsewhere Chopin seems to show that experiences can be simultaneously positive and negative (117). **Arner 1975:** The woman in the story ultimately (and timidly) rejects extremes of both pain and pleasure, including (symbolically) sexual pleasure (96). **Bonner 1975:** This is one of Chopin's several stories on taboo topics (283). **Rogers 1983:** Smoking represents freedom in this tale (29). **Skaggs 1985:** Here as elsewhere Chopin touches on the possibility of suicide, which she may have considered the ultimate form of self-control (42). **Ewell 1986:** Although the events it describes are simple, this story is important for its provocative subject, suggestive phrasing, dark sexuality, oriental mood, mellifluous language, symbolic overtones, and revelatory climax. It resembles writing of the French avant-garde, and the dark dream it describes perhaps reflects the hopelessness of most women's lives—a hopelessness reinforced by lack of freedom. Ironically, the dark vision makes the narrator seem less likely to depart again from prescribed routine (138–40). **Papke 1988:** This story presents a condensed version of *The Awakening* in imagery, events, characters, and themes (78–79). **Papke 1990:** This is one of four pivotal stories in Chopin's career in which she momentarily overcomes gloomy views of women's possibilities and instead presents resolute and confident female protagonists (60). In this story Chopin presents a distilled version of the plot of *The Awakening*. The conclusion of the story is puzzling but not pessimistic. The main character resembles the author herself and may symbolize Chopin's longing to be imaginative but self-possessed. The protagonist of the main character's dream, meanwhile, often resembles Edna from *The Awakening*, which Chopin composed soon after writing this tale (68–69). **Toth 1990a:** This was an unusual story for a midwestern female author (262–63) and was published in an adventurous journal (280; 296; 373–74). **Toth 1991:** Does this story reflect Chopin's own familiarity with drugs? (xiii). This is one of many of her late works that were first printed in *Vogue* (xiii–xiv). The imagery of this story is unusual for her time and place (xix). We can't be sure precisely how long it took Chopin to compose this work (xxii). Here and in other stories in *A Vocation and a Voice*, Chopin depicts an intriguing female character (xxv). **Davis 1992b:** This is one of many stories from *A Vocation and a Voice* that focus on suddenly altered perceptions. The changed outlook of the protagonist resembles that of Edna in *The Awakening*, and in fact this story was the last one Chopin finished before starting her novel. The two works are alike in imagery and atmosphere, and both reflect a new development in Chopin's writing. In the present tale Chopin juxtaposes the mundane and the exotic. The story may reflect the influence of opium consumption in Chopin's culture—a problem more common among women than among men, especially in the upper ranks of society (200–205). **Hoder-Salmon 1992:** Here as in *The Awakening*, Chopin associates smoking with a freedom usually reserved for males (136). The two works also share an emphasis on bee imagery (153). **Cothern 1994:** This is one of various stories in which Chopin used an internal narrator, a device which allowed her greater authorial distance both from the tale and from the dominant culture she may have been implicitly critiquing (124). **Cutter 1994:** Here as in some of her other late stories, Chopin creates a female voice that undercuts (often by mimicking) patriarchal language (17). The cigarettes, wrapped in yellow paper like the walls of Charlotte Perkins Gilman's famous story, allow a brief escape from the mundane constraints of typical female life, but even the dream shows the limits of a woman's freedom, especially since the woman in the dream is denied self-expression. The female narrator eventually renounces such fantasy and escapism, preferring instead a real (if covert) struggle against male domination (24–25). This is one of various works in which Chopin shows that subtle rebellion is often the most effective (34). **Day 1994:** Theme: how unconscious, pre-linguistic, suppressed impulses sometimes overflow into dreams (108). The tale is one of several showing a woman whose self-divisions cannot be healed (113–14). **Ewell 1994:** In this late work Chopin both alters and rises above standard literary conventions (169). In this tale the female dreamer must move away from other women into a conventionally male space, just as her dream is initiated by a gift from a male. Her rhythmic, repetitive dream enables a give-and-take between consciousness and the unconscious. The sensual and the linguistic combine and recombine in this dream (109–11). **Koloski 1994:** The story is included in a soft-cover collection of Chopin's fiction published in 1991 (28). **Bender 1996:** The dark tone of this story resembles the final tone of *The Awakening*. The story implies a Darwinian vision of conflict between the sexes. The image of the blue lily in this tale may imply an ideal androgyny and an absence of sexual strife (113). **Koloski 1996:** A French translation of *A Vocation and a Voice* gives the title of this story to the whole volume (46). **Toth and Seyersted 1998:** This story is mentioned in Chopin's account books (142–44, 150). **Toth 1999a:** This work typifies the lack of neat endings in Chopin's later writings (10). **Toth 1999c:** This tale, one of the unusual stories Chopin was able to publish in *Vogue* (172), was one of many somewhat dark stories intended for inclusion in *A Vocation and a Voice* (208). **Knights 2000:** This is one of several stories by Chopin published in *Vogue* despite the failure of *The Awakening* (xvii). In this work, Chopin untypically presents a female first-person narrator who encounters an unconventional experience through mysterious contact with a male (xvii). The setting of this tale is unusual in Chopin's fiction (xxxiii). Phrases here as in other works imply the narrator's presence (xlvi).

"Elizabeth Stock's One Story"

Written: 1898. Included in *A Vocation and a Voice* (1991).

An unnamed narrator tells about Elizabeth Stock, an old maid of thirty-eight, who died as if she had given up on life and simply gone to sleep. Visiting in Miss Stock's hometown one summer, the narrator stumbles upon a few pages written by Elizabeth. In the pages, Elizabeth explains that she has wanted to be a writer ever since she was a girl, but she admits that she has never been able to develop a good plot for a story. She writes that one day as she sat gazing out the window, she felt compelled to write an explanation of how she lost her position as postmistress of Stonelift. Her story goes like this: the mail is very late arriving one cold, rainy day. Although it is after dark when the mail finally arrives, she sorts it all, giving letters to those waiting for their mail. Nathan Brightman's girls had come for the mail that day, just as they did every day, but they went home hours earlier. Elizabeth admits that occasionally she glances at postal cards and, on this night, she notices that Mr. Brightman has received a card from a man in St. Louis saying that it is important for him to attend a meeting the next day. Elizabeth puts Mr. Brightman's mail aside and goes home to supper. After supper, as she is relaxing with a book, she begins thinking about Mr. Brightman's postal card. She knows that if he does not receive the card that very night, he will miss the meeting. Elizabeth gets up, dons her slicker and rubber boots, and climbs up the hill to Mr. Brightman's house through the freezing rain to deliver his mail. He praises her dedication to her position, continually thanking her while his family packs his bags. A few months later, Elizabeth receives a letter from Washington relieving her of her position as postmistress due to incompetence and negligence. She is shocked and the town is outraged, but as it turns out the position is given to the son of the man who sent the postal card to Brightman. Elizabeth is despondent and wishes she could simply go to sleep and never wake up. **(DR)**

***

Seyersted 1969a: The story may imply understated satire of "political favoritism" (214). **Peterson 1972:** This was one of the few stories Chopin composed during the time she was either completing or awaiting the appearance of *The Awakening* (244). Like most of the other stories she wrote during this period, this one differs from her earlier writing but does not point toward any obvious new development in her fiction (245). The story is atypical in structure and narration, resembling only the earlier works "La Belle Zoraïde" in the first instance and "Vagabonds" in the second. The narrator is oblivious to much of the irony surrounding her fate, and her trust in God seems especially ironic. In her lack of awareness, Elizabeth resembles the main character of "The Blind Man." Although the first-person narration is effective, the events and antagonist seem a bit contrived (247–50). This work, along with the other tales written at around the same time as the novel, suggest that Chopin was not pleased with her recent short fiction but had not yet found a satisfying new approach (256). **Rocks 1972:** The story reveals Chopin's own view that an over-emphasis on plot can hamper a beginning author. Chopin herself was less interested in describing events than in conveying impressions (112–13). **Arner 1975:** This is one of Chopin few "tales-within-a-tale"; it succeeds or fails according to the success or failure of Chopin's depiction of the title character. The story is partly handicapped by sentimentality, but it may also be the fiercest piece of social satire Chopin ever composed, particularly in its indictment of both Brightman (who shows gratitude to Collins but not to Elizabeth) and the government. Elizabeth's goodness and relative passivity ironically lead to her destruction. Thanks to its symbolic use of names, its contrasting tones, and its focus on quotidian life, the story is an unusually blatant piece of satire for Chopin to have composed (100–102). **Ladenson 1976:** In a story that focuses movingly on a woman of a lower class than Chopin herself, the title character is presented as a complicated human being, not a mere caricature. Elizabeth is undone by one of the very men she so loyally served (31). **Klemans 1981:** Although Elizabeth's natural instinct about how to write is correct, she is intimidated by a male who dissuades her from following it. She shows poor judgment in assessing the other males in her ironically-named town (40–41). **Fluck 1982:** This story illustrates Chopin's frequent tendency to associate regression with freedom (166). **Gilbert 1984:** This tale presents an affecting depiction of a woman from her own point of view (16). **Skaggs 1985:** This is one of several tales that explore the unpredictability of persons and events (46). **Ewell 1986:** Atypical in its structure and narrative voice, this story reflects Chopin's own thoughts on the challenges an author may face, including the difficulties of writing historical fiction. The opening sentences avoid maudlin pity, while the story gives Stock herself the voice she had sought for so long. The tone of that highly personal voice contrasts with the main narrator's objectivity, while the tale Stock finally tells is not conventional or contrived but is instead firmly rooted in her own experience. The story resembles other satirical works by Chopin, but its main importance derives from the title character, one of the most resolute, resilient, and autonomous of all of Chopin's heroines. The quirkiness of Elizabeth's literary style reflects her admirable personality and perceptive mind. She is more complex than she realizes, and her story illustrates the richness of much "ordinary" human life. Likewise, Chopin's own tale seems simple but is actually complex, revealing a willingness to take chances in characterization, structure, and tone. Chopin seems to have taken some real pride in this work (165–68). **Inge 1989:** This tale seems uncharacteristically maudlin, didactic, and unconvincing for a work by Chopin (106). **Toth 1990a:** This tale was influenced by a story by Bret Harte (315), although the dark conclusion of Chopin's narrative probably kept the tale from being accepted for publication (315). It was intended for inclusion in *A Vocation and a Voice* (374). Unlike others of her later stories, this one was preserved by the author (386). **Toth 1991:** The setting of the tale is the Missouri countryside (xiv). The dark tone may reflect Chopin's worries about her son, who was at war when she wrote the tale (xx). The story satirizes the assumption that women should suffer on behalf of others (xxi). This is one of several late stories by Chopin which reflect her interest in thought rather than mere plot (xxi–xxii). It is one of various stories in *A Vocation and a Voice* that seem to satirize contemporary class relations (xxiv) and that depict an intriguing female character (xxv). It is also one of several dark stories in the final collection (xxv). **Hoder-Salmon 1992:** Here as elsewhere Chopin links women and dreaming (112). **Thomas 1992:** Chopin may have been influenced by a St. Louis reviewer to write this story set in Missouri. It was one of the few pieces of short fiction Chopin composed in 1898 (40). **Cutter 1994:** Here as in some of her other late stories, Chopin creates a female voice that undercuts (often by mimicking) patriarchal language (17). The heroine here is one of Chopin's hardiest and most confident women, but for precisely this reason she is doomed. She is ultimately undone by official language as employed by the symbolic U.S. "male." She subverts standard assumptions about language and reading and she seeks to escape patriarchal control through her own writing, which does not fit conventional male patterns. She engages in a kind of feminine writing, and it is significant that she writes her story *after* being fired. She writes in a way that seems simple but is actually clever, not only because her writing seems to present no threat but also because she pretends to know less than she probably does. Ultimately the seemingly defeated Elizabeth has her say (28–31). This is one of various works in which Chopin shows that subtle rebellion is often the most effective (34). **Ewell 1994:** In this late work Chopin both alters and rises above standard literary conventions (169). **Koloski 1994:** The story is included in soft-cover collections of Chopin's fiction published in 1984 and 1991 (27–28). **Thomas 1995:** This is one of several stories in which Chopin mocks—and thus distances herself from—stereotypes of the woman writer (19). As her name may suggest, Stock writes mainly to make money, but Chopin's unblinking depiction of this female author may also be her most sympathetic presentation of such a character (25–27). Perhaps Chopin's nervous anticipation of the reception of *The Awakening* helped inspire this story, with its unconventional and ultimately unsuccessful central character (28–30). **Walker 1995:** Like much other writing by women, this tale begins by assuming that a woman writer is an outsider (6) and focuses on the protagonist's own life (9, 15). This tale demonstrates Chopin's awareness that writing inevitably was affected by gender—which is perhaps one reason that the patronizing narrator seems to be a male (16). Her name suggests an untapped well of possible tales (17), yet the story shows her difficulty in relating to the (male) literary tradition (18). She knows of no feminine tradition (20–21) and is more passive than one later (and real) woman writer (22). Her story shows that autobiography is always one available resource for marginalized writers (121). The tale is more complex than it seems (171–72), partly because it refutes the way she is understood by others (174–75). **Walker 1996:** Theme: the relations between women and writing (220). The town in this tale is reminiscent of the one in "Miss Witherwell's Mistake" (223). This is Chopin's most explicit depiction of the ways a writer's gender affects his or her work. The censorious narrator is a male (224). Although the title character's name implies her potential creativity, the fact that she is a woman prevents her from fulfilling the ambition her nephew can take for granted because he is a male. The story shows Chopin's awareness of the limits faced by any female author, including Chopin herself (225). **Toth and Seyersted 1998:** This story is mentioned in Chopin's account books (144, 151). **Toth 1999c:** The dark tone of this tale, which may have been influenced by recent rumors of war, made the story unlikely to achieve publication (203). It was one of several dark narratives intended for inclusion in *A Vocation and a Voice* (208). **Knights 2000:** This is one of various works in which Chopin juxtaposes an individual life with a larger social context (xviii–xix). Here as elsewhere Chopin implies the uncertainties of existence (xxvi).

"Emancipation"

Included in *Complete Works* (1969).

An animal is born in a barred cage. Having everything that it needs in the cage—air, light, food, drink, and a comfortable place to rest—the animal grows in strength and beauty and is content. The animal awakens one day to discover that the cage door is open. Fearing the unfamiliar, the animal wants to close the door, but it lacks the appropriate limbs to do so. Instead, the animal thrusts its head outside the cage and sees the world that it knows grow larger. The animal retires to its corner, but the thought of the Unknown prevents it from being able to rest.

The animal repeatedly goes to the door and sees more and more each time. It eventually takes a deep breath and springs out of the cage and into the Light. In the animal's mad flight, its race to experience the Unknown through its senses of taste, smell and touch, the animal tears its flanks, but takes no notice. The animal must hunt to satisfy its hunger and search at length, on tired limbs, for good water to slake its thirst. The animal, choosing to spend its life seeking and finding, experiencing joy and suffering, never revisits the cage with its door ajar. (JW)

***

Zlotnick 1968: Here as elsewhere Chopin demonstrates a strong interest in freedom (2). **Seyersted 1969a:** Perhaps the story reflects the young Chopin's own desire to taste adult freedoms (30–31). **Seyersted 1969b:** This story may reflect Chopin's early aspirations for a liberated life (29). **Leary 1970a:** This fable of liberation is one of Chopin's earliest works (v). **Rocks 1972:** Here as elsewhere, Chopin shows the complexities of liberty, including the pain and disappointments it can sometimes carry with it (116). **Bender 1974:** This early story anticipates important themes of *The Awakening* (258). **Seyersted 1974:** The plot of this very early story may be relevant to Chopin's own later decision to leave home and marry (9–10). The sense of adventure implied in this early tale contrasts with the sense of disillusionment suggested by some of Chopin's final stories (18). **Wolff 1979:** This tale foreshadows a major theme of her later fiction: the restrictions any choice inevitably imposes on life (208). **Jones 1981:** The title suggests the story's relevance to slavery (23), whether of blacks or of women (150). **Fluck 1982:** This story illustrates Chopin's concern with transgression (162). **Bonner 1983b:** Chopin endorses the central character's unconventional self-assertion (146). **Rogers 1983:** Like George Sand, Chopin focuses (in this work) on a symbol of freedom (33). **Gilbert 1984:** This early work suggests the rebellious side of Chopin's personality, especially since the escaped beast is depicted as a male (11). **White 1984:** This tale foreshadows *The Awakening* both in topics and in design. Edna is even compared at one point to an awakening animal (97–98). **Skaggs 1985:** In theme, imagery, and tone, this story anticipates some of Chopin's most important later works. It resembles the story of the choice made in Eden: although knowledge and freedom bring pain, they are valuable nonetheless (54–55). **Ewell 1986:** Chopin took precautions to save this work, which may have been her first piece of genuine fiction. The tale focuses on themes she would later explore much more fully, and perhaps it grew out of her own initiation into maturity and adult love (10–11). **Stepenoff 1987:** In this almost excessively transparent tale, an escaped bird discovers both the challenges and the satisfactions of freedom (452). **Inge 1989:** Composed just before Chopin turned twenty, this is the first of her still-extant stories. It deals in symbolic terms with one of the major topics of her fiction—the transition from imprisonment to liberty of spirit and the difficulties this valuable transition often entails (92). **Taylor 1989:** Both the title and theme of this story are relevant to Chopin's later interest in matters of race (157). **Papke 1990:** The story reflects Chopin's adventurous early reading. She wrote nothing after it for two decades (23), yet the work clearly anticipates *The Awakening* in its emphasis on risk, defiance, and the practical consequences of each, although the story is less realistic than the novel. The story endorses full participation in life, despite its pains, but its allegorical form weakens the work, especially because the subject is an animal whose potential development is necessarily limited and mostly due to chance. As befits a youthful author, the ending of the tale is also optimistic. The story is important, nonetheless, for its romantic treatment of themes Chopin would later confront more complexly, as in "Euphrasie" (34–37) or "Azélie" (61). **Toth 1990a:** This is Chopin's first extant story. It seems to have been influenced by a Victor Hugo tale and already reveals Chopin's interest in a central theme of her later work (97). **Guidici 1991:** This early work typifies Chopin's interest in freedom (34). **Black 1992:** This early tale implies Chopin's dread of confinement (99–100). **Dyer 1992:** Here as in *The Awakening*, cage imagery is important (42). **Mitchell 1992:** All living things, like the bird in this tale, instinctively yearn for liberty, which is not easily achieved (60–61). **Ewell 1994:** This early story implies that one of Chopin's motives as a writer may have been to escape from social and literary conventions and to explore reality as fully as possible for herself (157–58). **Koloski 1994:** The story is included in a soft-cover collection of Chopin's fiction published in 1984 (28). **Saar 1994:** Theme: the costs but also the value of liberation (67). **Walker 1994:** Because the creature here is not a female, the story may not be relevant to Chopin's own marriage (6). **Weatherford 1994:** This work was written much earlier than Chopin's other fiction (105). **Koloski 1996:** Chopin composed this tale before turning twenty (84). **Beer 1997:** This story experiments with the genre announced in its subtitle and responds well to close analysis while also being open to historical interpretation. Like Aesop's fables, this tale focuses on an animal, while the main title suggests a relevance to issues of slavery. The story encourages readers to ponder the paradoxes implied by both the title and subtitle, and the narrative implicitly refutes arguments favoring slavery. Chopin effectively uses complicated references to verb tenses to broaden the significance of the tale; the story shows both the necessity and the risks of freedom (67–70). **Benfey 1999:** The story may be relevant to the topic of slavery since it suggests that uncomfortable freedom is better than comfortable imprisonment (248). **Toth 1999c:** This tale, the first extant piece of fiction by Chopin, was influenced by the work of a French writer. It rejects the standard feminine image of the caged bird (51).

"A Family Affair"

Written: 1897. First published: 1898. Reprinted: 1899. Included in
***Complete Works* (1969).**

Madame Félicie Solisainte, who is "superabundantly fat," has been unable to leave her chair for two years. Servants, undertaking "an affair of importance," move her to and from her bed to the chair each day. Her time otherwise is spent supervising the movements in and out of her house from the window by her chair. She is preoccupied by the idea that she is being robbed "continuously and on all sides" by her servants, a notion that is nurtured by her servant, Dimple, a "very black girl of sixteen."

To be spared the cost of a housekeeper, Madame Solisainte decides to invite one of her nieces from New Orleans to live with her. The niece who decides to come is Bosey Brantonniere, who is preceded by her mother's written recommendation regarding Bosey's amiable temperament and housekeeping and managerial abilities. What the mother does not write is that none of her other girls can abide the notion of living with Tante Félicie, and that Bosey (or Bosé) has agreed to go only on an experimental basis with no "cast-iron obligation" to stay.

After the first greetings, Bosé informs her aunt that she will take all care and bother off of her aunt's shoulders. She promises, too, that she will have her aunt on her feet in less than two months.

Bosé has been informed by family members of Madame Solisainte's avarice and how she took possession "by the force of audacity alone" of Bosé's mother's rightful share of Bosey's grandmother's estate. Bosé cannot help thinking how it must have been while her grandmother was immobilized in her huge chair ("She lived many year' like you see me," confides Madame Solisainte) that Tante Felicie took charge of things. Rather than malice, however, Bosé feels sympathy for her afflicted aunt.

With Madame Solisainte similarly immobilized, Bosé has her moved to the front room, where she will have a "sweet, peaceful view" and be unable to monitor the comings and goings from the house. For Madame Solisainte's enjoyment, Bosé has Dimple, "staggering with arms full of books and periodicals," bring in to her a portion of the trunk of reading material, including French books sent by Bosé's mother.

After cleaning Tante Félicie's spectacles, Bosé then demands the household keys. Madame Solisainte's resistance is a furtive

grip on the bag of keys, which Bosé easily overcomes. Command-
ing Dimple to accompany her, Bosé sets off to investigate the
house and its holdings. Madame Solisainte, having never been
spoken to with "the authority which this young woman assumed,"
is stupefied. She attempts to retain some semblance of authority by
interrogating Dimple as to Bosé's actions. Dimple's answers only
increase her trepidation. While Bosé reorganizes the household
staff into a more efficient group, "upscales" the supplies, and puts
into service long-stored tablecloths and family silver, Madame
Solisainte obsesses over imagined thievery: "*Bon Dieu!* it won't be
a grain of sugar left, a bar of soap—nothing, nothing!" Her
expressions are reserved for Dimple because her outwardly timid
persona permits only "an occasional outburst like the flare of a
smouldering fire."

One morning not long after her arrival, Bosé takes extra care
with her aunt's toilet, powdering her face and scenting her with
cologne. Bosé puts fresh flowers on the table in the front room and
dusts and rearranges the books. An hour or two later, Bosé brings
in their neighbor Doctor Godfrey, a young and handsome man
with a "superabundance of animal spirits." Bosé explains she has
decided, after seeing the suffering her aunt endures at being put to
bed, that Madame Solisainte should be under a physician's care.

Madame Solisainte resists this idea, claiming that nothing can
help her just as nothing could help her mother. Her fate is to die in
her chair. She is also concerned about the doctor's bill for this visit
and is determined that he will visit no more. However, she grows
"sick with apprehension and uncertainty, unable to distinguish between his professional and social visits" as the doctor spends more
and more time with Bosé.

Pursuing her "avocation of the ministering angel," Bosé im-
provises more devices for her aunt's "comfort and entertainment":
visits by Madame Solisainte's old friends, visits by Bosé's new
friends, serving lemonade, red wine from Lablatte of New Orleans,
and cakes, lawn parties with musicians and Chinese lanterns, and
a ball at which Madame Solisainte appears in a custom-made silk
peignoir.

At risk of losing his practice because of the time he is spending
with Bosé, Godfrey asks her to marry him, and she accepts his
proposal but keeps the engagement a secret from her aunt while
she makes preparations for her marriage. When she announces her
engagement and imminent departure from the plantation, "[a]
beatitude, a beneficent joy settled upon Madame." Madame Soli-

sainte, with a "shrill protest," declines Bosé's offers to send one of her sisters in her place, and all morning Madame Solisainte feels like she "could have sung for the very joy" as she listens to Bosé's packing. At the time of their departure, she is "as suave as honey" to Godfrey since "in the character of a nephew he would not have the indelicacy to present a bill for professional services."

Bosé's final gesture is to return her aunt's keys to her with a summary of the accuracy of the financial transactions she undertook at Lablatte's and elsewhere. With the preface of "by the way," Bosé informs her aunt that she has made an equal division of her grandmother's silver, table linen, and jewelry, which she has sent on to her mother. Asserting first that this action was only fair and then asking if her aunt is certain she doesn't want Bosé's sister as a replacement, Bosé takes her leave.

Behind her, Bosé hears cries of "*Voleuse!*" ("*thief*" or "*filcher*"). Madame Solisainte's imagination is feverish with fantastic vandalism and robbery. She pounds her cane on the floor and calls for hours, but no one heeds her because the servants have accompanied Bosé to the station. Absorbed with "the most violent agitation, the most turbulent misgivings," she attempts to rise from her chair and succeeds after the third try. So intent is she on inspecting the contents of her press, which holds her gold, that she does not "think it strange or miraculous" that she is walking. When she eventually arrives at and unlocks the press, she is relieved to find all of her gold intact. However, half of the silver, the table linen, and the jewelry are gone.

When the servants return, they are astonished to find Madame Solisainte waiting on the front gallery. Dimple becomes hysterical and screams and cries out.

Madame Solisainte orders one servant to fetch the overseer, Richmond, and then she systematically undoes, through a series of fiats, all of the changes Bosé made in the household. All the while, she fumes, "I will 'ave the law!" **(EP)**

***

Bush 1957: This story mentions French writers of the kind Chopin and others in Louisiana read (235). This narrative is Chopin's only exclusively humorous tale (241–42). **Peterson 1972:** This was one of the few stories Chopin composed during the time she was either completing or awaiting the appearance of *The Awakening* (244). Like most of the other stories she wrote during this period, this one differs from her earlier writing but does not point toward any obvious new development in her fiction (245). This work is Chopin's single attempt at obvious humor. In theme it recalls

"Ma'ame Pélagie," but here the treatment is basically light. The main character is a caricature, but the treatment she receives partly mirrors her own treatment of her own mother. The story-line is fairly conventional, but the setting and protagonist give the tale some originality (245–47). This work, along with the other tales written at around the same time as the novel, suggest that Chopin was not pleased with her recent short fiction but had not yet found a satisfying new approach (256). **Rocks 1972:** This is one of many stories in which Chopin suggests that each person must decide whether it is better to be content with one's present condition or attempt to alter one's future. The results of either choice cannot be predicted. The story implies that sometimes pain provides an incentive for change (115–16). **Arner 1975:** In this tale Chopin avoids the pitfall of a sentimentally happy ending, choosing instead to offer a psychologically credible account of complex characters (133). **Davis 1982:** This seems to have been the only story Chopin composed during the period when she was devoting her fullest attentions to writing *The Awakening* (68). **Newman 1986:** Like many of Chopin's tales, this one suggests a view of marriage that seems to conflict with views implied by some of her other stories. This work seems to affirm traditional ideas about the value of matrimony (152). As in other tales, Chopin here contrasts real life with the stereotypes of fiction, especially in presenting the scheming Bosé (160–61). **Ewell 1986:** This tale—the first Chopin composed after finishing *The Awakening*—was immediately accepted for publication. It features a strong female protagonist and skillful ethical exploration, and it is all the more lively due to its descriptions of things and conduct. The young heroine cleverly manipulates people and situations to her own (and their) advantage, although our knowledge of her activities is filtered through the perceptions of her bed-ridden aunt. This lively and amusing tale ends with striking irony (164–65). **Inge 1989:** Although this tale does emphasize a distinctive setting, the details make the narrative seem plausibly convincing rather than merely quaint. As usual, it concludes with effective irony (108). **Toth 1990a:** This story mocks conventional tales about virtuous youth; it symbolizes Chopin's's rejection of typical fiction for young people. She was well paid for the narrative, which perhaps was partly inspired by circumstances in her own extended family (although this is uncertain [275–76]). The story was published shortly before a time when Chopin temporarily ceased writing (357). **Hoder-Salmon 1992:** Here as elsewhere Chopin shows her familiarity with real details of life on Grand Isle (123). **Cutter 1994:** As in some of her other later tales, Chopin here presents a strong woman (27–28). **Fusco 1994:** In this tale Chopin mentions Maupassant (a great influence) by name (140). **Koloski 1994:** The story is included in soft-cover collections of Chopin's fiction published in 1979 and 1992 (27–28). **Toth and Seyersted 1998:** This story is mentioned in Chopin's account books (141, 142, 151).

"Fedora"

Written: 1895. First published: 1897. *Included in Complete Works* **(1969) and** *A Vocation and a Voice* **(1991).**

Fedora insists that she drive to the station and pick up Miss Malthers. Fedora is thirty and feels superior to her siblings and the others. She has long ago formed her idea of the ideal man and has been unable to find a man who measures up to that ideal. She assumes the position of the mother and takes care of her brothers' and sisters' guests. They all consider her to be at least a hundred years old. One young man, Malthers, thinks she is about forty.

Fedora has known Malthers for eight years, since he was fifteen. She begins noticing his blue eyes, his smooth skin, and his strong, firm lips. She wants him by her constantly. Fedora is totally infatuated with Malthers. She wants to see his sister and to be near her also.

Malthers' sister is the only one to get off the train, but Fedora would have known her if there had been thousands. She possesses the same features as her brother. The two women get into the carriage and Fedora begins telling the sister that she wants her to feel completely at home and that she is sure they will become fond of one another. Fedora then puts her arm around Miss Malthers' shoulders. When Miss Malthers looks up at Fedora and to thank her, Fedora kisses her mouth with a long, penetrating kiss.

Miss Malthers is astonished and not too happy. Fedora picks up the reins and stares ahead the rest of the way home. **(DR)**

***

Peterson 1972: This is another late tale by Chopin that emphasizes irony. Lesbianism probably does not explain the title character's conduct; instead, she chooses an approved (if unusual) means to express a desire she must otherwise suppress. Here as in "Regret" and "Azélie," the realization of affection leads ultimately to alienation (182–84). **Rocks 1972:** As elsewhere, Chopin here shows that erotic desire often causes suffering, not simply pleasure (116). **Arner 1975:** Fedora's handling of the whip as she waits for the train has sexual overtones. Just as she had used the young man's clothes as part of her fantasies, so does she later use his sister. As the story concludes, Fedora handles the whip again, although Chopin keeps her meanings implicit (87–88). **Bonner 1975:** This is one of Chopin's several stories on taboo topics (283). **Wolff 1979:** This is one of many Chopin stories in which sexual attraction is an important topic (220). **Dyer 1980–81:** This is one of many stories by Chopin in which a female is aroused by contact with a male (10–11). **Dyer 1981c:** This story is one of Chopin's most effective studies of internal identity. The protagonist is briefly if vividly characterized, and her uncertainties are implied by her conduct in ways that are highly efficient. By making Fedora inarticulate, Chopin enhances our sense of her confusion (261). After initially establishing a sense of Fedora's firm identity, Chopin quickly undermines her—and our—certainty, but she does so mostly by showing rather than telling (262). The sister's presence gives Fedora a chance to express feelings she could not otherwise openly display, but she expresses those feelings in an excessive way (263–64). Meanwhile her dealings with the horse seem symbolic, both before and after the kiss (264–65). This is one of Chopin's best explorations of feelings that are either held inside or are expressed only indirectly (265). **Rogers 1983:** Here as elsewhere Chopin (like George Sand) explores the complexities of feminine sexuality. The tale deals with fairly unusual sexual self-expression, including incestuous overtones (35–36). **Dyer 1985:** In this as in other tales, Chopin relies on readers' stereotypes about unconventional characters in order to deal with topics she might not have been able to depict otherwise (81). **Newman 1986:** The title character here adopts, at an early stage, a self-destructive identity. The lesbian implications of the ending are less significant than the story's exploration of the injuries that can result from extreme self-involvement (161). **Skaggs 1985:** This is one of several tales emphasizing the strong influence of erotic desire. Fedora's final act seems an effort to harmonize these desires with her other important motives (46–48). **Ewell 1986:** The story had trouble finding a publisher immediately and was eventually published under a pseudonym, although the latter circumstance may have resulted simply from the fact that the story was published simultaneously with some other works that *were* explicitly attributed to Chopin. Even the name of the title character seems a bit unfeminine, and the story itself is fairly audacious in its treatment of issues of sexual impulse and identity. The story illustrates the price paid by those who struggle to control their sexual yearnings (114–15). **Toth 1990a:** The pseudonym under which Chopin published this story seems indebted to the name of a character in one of the favorite books of her youth (52). The story was rejected by the first magazine to which she sent it. It partly resembles her earlier tale "A Shameful Affair" as well as a manuscript entitled "The Impossible Miss Meadows." This mysterious tale may have been inspired by a real event. Although it was eventually published (288–90), it was probably at first turned down (296), perhaps because it was too unconventional (300). One character bears the same name as an acquaintance of Chopin (323). The story was intended for inclusion in *A Vocation and a Voice* (374). **Toth 1991:** The main character of this work resembles a friend of Chopin (xvii). The tale can be read from numerous psychological perspectives (xxii). This is one of various stories in *A Vocation and a Voice* that defy conventional expectations about sexuality (xxiii). Perhaps this story reflected a real-life, local incident (xxiii). **Davis 1992b:** This is one of many stories from *A Voca-*

tion and a Voice that focus on suddenly altered perceptions (200–201). **Day 1994:** Theme: how unconscious, pre-linguistic, suppressed impulses sometimes overflow into dreams (108). Here as elsewhere Chopin explores the theme of a divided woman, although in this tale bisexuality seems a possible solution (116). **Ewell 1994:** This is one of many stories by Chopin that show the dangers of ignoring the sexual or sensual aspects of human nature (168). **Koloski 1994:** The story is included in soft-cover collections of Chopin's fiction published in 1979 and 1991 (27–28). **Bender 1996:** Perhaps Chopin's Darwinism affected her depiction here of a woman who foolishly delays her selection of a mate, so that in the end she becomes a kind of parody of a dominant male. The theme of Darwinian selection is explicit here for the first time in Chopin's fiction (110–11). **Koloski 1996:** This story reflects Chopin's interest in opera (53) and may have been influenced by a contemporary play. Indeed, the title character is a role-player. The story concludes with one of the various uncertain kisses featured in Chopin's fiction. Fedora's behavior may be unclear to literally everyone, including herself (61–63; 86). **Toth and Seyersted 1998:** One of Chopin's friends resembled Fedora (130). This story is mentioned in Chopin's account books (141, 150). **Koloski 1999:** This was one of a number of effective tales Chopin composed before the publication of *A Night in Acadie* but which she did not include in that collection (xv–xvi). **Toth 1999c:** One important editor turned down this tale because he considered it uneventful (191–92). Recent readers have wondered whether the story's theme is lesbianism or redirected affection, but perhaps the tale in fact reflects an event in the life of Chopin's daughter (197–98).

"For Marse Chouchoute"

Written: 1891. First published: 1891. Included in *Bayou Folk* (1894).

When young Armand Verchette receives his instructions for the position of mail carrier from Cloutierville to the railway station three miles away, he is accompanied by his usual attendant, a little black boy called Wash. Sixteen-year-old Armand's nickname, "Chouchoute," aptly describes his personality, because he is a dear fellow. People can not help but like him because he is so open and cheerful, even though, unfortunately, he is also careless and forgetful. Indeed, Wash positively adores Chouchoute and his mother. He takes pride in being the young man's conscience to remind him of his duties. Also, he is impressed with Chouchoute's responsible job, which will provide thirty dollars a month. The money will make a great difference in the lives of Madame Verchette and her fatherless boy.

One fine spring night, as Chouchoute rides with the mail to the station, he passes a lighted cabin and hears the sound of fiddle music floating from inside. He remembers there is a ball taking place that night, and he can not resist going to the door for a moment just to see everyone. Now, Chouchoute is well-known in the community as a fine dancer. Of course, he is drawn into the group and dances in a few sets. Too soon, though, he hears a loud whistle and knows there is not time left to get the mail to the train. His heart pounds from fear and shame, and he envisions himself and his mother sinking back into poverty. Chouchoute bolts from the cabin, only to learn that his horse with the mail-bag is gone. Frantically, he mounts a nearby pony and rides at top speed to the station. The young manager tells him that his horse is safe in the nearby woods and that the mail-bag is on the train to New Orleans. "Thank God!" sighs Chouchoute. Alas, continues the station master, his poor little darkey has just about done himself in. He rode the horse beside the moving train, trying to get the mail sack on it, but when he hurled the bag into the car the horse shied and Wash was thrown against the train and then back onto the ground. When Chouchoute kneels beside the boy's pallet and looks into his dying face, Wash apologizes for taking the horse away like that. There was just no other way to meet the train with the mail. He hopes Ma'ame Verchette will know something to cure his head, he whispers, because "I boun' to git well, 'ca'se who—gwine—watch Marse—Chouchoute?" **(CY)**

***

Anonymous 1894 [*The Critic*]: The very simplicity and brevity of this tale contributes to its effectiveness (41). **Rankin 1932:** The town in this tale is based on Cloutierville, Louisiana, where Chopin lived during 1880–83 (98). The story was composed in a single day (March 14, 1891) and was mailed to a magazine for youth two days later. Its main character—a young disabled black boy—proves himself loyal and heroic. The work illustrates Chopin's narrative gifts and her innate talent for presenting subtle oppositions in an intriguing fashion (130). **Seyersted 1969a:** This is one of several tales in which Chopin depicts the devotion sometimes felt by freed blacks toward whites (79). **Potter 1971:** Unlike some of Chopin's other black characters, Wash in this tale seems mostly stereotypical. His motives seem simplistic, perhaps because this was originally a children's tale designed to emphasize the importance of fulfilling obligations. Nevertheless, Wash is not a person but a puppet (50–51). **Peterson 1972:** Although this story was first published in a magazine apparently intended for young readers, the journal's actual audience was broader than its title might suggest (61). This tale, though, is a bit maudlin and is simplistic in depicting characters. The moral and its presentation are conventional (62; 65). In this early tale, a 'Cadian ball is mentioned but is not made integral to the story, as it would be in the later "At the 'Cadian Ball" (98). **Bonner 1977:** Here as elsewhere Chopin treats her black characters as individual persons rather than as stereotypes (6–7). As elsewhere in *Bayou Folk*, Chopin here uses a sudden twist to create irony (9). The story illustrates Christian self-sacrifice (11). The white boy matures because of the black boy's self-sacrifice, but the story is too simplistic (11). **Lattin 1980:** This is one of various stories by Chopin featuring repeating characters (28). **Toth 1981:** Here and in some other early tales, the black characters fit the stereotype of the happy slave (202). **Bonner 1982:** This is one of various stories by Chopin that reflect the importance of selfless Christian love (119). **Skaggs 1985:** This is one of several stories dealing with the selfhood of exslaves. Although disturbing, the tale is also psychologically realistic (16–17). **Ewell 1986:** This was Chopin's first attempt to center a story on a black protagonist, but it is largely unsuccessful because of its maudlin tone and ethical simplicity (67). **Toth 1990a:** This story is set in Cloutierville, where Chopin lived for a time (140; 224), while the priest in the narrative may be based on one who lived in that town (147–48). The title character shares a name with an acquaintance of Chopin (150), and the reference in the story to dancing reflects life in Cloutierville (153). This was one of several stories from 1891 in which Chopin sought a friendly, interested readership, and it was one of four she published in the same young persons' magazine in that year (201). It was republished in a local Louisiana newspaper (201–2) and was a particular favorite of a later resident of Cloutierville (404). **Toth 1990b:** Here as in other works, Chopin mocks the priest of her local Louisiana parish (290). **Toth 1992:** As in some other writings, Chopin here creates characters whose names resemble those of real persons (16). **Ewell 1994:** Of the nearly ten stories Chopin wrote early in 1891, this was one of only three to be immediately accepted for publication (160). **Goodwyn 1994:** This is one of various stories in which Chopin depicts the stereotype of the loyal black (10). **Koloski 1996:** This is one of several children's stories by Chopin that depict the poor (71; 87). **Wagner-Martin 1996:** Here as elsewhere Chopin depicts an appealing, altruistic young male. Although the story is somewhat hard to take seriously, it is like many of Chopin's works in portraying an attractive black character (203). **Beer 1997:** Here as elsewhere Chopin focuses on blacks' loyalty to whites (35). **Toth and Seyersted 1998:** This story is mentioned in Chopin's account books (139, 148, 167). **Koloski 1999:** This is one of many stories by Chopin which either feature children or were written for them (xxii). Here as elsewhere she describes children's' responses to poverty (xxiii). **McCullough 1999:** This is one of various stories by Chopin whose underlying attitudes seem implicitly racist (319). **Toth 1999c:** The tale accurately describes the main street of Cloutierville (82). The name in the title may have been inspired by the name of one of Chopin's relatives (88). The entertainment described in the story was realistic (89), while the priest in the narrative was modeled on a local cleric (92). This kind of tale was favored by white editors of the time (169).

"A Gentleman from New Orleans"

Written: 1900. Included in *Complete Works* (1969).

Except for a few minor disagreements, Mr. and Mrs. Buddie Bénôite have a happy marriage, although Buddie can neither forgive nor forget the fact that his wife's family opposed their union. When the Bénôites and their children set off one day for a barbecue, Buddie leaves his sister Sophronie behind to look after the house, to take care of the elderly black servant, Aunt Crissy, and especially to keep an eye open for Mr. Sneckbauer, an important businessman from New Orleans whose visit has been expected for some time.

Sophronie throws herself into her housework and banters with Aunt Crissy until she notices a buggy in the distance. Excited and alarmed by the stranger's appearance, Sophronie does her best to make him feel at home, especially since she knows how much her brother is depending on the success of this visit. The stranger is mostly quiet, so Sophronie is relieved when he accepts her suggestion that he inspect her brother's brimming cotton fields.

When Buddie returns with his family later that evening, he is excited to hear that the anticipated visitor has arrived. He urges his wife and children to make themselves presentable, and he quickly gets himself ready for the visitor's return from the fields. When the man does walk up to the house, however, Buddie's wife dashes from the porch and tearfully embraces him. It is her father, whom she has not seen in years. Although Buddie had always threatened to shoot any member of her family who trespassed on his property, he is deeply moved by his wife's intense affection for her father. He welcomes the visitor and regrets his earlier hostility.

Buddie's father-in-law explains that his wife is seriously ill and is anxious to see her daughter. Although Sneckbauer, the businessman, also arrives later that night, Buddie's father-in-law is clearly the guest of honor, and Buddie makes plans for almost the whole family to visit his wife's sick mother immediately. **(RCE)**

***

Peterson 1972: This relatively ineffective tale for the young depends on the over-used plot device of confused perception. The story lacks both comedy and tension, and even the setting is uninteresting (260). **Dyer 1981a:** Gouvernail, a skeptical character present in some of Chopin's earlier work, would be inappropriate in this story (55). **Ewell 1986:** In its setting and theme this work is a throw-back to some of Chopin's earlier writings, but the story does contain innovations of characterization and plot. It exemplifies Chopin's comprehension of the difficulties women faced, but its most fascinating component is its treatment of father-daughter relations (177). **Toth 1990a:** Chopin wrote this story on the day she turned fifty. Its protagonists' last name resembles that of some of Chopin's relatives. She received forty dollars for the tale from a young person's magazine, although it never actually published the story it had purchased (373). **Hoder-Salmon 1992:** A statement in this story mocks an insufficiently independent woman (21). **Thomas 1992:** This is one of several works by Chopin written in 1900 that focus on sickness, death, or growing old (50). **Cutter 1994:** This story shows the dangers of feminine self-abnegation (31–32). **Koloski 1994:** This tale was included in an anthology of local color fiction published in 1941 and then reprinted nearly thirty years later (23). The story is included in a soft-cover collection of Chopin's fiction published in 1992 (28). **Koloski 1996:** This is one of Chopin's numerous works written for young people (87). **Thomas 1996:** This story is one of many in which Chopin depicts aged black females, often in stereotypical terms (216–17). **Toth and Seyersted 1998:** An early draft of this story was among a collection of Chopin manuscripts uncovered in the early 1990s (135). The story is mentioned in Chopin's account books (142, 146–47, 151). The newly uncovered manuscript closely resembles the already published text (246). This was one of several stories by Chopin that were accepted and paid for but never published (275). The slight differences between the two versions are briefly discussed (284). **Bell 1998:** A phrase in this tale reflects Chopin's awareness of how women could be constricted by marriage (243). **Toth 1999c:** A version of this tale was rediscovered in 1992 (166). The story had been purchased, but was not printed, by a young persons' magazine, perhaps because of alterations in personnel (229).

"A Gentleman of Bayou Têche"

Written: 1893. Included in *Bayou Folk* (1894).

It was not surprising that the artist staying at the Hallet planta-tion wanted to draw a picture of Evariste, a 'Cadian who hunted wild turkey and caught fish to sell to the folk in plantation houses along Bayou Têche. After all, Mr. Sublet was looking for examples of "local color" for a magazine, so when Mr. Sublet gave Evariste two dollars to return the next morning dressed just as he came out of the swamp, the latter went home to his cabin to carry the good news to his daughter Martinette. Martinette, in turn, took the two dollars and started for the store to buy some warmer clothes for herself. On her way, she detoured by Aunt Dicey's cabin to relate their good fortune. When she noticed Aunt Dicey was sniggering to herself, Martinette asked why she was laughing. Aunt Dicey said that she and her father were so simple. Did she not realize the man would put underneath the picture, "Dis heah is one dem low-down 'Cajuns o' Bayeh Têche?" Then Dicey related how Mr. Sub-let's young son tried to take her picture with a little black box yes-terday while she was ironing. She was insulted and told him she would hit him with the iron if he did not leave. Martinette decides that Aunt Dicey knows how the plantation people talk because her son, Wilkins, is the dining-room boy at Mr. Halle's. She slowly turns and trudges back home to Evariste with the truth about the picture. Sadly, he asks her to return the two dollars tomorrow, while he goes fishing.

The next morning Mr. Hallet notices Martinette standing out-side on the gallery. After Martinette is brought inside, she timidly tells him and his guests that her papa does not want his picture made. Just then, she catches knowing glances going from one man to another. Facing them all, she states boldly that her papa is not a low-down 'Cajun, and that he is not going to have that inscription written beneath his picture. As she is leaving, Evariste comes up the steps, carrying a small boy in his arms. He staggers over to Mr. Sublet and declares that he should not have let his son go out in a boat by himself. He relates how he was fishing and saw the boy paddle over to the deep end; then he saw the boat overturn and heard the child scream. Evariste jumped into the water and res-cued the boy, taking him to a friend's cabin, where he warmed the child and got him dry clothes. Now, Mr. Halley urges Martinette and Evariste to stay for breakfast, while Wilkins serves them contemptuously at the end of the table. All the while, Mr. Sublet, in his gratitude, begs Evariste to let him paint his picture and inscribe it "hero of Bayou Têche." Such extravagance embarrasses Evariste; he says he is no hero, and he refuses the offer. But Mr. Hallet, who understands the 'Cadian, requests Evariste to let Mr. Sublet draw his picture and says he knows Mr. Sublet will title it whatever Evariste wants. Pleased, Evariste makes a bargain. After careful thought, he announces that Mr. Sublet should put underneath his picture, "Dis is one picture of Mista Evariste Anatole Bonamour, a gen'man of de Bayou Têche." **(CY)**

***

Rankin 1932: The upright, self-respecting Acadian of this story is one of the kinds of people Chopin would have come to know during her time in Cloutierville (103). In efficient diction or mere snatches of talk, Chopin quickly sums up the strong emotions and subtle feelings of nobly motivated characters (140). **Bush 1957:** This is one of Chopin's many amusing tales. It makes us smile because of the protagonist's insistence on his social rather than his ethical stature (241). **Seyersted 1969a:** This is one of several tales in which Chopin depicts Cajuns as poor and even mocked yet also as worthy of respect (78). **Rocks 1972:** This story illustrates Chopin's skill at depicting the complexity of regional personalities rather than merely caricaturing them (113). **Arner 1975:** Evariste regards the term "Cajun" as a slur in this straightforward tale of local color (61). **Bonner 1977:** Here as elsewhere Chopin treats her local-color characters as individual persons rather than as stereotypes (6–7) and uses time-alterations as an important device (9). As in other *Bayou Folk* tales, the focus here on a threatened child helps resolve the plot (10). In this story Chopin illustrates the social and ethnic hierarchy of Louisiana (12). **Wolff 1979:** This story suggests Chopin's interest in complicated characters rather than in the simple charms of exotic places (211–12). **Skaggs 1985:** This is one of several tales depicting unusually independent girls. The daughter's decisiveness helps the father preserve his self-respect (12–13). The story in some respects resembles the later work "Ti Démon" of 1899 (63). **Skaggs 1988:** In this local color story, Martinette is the main focus (80). **Ewell 1986:** The story shows that even the poor can be dignified, despite economic and racial discrimination. The tale shows the limits of various points of view, even those of author and reader, and it also subverts some of the standard assumptions of "local color" writing, particularly its over-emphasis on setting. Chopin's ability to use the genre even while recognizing its limits may help explain why she ultimately stopped using this style (60–62). **Toth 1990a:** This was one of four previously unpublished stories included in *Bayou Folk*. It is part of a group of five near the conclusion of that collection that deal with adult dilemmas. The servant in the story resembles a real person Chopin knew. A reviewer mistook one detail of this story (223–25), which had once been turned down by *The Atlantic* (235). **Steiling 1994:** In this story Chopin reflects on her own use of "local color" conventions; she explores how those conventions can diminish both the artists who use them as well as their subjects. She employs irony to subvert stereotypes and tries to view local color artistry from the perspective of the persons it depicts. In this tale the artist is less ethically sophisticated than those he plans to paint. The story manages to provide local color while also critiquing the usual methods of such art (197–200). **Fetterley and Pryse 1995:** This tale generically resembles works by Mary Murfree and Sarah Orne Jewett. A black woman and a white female play fairly assertive roles in this work (409). **Thomas 1996:** This story is one of many in which Chopin depicts aged black females, often in stereotypical terms (216–17). **Beer 1997:** This story begins by showing Chopin's self-consciousness of the appeal of regional fiction (54). **Toth and Seyersted 1998:** This story is mentioned in Chopin's account books (149, 169). **Koloski 1999:** This is one of the few cheerful tales from the final pages of *Bayou Folk* (xv). **McCullough 1999:** The story implies that local color writing could often be patronizing, especially as a way for Northerners to view the South. Chopin undercuts stereotypes by making the daughter the protecting figure here. The story subverts standard generic, ethnic, and regional prejudices. It thus demonstrates how Chopin's writing could be conservative in some ways but progressive in others (198–200). The race of the title character and his daughter is not emphasized, but Aunt Dicey is black (318). Here as elsewhere Chopin makes her Cajun figures white (328). **Toth 1999b:** As Bernard Koloski has demonstrated, this was one of eight stories by Chopin that were frequently republished in the twentieth century (46). **Toth 1999c:** This was one of several submissions by Chopin turned down by one of the most prominent journals of the day (159). **Knights 2000:** This work, one of Chopin's most compelling, was produced during a particularly creative period—the fall and summer of 1893 (xv). Here as elsewhere Chopin depicts artists as strangers who unsettle local conditions (xxxiv). This story is one of Chopin's most complicated examples of artistic self-reflection (xxxv).

"The Godmother"

Written: 1899. First published: 1901. Included in *A Vocation and a Voice* (1991).

Tante Elodie worships her godson, Gabriel Lucaze. He is a good-looking young man whom she dotes on excessively. There is no one on earth whom she loves as much as she loves Gabriel. He loves her, not out of a sense of duty, but out of a true sense of devotion.

One night Tante Elodie dresses for bed and kneels beside her chair to say her prayers. While she is praying, she hears someone at the bedroom door. She opens the door and Gabriel comes into her room in a daze. His eyes are bloodshot. He is pale and his clothes are in a state of disarray. At first he cannot speak. Finally, he nervously tells Tante Elodie that he has killed a man.

He says that he had been playing cards at Symond's. He left there at ten o'clock to see a woman at eleven. The man was drunk and followed him because he wanted to go with Gabriel. He told Gabriel that if he could not go, no one was going and he barred the door with his body. Gabriel lunged at him with his knife and stabbed him. The man fell to the floor; he was dead.

Tante Elodie repeatedly tells Gabriel that he did not kill anyone. She runs around the porch to Madame Nicholas' door. She tells Madame that Gabriel has been with her all night and that he is very ill and needs medicine. She borrows some morphine from Madame to alleviate his stomach pains. She returns to her room and gives Gabriel a glass of brandy to calm his nerves. She brushes his hair, straightens his clothes, sews the top button back on his coat, bathes his face and hand, and sends him home to go to bed.

She gets dressed, throws a shawl over her head and walks to Nigger-Luke Cabin. She passes no one on her way to the scene of the crime. She enters the cabin and finds the body. She recovers Gabriel's knife and takes the man's watch and all his money out of his pockets. She feels like another being, not like herself at all. She does not mind her actions because she is doing all this to protect Gabriel.

She runs back to her house. As she falls face down on her bed she becomes sick. She hides the knife in the pocket of Gabriel's other coat. When she awakes the next morning, she moans and groans when she remembers the events of the previous night. She remains in bed for two days, too ill to get up.

Her friends visit her, carrying the news of the murder. She listens in great torment. Her beloved Gabriel does not come to visit her. She is deeply hurt by Gabriel's absence. She watches for him from her window and calls for him to come up to see her.

Tante Elodie tells Gabriel that there is no evidence to accuse anyone of the murder and that he should forget the whole thing. He takes off his coat, telling her to burn it. He goes to the closet and takes out his other coat, puts it on and leaves.

After it becomes obvious that there is no suspicion against him, Gabriel decides to go away. His emotions have completely changed. He is no longer in love with his girl and he has no desire to see Tante Elodie. Seeing Tante Elodie only reminds him of the incident. Finding the knife in his coat pocket, he knows that Tante Elodie is a part of the horrible crime. He cannot feel gratitude to her for saving him because now she seems more monstrous, more cold-blooded than he.

Two months later Tante Elodie appears to be shriveling away. She is very feeble. News comes to her that Gabriel is working on the railroad and later that he is working cattle on his father's farm. She listens. It is not Gabriel's crime that is killing her, but rather his indifference to her that has broken her heart.

A notice eventually reports that Gabriel is dead. He fell from a horse and was killed instantly.

Tante Elodie is alone on her porch until the stars come out to keep her from being alone. **(DR)**

***

Rankin 1932: Like Tante Elodie in this tale, Chopin was a favorite with her youthful acquaintances (141). **Peterson 1972:** This was one of the few stories Chopin composed during the time Chopin was either completing or awaiting the appearance of *The Awakening* (244). Like most of the other stories she wrote during this period, this one differs from her earlier writing but does not point toward any obvious new development in her fiction (245). The plot seems a bit sensational, and at first the emphasis is upon events. Later the focus shifts to the ironic results of the earlier behavior, particularly the ironic change in the godson's perception of his protector. Here as in other works by Chopin, alienation is a powerful theme (253–55). This work, along with the other tales written at around the same time as the novel, suggest that Chopin was not pleased with her recent short fiction but had not yet found a satisfying new approach (256). **Rocks 1972:** Chopin here shows the ills that can result from the attempt to deny reality (118). **Arner 1975:** Chopin uses the odd elements of this story as symbols to explore the impact of guilt. Although the tale seems a bit too artificial to be entirely convincing, it is an interesting examination of the impact of chaos upon a supposedly settled existence (95). **Skaggs 1985:** This is one of several tales emphasizing the strong influence of erotic desire, which in this case is as frustrated as Tante Elodie's yearning for motherhood (48–49). **Ewell 1986:** Composed shortly after "The Storm," this tale likewise focuses on an abrupt outburst of emotion and resembles a work by Dostoevsky in its emphasis on the relentless powers of the conscience. Chopin shows the sometimes paradoxical effects of love, while the inner destruction wrought by evil is reflected in the end in external details of the setting

(171–72). **Lattin 1978:** Here as often in her fiction, Chopin explores the theme of substitute motherhood (2). **Toth 1990a:** Chopin wrote this power-ful story during unusually cold weather. The godson resembles various persons she knew, while the godmother resembles Chopin herself in cer-tain ways, particularly in her moral relativism (326–27). The story was in-tended for inclusion in *A Vocation and a Voice* (374) and was one of the last stories Chopin sold (389). **Toth 1991:** The location of this tale is less impor-tant than its plot and themes (xiv). The story satirizes the assumption that women should suffer on behalf of others (xxi). This story, unusually, took many weeks to write (xxii). Here and in other stories in *A Vocation and a Voice*, Chopin depicts an intriguing female character (xxv). This is one of several dark stories in the final collection (xxv). **Hoder-Salmon 1992:** This story shows Chopin's familiarity with Louisiana death announcements (137). **Thomas 1992:** The work reflects Chopin's recent visit to Louisiana (47). **Fusco 1994:** Chopin here recounts the decline of two characters at once—an innovation on the typical pattern of single decline, for which she was indebted to Maupassant. Paradoxically, Elodie's desire to help her godson leads to their mutual corruption. Until the murder, she has experi-enced the pleasures, but not the pitfalls, of a kind of motherhood. Any contrivances of the plot are justified by the insights into character the tale offers. Elodie cannot cope with alterations in familiar relationships (an at-titude that affects her reactions both to slavery and to her godson's crime). The very lie that binds her to Lucaze also breaks their connections. Al-though Chopin does not make Elodie herself the narrator (as Maupassant might have done), she nevertheless does convey insights into Elodie's character while also offering an eventually bleak vision of life (163–66). **Koloski 1994:** This story appeared in a selection of Chopin's fiction pub-lished in 1991 (28). **Toth 1994:** This is one of several stories by Chopin that mention the Normal school in Natchitoches (12). **Thomas 1996:** This story undercuts the notion of a substitute mother's love—a notion implied by such a story as "Polydore" (208). **Beer 1997:** This story illustrates Chopin's typically unconventional approach to matters of race, religion, and sex. The story probes such issues as justice, hypocrisy, and competing kinds of obligations. Tante Elodie is racist, arrogant, calculating, and cynically aware of the community's prejudice. Chopin effectively uses irony and implication as tools of subtle social satire as she depicts the unwritten codes that structure society even as they destroy the person they seem to assist. Nostalgic romance is shown to be a distorting, corruptive, and ultimately self-destructive force (14–17). **Toth and Seyersted 1998:** This story is mentioned in Chopin's account books (142, 145–46, 151). It is one of several works in which Chopin describes women who are not naturally depressed but who do face particular problems (274). **Toth 1999c:** Chopin composed this bleak story while awaiting publication of *The Awakening* (207). It was one of several somewhat dark tales intended for inclusion in *A Vocation and a Voice* (208), and was one of only several for that collection that she set in Louisiana (229–30). Perhaps the story was influenced by Chopin's own worries about one of her sons (232).

"Going and Coming of Liza Jane"
See "The Going Away of Liza"

"The Going Away of Liza"

Written: 1891. First published: 1892. Included in *Complete Works* (1969).

When Abner Rydon goes to the Bludgitt train station on a wintry Christmas eve to pick up his mail, he encounters a few shriveled old men, "regulars" at the station. The thirty-year-old, with his square jaw set, his face stern, coolly stands up to his elders as they chide him at every turn, but when Si Smith mentions that a man had seen Abner's wife Liza-Jane in town a couple of weeks earlier, Abner strikes the old man to the floor and leaves the station. In his absence, the aged gossips heap blame on Abner for marrying a woman who was fond of mail-order paperbacks, who so longed for the city life depicted in them that she left the home of her husband and her live-in mother-in-law, vowing never to return.

Meanwhile, Abner is noticeably more relaxed and gentle in his cozy farm-house. He throws another log into the fireplace and tries to calm his mother's concerns about the winter blast that is pelting the house with sleet and snow. Abner tells his mother that he encountered Old Joseph, McBride, and Smith in Bludgitt, but he speaks only of their idleness. When Abner exclaims that the government ought to do something about it, mother Rydon reminds her son that what the old men do is their own business and then asks him to read aloud from the newspaper. As Abner is reading, his mother hears a noise at the door and opens it to the pale and gaunt figure of Liza-Jane. Mother and son express their astonishment as the force of the wind drives the prodigal into the farm-house. Mother Rydon tries to help Liza-Jane out of her wet shawl, but Abner, looking into his wife's fearful, beseeching face, stands aloof. When his mother demands to know what he's waiting for,

Abner looks into his mother's eyes for a long time and then takes the tattered shawl from his wife's shoulders. Upon seeing Liza-Jane's defenseless posture and half-closed, tear-laden eyelids, Abner kneels to remove the wet, torn shoes from his wife's feet. (JW)

***

Seyersted 1969a: This flawed, sentimental tale of failed liberation is nonetheless intriguing because Chopin here for the first time depicts a woman abandoning her marriage. The husband's name suggests his domineering character (110). The story was written at around the same time as "The Maid of Saint Phillippe," in which the heroine *does* succeed in achieving freedom (216). **Peterson 1972:** The resolution of this story is too simple and maudlin (70–71). **Rocks 1972:** This is one of many stories in which Chopin suggests that each person must decide whether it is better to be content with one's present condition or attempt to alter one's future. The results of either choice cannot be predicted (115). **Dyer 1981b:** In works like this, Chopin uses night imagery in highly predictable ways to emphasize doom and/or gloom (217). The plot, diction, ethics, setting, characterization, and imagery of this story are all predictable (218–19). **Stein 1984:** Here as elsewhere, Chopin presents a wife who ultimately is happy to submit to her husband (176). She has developed her ill-defined, abstract notions of an intense life from reading foolish fiction, but her husband is willing to take her back, and their future happiness seems implied. The wife's language makes her lofty ideas seem foolish, while the home to which she returns seems to symbolize domestic bliss (178–80). **Taylor 1989:** The story suggests the negative impact for women of reading romantic fiction (189). **Ewell 1994:** This was one of a number of stories Chopin wrote in early 1891 that focused on the dilemmas of women and that were at first rejected by publishers (160). **Saar 1994:** This story was turned down a dozen times (61). **Bender 1996:** Both the woman and man in this tale behave in ways Darwin might not have predicted (106). **Toth and Seyersted 1998:** This story is mentioned in Chopin's account books (139, 148, 168–69). **Taylor 1999:** In this minor work from the first stage of her career, Chopin shows the risks facing a woman on her own in a big city. Liza may even fall victim to exploitation there, which may be one reason for her return (23). **Toth 1999c:** Tales of conversion linked to major Christian holidays were popular and lucrative, as Chopin discovered when this story was published in newspapers nationwide (125). **Knights 2000:** This was one of the numerous works Chopin composed in 1891 (xv). This was Chopin's first effort to describe a wife quitting a marriage. Liza is connected in the tale with various kinds of differences from the normal or usual. The description of her departure draws on conflicting points of view, thus complicating the tale. Humor is juxtaposed with a more pious tone, but Chopin may undercut even the irony to some degree. By the end of the story we cannot be sure whether we should admire or question her return.

In this respect the story resembles "Athénaïse." The conclusion of the work is tantalizingly inconclusive (xxviii–xxix). Phrases here as in other works imply the narrator's presence (xlvi). **Toth 1999c:** One of Chopin's final tales set in Missouri, this narrative proved acceptable only because of its happy ending (125).

"A Harbinger"

Written: 1891. First published: 1891. Included in *Complete Works* (1969).

As an artist paints lovely women in the city during the dreary months of winter, he cannot stop thinking back on the time he spent in the hills a few months earlier. The summer had yielded Bruno not only his best paintings, but also delightful memories of Diantha, a beautiful, young woman, with golden hair and violet baby-eyes, who posed for him when he wished. Sighing over his easel, Bruno remembers how the summer breeze and the songs of birds filtered through the leaves of the trees on the wooded hillside where he and Diantha were together. He recalls with even greater pleasure how Diantha trembled and blushed, how her baby-eyes flashed, their innocence lost, at his good-bye kiss.

When summer comes at last, the painter readies himself to return to the hills. While he packs his paints and things, Bruno whistles and sings, stopping from time to time to wonder if the hillside will be as beautiful as in the summer past or if Diantha will blush and tremble again when he calls her his sweetheart.

Bruno maneuvers through the underbrush but stops short, before he gets to the wood's edge, at the sight of a group of people gathered in front of a little white church. Bruno's eyes scan the crowd, looking for Diantha. She is nowhere in sight. But when the church doors swing open, Bruno spies Diantha, looking like a lily in her bridal gown, standing beside her groom. After chastising himself for dreaming while another man was gathering his flower, Bruno, anxious to catch the next train out of town, turns on his heels and hurries down the hill. (JW)

***

Rankin 1932: This brief realistic tale provokes agreement with Chopin's assessment of Bruno as unwise (130). **Seyersted 1969a:** Theme: "activated passion" (108). **Arner 1975:** Imagery of nature emphasizes a woman's growing awareness in this rather trite and traditional narrative (126–27). **Dyer 1980–81:** This is one of many stories by Chopin in which a female is aroused by contact with a male (10–11). **Dyer 1981d:** Here and in numerous other works, Chopin uses physical setting to imply what a character is feeling. Her frequent use of this technique is open to various explanations (451–52). **Ewell 1986:** Although written from a male perspective, the story describes the growth of a woman's consciousness. Chopin makes effective use of setting and of contrasting tones (82). **Stepenoff 1987:** This minor early tale is typical of Chopin's apprentice writing in its imprecise setting and mawkish tone (455). **Toth 1990a:** This story, set in Missouri, was quickly accepted for publication, but by a journal with only a limited readership (200). **Bender 1996:** This is one of various stories in which Chopin's basically Darwinian outlook leads her to examine the problems caused by an insufficiently assertive male (107). **Beer 1997:** This story explores the shortcomings of a single-minded perspective. The opening suggests a predictable narrative, one confined to Bruno's point of view. The story illustrates Chopin's ability to use simple diction in ambiguous ways, particularly through the exact placement of key words. The tale is highly efficient and compact, and its concluding comment is subtle and potentially multivalent, although it suggests the limits of Bruno's perceptiveness (77–78). The frame structure here resembles the similar structure of "The Night Came Slowly" (80). **Toth and Seyersted 1998:** This story is mentioned in Chopin's account books (148, 174). In tone it has something in common with the "Doralise" fragment (272).

"Her Letters"

Written: 1894. First published: 1895. Included in *A Vocation and a Voice* (1991).

An unnamed narrator tells the story of a woman who locks herself in her room on a rainy day. She takes a bundle of letters from a nook in her writing desk. She is resolved to destroy them, but after cutting the twine holding them together, she watches as they scatter. They are of different sizes and shapes with addresses in two different handwritings, including the hand of a man with whom she had secretly been having an affair.

He returned the letters to her four years ago and they have been sustaining her ever since. The time has come for her to destroy them. She tosses a letter into the roaring fire, then a second, and a third. After disposing of the sixth letter, she stops and stares into the fire in disbelief at what she has done. She looks through the remaining letters, thanking God that she still has them.

The man who had written the letters had changed her life— had given her a reason to live. She tries to think of a way to keep her precious letters without hurting her husband.

She stacks the letters, tying them again with twine. She writes a note asking her husband to destroy them unopened after her death. She places the note on top of the stack and returns them to her desk.

One year later the woman is found dead on the floor of her room, clutching the key to her desk. Her husband finds the letters several months later. His first thought is to open them and read them, but he cannot go against her wishes. He throws the un-opened bundle into the river.

The unopened letters change his life, for now he is suspicious of all their former male friends. He feels that there is only one secret a woman would take to her grave. The secret torments him until he can stand it no longer. He goes back to the river and joins her and her secret for eternity. **(DR)**

***

Peterson 1972: This is one of Chopin's better explorations of human psychology. Although the plot may have been inspired by Maupassant, the presentation shows Chopin's own originality; she focuses less on revelations of fact than on revelations of character. The story may originally have been meant to end before the wife's death; such a design would have been effectively ironic. Here as elsewhere, Chopin explores the topic of alienation—a problem intensified by the husband's lack of religious belief. In the end, death is the only thing he can know for sure (139–42). This is the first story by Chopin to deal explicitly with unfaithfulness, and it is her first to present an unapologetic adulteress (142–43). **Rocks 1972:** Here as elsewhere Chopin shows that a loveless or oppressive marriage is unethical (119). **Arner 1975:** Similar in its dark tone to "The Story of an Hour," this work is also similarly ironic, especially since the husband seems interested in really understanding his wife only after she dies. Paradoxically, although his suspicions about her are correct, he cannot know that they are, and possibly his wife even intended to torment him in this way to repay him for her own frustrations. His suicide results not from regret for having treated her badly but from having lost his sense of her as his possession (88–90). Natural imagery helps lend this work part of its power (104). **Skaggs 1975:** In this tale Chopin illustrates the self-destructiveness of the male impulse to own women. The anonymous (and therefore more obviously universal) male is well-intended both before and after his wife's death, but even he cannot control the male urge to possess—a jealous urge that becomes especially strong (ironically) after his wife is dead (283–85). **Jones 1981:** This story states explicitly a theme Chopin also explores elsewhere: the male tendency to treat women as possessions (173). **Rogers 1983:** Here as elsewhere Chopin (like George Sand) explores the complexities of feminine sexuality (35). **Stein 1984:** The wife here has lacked the resolve to quit her marriage, and thus her yearning for independence expresses itself in a nearly-crazed sexual desire and also in a subliminal contempt for her husband. She may actually desire his death, if only subconsciously, and her lust for her lover may not be as ennobling as she assumes. His letters become almost fetishes for her, and her eating of them is almost strangely eucharistic. Her decision about the letters causes her husband extended torment, so that her hatred for him is as passionate as her lust for her lover, although she cannot admit the depth of her hostility (186–88). **Skaggs 1985:** This is one of a number of tales that touch on the possibility of suicide, which Chopin may have considered the ultimate form of self-control (42–44). This work resembles "A Shameful Affair" by exploring a female's burgeoning sensuality (58). **Ewell 1986:** The slightly maudlin heroine has lived a secret existence through the letters, and Chopin effectively uses uncertainty, suspense, irony, scenic echoes, and contrasts of internal and external settings when describing the predicaments the anonymous couple confront. The story explores the external and erotic tensions marriages often involve, and it may also reflect aspects of Chopin's own relations with men. Here as in other tales, inner personality is hidden or warped by social pressures (105–6). The story shows the costs of lacking freedom (183). **Papke 1988:** This story is significant not only because it shows how both sexes react to passion but also because its conclusion foreshadows that of *The Awakening*. The story explores the dark side of desire (77–78). **Inge 1989:** In this story Chopin deals with a woman's sexual desires with as much candor as she demonstrates in *The Awakening* and "The Storm." The puzzled husband feels stripped of a selfhood grounded in his sense of having possessed his wife (104). **Papke 1990:** Chopin here depicts masculine and feminine responses to intense feeling and anticipates important aspects of *The Awakening*. The crucial acts in the tale occur on similar days, and the husband's later behavior illustrates the bleakness of mundane existence and the sadness that results from deliberate ignorance. In this tale the yearning to fully fathom and commune with another person leads to suicide. The husband's attempt to reunite with his wife by plunging into the water merely guarantees their perpetual separation. Intense emotion, by itself, leads nowhere (66–67). **Toth 1990a:** This is one of several stories composed around the same time in which Chopin depicted strong-willed women (233). A phrase from the tale echoes one by Hamlin Garland (248). The story, which raises significant ethical questions, was published in *Vogue* (251–53). It is similar to a tale by Maupassant (272) and is one of several early stories by Chopin dealing with forbidden desire (279). It was intended for publication in *A Vocation and a*

Voice (374). **Toth 1991:** This is one of many of Chopin's late works that were first printed in *Vogue* (xiii–xiv). The story may have influenced a painting by a woman artist who was Chopin's friend (xvi). It is one of various stories in *A Vocation and a Voice* in which loyal husbands suffer (xxiii) and that focus on determined single-mindedness (xxiv). **Davis 1992b:** This is one of many stories from *A Vocation and a Voice* that focus on suddenly altered perceptions (200–201). **Cutter 1994:** Here as in some of her other late stories, Chopin creates a female voice that undercuts (often by mimicking) patriarchal language (17). The wife is a writer for whom the hidden letters are more important than either of the men in her life. The letters ultimately undermine the husband's confident perception of his wife, himself, and language itself. He kills himself because he cannot penetrate the secrets of his wife's existence; the letters show the power of language even when the author no longer exists (25–27). This is one of various works in which Chopin shows that subtle rebellion is often the most effective (34). **Koloski 1994:** This story was reprinted in a 1985 anthology of supernatural fiction as an example of the links between horror and relations between the sexes, especially in marriage (24–25). The story is included in a soft-cover collection of Chopin's fiction published in 1991 (28). **Lundie 1994:** Chopin's reference in this story to male possessiveness is relevant to some of her other and more famous tales (136). **Sempreora 1994:** The emphasis here on multiple perspectives may have been partly inspired by Chopin's recent translations of some short stories by Maupassant in which such an emphasis was lacking (87–88). **Koloski 1996:** This story bears comparison with "The Story of an Hour," especially because of their similar plots, settings, structures, and themes. The story also resembles others by Chopin, particularly in its emphasis on irreconcilable differences (63–65; 87). **Walker 1996:** This is one of many stories by Chopin in which the reading of correspondence is very significant. Such correspondence often symbolizes the power of the general written word (220). **Beer 1997:** Chopin did anticipate the publication of this fairly daring tale (41), which presents the two characters in distinct sections as a way of emphasizing their lack of mutual understanding. Imagery of an almost daring eucharistic intensity is used to describe the woman's attitude toward the letters, which become symbols of vitality. Chopin is careful, however, to focus most attention on the husband, even as she exposes the limitations of his perspective. By confining the focus on the woman to the first section, Chopin insulates her from any overt moral judgment, granting her a kind of ethical and narrative independence. Here as in other stories, Chopin compares erotic and spiritual ecstasy and shows the power of passion. She effectively delays and withholds information in the first part of the tale, thus postponing or frustrating any impulse we may feel to judge the wife. The husband ultimately cannot survive the realization that his wife escaped his narrow definition of her; his own identity depended on the limits he imposed on hers (45–48). Here as elsewhere, Chopin implies the dangers of obsessiveness (82). **Toth and Seyersted 1998:** One of

Chopin's friends may have been behind this tale (130). The story is mentioned in Chopin's account books (140, 150, 175–76). **Toth 1999c:** This was one of several stories from 1894 depicting marital tension (158). Its title character partly resembles a woman Chopin knew (181). **Knights 2000:** Here as elsewhere Chopin explores the dangers of solipsism (xxvi). This story implicitly questions the commercial values prevalent in Chopin's society (xxix).

"A Horse Story"

1898. Unfinished children's story. Included in *Private Papers* (1998). See also *A Vocation and a Voice* (1991).

Herminia rides her sad-looking sorrel pony to deliver eggs and garden vegetables to a local planter. The horse's coat is worn in places, while growing shabby in clumps in other places.

Ti Démon has a slight limp in his left fore foot, which Herminia ignores. The hills up to the planter's home are steep and Ti Démon often slips on the pine needles. After a while, he holds his leg up, doubled in pain. Herminia gets off his back to examine his foot. She finds no nail or stone, but realizes that because of his pain, he cannot go on.

Herminia ties Ti Démon to a tree and walks the remaining three miles to the planter's home. She knows that Madame Labatier will pay her well for the eggs and vegetables. Young Mr. Labatier might even offer to drive her home in his buggy!

Ti Démon looks around the forest, thinking how pleasant it would be only if he was not in pain. He wonders what will become of him if his suffering continues. He always thinks in his native language, which he learned in his youth in the Indian nation. He relaxes for several hours and the pain subsides.

He unties the rope and tries to rid himself of the saddle, but because he can only loosen it, it falls below his belly. He goes back home, but, finding no one there, he decides to go over to Solistan's house.

When Solistan looks up and sees Ti Démon covered with mud, sticks, and bark with his saddle hanging from him, he panics for fear that Herminia has been hurt. He has not realized how much she means to him until this moment.

Solistan jumps on his horse and rides out to find Herminia. He fears for what he will find at every turn. He finds her standing in front of the tree where she had tied Ti Démon, a look of confusion on her face.

After they get back to Solistan's home, he brings Ti Démon out to her. He tells Herminia that Ti Démon is old and worn out and suggests that she use his mare instead. When she replies that she cannot afford to feed an additional horse, Solistan tells her to shoot Ti Démon. Herminia is horrified at the thought and says that she would rather shoot someone passing by on the road than her old, faithful horse. Solistan suggests that she and Ti Démon come live with him and he will feed them both. She laughs at the prospect of marriage, saying they will talk about that later.

Hearing Solistan's unkind remarks about him, Ti Démon loses his sense of joy. When Solistan and Herminia marry the next fall, Ti Démon can only brood about his fate. He decides to determine his own fate and strike out for the Indian nation.

One winter's night Solistan tells Herminia that Raul was driving his cattle into Texas and came across Ti Démon lying dead in the road. Herminia exclaims that he was a good and faithful horse. Solistan agrees, but says that maybe his death was for the best. **(DR)**

***

Ewell 1986: Lively comedy characterizes this story, Chopin's only tale about an animal. Although the work is somewhat insubstantial and maudlin, the stubborn, self-assured, and unpredictable protagonist, with his varied language, lends the work real appeal (165). **Stepenoff 1987:** A St. Louis newspaper described Chopin's public reading of this moving little tale. The story shows Chopin's relapse into tamer fiction after having written *The Awakening* (463). **Elfenbein 1989:** Here and in other works, Chopin shows the impact of class prejudice; the heroine's attempt to transcend her class is ultimately defeated (119). **Toth 1990a:** This is a young person's story set in Louisiana (315) **Toth 1991:** It is unclear whether this story or another with a similar title is the one mentioned in a compilation by Chopin's earliest biographer (xxi). **Thomas 1992:** This was one of the few pieces of short fiction Chopin composed in 1898 (40). She was paid to read either this tale or a similarly named story to a local club. A newspaper praised it. Her work on this tale suggests that she had recovered from a recent illness (46). **Koloski 1994:** The story is included in a soft-cover collection of Chopin's fiction published in 1991 (28). **Koloski 1996:** This is one of the numerous stories Chopin originally composed for youthful readers (87). **Toth and Seyersted 1998:** This story is mentioned in Chopin's ac-

count books (144, 151). The version printed here (254–61) is the same as
that published in 1979 (245).

"An Idle Fellow"

Written: 1893. Included in *A Vocation and a Voice* (1991).

An unnamed narrator states that s/he is very tired from studying and learning. S/he is weary and in want of rest, so s/he sits
next to a friend, Paul, who is an idle fellow. Paul is listening to a
thrush singing for her mate to return. The narrator comments that
Paul is a strange fellow, turning away from instructions, gazing
instead at the clouds, and drinking the perfumes of the clover-field
and the rose-hedge. Paul and the narrator walk together down the
hill to where men, women, and children live. Paul looks into the
faces of people and reads their souls. The narrator decides to walk
with Paul because Paul knows the language of God, which s/he
has not yet learned. **(DR)**

***

Seyersted 1969a: The story may reflect Chopin's nostalgia for her dead
husband (55). The work was written at around the same time as "Madame
Célestin's Divorce." Like some of Chopin's other paired stories, these two
explore alternative roles for women—traditional and untraditional. The
speaker of the story seems passively to adopt traditional Biblical
(specifically, St. Paul's) attitudes toward women (114–15). **Rocks 1972:**
Here as elsewhere, Chopin implies that a balanced life results from a sympathetic knowledge of human and physical nature (115). **Bender 1974:**
Paul, the title character, typifies the kinds of Whitmanesque persons
sometimes found in Chopin's fiction who seem closely attuned to nature
(260). **Arner 1975:** Although Paul is mentally defective, Chopin seems to
find his rapport with nature more appealing than the sterile intellectuality
of the narrator. At the same time, her notion of nature is not unduly romantic (94–95). **Dyer 1983–84:** This is one of various stories by Chopin that
emphasizes the revelatory power of nature (75). **Skaggs 1985:** This is one
of several stories emphasizing the significance of religion—in this case a
kind of pantheism (39). **Ewell 1986:** This previously unprinted work was
the earliest tale Chopin intended to include in *A Vocation and a Voice*. It
foreshadows "The Night Came Slowly" in language and theme and emphasizes the contrasts between bookishness and exposure to the outdoors.
It seems typical of Chopin's mature writing in its tone and topics, particu-

larly in its allusions to romance, its stress on inner existence, and its concern with the natural and the divine (126–27). **Toth 1990a:** This story was turned down by seven different journals (215). Less well crafted than many of Chopin's works (220–21), it was intended for inclusion in *A Vocation and a Voice* (374). This is one of several late stories by Chopin which reflect her interest in thought rather than mere plot (xxi–xxii). **Davis 1992b:** This is one of many stories from *A Vocation and a Voice* that focus on suddenly altered perceptions (200–201). **Cothern 1994:** This is one of various stories in which Chopin used an internal narrator, a device which allowed her greater authorial distance both from the tale and from the dominant culture she may have been implicitly critiquing (124). **Koloski 1994:** The story is included in a soft-cover collection of Chopin's fiction published in 1991 (28). **Beer 1997:** This tale often resembles "The Night Came Slowly." It was turned down by numerous editors. It juxtaposes the perspectives of a scholar and an impassive observer, implying that the latter is more in tune with other humans. By the conclusion of the story, Paul's indifference to formal learning seems synonymous with a different (and perhaps deeper) kind of insight. Here as in other works, Chopin implies the risks involved in focusing too exclusively on one kind of perception. In her fiction, such exclusivity is inevitably destructive—as, for instance, in "Désirée's Baby" or "Her Letters." A standard feature of Chopin's short fiction is its emphasis on alternative points of view (82). **Ewell 1997:** This sketch seems to have had personal relevance to Chopin, who was much concerned with the conflict between natural experience and dogmatic teachings (107–8).

"The Impossible Miss Meadows"

Probably written: 1903. Included in *Complete Works* (1969).

Mrs. Hyleigh sends her second-best carriage to the train station to pick up Miss Meadows, "a person of no consequence whatever." Miss Meadows' visit is the result of the bishop's request to Mrs. Hyleigh. Miss Meadows, the orphan daughter of an impoverished English clergyman, suffers from "shattered nerves" after a long illness, so the bishop believes that a couple of weeks in the country at the Hyleigh estate will restore her to health. He assures Mrs. Hyleigh that her generosity will not be overlooked.

While sitting on the piazza of their summer home on a lake in Far Niente, Wisconsin, and awaiting Miss Meadows' arrival, Mrs. Hyleigh and her children debate whether their failure to meet her at the train station will displease the bishop. The older daughter, Mildred, remarks that they do enough "church work in town" and wonders where they will put Miss Meadows given that the Sheltons are arriving on Thursday. Max, the nineteen-year-old son, is more concerned with Mildred's use of slang and with his and his college chum's boredom at a Wisconsin summer resort.

Miss Meadows arrives and awkwardly and timidly descends from the carriage. Her clothes are shabby and ill fitting, and her features are "ordinary and uninteresting." Only her voice is not commonplace, but instead it is "rich and singy." After hasty introductions, Mrs. Hyleigh has Miss Meadows shown to her room, and, watching her go, she sighs, "She's impossible! utterly impossible!"

Mildred resents Miss Meadows' presence, but Evande (another sister) alters her clothes and promises to put some color in her cheeks by teaching her tennis and taking her driving and sailing.

Sitting together on the piazza the morning after Miss Meadows' arrival, Mrs. Hyleigh questions her about any relatives in America. Miss Meadows explains that her one relative, an uncle in the north of England, thought her chances would be better in America, so, with a tiny inheritance, she came to New York with a letter of recommendation to the bishop in Chicago. However, before she could reach her destination, she came down with typhoid, and now she is only capable of being a nursery governess.

Mrs. Hyleigh is "uncomfortably moved" by Miss Meadows' story, but she wishes she could help her at a time more convenient than the high social season at Far Niente. Feeling an obligation to return Miss Meadows to the bishop in better condition than she received her, Mrs. Hyleigh promptly promises that Evande will look after her and that the boys will see that she has a good time.

Playing inside, "the boys" overhear this promise of their services, fall on one another with a groan, and make a swift, silent exit out of the rear of the house. **(EP)**

***

Peterson 1972: The family's name is ironic, but even the heroine displays a tinge of pride. This story does show some skill in presenting personalities and in suggesting tension. The work is one of Chopin's better final pieces, most of which imply that her talent had begun to diminish (267–69). **Ewell 1986:** This uncompleted story is the last preserved piece of Chopin's fiction. Innovative in setting and characterization, it is nonetheless too fragmentary and unique to be very revealing (182). **Stepenoff 1987:** This was Chopin's last tale (448). Chopin wrote this work in a small St. Louis house not unlike Edna's "pigeon house" in *The Awakening*. The story may reflect her own sense of alienation from St. Louis society (463–64). **Toth 1990a:** Perhaps this was an early version of "Fedora" (289). **Thomas 1992:** This late tale, based on Chopin's vacations in Wisconsin, was left unfinished (54).

"In and Out of Old Natchitoches"

Written: 1893. First published: 1893. Included in *Bayou Folk* (1894).

Every weekday morning Mr. Alphonse Laballière pauses in his work to watch Mademoiselle Suzanne St. Denys Godolph cross the railroad trestle that spans the nearby bayou. He knows she is the teacher at the little school on his property and that she is the daughter of the stubborn old lady who refuses to sell any of her land, even though she has no money. Alphonse is a newcomer to Natchitoches parish who has bought a rich but run-down planta-tion and is now busy preparing it for raising cotton. Although he speaks pleasantly to the young lady each morning, she looks away without returning his greeting. This puzzles him, but Suzanne has her reasons. Everyone in the parish gossips about his letting a free mulatto family named Giestin live in the uninhabitable plantation house on the place. Madame Giestin even prepares his meals. Fi-nally, Giestin comes to Laballière at breakfast one morning and tells him about the talk in the town. Therefore, he says, his family must leave. In response, Laballière angrily takes little André Giestin with him to the schoolhouse and informs Mademoiselle St. Denys Goldolph that he has brought her a new pupil. In a shaking voice she reminds him that educating the colored population is not the purpose of the school. At the close of the day, she tells her pupils good-bye and walks back home. In the days that follow, La-ballière watches for the young teacher, but she crosses the trestle no more. At last, unable to stand it, he goes to her home to apolo-gize for his rude behavior. "She is at the time in New Orleans," her mother informs him.

Suzanne had found a position there and sought help from Hector Santien, her friend and distant relative, who had moved from Natchitoches to New Orleans. She requested that he find her suitable lodgings. When he met the train on her arrival, she hardly recognized Hector, since he was so elegant and so attentive. He had secured a room for her with Maman Chavan. Soon, he formed the habit of visiting them every Sunday morning for breakfast. Even though he went nowhere with them, he gave the two women tickets for the theater and the opera. But he always warned that there was no place in his heart for any woman. One Sunday, as Hector walks the ladies to vespers, they pass Alphonse Laballière on the street. Laballière tips his hat to Suzanne, but looks angrily at Hector. Then, Laballière calls on Suzanne that evening and tells her that her mother had sold him a piece of land. He also says that she has sent her daughter a message to return home to Natchitoches. Abruptly, Alphonse asks the name of the man who accompanied her that afternoon. He tells Suzanne that she must not walk in the New Orleans streets with Hector. In fact, he vows to wring Hector's neck if he ever catches the latter with Suzanne again. Even though Alphonse realizes his rashness at once and asks Suzanne's forgiveness, she refuses and walks past him without a glance.

Stunned but unconvinced, Suzanne sends for Hector and asks him if there is any reason that she should not be seen with him, and he replies, "Yes, there are reasons." Hector also advises her to return to Natchitoches. Later, Suzanne is not surprised to see Alphonse on the train going home. Without a word, he holds out his hand, and without a pause she takes it.

A few days later, as the elegant Hector walks down Canal Street, one young man says to a friend, "That's Deroustan, the most notorious gambler in New Orleans." **(CY)**

***

Reilly 1942: The effective ending of this tale shows the kind of skill displayed by the stories of O. Henry (131). **Seyersted 1969a:** Here as in other stories, Chopin does not treat desegregation as seriously as she treats other racial matters (94–95). The moment when Hector strokes Suzanne with the rose recalls the writing style of Alphonse Daudet (122). **Seyersted 1969b:** In this story Chopin seems to mock efforts at racial integration (26). **Potter 1971:** In this story integration is not Chopin's central focus, and the problems it momentarily creates are neatly resolved (46–47). **Peterson 1972:** The design of this story is flawed, while the plot implies that Chopin was not especially progressive in her views of race (104–5). **Arner 1975:** Here as elsewhere, the somewhat crude settings and characters contrast with an intriguing theme (56; 64). **Webb 1976:** As elsewhere, Chopin here uses a cyclical pattern to structure a story (14). **Bonner 1977:** Here as elsewhere, *Bayou Folk* reveals Chopin's talent for creating rich characters and for presenting, rather than announcing, their traits (6). The story illustrates the theme of affection vs. self-respect (10). Racial mixing is an important theme of the work (11–12). **Lattin 1980:** This is one of various stories featuring members of the intriguing Santien family (22). The tale also depicts other recurring characters, including Alcée Laballière (25) and the titular character of "Athénaïse" (28). **Dyer 1980–81:** This is one of various stories in which Chopin reveals a significant interest in the strong yearnings of males (15). **Jones 1981:** In this ambiguous tale, the white teacher who acts oppressively toward mulattoes is herself consigned, in the end, to a kind of oppression. Chopin obviously sides with the mulattoes and the more liberated whites (152). **Skaggs 1985:** This is one of several tales focusing on the interaction of affection and selfhood (17); it alters focus when it switches setting (18–19). **Ewell 1986:** Here as in other works, Chopin touches on characters she develops fully only in much later stories (20). She effectively uses a surprise ending, although the characters are somewhat simplistic and the story loses a bit of steam when it switches locales. Yet the personalities are lively and the themes intriguing, and although issues of race are dealt with only obliquely, Chopin does seem sympathetic to the plight of the mulattoes, just as she also seems to admire Alphonse's streak of independence (a common theme in her writing, even when social pressures ultimately stifle such autonomy). The description of Hector's manipulation of the rose typifies Chopin's frequently subtle yet highly evocative treatments of latent (and sometimes dark) sexual energy (57–58). **Gaudet 1986:** Chopin here reveals a credible knowledge of the self-respect felt by Louisiana mulattoes (49). **Toth 1990a:** Racial controversy is touched on here but is not the central focus (136). One of several stories by Chopin printed in the same month, it is erotically provocative (216) and contains an assertive woman. The tale, which was placed in a sequence with two others in *Bayou Folk* (224), was later syndicated (246). It foreshadowed "Athénaise" (274). **Robinson 1992:** In this story the low social ranking of mulattoes is stressed (xviii). **Bryan 1993:** Here as in other stories by Chopin, New Orleans is the setting for the most complicated phase of a character's development. Thus the city is associated with transformation, but her emphasis is usually on internal developments (55). As is true elsewhere in Chopin's writings, a woman in this story ventures into, but then returns from, New Orleans. In this tale the return coincides with a return to control by a conventionally respectable male (61–62). The story alludes to the all-male, all-white associations that were common in the city (187). **Koloski 1994:** The story is included in a soft-cover collection of Chopin's fiction published in 1992 (28). **Padgett 1994:** Here as elsewhere Chopin describes a woman who sees a male in angelic terms (103). **Koloski 1996:** This is one of various stories by Chopin in which violent death seems a possibility (12). The tale shares settings, themes, and characters with other works by Chopin, particularly in its focus on shocking behavior. It contains one of the most memorable passages in Chopin's fiction

(19–21; 35). It is one of her tales mentioning trains (52) and opera (57). **Beer 1997:** Because this story was syndicated, it reached a wider-than-normal readership, despite (or perhaps because of) its controversial contents. Chopin plays on different senses of the word "old" in the title, just as she plays with contrasting versions of masculinity by juxtaposing the uncomplicated Laballière with the enigmatic and provocative Santien. The ending seems deliberately anticlimactic, while the rose imagery seems intriguingly phallic (54–58). **Toth and Seyersted 1998:** This story is one of several works in which Chopin describes irascible, youthful males who cause themselves problems (125). It is mentioned in Chopin's account books (140, 149, 154, 156) and in her letters (206). **Bonner and Bonner 1999:** This is one of several works by Chopin that features St. Louis Cathedral in New Orleans (55). **Koloski 1999:** Here as in other stories by Chopin, the heroine ultimately achieves her goals (xiii). This work and others exemplify Chopin's complicated views of racial matters (xix–xx). **Taylor 1999:** In this work Chopin implies the temptation of urban life in New Orleans (27). **Toth 1999c:** This story sheds little light on Chopin's own racial views (77–78); its focus is chiefly on its main female character (150).

"In Sabine"

Written: 1893. Included in *Bayou Folk* (1894).

Grégoire Santien comes upon a crude log cabin in the Sabine parish on his way to Texas. An old Negro man is chopping wood. Grégoire asks him who the cabin belongs to and is told that it belongs to Bud Aiken.

The name sounds familiar to Grégoire. He tries to remember where he has heard the name when Aiken appears at the door. When Grégoire sees him he recognizes him as the man who married 'Tite Reine.

She was a beautiful girl whom Grégoire has known at the 'Cadian balls. She was nicknamed 'Tite Reine, which meant "little queen." Her father adored her.

Bud yells for her to come. She is out back feeding the pig. When she comes to the door, she is embarrassed at her appearance. Her dress is drab and worn and her shoes are in shreds. Her eyes are filled with tears.

Grégoire decides to spend the night; he wants to find out what is behind the look of desperation in 'Tite Reine's eyes. They make a bed on the porch for him. In the middle of the night 'Tite Reine awakens Grégoire and tells him that Bud is killing her. He beats her regularly and is working her to death, and he gets drunk often.

The next morning Grégoire announces that he is going to stay a week with his new friend, Bud. He brings in a bottle of whiskey and Bud is delighted. While 'Tite Reine picks cotton and cooks, Grégoire and Bud play cards and Bud drinks.

By nightfall Bud is drunk. He wakes up mid-morning the next day and yells for 'Tite Reine. She does not come. There is no coffee on the stove. He cannot see her in the cotton field. He yells for the Negro, asking him where his wife is. The Negro answers that she is gone back home on Grégoire's fast horse. Bud says he will catch her on his old horse, but the Negro says that Grégoire has taken Bud's old horse. **(DR)**

***

Rankin 1932: The whole tale sparkles with comedy (139). **Reilly 1942:** The effective ending of this tale is comparable in skill to the conclusions of stories by better-known writers (131). **Bush 1957:** This is one of the few stories by Chopin that focuses on a genuinely malevolent character (242). **Zlotnick 1968:** This is one of many stories in which Chopin implies ambivalent, unconventional responses to marriage (2). **Seyersted 1969a:** The story was unproblematic to contemporary editors because the woman abandons her marriage only after being abused (55). **Berthoff 1970:** This work reveals Chopin's talent for effective description of physical traits (xvi). **Potter 1971:** This story contradicts the stereotype of a black man threatening a white woman. Here, instead, the black man protects her, although we are never told if he is punished as a result. Nevertheless, in Uncle Mortimer Chopin has created a highly unusual black character (47–48). **Peterson 1972:** This is one of six tales Chopin composed between the summers of 1893 and 1895 in which she focuses on altruism (124). Here as in most of the others, she manages to avoid a maudlin tone. Earlier critics have perhaps neglected the comic aspects of the story and have thus simplified it. Chopin plays with chivalric conventions of the damsel in distress; all of the main personalities fit well-worn patterns, but the rural Louisiana setting gives the familiar story a clever twist. The story is more witty than has been suspected (125–27). **Rocks 1972:** Here as elsewhere Chopin shows that a loveless or oppressive marriage is unethical (119). **Arner 1975:** Readers familiar with Chopin's novel *At Fault* are best positioned to understand this story, since Grégoire appears in both. Paradoxically, he shares some traits with Bud Aiken (57–58). **Skaggs 1975:** This story is less finely crafted than "Désirée's Baby" or "At the 'Cadian Ball"; its picture of Chopin's frequent theme of male dominance is more blatant (281). **Bonner 1977:** Here as elsewhere Chopin treats her local-color characters as individual persons rather than as stereotypes (6–7). This is one of several stories from *Bayou Folk* in which travel is a key device of plot (8). The story shows love sapped by a harsh setting (10–11). **Taylor 1979:** This is one of many tales in which a woman triumphs, if only briefly (xvi). **Wolff 1979:** This tale is one of Chopin's many realistic variations on the theme of marriage (213). **Lattin 1980:** The resonances of this story are more complex when it seems to allude to Chopin's novel *At Fault*, in which Grégoire Santien also appears (22–24). **Baym 1981:** This story illustrates Chopin's frequent emphasis on the larger community as opposed to the isolated self (xxvi). **Stein 1984:** This is one of a number of works in which Chopin deals with the need to seek self-fulfillment, no matter what its consequences (189). Although this story resembles "A Visit to Avoyelles" in focusing on a boorish husband, here the wife leaves with the handsome man who comes to her aid. By stressing (and even over-stressing) the husband's bad behavior, Chopin attempts to make the wife's decision more credible. The husband even robs her of a proper name, but his tendency to call her "Rain" fits her present tearfulness. In this story as in "A Visit," Chopin implies that the crucial matter in determining whether a marriage should last is whether the partners find the relationship fulfilling (189–90). **Aherne 1985:** Here Chopin shows her mastery as a writer about affection (82). **Skaggs 1985:** This is one of several tales focusing on the interaction of affection and selfhood (17; 19). Our satisfaction that the woman flees her current fate obscures much thought about her future (19). **Ewell 1986:** Characters from this tale appear much earlier in Chopin's fiction (20–21). The story, which almost continues where *At Fault* left off, shows Chopin's oblique handling of social topics and her ability to sustain intrigue (partly by manipulating point of view). Bud Aiken darkly resembles characters in southwestern comic writing; he makes an effective contrast to Grégoire, whose ethical complexity may reflect his recent experiences in *At Fault*. Chopin likens the oppressed woman to the oppressed black, although neither character completely escapes seeming stereotypical. The possibility of an erotic dimension to the relation of the black man (Mortimer) and white woman ('Tite Reine) is undercut by Mortimer's designation ("Uncle"), but Chopin does make him superior to the white man, Aiken, in both ethics and wit. Yet Chopin's satire of social traditions remains, in this story at least, mostly implicit (58–60). The experiences of 'Tite Reine's sister are later described in "Mamouche" (95). **Elfenbein 1989:** Here as elsewhere when depicting persons of color, Chopin shows how such persons could both be victimized by stereotypes and use them to their own advantage. In this story it is the black man who behaves most valorously in relation to the white woman. Stories like this help suggest why some white females organized to oppose lynchings (118–19). **Inge 1989:** The story offers complicated insights into the minds and mutual relations of its characters, some of whom appear in other works by Chopin, including *At Fault*. Bud Aiken and Grégoire share important traits (including violent tendencies), and although Chopin is mainly interested in the inner transformation of 'Tite Reine, she also explores masculine habits of mind. Parallels even exist between Aiken and his horse, which comes to symbolize his confidence as a male. In the end, however, Aiken's arrogance is undercut by his horse, his wife, her lover, and even a neighboring black to whom Aiken had thought himself superior (99). **Taylor 1989:** This is one of various stories by Chopin that emphasize a female's concluding feeling of triumph (179). **Toth 1990a:** This was one of four new stories included in *Bayou Folk* (223), where it appears in a sequence with two other tales. Of that trio, this story features the most assertive woman (224), and it also depicts a mean, repulsive husband (225). Ironically, one reviewer found the narrative amusing (228). Although it was turned down by a major magazine (235), it was later syndicated (246). It is one of Chopin's early stories focusing on forbidden desire (279). **Robinson 1992:** Here as in other works, Chopin shows an interest in persons of diverse cultures—American, Cajun, and Creole. Bud, the American, is self-centered in a way that few Cajun or Creole males seem to be. The American and Creole men in this story symbolize the contrasts between the two cultures. Even the Creole's clever final triumph symbolizes the greater thoughtfulness characteristic of his kind of people (xv–xvi). **Dyer 1993:** One critic from the 1960s saw the theme of female self-assertion in this story as foreshadowing *The Awakening* (22). **Shurbutt 1993:** This is one of various stories in which Chopin challenges a stereotype about women (22). **Fusco 1994:** The story explores the oppression of married women; in form and content it resembles a tale by Hamlin Garland. No particular event in the story is given special emphasis, and even the escape can be anticipated by the reader (if not by Bud). Chopin mocks Bud, creates sympathy for 'Tite Reine, and provides the wished-for happy ending. Although Santien wins a married woman from her husband, her new relationship with her rescuer merely transfers her to another man and thus does not greatly disrupt conventional values (147–48). **Koloski 1994:** The story is included in soft-cover collections of Chopin's fiction published in 1979, 1981, and 1992 (27–28). **Gunning 1995:** In this story Chopin seems less concerned to depict a black man favorably than to assert the freedom and racial dignity of a white woman and offer a new vision of white male heroism (67; 72–76; 82). **Bender 1996:** In this story Chopin alters the initial Darwinian situation (in which the male is dominant) by making the woman triumphant in the end; even her name suggests her eventual victory (108). **Carr 1996:** Bud embodies the stereotype of the shiftless, abusive Cajun (54–55). **Koloski 1996:** Topics of this story include abuse (11), the Santien family (20), rescue, journey motifs, and links between a black man and white woman (23–24). The heroine here resembles the one in "A Night in Acadie" (52). **Walker 1996:** The heroine's illiteracy reflects her general lack of power (219). **Beer 1997:** Here as in other stories Chopin depicts the oppressiveness of a partner's presence and confronts the need for romantic freedom, even as she is careful at the end to show Grégoire and Tite Reine moving in opposite geographical directions. (42). Although the topic of the story was controversial when Chopin wrote, the tale was syndicated to a broader-than-usual readership.

Chopin subtly introduces geographical information in order to prepare for the ending. This conclusion is unusual in her works because it resolves the central conflict, but it does so in a way that subverts conventional values (54–55). **Toth and Seyersted 1998:** This story is mentioned in Chopin's account books (149, 154, 168) and in her letters (206). **Koloski 1999:** Here as in other stories by Chopin, the heroine ultimately achieves her goals (xiii). **Toth 1999a:** This is one of Chopin's most unconventional tales and thus would not have appealed to traditional editors (9–10). **Toth 1999b:** The abusive husband in this often-overlooked story resembles Chopin's father-in-law. Although the wife here has the sympathy of the black servant, his role is mainly passive. Even so, this is the only story of its kind, time, and place that shows a battered wife achieving freedom. Perhaps it reflects Chopin's own success in leaving a potentially abusive relationship. Perhaps this is one of Chopin's two most revolutionary pieces of fiction (48), although its full implications are disguised by its use of local color conventions (49). **Toth 1999c:** This story resembles events in the lives of Chopin's mother-in-law and husband (63), while the husband in the tale resembles a man Chopin knew (108). The story proved unacceptable to magazines (146) and seems not to have been correctly comprehended by a local reviewer (149). Chopin's main focus here is on the woman (150), although her depiction of the black male was unconventional. This is the only printed tale of its time that describes an abused woman who gets away. Perhaps the narrative reflects Chopin's own experiences with the two most important men of her adult life, particularly her admiration for her own virtuous husband (152–53). The story was rejected by a major journal (159). Like another of Chopin's tales, this one proved difficult to publish (170). **Gibbons 2000:** This story reveals not only Chopin's progress away from local color conventions but also her continuing allegiance to them. The figurative language is still often (but not always) hackneyed; the characters are often largely (but not entirely) stereotyped; and the tone is still greatly (but not completely) sentimental. This work, like several others, represents a potential turning point in Chopin's career (xxxii). **Knights 2000:** This work, one of Chopin's most compelling, was produced during a particularly creative period—the fall and summer of 1893 (xv). This is one of various works in which Chopin juxtaposes an individual life with a larger social context (xviii–xix). Here as in other works, Chopin subverts romantic expectations (xxi). Also as elsewhere, Chopin explores the dangers of solipsism (xxvi). Chopin's sympathetic depiction of the assertive black character here was written at a time of particular persecution of black males suspected of being too familiar with white women (xxxi).

"Juanita"

Written: 1894. First published: 1895. Included in *A Vocation and a Voice* (1991).

An unnamed narrator tells the story of Juanita, a large, shy woman who dresses as "Mother Hubbard." Her face and mouth have a sensuous beauty, although she cannot be called a beauty. It is amazing that in spite of her unattractiveness, she has admirers.

Juanita enjoys the attentions of many suitors. There is much speculation among the townspeople as to whom Juanita will choose. Suddenly a man appears who is poor, shabby, and one-legged. Her attention to the one-legged man first becomes evident when she solicits the town to buy him an artificial leg, and the attention grows. One day Juanita becomes a mother. She says that the father of the baby is her husband, the one-legged man.

Juanita turns her back on the townspeople and turns all her attention to the one-legged man. She puts her husband on a dejected-looking pony and leads him everywhere. They travel into the woods in this manner, where they can love each other away from the prying eyes of the town. The only spectators are the birds and squirrels.

The narrator never expected Juanita to be more respectful than a squirrel anyway. **(DR)**

***

Rankin 1932: This story is effective in its presentation of ideas and feelings (163). **Zlotnick 1968:** This is one of many stories in which Chopin implies ambivalent, unconventional responses to marriage (2). **Seyersted 1969a:** Based on a real woman Chopin knew, the story illustrates her willingness to describe reality as she saw it (90). This is one of only four stories by Chopin demonstrably taken directly from life (217). **Berthoff 1970:** This work foreshadows a much later piece by Carson McCullers (xv). **Arner 1975:** This subtly comic tale implies that deep desire will triumph over any conventional restrictions (94). **Davis 1982:** As in various later tales, Chopin here deals with erotic desire as a force of nature leading to many possible effects on people's lives (66). **Dyer 1985:** In this as in other tales, Chopin uses the prejudices of her readers in order to depict feminine sensuality in permissible terms. The narrator is presented ironically, and further complexity of perspective is achieved by Chopin's decision to link this tale with "The Night Came Slowly" (77–80). **Skaggs 1985:** Theme: erotic attraction is an enigmatic but perfectly natural power (40). **Ewell 1986:** The story contrasts conventional ethics with impulsive choice and features Chopin's skill at depicting the bizarre, the charming, and the natural in tones of ambiguity (93). Like the title character in "Azélie," Juanita takes little initiative and shows little concern with customary notions of right and wrong (97). This is one of several late stories in which Chopin innovates in her use of narrative perspective (101). **Toth 1990a:** This tale, with its jocular conclusion, was the first by Chopin in several years to take place in Missouri. Although based on a real person, the tale may have been an experiment for its author, who waited months before submitting it (along with another narrative) to an east-coast journal (232). It is one of various stories by Chopin focusing on forbidden desire (279). One of her most avant-garde narratives (306), it was intended for inclusion in *A Vocation and a Voice* (374). **Toth 1991:** The setting of the tale is the Missouri countryside (xiv). This is one of various stories in *A Vocation and a Voice* that defy conventional expectations about sexuality (xxiii). **Dyer 1993:** One critic from the 1960s saw the theme of female self-assertion in this story as foreshadowing *The Awakening* (22). **Cothern 1994:** This is one of various stories in which Chopin used an internal narrator, a device which allowed her greater authorial distance both from the tale and from the dominant culture she may have been implicitly critiquing (124). **Koloski 1994:** The story is included in a soft-cover collection of Chopin's fiction published in 1991 (28). **Bender 1996:** Here as in other stories, Chopin disrupts the usual Darwinian expectation that the male is dominant, just as she also undercuts Darwin by showing that women do not always select wealthy or prominent mates. In Chopin's view, Darwin over-emphasized competition between men and under-emphasized conflict between the sexes. Yet even Juanita is rather sexually conservative (108–9). **Beer 1997:** Chopin seems as interested in the diverse reactions to Juanita as she is in Juanita herself. She effectively uses passive voice to emphasize these varied responses. Chopin seems uninterested here in passing ethical judgment (78–80). **Toth and Seyersted 1998:** This story is mentioned in Chopin's account books (149) and diary for 1894 (190). **Toth 1999c:** This work, written in the aftermath of a bout with melancholy, was the first in several years to take place in Missouri. It depicts unconventional characters in a somewhat scandalous relationship and was published in a minor journal (157–58).

"The Kiss"

Written: 1894. First published: 1895. Included in *Complete Works* (1969).

Brantain sits in the shadows of the dark room which is lit only by the fireplace. The darkness allows him to stare at the beautiful brunette girl sitting by the fire. She knows that he loves her, but she is waiting for him to declare himself. She will accept him. Brantain is not handsome, but is enormously rich; his wealth can give her the lifestyle she desires.

The door opens and a young man who is well known to Brantain enters the room. He strides over to the girl; she turns her face toward him and he leans down and gives her a lingering kiss on her lips. He does not see Brantain in the darkness. Brantain and the girl stand up and the newcomer stands between them. Brantain excuses himself from the room.

The next time she sees Brantain, she asks to have a word with him. Taking him aside, she explains that Mr. Harvy is like a brother to her because he is her brother's dearest friend. Brantain is hopeful about the relationship again. Mr. Harvy is a guest at the wedding. He walks up to the girl and tells her that her husband sent him over to kiss her. Her eyes look tenderly at him and her lips invite his kiss, but he does not kiss her. Instead he tells her that he no longer kisses women because "it's dangerous."

Nevertheless, she has Brantain and all his money. She should not expect to have everything. **(DR)**

***

Seyersted 1969a: Although Nathalie's eventual disappointment is unsurprising for a story of this time, Chopin's non-judgmental, objective presentation of unfaithfulness is unconventional, and the final sentence typifies her skillful deftness (111). **Leary 1970a:** This tale depicts feminine self-assertion in a manner unusual for its day (xii). **Leary 1971:** This story was unusual for its time in its explicit focus on feminine liberty and scheming (168). **Peterson 1972:** The comic tone and ethical agnosticism of this story suggest that Chopin herself was feeling a greater degree of aesthetic autonomy (139). The tone of this work is less serious than in some of Chopin's other writings about infidelity (142–43). The story illustrates her tendency during this period to treat unusual topics in an objective tone (161). **Rocks 1972:** Here and elsewhere Chopin describes a somewhat selfish decision that nevertheless harms no one (118). **Arner 1975:** The cat is used to suggest Nathalie's sexuality, and the conclusion of the tale suggests that Nathalie will find a substitute for Harvey (90–91). Chopin does not censure Nathalie, depicting her instead as a woman who knows how to play the marriage game—which is biased in favor of male power—to her own advantage (92). **Ladenson 1976:** Here as in *The Awakening*, a woman's unconventional emotions are presented as being even stronger than a man's (30). **Skaggs 1985:** This is one of several tales that explore the unpredictability of persons and events (45–46). **Ewell 1986:** The story describes the bitter alternatives women sometimes confront. The somewhat crude Nathalie is willing to accept material comfort rather than romantic bliss, but her manipulative nature provokes our scorn. The tale juxtaposes caustic observation with sophisticated comedy (103–4). **Toth 1990a:** This was one of Chopin's earliest stories dealing with forbidden desire (279). It was intended for inclusion in *A Vocation and a Voice* (374). **Brown 1991:** The heroine here achieves a merely temporary balance of social expectations and personal desire (126). **Toth 1991:** This is one of many of Chopin's late works that were first printed in *Vogue* (xiii–xiv). In this tale Chopin mocks materialistic women (xvi). The wry tone of this story is typical of many tales in *A Vocation and a Voice* (xxii). This is one of many stories in *A Vocation and a Voice* in which love fails because of bad timing (xxiii), which seem to satirize contemporary class relations (xxiv), and which depict an intriguing female character (xxv). **Fusco 1994:** This is one of several stories by Chopin whose title resembles that of a story by Maupassant (140). **Koloski 1994:** The story is included in soft-cover collections of Chopin's fiction published in 1970, 1976, 1979, 1981, and 1991 (27–28). **Bender 1996:** Chopin's Darwinism may have influenced her portrayal here of a woman who chooses a mate for unwise reasons (110). **Koloski 1996:** As with several other tales in *A Vocation and a Voice*, the setting of the story is unspecified (54), although the meaning of the act mentioned in the title is clear (63). **Toth and Seyersted 1998:** This story is mentioned in Chopin's account books (140, 149) and diary for 1894 (191). **Toth 1999c:** This was one of various stories about infidelity that Chopin did not send to standard magazines (171). It was first printed in *Vogue* (172) and was later intended for inclusion in *A Vocation and a Voice* (208). **Knights 2000:** This story, like others by Chopin, gains added interest when read in the context of the materials with which it was originally published (xix). This story, written not long after "Regret," implies a view of marriage that contrasts with the one presented in that tale (xxi).

"A Lady of Bayou St. John"

Written: 1893. First published: 1893. Included in *Bayou Folk* (1894).

Madame Delisle is very beautiful, very young, and very lonely. Her husband, Gustave, is away in Virginia fighting with Beauregard. Madame is such a child that she can not comprehend the importance of this tragedy that is enveloping the whole civilized world; she just knows that her own little world is stripped of its joyousness. Why, she can not even go to sleep now without old black Manna-Loulou's bedtime story.

One day, her nearby neighbor, Sépincourt, stops to talk with her. He is a young Frenchman who is not involved in this war between brothers. His pleasant brown eyes comfort Madame Delisle as a gentle hug comforts a sad child. As the summer progresses, their empathy grows until Madame Delisle begins watching every day for his slender figure approaching languidly up the walk. They sit on the gallery, sipping coffee and discussing everything. They read Gustave's infrequent letters together and sigh over them and the war. Finally, it seems to Madame Delisle that she can no longer remember her living husband; he has become like a distant figure in a mist.

One day, Sépincourt looks at her and suddenly suggests that they go to Paris and get away from this sad country. Madame Delisle is frightened and runs into the house, leaving him alone. That night, however, she does not want to hear Manna-Loulou's story; instead, she wants to be alone and to think. Madame Delisle has changed; in fact, she has become a woman who is capable of love or sacrifice. When she refuses to see Sépincourt the next day, he sends her a note begging permission to call and apologize. However, one look in her face tells him to forget forgiveness and declare his love. When he asks if she will go away with him, she whispers, "Anywhere, anywhere." But their plans are not to be. That night a messenger brings Madame Delisle a letter from Beauregard, informing her that Gustave has been killed.

Early in the new year, Sépincourt decides that it is not too soon for him to return to Madame Delisle and declare his love again. He finds her dressed in heavy mourning, sitting in front of Gustave's portrait, which is adorned with his scarf, sword and a veritable bank of flowers. She now treats Sépincourt as a casual acquaintance and argues that surely he must understand that his plans are no longer possible. Henceforth, her heart, soul and very life belong to another. In fact, she vows, she now sees her dear husband in every circumstance; his nearness surrounds her everywhere and his memory will fill the remainder of her life.

Finally, there is nothing for Sépincourt to do but take his leave. Try as he might he can never understand a woman's heart. Many years later, Madame Delisle still lives on Bayou St. John. She is old now but very pretty. Gustave's memory still fills her days, and she has never once failed to have an annual high mass said for the eternal peace of his soul. **(CY)**

Rankin 1932: By using efficient diction or mere snatches of talk, Chopin quickly sums up the strong emotions and subtle feelings of nobly motivated characters (140). **Reilly 1937:** This is one of various stories in which Chopin deals subtly with the ambiguities of affection (72). **Reilly 1942:** This story illustrates Chopin's typically deft and sometimes implicit handling of the complexities of love (133–34). **Arms 1967:** This work takes an unusual approach to depicting opposed views, finding humor in the stubbornness of feelings subjected to stress (223). **Seyersted 1969a:** The story did not trouble contemporary editors because the heroine never does commit adultery, although she is briefly tempted (55). Madame Delisle's temptation, though, suggests that Chopin is moving toward a non-judgmental depiction of feminine infidelity (111). **Leary 1970a:** This is one of many works in which Chopin depicts the ambiguities and complexities of love (x). **Leary 1971:** Theme: the complexity of feminine affection (166–67). **Peterson 1972:** The stories Chopin wrote for *Vogue*, such as this one, tend to be more daring than her other works, perhaps because *Vogue*'s editors made few demands. The woman's growing passion here resembles the kind described in Flaubert's *Madame Bovary*, while her eventual renunciation resembles that of a nun. Chopin nicely refuses to explain her heroine's decision, although she implies, here as elsewhere, that having a purpose can be more fulfilling than satisfying a desire (130–33). This work is a little less risky than some of Chopin's later writing about marriage (142). Here as elsewhere, Chopin offers an interesting study of the human mind (273). **Rocks 1972:** Chopin here typically shows that people often freely choose not to alter their circumstances; they elect to renounce other options, but the choice is theirs and no decision is externally imposed (118). Here Chopin reveals the possible rewards of resisting temptation (119). **Arner 1975:** This story treats a theme similar to that of "Madame Célestin's Divorce," although in a darker tone, and Madame Delisle and her paramour are both defective in their own ways. This work is significant as a precursor of *The Awakening*, partly because its heroine is motivated (even in the end) less by ethics than by personal idiosyncrasies (59–60). **Solomon 1976:** Madame Delisle suffers in this tale much as the title character does in "La Belle Zoraïde," a story in which Madame Delisle also appears (xv). **Bonner 1977:** The story shows the ambiguities of love (10). This story foreshadows Chopin's focus later in her career on autonomous women (13–14). **Lattin 1980:** This is one of various stories by Chopin that seems richer because it uses characters who appear elsewhere (20; 29–31). **Davis 1982:** Like many other stories in *Bayou Folk*, this one focuses on human affection, although Chopin uses irony to raise a number of questions about this theme that the story leaves tantalizingly unresolved (64). **Rogers 1983:** Here as elsewhere, Chopin, like George Sand, depicts the complexities of marriage (32). **Stein 1984:** This story depicts a woman who chooses a kind of living death rather than pursue full adulthood. Her final decision, like her behavior throughout the story, is unattractively immature and self-centered. If she had gone to Paris she at least might have faced some complications that might have helped her grow up. By the end of the tale, she seems the only one of Chopin's heroines who is unlikely ever to change or develop (188–89). **Aherne 1985:** The title character is one of the many fascinating women Chopin depicted (although she did less well in characterizing men [84]). **Dyer 1985:** Although this tale seems similar to others by Chopin focusing on nostalgia, it also hints at feminine sensuality (74–75). **Newman 1986:** Like many of Chopin's tales, this one suggests a view of marriage that seems to conflict with the views implied by some of her other stories. This work eventually seems to affirm traditional ideas about the value of matrimony (152). Like the titular character of "La Belle Zoraïde," Madame Delisle here finally turns from reality to fantasy (161). **Skaggs 1985:** This is one of several tales focusing on the interaction of affection and selfhood (17). The ending of this story resembles that of "La Belle Zoraïde": both title characters retreat into fantasy (20–21). **Ewell 1986:** Although this tale comes last in *Bayou Folk*, it was published earlier than its companion-piece, "La Belle Zoraïde." It sums up a central theme of the whole volume: how romanticism can stunt personal development. The title character never escapes immaturity; she plays at romance until offered the reality of marriage, which she then rejects in favor of a different kind of fantasy. She lacks a first name as well as much of an independent identity, and her stilted narcissism contrasts with Zoraïde's efforts to achieve full selfhood (73–74). **Martin 1988a:** This is one of various stories in which Chopin investigates conflicts between strong, often sexual feelings and the conventional ethics of society. The tale is frank in its treatment of desire and its results (4). **Elfenbein 1989:** Madame Delisle shows many of the same traits here as in "La Belle Zoraïde" (132). In both cases she is devoted to a conventional routine (135). **Inge 1989:** Madame Delisle's apparent fixation on her own attractiveness actually reflects her yearning for sensual affection. Meanwhile, her imaginative needs are fulfilled first by Manna-Loulou's stories and then by the fantasies supplied by her visitor. After she and Sépincourt soon run out of ideas to discuss, their relationship quickly turns physical, but Madame Delisle's daringly romantic self-image is at variance with her timid behavior. Her husband's death allows her to make him the focus of her imagination, which seems to recoil from real sexual expression. She is a character of real mental complexity (98). **Toth 1990a:** Chopin's mother, like the woman in this tale, was a respected widow (32). This is one of several stories in which Chopin depicts the Civil War in a harsh light (70). Perhaps she set the narrative in New Orleans as a marketing tactic (216). On the day it first appeared in print, she composed a companion piece—"La Belle Zoraïde" (221). Both tales are one of five on adult dilemmas placed at the end of *Bayou Folk* (224). This story was particularly praised by one reviewer for its insight into feminine psychology (228), and it is one of Chopin's early tales dealing with forbidden desire (279). **Brown 1991:** Here as in other works by Chopin, a child-like woman briefly feels a sensual awakening, only to withdraw both mentally and physically. Madame Delisle never achieves the self-awareness attained by Edna in *The Awakening*, and initial readers probably missed the submerged irony of Chopin's story as well as its deliberate ambiguities (121–26; 131). **Guidici 1991:** Here as elsewhere in Chopin's fiction, a husband's death enhances his wife's power. Her devotion to his memory does not subvert the freedom she now enjoys (29–30). Chopin herself achieved a similar autonomy through her own husband's death (33). **Toth 1992:** Here as elsewhere, widows in Chopin see possibilities in their changed circumstances (16–17). In this story as in others, the experiences of the main female may be relevant to the experiences of Chopin's married mother (21–22). **Bryan 1993:** The links between this story and in "La Belle Zoraïde" imply parallels between the situations of Zoraïde and Madame Delisle (55). **Larsson 1993:** Several characters here also appear in "La Belle Zoraïde" (2:537–38). **Shurbutt 1993:** Chopin's final comments here offer an ironic perspective on traditional views of marriage (19–20). **Koloski 1994:** The story is included in soft-cover collections of Chopin's fiction published in 1970, 1976, and 1979 (27). **Gunning 1995:** The story depicts a privileged white woman whose adherence to old ideals restricts her own freedom (76–77). **Koloski 1996:** When the story is read as part of *Bayou Folk*, certain potential objections to its tone and characterization vanish. Chopin views both major characters with a kind of distanced irony (27–30). **Walker 1996:** Madame Delisle in this story, like Edna in *The Awakening*, is passive in her approach to fiction (219). **Toth and Seyersted 1998:** This work, which is mentioned in Chopin's account books (140, 149, 163), provides examples of the French spoken in New Orleans in her day (226). **Bonner and Bonner 1999:** This story shows Chopin's familiarity with Bayou St. John, which was on the outer edge of New Orleans (58–59). **Brown 1999:** Sépincourt is one of the socially and politically unconventional men whom Chopin often features in her fiction (72). However, until he encounters Madame Delisle, he remains generally willing to conform (72–73). Here as elsewhere Chopin depicts the woman's traditional role as static and passive, whereas the conventional male role seems more active and assertive (73). **Koloski 1999:** This tale, like some other stories near the end of *Bayou Folk*, is gloomy in atmosphere; the joy often expressed in the earlier tales has vanished. Instead, these later works show the malign influence of the past rather than focusing on a hopeful tomorrow (xv). **Toth 1999a:** This is one of many tales whose themes early critics failed to connect to Chopin's own life and views (3). Like some of Chopin's other most currently popular works, it first appeared in *Vogue* (9). **Toth 1999c:** Like other successful stories by Chopin about the Civil War, this one focuses on a woman (33). It deals with a female's extra-marital desire, a theme Chopin also explores elsewhere (97). Its descriptive techniques may have been influenced by paintings she had recently viewed (138). Reviewers may have failed to comprehend the tale (150), particularly its implications concerning marriage (152). It was one of the unconventional stories first printed in *Vogue*

(172), and the attitude toward the past expressed by the main character may reflect Chopin's own views (202). **Knights 2000:** This work, one of Chopin's most compelling, was produced during a particularly creative period—the fall and summer of 1893 (xv). Here as elsewhere, Chopin satirizes inadequate responses to life's complexities (xxiv).

"A Lady of Shifting Intentions"

1895. Mostly destroyed or lost. Rediscovered fragment included in *Private Papers* (1998).

... Stetson, excited to be revisiting his family home, has brought his friend Beverly with him. As Stetson runs upstairs to see his mother, the other young man remains in the parlor, building a blaze in the fireplace. Suddenly Bess, Stetson's sister, enters the house. Beverly hesitantly introduces himself. When the sister runs upstairs to greet her brother, Beverly sinks back, disillusioned, into his chair.... **(RCE)**

***

Ewell 1986: Like other stories Chopin wrote at this time, this work focuses on unstable feelings (112). **Toth and Seyersted 1998:** This story is mentioned in Chopin's account books (149, 161). A fragment of this story was discovered in the early 1990s and is reprinted here (246–47).

"Lilacs"

Written: 1894. First published: 1896. Included in *A Vocation and a Voice* (1991).

Each year, as soon as the lilacs are in bloom, Adrienne Farival travels back to the convent where she was raised, her arms full of fresh lilac blooms. The sisters and the Mother Superior welcome her with open arms. She carries with her an extravagant gift to express her love and respect; each year the Mother Superior chides Adrienne for her extravagance. Adrienne answers that coming to the convent each year is the greatest pleasure she has in life. She spends her days walking in the gardens, attending services, and refreshing her spirit.

When Adrienne returns to Paris, her life returns to normal. She sits in her armchair wearing a negligee. Music sheets are scattered over the floor and the open piano. Her maid is complaining that Adrienne's manager is upset because she left without telling him that she was going. He feels that he is ruined because the public will not be happy with someone else playing the role that Adrienne made famous.

The next year Adrienne leaves Paris to go to the convent, again not telling her manager that she is leaving. This year there is a different manager. When she reaches the convent there is no one in the windows to see her arrive. She rings the bell. The door is opened slightly by a lay sister with downcast eyes and red cheeks. She pushes a box toward Adrienne, saying that the Mother Superior has ordered her to do so. Adrienne is shocked; she does not understand this cold reception. She opens the enclosed letter that banishes her forever from the convent. She leans her forehead against the door and weeps, for she has lost her haven of peace, the place she visits to refresh her soul. She leaves.

The lay sister comes out of the door and sweeps away the fallen lilac blooms. **(DR)**

***

Rankin 1932: This narrative is tasteful, refined, and affectionately detailed; it comes close to being flawless. It abounds in emotions, drama, affection, dilemmas of the soul, and the dark force of distrust. The phrasing is highly efficient and the whole work gives an impression of skillful craftsmanship. The story seems full of vitality and is credible in its presentation of setting, circumstances, and mood. The two locations are effectively presented and the characters brim with vitality. The story deals with conflicting senses of ethics and shows the devastating impact such conflict can have on third parties. The admirably free-spirited opera singer is juxtaposed with the inhibited, straight-laced senior nun, and the implied conflict between them leads to severe pain. Nearly all the nuns are effectively drawn, as are the ancient gardener and Sophie the maid. The story's richly complex emotions and characters seem both life-like and unexpected, partly because they combine the comic and the tragic (166–67). **Arms 1967:** Rankin responded too sentimentally to this fairly straightforward tale, which is one of the three most successful stories included in Chopin's final (unpublished) collection. Chopin imposes no interpretation on the events she describes but does make them clearly comprehensible (225–26). **Seyersted 1969a:** Theme: implied sexual affairs by a woman (70) who is partly ostracized as a result (111). The story, although rejected by the first journal to which Chopin submitted it (73), is one of her most successful, especially in presenting character (123) and using flower symbolism (132). Yet even this fine a story is sometimes marred by clumsy diction (130). Chopin noted in a journal that she could not remember what inspired the tale (217). **Berthoff 1970:** This unsettling tale is one of Chopin's finest works (x). **Peterson 1972:** The sentence beginning "Once within the convent" is an example of the occasional clumsiness of Chopin's writing (9). This is the first work in which Chopin juxtaposes religious and secular lifestyles, although "Madame Célestin's Divorce" had skated close to the issue (147). Two slight early hints suggest that Adrienne's life in Paris may not be what the nuns assume, but the contrast is eventually reinforced by a switch in floral imagery. The contrasting settings are reinforced by the contrast between Adrienne and the abbess, who eventually shows the visitor little Christian compassion. Although Adrienne is not without faults, she nonetheless adds something to the convent, but she is ultimately discarded as easily as her flowers. The convent is idyllic but static and somewhat dead (147–51). **Rocks 1972:** Here as elsewhere, Chopin demonstrates the complexities liberty can involve and shows that true liberty often entails a responsible concern for others (117). **Arner 1975:** As in "A Vocation and a Voice," a cloister is associated here with a measure of unreality. Thanks in part to its highly evocative final sentence as well as its general skill, this is one of Chopin's most successfully crafted tales (84). **Bonner 1975:** This is one of the most intriguing of Chopin's stories set in Europe. It implies a growing erotic attachment between Adrienne and Sister Agatha (281–83). **Wolff 1978:** This is one of many stories by Chopin dealing with the instability of human experience (126). **Howell 1979b:** This story makes clearer than much of Chopin's local color writing her key ideas about human life (105). Although one might assume that Chopin is using this tale to satirize the Catholic church, in fact her focus is on the internal ambivalence of the main character. The story is typically subtle and implicit, especially in suggesting the heroine's divided mind (106–7). The convent itself has a sensuous appeal and in some ways is more deeply satisfying than her other life. Mme. Farival hopes to enjoy both forms of life, but the two cannot be reconciled (107–8). She resembles Edna in *The Awakening*, but Chopin leaves her ultimate destiny unclear. Chopin herself was a never a moral relativist; she acknowledges the sensual impulse but never rejects the importance of spirituality. She is more interested in depicting tensions than in resolving them (108). **Taylor 1979:** This was one of several tales Chopin had difficulty publishing (viii). Like some of her other works, it subtly suggests the shortcomings of Catholicism (x). Although the story involves female suffering, it also shows how nearly all persons are handicapped by social conventions (xviii). **Bonner 1982:** This is one of several stories by Chopin in which Christianity is an important aspect (125). **Davis 1982:** As in a number of her later works, Chopin here deals with erotic desire as a force of nature leading to many possible effects on people's lives (66). **Lattin 1982:** In this story Chopin tragically suggests that renewal is sometimes impossible (228). **Rogers 1983:** Like George Sand in some of her fiction, Chopin here focuses on ambivalent women (38). Also like Sand, she seems to imply that physical pleasure is often a hidden motive underlying religious devotion (38). **Gilbert 1984:** This story offers an affecting tale of the bond shared between two distinctly different females (17). **Newman 1986:** The main character embodies conflicting cultural stereotypes, thereby living a double life. Chopin treats the Mother Superior with some irony, implying that even the nun, like Adrienne, is preoccupied with men (specifically, the statue of St. Joseph). Adrienne seems more whole, however, than the rigid Mother Superior (162). **Skaggs 1985:** This is one of several stories emphasizing the significance of religion (39). The tale resembles "Two Portraits" by implying opposed but equally incomplete styles of life (41–42). **Ewell 1986:** This story was turned down by numerous publications before finally being accepted two years after Chopin composed it. It concerns alternating points of view and the attempt to harmonize autonomy and responsibility. Chopin highly valued the work, which is her only story completely set in France. Its two locales reveal different aspects of Adrienne Farival's lively if somewhat immature personality. By the end of the tale our view of her changes, as does that of the nuns, whose rejection of her seems painful but just. Not long after finishing this story Chopin recounted her own disturbed and disappointing visit to a convent—a place she seems to have found confining and unreal. The story's final image of the fallen flowers suggests Adrienne's loss of innocence, but it also suggests the loss the nuns will sustain by her absence. Here as in other works, Chopin sees a link between the natural and the genuinely divine (91–92) and explores tensions between flesh and soul, artifice and simplicity (98). Basic desires for sensual love are juxtaposed with an inflexible system of ethics (105), and in some respects Adrienne resembles Edna of *The Awakening* (144). As in some of her other works, Chopin here illustrates the occasional costs of liberty (183). **Martin 1988a:** This is one of various stories in which Chopin depicts a passionate woman without censuring or penalizing her in order to court the approval of readers (6). **Inge 1989:** In this tale, with its efficient A/B/A organization, the initial journey to the convent implies Adrienne's return to a sexually less complicated but more rigid life than she experiences in the city. Chopin, like William Blake, implies that all humans (even nuns such as the young Agathe) yearn for both innocence and experience and also for a way of uniting the two. Although the mood of the middle section is perhaps too light, the story does intriguingly explore a favorite topic of nineteenth century writers (103–4). **Taylor 1989:** This was one of Chopin's most unconventional tales (153). It alludes to work by continental women writers and emphasizes tensions centering on erotic yearnings (153–54). The heroine resembles but also differs from the title character of a work by Madame de Staël, while the lilac symbolism resembles that of Walt Whitman (154). **Papke 1990:** This is one of several tales in which Chopin treats conflicts between personal yearnings and communal obligations, between self-fulfillment and communally approved self-denial (60). **Toth 1990a:** In this story Chopin drew on her own experiences in a convent school (44–45). Her best friend in youth had become a nun, and Chopin was friendly in later life with other nuns (238). One of several stories by Chopin focusing on romance outside of marriage, this tale was published in *Vogue* after being rejected for publication in a book (296). It was intended for inclusion in *A Vocation and a Voice* (374). **Vanlandingham 1990:** Chopin sought—earnestly but unsuccessfully—to have this work published in an avant-garde journal (162). **Toth 1991:** Various activities mentioned here reflect Chopin's own childhood behavior (ix). Paris is one setting of this tale (xiv). Although the story shows Chopin's attractions for some aspects of religion, her own visit to a convent a few days after composing this piece left her critical of such an existence (xix). This story, unusually, took several days to write (xxii). This is one of several stories in *A Vocation and a Voice* in which Chopin presents complex views of religion (xxiii) and depicts an intriguing female character (xxv). **Ellis 1992:** Here as in "A Vocation and a Voice," Chopin explores the tensions between religious and non-religious lives (228). **Dyer 1993:** Here as in *The Awakening*, Chopin significantly describes a parrot (37). **Ellis 1994:** This is one of several stories by Chopin that uses a three-part structure perhaps influenced by, and certainly similar to, the sonata form in music (147). **Ewell 1994:** Soon after Chopin's success as a local color writer was assured, she composed this narrative, which turns away from local color conventions. Unlike much of her local color fiction, however, this tale was not immediately accepted for publication (165). **Koloski 1994:** The story is included in soft-cover collections of Chopin's fiction published in 1979, 1984, and 1991 (27–28). It was one of six stories by Chopin included in an important 1994 college text (29). **Padgett 1994:** This story draws on Biblical imagery of the Annunciation to ridicule both the exclusively secular and exclusively ascetic spheres, which reflect divisions in the lives of women in Western Christian culture. The story laments the split between spiritual and physical and the ways this split prevents unity between and within women. Ironic parallels exist between the two supposedly contrasting environments the story depicts. In the end of possibility of communion is frustrated (97–106). **Fetterley and Pryse 1995:** Adrienne's banishment foreshadows Chopin's own ostracism following the publication of *The Awakening*. Nevertheless, the story does indicate the sensual nature of women (410). **Koloski 1996:** Set in France (54), the story features a main character perhaps based on the actress Sarah Bernhardt but also resembling other characters Chopin had created. Adrienne is extremely perceptive, desires stability, and is as important to Agathe as the latter is to her. Perhaps the story was also influenced by a recent novel by Zola and also by Chopin's own experiences with religious schooling (58–60). The story exemplifies Chopin's interest in duality (64), and the heroine has the same last name as two characters in *The Awakening* (86). **Ewell 1997:** Chopin particularly valued this story, which was rooted in personal experience. The final emphasis on rigid dogma hurts both the nuns and their visitor by depriving both of affection and by cheating the nuns of exposure to what is natural (109–10). **Toth and Seyersted 1998:** This story is mentioned in Chopin's account books (141, 149, 170, 173), diary for 1894 (181), and letters (209). **Koloski 1999:** This was one of a number of effective tales Chopin composed before the publication of *A Night in Acadie* but which she did not include in that collection (xv–xvi). **Toth 1999a:** This is one of various stories in which Chopin describes independent, capable women—the kind she knew from her own childhood (4). **Toth 1999c:** This is one of only a couple of stories Chopin set in Paris (61). A lengthier tale than was usual for Chopin, it favorably depicts an all-female environment but was turned down by many magazines until it was eventually printed in a New Orleans newspaper, whose readers may have been among the few Americans with an interest in a French convent (175–76). This narrative is one of the somewhat dark tales intended for inclusion in *A Vocation and a Voice* (208). **Knights 2000:** This story, which presents a positive view of an unconventional life, was rejected even by one of the journals to which Chopin could usually reliably turn (xvii).

"Lilies"

Written: 1892. First published: 1893. Included in *A Night in Acadie* (1897).

A small boy named Mamouche thinks it will be amusing to let down the fence that surrounds Mr. Billy's crops and let Ma'me Angèle's calf, Toto, in to play among the cotton and corn. After doing exactly that, Mamouche decides it will be fun to watch Mr. Billy's response when he discovers Toto in his fields, so he warns one of Mr. Billy's men that Toto is in the middle of the crops.

Mr. Billy is furious. He storms over to Ma'me Angèle's door, threatening to kill Toto if he ever gets into his fields again. Ma'me Angèle is busy trying to finish an Easter dress for a customer and does not have time to devote to the mishap. Her young daughter, Marie Louise, is impressed by Mr. Billy's anger. She goes out into the yard and scolds Toto. All afternoon she tries to think of how she and her mother can repay Mr. Billy for the cotton and corn ruined by Toto. They have no money or enough cotton or corn to replace what was lost. She finally decides that she can soothe Mr. Billy's anger by taking him some of the beautiful Easter lilies growing along the side of their house.

The next day Marie Louise goes out and cuts a huge bouquet of lilies to take to Mr. Billy. The bouquet is so large that when Marie Louise picks it up she can hardly be seen around it. She goes straight to Mr. Billy's house. He is having his dinner alone and is touched by the child's gift. He has a place set for her at this table.

As long as the lilies last, Mr. Billy thinks of Marie Louise. As soon as they wither, he puts on his suit and goes to apologize to Ma'me Angèle and to pay a first visit to her and to Mamzelle Marie Louise. **(DR)**

***

Rankin 1932: Mr. Billy seems convincingly life-like, while Marie Louise, Mamouche, and Pompey act exactly as one would expect such persons to behave (169–70). **Peterson 1972:** Here as elsewhere Chopin focuses on transformation, but the imagery and alteration are both subtler than in "After the Winter." The ending also seems more credible (80–81). Here as elsewhere, Chopin uses children symbolically but also somewhat simplistically (103). **Arner 1975:** In this tale marriage is finally implied if not described. Affection is shown as a means to reconciliation in a story that is a bit facile but not without merit (65–66). **Lattin 1980:** This is one of various stories by Chopin featuring repeating characters (28). **Davis 1982:** As in other stories, Chopin here uses imagery of springtime and religion to reinforce a theme of secular, personal rebirth (66). **Lattin 1982:** Like other stories by Chopin, this one features an alienated, stunted character who eventually and somewhat easily achieves integration (224–25). **Skaggs 1985:** This is one of many stories by Chopin that shows a real familiarity with children and their effects on others. Mamouche plays a role here not unlike his role in the story that bears his name (27). **Ewell 1986:** Generally delicate in tone but also effective in its use of hyperbole, the story also uses contrasts well. Its original title had underlined its gentle satire on materialism (95). **Toth 1990a:** This is one of Chopin's more conventional children's stories (207). It was one of four tales by her published in just one month (215). This tale later appeared in *A Night in Acadie*, in which all the stories are set in Louisiana (298). **Koloski 1994:** The story is included in a softcover collection of Chopin's fiction published in 1992 (28). **Koloski 1996:** The racial stereotypes in this story may trouble present-day readers, who may find them surprisingly insensitive coming from Chopin (44). This was one of her tales for youth (66). **Toth and Seyersted 1998:** This story is mentioned in Chopin's account books (140, 148, 163). **Koloski 1999:** This is one of many stories by Chopin which either feature children or were written for them (xxii). Here as elsewhere she describes grown-ups who find connection with others (xxiii).

"A Little Country Girl."

Written: 1899. Included in *Complete Works* **(1969) and in** *Private Papers* **(1998).**

While scouring a tin milk-pail, Ninette is taunted by Black Gal because she is going to the circus while Ninette is not. When Black Gal leaves, Ninette's emotions give way to tears. Her obstacle to the circus is her grandparents, the Bézeaus, who refuse to let her go. Her frustration and resentment cause her to curse aloud the circus goers with a wish for rain—a great deal of it. Her grandmother overhears Ninette's jinx and remonstrates with her. She reminds Ninette that rain would ruin her grandfather's acres of standing cotton and that he is already angry enough because the cotton-pickers have left early to attend the circus.

Believing that some miracle might yet secure her attendance at the circus, Ninette is prompted by "the white-winged goddess," or Hope, to prepare her clothes and person in the event of such a miracle. As the crowd of circus-goers passes by, Ninette, though distracted, concentrates on her task of shelling peas while offering "inward supplications that something might happen."

A neighbor, Monsieur Perrault, whom the Bézeaus hold somewhat in awe, stops with his family-laden wagon and insists that Ninette attend the circus with them. To Ninette's astonishment, her grandmother gives permission, and her grandfather gives her money for the circus. She happily boards the wagon and takes the Perrault baby in her arms.

Ninette continues to hold the baby as she explores the exotic offerings and entertainments of the circus. She considers the baby something to which she might communicate her excitement.

During the circus performance, a sudden storm arises, destroying the tent. The rain is a deluge. Clutching the baby, Ninette prays on her knees for a safe return home and for safety for her, the baby, and everyone at the circus. Perrault discovers her at prayer, half covered by the fallen tent.

Believing that her curse caused the calamity, Ninette is morose for days. She confides in Grandmother Bézeau, who asks the priest to talk with Ninette. The priest at first jests with her about her "powers," and then he scolds her for her presumptuousness. As a result, Ninette feels ashamed.

Perrault, however, convinces the Bézeaus that Ninette's condition is the result of spending too much time with old people and that she must associate with individuals of her own age to prevent "terrible consequences" to her intellect. Apparently convinced, the Bézeaus allow Ninette to attend a birthday party at the Perrault home the next day, and Grandfather Bézeau says that if it is necessary, he will pay for her to have "a suitable toilet for the occasion." **(EP)**

***

Peterson 1972: This work for children was composed around the same time Chopin wrote her audacious tale "The Storm" (10). It was one of the few stories she composed during the time she was either completing or awaiting the appearance of *The Awakening* (244). A work for the young, the tale is not especially impressive (245); it is significant only because it was the last piece of short fiction she completed before the novel was published (255–56). At least in this story Chopin created a credibly flawed child (256). This work, along with the other tales written at around the same time as the novel, suggest that Chopin was not pleased with her recent short fiction but had not yet found a satisfying new approach (256). **Ewell 1986:** The composition of this story immediately preceded public response to *The Awakening*. It effectively describes children's hopes and disappointments. Although Chopin received payment for the piece from a young persons' magazine, the story seems never to have appeared in print during her lifetime. Perhaps this fact can be explained by the hostile response that greeted *The Awakening* (172–73). **Toth 1990a:** This story, which reflects Chopin's experiences with festivities in rural Louisiana (153), was the final local-color tale she composed before writing *The Awakening* (326–27). Many months passed before she wrote another story (357). Despite poor reviews of her novel, this story was accepted, paid for, and advertised (but not published) by a young persons' magazine (373). **Thomas 1992:** This work reflects Chopin's recent visit to Louisiana (47). **Koloski 1994:** The story is included in a soft-cover collection of Chopin's fiction published in 1992 (28). **Koloski 1996:** This is one of several children's stories by Chopin that depict the poor (71; 87). **Toth and Seyersted 1998:** An early draft of this story was among a collection of Chopin manuscripts uncovered in the early 1990s (135). It is mentioned in her account books (142, 146, 151) and in her letters (210). The newly discovered manuscript strongly resembles the already published version, although slight differences make it worth reprinting here (275–83). **Toth 1999a:** An early version of this tale was rediscovered in 1992 (8). **Toth 1999b:** A newly uncovered version of this story helps demonstrate Chopin's habits of revision (49). **Toth 1999c:** Perhaps this story was influenced by Chopin's memories of her own childhood (8). She would have been familiar with circuses from her time in Cloutierville (89). A version of this story, discovered in 1992, shows evidence of revision (166–67). The story was composed at around the same time as "The Godmother" (207). A young persons' magazine purchased but never published the tale, perhaps because of an alteration in personnel (229).

"A Little Free-Mulatto"

Written: 1892. Included in *Complete Works* (1969).

M'sie Jean-Ba', in his appearance and dress, could easily pass for a white man. But he and his wife, Ma'ame Jean-Ba', are so proud that they will not enjoy the white man's privileges. Nor will they associate with the blacks who live on the plantation, where M'sie Jean-Ba' works as a contracted laborer.

The Jean-Ba's' prejudice against the whites and the blacks makes life difficult for their little daughter. As a baby, Aurélia is content to play by herself, but as she grows older, she desires the companionship of other children, regardless of their color. However, Aurélia's parents will not allow her to play at the big house with the white children or at the cabins with the black children. As she spends her days confined in the house with nothing more to do than fixing her hair and learning to spell or patch quilt pieces, the little girl's spirit begins to wane.

M'sie and Ma'ame Jean-Ba' notice the change in Aurélia and watch her carefully. Unable to bear his daughter's decline, M'sie Jean-Ba' moves his family after his contract expires. Their new home is a paradise to Aurélia, for she is able to make and receive visits, go to school, attend Sunday devotions, and ride ponies with mixed-race children just like herself on "L'Isle des Mulâtres." **(JW)**

***

Seyersted 1969a: One of the few stories by Chopin that focuses seriously on the issue of integration, the tale implies that she may not have favored this solution to racial problems and that she may have considered prejudice a universal phenomenon that was not confined to whites and that was perhaps even less intense among the ones in this story than among certain of the tale's mulattoes (95–96). After the story was rejected by four different potential publishers, Chopin ceased submitting it (214). **Seyersted 1969b:** Here as in her other stories about race, Chopin's focus is more on individual psychology than on social contexts (26). **Peterson 1972:** If this piece had not been written for a young audience, it might almost seem satirical; instead, its main focus seems to be on an unusual situation (60–

61). **Jones 1981:** Ironically, the satisfaction eventually achieved by the title character is sharply circumscribed (150). **Ewell 1986:** This story was Chopin's first effort to deal directly with matters of race, particularly the widespread nature of racial chauvinism and the hurt it can cause. Nonetheless, the story implies Chopin's own support for racial separatism, and the speech of the mulattoes here seems designed to weaken our respect for them (68). This story was never printed during Chopin's life (100). **Gaudet 1986:** Critics have not appreciated the importance of the ethnic group Chopin depicts here, particularly its history (46). This story reveals that Chopin knew their culture, even though they themselves disliked the term "mulatto." Per Seyersted over-estimates the white racism implied in this work. The tale shows the sometimes self-defeating self-regard of this group, who considered themselves superior to blacks (49). **Elfenbein 1989:** Here as in other stories featuring black characters, Chopin seems to focus less on race itself than on sexual politics (119). **Taylor 1989:** In this and other stories, potentially major problems are resolved fairly easily and without extreme conflict (166). **Toth 1990a:** Like many other persons with a similar background, Chopin seems to have assumed that mulattoes preferred the company of mulattoes (136). This children's tale was not accepted for journal publication (207). **Bender 1996:** Chopin's Darwinian views help explain this story, which links subservience by race and by gender (107). **Koloski 1996:** This is one of Chopin's children's stories and explores the desire for selfhood and safety (71–72; 87). **Thomas 1996:** Although this story deals with liberated blacks, Chopin did not often depict such characters in great detail (209). **Beer 1997:** Liberty is a central theme of this tale (70), which focuses on a family trapped between rigid categories until they escape to a "paradise" where only one category exists. Ironically, freedom becomes possible only by a further retreat into difference and isolation. Here as in other tales, Chopin presents a paradigm of Southern race relations (72–74). Typically, even the name of "M'sie Jean-Ba" suggests his ambiguous social status (88–89). **Toth and Seyersted 1998:** This story is mentioned in Chopin's account books (149, 162). **Toth 1999c:** Perhaps this story was influenced by Chopin's own dealings with blacks as a young girl (8).

"The Locket"

Written: 1897. Included in *Complete Works* (1969).

Divided into two parts, this story takes its name from a locket shared by two sweethearts, Edmond and Octavie. An "old fashioned golden locket," it is a keepsake given to Edmond by Octavie.

It contains miniature portraits of her parents with their names and the date of their marriage. The locket is Octavie's "most precious earthly possession." In the first part of the story, Edmond, a Confederate soldier, is lying by a campfire, reading a letter from Octavie. His three fellow soldiers tease him about the locket, suggesting that it is "hoodoo business" or a talisman. Edmond takes the jests good-naturedly while dealing with the feelings of homesickness and heartsickness that the letter has stirred within him. His memories of parting from Octavie cause him to bury his face in his arm and to remain motionless until he falls asleep.

He dreams of a serpent coiling around his neck. When he tries to remove it, it eludes him. Then his dream turns to clamor as the small camp erupts into scrambled movements. One of the soldiers bellows at Edmond to get his duds.

Overhead a black bird asks, "What's it all about?" The bird, wise and old, watches the commotion of battle all day and concludes that he is watching children play a game, which he can decipher if he watches long enough. When he gains understanding, he flies away toward the plain. As the bird flies, a priest, whose duty is to bring comfort to dying soldiers, is making his way across the plain with a Negro. The priest discovers one soldier, "a mere boy," lying lifeless on the plain, his face to the sky. Around the young soldier's neck is a golden chain and locket, which the priest, his old eyes teary, removes. While an angelus rings nearby, the priest and the Negro kneel and recite the evening benediction and a prayer for the dead.

The second part of the story begins with Octavie out for a spring morning ride with her old friend and neighbor, Judge Pillier, who is also Edmond's father. Octavie is dressed in black, wears a veil, and carries the locket within the folds of her bodice. The locket was recently returned to her by the priest along with a letter, which she has read a hundred times. She read it just that morning, and as she rides with Pillier, she is seized by emotions of rebellion, resistance, and disbelief. She resigns herself to becoming "old and quiet and sad like Aunt Tavie."

Pillier asks Octavie if she will remove her veil, for it seems incongruent with the beauty of the spring day. Octavie complies, and Pillier requests that she not put it on again.

Approaching Pillier's house, he asks her if a spring day like this one might not create a miracle, even bring back the dead. Octavie first finds herself in a dream-like state and then finds herself in Edmond's arms.

When Octavie later produces the locket with a questioning look, Edmond explains that his messmate stole it from him the night before the battle. **(EP)**

***

Seyersted 1969a: The story may have been rejected because its depiction of battlefield corpses was too graphic (77). **Peterson 1972:** This story was turned down for good reason: it is not especially skillful. Chopin's motives for writing seem to have been mainly financial, and the soldiers' conversation seems especially unsuccessful. Nonetheless, despite the weaknesses of this work, Chopin would shortly begin writing her great novel (171). **Ewell 1986:** Although Chopin trimmed the original opening of the story and tightened other sections, it seems to have been rejected by the nine or ten publications to which she submitted it. The two protagonists are not described in much detail, and the story line depends on the device of mistaken identity, which is used more effectively in "The Story of an Hour." The military descriptions, however, are effective, as is the use of parallels and the imagery of seasons, by which Chopin underscores the foolishness of conflict. Octavie's ambivalent pain, set against a background of seasonal renewal, is similar to the confused responses of the birds: both reactions exemplify the paradoxes of romance and battle and thereby foreshadow the final comic twist (136–37). **Toth 1990a:** This is the only tale in which Chopin depicts warfare directly (70); its description of battlefield vultures was realistic (165). The bleak tone of the story, plus the fact that its author was a woman, may help explain why it was so often rejected during a period of American enthusiasm for war (282). **Fusco 1994:** This is one of several late stories in which Chopin tricks her audience (153). **Koloski 1994:** This story was included in a 1988 anthology of women's tales about the Civil War. Many of these works depict new roles for women, but Chopin's shows how females are encouraged to de-emphasize the realities of conflict (25). The story is included in a soft-cover collection of Chopin's fiction published in 1981 (27). **Toth and Seyersted 1998:** This story is mentioned in Chopin's account books (143, 150). **Benfey 1999:** Here as elsewhere Chopin deals with the theme of return, linking it to revival and rejuvenation (235–36). **Toth 1999c:** No publisher was interested in this dark piece (32).

"Loka"

Written: 1892. First published: 1892. Included in *Bayou Folk*
(1894).

Loka is a half-breed Indian girl who appears in Natchitoches
one day, begging for food at the side door of an oyster saloon. The
owner puts her to washing glasses, but that job does not work out,
since she breaks too many, some accidentally and some over the
heads of customers. In exasperation Frobissaint, the owner, grabs
her and takes her before the Band of United Endeavor, a group of
the leading ladies in town who help the underprivileged. The girl
tells them she is called Loka, but she does not know her age or
where she belongs. Loka is not pretty; she is big-boned and
clumsy, dressed in rags, and even dirty. The Band finally decide to
place her with the Padues, a respectable 'Cadian family with many
small children. There Loka will work and be trained in good
morals, too.

Loka is afraid she will step on one of the Padue children, since
they are so little and lively and her feet are so big. But she falls in
love with Bibine, the baby, who can not run under her feet.
Madame Padue, however, does not fall in love with Loka. Loka
can not speak French, and she is too slow for the madame's taste.
Yet Monsieur Padue, who is more easy-going than his wife, reminds her that the girl is only a child.

One day, Loka is instructed to care for Bibine while the rest of
the family go to town shopping. After Loka finishes her chores, she
watches Bibine play in his swing until he falls asleep. Then she
leans back in her rocking chair and gazes at the field and river before her and the deep woods beyond. She begins to day-dream
about her past life with the Indians. Even though she had often
been beaten and was made to cheat and lie, it was a life with which
she was comfortable. Loka stands up, longing to run away, but one
look at Bibine convinces her that she can not leave him.

Later that day, when the Padues return, there is no sign of either Loka or Bibine. Madame Padue panics, sending everyone
looking in different places. Still, no Indian girl and no baby can be
found. Finally, François calls from the top of a tree that he sees
Loka in the melon patch. Monsieur Padue rides down and returns
with Bibine in his arms, and Loka is trudging behind. Madame
Padue is so distraught that she will not listen to Loka's explanation
that the two had just taken a little walk in the woods. She screams

that she is going to send Loka straight back to the Band that sent her there. Loka pleads that only Bibine kept her from running back to Bayou Choctaw and a life of stealing and lying that day: "Don' sen' me 'way frum Bibine!" Monsieur Padue leads Loka away, promising that he will straighten things out. A little later he returns to confront Madame Padue. He reminds her that he, not she, is the master in the house. Moreover, he tells her she must listen to the truth for once. She has been too hard on Loka, who is not a bad girl. Also, Loka has told them that the only thing that saved her from temptation today was little Bibine. Madame Padue can not take Loka's guardian angel away from her. Placing his hand softly on his wife's head he says, "We got to rememba she ent like you an' me, po' thing; she's one Injun, her." **(CY)**

***

Rankin 1932: Loka reflects the kind of person Chopin probably met during her time in Cloutierville (103). The tale stirred response when published in a magazine for youth on December 22, 1892 (133). **Peterson 1972:** Although this story is less effective than "Beyond the Bayou," it is also less maudlin. Although the ending is a bit stagy, the preceding tensions are real. The tale juxtaposes two lifestyles and shows that their impact on persons are more important than their supposed ethics. Chopin here avoids the simple didacticism of some of her earlier works, although the story might have proved offensive if the heroine had been white. The ending, though, is possibly ironic, even though the tale generally follows Chopin's early emphasis on final resolutions of problems (66–69). **Rocks 1972:** This is one of many stories in which Chopin suggests that each person must decide whether it is better to be content with one's present condition or attempt to alter one's future. The results of either choice cannot be predicted. The story implies that pain sometimes provides the incentive for change. Here as elsewhere in Chopin's fiction, a female is forced, by facing restrictions, into a new level of self-consciousness (115–16). The story demonstrates the complexities liberty can involve and shows that true liberty often entails a responsible concern for others (117). **Arner 1975:** This story shows additional progress in Chopin's ability to depict thoughts and feelings, particularly by emphasizing the recollections of the title character. Loka's agonizing choice, however, is still presented from an external point of view, and the curiosity Chopin arouses in us near the end is purchased at the cost of a damaging shift of focus away from Loka herself. Yet the story does use symbols of nature effectively if somewhat simplistically (24–25). The closing sentences are among Chopin's best. Baptiste's restrained, somewhat amusing reimposition of his male authority, like Loka's strong desire for freedom but her ultimately stronger attraction to motherhood, suggests that natural impulses need not be uncivilized. Baptiste's yearning for freedom is simply more sublimated than Loka's (48–50). As in "Athénaïse," a woman is reintegrated into society by her love of a child (55). **Bonner 1977:** In this story, intense affection prompts a renunciation of freedom (11). The story shows the struggle between self-concern and concern for others (11). In this story Chopin illustrates the social and ethnic hierarchy of Louisiana (12). **Lattin 1980:** This story is one of many in which Chopin presents recurring characters—in this case Alphonse and Suzanne Laballière (25). **Fluck 1982:** This story illustrates Chopin's frequent tendency to associate regression with freedom (166). **Dyer 1983–84:** This is one of various stories by Chopin in which characters gain insight, win resolve, and feel freer after experiencing nature (75). In this story nature seems both liberating and dangerous, and although Loka's memories of people from her natural past seem ambiguous, her feelings about the natural world itself are far more positive. Both the Indian girl and the white husband yearn for some measure of freedom (76). Loka's response to nature is primarily non-intellectual (77). The natural imagery here resembles Chopin's use of sea imagery in *The Awakening* (80–81). **Aherne 1985:** This is one of Chopin's stories that emphasize children (83). The title character is one of the many fascinating women Chopin depicted (although she did less well in characterizing men [84]). **Dyer 1985:** In this as in other tales, Chopin relies on readers' stereotypes about unconventional characters in order to deal with topics she might not have been able to depict otherwise (80). **Skaggs 1985:** This is one of several tales depicting unusually independent girls. Although her sense of self is threatened on several levels, she nonetheless ultimately makes a noble choice (12–14). **Ewell 1986:** This is the only tale in which Chopin focuses on an American Indian protagonist. Although the story features memorable speeches and a nice touch of satire in its subtle mockery of female do-gooders, it is handicapped by its reliance on racial caricature. Native American culture seems equated with brutality and lies, and Loka herself seems both wild and unintelligent. Nonetheless, the story does nicely portray Loka's ambiguous response to her new life and shows the strong appeal of nature (69). Here as in "The Maid of Saint Philippe," Indian life is associated to some degree with liberty (81). **Inge 1989:** Whereas motherly feelings lead the main character of "Beyond the Bayou" to an experience of liberation, here they prove ultimately confining. Loka exemplifies a common human impulse to return to nature. Paradoxically (according to Baptiste, in any case), her attraction to motherhood may prevent her from returning to a life of abuse. In the final scene Baptiste reclaims a male power that Chopin seems to associate here with the safety and stability offered by a patriarchal society. Although her existence in the wild gave Loka a broader taste of life than was true of her time with the Cajuns, ultimately she chooses the obligations to society that come with maturity, even if those obligations necessarily narrow her range of options (95). **Toth 1990a:** This story, which realistically describes a device for infant care (152), may also reflect Chopin's personal disenchantment with female "do-gooders" (210). Certainly the story is her sharpest depiction of women from Cloutierville, and the title character of this perhaps deceptively conventional narrative bears a name similar to that of a local woman (213–14). The narrative is one of only a few by Chopin depicting exemplary husbands (224) and was highly praised by one male reader (328). **Robinson 1992:** This is one of many stories by Chopin that depict harmony between ethnic groups—a harmony that was not entirely unknown or unrealistic following the Civil War (xix). **Koloski 1994:** The story is included in a soft-cover collection of Chopin's fiction published in 1992 (28). **Saar 1994:** Here as elsewhere in Chopin's fiction, an initially assertive woman eventually succumbs to a conventional woman's role (68–69). **Toth 1994:** Loka is a parody of a woman with whose husband Chopin had an affair (11). **Bender 1996:** Chopin's Darwinian views help explain the story's depiction of Loka as almost a savage (107). **Koloski 1996:** Laballière appears elsewhere in Chopin's fiction (21). One of Chopin's children's tales focusing on female adolescents coming of age, it also deals with the desire for selfhood and safety (71–72; 87). **Toth and Seyersted 1998:** This story alludes unflatteringly to the wife of a man with whom Chopin was involved (126). The work is mentioned in Chopin's account books (139, 149, 159). **Koloski 1999:** This is one of many stories by Chopin which either feature children or were written for them (xxii). Here as elsewhere she describes a feminine adolescent's maturation (xxiii). **Toth 1999b:** The title character, based on the wife of a man with whom Chopin was involved, is depicted as unattractive, unappealing, and unintelligent (47). **Toth 1999c:** This story shows Chopin's familiarity with the care of infants in Louisiana (89), but it also suggests her contempt for a specific romantic rival (99; 108) as well as for women's organizations (127; 141). The work was quickly accepted by a young persons' magazine, but it probably contains jabs at both a former lover and his wife, and it presents perhaps the least attractive woman Chopin ever depicted. The woman on whom the title character was based never forgave Chopin for ruining her marriage (141). Writing the story, however, seemed to help Chopin put the past behind her and allowed her to focus on her craft (142). This is the only story in *Bayou Folk* depicting an affectionate husband (151), although, like many of her other tales, it emphasizes the kindness of women (154).

"A Louisiana Snow"
See "A December Day in Dixie"

"Love on the Bon-Dieu"

Written: 1891. First published: 1892. Included in *Bayou Folk*
(1894).

A young girl waits all afternoon on the veranda of Père Antoine's cottage adjoining the church. It is Easter eve and the priest
is occupied hearing confessions. The girl is thin and frail; in fact,
she looks undernourished, and her clothing seems cheap. She
holds in her lap a package of eggs wrapped in a bandana. Still, she
has good features, pretty light brown hair, and gray eyes that look
out with interest at the people passing in the street. A strong,
handsome young man with a kind face stops by several times
looking for the priest. Finally, he sits down and talks with the girl.
He soon discovers that she lives on the Bon-Dieu river, past his
own place.

When Père Antoine arrives, he calls the young man Azenor
and the young girl Lalie. He teases Lalie about her ill-tempered
grandmother, but she makes no comment. She simply asks the
père to write a note to a store owner so that he will sell her new
Easter shoes on the promise of her weekly payment with eggs.
Père Antoine is glad to do this, but he feels no special concern for
her. After Lalie leaves, the priest tells Azenor that her grandmother
mistreats the child. Why, there is gossip that she even beats her.

The next morning at church, Azenor stands and watches the
people as they come in. All the young girls are finely dressed, and
every one of them carries a basket filled with colored Easter eggs—
everyone except Lalie, that is. She wears the same clothes she had
worn the day before, with a veil instead of a hat, and she carries no
Easter basket. After the service, all the young people gather in a
friendly cluster, but no one speaks to Lalie. Azenor goes over to
her. Saying that she must have forgotten her eggs, he hands her his
"pretties'" one. When he returns to the others, they chide him for
talking to such a low, dishonest person, but he is angered by their
comments.

After that, Azenor begins noticing Lalie. Indeed, he walks with
her each Sunday after mass. He shows her a short-cut home across
his cotton-field, and one Sunday, she happily tells him she has a
job as a field hand. Although he begs her not to do this, she is
proud of the work. When she is not at church the next Sunday,
Azenor asks Père Antoine about her and is told that Lalie is sick.
He leaves at once and goes straight into the woods where he had

seen Lalie go. When he finds what must be her cabin and knocks on the door, he hears no response. Then, he looks through a window and sees Lalie lying on a shabby bed, gravely ill. He goes inside and kneels beside her bed, torn with grief to see her so sick and neglected. He is angry as well—angry at himself, at Père Antoine, and at everyone in the village. They all had known she was mistreated, but because she did not complain they felt her suffering was not too bad. He knows she must be taken out of this place if she is to live, so he lifts her in his arms. When her hand comes from beneath the pillow, his Easter egg rolls from it. Immediately, the truth strikes him. Lalie and Azenor are bound together; she loves him as he loves her. No need now to go from house to house searching for someone with Christ-like love to care for Lalie; he will take her home and care for her himself. He walks all the way, carrying her in his arms, until he places her on his own couch. Cautioning his housekeeper to attend to Lalie closely while he goes for the doctor, Azenor adds, "She is goin' to live! Do you think I would let my wife die?" **(CY)**

***

Anonymous 1894 [*The Critic*]: This story is even richer than some of the others with which it was first collected (41). **Rankin 1932:** Characters and events in this story may have been loosely inspired by Chopin's time in Cloutierville (103). The tale was eventually published in a then-new forum for short fiction (133). **Bush 1957:** Like some of Chopin's other best stories, this one focuses on love—in this case on its transforming powers. Lalie is one of Chopin's best creations, partly because of the author's manipulation of perspective. As in other works, a period of potentially tragic ambiguity is suddenly resolved in a way that satisfies the protagonist (245–47). **Peterson 1972:** The maudlin ending of the tale is appropriate to the relatively light tone of this piece (71). **Rocks 1972:** Here as elsewhere Chopin shows the complexities but also the rewards of marriage as well as its superiority to remaining single (118). **Arner 1975:** This story illustrates the weaknesses that often resulted from Chopin's over-reliance on local-color techniques. The characters are depicted in psychologically superficial ways, and the influences of their environment seem to pose no real problems to the people who populate the story (20). The shortcomings of this tale are typical of many of Chopin's early stories about love and marriage. Here as elsewhere, the somewhat crude settings and characters contrast with an intriguing theme (55–56; 64). **Ringe 1975:** This story illustrates the range of social classes depicted in Chopin's fiction (159). **Bonner 1977:** This is one of several stories from *Bayou Folk* in which travel is a key device of plot (8). The story shows the evolution of love (10). The story shows the struggle between self-concern and concern for others (11).

Wolff 1979: This tale is one of Chopin's many realistic variations on the theme of marriage (213). **Lattin 1980:** This is one of various stories by Chopin featuring repeating characters (28). **Baym 1981:** The story exemplifies Chopin's depiction of Cajuns (xix). **Dyer 1981b:** Although imagery of darkness may at first seem to be used fairly conventionally in this tale (as a symbol of evil), other aspects of the imagery are less predictable and contribute to the characterization of Azenor, particularly of his hesitation (219; 221). The night imagery is effectively ambiguous and disturbing and relates well to Azenor's own thinking (222). **Bonner 1982:** This is one of various stories by Chopin that emphasize the specifics of Christian religious practice (123–24). **Davis 1982:** The instantaneous affection the tale describes seems more credible because the story is set in a tiny place where most of the characters already know one another (64). **Rogers 1983:** The heroine of this tale resembles a particular character created by George Sand (40–41). **Aherne 1985:** This is the most affecting tale in *Bayou Folk*. It illustrates Chopin's profound appreciation of the importance of Catholicism for the Louisiana folk she described. Here as elsewhere, she also emphasizes how poor those folk often were. The priest in this work is completely attractive (83). **Skaggs 1985:** This is one of several tales focusing on the interaction of affection and selfhood (17). As elsewhere, Chopin here explores mental problems (17). **Ewell 1986:** This story explores the complexities of affection by focusing on its uncertainties. Although the tale is not told especially smoothly, it nicely depicts the challenges lovers face and the problems caused by being poor. A number of characters are effectively drawn, particularly the grandmother, the servant, and the priest (76). **Toth 1990a:** The priest in this story was modeled on a cleric from Cloutierville whom Chopin respected but whose shortcomings may be implied here. The story realistically depicts encounters between men and women in rural Louisiana (168). It is typical of Chopin's popular local color writing but already shows an interest in potentially touchy topics (201–2). The merchant in this tale was based on a real person (224). **Toth 1990b:** Here as in other works, Chopin mocks the priest of her local Louisiana parish (290). **Toth 1992:** Here as elsewhere Chopin creates characters whose names resemble those of real persons (16). **Shurbutt 1993:** This is one of a few stories in which Chopin seems to accept conventional views of the relations between the sexes (22). **Cutter 1994:** Lalie typifies the often reticent women Chopin depicted early in her career (19). **Ewell 1994:** This was one of Chopin's early stories that helped make her aware of the market for local color fiction (160). It exemplifies the ambiguous role that such fiction played in the national culture of the time (160–63). **Koloski 1994:** The story is included in soft-cover collections of Chopin's fiction published in 1981 and 1992 (27). **Bender 1996:** In this tale, nature eventually assumes the role of "good god" by leading the male to act with an assertiveness Darwin would have predicted (106–7). This is one of various stories in which Chopin's basically Darwinian outlook leads her to examine the problems caused by an insufficiently assertive male (107). **Koloski 1996:** The tale is set on a holiday and is one of several children's stories by Chopin that depict the poor (11; 71; 87). **Wagner-Martin 1996:** As in many of her tales, Chopin here depicts an altruistic young man—this time in a somewhat melodramatic context (202). Here, too, she typically portrays an appealing black female (203). **Toth and Seyersted 1998:** This story is mentioned in Chopin's account books (139, 148, 172). **Koloski 1999:** This is one of many stories by Chopin which either feature children or were written for them (xxii). **Toth 1999c:** The priest in this story is based on one Chopin knew (92), while the tale shows that in Louisiana even a church could be the scene of a romantic rendezvous (96). One character shares the name of a local acquaintance of Chopin (140). The story depicts the follies of love (151) but presents women in an attractive light (154). **Gibbons 2000:** This work is a standard local color tale. Both the hero and the heroine are stereotypes, as are many of the other characters. Nature imagery is amateurishly used. The story explores no psychological depths and challenges no conventional expectations (xxx–xxxi).

"The Lover of Mentine"
See "A Visit to Avoyelles"

"Ma'ame Pélagie"

Written: 1892. First published: 1893. Included in *Bayou Folk* (1894).

When the war began, Côte Joyeuse was a majestic brick mansion styled after the Pantheon and surrounded by a grove of live oak trees. Thirty years later, however, the great house is in ruins, with only the walls and the huge round pillars still standing. The lives of the inhabitants are in ruins too. Ma'ame Pélagie, who is called "Ma'ame" even though at fifty years of age she is still unmarried, now lives in a three-roomed log cabin nearby the ruins. Mam'selle Pauline, her thirty-five-year-old sister, whom Ma'ame Pélagie still considers a child, shares the cabin. She also shares Ma'ame Pélagie's dream of restoring the old home to its former grandeur and regaining their lost gracious lives. In order to achieve this dream the two have lived like paupers and saved every bit of money they possibly could. When they sit outside on pleasant afternoons, drinking their coffee and savoring their plans, Ma'ame Pélagie would ask Mam'selle Pauline if she were willing to do this and always received the same reply: "Just as you please." Their brother, Léandre, the only son of the house, had left the management of the plantation to his older sister and gone into the business world. Now, all these years later, he was sending his motherless daughter to stay with her aunts at Côte Joyeuse. Ma'ame Pélagie calms Mam'selle Pauline's doubts about La Petite by saying the girl is a true Valmêt and will sleep on a cot and live as they do; her father would have told her about their lifestyle.

When La Petite arrives, with her pink cheeks and eyes that mirror a quiet joy, she fits herself into her aunts' restricted world. Yet she brings strong feelings of another alien world into their dreamlike existence. She often helps Mam'selle Pauline with the household duties, chattering all the while about her past life. Mam'selle Pauline fairly blossoms with this companionship, but although La Petite seems to return her affection, she becomes quiet and thoughtful. Finally, she tells Ma'ame Pélagie and Mam'selle Pauline that despite her love for them, she can no longer live as they live at Côte Joyeuse. Ma'ame Pélagie feels a certain inner satisfaction at this confession, but Mam'selle Pauline is inconsolable. At last, Ma'ame Pélagie promises her sister that La Petite will not go away.

That night, Ma'ame Pélagie walks to the ruins and reminisces about the life before the war. She remembers that she had pledged to herself that Pauline must not get hurt. She thinks of the night that Felix came home with her to speak to her father, but news of the war shattered their pleasant dreams. Then the men were gone, and the enemy came and set fire to the mansion, forcing Pélagie to flee while carrying Pauline in her arms, wrapped in a blanket. Now, hugging one of the big pillars, Ma'ame Pélagie vows aloud that Pauline must not be hurt.

By the time a year has passed, everything has changed at Côte Joyeuse. The ruins are gone and so is the log cabin. Instead there is an attractive wooden structure resting on a solid brick foundation, situated out in the open in the sunshine. More than that, the new home is filled with the laughter of young people, and Léandre comes often, using it as his country home. La Petite plays the piano, and Pauline grows younger every day. Only Ma'ame Pélagie continues her old ways. She always wears black, and she has aged by years since the night she gave up her dream in order to protect Pauline. Ma'ame Pélagie could force her body to walk in the light of this new life, but she could not take her soul from the shadow. (CY)

***

Rankin 1932: This tale is an excellent depiction of a woman whose constricted life is dominated by a fantastic hope. With a delicacy that is not maudlin, Chopin explores the destructiveness of war and the force of fantasy (135). The story uses the Civil War merely as background rather than emphasizing it strongly (140). **Seyersted 1969a:** In her only story focused on the plantation myth, Chopin subtly sympathizes with the younger women rather than with their nostalgic elder (94). **Seyersted 1969b:** The story suggests the importance of focusing on the future, not dwelling on the past (26). **Peterson 1972:** This story focuses on contrasting lifestyles and conflicting personal values. The title character is persuasively depicted. The skillful ending is marred by extraneous commentary. Nonetheless, Chopin shows progress in this tale by refusing to provide a concluding lesson. Each lifestyle is given its due, and the apparent resolution is effectively ambiguous (105–8). **Rocks 1972:** Here as elsewhere Chopin shows the price one often pays for one's obsessions (117). **Arner 1975:** Images of buildings are effectively used throughout the story. The title character resembles some characters in Faulkner in her obsession with the past, but Chopin shows some sympathy for her dreams, and in the end the new house (representing family and the present world) is constructed atop the foundation of the old (45–47). **Ringe 1975:** This tale is relevant to Chopin's novel *At Fault*, not only because both works share several characters but also because the story illustrates the effects of the Civil War on the society the novel describes (158). **Bonner 1977:** This is one of only three stories in *Bayou Folk* in which the author comments (7). Here as elsewhere in the collection, Chopin uses time-alterations as an important device (9). As in other *Bayou Folk* tales, the focus here on a threatened child helps resolve the plot (10). The story illustrates Christian self-sacrifice and shows the struggle between self-concern and concern for others (11). The story explores the topic of the young vs. the old (13). This is one of the best stories in *Bayou Folk* (13). **Lattin 1978:** Here as often in her fiction, Chopin explores the theme of substitute motherhood (2). **Taylor 1979:** Although this story involves female suffering, it also shows how nearly all persons are handicapped by social conventions (xviii). **Lattin 1980:** This is one of various stories featuring members of the intriguing Santien family (21). **Dyer 1981b:** In this work Chopin uses night imagery more effectively than in some earlier works, employing it subtly to characterize the title character and her change of mind. Night is linked with the past, but the overtones are complex rather than simplistic. The disappearance of the moon symbolizes her new perception (219–20). **Jones 1981:** This tale is Chopin's only explicit treatment of the South before and after the Civil War. It manages to present the attractions of the old way of life while still showing the need to move on (152–53). **Bonner 1982:** This is one of various stories by Chopin that reflect the importance of selfless Christian love (119). **Lattin 1982:** In this story Chopin tragically suggests that renewal is sometimes impossible (228–29). **Aherne 1985:** The title character is one of the many fascinating women Chopin depicted (although she did less well in characterizing men [84]). **Dyer 1985:** This is one of several tales by Chopin about extreme nostalgia (74). **Newman 1986:** As in other tales, Chopin here contrasts real life with the stereotypes of fiction (161). **Skaggs 1985:** This is one of several stories featuring characters whose lives and minds have been disrupted by the Civil War (15). **Ewell 1986:** This is Chopin's one developed depiction of the widespread Southern ideal of the happy days before the Civil War. Its title character is one of Chopin's most forceful people, although she now seems fixated on a bye-gone time. Imagery of buildings is used to reinforce the main choice the protagonist must confront: her and her sister's lives are now as confined as their small cabin. Pélagie's dream is effectively described, creating a striking contrast between remembered glory and present decay. After the dream, however, she is motivated by affection (symbolized by the planet Venus) to build a new life and home for her sister and niece. The story shows the kinds of losses women can suffer during war (significantly, Pélagie's brother long ago gave up on the old life and the old home). Chopin depicts the two sisters with compassion but (unlike other authors) does not romanticize the past. It is gone for good, and to focus on it too much is to rob the present of its potential. Although Pélagie fades rapidly after she relinquishes her memories, she is nonetheless surrounded by vitality (65–66). This story was added to *Bayou Folk* when "Mamouche" could not be included (95). **Papke 1988:** Here as elsewhere Chopin scrutinizes conventional views of women by setting them in a complex social and historical context (73–74). **Inge 1989:** Although she is a spinster, the title character is aptly called "Madame" because she is wedded to her ideal, which hampers her life even after she finally rejects it (95). Her mind is locked into a pattern that she affirms even while seeming to abandon it, since she still remains obsessed with her almost-maternal commitment to her sister. Chopin's narrative stance is less distanced in this story than it would be in some of her later, more successful tales, but this work is significant in revealing Chopin's interest and skill in depicting the thoughts and feelings of her characters (96). The title character is especially well drawn; her inconsistent impulses are credibly depicted (96–97). **Papke 1990:** Chopin here rejects an optimistic conclusion. She shows the oppressive aspects of conventional ideals of feminine behavior (60). Although this tale is less complex than "Désirée's Baby," their endings are similar. The title character embodies traditional views of women, and she never completely gives them up but finally remains controlling and isolated despite her limited change of mind. She dominates her sister as she strives to be part of a long-gone, cocoon-like community—an aspiration that distorts her perceptions of others. Her sister's change of heart leaves Pélagie with no one to control, no one who will function as her mirror. Although Pélagie adapts superficially, in the end she remains remote and obsessed with self-destructive, willful ignorance. Her fantasies are sometimes both romantic and rooted in meanness, racism, and oppression, and even her notions of self-sacrifice are fundamentally selfish. She chooses to remain trapped in a completely negative existence, even after giving up her almost predatory control of her sister and niece. The niece, however, perhaps symbolizes Chopin's optimistic view of women as potentially active agents of positive change, while Pauline prefigures feminine characters in Chopin's later fiction who awaken and grow (56–60). **Toth 1990a:** This is one of several stories in which Chopin depicts the consequences of the Civil War in bleak terms (70), and Chopin herself knew of such consequences (142). Here she tells one of her most somber stories of Louisiana life and was perhaps influenced by memories of a ruined mansion she once knew (214–15). This story was placed with four others on adult dilemmas at the end of *Bayou Folk* (224). **Koloski 1994:** The story is included in soft-cover collections of Chopin's fiction published in 1979 and 1981 (27). **Koloski 1996:** This tale both resembles and differs from "A No-Account Creole," particularly in its outcome. Both stories center on a home and on the impact of a visitor associated with new possibilities. The house becomes symbolic of the title character's choices and fate; perhaps Chopin intended this story to be read along with "A No-Account Creole" (15–19; 21; 24). The motif of the visitor may reflect Chopin's reading of George Sand (84). **Toth and Seyersted 1998:** This story is mentioned in Chopin's account books (140, 149, 154–55). **Koloski 1999:** This story features several motifs common to Chopin's fiction: construction of a house, a significant visitor, the appeal of days gone by, and the effort to achieve equilibrium (xiv–xv). **McCullough 1999:** The central character here represents the past of both her gender and her region (316). **Toth 1999c:** Like most of Chopin's best Civil War tales, this one focuses on female characters (33). Chopin later knew a woman who lived on the plantation the story describes (137). This was one of the darker tales included in *Bayou Folk* (151), although it does present the generous side of women (154).

"Madame Célestin's Divorce"

1893. Included in *Bayou Folk* (1894).

Lawyer Paxton always sees Madame Celéstin sweeping her gallery. He thinks she looks pretty, and he also enjoys leaning over her fence to talk with her. Madame Celéstin enjoys their conversations, too. Holding her train in one hand and balancing her broom gracefully with the other, she discusses her troubles with him. Everyone in Natchitoches parish knows of her troubles. For instance, they all know that she supports her two little ones by taking in sewing, giving music lessons, and doing other labor. Madame Celéstin fairly glows with satisfaction at Paxton's praise. Besides, she adds, she has not seen her husband in four months nor received any money from him in all that time, either.

When Paxton accuses her husband of deserting her and hints that he would not be surprised to learn he has even mistreated her, Madame Celéstin replies, "Well, you know, Judge, a man that drinks—w'at can you expec?" Lawyer Paxton advises her not to stand it any longer and says the divorce court is there to remedy her situation. Madame Celéstin remembers that he has mentioned divorce before, but now she is going to think about it. Every day when he passes, the two discuss the divorce, and lawyer Paxton grows deeply concerned with the subject. Of course, her family are all opposed to a divorce, since they are Catholic Creoles. She will just have to face their opposition and be brave, Paxton advises. Although she plans to consult her confessor, she also vows that no confessor in the world can stop her. A few days later, Paxton finds her waiting for him with fresh determination in her eyes. Madame Celéstin relates how the confessor has just washed his hands of so big a scandal and said she must see the bishop. Paxton grows anxious and stutters that she must not let the bishop change her mind. "You don't know me yet, Judge," she laughs. When she reports on her conference with the bishop, lawyer Paxton holds on to the pickets of her fence, eagerly listening. She says that the bishop was so eloquent she had to cry, but she is resolved to follow through with her plans.

Soon a change becomes noticeable in lawyer Paxton. He begins to wear his Sunday coat to the office. He shines his shoes and is particular about his tie. He even grooms and trims his whiskers with special care. Then he begins to daydream as he walks about town. He decides it is time for him to take a wife, and that no woman can fill that position except Madame Celéstin. If Natchitoches will not accept them, there are other places to live.

His heart leaps one morning as he passes her house and sees her sweeping the walk right near the hedge. She looks unusually pink and fetching as she twirls the broom handle in her hand and looks up at him. Then, hesitating, she tells lawyer Paxton she reckons he should forget about her divorce. "You see, Judge, Celéstin came home las' night. An' he's promise me on his word an' honor he's going to turn ova a new leaf." **(CY)**

***

Beale 1911: For composing this tale, Chopin deserves a lofty place in the history of American short fiction (63). **Pattee 1923:** Célestin typifies the complexity and vitality of Chopin's characters, while the very ending of the story—so unexpected, conclusive, and yet credible—illustrates the skill with which Chopin often crafted her finales (326). **Reilly 1942:** This story illustrates the tendency of Chopin's heroines to remain loyal once they have made a romantic commitment (132–33). **Fletcher 1966:** Here as in other stories focused on Creole women, Chopin's heroine demonstrates a typical fidelity despite her sufferings (127). **Arms 1967:** This work takes an unusual approach to depicting opposed views, finding humor in the stubbornness of feelings subjected to stress (223). **Seyersted 1969a:** The story, written at around the same time as "An Idle Fellow" (which has a distinctly different emphasis), depicts a Catholic woman willing to consider risking condemnation to achieve freedom (110–11). The story represents a high-point of Chopin's artistry, and the sudden final turn-about is entirely consistent with the main protagonist's inconsistent character, which is treated by Chopin with efficiency, distance, and wit (122–23). **Leary 1970a:** This tale is extremely simple but also subtle and convincing, especially as a study in character (ix). **Leary 1971:** This tale typifies the tendency of Chopin's stories to be rather basic in plot but often highly complex in depicting persons (165–66). **Peterson 1972:** This very fine realistic work was composed around the same time Chopin turned out less accomplished pieces (10). It is one of her most effective pieces focusing on a personality. Here as elsewhere, Chopin shows how people perceive experience from their own points of view, and she also shows how persons often follow their heads rather than their hearts. The ultimate change in the heroine's complexion, however, suggests that her decision is not entirely based on logic. The story ends on a skillful note of irresolution (116–17). This story is one of Chopin's finest (120). **Rocks 1972:** Here as elsewhere Chopin shows the complexities but also the rewards of marriage as well as its superiority to remaining single (118). **Seyersted 1974:** This work and others justify Chopin's reputation as a superb writer of local color fiction (11). **Arner 1975:** Chopin here shows the strong force of affection, even in a woman capable of resisting male power (57). **Solomon 1976:** This tale illustrates Chopin's frequent focus on diverse kinds of courting (xv). **Bonner 1977:** Here as elsewhere in *Bayou Folk,* Chopin uses a sudden twist to create irony (9). The story treats potential adultery in a comic way (11). The story explores the topic of secular vs. religious views of divorce (13) and foreshadows Chopin's focus later in her career on sexual attraction (13–14). **Howell 1979b:** Here as elsewhere Chopin makes no obvious religious argument; instead, the Creole cultural solidarity holds firm and the American lawyer loses (105). **Taylor 1979:** This is one of several of her stories that subtly suggest the shortcomings of Catholicism (x). The title character's sudden change at the end reflects a general tendency of Southerners to adapt to the demands of nature (xii). **Wolff 1979:** This tale stands in intriguing contrast to "The Story of an Hour," but here as in that tale Chopin does not moralize on the topic of marriage (213). **Lattin 1980:** This is one of various stories by Chopin featuring repeating characters (28). **Dyer 1981a:** This is one of several stories by Chopin that use repeating male professional characters, thus adding depth and continuity to her fiction (54). **Bonner 1982:** This story reflects Chopin's often comic attitude toward the intricacies of Catholic worship (123). **Stein 1984:** Here as elsewhere, Chopin presents a wife who ultimately is happy to submit to her husband (176). The circumstances here resemble those in "A Visit to Avoyelles." Madame Célestin seems most fulfilled when she is fulfilling the feminine stereotypes of her culture. The description of her hands may imply the sadistic aspects of her marriage, but she finally seems content with the relationship, and Chopin does not judge her choice but instead merely reports it (178). **Aherne 1985:** The story illustrates Chopin's range in depicting female characters (82). **Newman 1986:** Like many of Chopin's tales, this one suggests a view of marriage that seems to conflict with the views implied by some of her other stories. This work eventually seems to affirm traditional ideas about the value of matrimony (152). Like other works by Chopin, this one explores the interaction of affection and selfhood (17). The title character is identified only as a wife; her freely bestowed love, not social pressures, finally determines the outcome (21). **Ewell 1986:** Chopin's talent for creating complicated and understated conclusions appears in this superb tale. As in "A Visit to Avoyelles," the chief male character here seeks to save a woman who ultimately remains elusive. Effectively narrated in a quick sequence of vignettes, the story contrasts the personalities of its two main characters, with the tone of each of their exchanges becoming increasingly more serious. Célestin's handling of the almost-phallic broom symbolizes her relationship with the lawyer, while her improved complexion at the end of the story implies her returned husband's sexual skills. As readers we empathize with Paxton and feel the final disappointment that he himself never vocalizes. Both he and Célestin illustrate the power of romantic hope. Ironically, the unconventional woman behaves in the end as social convention dictates, but she does so for reasons (largely erotic) of her own. The story thus achieves subtle complexity of theme (74–76; 78). **Martin 1988a:** This story reflects

Chopin's growing interest in liberty, both in her fiction and in her own life. The work exhibits her frequent explorations of the conflicts between selflessness and self-fulfillment (6). **Inge 1989:** This is one of Chopin's most successful tales. It shows striking candor and skill in depicting an autonomous woman whose constant act of sweeping implies her strengths of character (97). Ultimately, however, she finds her husband erotically preferable to the less sensual lawyer (97–98). **Toth 1990a:** This is one of several stories in which Chopin explores female extramarital temptation (168). It also contains one of her sharpest depictions of official Catholic attitudes toward marriage and perhaps was influenced by her own recent personal life. Although the story somewhat half-heartedly reaffirms marriage, it was still turned down by the magazine to which Chopin sent it (220). This tale was one of four previously unpublished stories included in *Bayou Folk* and is one of five near the end of that collection that focus on adult dilemmas (223–24). This is one of almost ten stories Chopin wrote in four years that deal with potential infidelity (279). **Guidici 1991:** Here as elsewhere a Chopin heroine fails to seize the opportunity for greater autonomy (31). **Shurbutt 1993:** Here as in other tales, Chopin offers an ironic perspective on the convention of the male as savior (21). **Koloski 1994:** This story was reprinted in two early anthologies—one published in 1927 and the other in print from 1930 to 1982. Neither anthologist explains why he chose this story in particular, although both make passing comments about Chopin's general traits (21). The story is included in soft-cover collections of Chopin's fiction published in 1970, 1976, 1979, and 1992 (27). **Fetterley and Pryse 1995:** This story, like others by Chopin, challenges the emphasis on New England in local color writing. The lawyer misinterprets the title character, who chooses her own path (409). **Koloski 1996:** This clever, alluring tale features a single setting, engaging characters, a symbolic broom, erotic undertones, and significantly contrasting personalities. In the end Madame Célestin remains circumscribed (26–27) within a symbolic boundary (68). **Toth and Seyersted 1998:** This story is mentioned in Chopin's account books (149, 158). **Toth 1999b:** As Bernard Koloski has demonstrated, this was one of eight stories by Chopin that were frequently republished in the twentieth century (46). **Koloski 1999:** This is one of Chopin's tales focusing on a woman's concerns and restraints (viii). Here as in other stories, Chopin depicts a character who reacts to a symbolic boundary (viii). The story is appealing and clever, and the fence is effectively emphasized, as is the symbolically erotic broom (xiv).

"Madame Martel's Christmas Eve"

Written: 1896. Included in *Complete Works* (1969).

Alone on Christmas Eve in her house, which "betokened taste as well as comfort and wealth," Madame Martel is one of those women "who make a luxury of grief." She has mourned her husband for six years, and she sits by the fire, dressed in black, holding his ambrotype in her hand, and wiping away tears with a "fine, black-bordered cambric handkerchief."

Her children are occupied elsewhere. Having "learned by experience that his mother preferred to be alone at this season," her son, Gustave, is spending the holidays with a college friend in Assumption. Her oldest child, Adélaïde, is visiting her uncle Achille in Iberville, "where there was no end of merrymaking all the year round." Young Lulu, too, was away for a few days at a friend's home across town.

Madame Martel's feelings of grief are so persistent that they begin to make her feel "nervous and unstrung." She even imagines her dead husband's presence in the house. "Suffocating with memories," she decides to take a walk.

After she has spent some time walking, her grief dissipates, but it is replaced by "a terrible loneliness." Her husband is gone, and now the children seem to be slipping away, too. As she thinks about this, her heart "suddenly turn[s] savage and hungry within her … for some expression of human love." Recalling that Lulu is nearby, she resolves to see her and to bring her daughter home with her.

As she walks resolutely toward the house where Lulu is staying, people make way for her or become silent as she passes by: "People respected her as a sort of mystery; as something above them, and to be taken very seriously."

Madame Martel's entrance into the festive atmosphere of the house, which is full of people, has an "instantaneous, depressing effect upon the whole assembly." The piano stops playing; the Convent girls stop waltzing; the old people stop talking, and the young ones stop laughing. However, this halt is only temporary as Madame Martel is quickly besieged by well-wishers.

Using as a pretense her child's illness that morning, Madame Martel explains that she only came to retrieve Lulu, but the guests will not hear of it. One guest, "a comfortably fat old lady with a talent for arranging matters," suggests that Madame Martel would never be so selfish. Not wanting to "afflict others with her own selfish desires," Madame Martel relinquishes her request for Lulu and leaves the party.

As she walks home alone, Madame Martel is plagued by the morbid mantra: "I have driven love away." She resolves to return to her thoughts, letters, and tears.

Mounting the stairs to her home, she notices that the downstairs room appears brighter than it did when she left it. Looking in the front window, she gasps. She thinks she sees her husband sitting by the fire. Though his face is turned away from her, "the poise of his head, the sweep of his arm and set of his shoulder" is familiar.

However, she disbelieves her eyes and speculates that she is losing her mind. She determines to go in, place her hand on the apparition's shoulder, and thereby dispel it. Before she can touch "her ghastly visitant," however, he rises from the chair. Madame Martel totters, and he catches her in his arms.

The apparition turns out to be Gustave, who has returned from Assumption to be with his mother on Christmas Eve despite his usual instinct to give her solitude at this time of year. Madame Martel asks Gustave to confess that he knew she wanted him. He denies this, asserting instead his selfish desire to be with his mother on Christmas Eve. He discounts her remark about a lack of festivity, saying that they may not be festive, but they will be happy. Madame Martel is "very, very happy" as she rubs her cheek against his coat sleeve and feels the "warm, firm pressure of his hand." **(EP)**

***

Seyersted 1969a: The protagonist's love of her dead husband and her fear of seeking any satisfactions aside from her memories of him may reflect Chopin's own ambivalent feelings about widowhood (72). The story illustrates the tendency among many of Chopin's characters to take intense pleasure in parties (76). **Peterson 1972:** This is one of the more intriguing of Chopin's late tales featuring a somewhat maudlin conclusion. The protagonist moves through a landscape full of contrasting symbols of mortality and vitality. If the story had ended at the party, it might have been as effective as "Regret." Instead, as in many of the late stories, the conclusion is marred by a sentimental, comforting resolution (166–68). **Rocks 1972:** Here as elsewhere Chopin shows that people often freely choose not to alter their circumstances; they elect to renounce other options, but the choice is theirs and no decision is externally imposed (118). **Bonner 1982:** This is one of several stories by Chopin that are centered on Christmas (124).

Skaggs 1985: In some respects the depiction of widowhood in this story may reflect the experiences of both Chopin's mother and perhaps even Chopin herself, although in the latter case differences seem more important than similarities (59). **Ewell 1986:** Chopin neglected to publish this story in *Bayou Folk*, perhaps because it hit too close to home. In exploring a fragile mind, the tale resembles two by Maupassant that Chopin had translated, but she implicitly censures (rather than indulges) her character's gloom. The protagonist's renewed attention to her children illustrates Chopin's own movement toward realism and away from self-indulgent sentiment (116). **Toth 1990a:** Although a young persons' magazine paid Chopin for this story, the journal did not actually publish the tale, perhaps because it seemed too serious (282–83). **Toth 1992:** Unusually, Chopin here presents a widow paralyzed by sadness (16). **Fusco 1994:** This was the first significant story in which Chopin used a plot structure emphasizing movement from bad to good to bad fortune. She wrote it while translating stories by Maupassant, although her ending is less bleak than his tend to be. The title character moves from isolation to hope and back to isolation, but in the end she is less alone than a character created by Maupassant might have been (167–69). She wins a clearer perception of the importance of family (171–72). **Koloski 1996:** This is one of several children's tales by Chopin set on a holiday (71; 87). **Toth and Seyersted 1998:** This story is mentioned in Chopin's account books (141, 150).

"A Maid and Her Lovers"
See "A No-Account Creole"

"The Maid of Saint Phillippe"

Written: 1891. First published: 1892. Included in *Complete Works* (1969).

Marianne is a seventeen-year-old French girl who lives in the colonial village of Saint Phillipe with her father, Picoté Laronce. Returning from a hunting excursion with her rifle and buckskin trappings, she looks more like a boy than a girl. When she arrives at the village tavern, she sees a group of men talking excitedly on the front porch; her father is among the number, but he is silent and holds himself aloof. Marianne asks her friend Jacques Labrie what the commotion is about. He tells her that the English will soon overtake nearby Fort Chartres and that everyone in the town, save her father, would rather salvage what building materials they can from their houses and move to St. Louis than live under English rule. Although Picoté Laronce claims that he does not want to leave his mill behind, Marianne knows that he wants to remain near his wife's grave. The young girl decides to stay with her father, and the two are left alone when the rest of the villagers strip and abandon their homes a week later. Hearing that they are living a life of solitude, Captain Alexis Vaudry rides up from Fort Chartres and asks the Laronces to return with him to their homeland, but his efforts are to no avail.

A short time later, Marianne returns from her hunting and discovers that her father has died under the maple near her mother's grave. Marianne draws strength from the awareness that she is now free to follow her own will. That night, she lovingly gathers her father's body into the house and weeps over his passing. On the following day, Marianne finds Captain Vaudry and others to help her bury her father under the maple tree. A few of the friends who come to the girl's aid in her time of need insist that she come to live with them. Captain Vaudry, for one, even proclaims his love for her and offers to give her a life of luxury in France, but, having tasted freedom, Marianne cannot bear the thought of marrying and becoming a mother to "slaves." Marianne herself refuses to be ruled by the English in Saint Phillippe, the Spanish in St. Louis, and the French in her native homeland. Because she will be in bondage to no one, Marianne literally turns her back on all the offers extended to her and leaves St. Phillippe to live with the Cherokees. **(JW)**

***

Rankin 1932: The story may have reflected tales Chopin heard as a child from her great-grandmother. Historically-based fiction had come into fashion in the 1890s, and this work was part of Chopin's response (14–15). It was printed in a venerable journal in November 1892 (133). **Zlotnick 1968:** This is one of many stories in which Chopin implies ambivalent, unconventional responses to marriage (2). **Seyersted 1969a:** This tale, the only one by Chopin rooted in historical research, fails badly (82), although Marianne does exemplify the kind of Chopin heroine who asserts independence (110). Chopin felt that the writing of this story had been full of unnatural effort (117). It was composed at around the same time as a strikingly different story, "The Going Away of Liza" (216). **Leary 1970a:** This story is more successful than "Wiser Than a God," despite its often hackneyed phrasing (xi). **Leary 1971:** Although this story is more skillfully written than "Wiser Than a God," its thought and phrasing are often stale (168). **Peterson 1972:** The heroine rejects both political and personal constraints, but the tale lacks a certain interest, the conclusion provides too pat an ending, and the heroine seems unconvincing and finally tedious (76–78). **Rocks 1972:** This is one of many stories in which Chopin suggests that each person must decide whether it is better to be content with one's present condition or attempt to alter one's future. The results of either choice cannot be predicted (115). The story shows that people often freely choose not to alter their circumstances; they elect to renounce other options, but the choice is theirs and no decision is externally imposed (118). **Arner 1975:** Although in this tale Chopin seems to have felt restricted by the need to describe setting accurately rather than to depict character insightfully, even this work has real merits. Chopin shows some talent for setting an individual life against a historical and national panorama: Marianne's rejection of domination is likened to America's, and even in her devotion to her father she assumes a traditionally male role (124–25). **Ladenson 1976:** This is perhaps the most daring of Chopin's tales and is certainly one of the most open works of nineteenth-century American fiction in its emphasis on women's autonomy and liberation. It has attracted little (or misguided) commentary. The heroine here resembles Joan of Arc, although Marianne's struggle is more personal. Like many women Chopin depicts, she is linked with nature, although she is also identified with the laboring class. She is Chopin's most radical woman, for she insists on both political and sexual freedom, and she is freer from class restraints than other Chopin heroines (25–26). **Fluck 1982:** This story shows that depicting emancipation could not guarantee the aesthetic success of a tale, since this is one of Chopin's least successful works (159). **Bonner 1983b:** Chopin endorses the heroine's unconventional self-assertion (146). **Rogers 1983:** The heroine of this story resembles one created by George Sand. Both characters, in turn, resemble Joan of Arc (40–41). **Stein 1984:** This is one of various tales in which Chopin describes the need to be true to oneself (207). **Skaggs 1985:** This relatively unsuccessful work focuses on a woman's desire for liberty (57). **Ewell 1986:** Although this story represents a new direction in Chopin's writing (it is her only effort at historical narrative), it is not entirely successful. Neither the dialogue nor the characterization seems convincing, probably because Chopin felt uncomfortable with this kind of writing. Friends may have urged her to make the attempt, and in a later essay she recounted her struggles with this project. Nevertheless, the gender-bending title character is interesting, especially in the way she uses virginity to preserve her freedom. Even though her hackneyed final choice seems to ensure a life of loneliness, it also illustrates Chopin's habit of linking nature and liberty and implies that female freedom may be unconventional but is not unnatural (80–81). **Gaudet 1986:** This story's failure

may reflect the fact that it was written to satisfy criteria for a literary contest (45). **Papke 1990:** Most of the stories Chopin wrote during this year
seem fairly predictable, perhaps because she was focusing most of her attention on calling attention to her novels. This tale, though, is one of several from this period that present unusual female protagonists (52). **Toth
1990a:** Perhaps the atmosphere and main character of the story were inspired by Chopin's knowledge of her feminine pioneer ancestors (40). After being turned down only a few times, the story was accepted. It was
only the second Chopin had written about a young woman who refuses to
marry, and it was her only narrative based on stories she had heard from
her great-grandmother. She later told why she never again undertook another historical fable, even though such fiction was widely read. Despite
her labor, others did not feel the story had succeeded (200–201). She
herself probably considered the plot and methods of the story old-
fashioned (205), but the work anticipates one of her later narratives,
"Charlie," in its focus on an assertive, tomboyish female (376). **Guidici
1991:** Marianne resembles the hunting goddess Artemis. She prefers
independence to marriage but realizes that the men courting her will find
fault with any reason she might give for refusing them. Because she lives
on the frontier, her options are more flexible than if she lived in a
structured community (27–28). **Toth 1992:** Here as elsewhere Chopin
presents a female figure who is most forceful when she is independent.
The story may have been influenced by the life of a distant relative of
Chopin (17–18). The experiences of the main female may also be relevant
to the experiences of Chopin's married mother (21–22). Here as elsewhere
Chopin shows a woman whose isolation makes freedom possible, if only
temporarily (23). In this early story Chopin could be relatively optimistic
about the prospects for feminine independence (24). **Ewell 1994:** This was
one of a number of stories Chopin wrote in early 1891 that focused on the
dilemmas of women and that were at first rejected by publishers (160).
Koloski 1994: The story is included in a soft-cover collection of Chopin's
fiction published in 1970 (27). **Saar 1994:** Although this story was quite
important in Chopin's development, it has received little analysis (59). The
tale offers some of her most unconventional views about women, partly
because it appropriates methods and topics often used by established
white American male authors (62–63). Such topics included an emphasis
on rugged individuality and the frontier, but Chopin's radical gesture was
to make the protagonist a woman (63–64). The rejection the story suffered
helped Chopin realize that further use of conventionally male stories was
pointless; she therefore turned in a distinctive direction that emphasized
feminine liberation (65). The titular character here is unusual in Chopin's
fiction because of her "masculine" traits, especially since such traits
remain unchanged and are not punished or regretted (67). She rejects
marriage but does not seem unhappy as a result (69). Chopin reverses the
conventional emphasis on the woman as a threat to a man's freedom (70).
The story may have reflected her own life (70–71) even as its poor

reception helped redirect her art (71–72). **Bender 1996:** The girl in this tale behaves with a freedom Darwin might not have predicted (106). **Koloski 1996:** This is one of various stories for young people depicting the maturation of adolescent girls (71; 87). **Toth and Seyersted 1998:** This story is mentioned in Chopin's account books (139, 169–70). **Benfey 1999:** Biographical information suggests that the plot of this tale may reflect Chopin's experiences with the White League in New Orleans, which had forcefully resisted Reconstruction. The story also links oppression and motherhood (250–51). **Toth 1999a:** This is one of various stories in which Chopin describes independent, capable women—the kind she knew from her own childhood (4). **Toth 1999c:** This tale failed to win a contest for folk fiction (125). It may have been based on the experiences of a distant ancestor; certainly it depicts marriage in an unapproving light (182). **Knights 2000:** This was one of the numerous works Chopin composed in 1891 (xv). This is one of various works in which Chopin juxtaposes an individual life with a larger social context (xviii–xix). This tale may be more complex in its engagement with previous writing (especially *Evangeline*, by Longfellow) than has been previously assumed. The story also calls into question easy assumptions about civic economic advancement; the heroine chooses to preserve her freedom rather than sacrificing it on behalf of the community. The heroine rejects the values dominant during the years when Chopin wrote the tale (xxix).

"Mamouche"

Written: 1893. First published: 1894. Included in *A Night in Acadie* **(1897).**

Mamouche is brought into Dr. John-Luis' sitting room by Marshall. He is soaking wet from the rain. When Dr. John-Luis asks him his name and where he comes from, he learns that Mamouche is the grandson of Théodule Peloté and Stéphanie Galopin Pelote who are old friends of his.

Dr. John-Luis spends the evening reminiscing with Mamouche about the latter's grandparents. The next morning Mamouche is gone when Dr. John-Luis awakens.

A few days later, Dr. John-Luis tells Marshall that he would like to find a young lad to teach to seek knowledge, to train to work hard and lead an honest, decent life. He will leave his property and wealth to the boy in return for the boy's company and for caring for him in his old age. He tells Marshall to find him such a boy. After spending an evening with several candidates, the doctor gives up his search for he can find no one that makes him feel the way Mamouche did that one night.

There have been many mischievous happenings around lately. Someone took Dr. John-Luis' gates off the hinges, let cows out of pastures, and took down fences, to name a few. Dr. John-Luis offers a reward for the culprit. A man comes to the door with Mamouche, saying that he is the guilty one. Mamouche admits that he is indeed guilty of all the mischievous actions. The doctor pays the man and sends him away. He asks Mamouche why he left his house in the night like a criminal. Mamouche begins to cry and tells him that he felt bad because the doctor had treated him so kindly.

Dr. John-Luis tells Mamouche that he understands how the grandson of Théodule Peloté could do such mischievous things and that he also understands that the grandson of Stéphanie Peloté could never be a thief. He then tells him that he wants Mamouche to live with him and be like his very own child.

The next morning the doctor asks Marshall what the boy is doing. Marshall says that he is saying his prayers and Hail Marys as his grandmother taught him to do. Dr. John-Luis says that Mamouche has his grandmother's eyes and her intelligence. He says that she was a clever woman, and the only mistake she ever made was marrying Théodule Peloté. **(DR)**

∗∗∗

Gilder 1898: This story demonstrates Chopin's knowledge of real emotions (50). **Potter 1971:** Like some other stories in *A Night in Acadie*, this one depicts a black man with his own views about religion (56). **Peterson 1972:** Although the premise of this young persons' tale is a bit maudlin, the title character is not excessively romanticized, the doctor is not completely altruistic, and the black servant adds a touch of understated comedy. The adoption is credibly presented; there are no abrupt shifts in plot; and no one is unbelievably virtuous. The story shows how much Chopin had advanced since composing such stories as "A Wizard from Gettysburg" or "A Rude Awakening" (99–101). Here as elsewhere, Chopin uses children symbolically but also somewhat simplistically (103). In this tale Chopin manages to avoid an extremely maudlin tone (104). **Lattin 1980:** This is one of various stories by Chopin featuring repeating characters (28). **Skaggs 1985:** This is one of many stories by Chopin that shows a real familiarity with children and their effects on others. Mamouche plays a role here not unlike his role in "The Lilies" (27). **Ewell 1986:** The title character's name means "my fly speck"; his sister appears in "In Sabine." Both tales were scheduled to be printed in *Bayou Folk,* but sluggish magazine publication of "Mamouche" caused Chopin to drop the story from the collection. The comic tone of the tale partially rescues it from its maudlin plot, and although the characters are not especially complex, they serve Chopin's purpose of teaching a rather simple lesson about age and youth (95–96). **Toth 1990a:** This tale later appeared in *A Night in Acadie,* in which all the stories are set in Louisiana (298). It was praised by one reviewer for its psychological insight (300). **Robinson 1992:** In this story, racial identity becomes an explicit question, thereby showing the difficulties of making clear distinctions in Louisiana society (xviii). **Koloski 1994:** The story is included in a soft-cover collection of Chopin's fiction published in 1992 (28). **Carr 1996 :** This is one of various stories in which a Creole adopts a Cajun, usually improving him in the process (55). **Koloski 1996:** The racial stereotypes in this story may trouble present-day readers, who may find them surprisingly insensitive coming from Chopin (44). This is one of Chopin's children's tales that feature the poor (71; 87). **Tuttleton 1996:** Even the title of this tale implies its regional focus (182). **Beer 1997:** The servant's question about identity suggests the crucial focus on race in the culture this tale describes (30). **Toth and Seyersted 1998:** This story is mentioned in Chopin's account books (140, 149, 157). **Koloski 1999:** This is one of Chopin's tales that focuses on a male (viii). Here as in other stories, Chopin depicts a character who reacts to a symbolic boundary (viii). This is one of various stories by Chopin in which children inaugurate a transformation (xvii–xviii). This is one of many stories by Chopin which either feature children or were written for them (xxii). Here as elsewhere she describes grown-ups who find connection with others (xxiii). **Toth 1999c:** This is one of various stories by Chopin in which youthful men attempt to evade mature feelings (194). The title character was badly misdescribed by one reviewer, perhaps in order to caricature Chopin's writing (196–97).

"A Matter of Prejudice"

Written: 1893. First published: 1895. Included in *A Night in Acadie* (1897).

Madame Carambeau lives in her large house in the French quarter. With her lives her widowed daughter, Cécile, and Cécile's young son, Gustave. Madame does not like dogs, cats, organ-grinders, white servants, children's noises, Americans, Germans, people of a faith other than hers, and anything not French. She has not spoken to her son, Henri, in ten years because he chose to marry an American girl.

Madame runs her household with a stern hand, except for once a year when Gustave has his birthday party. Today she retreats to her garden to stay as far away from the children as possible. All of a sudden she hears footsteps and screams coming in her direction. A little girl runs and jumps into her lap to save herself from the little boy chasing her. She does not jump down when the threat of being chased is gone, remaining instead in Madame's lap. Her breathing is quick and irregular. Being a skilled nurse, Madame immediately makes the child comfortable in her lap and begins rocking her and singing softly to her. When the child falls asleep Madame takes her and puts her in Madame's own bed. She takes the hot clothes off the child and tells the maid to get something soft and cool for the child to sleep in. It does not matter that the child is American, for Madame has no prejudices when it comes to nursing. She treats all patients with equal care.

When the child's nursemaid comes to call for her, Madame sends a note home saying that the child is ill with a fever and will be cared for at her home. After the child returns to health and goes home, Madame cannot forget the touch of the small arms and the hot lips that kissed her. This causes her to do some soul searching.

On Christmas morning she tells her driver to take them to one of the American churches. After church she tells the driver to take them to the home of her son. When they arrive at Henri's home, she is welcomed with open arms. Henri's wife comes in leading their daughter by the hand. It is the American child that Madame nursed at Gustave's party. They all drive back together to Madame's house for Christmas dinner. **(DR)**

***

Rankin 1932: The presentation here of Madame Carambeau may reflect Chopin's own humorous frustration with the disapproving attitudes of some of her own in-laws (81–82). **Reilly 1937:** Here as elsewhere, motherhood is an important theme in Chopin's fiction (73). **Reilly 1942:** Here as in some of her other best works, Chopin focuses on the feelings natural to mothers (135). **Fletcher 1966:** In this tale a woman's maternal instinct helps her overcome the pride that estranged her from her son (129). **Seyersted 1969a:** This story is the only one by Chopin centered on the conflict between the new American and old Creole cultures (81). It illustrates her developing skill in characterization and irony, especially in its conclusion (121). **Peterson 1972:** The abrupt change in this story seems a bit unrealistic (10). This is the least successful of eleven stories Chopin composed in eleven months beginning in July 1892. It represents no advance on her very earliest tales (98). Although the conclusion is predictable, it is not felicitously presented. The fence symbolism is too obvious, and the description of the child is too maudlin. The touch of irony in the concluding sentence cannot repair the earlier lack of skill. The story illustrates the frequent unevenness of Chopin's art—an unevenness caused in part by her descriptions of children (101–3). **Arner 1975:** Like many stories by Chopin, this one is deep neither in theme nor in ultimate meaning, but it is nonetheless effective because of its insightful characterization, its skillful structure, its careful plot, and its subtle juxtapositions of youth and age (72–73). **Lattin 1978:** The main character here is Chopin's only female outside *The Awakening* who obviously feels no affection for children (4). **Baym 1981:** The main characters exemplify the often conservative nature of Creole life (xx). Here as in other tales, Chopin provides a morally complex and appealing conclusion (xxv). **Bonner 1982:** This is one of several stories by Chopin that are centered on Christmas (124–25). **Lattin 1982:** Like other stories by Chopin, this one features an alienated, stunted character who eventually and somewhat easily achieves integration (224–25). **Skaggs 1985:** This is one of many stories by Chopin that shows a real familiarity with children and their effects on others (27). **Ewell 1986:** This tale is far superior to "Mamouche" in depicting relations between the young and old. The story reflects the influence of G.W. Cable in contrasting the "French" and "American" cultures of New Orleans, and the story resembles Chopin's own later work "Regret" in showing the beneficial effects of children. The potentially ambiguous irony of Madame's final comment is superb (96). **Toth 1990a:** The prejudiced main character may have been modeled in part on Chopin's father-in-law (122). She may have set this story in New Orleans to help it sell (216); later it appeared in *A Night in Acadie*, in which all the stories are set in Louisiana (298). **Robinson 1992:** This story reflects Chopin's own strongly French family background (x). **Goodwyn 1994:** This is one of various stories by Chopin that illustrate the importance of cultural differences (even in shaping race relations) while also demonstrating the value of a post-colonial perspective on her fiction (5–6). **Koloski 1994:** The story is included in soft-cover collections of Chopin's fiction published in 1981 and 1992 (27–28). **Koloski 1996:** This affecting tale features symbolic houses; a matriarch who is always in control of herself and others; and generational relations that fit standard sociological patterns. The little girl reconciles extremes (32–34). This is one of Chopin's tales for youth that centers on a holiday and is especially effective (71–72; 87). **Beer 1997:** This story shows that cultural tensions can be as significant in Chopin's fiction as racial divisions and that blacks can even become complicit in their own subjugation (29–30). **Toth and Seyersted 1998:** This story is mentioned in Chopin's account books (140, 149, 159). This is one of several stories in which Chopin describes women who are not depressed by nature but who do face particular problems (274). **Benfey 1999:** This story demonstrates the positive attitudes toward black nurses felt among many families in New Orleans after the Civil War (151). **Bonner and Bonner 1999:** Madame Carambeau's decision to attend a service at New Orleans' cathedral for speakers of English is significant (60). Chopin also uses architectural details to suggest the symbolic contrasts between the French and American sections of New Orleans (63). **Koloski 1999:** This is one of Chopin's best stories and appears in one of the best, most convincing, and most charitable collections of short fiction published in her time and place (xvi). This is one of various stories by Chopin in which children inaugurate a transformation (xvii–xviii). Here as in other works, Chopin explores how society shapes perceptions of reality, but she also shows here how society is changing (xviii). This is one of many stories by Chopin which either feature children or were written for them, although its themes seem quite mature (xxii). Here as elsewhere she describes grown-ups who find connection with others (xxiii). **McCullough 1999:** This story explores ethnic tensions among whites while also showing how those tensions are ultimately overcome. The story would thus appeal to white desires, even while Madame's conduct can be read as affirming both her ethnic identity and her status as a noble Creole (224–25). **Taylor 1999:** This is one of the few works by Chopin that suggests the ethnic tensions of life in New Orleans (25). **Toth 1999a:** The ending of this story is more conventional than is true of some of Chopin's later tales (10). **Toth 1999c:** Like many of Chopin's stories, this one depicts the inner transformation of an older woman (194). **Gibbons 2000:** This story reveals not only Chopin's progress away from local color conventions but also her continuing allegiance to them. The figurative language is still often (but not always) hackneyed; the characters are often largely (but not entirely) stereotyped; and the tone is still greatly (but not completely) sentimental. This work, like several others, represents a potential turning point in Chopin's career (xxxii). The potential success of this story is immediately apparent, especially in the depiction of the central character. Nevertheless, the rest of the tale, and the other characters, are less appealing, and the conclusion is disappointingly conventional. Even so, the old woman here prefigures the complexity of Edna in *The Awakening* (xxxii–xxxiii). **Knights 2000:** This work, one of Chopin's most compelling, was produced during a particularly creative period—the fall and summer of 1893 (xv). Even in this work for a fairly conventional magazine, Chopin shows a willingness to confront an unusual theme (xviii). A phrase in this story illustrates Chopin's occasional tendency to make ethical points too explicitly (xxvi–xxvii). When originally published, this tale was printed with "local color" stories by other writers (xxxii). As in other works, Chopin here emphasizes sites of urban privacy (xxxiii). Although Chopin relies in this story on narrative conventions emphasizing a character's transformation, she also shows genuine respect for both of the cultures she depicts (xxxv).

"Melancholy"

Fragment. Included in *Private Papers* (1998).

... As Edouward de Savignole stands beneath the stars on a dark Parisian night, he reflects on his life-long loneliness and sense of isolation. What could explain his persistent alienation from others? .... **(RCE)**

***

Toth and Seyersted 1998: This previously unknown work, which is unlike any of Chopin's published works and which may therefore have been begun but then put aside (132), was among a collection of her manuscripts uncovered in the early 1990s (135). It was borrowed (but not returned) by Chopin's earliest biographer (245). Like other works by Chopin, this one focuses on a morose, angry male misfit; perhaps it was influenced by fiction by Maupassant. In certain respects it foreshadows *The Awakening* (274). **Toth 1999b:** This fragment demonstrates Chopin's willingness to give up on work she found unsatisfying (49). **Toth 1999c:** Chopin gave up her efforts to finish this tale, which features a sad man and may therefore have seemed unlikely to be purchased for publication (167).

"A Mental Suggestion"

Written: 1896. Included in *A Vocation and a Voice* (1991).

Don Graham, a college professor, makes a psychic suggestion to his friend Faverham that when he next sees Pauline he will think that she is charming, attractive, and captivating. Pauline is Graham's fiancée, but Faverham detests her. Graham often makes insignificant "mental suggestions" to Faverham, but this time his suggestion is on a larger scale. Graham must go back to town, leaving Pauline at the resort to find companionship on her own. Graham thinks that if Faverham finds Pauline charming and attractive then he will be an appropriate companion for her. The next morning when Faverham sees Pauline, he immediately realizes how interesting, charming, and beautiful she is and the two become inseparable.

Pauline's letters to Graham detail how much fun she and Faverham are having, finally insisting that Graham come back because she is at the "mercy of her emotions." When Graham returns to Cedar Branch, Pauline breaks the engagement. Graham, feeling that Faverham is in love with Pauline only because of the "suggestion," is perplexed over the predicament, but decides to let it work itself out.

Pauline and Faverham are married a few months later. Graham visits them in the first few months of their marriage, finding them ecstatically happy. Graham's mind is in turmoil, wondering how long it will be before the suggestion wears off and Faverham reverts back to his original feelings for Pauline. He cannot stand the anxiety any longer, so he "suggests" to Faverham that Pauline is still the woman she was six months ago. Faverham immediately embraces Pauline, kisses her face all over, and proclaims his love for her. After witnessing this outbreak of emotion, Graham leaves to contemplate what happened. He decides that six months ago was when he suggested that Pauline was charming, attractive, and captivating, but evidently after the suggestion, love grew on its own. As Graham looks up at the stars he realizes that love and life are the supreme power. **(DR)**

***

Seyersted 1969a: Themes: hypnotism (112) and the common desire of men to dominate and of women to be dominated (148). **Peterson 1972:** Here as in "A Morning Walk," Chopin mocks mere logic, but here again she also seems unsubtle (170). As in some of her other late stories, the protagonists seem too simple (198). **Rocks 1972:** Here as elsewhere Chopin shows the complexities but also the rewards of marriage as well as its superiority to remaining single (118). **Arner 1975:** This story is especially intriguing because of its depiction of the cool, controlling scientist, who turns his back on life and whose one-time fiancée blossoms when she marries another man (92–93). **Skaggs 1985:** This is one of several tales emphasizing the strong influence of erotic desire (46). **Ewell 1986:** In this story hypnotism symbolizes compulsive behavior, and the tale may reflect Chopin's own interest in—and occasional skill at—strange mental powers. Although Chopin shows the effects such powers might exert on material objects, she also suggests their limitations when human emotions are involved. The manipulative Graham resembles the male protagonist in Hawthorne's "The Birthmark": both disguise their emotion behind a mask of scientific objectivity. **Toth 1990a:** Magazines repeatedly rejected this tale of strange mental powers—powers Chopin herself had some reason to find credible (281–82), even though she made slight fun of them here (357). This tale was intended for inclusion in *A Vocation and a Voice* (274). **Toth 1991:** The scholar described here resembles ones Chopin knew in her youth (ix). The main character resembles a friend of Chopin (xvii). This story may reflect (and mock) the intellectual interests of Chopin's friends and may also reflect her own interest in mental telepathy (xvii). This may be one of only two stories in *A Vocation and a Voice* with conventionally happy endings (xxii). This is one of many stories in *A Vocation and a Voice* in which love fails because of bad timing (xxiii). **Davis 1992b:** This is one of many stories from *A Vocation and a Voice* that focus on suddenly altered perceptions (200–201). The tale shows how exotic perceptions can alter relations between the sexes, and in this respect the work is relevant to *The Awakening* (204). **Hoder-Salmon 1992:** A comment in this story implies Chopin's approval of an independent woman (21). **Koloski 1994:** The story is included in a soft-cover collection of Chopin's fiction published in 1991 (28).

"Millie's First Party"

Written: 1901. Lost.

Peterson 1972: Chopin probably wrote this work with the idea of submitting it to *Youth's Companion* (265). **Ewell 1986:** This is one of several nonextant stories mentioned in Chopin's records (190). **Toth 1990a:** This narrative for young people was one of three that Chopin wrote in as many days (386). **Thomas 1992:** This story was one of three works that may have been written over three days in 1901 (53–54). **Toth 1999c:** This was one of a trio of tales for youth that Chopin suddenly composed quite quickly (235).

"Miss McEnders"

Written: 1892. First published: 1897. Included in *Complete Works* (1969).

Having an abundance of money at her disposal, Georgie McEnders, a twenty-five-year-old woman of unquestionable character, also has enough leisure time to pursue her interests in philanthropy and morality even as she makes preparations, to exacting standards, for her own upcoming wedding. Prior to her speaking engagement at the Woman's Reform Club and her meeting with a committee of ladies who hope to investigate the morality of St. Louis' factory-girls, Miss McEnders makes a surprise visit to the home of Mademoiselle Salambre, a woman hired by a local clothier's shop to sew the bride-to-be's delicate lingerie, because she has heard a few gossips suggest that the woman is of dubious character.

The young woman is not taken aback when a gruff German woman points the way to Mlle. Salambre's upstairs apartment. However, once inside the apartment, Georgie is disturbed by her "employee's" haggard appearance and unkempt home, though she says nothing at first. When she discovers that Mlle. Salambre lied when she said the child on the floor was her neighbor's, Miss McEnders rebukes the woman for her dishonesty and questions why she calls herself "Mademoiselle" rather than "Madame," since she is a mother. The latter explains that it is easier to find employment that way and charges that Miss McEnders doesn't know anything about life. The young woman again rebukes the seamstress and immediately goes about her business of doing good.

As soon as Georgie has a moment's break, she sets about the task of making sure the seamstress is punished for her dishonesty. She writes a letter to the clothier shop and demands that her materials be returned to her at once. Two days later, the worker makes an unexpected visit to Miss McEnders' home. The latter explains that she has acted according to her duty to do God's will and that the seamstress is merely reaping God's just punishment. The poor woman, however, chides Georgie for preaching a sermon to such a small audience and says that she doesn't want her work or her money. After she looks around the room, the seamstress boasts that her own parents are honest, even if they are as poor as rats, and then she attacks the corrupt morals of Georgie's father and her fiancé, Meredith Holt.

Although she is due to meet with her ladies' group, Miss McEnders decides to make sure her own house is in order first. She acts on the worker's challenge to ask people on the street how her father got his wealth. The elderly gentleman whom Georgie first stops refuses to answer her question; the second passerby, a plumber, tells her that Horace McEnders made the majority of his money operating a Whisky Ring; the third, a newspaper boy, says that Mr. McEnders built his large house with stolen money. Georgie is suddenly and painfully aware that she is the last person in the whole community to know the truth behind her family's fortune. She silently returns to her bedroom, throws a box of white flowers, just arrived from her fiancé, into the fireplace, and sinks into a chair, weeping bitterly. **(JW)**

***

Seyersted 1969a: This story of growing awareness took five years to find a willing publisher (55). Chopin's single tale chiefly designed to expose social and moral posturing, it reflects her personal familiarity with a St. Louis social improvement club, explores issues of hypocrisy and disillusionment (96–97), and uses flowers as effective symbols (132). **Seyersted 1969b:** Although Chopin was probably not sympathetic to the materialism of her day, she was not a self-conscious reformer. In this story, the closest she comes to such fiction, the reformer herself is the subject of satire (26). **Leary 1970a:** Here as elsewhere Chopin depicts a woman's process of self-understanding (xi). **Leary 1971:** Here, more explicitly than in some of her local-color writing, Chopin treats the awakening of a young woman (168). **Peterson 1972:** The opening section focuses on contradictions in Georgie's life—contradictions she seems genuinely not to notice. The discussion of the two photographs robs the story of much surprise; instead we concentrate mainly on the heroine's responses. The story is fairly unsubtle, but the ending is the first one in which Chopin emphasizes tension rather than dissolving it (92–96). Here as elsewhere Chopin spotlights one character whose changed perspective ends the tale (114–15). **Rocks 1972:** In this story Chopin shows her mistrust of persons who tend to think in abstract terms—especially of abstract social reformers (114). **Arner 1975:** This story suggests Chopin's misgivings about smug moralists and her compassion for persons who violated rigid sexual standards (127–28). **Taylor 1979:** This was one of several tales Chopin had difficulty publishing (viii). **Jones 1981:** Although social reform provided an outlet for assertive women in Chopin's day, this story shows her own disregard for such smug efforts. The tale celebrates honest labor as the basis of self-worth, just as it also endorses the kind of self-reliance and maturity that could not be won by devotion to a public cause (147–48). Works by Ellen Glasgow resemble this story by Chopin (235). Although the title character sees herself in symbolic terms, Chopin undercuts this self-perception by providing realistic detail (360). **Fluck 1982:** This was one of the various unconventional, innovative stories by Chopin that were often turned down for publication (163). **Lattin 1982:** This is one of several stories by Chopin in which self-assured characters must learn their limitations in order to achieve true self-understanding (225–26). **Burchard 1984:** This story implies Chopin's disregard for feminine idealists (36–37). **McMahan 1985:** Here as elsewhere Chopin depicts a woman who marries after not having given the matter much thought (32). **Ewell 1986:** This tale, one of her few not set in Louisiana, was difficult to publish, and when it was printed it appeared under a pseudonym. Possibly its satire inhibited publication; its tone may reflect Chopin's friendship with "muckraking" journalists. The tale severely attacks many kinds of falseness and pretension. Although Georgie is perhaps too easy a target, Chopin shows some compassion for her eventual honesty. The image of Georgie tossing her flowers into the filthy fireplace is highly symbolic. Meanwhile, even Mademoiselle Salambre's falsity is comprehensible in view of her real social circumstances. Neither of these women can claim to be pure; only the man, Meredith Holt, escapes the bind that traps the females. The story reflects Chopin's skepticism about both moralizing and romantic posturing. She preferred reality rather than impossible standards or deluded ideals (82–84). **Stepenoff 1987:** In this story set in St. Louis, Chopin exposes moral ignorance and pretension (460–61). **Papke 1990:** This is one of various works in which Chopin shows how women sometimes contribute to feminine oppression (59). **Toth 1990a:** The story reflects Chopin's girlhood familiarity with sewing (46), while the pseudonym under which it was published echoes Chopin's youthful reading (52). She wrote the story shortly before resigning from a local women's group (210), and the narrative perhaps mocks the social theories of Henry George (258). The tale, which resembles one by a Norwegian author (287), was so strongly satirical that Chopin had trouble for four years in finding a journal willing to publish it. After it finally was printed, a St. Louis journalist noted parallels between Chopin's fiction and the lives of some prominent local residents, including a chief financial backer of the magazine in which the story appeared. Apparently Chopin intended this personal satire, since she did not publish the story under her own name (290–92). **Koloski 1994:** The story is included in soft-cover collections of Chopin's fiction published in 1970, 1976, and 1979 (27). **Bender 1996:** Georgie is a minor version of Henry George. The story implies Chopin's skepticism that social reform movements could transform human nature. Instead, she believed (with Darwin) that change would only evolve slowly and would be reflected and effected through the lives of individuals (105). **Tuttleton 1996:** Partly because this story mocks feminists, it is not a favorite of modern-day women's rights advocates (193–94). **Toth and Seyersted 1998:** This story, one of various works in which Chopin mocks clubs for females (131), is mentioned in Chopin's account books (141, 149, 161) and in her letters (203). **Toth 1999c:** After resigning from a women's club, Chopin satirized them in this story (127), which she published under an assumed name because the tale also mocked a local woman who owned the newspaper in which the story was printed. This fact was made public in another paper by one of Chopin's friends (197–99). The assumed name may have been borrowed from a French painter (216). The paper owned by the woman Chopin had mocked later criticized *The Awakening* (221). **Knights 2000:** This story was rejected even by one of Chopin's most reliable sources of publication, perhaps because the subject-matter would have offended upscale readers (xvii). Here as elsewhere Chopin focuses on a moment of self-realization (xix). This story implicitly questions the commercial values prevalent in Chopin's society (xxix).

"Miss Witherwell's Mistake"

Written: 1889. First published: 1891. Included in *Complete Works* (1969).

Frances Witherwell delights in sending weekly writings to the Boredomville *Battery*. The editor prints the old spinster's contributions and the staff allows her to proofread them for typesetting errors because she possesses exacting working methods, not to mention a financial interest in the newspaper. Miss Witherwell's weekly routine is disrupted by a letter from her brother Hiram, who asks that his sister receive his daughter Mildred into her home. The letter explains that the nineteen-year-old has made the mistake of falling in love with a young man, who has all of the qualities a father could hope for in a son-in-law save wealth, and that even though the young man has himself gone away, Mildred needs some time away from home to take her thoughts off of love.

When Mildred arrives, she tells her aunt that she has not come to her home for pleasure. Instead, she wants to do something useful with her time so that she can forget about her past joys and sorrows. Having noticed that Mildred takes daily walks regardless of the weather, Miss Witherwell asks her niece to go by the newspaper to proofread her letter for the week when bad weather hits. As Mildred is proofreading her aunt's letter, she discovers that Mr. Wilson, the new assistant editor her aunt spoke of, is none other than Roland Wilson, the man she loves. She gets Roland's attention and the two greet each other with as much decorum as possible, given the circumstances. From that day on, Mildred goes to the newspaper every week on her aunt's behalf.

Though months pass, Miss Witherwell's niece seems content to stay in Boredomville, which is interpreted as a good sign by all. One day Mildred says that she is working on a story and needs her aunt's help to end it. When Miss Witherwell unknowingly hears her niece's autobiographical love story and must decide whether the "two lovers" should marry or not, the old woman urges her niece, "Marry them, most certainly, or let them die." Mildred promptly marries Roland, and brings him home so that he can tell Miss Witherwell how her niece's story ends. Roland becomes the editor in chief of the *Battery*. Mr. Witherwell grows to accept and appreciate his new son-in-law, and Miss Witherwell, who is enjoying brighter days with family nearby, seems proud of her "lucky mistake." **(JW)**

***

Rankin 1932: The tale, written in November 1889 (116), exemplifies Chopin's skill, wit, humor, and talent at creating characters (132). **Seyersted 1969a:** Chopin later outgrew a flaw this story illustrates: unlikely plot developments (121). **Taylor 1979:** Chopin here mocks contemporary critical condemnation of realistic fiction (ix). **Rocks 1972:** This story shows the importance of seeing reality as it is and of not being misled either by sentimentalist or determinist works of art (112). **Newman 1986:** Like many of Chopin's tales, this one suggests a view of marriage that seems to conflict with the views implied by some of her other stories. This work seems to affirm traditional ideas about the value of matrimony (152). Chopin's ironic depiction of Miss Witherwell sets reality against the fantasies of fiction (160). **Skaggs 1985:** This tale was intended for a broad audience (56). **Ewell 1986:** Although rejected by the prominent journals to which Chopin first submitted it, the story does show progress in coherence and point of view while also exploring the relations between fiction and reality. Although its social satire is somewhat undermined by its happy ending, the tale does successfully lampoon the devices of romantic fiction. In many respects this work improves on her recent novel, *At Fault* (47). **Toth 1990a:** Like many of Chopin's early tales, this story (which was turned down six times before being accepted) focuses on a professional woman (181–82). **Cutter 1994:** Miss Witherwell's writing contrasts with the kind described in "Elizabeth Stock's One Story" (30). **Ewell 1994:** This is one of several stories by Chopin in which she seems to ignore the marketability of local color fiction (160). **Koloski 1994:** The story is included in a soft-cover collection of Chopin's fiction published in 1979 (27). **Thomas 1995:** This is one of several stories in which Chopin mocks—and thus distances herself from—stereotypes of the woman writer (19). The tale mocks the restrictions under which feminine authors were constrained (or chose) to operate, but perhaps it also uneasily implies Chopin's own sense of constraint (20–23). The story satirizes both Miss Witherwell and her popularity, thereby implying the kind of author Chopin did *not* want to be (27). Ironically, however, one of Chopin's own final stories ("Polly") is the kind of tale Miss Witherwell might very well compose (29). **Walker 1996:** Theme: the relations between women and writing (220). The title character is associated with a vulgar, commercial kind of writing (222–23). Chopin uses the tale ironically to comment on the contrasts between romantic and realistic fiction. The title character symbolizes convention-bound female authors (223). **McCullough 1999:** This work shows Chopin's sympathy for fictional realism and her skepticism about romantic conventions (192). **Toth 1999c:** Chopin mocks an assertive woman here, but the mood of the tale is not entirely comic (112).

"Mrs. Mobry's Reason"

Written: 1891. First published: 1893. Included in *Complete Works* **(1969).**

Editha Payne is not particularly young or beautiful when John Mobry asks her to marry him, so everyone wonders why she refuses to accept his proposal for a full three years. Twenty-five years pass before anyone knows the answer to the question. Editha Payne and John Mobry marry and have two children, Edward and Naomi; it is Mrs. Mobry's will that neither of her children marry. In spite of his mother's opposition, Edward leaves her side and marries when he is of age. For this reason, Mrs. Mobry warns John's nephew Sigmund, a medical student who is living with the family over the summer, that they do not want their beautiful eighteen-year-old daughter to marry when she sees that Naomi and Sigmund are enjoying each other's company.

Realizing that Naomi has not promised to remain single and thinking that his aunt is just set in her ways, Sigmund is not discouraged. On the contrary, Mrs. Mobry's warning seems to increase her nephew's desire for Naomi. When Sigmund is not studying, he and Naomi spend a great deal of time together— walking, floating on the Meramec river in Naomi's boat, and reading from romance literature.

Always attentive to her daughter's health and happiness, Mrs. Mobry is the first to notice that her daughter is listless. When Mrs. Mobry expresses her concern, Naomi attributes her sluggishness to the summer's heat. Mrs. Mobry becomes alarmed when her daughter leaves the house early one morning and does not return. Sigmund becomes worried, too, and he searches for Naomi in all of their haunts. By the time he finds Naomi resting in her boat under the willows, the sun is fierce. He calls to her, and she comes immediately. Sigmund rebukes her for being gone so long. In response, Naomi takes hold of her cousin and tells him that she wants a kiss, and the two kiss passionately. Afterwards, Sigmund realizes by her conversation and the look in her eyes that there is something wrong with Naomi. He takes her back to the house and explains to his aunt that Naomi must be ill. At first, Mrs. Mobry denies that her daughter is ill, but later that night she confesses, weeping at her husband's feet, that mental illness has plagued her family for generations. That is why she had initially refused to marry and why she had forbidden her children to marry. Mrs.

Mobry laments that Edward now has a son and that future generations will curse her for accepting John Mobry's offer of marriage. **(JW)**

***

Rankin 1932: This tale is serious and intriguing (134). **Seyersted 1969a:** The story's provocative topic—inherited insanity—may have made editors unwilling to publish it (54), yet Chopin seems less interested here in genetics than in causes of growing affection (108). **Leary 1970a:** This story is less subtle than some of Chopin's other works (xi). **Leary 1971:** This tale is a bit tedious and unwieldy (168). **Peterson 1972:** This is the first story by Chopin in which she does not rely on a somewhat maudlin conclusion. The tale has Gothic touches reminiscent of Poe, although it lacks Poe's mastery of tone and incident. Alienation is an important motif here, but neither the title character nor others are characterized sufficiently fully. The story therefore lacks a certain interest (74–76). **Arner 1975:** Some of the earlier titles Chopin considered for this tale would have fit it better than the rather vague one she finally chose. The Ibsenesque story—perhaps the gloomiest, most fatalistic piece Chopin ever wrote—explores the enduring consequences of evil acts. Paradisiacal symbolism and musical imagery help underscore the irony of the tale, particularly in its dark view of marriage (121–23). **Lattin 1978:** This is one of various stories in which Chopin describes the genuine complications that can result from real (rather than merely imagined or potential) motherhood (2). **Taylor 1979:** This tale, resembling Ibsen's "Ghosts," was one of several of Chopin's works which was at first rejected for publication (viii). **Wolstenholme 1980:** In this story Chopin explores a topic also confronted by Henrik Ibsen and Richard Wagner: how parental actions can determine children's fates. Names, topics, and incidents in the story resemble details of Ibsen's *Ghosts* and Wagner's *Ring Cycle*. The story is flawed because of its contrived conclusion, but it does show how fate can affect even ordinary lives (540–43). **Fluck 1982:** This story illustrates the possibility that transgression—an important theme in Chopin's fiction—may eventually prove destructive (160–61). This was one of the various unconventional, innovative stories by Chopin that were often turned down for publication (163). **Dyer 1985:** In this story as in others, Chopin exploits the prejudices of her readers about the insane in order to depict a female sensuality she considered far more widespread (69–73). **Skaggs 1985:** The story may reflect not only current biological thinking but also the influence of scripture (56–57). **Ewell 1986:** The story went through five distinct titles and was submitted fifteen different times before finally being accepted. It alludes to worries at the time about venereal disease, but it also examines destructive feelings and their links to music. The heroine's physical desires eventually undermine her mental stability, leading to a somewhat overblown ending that is not entirely effective in rebuking sexual impulses. Nonetheless, the story complexly handles topics prominent elsewhere in Chopin's works (48). **Toth 1988a:** Here as elsewhere, Chopin shows her awareness of the complex experience of motherhood (56). This was one of various stories by Chopin printed in a New Orleans newspaper (60). **Inge 1989:** Chopin had given this story a series of intriguing names before settling on the present title. Her exploration here of deterministic forces, including drives and handicaps rooted in human biology, anticipates her similar focus on such forces in *The Awakening* (93). **Toth 1990a:** This is one of several tales in which Chopin describes the various emotions motherhood entails (128). Probably because the story dealt with a sexually transmitted disease, it was turned down more frequently than any other narrative she wrote. Its composition was probably encouraged by the mother of T.S. Eliot, and the success of a recent British novel about syphilis may finally have helped Chopin find a publisher for her story. The tale even resembles the novel in various ways, and it seems generally indebted to European influences, despite its local setting (198–99). The story illustrates the increasing seriousness of Chopin's writing (206) and was one of four of her tales published in a single month (215–16). **Guidici 1991:** Here as elsewhere a Chopin heroine fails to seize the opportunity for greater autonomy. Mrs. Mobry should steadfastly have refused marriage (31). **Hoder-Salmon 1992:** The story most obviously shows Chopin's sensitivity to sound (149). **Cutter 1994:** Here as in other early stories, Chopin describes women whose efforts to express opposition are promptly silenced or suppressed (17). The mother in this story is submissive toward men and tries to breed the same submissiveness in her daughter, but when the daughter resists and becomes both sexually and linguistically liberated, she is considered crazy. Her rebelliousness, however, may still prove subtly subversive (23–24), although her language is less potent than the kind described in "Elizabeth Stock's One Story" (31). Naomi's extreme independence is ultimately self-defeating (34). **Ewell 1994:** This was one of a number of stories Chopin wrote in early 1891 that focused on the dilemmas of women and that were at first rejected by publishers (160). **Koloski 1994:** The story is included in a soft-cover collection of Chopin's fiction published in 1970 (27). **Saar 1994:** This was the story by Chopin most often turned down by publications (62). **Beer 1997:** Emily Toth reports that this story was turned down more than any other Chopin wrote, despite the author's established status. The long lag-time between composition and publication was not unusual (2–3). She was paid five dollars for this story (6). **Green 1999:** Martha Cutter uses this tale to illustrate the suppression of feminine self-expression (22). **Toth 1999c:** This was one of various tales by Chopin focusing on the emotions of a mother (70). This narrative, the first by Chopin to reflect her reading of Maupassant, was also the one most frequently turned down by editors. The work deals with the insanity syphilis can cause. Eventually it was accepted after an English novel on the same topic became popular. Chopin may even have made the names of her characters resemble those in the novel (124–25). The story was printed in a newspaper owned by an acquaintance (133). **Knights 2000:** This was one of the numerous works Chopin composed in 1891, although it was often turned down by publishers (xv).

"Misty"

Fragment. Included in *Private Papers* (1998).

... The world is full of many potential stories.... Brief, confused fragment of a tale.... However, the story failed to please a visiting friend.... **(RCE)**

***

Toth and Seyersted 1998: This fragment was among a collection of Chopin manuscripts uncovered in the early 1990s (135). It was among a group of papers borrowed but not returned by Chopin's first biographer (245). It is an early version of an essay on fiction-writing Chopin eventually published in a major national magazine (272–73).

"The Mittens"

Writen: 1892. Destroyed.

Toth 1990a: Chopin apparently thought so little of this story that she destroyed it (207). **Toth and Seyersted 1998:** This work is mentioned in her account books (148, 162).

"A Morning Walk"

Written: 1897. First published: 1897. Included in *Complete Works* (1969).

Archibald, a man of forty, has been up for hours. It is spring and he starts out for a walk, purely for the exercise. Spring is nothing new to him, but for some reason this morning he notices the color of the blossoms, their aromas, the butterflies and the grasshoppers. Ahead of him is a pretty, healthy girl of twenty carrying a bunch of white lilies.

She bids him good morning and he responds, "Good morning, Jane." The girl laughs and tells him that she is Lucy and says that he calls her by a different name every time he sees her. She is one of the girls who has grown up with his nieces. He offers to carry her flowers.

They walk along together to the church, but rather than handing her the flowers and leaving, he follows her into the church and sits down beside her in the pew. His presence causes wonder and whispers. During the service he is inattentive until the minister says, "I am the Resurrection and the Life." He pauses and repeats himself.

These words creep into Archibald's consciousness; he absorbs the words and preaches his own sermon to himself as he gazes out the window. **(DR)**

***

Peterson 1972: Here the rejection of logic and reason is blatant. Like "Beyond the Bayou" and "After the Winter," this work emphasizes rejuvenation, but the story is too plainly moralistic and contrived, and even its message seems uncharacteristically simple (165–69). Here as in some of her other late stories, Chopin's protagonists can seem too simple (198). **Rocks 1972:** Here as elsewhere, Chopin implies that a balanced life results from a sympathetic knowledge of human and physical nature (115). **Arner 1975:** The main male character here undergoes a profound awakening to self and nature similar to the kind granted to the protagonists of some of Chopin's finest works (93). **Dyer 1980–81:** This is one of various stories in which Chopin reveals a significant interest in the strong yearnings of males (15). **Bonner 1982:** This is one of various stories by Chopin that emphasize the specifics of Christian religious practice (123). **Lattin 1982:** Like other stories by Chopin, this one features an alienated, stunted character who eventually and somewhat easily achieves integration (224–25). **Dyer 1983–84:** This is one of various stories by Chopin in which characters gain insight, win resolve, and feel freer after experiencing nature (75). At first Archibald seems a sterile intellectual, but his encounter with nature opens his eyes to a richer sense of life's beauty (79–80). The natural imagery here resembles Chopin's use of sea imagery in *The Awakening* (80–81). **Skaggs 1985:** This is one of several stories emphasizing the significance of religion. Although the protagonist is familiar with nature, he remains blind to its divinity until both his senses and his spirit are stirred. The bond he then feels with nature is of a sort never achieved by Edna in *The Awakening* (40).

Ewell 1986: This story deals with two of Chopin's recent favorite topics: religion and the nature. The male protagonist resembles other scientists in early Chopin stories such as "A Mental Suggestion" or "A Point at Issue." Nature interests him without affecting him deeply. Nonetheless, he suddenly finds himself erotically fascinated by a girl whose name (Lucy) associates her with enlightenment. As in "A Vocation and a Voice," sexual desire serves here as a prelude to religious awakening, although Chopin carefully avoids excessive emotion when describing the latter experience. As with characters in other works by Chopin, Archibald's new vision is linked to Easter, but his vision is pantheistic rather than narrowly dogmatic. His awakening takes place in a church but signals a far deeper renewal (137–38). Chopin's emphasis here is on an inner spirituality (162), and she links physical desire with a person's deepest sense of selfhood (183). **Toth 1990a:** Chopin was easily able to publish conventional holiday tales like this one (275), which was intended for reprinting in *A Vocation and a Voice* (374). **Toth 1991:** The scholar described here resembles ones Chopin knew in her youth (ix). This may be one of only two stories in *A Vocation and a Voice* with conventionally happy endings (xxii). This is the most conventional (and marketable) religious story in *A Vocation and a Voice* (xxiv). **Davis 1992b:** This is one of many stories from *A Vocation and a Voice* that focus on suddenly altered perceptions (200–201). **Fusco 1994:** This was one of several stories by Chopin whose title resembles that of a story by Maupassant (140). **Koloski 1994:** The story is included in a softcover collection of Chopin's fiction published in 1991 (29). **Koloski 1996:** This story resembles "After the Winter" in its emphasis on renewal through Christian fellowship (50), yet the primary source of harmony in this tale (and elsewhere in Chopin) is not religious (65–66). One critic has stressed the search for self as a central motif of this narrative (87). **Ewell 1997:** This tale, written not long before Chopin composed *The Awakening*, offers her clearest exploration of the links between nature, sexuality, and mystical perception. The heroine's name suggests that she is an agent of illumination whose sexuality stimulates the protagonist to a clearer perception of existence. The focus of the tale is not on religious transformation *per se* (while in church, Archibald is still focused more on nature than on the service) but on a deeper change. He comes to appreciate a unity that transcends any narrow dogma (112–13). **Toth and Seyersted 1998:** This tale, also entitled "An Easter-Day Conversion," is mentioned in Chopin's account books (141, 150) and is one of several stories in which she describes morose, angry male misfits (274).

"Nég Créol"

Written: 1896. First published: 1897. Included in *A Night in Acadie* **(1897).**

Chicot is a poor, crippled, black man who makes his meager living by doing odd jobs for the vendors in the French market. He seldom receives money for his work, but usually barters for goods. His former master was a prominent man of the city. Chicot often brags about his master and his descendants who, according to Chicot, are rich, cultured, famous, and powerful.

There is only one person in the world who cares about Chicot's existence. That person is Mamzelle Aglaé Boisduré. She is seventy-five-years-old and lives on the top floor of an old boarding house. Fifty years ago she played minor roles in a company of actors, a career that put her grandmother in her grave.

Every day Chicot goes to Mamzelle's house and shares his daily earnings with her. She suffers from poor health, and every day she complains about everything around her and how bad she feels. One day when Chicot arrives, she is so ill that she cannot complain. All she can do is moan. If Chicot could better her life by giving up his own, he would gladly do it. He is totally devoted to Mamzelle.

One day Chicot's earnings are especially good; he has an unusual amount of dainties from the market. He hurries to see Mamzelle. When he arrives he is told that she died during the night. All the arrangements have been made for the funeral.

The next day one of the vendors asks Chicot if the Boisduré woman who died as poor as a church mouse is related to the family he always talks about. He answers no because his family is wealthy with high social standing. When the funeral procession passes by he does not even turn his head to look. **(DR)**

***

Anonymous 1897 [*Post-Dispatch*]: This is one of various stories by Chopin that seems appealing because of its subtle depiction of altruism. Here as often in her writing, Chopin achieves a spiritual epiphany in the conclusion (47). **Gilder 1898:** This is a moving account of altruism (50). **Reilly 1937:** This is one of various stories in which Chopin deals subtly with the ambiguities of human emotions (72–73). **Reilly 1942:** The ending of this tale is effectively ironic (131). This is one of various tales in which Chopin deals subtly with the ambiguities of affection (134). **Bush 1957:** Here as in other stories, Chopin depicts loyal slaves (243–45). **Seyersted**

1969a: The story shows Chopin's ability, by inserting an unexpected twist, to transcend the literary stereotype of the loyal black servant (79). **Leary 1970a:** This is one of many works in which Chopin depicts the ambiguities and complexities of love (x). **Leary 1971:** Theme: altruistic affection (160). **Seyersted 1969b:** The tone of this work typifies that of conventional maudlin attitudes toward loyal freed slaves (26). **Potter 1971:** Chicot is a skillfully individualized black who cannot escape the impact of having once been a slave: he is obsessed with the past and lacks any real sense of independent selfhood. He is a sad example of the tragic impact of slavery (54). Nonetheless, our sense of his individuality is enhanced by his distinctive religious attitudes (56). **Peterson 1972:** This is one of Chopin's better final tales, partly because it emphasizes character rather than incident. The irony seems more natural than in some of the other late stories (166). Chopin here avoids the stereotypes of a "devoted slave" narrative by focusing on the tensions between the main characters (186–88). This story illustrates Chopin's impulse to describe life objectively (199). **Arner 1975:** As in "Cavanelle," Chopin here explores selfless devotion in a way that does not merely reaffirm the stereotype of the faithful former slave. The characters seem alive, real, and intriguingly complex, particularly the title character, who seems at once both foolish and angelic. Although the story is thin in plot and lacking in drama, it is nonetheless both moving and memorable (75–76). **Webb 1976:** This is one of various works by Chopin that center around movements into and away from New Orleans (6). This story's brevity and skillful design make it worth reprinting. Chopin here varies her frequent use of cyclical structures by setting the entire tale inside New Orleans. In addition, the cyclical movement occurs not just once but every day. The protagonist's nicknames include "black Creole" and "stump" (Chicot). He has become the center of his old mistress' mental and practical life (12–13). He moves over and over from the market to his mistress to his shack and then back, until the mistress' illness alters this familiar pattern (13). In the final scene he proves too weak, because of self-concern and egotism, to continue his devotion. Instead he betrays his mistress, and we perceive him more clearly than he perceives himself (14). **Jones 1981:** Although the story may seem to present the title character in a stereotyped way, Chopin achieves complexity by making him the central focus and by making him more appealing than the white mistress he serves (151). **Davis 1982:** This is one of Chopin's most effective treatments of a theme common in her fiction: inner and outer existence. Chicot manages to reconcile his personal desires with his responsibilities to society (65–66). **Gilbert 1984:** Here as elsewhere Chopin presents a lower-class male who shows affection for an upper-class woman (16). **Grover 1984:** This tale is excellent because Chopin avoids caricature when depicting a black man (32). **Skaggs 1985:** This is one of several tales emphasizing altruistic self-denial (30) and featuring a black character concerned with social class (60). Both he and his former owner take ironic pride in a long-gone status that once defined (and still does define) the identities of both

(30). **Ewell 1986:** The story shows how being poor can affect a person's sense of self. Chicot transcends any caricature of an ex-slave and is one of Chopin's last and best depictions of a black person. His somewhat comic concern with dignity (a concern he has in common with the former slave-owner he serves) ironically earns our respect. Both characters embrace unconventional behavior in order to affirm themselves, yet the story also shows that genuine compassion can and does exist. The title character's refusal to witness the old woman's funeral exemplifies, paradoxically, his respect both for her and for himself (121–22). Like other stories written by Chopin at around this time, this tale implies a powerful social message (127) and reveals her ambivalent vision of human existence (183). **Manders 1990:** Here as in several of her other stories featuring blacks, Chopin presents a variation of the conventional figure of the "wretched freeman"—the erstwhile slave who allegedly had benefited from subjection (37–39). She interestingly implies that the emotional attachments that blacks developed toward whites during slavery helped perpetuate their dependence after they were freed (41). Unlike some of the writings of Grace King, the present tale manages to transcend narrow stereotypes and depict blacks with a certain measure of psychological complexity (42). The disagreements between the title character and the mistress he serves are unusual in such stories, and their tensions are exacerbated since each also reminds the other of life's disappointments. Chicot also transcends the stereotype because he is able to cope with life after his mistress dies. Here and elsewhere Chopin manages to create a black character who is more than a mere caricature (43–44). **Toth 1990a:** This was one of only several stories by Chopin published in the prominent magazine *The Atlantic* (235). Here as in her other tales, disabled characters are depicted with dignity (260) and thus help Chopin's story differ from the works of some other writers (269). The tale, which treats a conventional plot with unusual seriousness (274), was reprinted in *A Night in Acadie* (298) and was praised by one conservative critic (300). Another reviewer praised the subtle revelation at the conclusion of the narrative (303). **Boren 1992:** This story exemplifies Chopin's interest in multi-ethnic social stratification (6). **Toth 1992:** Like other stories Chopin published in *The Atlantic*, it shows an oppressed person submitting to oppression (19–20). **Bryan 1993:** The emphasis on the poor in this story contrasts with the focus on the wealthy in *The Awakening* (55). Chopin emphasizes the multicultural nature of the French Market, and she makes the black character the central focus (55–58). This is one of the relatively few tales in which Chopin explicitly deals with matters of race and with other social concerns (62). **Goodwyn 1994:** This is one of various stories in which Chopin depicts the stereotype of the loyal black (10). **Koloski 1994:** This tale was included in an anthology of local color fiction published in 1941 and then reprinted nearly thirty years later (23). The story is also included in a 1970 soft-cover collection of Chopin's fiction (27). **Castillo 1995:** Chopin transcends local color conventions by making the title character a real individual, not a stereotype. He shows genuine concern for the woman he helps (85–86). **Koloski 1996:** This was one of a trio of stories by Chopin accepted by *The Atlantic*, but it has not received much analysis. Perhaps it has been considered too simple in plot or too stereotypical in its presentation of the title character. However, the story superbly shows a weak, oppressed person achieving selfhood through self-sacrifice and integrity. Names are significant in this subtle tale of post-bellum race-relations with its memorable title character (42–45) and sensitive multiculturalism (47). "After the Winter" both resembles and differs from the present tale (50). **Tuttleton 1996:** Even the title of this tale implies its regional focus (182). **Beer 1997:** Chopin here uses the standard post-Civil War story of black loyalty to whites (35). **Toth and Seyersted 1998:** This story is mentioned in Chopin's account books (141, 150). **Koloski 1999:** This is one of Chopin's best stories and appears in one of the best, most convincing, and most charitable collections of short fiction published in her time and place (xvi). The present work is one of Chopin's best partly because it depicts with such sympathy a black person who shows enormous resolution and self-respect. Here as elsewhere, Chopin implicitly commends one person's fidelity to another, but here as in "Tante Cat'rinette" the faithfulness of a black toward a white is especially long-lasting (xviii–xix). This work and others exemplify Chopin's complicated views of racial matters (xix). Chopin here shows affection that exists across color lines, and she presents racial issues objectively (xx). **Toth 1999b:** As Bernard Koloski has demonstrated, this was one of eight stories by Chopin that were frequently republished in the twentieth century (46).

"The Night Came Slowly"

Written: 1894. First published: 1895. Included in *A Vocation and a Voice* (1991).

An unnamed narrator states that he has no interest in humans or their significance. He is told that it is better to study men than books, but he is not interested in either. Nothing speaks to him like a summer night.

He lies under a maple tree, watching the night approach. The night is full of mystery that charms him. The katydids sing him to sleep and the wind ripples through the leaves.

A man's voice breaks the spell of the necromancer. The man has red cheeks, bold eyes, coarse manner, and coarse speech; he brings his "Bible Class" with him. The narrator wonders what men know of Christ; he would rather ask the stars about Christ, for they have seen him. **(DR)**

***

Seyersted 1969a: The story is closely based on an autobiographical passage recorded in Chopin's diary (209; 217). **Arner 1975:** This tale, related in ideas and otherwise to "Juanita," implies the littleness of humanity in relation to nature and suggests that nature is an enigma to be contemplated rather than solved (93–94). **Dyer 1981b:** This personal piece reflects Chopin's own attraction to the evening hours (216). **Dyer 1983–84:** This is one of various stories by Chopin that emphasize the revelatory power of nature (75). **Dyer 1985:** By linking this tale with "Juanita," Chopin implies sympathy for Juanita's sensuality (79–80). **Skaggs 1985:** This is one of several stories emphasizing the significance of religion—in this case a kind of pantheism (39). **Ewell 1986:** This tale shows Chopin's frustration with the shallow ethics often promoted by churches. It contrasts mystical, natural beauty (a true source of the divine) with the egotism of rigid dogma (92–93). This sketch shows Chopin's openness to new forms, styles, and subjects (101), in some ways resembling "An Idle Fellow" (126). **Toth 1990a:** This meditation may have been prompted by recently published criticism of Chopin. She did not submit the narrative at once but instead waited nearly a year before sending it, along with "Juanita," to an east-coast magazine, which quickly accepted both stories (231–32). The work, which resembles one by Maupassant (272), was intended for inclusion in *A Vocation and a Voice* (374). **Toth 1991:** This is one of several late stories by Chopin which reflect her interest in thought rather than mere plot (xxi–xxii). It is one of several stories in *A Vocation and a Voice* in which Chopin presents complex views of religion (xxiii). **Davis 1992b:** This is one of many stories from *A Vocation and a Voice* that focus on suddenly altered perceptions (200–201). **Fusco 1994:** Emily Toth sees resemblances between this tale and Maupassant's "Solitude" (141). **Koloski 1994:** The story is included in a soft-cover collection of Chopin's fiction published in 1991 (28). **Bender 1996:** The story emphasizes the narrator's rejection of conventional thought, whether religious or scientific (109). **Koloski 1996:** This story typifies Chopin's sardonic presentation of religion in *A Vocation and a Voice* (66–67). **Beer 1997:** This narrative, which can be seen as a lyric (67), should be considered alongside "Juanita," its companion-piece. Both tales reject superficial claims to knowledge and shallow ethical assessments, emphasizing instead the value of feelings. Chopin here uses a story-within-a-story, with the inner tale emphasizing sensuality without ever quite excluding social distinctions. The second paragraph resembles Whitman's poetry in moving from the local to the universal while recording the observer's responses, which constitute the story's main "plot." Like Juanita, the speaker here feels oppressed, yet unlike Juanita she is obliged to speak. The lyric interlude is inevitably brief and circumscribed by social pressures (78–82). **Ewell 1997:** This sketch seems to have had personal relevance to Chopin, who was much concerned with the conflict between natural experience and dogmatic teachings. The language describing the wind is especially indicative of the value she placed on the senses (108). **Toth and Seyersted 1998:** This story is mentioned in Chopin's account books (149) and in her diary for 1894 (189). **Toth 1999c:** The dark tone of this piece may have been influenced by public criticism recently leveled against Chopin (157).

"A Night in Acadie"

Written: 1896. Included in *A Night in Acadie* (1897).

Telèsphore is twenty-eight and realizes his need for a wife. The trouble is that he cannot decide which of the girls he knows he wants to marry. Sometimes he likes a change of scenery in which to contemplate his dilemma. He boards the train and heads for Marksville. At the station he notices a girl who is also boarding the train. He watches her and offers her his seat on the shady side of the train.

She accepts his offer and he sits beside her. They talk all the way to Marksville. She asks him if he is going to the ball. He knows nothing of the ball, but decides right then that if she is going to be there, then he will go. They get off the train and Telèsphore walks her to her cousin's house where she is staying.

When Telèsphore arrives at the ball there are people coming from all directions. Zaïda's cousin pulls up and lets her off the wagon at the front door. She is a vision, dressed in white from head to toe, with orange blossoms in her hair. One of the old ladies tells her that she looks just like a bride.

Telèsphore dances with Zaïda as often as possible. About midnight she asks him to see if her cousin is back in the card room. Jules is happily playing cards, so Zaïda walks out to the wagon with Telèsphore following at her heels. She gets in the wagon and starts to pull off. Telèsphore jumps in with her, asking where she is going. At first she is silent, but finally says that she is going to get married. Telèsphore is crushed. They get to the justice of the peace's house, but André Pascal, the intended groom, is not there. He finally arrives late and is half drunk. Zaïda is furious and tells him that she will not marry him. When he sees Telèsphore they begin to fight. They fight until André leaves. Telèsphore takes Zaïda back home. He is happy. **(DR)**

***

Rankin 1932: This story reflects Chopin's own thinking at the moment (163). **Seyersted 1969a:** To win the story's acceptance by the editor of a prestigious magazine, Chopin made the heroine more passive at the end, thus subverting the character's consistency (68–69). The conclusion Chopin first composed no longer exists (209). **Leary 1970a:** The young male in this story is treated by Chopin with gentle irony. His behavior is largely reactive, and the conclusion is nicely ambiguous (ix–x). Here as elsewhere, local color conventions help make the theme of feminine self-assertion more palatable to Chopin's readers (xi). **Leary 1971:** This story exemplifies Chopin's tendency to present her characters from a delicately amused and ironic perspective, as in her presentation of the male protagonist, who, by seeking to avoid romantic entanglement, collides with it (166). Here the popular local-color personalities and setting may have provided cover for Chopin's exploration of her favorite theme: women's yearning for freedom (167). **Peterson 1972:** The sentence beginning "He noticed that they were handsome eyes" is an example of the occasional clumsiness of Chopin's phrasing (9). In this story as elsewhere, Chopin uses sentimental conventions to subvert sentimentalism. Although the outcome of the tale is predictable, the prose gives pleasure. By the end of the story the main character has been subtly transformed. Authorial comments complicate the romantic tone of the piece, while the final battle is given an ironic setting (184–86). This story illustrates Chopin's impulse to describe life objectively (199). **Rocks 1972:** Here as elsewhere Chopin describes the passionate nature of courtship in Louisiana (118). **Arner 1975:** Here as in some other tales in the collection of the same name, Chopin risks being accused of shallow, if idiosyncratic, characterization. Nonetheless, the tale is effective in narration, plot, and credibility, showing affection as a potentially if not ultimately disruptive social influence. Chopin manages to breathe some new life even into old truisms here (64–65). **Taylor 1979:** This was one of several tales Chopin had difficulty publishing (viii). **Lattin 1980:** This is one of various stories by Chopin featuring repeating characters (28). **Baym 1981:** In this tale as in others, Chopin adapts the objective narrative style of Maupassant to a society whose ethics are basically healthy even as she also manages to communicate her own regard for her characters (xxv). **Fluck 1982:** This was one of the various unconventional, innovative stories by Chopin that were often turned down for publication (163). **Skaggs 1985:** This is one of several stories by Chopin that explore romance, often of an odd variety (32). The heroine here in some ways resembles not only Edna in *The Awakening* but also Calixta in "At the 'Cadian Ball" and "The Storm," especially in their self-assertiveness and independence (32–33). **Ewell 1986:** Although Chopin amended the story for a major magazine, seeking to make it more ethically and aesthetically acceptable, it was nevertheless turned down. Its current conclusion (emphasizing Zaïda's submission) therefore seems not to fit very well with the narrative—perhaps because Chopin changed the ending to make the story more conventionally palatable. Even so, the tale is superbly written, especially when describing the heroine. Touches of irony and understated comedy give the story an effectively ambiguous tone (117–18). **Gaudet 1986:** The geographical setting of this story is quite precise and implies Cajun characters (50). **Martin 1988a:** Although Chopin revised this work by disciplining a wayward character in order to make the tale more morally palatable, the story was still rejected by one editor (7). **Elfenbein 1989:** The rejection of "The Story of an Hour" by a major magazine encouraged Chopin to alter the present tale to make it more acceptable (125). **Toth 1990a:** Zaïda in this tale is similar to a character from Chopin's youthful reading (52), and the story also reflects the popularity of card games in Cloutierville (153). Although Chopin tried to tone down Zaïda's character to please an editor, she could not make the story conform to his conventional expectations (283). When the story was published in book form, it was given its present title, which is more intriguing than the original one (297); like the other stories in *A Night in Acadie*, this one is set in Louisiana (298). The tale was later reprinted in digest form, and one critic suggested an alternative ending to the story (328). Chopin once read the narrative at a ladies' club meeting (308). One male reader particularly praised this tale (328). **Vanlandingham 1990:** Chopin altered this story and another to satisfy the same editor, but she never again responded to such editorial pressure (161). **Guidici 1991:** This is one of many stories by Chopin that center around rejected marriage proposals. These rejections give the women greater autonomy (28–29). **Robinson 1992:** This story is typical of Chopin's work in presenting Cajuns—especially Cajun females—as more free-spirited than their Creole counterparts (xiii). Here as in other stories, Chopin depicts a woman who lacks social status but who nonetheless enjoys real power. Only the squeamishness of Chopin's editor prevented Zaïda from achieving the audacious goal she had set for herself in the original version of the story (xix). **Shurbutt 1993:** This is one of a few stories in which Chopin seems to accept conventional views of the relations between the sexes (22). **Cutter 1994:** Although Zaïda in some ways seems assertive and unconventional, eventually she becomes passive and reticent, perhaps because Chopin's editors wanted her that way (20). **Koloski 1994:** The story is included in soft-cover collections of Chopin's fiction published in 1970, 1981, and 1992 (27). **Bender 1996:** This is one of various stories in which Chopin's basically Darwinian outlook leads her to examine the problems caused by an insufficiently assertive male (107). The tale exemplifies Darwinian ideas about competition between males, the power of natural instincts, and the predominance of sexual desire over love (112). **Koloski 1996:** Here as elsewhere Chopin presents characters who lack learning (11) and also describes Acadian festivities (20). This tale establishes the key traits of the volume in which it appears. The dance provides opportunities for social experimentation and for making and dissolving relationships. The plot is uncomplicated, and the story resembles others by Chopin in its heroine, its focus on a train, its depiction of impoverishment, and its diction, although it differs from her other works in emphasizing physical conflict. This tale, the introductory story of *A Night in Acadie*, resembles the initial stories in *Bayou Folk* and *A Vocation and a Voice*, and its heroine's name may reflect Chopin's knowledge of opera (51–53). She altered the conclusion of the work at the prompting of an editor (85). **Toth and Seyersted 1998:** This story is mentioned in Chopin's account books (142, 150). In a letter Chopin mentions that the story was once called "In the Vicinity of Marksville" (209). **Brown 1999:** As in "A No-Account Creole," Chopin here contrasts two types of men who compete for a woman. Telèsphore, like other males in Chopin's fiction, undergoes a kind of awakening thanks to his contact with an unconventional woman (80–81). **Koloski 1999:** This is one of several tales in *A Night in Acadie* that focus on a transforming journey (xvi). It forms an effective link with the tales published in *Bayou Folk*, particularly with "A Visit to Avoyelles." It shows the economic and social constraints Chopin's characters often suffer in their quests for personal fulfillment. The description of Zaïda's slippers here is especially clever. In plot the story resembles the later "In Sabine," but in both cases the heroine's life is improved merely by accident (xvi). **McCullough 1999:** Zaïda's race is not emphasized, but the cook is black (318). Regional identities are important in this tale, especially in characterizing the heroine. In certain respects the story reinforces ethnic, even racist, stereotypes. The tale may seem to challenge some prejudices about women, but it implicitly supports others. The revised ending undercuts some of the story's original subversiveness, thereby weakening the characterization of the heroine. Here and elsewhere Chopin's depiction of Cajun women is ambivalent and elastic. The revision robs Zaïda of some of her ethnic otherness, but it cannot erase that otherness completely. Hence the revised ending is less consistent with the rest of the story (205–9). **Toth 1999c:** A character in this tale may have been influenced by Chopin's childhood reading (20). The story reflects her own interest in card-playing when she lived in Cloutierville (89). This is the most unusual story included in Chopin's second collection. Its defects may have resulted from her efforts to please conventional tastes. She toned the work down to mollify an editor, although he still rejected the story. Ironically, when it was finally published a reviewer suggested that a better ending would have been the one Chopin had suppressed (194–95). **Gibbons 2000:** Although the heroine of the story proves far more submissive and accommodating than Edna in *The Awakening*, the skill of the story—especially in language, characterization, and plot—foreshadows the success of the novel (xxxix–xl).

"A No-Account Creole"

Written: 1888. Rewritten: 1891. First published: 1894. Included in *Bayou Folk* **(1894).**

Wallace Offdean is a young man questioning his existence. He has graduated college, traveled at home and abroad, enjoyed society and his clubs, and worked in his uncle's commission-house. He has just turned twenty-six and received his inheritance, and now he is undecided about what he wants out of life and what to do next.

When his uncle's firm needs someone to look after a piece of run-down land on the Red River in north Louisiana, Offdean volunteers, hoping that being away from New Orleans will give him the opportunity to do some soul-searching.

The piece of land is known as "the old Santien place," for it was once owned by Lucien Santien. It was worked with a hundred slaves and produced much wealth for Santien. Then the war came and ruined the thousand-acre plantation. Santien could not overcome the damages of the war, nor could his three sons. Eventually the New Orleans creditors, Harding and Offdean, took the run-down plantation.

Of the three sons Placide, the middle son, tries to keep a foothold on the place. He travels often, but never further than a half day's distance from the place. Some farming is still done by several ex-slaves. The house is in such bad condition that half the rooms are useless because the roof leaks badly when it rains. The brick pillars holding the veranda roof are crumbling and the rails are broken. The slave quarters are in even worse condition.

Wallace Offdean sits on the veranda, oblivious to the run-down condition of the house. He sees only beauty in the openness of the land. Next to him, a flowering vine with huge yellow, fragrant blooms fills his senses with beauty and peacefulness. The plantation manager, Pierre Manton, sits with him, telling him about the workings of the place. Pierre mentions that his daughter, Euphrasie, is coming home today and that she is the one who has been writing the letters to Harding and Offdean about the condition of the plantation.

Placide does not feel good about Euphrasie's interest in the plantation, but she feels strongly that it is shameful for a company as large as Harding and Offdean not to bring the place back to its original state of grandeur. Placide could make all the repairs himself, for he is talented as a blacksmith, carpenter, and painter. However, he uses his skills not on the plantation but in the surrounding towns, particularly Orville, where he owns a small home. He spends a great deal of time on his little home because in the spring he will marry Euphrasie and bring her here to live.

Placide believes that he fell in love with Euphrasie when he was six years old. Pierre, his father's overseer, allowed Placide to hold his infant daughter in his arms. She was the first white baby Placide had ever seen. He can marry any girl he pleases, but he wants Euphrasie, even though everyone else feels that she is beneath him.

Euphrasie arrives at the plantation and Offdean realizes that she is the girl he helped to a high position on the balcony of his club on the last Mardi Gras night. He had wondered then who the beautiful girl was.

After two weeks has passed, Offdean feels very much at home with Pierre and Euphrasie on the plantation. Every afternoon he and Euphrasie ride on horseback into the woods to mark trees to be cut down. Offdean learns everything he can about the condition of the place and how he can improve it. As he and Euphrasie ride past the slave quarters, old LaChatte tells another woman that nothing good will come of Offdean "caperin' roun' Miss 'Phrasie." She tells the story of Placide holding a gun on her once, insisting that she make him some croquignoles.

When Offdean gets back to his office in New Orleans, he can think of nothing else than the plantation and its improvements. His interest in the place consumes him. One day he gets a letter from Euphrasie saying that she is coming to New Orleans for Mardi Gras.

He is delighted with the news, hoping that he can return some of the hospitality that was extended to him by Euphrasie and her father. He makes all sorts of plans for the two of them, but when Euphrasie arrives the Duplans already have everything planned for her. Offdean has no time alone with her, so he writes her a note, asking for a meeting to discuss matters of the plantation. She agrees to see him the day before she leaves to go home.

The meeting goes well. It is obvious that they are in love. When Offdean leaves, she goes to the window to watch him. Placide comes in the room and finds her. She is confused, for she is inexperienced in matters of the heart.

Spring arrives and Placide is busily making the finishing touches on his house. After Euphrasie left New Orleans, Offdean admitted to himself that he loved her, but because his future is un-certain he feels he cannot ask her to marry him. After weeks of dreaming of her and constantly thinking of her, it suddenly comes to him that he can buy the plantation with his inheritance and that he and Euphrasie can marry and be forever happy on the land they both love.

Placide had arrived at the plantation that morning and is rest-ing in his room after traveling all night. His marriage to Euphrasie is expected to occur in a few days. He hears Euphrasie walk to a chair on the veranda outside his room. He lies on his bed, listening.

Offdean arrives and finds Euphrasie sitting on the veranda with her sewing. He immediately expresses his love for her, tells her his plan, and asks her to be his wife. She answers that she does not love him and asks him if he knows that she and Placide will be married in two days. She is almost whimpering. Offdean is shocked, but tries to recover, saying that had he known, he never would have spoken this way to her. He asks for her forgiveness. As he leaves, she sobs. She goes to her room and locks the door.

Placide hears everything. Upon hearing her lock her door, he rises, puts on his boots, and takes his pistol from the dressing table. He leaves the house quietly. He has only one thought: to put an end to the man who has come between him and his beloved. He catches up with Offdean. He could shoot him in the back, but he wants Offdean to know who ended his life and why. When he con-fronts Offdean, Offdean tells him that he must be crazy to spoil his own happiness with murder. He says that he thought Creoles knew how to love a woman and that is to consider her happiness first of all. Offdean says that he is leaving tomorrow and vows that they will never see him again. He turns and rides away. Placide thinks about what Offdean said and puts his gun away.

Offdean rises early the next morning. Euphrasie is in the hall with Pierre, who is walking slowly with his head bowed. Eu-phrasie asks him if Placide is up and he starts telling her that Placide left in the night, telling Pierre that he was going to Orville to paint Mr. Luke Williams' place. He also told Pierre to tell Eu-phrasie that he knows what will make her happy. Pierre exclaims that he always knew that Placide was "a no-account creole." Eu-phrasie tells Pierre not to talk like that about Placide because he has saved her life.

The news in the town is that Placide has been jilted by his fi-ancée and the wedding is off. The news is being broadcast by Placide. **(DR)**

Anonymous 1894 [*Review of Reviews*]: This is the longest tale in *Bayou Folk*, an unusually strong collection full of varied emotions, straightforward prose, and effective dialect—a book comparable to the works of the best French writers (44). **Rankin 1932:** Wallace Offdean is based on Chopin's own husband's experiences in the cotton business in 1870 (95–96). The title of the tale went through four variations, ending in one that refers ironically to the main male character (114). The story was very well received by the editor who eventually published it (135–36). **Reilly 1942:** This story illustrates the tendency of Chopin's heroines to remain loyal once they have made a romantic commitment (132–33). **Fletcher 1966:** This tale typifies the emphasis on fidelity often exemplified by Chopin's Creole women (127). **Seyersted 1969a:** The experiences of Chopin's own husband may be reflected in those of young Wallace Offdean in this earliest of her tales (37–38), which was originally entitled "Euphrasie" (50). After showing the story to a trusted male friend in 1890, Chopin rewrote it and retitled it and early the next year submitted it to a prominent magazine, whose editor suggested clarifying characterization in ways Chopin considered helpful. After she revised the story, it was gladly accepted (55–56), perhaps in part because she had softened the character of the heroine (68). Like other stories by Chopin, this one features a poor Creole whose fortunes have been damaged by the Civil War, although his fate is partly due to his own lack of drive. Nonetheless, this is one of Chopin's few tales in which Northerners and Creoles are brought into explicit contact (77). Euphrasie is a passive woman willing to accept a fate she would like to avoid and unwilling even to kiss the man she truly loves (a reluctance Chopin subtly criticizes). When revising the story, Chopin tightened it and changed the title to focus on one of the males (103–4). Although Euphrasie is submissive, she is not stereotypically maudlin; Chopin's tone is unusually distanced and objective (105). **Leary 1970a:** Here as in other works by Chopin, plot is less important than motivation and character. Chopin depicts her people honestly and without becoming maudlin. The story is thus completely convincing (ix). **Leary 1970b:** This is one of Chopin's two best and most detailed tales (140). **Leary 1971:** The story is typical of Chopin in its colorful setting, its focus on a city dweller visiting the country, and its emphasis on a woman's latent desire for emancipation. Here as so often, however, plot is less significant than meaning. The story avoids becoming maudlin; instead it delicately explores the complexity of the human psyche (165). **Peterson 1972:** This story is much longer than most by Chopin, and in its weaknesses it resembles her early novel, *At Fault*. Although the basic plot is familiar, Chopin manages to keep it fairly fresh, partly by making Euphrasie relatively assertive (in fact, she may have been even more so in the first version). Also atypical is the fact that the businessman wins the romantic contest (81–83). Even so, the story eventually relies on typical plot devices to produce its somewhat maudlin conclusion, but Chopin creates some effective scenes in the process (83–85). The story is over-populated with unintegrated characters who add some spice but do not greatly advance the plot. Meanwhile, the main characters tend to exist in isolation, with most of the tension occurring within Euphrasie. All in all, though, this is one of Chopin's more successful early stories (85–88). It illustrates her skill in characterization (96). **Rocks 1972:** Here as elsewhere Chopin describes the passionate nature of courtship in Louisiana (118). **Seyersted 1974:** This story depicts a conventionally selfless, passive woman whose fate is determined by the men in her life (11–12). **Arner 1975:** Here as elsewhere, the somewhat crude setting, plot, and characters contrast with an intriguing theme. Structure and dialogue are effective but the resolution is somewhat timid and unconvincing. Nonetheless, this work anticipates, in important ways, Chopin's often more candid treatment of similar subjects later (56–57). **Skaggs 1975:** This is Chopin's earliest tale focusing on masculine possessiveness, which she seems to have considered especially typical of the hierarchical culture of the South. Here, though, Chopin contrives to prevent the kind of unhappy marriage she later explored in *The Awakening* (277). **Bonner 1977:** Here as elsewhere Chopin treats her local-color characters as individual persons rather than as stereotypes (6–7). Here as elsewhere in *Bayou Folk*, Chopin divides a story into distinct sections (8–9). The story shows the tensions often inherent in love (10). The story explores the topic of the rural vs. the urban (13). **Taylor 1979:** This was one of several tales Chopin had difficulty publishing (viii). **Lattin 1980:** This is one of the stories in which Chopin describes members of the Duplan family, her least intriguing and least dramatic group of repeating characters. However, this story also depicts members of the more interesting (because less stable) Santien family, and it offers many details about them (21). Other repeating characters also appear in this tale (25; 28). **Lattin 1982:** This is one of several stories by Chopin in which self-assured characters must learn their limitations in order to achieve true self-understanding (225–26). **Grover 1984:** This is one of a surprising number of Chopin's tales in which men are appealingly depicted (30–31). Although Euphrasie is a Cajun, the fact that she has been raised by Creoles makes her eligible to marry one (31). **Aherne 1985:** This is one of many stories by Chopin that involve conflicting affections. The outcome is ambiguous (81). **Skaggs 1985:** This is one of several tales focusing on the interaction of affection and selfhood (17–18). **Ewell 1986:** The first version of this story may already have contained the seeds of Chopin's later full-blown depiction, developed in several works, of the Santien family (20–21). This was the first of her tales to be published in *The Century*, a very prominent national magazine (24), from which she received a substantial payment and welcome praise (although the story did not actually appear for almost two-and-a-half years [54–55]). This was a rewritten version of her very first story, which she had earlier entitled "Euphrasie" and then "A Maid and Her Lovers." Chopin herself thought the pace of the tale was slow, but she also considered all its material essential. The protagonists are all complexly and coherently depicted, while the less important characters are effectively comic but also essential to the plot. Many of the protagonists foreshadow character-types Chopin would also explore in her later writings, although Euphrasie herself sometimes seems inconsistently portrayed. This is much less true of the men, whose tensions symbolize regional strife while also implying Chopin's understated mockery of overblown Southern idealism. Offdean represents the rise of new cultural forces, while Placide seems mired in a decaying past. Nonetheless, his final generous impulse wins our respect, even if it seems a bit contrived. The title is richly ambiguous, since it both does and does not accurately describe the complexity of Placide, who represents values Chopin cannot fully respect (55–56). **Martin 1988a:** Although Chopin revised this work by disciplining a wayward character in order to make the tale more morally palatable, the story was still rejected by one editor (7). **Papke 1988:** This early tale shows a woman who accepts male power and who therefore resembles Adèle in *The Awakening* (73). **Inge 1989:** Important themes include the potential of affection, and of a natural setting, to transform the soul; the selflessness of real affection; and the often paradoxical impact of claims to cultural superiority. This tale, one of Chopin's most lengthy, illustrates her developing capacity to use descriptions of environment as a way to illuminate characters' psyches. The dilapidated estate here implies the inner chaos felt by Euphrasie and Offdean. Just as Offdean helps organize the estate, so his own emotions become better integrated thanks to his affection: as the estate is transformed, so is his spirit. In this tale, matrimony seems to hold out the hope of genuinely mutual freedom, although in Placide's case a truer comprehension of love involves abandoning his hope for marriage (94). **Taylor 1989:** Chopin's revision of this tale shows that she sometimes responded to editorial influence in order to win approval (149). Although this work foreshadows *The Awakening*, it is less radical than the novel (179). It anticipates the latter work by emphasizing the ubiquity and force of erotic yearnings and by stressing unusual matters, including social and sexual instability and cultural change. Although the heroine seems to achieve some liberty by the end of the tale, our final glimpse of her suggests that she is still subordinate to a man (179–80). Euphrasie's attitude toward marriage is largely conformist, partly because her practical alternatives are few (182). **Papke 1990:** Chopin's decision to change the title of this story and thus de-emphasize its feminine protagonist reveals her willingness to adapt to conventional social pressures. Ironically, the action by Euphrasie that stimulates the plot takes place before the story itself begins, so that the focus of the tale is thrown even more onto the two major male characters. Euphrasie herself remains fairly static, passive, and bland. Honor, rather than romance, is the tale's central theme, and it is Placide who emerges as the most conventionally honorable character. Euphrasie, meanwhile, is one of Chopin's few heroines who conforms to conventional expectations of women's uncomprehending passivity. In some respects she reflects

Chopin's own lack of daring at this point in her career, although even in depicting Euphrasie so passively, Chopin perhaps occasionally implies a more radical view of feminine existence (36–38). **Toth 1990a:** In certain respects Offdean here is comparable to Chopin's husband (92–93). The story shows Chopin's familiarity with the ways men and women often mingled in Louisiana society (168). The story began as a novella, but Chopin trimmed it after allowing a friend to read it. When it appeared in a national magazine, Chopin was already a well-known local-color writer (177–78). The story had been rejected by various other journals because of its length, but to help ensure its acceptance by the *Century* she revised it according to the editor's suggestions and received handsome payment for her efforts (203–4). When the tale was reprinted in *Bayou Folk*, it was grouped with two other tales treating members of the same extended family (224). A St. Louis publication praised the story (234), which had taken Chopin longer to compose than most of her tales (245). Although Placide is racially abusive, Chopin presents him with some sympathy even as she implies the need for a new kind of white cultural supremacy represented by Euphrasie and Offdean (61–63; 67). **Vanlandingham 1990:** Chopin was willing to alter this story so it could appear in a major journal, but the magazine did not print it for over two years (160–61). **Brown 1991:** The story anticipates *The Awakening* in its focus on a sheltered woman's sudden sensual longings (119–20). **Guidici 1991:** This is one of many stories by Chopin that center around rejected marriage proposals. These rejections give the women greater autonomy (28–29). **Robinson 1992:** The Creole preoccupation with self-respect and family status is a major focus of this tale. Euphrasie is a perplexing figure: attractive both physically and ethically, she nonetheless has unconventional ideas. These propel the story line, yet she herself takes little personal initiative, partly because she is constrained by social tradition. Placide's act of renunciation helps save the life of Offdean and also helps transform the inner lives of both himself and Euphrasie. Partly the story illustrates changes taking place in the contemporary social hierarchy, but partly it examines the intricacies of Creole culture, particularly the social mobility reflected in the rise of a person like Euphrasie, whose attractiveness allows her to overcome her racial heritage (which was probably somewhat mixed [xvi–xvii]). **Toth 1992:** Perhaps this story took an unusually long time to compose because it was one of Chopin's earliest (18). **Cutter 1994:** Euphrasie typifies the often reticent women Chopin depicted early in her career (18–19). **Ewell 1994:** In setting and topics, this early tale foreshadows much of Chopin's later writing. At an editor's prompting she changed the title's focus from a female to a male character, and the new title also made the story more obviously marketable as a piece of local color fiction (159). Here as elsewhere Chopin explores how women respond to social convention—an exploration partly prompted, it seems, by her own experiences as a middle-aged female (169). **Koloski 1994:** The story is included in soft-cover collections of Chopin's fiction published in 1970 and 1992 (27–28). **Gunning 1995:** The focus here is less on Euphrasie than on Placide, whose motives reflect the violent ethic that resulted in slavery. Chopin, however, largely ignores race in this story, concentrating instead on depicting Placide as a victim of the social changes wrought by the Civil War. Ironically, Placide's status in the story is not unlike the status of blacks in Southern life, and the tale seems to justify the rise of a new but still culturally prejudiced South based on cooperation between whites from the country and the city. Like much of Chopin's other local-color fiction, this story is rooted in the dominant racial ideology of the time (61–67). **Bender 1996:** In this story Chopin suggests that Darwinian principles of male sexual competition might be softened if men heeded the desires of women (105–6). **Koloski 1996:** This story, one of several by Chopin that depict violence (11–12), was her first published tale and took three years to complete. Like other works of hers, it uses a house to symbolize new possibilities, and it presents its heroine as a stoic realist, not a nostalgic dreamer. Both she and Offdean seek stability and moderation—ideals that often elude other characters Chopin created. This work differs significantly from "Ma'ame Pélagie," despite its similar theme (14–19). This story shares characters and other elements with various other stories by Chopin (20–24; 35; 53) and features such motifs as a symbolic house (15–18; 24; 51), an ambiguous kiss (62), important boundaries (87), allusions to opera (57), significant outsiders (21), and matters of voice (55). **Wagner-Martin 1996:** Here as elsewhere Chopin depicts an energetic, determined female (197). However, the tale also features the men of the Santien clan (198) as well as an appealing black woman of the sort presented elsewhere in Chopin's fiction (203). **Beer 1997:** This is one of Chopin's few stories that was shaped substantially by the responses of friends and editors, whose advice she sought (11). It is one of several tales in which she deals with the need for romantic freedom and depicts the oppressiveness of a partner's presence (42). **Toth and Seyersted 1998:** This story, one of Chopin's earliest published tales (127), is mentioned in her account books (139, 148, 153, 165) and letters (202, 203). **Bonner and Bonner 1999:** This story shows Chopin's familiarity with the business district of New Orleans (57–58). The streetcars mentioned in this story help establish the status of the streets on which they run (63). **Brown 1999:** Here as in other works, Chopin presents two contrasting types of men. Their interactions lead each to important discoveries about themselves and to significant changes in their views and behavior (78–80). **Bryant 1999:** Here as elsewhere Chopin combines interests in ethnicity, gender, and economic status (31). In this tale black characters are denied a voice and are linked with animals and material possessions, and Chopin seems to approve these associations. La Chatte not only fits the "mammy" stereotype but is also intimidated by a young white male (46–47). **Koloski 1999:** Euphrasie, like many figures Chopin created, tends to follow her instincts. Offdean seeks a well-tempered life of intelligent moderation (xii). Here as in other stories by Chopin, the heroine ultimately achieves her goals (xiii). This story features several motifs common to

Chopin's fiction: construction of a house, a significant visitor, and the effort to achieve equilibrium (xiv). **Toth 1999c:** This story shows how a romantic rendezvous might be arranged in Cloutierville (96). This was the first work Chopin wrote with the intention of submitting it to be printed, and its male characters may resemble men Chopin knew (104–5). She worked on the story for several years, but it was repeatedly turned down before being purchased by a major magazine that requested further revisions. Chopin mainly complied, although the heroine of the tale seems a bit lackluster. Nevertheless, Chopin was very well paid, and her success sparked further creativity (131–32). She actually visited the editor of the journal and perhaps prompted him to speed the story's publication (134). Later, though, the magazine turned down many of her submissions (136). When the tale was printed in *Bayou Folk*, the publisher asked her to make it one of the first three stories (150). It is one of many works in that collection that depict women very favorably (154).

"Octave Feuillet"

Written: 1891. Lost.

Ewell 1986: This is one of several non-extant stories mentioned in Chopin's records (190). **Toth 1990a:** This story, one of sixteen Chopin composed in 1891, was one of two of that number that were lost or discarded (198).

"Odalie Misses Mass"

Written: 1895. First published: 1895. Included in *A Night in Acadie* (1897).

Odalie and her family are on their way to mass, but she insists that they stop at Aunt Pinky's so the elderly woman can see how Odalie looks all dressed up. Aunt Pinky is old and shriveled. Odalie asks where Pug is. Pug has gone to church, as it appears that everyone else has done. Finding no one else around who can stay with Aunt Pinky, Odalie tells her family to go on to church without her. She is afraid that Aunt Pinky might fall and hurt herself if left alone.

Odalie sits down in a rocking chair close to Aunt Pinky and begins to rock. Aunt Pinky begins to repeat previous conversations; Odalie moves her chair closer to Aunt Pinky's knee and Aunt Pinky caresses the girl's curls and her shoulders as she talks.

Aunt Pinky asks Odalie if she remembers events of long ago. Odalie realizes that Aunt Pinky thinks that she is Paulette. Odalie goes along with the old woman even though she has heard all these stories many times. The two spend the time reminiscing until Odalie is awakened by her mother. Odalie tells her mother that she fell asleep and that so did Aunt Pinky. Her mother replies that yes, Aunt Pinky is asleep. She walks quietly out of the cabin and out of the presence of the dead. **(DR)**

***

Gilder 1898: This is a moving account of altruism, in this case of a white toward a black (50). **Seyersted 1969a:** An important theme is the devotion of whites to blacks (79). **Potter 1971:** Once more, as in "The Bênitous' Slave" (a story with which this one even shares some characters), Chopin shows the devastating impact of slavery on individual lives. The main characters in both tales, mired in the past and unable to adapt to liberty, meet death while still mentally enslaved. Although the story might conceivably be read as presenting a benign view of slavery, the impact of that system on Pinky's life destroys her capacity for real human affection (52–53). **Bonner 1982:** This is one of several stories by Chopin in which Christianity is an important aspect (125). **Davis 1982:** As in other stories, Chopin here uses imagery of springtime and religion to reinforce a theme of secular, personal rebirth (66). **Skaggs 1985:** This is one of many stories by Chopin that shows a real familiarity with children and their effects on others (27–28). **Ewell 1986:** This story is fairly traditional in topic and method. Although it does invert the standard plot stressing blacks' affection for whites, it also poorly explains Odalie's conduct. Likewise, Aunt Pinky's wandering thoughts, though expressed and somewhat affecting, are largely unsurprising (107). **Manders 1990:** Here as in several of her other stories featuring blacks, Chopin presents a variation of the conventional figure of the "wretched freeman"—the erstwhile slave who allegedly had benefited from subjection. However, her focus on former domestic slaves, rather than on the more abused field-workers, makes her depiction more credible (37–40). Both the elderly black and the young white are depicted here as innocently childlike, but such pairing contributes to the complexity of the tale (40). The young woman matures by experiencing the old woman's death, and although the story sentimentalizes the physical punishments slaves suffered, it achieves value by exploring an example of the existential loneliness of the elderly (40–41). **Toth 1990a:** This is one of various stories in which Chopin shows respect for elderly women (40). It was unusual for its time in depicting a friendship that crossed racial and generational divisions. Perhaps because it was unusual, the story was turned down by *The Century* (251). It was included in *A Night in Acadie* (298) and was praised by one reviewer (300). **Robinson 1992:** This is one of many stories by Chopin that depict harmony between the races—a harmony that was not entirely unknown or unrealistic following the Civil War (xix). **Goodwyn 1994:** This is one of various stories by Chopin depicting the loyalty of whites to blacks (10). **Koloski 1994:** The story is included in a soft-cover collection of Chopin's fiction published in 1992 (28). **Fetterley and Pryse 1995:** Here as elsewhere in Chopin's fiction, a black female is a major character but mostly fits a cultural stereotype (409). As in other stories, Chopin depicts a young person's concern for an older one. Often the compassionate person is not an adult woman, although that was often the case in New England fiction (410). **Koloski 1996:** This is one of several stories in which Chopin's depiction of African-Americans seems stereotypical and potentially troubling, although Richard Potter argues that Chopin here and elsewhere individualized her black characters (44–45). **Thomas 1996:** This story is one of many in which Chopin depicts aged black females, often in stereotypical terms (216–17). **Beer 1997:** In this story Chopin reverses the standard emphasis on the loyalty of blacks to whites (35). **Koloski 1999:** Here as elsewhere, Chopin implicitly commends one person's fidelity to another (xviii–xix). **McCollough 1999:** Although this story shows some cooperation between the races, its underlying implications still seem basically racist (319). **Toth 1999a:** This is one of Chopin's most unconventional tales and thus would not have appealed to traditional editors (9–10). **Toth 1999b:** In its social implications, this story may be one of Chopin's two most revolutionary pieces of fiction (48). **Toth 1999c:** This unusual story reverses standard depictions of race relations (12), and it typifies Chopin's tendency to focus on harmony between young people and their elders (16). The title character is as old as Chopin was when her great-grandmother passed away. Chopin had trouble finding a publisher for the work, and the newspaper that did eventually print it gave her no compensation. The diction can strike modern audiences as saccharine or racially offensive, but the latter reaction shows a failure to perceive Chopin's view that women of different races can enjoy mutual affection. The title character is willing to give up her desire for social commendation out of loyalty to Aunt Pinky. Mutual regard of the sort this tale displays is unusual even today (169–70).

"Old Aunt Peggy"

Written: 1892. Included in *Bayou Folk* (1897).

When the war was finished, old Aunt Peggy went to Monsieur and declared that she would never leave him and the Madame. Even though she was getting old and weak, and she knew she did not have many days left here in this place of grief and sadness, she wanted nothing but a little spot on his plantation where she could sit down and wait peacefully for her end. Her love and loyalty struck responsive chords in these two decent people. So when they made the necessary changes after the surrender, they provided Aunt Peggy with a nice cabin, furnished with all she needed—even a rocking chair where she could sit and, as she said, wait for her end.

Aunt Peggy has been rocking for a long time now. About every two years, she shuffles up to the house and delivers a routine speech. She asks to take a last look at everyone. She wants to see Monsieur and Madame, the children big and small, the pictures and photographs, and the piano. She wants to see everything one more time before she goes "stone-bline." Then, as always, she returns home with an apron loaded with gifts. Monsieur has long ago lost the qualms he once felt about supporting a woman in idleness. His feeling for Aunt Peggy has grown into wonderment—amazement at the advanced age an old black woman can reach when she is determined to live. Why, she says she is a hundred and twenty-five now. That may not be true, though. She could be older. **(CY)**

***

Rankin 1932: The title character represents one of the kinds of people Chopin would have met during her time in Cloutierville (103). Although extremely short, this work is far better than many unnecessarily long tales by other writers (138). **Bush 1957:** This is one of Chopin's many amusing tales, partly because of its gentle irony (241). **Arms 1967:** Like "Beyond the Bayou" and "The Return of Alcibiade," this tale balances emotionalism and realism (223). **Arner 1975:** This tale is comparable to "The Bênitous' Slave," which focuses on an old black male (62). **Bonner 1977:** In this story and others, Chopin quickly describes a personality. Such brief and usually comic tales are often interspersed with longer, darker stories in *Bayou Folk* (9–10). **Taylor 1979:** Although Chopin's depictions of blacks are often simplistic, romantic, or patronizing, this tale is an exception (xiii). **Toth 1981:** Here and in some other early tales, the black characters fit the stereotype of the happy slave (202). **Skaggs 1985:** This is one of several stories featuring characters whose lives and minds have been disrupted by the Civil War (14–15). It is also one of several stories dealing with the selfhood of ex-slaves; its tone is fatalistic (16). **Ewell 1986:** This piece in some ways resembles "The Bênitous' Slave" but is less well developed (even though also more vital). The title character's premonitions of death are described with effective humor, and the final twist typifies Chopin's stimulating style (67). **Skaggs 1988:** This story is typical of Chopin's local color tales focusing on African-Americans (80). **Toth 1990a:** This is one of various stories in which Chopin shows respect for elderly women (40). It was one of three tales she composed in two days and which were all immediately purchased for publication (206–7). However, the tale had not been published before appearing in *Bayou Folk* (223). **Goodwyn 1994:** This story illustrates the ways the African-American characters in Chopin's fiction often subtly subvert racist values even while seeming to affirm them (4). **Koloski 1994:** The story is included in soft-cover collections of Chopin's fiction published in 1979 and 1992 (27–28). **Koloski 1996:** This is one of many stories Chopin wrote for children (87). **Thomas 1996:** This story is one of many in which Chopin depicts aged black females, often in stereotypical terms (216–17). **Beer 1997:** Here as in other stories by Chopin, black characters speak in subtly subversive ways (28). Liberty is a crucial theme, as is the clever use of language and symbols. Aunt Peggy realizes that she, ironically, helps confirm the status her former owners once enjoyed, and she exploits their nostalgia for her own benefit. Although Chopin generally doesn't describe material objects, she uses them here for their symbolic significance (70–73). This was one of three stories Chopin composed in only two days, according to Emily Toth (85). **Benfey 1999:** This story demonstrates Chopin's skill in using the theme of return (284). **Koloski 1999:** This is one of many stories by Chopin which either feature children or were written for them (xxii). **Toth 1999c:** This story shows the respect a white youth feels for an elderly black woman (16). However, it also shows the negative impact the Civil War could have on African-Americans, even as it also shows the generosity of women (154). **Knights 2000:** Although this story can be read as a condescending depiction of the title character, it can also be interpreted (as by Janet Beer) as subverting the prejudices of the white characters (xxxi).

"One Day in Winter"
See also "A December Day in Dixie"

Ewell 1986: This is an abbreviated retelling of "A December Day in Dixie." An accompanying note to an editor suggests some doubt about the story's success. The tale describes how snow, like the imagination, can briefly alter our perceptions and behavior (176).

"Ozème's Holiday"

Written: 1894. First published: 1896. Included in *A Night in Acadie* **(1897).**

Ozème is always busy. There is always something that needs his attention. One week each year he takes a holiday. This year he gets all dressed up and plans to go visiting along the Cane River. He counts on arriving at the Fédeaus' around noon and having lunch with them, hoping they will ask him to stay the night. Then to the Beltrans' to stay a night or two. On then to Tante Sophie and Cousin Victoire, and finally to Cloutierville before he retraces his steps and returns home.

The Fédeaus are not at home, so he decides to take a short cut to the Beltrans' home, thinking he will keep an eye out for Aunt Tildy's cabin somewhere along the way. When he sees her cabin, he also sees that the cotton is ready to be picked, with some of it already falling on the ground. Aunt Tildy is glad to see him. The first thing he asks her is why she is letting her crop of cotton go to waste. She explains that Sandy is sick in bed and she has a hurt hand.

Ozème considers the situation and tells Aunt Tildy that he will give Sandy a dose of quinine that night and will stay to see how it does him, but at daybreak he must be on his way. In the morning Sandy is better, but not well enough for Ozème to leave before noon. He asks Aunt Tildy for the cotton sack and goes out to pick cotton. By noon he has picked fifty pounds. He decides to stay the rest of the day and that night too. If Sandy is not better in the morning, he will go for the doctor.

Sandy is much better the next morning, but Ozème does not feel comfortable leaving him in Aunt Tildy's care, so he stays one more night.

One the third day it looks like it might rain, causing a substantial loss to Aunt Tildy on her cotton crop. Ozème goes again to the cotton field; this time he takes Aunt Tildy with him. On the fourth day rain still threatens, so again he and Aunt Tildy go to the fields.

The next night the rain comes, but Ozème and Aunt Tildy have all the cotton picked and put away. He leaves the next morning.

When Ozème arrives back home, everyone asks him how his holiday was and where he went, because nobody in Cloutierville has seen him. He answers that he was tired of things on the Cane River so he went to the back woods and camped out. **(DR)**

***

Anonymous 1897 [*Post-Dispatch*]: This is one of various stories by Chopin that seems appealing because of its subtle depiction of altruism (47). **Rankin 1932:** This small tale is comically moving. Ozème's conflicting impulses are depicted in a way that seems both appealing and true to life (169). **Reilly 1942:** Here as elsewhere, Chopin's talent for effectively ending a story protects the work from seeming sentimental or unconvincing (131). **Bush 1957:** In this tale Chopin reverses her common focus on a loyal slave by showing a white man's generosity toward blacks (245). **Seyersted 1969a:** This is one of Chopin's very best stories, especially in its deft, efficient depiction of character. Ozème is probably a Cajun of middle social status whose interactions with Aunt Tildy become increasingly complex in tone. His response combines humor, subtle antagonism, self-concern, generosity, and social self-consciousness (123–25). **Potter 1971:** Here as in other stories, Chopin makes her main black character seem a complex person rather than a mere stick figure. Aunt Tildy wins our regard because of her self-respect and self-assertion and is in fact one of Chopin's most commendable creations. Her individuality is enhanced by her distinctive religious attitudes (55–56). **Peterson 1972:** This is one of six tales Chopin composed between the summers of 1893 and 1895 in which she focuses on altruism. In this work she nicely avoids the sentimental tone that could have handicapped the story (124–25). **Rocks 1972:** Here as elsewhere, Chopin demonstrates the complexities liberty can involve and shows that true liberty often entails a responsible concern for others (117). **Seyersted 1974:** This work and others justify Chopin's reputation as a superb writer of local color fiction (11). **Berggren 1977:** Here and elsewhere Chopin shows that life often seems meaningless unless one has a vocation—a selfless dedication to a larger purpose. Stories such as this show the personal rewards of altruism. This story also shows that men, not only women, can feel enriched by helping others (1). **Lattin 1980:** This is one of the stories in which Chopin describes members of the Duplan family, her least intriguing and least dramatic group of repeating characters (21). Other repeating characters also appear in this tale (25; 28). **Baym 1981:** The story exemplifies Chopin's interest in race relations (xix). Here as in other tales, Chopin provides a morally complex and appealing conclusion (xxv). **Bonner 1982:** This is one of various stories by Chopin that reflect the importance of selfless Christian love. The story's comic touches prevent it from seeming too maudlin (119–20). **Davis 1982:** This is one of Chopin's most effective treatments of a theme common in her fiction: inner and outer existence. Ozème manages to reconcile his personal desires with his responsibilities to society (65–66). **Grover 1984:** This is one of a surprising number of Chopin's tales in which men are appealingly depicted (30–31). The tale is one of Chopin's finest, especially thanks to its skillful depiction of character (33). **Skaggs 1985:** This is one of several tales by Chopin emphasizing altruistic self-denial. Although generous, the title character is also thoughtless in scheduling his vacation and dishonest (because of pride) when explaining how he has spent his time (30–31). **Ewell 1986:** As in other tales, Chopin here focuses on generosity. The title character is one of her most appealing free spirits, but he also has a powerful commitment to ethical behavior. The tone of the story is comically complex (104); the work provides a humorous treatment on the theme of a divided self—a theme elsewhere treated in darker terms (106–7). **Gaudet 1986:** Ozème is probably a mulatto, not a Cajun (as Per Seyersted suggests). The colors of his eyes and hair support this interpretation. The area he visits was inhabited by mulattoes, and he speaks to Aunt Tildy as a mulatto might speak to a black. The area in which the story is set was not a Cajun enclave (50). Ozème is also more industrious than the Cajuns usually depicted in Chopin's works, and a Cajun would have been unlikely to visit the mulatto-populated area he visits (50). The story probably shows a mulatto helping a black—which may help explain his later embarrassment. He temporarily allows altruism to triumph over ethnic solidarity (50–51). **Elfenbein 1989:** Although Seyersted has denied that Ozème is a free mulatto, the character is clearly free of common prejudice. Chopin's imprecision here about racial categories actually does justice to the complexity of the racial situation (120–21). **Toth 1990a:** This is one of various stories in which Chopin, departing from convention, shows the devotion of whites to blacks. It was accepted by *The Century* magazine (251), was included in *A Night in Acadie* (298), was singled out for praises by one reviewer (299), and was commended by another for lacking smugness (303). **Robinson 1992:** This is one of many stories by Chopin that depict harmony between the races—a harmony that was not entirely unknown or unrealistic following the Civil War (xix). **Goodwyn 1994:** This is one of various stories by Chopin depicting the loyalty of whites to blacks (10). **Koloski 1994:** The story is included in soft-cover collections of Chopin's fiction published in 1981 and 1992 (27–28). **Fetterley and Pryse 1995:** Here as elsewhere in Chopin's fiction, a black female is a major character but mostly fits a cultural stereotype (409). Ozème is typical of some of Chopin's caring, compassionate Cajun males, who are generally less sexually appealing than Creole men (409–10). **Koloski 1996:** Here as elsewhere Chopin depicts members of the Laballière family (21) and also describes travel (23). **Thomas 1996:** This story is one of many in which Chopin depicts aged black females, often in stereotypical terms (216–17). **Beer 1997:** In this tale Chopin reverses the standard narrative of blacks who are loyal to whites (35). **Koloski 1999:** This is one of Chopin's tales that focuses on a male (viii). Here as elsewhere, Chopin implicitly commends one person's fidelity to another (xviii–xix). **McCollough 1999:** Although this story shows some cooperation between the races, its underlying implications still seem basically racist (319). **Toth 1999c:** The title character exchanges sloth for generosity but by doing so becomes a bit boring (136). Because the story makes the white male look good, it proved acceptable to a mainstream journal (169). **Gibbons 2000:** This story reveals not only Chopin's progress away from local color conventions but also her continuing allegiance to them. The figurative language is still often (but not always) hackneyed; the characters are often largely (but not entirely) stereotyped; and the tone is still greatly (but not completely) sentimental. This work, like several others, represents a potential turning point in Chopin's career (xxxii).

"A Pair of Silk Stockings"

Written: 1896. First published: 1897. Included in *Complete Works* (1969).

Mrs. Sommers is a single working mother. When she finds an unexpected fifteen dollars, her self-sacrificing instinct immediately comes into play as she ruminates over what she might do with the money for the benefit of her children. While she considers these options, her hand inadvertently comes into contact with a pair of silk stockings. Because the stockings are on sale, she decides to buy a pair, and this act intoxicates her with the power of self-gratification, an energy that has been repressed in her by years of self-denial. After the purchase of the stockings, Mrs. Sommers, who usually "knew the value of bargains," buys pointed-tipped boots, long-wristed gloves, two high-priced magazines, a restaurant meal, and a theater ticket. Following her self-indulgent afternoon, she catches the cable car to return to her routine existence. But as she rides, Mrs. Sommers wrestles with the poignancy of her everyday situation and a "powerful longing" that her buoyed feelings from the afternoon might never end. **(EP)**

***

Rankin 1932: This tale may reflect Chopin's own financial worries at one point in her life, and Mrs. Sommers resembles Chopin herself in this realistic account of female existence. Its subtle humor prevents it from seeming maudlin (107–12). **Zlotnick 1968:** This is one of many stories in which Chopin implies ambivalent, unconventional responses to marriage (2). **Seyersted 1969a:** While in other stories Chopin focuses on women who consider their own needs first, here the emphasis is on a devoted mother (111–12). **Peterson 1972:** Despite her unconventional behavior, Mrs. Sommers never loses our regard (176). **Rocks 1972:** Here and elsewhere Chopin describes a somewhat selfish decision that nevertheless harms no one (118). **Arner 1975:** The snake-like stockings tempt Mrs. Sommers; the visit to the theater suggests the illusion to which she has succumbed; and the street car ride symbolizes both her last bit of solipsism and her inevitable return to earth. Like many of Chopin's best stories, this one is economical and subtle, especially in its conclusion (132–33). **Solomon 1976:** The story depicts the conflict between the heroine's inner appreciation for fine things and the outer pressures of financial limitations, and this conflict makes her final thoughts painfully touching (xviii–xix). Here as in "Regret," Chopin emphasizes bodily pleasure as a main human motive (xix). **Bonner 1983b:** Chopin endorses the heroine's unconventional self-assertion (146). **Gilbert 1984:** This tale presents an affecting depiction of a woman from her own point of view (16). **Skaggs 1985:** Chopin pronounces no judgment on the protagonist, who in fact provokes our sympathy (59–60). **Ewell 1986:** This story, a brief triumph, effectively blends social satire with insightful characterization. Chopin plunges immediately into the midst of Mrs. Sommers' mind and circumstances, using the story to show the impact of finances on the protagonist's sense of identity. Although Chopin depicts Mrs. Sommers as a determined and resourceful woman, she also sometimes mimics, through her sentence-structure, the character's uncertainty. The story focuses not on her struggles with other shoppers but on her deeper internal struggles. Like Edna in *The Awakening*, Mrs. Sommers eventually abandons self-restraint. The fact that she ends up in a theater suggests the element of impermanent fantasy in her current behavior. Chopin leaves the nature of Mrs. Sommers' final regret tantalizingly unclear. This is a story tinged with pain (118–21). It implicitly criticizes social ills (127) while also showing the toll exacted by the attempt to live a worthy life (183). **Stepenoff 1987:** This story is unusual for its day in focusing on urban life. Unlike "The Blind Man," this tale explores the pleasures of city life (458). **Valentine and Palmer 1987:** Ironically, Mrs. Sommers struggles for personal identity without violating conventional standards of proper womanhood. Chopin implies the need for a balance between self-indulgence and self-sacrifice. Mrs. Sommers shows concern for others even during her spending spree, and the dynamic narrator shows similar concern for Mrs. Sommers. Eventually Mrs. Sommers herself becomes the active force in the story, and the tale comes to a balanced, ambiguous conclusion (59–66). **Bonner 1988:** This story is often anthologized as an example of Chopin's works focusing on women's issues (100). **Martin 1988a:** This story reflects Chopin's growing interest in liberty, both in her fiction and in her own life. The work exhibits her frequent explorations of the conflicts between selflessness and self-fulfillment (6). **Papke 1988:** This tale, which resembles "The Story of an Hour" in character, plot, and themes, offers a darker picture of motherhood than is found in some of Chopin's other works. Like Mrs. Mallard, Mrs. Sommers enjoys only a brief respite from her duties (76–77). **Inge 1989:** Chopin here offers a wry, brisk depiction of her protagonist's complex mind. As in the Garden of Eden, the woman in this story gives into temptation, partly in response to a desire for a better life. After indulging herself, however, she seems pained (106). **Michaels 1990:** In this exceptionally fine story, yearning is connected with a sense of the distinctness of the body (496). The heroine here foreshadows Edna in *The Awakening*; both women are depicted as consumers. The story in some respects resembles Theodore Dreiser's most famous novel (499–500). **Papke 1990:** This tale, which in some respects resembles "The Story of an Hour," treats the negative aspects of maternity. The main character is a conventional woman, worn down by self-denial, whose repressed (and sensual) self suddenly awakens, only to collapse again when she faces reality (65–66). **Toth 1990a:** Although Chopin's story resembles one by Hamlin Garland, Garland shows less sympathetic understanding of his main character's motives (248). Chopin's narratives would have helped the prosperous readers of *Vogue* (where the tale was first published) to comprehend the experience of someone less comfortable than themselves (281). **Davis 1992a:** Like Edna in *The Awakening*, the main character here develops a sense of self-worth by the careful use of money—in this case to enhance her sense of the beauty of life (148). **Toth 1992:** Although Chopin rarely depicts fathers, she did describe (as here) self-assertive mothers (23). **Dyer 1993:** One critic from the 1960s saw the theme of female self-assertion in this story as foreshadowing *The Awakening* (22). **Shurbutt 1993:** This is one of various stories in which Chopin challenges a stereotype about women (22). **Ewell 1994:** Like the main character of this tale, Chopin herself knew well the obligations created by small children (166). **Koloski 1994:** This story, reprinted in a 1981 collection of feminist fiction, was chosen partly because it shows Mrs. Summer's gradual development of individuality (24). The story is included in soft-cover collections of Chopin's fiction published in 1976, 1979, 1981, and 1984 (27–28). This work also often appears in college textbooks (28–29). **Koloski 1996:** This uncollected tale, with its theme of the experiences of women (xii), emphasizes the force of impulsive motives and ends with ambiguous regret (73–74). The main character satisfies her yearnings, but not without cost—a motif Chopin also explored elsewhere (78). **Koloski 1999:** This was one of a number of effective tales Chopin composed before the publication of *A Night in Acadie* but which she did not include in that collection (xv–xvi). **Toth 1999c:** Ironically, this tale was first published in a magazine that catered to wealthy readers (172). **Knights 2000:** Here as elsewhere Chopin focuses on a moment of self-realization (xix). Here as elsewhere Chopin presents a character who wanders both physically and mentally (xxxiv).

"A Point at Issue!"

Written: 1889. First published: 1889. Included in *Complete Works* (1969).

Eleanor Gail typically ignores what is deemed acceptable behavior for young women in Plymdale, so she marries Charles Faraday without pre-announcement or fanfare and then regrets making a public announcement of her marriage in the local newspaper the very day it is published. The townsfolk criticize Eleanor for ignoring the prescribed path for brides-to-be and suggest that if her past behavior is any indication, her marriage is sure to fail. However, her husband, a mathematics professor, believes that she is the ideal woman for him, for even though she lacks a proper education, she has the ability to think independently and logically.

Agreeing that their marriage is held together not by exacting "so-called marriage laws," but by trust and an open mind toward reciprocal freedom, Charles and Eleanor decide to live apart following their three-month honeymoon to Europe so that Eleanor can learn French in Paris. Rumors begin to fly about the town when Charles returns from his vacation to France without his new, headstrong bride.

During the time that they are apart, Charles and Eleanor correspond with each other quite frequently by sending letters and newspaper clippings through the mail. In one letter, Charles offhandedly writes at some length about the affection he has for his friend Beaton's lovely daughter Miss Kitty, who has recently returned from boarding school and is full of life. Charles does not understand why Eleanor sends him a cold letter some time later, but he forgets all about the incident when he receives a flood of passionate letters from her.

A few months later, in an effort to control her unstable emotions, Eleanor busies herself with preparations for her husband's arrival. The distraught woman's emotions overcome her reason at last, and she is racked by sobbing. Oblivious to her earlier distress, Charles finds his wife even more attractive than ever. His love soon turns to jealousy and suspicion, for Charles sees his wife with a man, whom she dismissively refers to as "no one special," on two different occasions. After the second occasion, Charles does not know whether to leave and never look back or to confront Eleanor, but he does not have to do either. Eleanor presents a painting of herself to Charles and introduces the mystery man as the artist. Charles is thrilled, and he rewards the artist handsomely. He is even more elated when Eleanor announces that she is ready to go home. In between kisses, Charles asks Eleanor why she sent the cold letter months earlier. When she answers that she was jealous of Kitty Beaton, Charles cannot believe it. Eleanor explains "that there are certain things which a woman can't philosophize about." Forgetting his own irrational, distrusting jealousy just a few moments earlier, Charles thinks to himself that he cannot blame his wife for being a woman. **(JW)**

***

Rankin 1932: This was Chopin's first published story (115). **Seyersted 1969a:** Although the couple in this work hold unconventional ideas about marriage, they eventually feel the need to conform to more traditional patterns of behavior (52). The story shows how jealousy can complicate lofty ideals, but whereas the wife gains some wisdom from the experience, the husband slips into old chauvinistic condescension. Chopin perhaps implies a connection between marriage and a woman's intellectual death, and although she seems to sympathize with the couple's original ideals, and particularly with the wife's desire for freedom, she also shows the difficulty of practicing such ideals and suggests that Charles, like many men, over-estimates his wisdom (105–7). Eleanor, who seeks equality with a man, is highly unusual among Chopin's heroines, who tend either to seek freedom or to accept submission (114). Chopin did not include this story in her planned third collection, perhaps assuming that such a work might cause the volume to be rejected (223). **Peterson 1972:** The somewhat maudlin conclusion of this tale is appropriate to the relatively light tone of the piece. Chopin uses nice irony in the way she places the wedding announcement and also in the way she characterizes the two protagonists (71–74). **Rocks 1972:** Here as elsewhere Chopin shows the complexities but also the rewards of marriage as well as its superiority to remaining single (118). **Seyersted 1974:** The heroine here is initially able to be a real partner, rather than simply an antagonist, in her relations with men. Eventually, however, the marriage depicted here takes a more conventional course (12). **Arner 1975:** In this early story, Chopin's ability to treat human psychology was still rather simplistic and ineffective; the story reveals various failures of artistic skill and tone (21–23). The crisis described in this story is less effectively presented than a similar one in *The Awakening*; the latter description is more psychologically complex (26–28). Flaws of characterization evident in this story also appear in Chopin's early novel *At Fault* (41). Published in 1899 [sic; the correct date is 1889], the story is simplistic in theme and in other ways but has interesting points of comparison and contrast with *The Awakening* (119–20). **Bonner 1975:** This is one of several stories that demonstrate Chopin's interest in Europe (281–83). **Solomon 1976:** This early story is important not only because it foreshadows many of Chopin's favorite themes but also because of the optimistic ideal of marriage it describes (vii–viii). **Wolff 1979:** This early tale is too simple in structure and characterization; it lacks vitality and force, although it does deal with some of her characteristic themes (208–9). **Davis 1982:** Eleanor's unusual views of marriage are symptoms of her unusual views of herself, and in this sense the story typifies much of Chopin's later fiction. The tale contrasts superficial emancipation with the struggle for true liberty (61–62). **Bonner 1983b:** Chopin endorses the central characters' unconventional self-assertion (146–47). **Rogers 1983:** Here as elsewhere, Chopin, like George Sand, depicts the complexities of marriage (32). **Stein 1984:** This story shows Chopin's habit of neither supporting nor indicting marriage *per se*; instead she examines whether any particular marriage leads to self-fulfillment. The present tale, which affirms marriage, was written not long after "Wiser Than a God," which had not; in each case the main issue is not marriage as such but whether a marriage is satisfying (166). In "A Point at Issue!" a couple try to over-control their natural impulses through rational decision-making and allegiance to abstract ideas. The placement of their wedding announcement does not connect marriage to death but rather implies that marriage is a natural part of life. Chopin does not really criticize or mock her characters' final choices here but simply describes how each of them eventually accepts customary roles (167–70). **Rowe 1985:** This early story explores the ways marriage might inhibit feminine development (230). **Skaggs 1985:** Although the story focuses on an independent and resolute heroine, it shows how marriage compromises feminine selfhood (56). **Ewell 1986:** Chopin here explores how an effort to escape the limits imposed on women by marriage creates complexities of its own. Ironically, the main difficulties are not imposed from without but arise from within. Even though the story has an intriguing plot, however, its conclusion seems a bit amateurish, and the work also seems somewhat flawed when describing Eleanor's strong emotions and when depicting the Beaton sisters (45–46). This tale is one of several suggesting how attempts to control emotions only make them more intense (183). **Martin 1988a:** This story investigates the conflicts between aesthetic ambition and societal tradition (4). **Papke 1988:** This early story depicts an ambivalent woman who therefore resembles Edna in *The Awakening* (73). **Inge 1989:** The story perhaps implies that humans may be innately incapable of escaping traditional conceptions of affection and matrimony (92). **Taylor 1989:** Here as elsewhere Chopin deals openly with feminist topics (153). The story alludes to Paris's associations with immoral behavior (191).

Papke 1990: Focusing on a woman torn between conflicting desires (36), the story depicts a couple who idealize each other in differing ways but whose deeper differences—between his traditional views and her unconventionality—lead to the breakdown of their relationship. Eleanor is the more adventurous character in every sense, while Charles is not only possessive but finally more self-possessed. Chopin flirts with unconventional possibilities but shows how elusive they often remain and how limited women's options are. This tale exemplifies Chopin's growing rejection of optimistic conclusions (40–42; 50). **Toth 1990a:** This tale of an unconventional but also unsuccessful romance may reflect Chopin's own skepticism about the possibilities of such relationships. The story, which was immediately accepted, subtly mocks both its female protagonist and also impractical styles of feminism (181). This was the first of Chopin's short narratives to appear in print (219). **Vanlandingham 1990:** This was one of Chopin's first stories accepted for publication (160). **Guidici 1991:** Here as in other works by Chopin, disruption of a marriage gives a woman greater power. Chopin here implies that sophisticated males promote their wives's talents rather than discouraging them (30). **Hoder-Salmon 1992:** Chopin was thirty-nine when this story was published (19). **Larsson 1993:** This story demonstrates Chopin's interest in autonomy for women as well as her skepticism about conventional marriage (2: 537). **Shurbutt 1993:** This is one of various tales in which Chopin depicts an unconventional marriage (21–22). **Skredsvig 1993:** This early work typifies many of Chopin's themes and tactics. A sociolinguistic analysis of the tale highlights the ways in which issues of culture and gender affect the use of language. In certain respects the story seems to endorse traditional views of the different roles of men and women. Eleanor is subjected to greater social supervision and judgment than Charles, and even Charles's interest in her is primarily egotistical. Despite its length, the story does not feature much speaking. Although Eleanor seems to thrive in Paris, her speech and conduct change when Charles returns, especially in their final discussion. At the same time, Eleanor subtly tries to assert her independence. Chopin's choice of an objective, reportorial point of view is significant, yet her own language is partly colored by gender stereotypes. Charles may seem in the end to have asserted control, but Eleanor achieves some of her own objectives. Eleanor evolves whereas Charles does not (77–85). **Ewell 1994:** This is one of several stories by Chopin in which she seems to ignore the marketability of local color fiction (160). **Koloski 1994:** The story is included in a soft-cover collection of Chopin's fiction published in 1976 (27). **Juneja 1995:** Here as elsewhere, Chopin explores the theme of liberty in marriage (118). **Baxter 1996:** This story lends itself to a creative writing exercise for students (240). **Toth 1999c:** This was one of only several stories Chopin set in Paris (65). It presents her single depiction of a self-avowed feminist. The story alludes to the disapproving comments Chopin herself had provoked in Louisiana even as it adopts a wry view of its characters and of life (111–12). The story was first published in a newspaper run by a

St. Louis acquaintance of hers (134). **Knights 2000:** This is one of various works in which Chopin shows a woman rejecting the limits of conventional marriage (xviii). Some recent readers have been disappointed by Chopin's failure to show more overt sympathy with the feminists she presents in stories like this one (xx). Here as elsewhere, Chopin shows her awareness of the ways individual lives are implicated in historical and cultural contexts—contexts her stories often challenge (xxvii). This is one of various stories by Chopin that have been (and can be) read in widely divergent ways—either as endorsing or subverting conventions (xxvii–xviii). The ambiguities of this work resemble those of "A Respectable Woman" (xxviii). Here as elsewhere, either editors or Chopin herself added a subtitle to the first version of this work to tone down its impact (xlvi–xlvii).

"Polly"

Written: 1902. First published: 1902. Included in *Complete Works* (1969).

Polly McQuade's pet peeve is to receive mail at her place of employment, the real estate office of Lord & Pellem in St. Jo, where she works as an assistant bookkeeper. She prefers instead to receive mail at her boardinghouse, where she may read letters unhurriedly and in private. She particularly looks forward to George's weekly letter, which always intimates marriage "when Ferguson opens up in St. Jo." The day she finds a "businesslike letter" on her desk when she arrives at work, she decides to take the letter with her to lunch so that she may enjoy some privacy while reading it. She discovers that the letter is from her Uncle Ben, who shares with her the news that he has "struck it rich in a small way." The letter is accompanied by a check for one hundred dollars, payable to Polly; Uncle Ben admonishes her to spend "every red cent of it" rather than put it into savings. He promises her that when Ferguson opens in St. Jo, he will send her another check for the same amount.

Buoyed by this generosity, Polly returns to the office and asks for the afternoon off so that she may honor her uncle's request. She shops expeditiously because her frequent window-shopping has given her a previously-made mental shopping list. Along with purchases of domestic items, such as dishes and sitting-room accessories, she orders some groceries and a large amount of coal for her mother, who lives in the nearby town of Filmore. Polly's shopping is completed when she buys gifts for her family and sends them a telegram to inform them of her arrival that weekend.

At her mother's Polly is giddy with high spirits and laughter. Her young sister, Phoebe, tells Polly of the local gossip concerning their mother's change in fortune, while Isabel, the sensible older sister, scolds Polly for her lack of practical purchases, such as a coat or other clothing. Polly, however, is not affected by Isabel's criticisms. Like the guests invited by Isabel—among whom George is to be one—Polly is fascinated by the "solid comfort" of her recent windfall.

As the hours pass, however, Polly's spirits lag because George has not arrived. Just when she decides to plead a headache and excuse herself, she hears the beat of his horse's hooves. Upon his entrance (he explains that he was delayed by business), he looks to Polly like all the "heroes of romance." He bypasses the newly-bought bounty, goes directly to Polly, and takes her hand in front of the guests. He tells Polly that he has great news: Ferguson is going to open up in St. Jo in January.

While the others congratulate Polly, Isabel asks her if she wishes now that she had the check back. Polly answers no, because if she did, she would have had to hear George's proposal in a letter rather than in person.

A month after the party, Lord & Pellem regrettably lets Polly go. The senior partner presents her with a gift on behalf of the firm: a brass tea kettle containing a month's salary. The tea kettle is accompanied by the humorous command: "'Polly put the kettle on!'" **(EP)**

***

Seyersted 1969a: This was Chopin's last story to be published during her lifetime and seems ironic in its focus on a compliant woman and in its closing sentence (185). **Peterson 1972:** This tale for young people seems rather routine. One almost wonders whether Chopin was mocking the genre, but the story itself provides no evidence for such a reading (266–67). **Berggren 1977:** The conventional behavior of the heroine of this story for young people suggests that Chopin became less daring after writing *The Awakening* (1). **Dyer 1981a:** Gouvernail, a skeptical character present in some of Chopin's earlier work, would be inappropriate in this story (55). **Dyer 1984:** This story is typical of many of Chopin's final works in its superficial use of imagery. The concluding sentence of the tale—Chopin's last published words ever—is especially unfortunate (190). **Ewell 1986:** As elsewhere, Chopin here shows how a woman gives up a career for marriage. The title character, nevertheless, differs from previous women Chopin had described, but although the work is skillful it also seems a bit insubstantial—an impression emphasized by its ending (181–82). **Toth 1990a:** This story, one of Chopin's few late optimistic tales (386), was published in a magazine for young readers (389). **Davis 1992a:** Like Edna in *The Awakening*, the main character here develops a sense of self-worth by the careful use of money—in this case to bring joy to others and thus to herself (148). **Thomas 1992:** This unsophisticated piece was Chopin's last published tale (54). **Ewell 1994:** This is one of various late works in which Chopin pulls back from the unconventional, perhaps in reaction to the poor reception of *The Awakening* (169–70). **Thomas 1995:** Ironically, this conventional tale is the kind of women's writing from which Chopin had earlier sought to distance herself (29). **Koloski 1996:** This work, Chopin's final printed story, resembles many of her other stories for children by depicting the poor (71; 87). **Toth 1999c:** This story (also known as "Polly's Opportunity") was Chopin's final published work (236). **Knights 2000:** This was one of many works by Chopin published in one of the best-established U.S. family magazines (xvi).

"Polydore"

Written: 1895. First published: 1896. Included in *A Night in Acadie* (1897).

It is often said that Polydore is the stupidest boy around. His mother died after making his godmother, Adélaïde, promise to raise him. Adélaïde takes Polydore into her home, where she lives with her father.

One evening Polydore decides that he does not want to get out of bed the next morning. He gives no thought to the implications or results of his desire. When the servant calls to wake him the next morning, he says that he is sick and cannot get out of bed. To his surprise, Adélaïde comes upstairs to his room to see about him. She sees that he has no fever, so he says that his leg is hurting. She pulls back the cover and declares that his leg is swollen. Polydore stays in bed all day with his leg elevated.

The following afternoon Polydore limps downstairs and is seated in an easy chair on the shady side of the porch. Adélaïde is returning from a long ride in the hot sun on an errand that would have been given to Polydore if he had not been sick. She is sweating profusely and is exhausted from the ride.

That night Adélaïde goes to bed without eating super. She has a headache, but thinks she will feel better in the morning. She does not. She gets sicker and sicker. Her father sends for the doctor and her married sister. The doctor decides to stay with his patient because he is not sure if she will live or die. Polydore watches all the activity and feels guilty. He knows that if Adélaïde dies, it will be his fault.

A week or two later Adélaïde is recuperating. Polydore comes in and tells her that he has been to confession and that the priest told him that he needs a whipping as part of his penitence. Even though he confessed to the priest, he still feels the burden of Adélaïde's illness. He drops to his knees, buries his face in her skirt, and sobs the story into her skirt. She realizes for the first time that she loves Polydore like a mother and tells him, "Neva mind." **(DR)**

***

Bush 1957: This story resembles "Regret," especially since both works focus on the kind of tough rural spinster often found in Louisiana fiction of this era (255). **Gilder 1898:** This story demonstrates Chopin's knowledge of real emotions (50). **Seyersted 1969a:** Aunt Siney illustrates Chopin's occasional tendency to depict blacks as superstitious (78). Some repetitious phrasing illustrates one occasional problem of Chopin's style (130). **Peterson 1972:** Here as in other comic tales Chopin wrote around this time, the happy ending is foreshadowed and predictable and therefore unobjectionable (127). **Rocks 1972:** Here as elsewhere, Chopin demonstrates the complexities liberty can involve and shows that true liberty often entails a responsible concern for others (117). **Skaggs 1985:** This is one of many stories by Chopin that show a real familiarity with children and their effects on others, particularly maternal figures (27–28). **Ewell 1986:** Although this story focuses on a youthful con-man who resembles Huck Finn, it also shares with the nearby "Regret" a concern with maternal instincts. Like other stories written for the young, this one teaches a lesson, but it also more subtly suggests the all-important power of human affection (107). **Gaudet 1986:** This story shows Chopin's familiarity with the folk beliefs of Louisiana blacks (45–46). **Toth 1990a:** This tale later appeared in *A Night in Acadie*, in which all the stories are set in Louisiana (298). **Toth 1990a:** This story, included in *A Night in Acadie* (298), was praised for its psychological insight (300). Chopin later read the tale at a ladies' club meeting (308). **Koloski 1994:** This story was reprinted frequently between 1925 and 1960 in an influential anthology. Although the anthologist praised many aspects of Chopin's writings, he did not specifically say why he chose this particular work for inclusion (20–21). **Carr 1996:** This is one of various stories in which a Creole adopts a Cajun, usually improving him in the process (55). **Koloski 1996:** This is one of Chopin's many stories for children (87). **Thomas 1996:** Theme: both the liberation and lack of freedom for women (208). **Koloski 1999:** This is one of various stories by Chopin in which children inaugurate a transformation (xvii–xviii). It is one of many stories by Chopin which either feature children or were written for them (xxii). Here as elsewhere she describes grown-ups who find connection with others (xxiii). **Toth 1999c:** This is one of several stories in *A Night in Acadie* in which youthful men try to evade grown-up feelings (194).

"A Poor Girl"

Written: 1889. Destroyed.

Rankin 1932: The tale, approximately 7000 words in length, received mixed responses from the first editor to whom Chopin submitted it. He found it intriguing and well written but called its plot "not desirable," promising to reconsider if Chopin were willing to make alterations (115). **Seyersted 1969a:** Negative responses to the plot from two male editors led Chopin to destroy the work (52). It thus illustrates her habit of being commended for her skills but censured for her topics (198). **Ewell 1986:** When the story was criticized first by an editor and then by a friend and was also rejected for publication, Chopin destroyed it (29). **Martin 1988a:** In this early work Chopin tried to imitate the realism she admired in other contemporary American authors (4). **Vanlandingham 1990:** This story was turned down by an editor because of its plot (160). **Toth 1990a:** Chopin eventually abandoned this early novella (181). It had received a mixed response from a male friend to whom she had shown it (190). Similarly, a magazine to which she had submitted it had praised its style yet rejected its content but promised to consider a revision (219). **Toth 1999c:** Chopin had given the title of this work to an early tale she had tried to compose (109).

"The Recovery"

Written: 1896. First published: 1896. Included in *A Vocation and a Voice* (1991).

At the age of thirty-five, "possessing something of youthfulness," Jane has her sight fully restored after fifteen years of living in "darkness with closed lids." Wishing to be alone when her sight returns, she first surveys the rural landscape around her and the "blue unfathomable June sky." Her joy and gratitude for seeing and experiencing this beauty again leave her almost speechless. She then turns her attention to the "dear, dumb companions" which comforted her during her years of blindness. Among these items are furniture—her mahogany table in particular—the carpet and draperies, a crystal vase, and a French clock with its "pompous little bronze figure of a last-century gentleman," which she greets like an old friend and tenderly wipes clean.

Her mirror, however, arrests her joyous return to sightedness. At first she mistakenly identifies her own reflection as that of her mother. Looking into the eyes in the glass, she eventually realizes, with "all the crushing weight of the accumulated wisdom of the years," that the aged reflection is her own. The next day she takes a walk with Robert who, despite her refusal to marry him, has remained devoted to Jane throughout the years of her blindness. Though five years older than Jane, Robert remains "a man of splendid physique." Jane is somber, introspective, and relatively silent as they progress.

Eventually Robert leads Jane to a bench, takes her hand, and again expresses his love for her and his desire to marry her. Robert's earnest pleas add to the confusion she now feels in a sighted world. "I must go back into the dark to think," she says. Turning half away from Robert, she covers her eyes with her arm, but the darkness she finds there is no refuge. "The blessed light had given her back the world, life, love; but it had robbed her of her illusions; it had stolen away her youth." As Robert draws near to Jane, pressing his face close to hers for his answer, all he hears is a "little, low sob." **(EP)**

***

Seyersted 1969a: Perhaps Chopin, whose eyes had been opened by modern science and who had therefore lost some of the comforting beliefs of her youth, may occasionally have sympathized with the heroine's desire to return momentarily to a less complicated view of the world (195). **Pe-terson 1972:** The theme of the story is a bit too obvious despite its appealing irony (175–76). **Rocks 1972:** This is one of many stories in which Chopin suggests that each person must decide whether it is better to be content with one's present condition or attempt to alter one's future. The results of either choice cannot be predicted (115). **Arner 1975:** The story explores such themes as how literal and metaphorical perceptions affect our lives and happiness and how we may sometimes prefer imagined ideals to accurate understanding (99–100). **Ewell 1986:** The title seems ironic in this story about the effects of time on human perception (116–17). **Toth 1990a:** Here as in various other stories she published in *Vogue*, Chopin writes about loss and alienation (280). Perhaps this tale, like "The Blind Man," was influenced by possible difficulties with her own sight (286). The story was intended for publication in *A Vocation and a Voice* (374). **Toth 1991:** This is one of many of Chopin's late works that were first printed in *Vogue* (xiii–xiv). This is one of many stories in *A Vocation and a Voice* in which love fails because of bad timing (xxiii) and which focus on determined single-mindedness (xxiv). **Davis 1992b:** This is one of many stories from *A Vocation and a Voice* that focus on suddenly altered perceptions (200–201). **Koloski 1994:** The story is included in a soft-cover collection of Chopin's fiction published in 1991 (28). **Toth 1999c:** In this unconventional, unpredictable tale, Chopin satirized the naive attitudes of the young concerning personal appearance (172). It is one of the darker tales scheduled to appear in *A Vocation and a Voice* (208).

"A Red Velvet Coat"

Written: 1890. Manuscript lost.

Ewell 1986: Chopin notes that this story was sold to a magazine, but apparently it was never published (48). **Toth 1990a:** Chopin composed this tale for young people while living in St. Louis (194).

"A Reflection"

Written: 1899. Included in *Complete Works* (1969).

In this four-paragraph meditation, an unnamed narrator describes the sense of alienation that accompanies one who lives an "examined life." She sees herself as separate from, and an observer of, the "vital and responsive energy" of the "moving procession of human energy," which is "greater than the stars." Though the alienation brought about by her status as a contemplative observer is enough to make her weep, the narrator acknowledges that she has little choice. To join the procession would mean her death amidst the "crushing feet, the clanging discords, the ruthless hands and stifling breath." She implies that this procession is ultimately unnatural, for it is only along the roadside that the elements of nature exist: grass, clouds, and "a few dumb animals." Thus, though painful in its solitude, the place of the contemplative observer, the narrator implies, is actually the natural place in the human drama. This notion is suggested again in the final line by the narrator's use of the Roman salutation *"Salve!"* (or *health*) before her resolution: "Let us be still and wait by the roadside." **(EP)**

***

Rankin 1932: The tone of exhaustion conveyed in this quick meditation may reflect Chopin's personal feelings of discouragement at the time, but eventually she got beyond this state of mind (190–91). **Arms 1967:** In this piece of slightly unfocused thinking, Chopin seems to imagine a simplistic harmonization of contradictions—an ideal she generally resists elsewhere in her writings. This desire for a lofty harmony perhaps helps explain why some of her stories are unsuccessful, although this tale itself ends by accepting things as they are (227–28). **Seyersted 1969a:** The story may reflect Chopin's own sense of having been damaged by hostile critics (180–81). **Peterson 1972:** This work has often been read for its personal relevance to Chopin, but it deals with a broader theme of perennial interest to her: the conflict between the desire for liberty and the desire for community (257–59). The work is one of Chopin's better final pieces, most of which imply that her talent had begin to diminish (269). **Seyersted 1974:** This work reflects Chopin's deep disappointment at the reception of *The Awakening* (17). **Arner 1975:** Here Chopin seems to speak fairly openly of her own disappointments with the recent negative reception of *The Awakening*—a reception she greeted with ambivalence (138–39). **Gilbert 1984:** This essay reflects Chopin's sense of being passed by in the aftermath of the failure of *The Awakening* (9). **Ewell 1986:** This work seems to ponder the isolation of the artist, whose role as an observer cuts him off from being a full participant but perhaps also gives him a larger perspective (174). **Martin 1988a:** In this piece of non-fiction prose, Chopin revealed her sadness at the hostile reception of *The Awakening* (10). **Toth 1990a:** In this serious-minded meditation, Chopin reveals her own feelings more openly than she usually did (362–63). **Hoder-Salmon 1992:** This piece reflects Chopin's disappointment at the failure of *The Awakening* (22). **Koloski 1994:** The story is included in a soft-cover collection of Chopin's fiction published in 1981 (27). **Thomas 1992:** This piece of autobiography was cut by Chopin from a published essay because it was too personal. Its tone is weary but ironic (48). **Dyer 1993:** The phrase about a procession in this piece echoes a phrase from *The Awakening*, and in both cases the implications are similar (44). **Thomas 1995:** Ironically, this sketch suggests Chopin's own sense of being neglected like the other female writers she sometimes mocked (30). **Toth 1999c:** This piece, perhaps implying Chopin's frustration with reactions to *The Awakening*, was never submitted to a journal (226).

"Regret"

Written: 1894. First published: 1895. Included in *A Night in Acadie* (1897).

Aurélie is an independent woman of fifty who never thought of marrying. She was proposed to when she was twenty, but declined and has never regretted her decision. She lives alone except for the Negroes who live in her cabins and work for her. She is quite content.

One morning her neighbor, with her four small children, comes to Aurélie's house in a state of bewilderment. She has received news that her mother is gravely ill in another parish; meanwhile, Léon, her husband, is away in Texas. She has no one to leave her children with except Aurélie.

Aurélie knows absolutely nothing about caring for children, but she learns quickly. She learns that the baby does not like to be addressed in a loud voice and that at night the children all have to have their feet bathed before putting on their night clothes and getting into bed. She learns that the little boy will not go to sleep until he hears a story. Aurélie confesses to Aunt Ruby that tending to children is an exhausting job.

Aurélie begins doing things she has not done in years, such as wearing her white aprons and mending torn slips and waists. She gets used to hearing laughter, chattering, and crying around the house, and she gets used to sleeping with the baby's hot little body next to hers.

In two weeks the neighbor returns to gather her children. Her mother is well and she is thrilled to see her children again. The children are excited to see their mother. After they leave Aurélie looks around at the disorder the children have left behind. She does not begin to straighten things immediately. She bends her head and cries while her dog licks her hand. **(DR)**

***

Gilder 1898: This story would seem psychologically accurate no matter where it was set (50). **Reilly 1937:** Here as elsewhere, motherhood is an important theme in Chopin's fiction (73). **Reilly 1942:** This story illustrates Chopin's ability to create complex characters in only a few words (131). Here as in some of her other best works, Chopin focuses on the feelings natural to mothers—feelings which appear even in the somewhat egocentric heroine of this work (135). **Bush 1957:** This story epitomizes much that is best in Chopin's fiction. It is not full of events; it contains no unexpected jolt; its style is simple. The final twist not only enriches the plot but also provides insight into character. Language is used efficiently; the opening paragraphs quickly provide crucial information about the protagonist's present and past while also foreshadowing her future (248). The two main women are subtly individualized and contrasted, and the story shows an effective use of implication. Depiction of setting is nicely delayed, quickly achieved, and sensually evocative (249). The description of the children's behavior is concrete and has a nice touch of comedy (251). The reference to the cook helps vary the tone, then the description of the children becomes more intimate, but Chopin does not spell out the transforming effect the young ones are having since that effect is occurring beneath the surface of the protagonist (252). The reappearance of the mother generates an effectively ambiguous response. Chopin also nicely juxtaposes loud sound with sudden silence when the children leave (253). In the concluding section the protagonist comes to a self-understanding that has been subtly foreshadowed, and the deeper meanings of this section are delicately suggested through symbolism and significant action. The structure of the story is basically cyclical, but the main movement is internal (254–55). Nonetheless, the final tone is not dark, since the protagonist paradoxically benefits from her sorrow by achieving a deeper insight into self and life. The tale resembles Chekhov's "Grief" and Chopin's own "Polydore," and it may also have been influenced by a spinster portrayed by Grace King (255). **Fletcher 1966:** In this tale Chopin describes the sadness of a foolishly unmarried, oddly isolated woman who tries to find satisfaction in a career rather than in raising children. The story implies that Chopin was at least partially sympathetic to conventional views of a woman's role in life (128–

29). **Zlotnick 1968:** Here as elsewhere Chopin suggests that errors are a necessary price of freedom (4). **Seyersted 1969a:** The heroine, at first self-involved, learns to care about others (112) in this story whose real artistry (115) makes it one of Chopin's ten or so best works (123). She adopts and adapts a topic of the sort Maupassant had explored in "La Reine Hortense" and then excels the French master in skill, subtlety, and profundity, producing a genuinely powerful work that is quite complex in tone, mixing (for example) humor and detachment. A surviving early draft permits study of Chopin's revisions, which were minor but effective. Although the character of Aunt Ruby at first seems inconsistent with the rest of the tale, she later seems to fit, and the moving ending of Chopin's story exemplifies its general superiority to Maupassant's narrative. The transformed feelings of Chopin's heroine seem more credible than those of Maupassant's central figure, and Chopin's story is more efficient and understated and reflects her greater comprehension of children. This work shows Chopin's solid growth as a writer (125–30). **Seyersted 1969b:** This story typifies the confident writing Chopin did following the success of *Bayou Folk*. Like many works from this period, it depicts a strong woman in the process of self-discovery (27). The tale typifies Chopin's tendencies to focus on a seemingly minor moment in a person's life and to describe both the person and the moment directly and in a way that leads to an ending that seems fated. The work displays her typical psychological penetration, her mastery of shape and structure, her clear and exact diction, and her delicacy and subtlety. Also typical is the understated force of the work's conclusion, as well as the tale's almost French efficiency, its discreet comedy, and its capacity for compassion despite its apparent reticence and detachment (31). **Peterson 1972:** Here as elsewhere, Chopin uses children symbolically but also somewhat simplistically (103). Here as in other stories Chopin composed between the summers of 1893 and 1895, the emphasis is upon alienation—in this case the alienation that results from self-discovery when change is no longer possible (122–23). Although in some respects the work recalls such earlier stories as "A Matter of Prejudice" and "The Lilies," here as in other more recent works Chopin describes a painful revelation. The final lines suggest alienation and eventual death (145–47). **Rocks 1972:** Here as elsewhere Chopin shows that desire often causes suffering, not simply pleasure (116). **Arner 1975:** The story illustrates the tragedy of an isolated life (72). **Solomon 1976:** This touching story is affecting not only to childless women but to women whose children have matured and gone away (xvi–xvii). This story's focus on the ironies of life can profitably be compared to that of a later story, "A Pair of Silk Stockings" (xviii). There as here, Chopin emphasizes bodily pleasure as a main human motive (xix). **Taylor 1979:** This is one of several tales that emphasize the power of the maternal role (xvi). **Baym 1981:** The main characters here exemplify the often conservative nature of Creole life (xx). **Davis 1982:** As in other stories by Chopin, the main character is revitalized by contact with the young (66). **Rogers 1983:** As this story illustrates,

Chopin, more than George Sand, emphasizes maternity in her fiction (36). **Burchard 1984:** Although the story deals with the common human problem of facing irreversible choices in life, it also confronts the limits placed on women in particular. The heroine's sudden breakdown—after years of independence—implies that Chopin believed that women have an innate maternal instinct. Here as elsewhere Chopin depicts a seemingly autonomous woman who eventually shows her need for a family (39–40). **Newman 1986:** Like many of Chopin's tales, this one suggests a view of marriage that seems to conflict with the views implied by some of her other stories (152). **Skaggs 1985:** This is one of many stories by Chopin that show a real familiarity with children and their effects on others, particularly because of their individual needs. At the conclusion, the old woman not only misses the children but mourns the loss of her earlier sense of self-sufficiency (27–29). **Ewell 1986:** This story resembles "A Matter of Prejudice" in showing how children can alter adult perceptions (96). The tale explores the price (particularly the sensual price) a person pays for independence. Physical contact with the children changes the woman's outlook on her life. Effective use of animal imagery and evocative details of setting help lend the story power. Although Aurélie's experience is in some ways the reverse of that of Louise Mallard in "The Story of an Hour," the mere fact that she survives suggests the value of autonomy (102–3). Here as in other stories by Chopin, understanding one's physical needs seems important to attaining full selfhood (183). **Stepenoff 1987:** The house in this story resembles Chopin's own home in Cloutierville. Perhaps the tale reflects Chopin's own regret about her children leaving home (453–54; 466). **Papke 1988:** This story offers a more affirmative view of motherhood than Chopin provides elsewhere (76). **Toth 1988a:** Here as elsewhere, Chopin shows her awareness of the complex experience of motherhood (56). **Inge 1989:** Chopin's skill, delicacy, efficient use of speech, effective use of setting to emphasize character, and combination of objectivity and good will all make this a superb example of her art (100). **Papke 1990:** This tale emphasizes maternal strength (64). **Toth 1990a:** The story reflects Chopin's complex attitudes toward motherhood (128). This tale later appeared in *A Night in Acadie,* in which all the stories are set in Louisiana (298), and was praised by one reviewer (300) and by a male poet (328). **Robinson 1992:** In this story a mulatto is shown to enjoy the same social standing as a white person (xviii). **Shurbutt 1993:** Here as elsewhere Chopin complicates our views of marriage (19). **Ewell 1994:** This is one of many stories by Chopin that show the dangers of ignoring the sexual or sensual aspects of human nature (168). **Fusco 1994:** This was one of several stories by Chopin whose title resembles that of a story by Maupassant. Critics have disagreed about the extent to which the story is modeled on another tale by Maupassant (140–41). **Koloski 1994:** This story was included in a 1989 anthology of fiction on American families (25–26). The story was also included in soft-cover collections of Chopin's fiction published in 1976, 1979, 1981, and 1992 (27). **Saar 1994:** Although this is one of

Chopin's few stories depicting a female with "masculine" traits, those traits do not remain unchanged (67). **Koloski 1996:** The central character, who is described in masculine terms, realizes that her own decisions have led to her current pain (47–48). Per Seyersted links this tale to one by Maupassant (85). **Thomas 1996:** This is one of various stories in which Chopin juxtaposes contrasting women (208). **Toth and Seyersted 1998:** This story is mentioned in Chopin's account books (140, 149, 175) and in her diary for 1894 (191). This is one of several stories in which Chopin describes women who are not depressed by nature but who do face particular problems (274). **Ewell 1999:** Theme: maternity. **Koloski 1999:** This is one of Chopin's tales dealing with a moment of realization (viii). It is one of various stories by Chopin in which children inaugurate a transformation (xvii–xviii). **Toth 1999a:** This is one of various stories in which Chopin describes independent, capable women—the kind she knew from her own childhood (4). **Toth 1999c:** This is one of many stories in which Chopin depicts varied maternal feelings (70). The main character's movement from isolation to generosity makes her a bit boring but also made her appealing to the editors of a mainstream journal (136). Yet her internal transformation gives the story some resonance (194). **Gibbons 2000:** This story foreshadows *The Awakening* in its emotional complexity. The tone of the tale is complicated, and both the heroine and her fundamental change are involving and appealing (xxxvii–xxxviii). **Knights 2000:** This story, written not long before "The Kiss," implies a contrasting view of marriage than is presented in that tale (xxi). Chopin altered this tale, cutting the word "darkie" (xxxi).

"A Respectable Woman"

Written: 1894. First published: 1894. Included in *A Night in Acadie* **(1897).**

Mr. Baroda had invited his friend, Gouvernail, to spend a week or two with him and his wife on their plantation. Mrs. Baroda is not too happy about this because she does not even know Gouvernail. Although she expects not to like him at all, she finds Gouvernail quite likeable after all.

Agitated, Mrs. Baroda asks her husband when Gouvernail will be leaving. He replies probably in another week. She announces that she is going to the city in the morning to have her spring gowns fitted and asks her husband to let her know when Gouvernail is gone. She will be staying with her Aunt Octavie.

That night she is sitting alone on a bench at the edge of the walk. Gouvernail appears and sits down beside her. He talks freely, but she is not listening to his words. She wants to reach out and touch him and hug him close to her. She gets up and goes inside. She leaves early the next morning for the city.

Later in the year she suggests to her husband that they have Gouvernail out again in the summer. Her husband tells her that he is glad she has overcome her dislike for Gouvernail. She assures him that she has overcome everything. **(DR)**

***

Anonymous 1897 [*Post-Dispatch*]: A comment in this story illustrates Chopin's subtle irony (48). **Rankin 1932:** This tale abounds in delicate implications, especially concerning its characters' minds (162). **Bush 1957:** The sudden change in the heroine here resembles the similar change in "Athénaïse," a story which also features Gouvernail. Presumably by the following year Mrs. Baroda has reined in her temptation, but the story suggests that the keynote of her personality is her unpredictability (260–62). **Arms 1967:** This is one of the five most successful tales included in *A Night in Acadie*, partly because its tone is non-moralistic and its view of truth is complex. Gouvernail had also been a character in "Athénaïse," and in some of its themes the story anticipates *The Awakening* (224). **Zlotnick 1968:** This is one of many stories in which Chopin implies ambivalent, unconventional responses to marriage (2). **Seyersted 1969a:** Although the story avoids describing actual infidelity by the wife, its closing words are rich with implication (111). **Berthoff 1970:** This work anticipates later writing by Sherwood Anderson (xvi). **Leary 1970a:** This story, risky for its time, is also effectively subtle (x). It reveals Chopin's familiarity with Whitman's poetry and implies her assumption that readers also knew his verse (xiii). **Leary 1970b:** This is one of Chopin's best tales (140–41). It reveals Whitman's freeing impact on Chopin (141). **Leary 1971:** This tale seems especially bold for its time. Gouvernail also turns up momentarily in *The Awakening* and is developed even more fully in "Athénaïse" (167). **Peterson 1972:** The treatment of the complexities of marriage is richer here than in some of Chopin's early writings (12). Here as in other stories Chopin composed between the summers of 1893 and 1895, the focus is on the ways a character can experience alienation—in this case, alienation caused by the conflict between social dictates and personal desires (122). Significantly, the wife is never identified by a first name; she is intrigued by Gouvernail because his aloofness seems to challenge her femininity. The final line is intriguingly ambiguous. The two words of the story's title imply the alternative choices facing Mrs. Baroda (135–37). This work is a little less risky than some of Chopin's later writing about marriage (142). **Rocks 1972:** Here as elsewhere Chopin shows that people often freely choose not to alter their circumstances; they elect to renounce other options, but the choice is theirs and no decision is externally imposed (118). The story shows the complexities but also the rewards of marriage as well as its superiority to remaining single (118). Here Chopin shows the possible rewards of resisting temptation (119). **Arner 1975:** Here as in many of Chopin's stories, the title seems significant. This tale has deeper resonance than some of Chopin's local-color works (20). It illustrates the progressively darker view of marriage exemplified by the tales in *A Night in Acadie* (64). The story draws on one of the most erotic portions of Whitman's "Song of Myself," and, as in *The Awakening*, Chopin here contrasts conventional expectations with a married woman's personal yearnings. Those yearnings are subtly emphasized at the very end (69). **Solomon 1976:** This is one of several tales by Chopin depicting women at various points of the life cycle (xvi). The tale concludes with appealing complexity and uncertainty (xvii). **Lattin 1978:** Here as elsewhere, when Chopin presents pregnancy and/or motherhood as a positive experience, the experience is usually limited (1–2). **Howell 1979a:** The plot of this story resembles that of *The Awakening*, although the story is obviously less psychologically probing than the novel. Here as elsewhere Chopin used an ambiguous conclusion (215–16). **Taylor 1979:** This is one of many tales in which a woman triumphs, if only briefly (xvi). **Lattin 1980:** Our knowledge of Gouvernail in this story helps us understand his behavior in Chopin's other fiction—and vice versa (31–35). **Dyer 1980–81:** This is one of many stories by Chopin in which a female is aroused by contact with a male (10–11). However, readers who know only this work and a few other of Chopin's more famous writings may fail to realize her significant interest in *male* (not simply female) passions (15). **Baym 1981:** This is one of Chopin's few short stories in which a woman feels torn between her individuality and social expectations (xxx). **Dyer 1981a:** Readers who recall this story will more fully appreciate the appearance of Gouvernail in *The Awakening* (47–49; 54). **Dyer 1981b:** Chopin's use of night imagery here is especially subtle and complex (222). Gouvernail's allusion to Whitman both implies and arouses sexual desire (222–23). Here as in "Athénaïse," Gouvernail plays a part in a story focusing on marital discord (223). This story is one of Chopin's most accomplished in its use of night imagery (228). **Dyer 1981d:** Here and in numerous other works, Chopin uses physical setting to imply what a character is feeling. Her frequent use of this technique is open to various explanations (451–52). **Davis 1982:** In this intriguingly puzzling tale, the uncertain ending prevented Chopin's readers from being scandalized in the way they later were by *The Awakening* (65). **Fluck 1982:** This story illustrates Chopin's effort to balance the desire for transgression with the demands of social respectability. The two men are associated with contrasting traits, and for the first time Chopin leaves the female protagonist's decision unclear (162). **Bonner 1983b:** Imagery of light and darkness suggests the ethical issues at stake, while color imagery (particularly that of the lighted cigar) suggests sexual temptations (144–45). **Stein 1984:** This is one of a number of works that deal with the need to seek self-fulfillment, no matter what its consequences (189). Although this story is not very substantive, it does foreshadow *The Awakening*, particularly since it depicts a woman who seems unable to reject newly aroused needs. As in the novel, the heroine here does not at first recognize how constrained she is by her marriage and her patronizing husband (190). Her fascination with Gouvernail suggests her inner urge to be challenged; her initial tendency to view him with prejudice shows how insecure she feels in her present way of life. He symbolizes her need to question her existence; she finds his self-assurance unfamiliar and therefore intriguing (190–91). He does not treat her condescendingly as her husband does. Although the precise meaning of her very last words is technically unclear, they fairly obviously imply that she has now thrown off the restraints of respectability. What is less clear (and therefore more intriguing) is how unrestrained she will be and what consequences will result (191–93). **Dyer 1985:** In this as in other tales, Chopin deals indirectly with topics she might not otherwise have been able to discuss (81). **Rowe 1985:** The story may have bothered its first readers because Chopin did not express disapproval of her heroine (231). **Skaggs 1985:** This is one of several stories by Chopin that explore romance, often of an odd variety. Although Mrs. Baroda seems neither romantically unsophisticated nor sexually unfulfilled, she still feels tempted by infidelity, merely from erotic desire. In the end she seems willing to take a chance on throwing away everything merely to satisfy this impulse (35–36). **Ewell 1986:** Gouvernail appears in other works by Chopin (21). In the present work, however, Chopin treated sensual appetite even more explicitly than before, and this tale provides what may be her most provocative ending. This conclusion, however, is skillfully foreshadowed. One theme of the story is the way conduct is shaped by perspective, and this theme enhances (and is enhanced by) the complex and subtle depictions of Mrs. Baroda and Gouvernail. The work is full of rich potential ironies and strongly insinuates the power of erotic attraction, while the objective narrative tone shows Chopin's mastery of her art (98–99). In the later story "Athénaïse," the tables are turned on Gouvernail (108). Themes explored in this work are also touched on in Chopin's poetry (160) and in her other prose fiction (183). **Lattin 1988:** Here as elsewhere in Chopin's fiction, Gouvernail is present when an attractive woman is undergoing a change of perspective (44). **Elfenbein 1989:** Here as elsewhere Chopin describes the erotic yearnings of respectable white women, although she realized the difficulties such tales might foment for her (125). White women such as the one described here tend to be more complicated characters, but less clearly victimized, than the women of color Chopin elsewhere describes (126). **Inge 1989:** Chopin handles the topic of potential infidelity with unusual daring, especially since the wife here seems generally satisfied with her husband (although there is perhaps a hint of sexual dissatisfaction). She seems erotically stirred by the visitor, and her refusal to wear the white scarf he offers her suggests her eventual rejection of the pledges she made when she married

(99–100). **Taylor 1989:** This is one of various stories by Chopin that emphasize a female's concluding feeling of triumph (179). Here as elsewhere she links feminine sexuality with the reading of continental realist fiction (189). **Toth 1990a:** This is one of various stories by Chopin about extramarital temptation (168). It was written during a time when Chopin was creating other assertive female protagonists (233). Gouvernail also takes part in other works by Chopin (275). This narrative, with its daring ending, was published in *Vogue* (like many of Chopin's more unconventional stories (279). It was reprinted in *A Night in Acadie* (298). **Brown 1991:** Here as elsewhere Chopin depicts a woman inhibited by her Creole culture; she expects little of herself and of her visitor. By the end of the tale, however, Mrs. Boroda seems on the verge of balancing social expectations and personal desires (125–26). **Dyer 1993:** One critic from the 1960s saw the theme of female self-assertion in this story as foreshadowing *The Awakening* (22). Gouvernail's appearance in this tale helps us interpret his significance in the novel (68). **Koloski 1994:** The story is included in soft-cover collections of Chopin's fiction published in 1970, 1976, 1979, 1981 (27). This work also often appears in college textbooks (28–29). **Lundie 1994:** Here as elsewhere Chopin shows a white woman feeling sexual desire, but rarely in her fiction do white women act on that desire in the way or to the degree that black women do (136). **Thomas 1995:** Given the self-assertiveness of this story's main female character, one might have expected Chopin to show more sympathy for other women who (like herself) dared to publish fiction (29). **Bender 1996:** In her unconventional desires Mrs. Boroda foreshadows Edna in *The Awakening*, but Chopin was not yet ready to depict a sexually adventurous mother. Nonetheless, Mrs. Baroda's sexual yearnings have nothing to do with reproduction—an idea that challenged Darwinian dogma (109–10). **Berkove 1996:** In this story as elsewhere Chopin treats sexual relations from an ethical point of view (194). **Koloski 1996:** This story and its heroine are among Chopin's most effective creations (xii–xiii). Gouvernail, who is likewise noteworthy, appears in other stories by Chopin and acts as a catalyst here. Everything is perceived, however, from Mrs. Baroda's perspective, and the final words typify Chopin's talent for effective conclusions (35–36). In this tale and elsewhere, Gouvernail is one of Chopin's most thoughtful and discerning characters (39). The train in this story is a means of avoiding an encounter rather than (as is often true elsewhere) of experiencing one (52). Voice is a strong presence here as in other Chopin stories (55), although the allusion to Whitman is a technique Chopin does not often employ elsewhere (60). This is one of several stories containing a puzzling kiss (62). **Beer 1997:** This is one of several stories by Chopin in which a woman rejects the assessments that others, including the story's readers, attempt to impose on her (48). In some respects this tale resembles "A Shameful Affair," in which another woman is puzzled and aroused by another distant male. The final line of this narrative can be interpreted in at least three different ways. Nonetheless, the marriage the story depicts has been permanently altered no matter how one chooses to read the ending. Sexual desire has disrupted our sense of the stability of the title character's life, and she will never again seem to be quite the same woman she seemed at first (50–51). **Brown 1999:** In this story as elsewhere, Gouvernail is contrasted with more conservative or predictable men (71–72). However, he apparently does not voice his deepest views until he meets Mrs. Baroda. Here as elsewhere, Chopin depicts the traditional woman's role as static and passive, whereas the conventional male role seems more active and assertive (72–74).Whereas Gouvernail is the one awakened in "Athénaïse," in the present story he provides the stimulus for another person's awakening (75). **Koloski 1999:** This is one of Chopin's tales focusing on a woman's concerns and restraints (viii). This is one of Chopin's best stories and appears in one of the best, most convincing, and most charitable collections of short fiction published in her time and place (xvi). This is one of several tales in *A Night in Acadie* that focus on a transforming journey (xvi). In certain respects this tale resembles "Athénaïse," which is placed near the beginning of *A Night in Acadie* (while the present story is placed near the end), particularly in their similar emphasis on Gouvernail, who in both cases perceives the heroine more clearly than the heroine does. It is rare for Chopin to make a male so perceptive (xxi–xxii). **Toth 1999a:** This is one of many tales whose themes early critics failed to connect to Chopin's own life and views (3). Like some of Chopin's other most currently popular works, it first appeared in *Vogue* (9). **Toth 1999c:** This is one of various stories by Chopin dealing with feminine extra-marital temptation (97). It was one of several on this theme written during the same year (158). Gouvernail in some ways resembles a man Chopin knew (186). Her focus on the female protagonists' inward transformation gives the story greater resonance (194). **Gibbons 2000:** The style of narration fits the personality of the heroine, whom the reader immediately perceives ironically. The story progresses with stunning rapidity and vitality and is Chopin's first entirely credible narrative, especially because of its transcendence of local color stereotypes. By subtly suggesting the desire that drives the heroine, Chopin also penetrates into territory that was culturally taboo. No other woman like Mrs. Baroda exists in Chopin's previous fiction, although she *does* foreshadow the heroine of *The Awakening* (xxxv–xxxvi).

"The Return of Alcibiade"

Written: 1892. First published: 1892. Included in *Bayou Folk* **(1894).**

Because Fred Bartner's buggy is in need of repair, he stops at the plantation of old Monsieur Jean Baptiste Plochel, who has the best blacksmith in the parish.

Monsieur Plochel lost his son in the war years ago. When Alcibiade left to go to war, he told his father that he would be back home for Christmas dinner. Every Christmas the old man anxiously waits for his son's return.

It is Christmas day, and as Bartner walks up to the house the old man and his granddaughter Esmée come out on the veranda. The old man throws his weak, frail arms around Bartner, exclaiming, "my son, my son." Esmée explains the situation to Bartner with tears in her eyes.

After some thought Esmée asks Bartner to pretend to be her Uncle Alcibiade so that the old man can finally have his dream come true. At first Bartner hesitates, but Esmée's charm wins him over to the charade. They have a wonderful Christmas dinner. Afterwards Esmée helps her grandfather to the veranda, where he likes to nap in the sun. Occasionally he calls for Alcibiade to come to him so that he can tell him something. Bartner answers him and goes to sit with the old man. Sometimes the old man forgets what he wants to say. Later he tells Bartner that he thinks he will take a nap.

Bartner and Esmée take a long walk. When they return they find that the old man has died peacefully in his sleep. **(DR)**

***

Anonymous 1894 [*The Critic***]:** The very simplicity and brevity of this tale contribute to its effectiveness (41). **Rankin 1932:** The town in this tale is based on Cloutierville, Louisiana, where Chopin lived during 1880–83 (98). **Reilly 1942:** Here as elsewhere, Chopin almost always depicts old people in the presence of the young and shows the complex relations between members of the two groups (132). **Seyersted 1969a:** Chopin altered McFarlane's original name when she revised the story (211). **Arms 1967:** Like "Beyond the Bayou" and "Old Aunt Peggy," this tale balances emotionalism and realism (223). **Peterson 1972:** In this tale Chopin manages to avoid an extremely maudlin tone (104). **Arner 1975:** Like several other stories set after the Civil War, this one uses mental disturbance symbolically. Although generally very strong, this tale is damaged by its complacent ending (44). **Bonner 1977:** This is one of only three stories in *Bayou Folk* in which the author comments (7). Here and elsewhere in Chopin, mental illness is a major theme (10). The story shows vanished love leading to mental breakdown (11). **Rogers 1983:** Esmée's name is similar to the name of a character in a novel by George Sand (41). **Dyer 1985:** This is one of several tales by Chopin about extreme nostalgia (74). **Skaggs 1985:** This is one of several stories featuring characters whose lives and minds have been disrupted by the Civil War (16). **Taylor 1989:** This story alludes to a famously mean slave-owner (144). **Toth 1990a:** This is one of several stories in which Chopin examines the devastating impact of war (70). The tale reflects the conditions of winter in Louisiana (325). **Toth 1999c:** This is one of several tales in which Chopin describes the tragic effects of the Civil War (32). It features one of the few gentle men presented in *Bayou Folk*, although he turns out to be demented (151). It also features one of Chopin's frequently generous women (154).

"Ripe Figs"

Written: 1892. First published: 1893. Included in *A Night in Acadie* (1897).

Maman-Naínaine tells Babette that she may visit her cousins in south Louisiana when the figs are ripe. Babette watches the figs slowly change from hard, green, tiny balls to plump, luscious, purple figs. Every day she checks on them until finally they are ripe. She carries a plate covered with bright green leaves and ripe figs to Maman-Naínaine, telling her godmother she thinks the figs have taken long to ripen. Maman-Naínaine disagrees, but she tells Babette to give her love to her cousins and to tell her aunt that she should look for Babette again when the chrysanthemums are in bloom. **(DR)**

***

Seyersted 1969a: This very short tale illustrates Chopin's typical focus on personalities and moods rather than mere happenings and exemplifies her tendency to see meaning even in tiny details. The subtlety and imagery of the tale make it almost a poem (122). **Peterson 1972:** Here as elsewhere, Chopin uses children symbolically but also somewhat simplistically (103). **Gardiner 1982:** This sketch is appealing partly because it is brief and seems simple yet nonetheless provides rich description. Chopin effectively uses balanced contrasts, imagery of nature, and cyclical structures (379–

82). **Skaggs 1985:** This is one of many stories by Chopin that shows a real familiarity with children and their effects on others. The work effectively illuminates the ways that older and younger persons experience time (27). **Toth 1990a:** The emphasis on seasonal time may reflect the influence of Chopin's early reading (52). The national publication of the tale contributed to her renown (207). This tale later appeared in *A Night in Acadie*, in which all the stories are set in Louisiana (298). **Branscomb 1994:** Because figs are associated with sexuality and chrysanthemums with death, the godmother's final allusion to All Saints Day suggests that a religious perspective must balance the girl's involvement in natural rhythms (165–67). **Koloski 1996:** This brief tale typifies the works of *A Night in Acadie* in its emphasis on the way society shapes perceptions of nature. Like many of Chopin's characters, the godmother here is confident of her own perspective (31–32). Like other children's stories by Chopin, this one features a person who is idiosyncratic but beneficent (71). It is one of Chopin's most effective tales for the young (72; 87). **Beer 1997:** This extremely straightforward story emphasizes seasons to symbolize important phases of human life. The delicate, understated narrative juxtaposes the viewpoints of the young and the old concerning time. Because the figs are part of nature, they can symbolize distinct and different chronological moments (87). **Koloski 1999:** This is one of Chopin's best stories and appears in one of the best, most convincing, and most charitable collections of short fiction published in her time and place (xvi). Here as in other works, Chopin explores how society shapes perceptions of reality and power (xviii). This is one of many stories by Chopin which either feature children or were written for them, although its themes seem quite mature (xxii).

"Roger and His Majesty"

Written: 1891. Destroyed.

Toth 1990a: This story, one of sixteen Chopin composed in 1891, was subsequently lost or destroyed (198).

"A Rude Awakening"

Written: 1891. First published: 1893. Included in *Bayou Folk* **(1894).**

Sylveste Bordon is an extremely lazy man. He has four hungry children, one of whom is only two years old and is ill. His oldest child, Lolotte, tries her best to keep the family fed. Sylveste never worries that his children are hungry or that he does not provide for their needs.

Sylveste comes home with Monsieur Joe Duplan's wagon and mules and tells Lolotte that he has a job driving the wagonload of cotton to the landing tomorrow. Lolotte is thrilled that there will be some money for food. Early the next morning Lolotte awakens and listens for the sound of the wagon leaving, but she hears nothing. She gets out of bed and looks for her father. He is gone, and so are his fishing pole and pail.

All Lolotte's dreams of food for the family are crushed. She decides to take the wagon and drive the load of cotton to the landing herself. She calls Aunt Mitty to watch the children, climbs up on the wagon, and drives off.

When Sylveste returns, he is upset that Lolotte has taken the wagon. She does not return that night. The next day one of Duplan's slaves comes to the cabin to tell them that the wagon was found smashed and the mules are gone, but there is no sign of Lolotte.

Sylveste is heartbroken. He grieves and does not know what to do with himself. He asks Duplan to give him some work. He becomes the hardest worker, being the first in the fields in the morning and the last to leave at nightfall. Everyone believes that Lolotte was thrown from the wagon in the water and drowned. Duplan is the only one who does not give up hope that she is alive.

One day Duplan comes to Sylveste and tells him to come to his house because he has something to show him. Lolotte, who had been secretly rescued and hidden by Duplan, is sitting in a chair, pale and small. Sylveste is ecstatic. Duplan tells him that he has one more chance to take care of his family. Sylveste answers that God wants to help him and so he is going to try his best to care for his children. **(DR)**

***

Anonymous 1894 [*The Critic*]: The very simplicity and brevity of this tale contribute to its effectiveness (41). **Seyersted 1969a:** Members of the Duplan family appear in many other tales by Chopin (78). Aunty Minty is generous in a way that fits the stereotypical image of blacks during the time Chopin wrote, but she transcends the stereotype by also being shrewd and blunt (80). **Peterson 1972:** Although this story was first published in a magazine apparently intended for young readers, the journal's actual audience was broader than its title might suggest (61). Here as elsewhere Chopin relies on amnesia to tell her story, and she also provides a very clear moral. The self-confident, self-assertive blacks provide the greatest interest (63–64). **Rocks 1972:** Here as elsewhere, Chopin demonstrates the complexities liberty can involve and shows that true liberty often entails a responsible concern for others (117). **Arner 1975:** This brief and amusing tale has been highly praised (61–62). **Webb 1976:** Here as elsewhere Chopin uses a cyclical pattern to structure a story (14). **Bonner 1977:** Here as elsewhere in *Bayou Folk*, Chopin uses a sudden twist to create irony (9). As in other *Bayou Folk* tales, the focus here on a threatened child helps resolve the plot (10). **Lattin 1980:** This is one of the stories in which Chopin describes members of the Duplan family, her least intriguing and least dramatic group of repeating characters (21). **Aherne 1985:** The story illustrates Chopin's range in depicting female characters. Its conclusion is ambiguous (82). Lolotte is one of the many fascinating women Chopin depicted (although she did less well in characterizing men [84]). **Skaggs 1985:** This is one of several tales depicting unusually independent girls. By the end of the story, both father and daughter have assumed more fitting roles than either possessed at the start (12–13). **Gaudet 1986:** Here a Cajun character is shown outside of Cajun country (50). **Elfenbein 1989:** In this tale, Chopin raises the issue of race explicitly, but only at the very end (121). **Papke 1990:** Most of the stories Chopin wrote during this year seem fairly predictable, perhaps because she was focusing most of her attention on calling attention to her novels. This tale, though, is one of several from this period that present unusual female protagonists, most of whom defy social rules but do so for sensible purposes and therefore seem less defiant than they may first appear (52). **Toth 1990a:** This was one of several stories from 1891 in which Chopin sought a friendly, interested readership. It was printed in a magazine for youth (201) and may allude to real persons from Cloutierville (202–3). Chopin received substantial payment for this tale (204). **Robinson 1992:** This rather maudlin tale is at the opposite end of the spectrum from Chopin's later revolutionary story "The Storm" (xii). **Ewell 1994:** Of the nearly ten stories Chopin wrote early in 1891, this was one of only three to be immediately accepted for publication (160). **Koloski 1994:** The story is included in a soft-cover collection of Chopin's fiction published in 1992 (28). **Saar 1994:** Here as elsewhere in Chopin's fiction, an initially assertive woman eventually succumbs to a conventional woman's role (68). **Carr 1996:** Here as elsewhere Chopin presents Cajun males in a condescending fashion (53–54). **Koloski 1996:** The tale is set on a holiday and is one of several children's stories by Chopin that depict the poor (11; 71; 87). **Wagner-Martin 1996:** Here as elsewhere Chopin depicts an energetic, determined female (197) as well as an appealing black woman (203). **Beer 1997:** Here as in "A Very Fine Fiddle," Chopin depicts an irresponsible father whose life suddenly alters (85). **Koloski 1999:** This is one of many stories by Chopin which either feature children or were written for them (xxii). Here as elsewhere she describes a feminine adolescent's maturation (xxiii). **Toth 1999c:** This tale satirized a man Chopin knew from Cloutierville (140). It was one of the several dark works included in *Bayou Folk* (151).

"A Scrap and a Sketch"
See "Juanita" and "The Night Came Slowly"

Toth 1999c: An east coast journal published two brief pieces by Chopin under this collective title (158).

"A Sentimental Soul"

Written: 1894. First published: 1895. Included in *A Night in Acadie* **(1897).**

Mamzelle Fleurette owns a little store across the street from the locksmith's store. Every evening the locksmith, Lacodie, comes in and buys a newspaper from Mamzelle. One evening he does not come in and Mamzelle Fleurette is cross and irritable. The next morning she realizes that she is in love with Lacodie.

This will never do because Lacodie is married. Mamzelle goes to confession and tells the priest that she is in love with a married man. The priest tells her that she must forget about Lacodie by praying and keeping him out of her mind. She takes his picture out of her prayer book. She decides to avoid him in the store. The next day Lacodie's wife, Augustine, comes in to buy the paper. She tells Mamzelle that Lacodie is ill. Augustine does not come for a paper the next two days. On the third day Mamzelle takes a paper to her and goes in to see Lacodie. He looks horrible and terribly sick. A few days later Lacodie dies.

Mamzelle confesses to the priest that she is still in love with Lacodie. He tells her that she must forget Lacodie and pray for forgiveness.

Less than a year later Augustine marries Gascon. Mamzelle goes to a new church and confesses to a new priest, never mentioning Lacodie or her love for him. She goes home and takes his picture out and puts it in a frame and hangs it on her wall. She does not care if Gascon's wife sees it or not. **(DR)**

***

Reilly 1937: This is one of various stories in which Chopin deals subtly with the ambiguities of affection (72). **Reilly 1942:** This story illustrates Chopin's ability to create complex characters in only a few words (131–32). This is one of various tales in which Chopin deals subtly with the ambiguities of affection (134). **Bush 1957:** This is one of various fine stories by Chopin about unmarried women. It seems to have been influenced by Flaubert's "A Simple Heart." Both works explore the psychologies of seemingly uncomplicated persons. Chopin effectively blends sadness and humor (255–57). **Seyersted 1969a:** The heroine here resembles heroines in other Chopin stories who are willing to take independent stands (111). **Fletcher 1966:** As in some of her other stories about Creole women, Chopin here emphasizes feminine fidelity (127–28). **Peterson 1972:** Here as elsewhere Chopin depicts the inflexibility of organized religion. Lacodie's simple respect for Mamzelle Fleurette as a person inspires her affection. The comedy of the tale derives from her response to her new feelings, yet the story effectively blends comedy with sadness and encourages sympathy for the heroine, whose final devotion gives meaning to her life (151–55). **Rocks 1972:** This is the one tale in which Chopin expresses a clear antipathy to the clergy. The story also shows that women can be just as single-minded in romance as men (118–19). **Arner 1975:** Here as in "Azélie," Chopin explores the more disturbing aspects of desire, which in this case finally leads to a significant if hidden rebellion and a fuller sense of personal if private independence (68). **Bonner 1983b:** The story explores prohibited desire (143–44). **Skaggs 1985:** This is one of several stories by Chopin that explore romance, often of an odd variety (33). The woman's looks and dress symbolize her inhibited life, but the description of her growing affection is the most appealing Chopin ever offered of that process. The heroine's desire for freedom is a significant aspect of this tale (33–34). **Martin 1988a:** This story reflects Chopin's growing interest in liberty, both in her fiction and in her own life. The work exhibits her frequent explorations of the conflicts between selflessness and self-fulfillment (6). **Inge 1989:** Although Chopin has a bit of fun at her heroine's expense, her point of view is not caustic, and the story is also intriguing because of its focus on complicated questions of ethics and the tensions between flesh and spirit. Chopin seems to mock the religious view that these tensions can never be resolved; she allows her heroine to achieve a kind of compromise (100). **Toth 1990a:** Chopin knew from her husband's own illness the ravages of malaria (158). A character in the story resembles a woman Chopin mentioned in a notebook (233). The story may reflect the influence of Zola; its main character may foreshadow a character in *The Awakening*, and its skepticism about organized religion may reflect Chopin's own opinions (250–51). This was one of several stories Chopin wrote about extra-marital desire (279) and about the growth in women's consciousness. It later appeared in *A Night in Acadie*, in which all the stories are set in Louisiana (298). **Shurbutt 1993:** This is one of various stories in which Chopin challenges a stereotype about women (22). **Koloski 1996:** The heroine of this tale achieves, by the end, an unusual kind of freedom (49–50). **Thomas 1996:** This is one of various stories in which Chopin juxtaposes contrasting women (208). **Benfey 1999:** Because the doctor in this story resembles a prominent figure in the New Orleans White League, the death of the main male character may symbolize the demise of Reconstruction in that city. In any case, the story suggests Chopin's liberal attitudes toward marriage (251). **Bonner and Bonner 1999:** This is one of several works by Chopin that features St. Louis Cathedral in New Orleans (55). **Toth 1999c:** The male protagonist here resembles a French novelist Chopin disliked, while the main female figure foreshadows a character in *The Awakening* (169). By disposing of Lacodie, Chopin exacted a kind of revenge on the offensive novelist (168–69). Probably because the tale implies adulterous feelings, it was rejected by various mainstream journals (171). Chopin's focus on the woman's inward transformation adds resonance to the work (194).

"A Shameful Affair"

Written: 1891. First published: 1893. Included in *Complete Works* (1969).

Mildred Orme leaves her family at Narragansett to enjoy a time of repose and reflection at the Kraummer's farmhouse, which is nestled among the rolling hills bordering the Meramec river. Well aware of her affluence, beauty, and intelligence, the young woman of twenty holds a rather high opinion of herself. For this reason, she will not so much as look at the farmhands who daily pass by the swing, where she sits reading Browning and Ibsen. One day a farmhand retrieves a piece of paper she has dropped. As she looks for the chance to give him a condescending smile over the next few days, Mildred notices that the farmhand is handsome and that he never looks her way. Having snubbed the advances of half a dozen farmhands already, she does not care that this farmhand pays her no attention at first. However, before the summer is over, she is pursuing him.

Mildred asks Mrs. Kraummer about the farmhand. She replies that one might say he is a tramp, but she assures the young woman that he is a good worker and a quiet person, not someone to be feared. Pretending to prove her courage, Mildred tells Mrs. Kraummer that she would like the farmhand to drive her to church the next day. When Aber sends back word that he is going fishing and can't drive her to church, Mildred becomes incensed. She is even more unsettled when he passes by later that day and looks at her for the first time.

The next day, instead of going to church or staying in to write letters, Mildred makes her way down to the river where Aber is fishing. After watching him stare patiently at his line for a while, she asks if she might hold the pole. Within a short time, she has a bite, and the farmhand rushes to her side to help her. Close to her lovely hair, cheeks, and eyes, Aber cannot resist holding Mildred and kissing her. Mildred is lost in the moment, for she cannot tell whether Aber kisses her once or ten times. When she recovers herself, Mildred sees the farmhand disappearing up the path through the woods.

Mildred is stunned by Aber's boldness, and she feels guilty because she thoroughly enjoyed his kiss. Nothing can make her feel better about herself, not even the letter she receives from a friend, a letter which makes her realize that the man she took as a tramp, a farmhand, and a boor is actually Fred Evelyn, an adventurous young man who is working as a laborer on the Kraummer farm only to experience a side of life he has never known. "Aber" later meets Mildred in the middle of a narrow path through a wheat field and apologizes for his forwardness. Mildred says that she wants to forget that the whole thing ever happened and that she can only forgive him when she has forgiven herself. As she walks slowly away, the young man's throat becomes flush as the meaning of her parting words sink in. (JW)

***

Rankin 1932: This tale, not set in the South, contains elements of comedy and romance (134). Seyersted 1969a: This story had difficulty finding a publisher at first, perhaps because of its heroine's frank emotions (54).

Mildred is one of the first main female characters in Chopin's fiction to be stirred both in spirit and in body, but she reacts to the kiss differently than some feminine protagonists in other recent fiction: she fails to fault the male, and she vows not to change her conduct. In a concession to standard thinking, however, Mildred does seem a bit ashamed of her own reaction to the kiss (109), although she made no effort to refuse it (142). Chopin excluded this tale from her planned third gathering of stories, probably because she assumed it would lead a publisher to reject the book (223). **Seyersted 1969b:** Mildred typifies the kind of women Chopin often depicted—women who violated conventional contemporary views of ideal feminine behavior. Mildred is self-assertive rather than passive (27). **Leary 1970a:** This tale depicts feminine self-assertion in a manner unusual for its day (xii). **Leary 1971:** This story was unusual for its time in its explicit focus on feminine liberty and scheming (168). **Peterson 1972:** In theme this story resembles "A No-Account Creole," since both focus on the tension between personal desire and impersonal ethics. Mildred, surrounded by a suggestively symbolic landscape, tries at first to assert social superiority over the indifferent farmhand, but the narrator's explanation of the cause of her romantic temptation seems simplistic (88–90). Revelation of the farmhand's real social status may have been meant to placate offended readers, and his own apology brings the tale to a fairly conventional conclusion (90–91). The story is tamer and much less radical than Per Seyersted suggests, although this is the first tale in which Chopin focuses on feminine physical desire. The nature of that desire is also commendably complex, although the story's larger complexities are never fully resolved (91–92). This tale illustrates Chopin's taste for complications and the unexpected (96). Here as elsewhere Chopin spotlights one character whose changed perspective ends the tale (114–15). **Rocks 1972:** Here as elsewhere Chopin shows that erotic desire often causes suffering, not simply pleasure (116). The story shows how a taste of liberty can often enhance one's larger sense of being constrained (117). **Arner 1975:** Although the plot seems a bit contrived, the contrivance contributes to Chopin's aim of mocking Mildred's hypocrisy and shallow sense of freedom (125–26). **Ladenson 1976:** Here as in *The Awakening*, a woman's unconventional emotions are presented as being even stronger than a man's (30). **Taylor 1979:** This is one of many tales in which a woman triumphs, if only briefly (xvi). **Dyer 1980–81:** This is one of many stories by Chopin in which a female is aroused by contact with a male (10–11). However, readers who know only this work and a few other of Chopin's more famous writings may fail to realize her significant interest in *male* (not simply female) passions (15). **Dyer 1981d:** Although this story was written almost a decade before *The Awakening*, it anticipates the novel's emphasis on sensual realization. Similarly, it also emphasizes the symbolic use of setting, since the farm is associated with abundant vitality. Such symbolism is important in each third of the story. Mildred is less self-aware than she assumes, and she feels smugly superior to the farm hands. Her quickening response to

Fred, however, is foreshadowed by the fertile setting. She becomes increasingly linked to the ripening wheat, and her frustration with Fred's fishing parallels her own sexual tension. Fred eventually responds to Mildred's own enthusiasm. In section three, the wheat fields once again provide a symbolic setting. By this point in the story Mildred knows herself better than she did at the beginning (449–52). **Fluck 1982:** This story illustrates Chopin's effort to balance the desire for transgression with the demands of social respectability. Although the heroine attempts to respond to her new feelings with dignity, she must still suppress them. This was one of the various unconventional, innovative stories by Chopin that were often turned down for publication (161–63). **Burchard 1984:** This is the most successful tale in which Chopin describes a growing sensual self-consciousness, but even here the woman (typically) suffers because of her self-assertion. The story is carefully designed, but its conclusion is typically ambivalent: rarely does Chopin allow her heroines to enjoy uncomplicated passion (41–42). **Stein 1984:** This is one of various tales in which Chopin describes the need to be true to oneself (207). **Newman 1986:** As in other tales, Chopin here contrasts real life with the stereotypes of fiction (160). **Skaggs 1985:** This tale, which surpasses the recent story "The Maid of St. Phillippe" in quality, depicts a woman who, although somewhat self-centered, at least has some sense of self. The work resembles "A Harbinger" by exploring a female's burgeoning sensuality (58). **Simpson 1986:** Chopin employs images of nature that suggest fertility and sensuality in order to suggest the heroine's confrontation with her submerged sexual nature. She tries to deny her yearnings for Fred, but nature surrounds her just as it does the man-made farmhouse she eventually must leave. As she immerses herself in nature, so she is immersed in her sexual feelings. At the river she puts aside the book (associated with civilization) and grasps the fishing pole (a phallic symbol) Fred hands her. Suppressing her desires once more, however, she returns to the shelter of the house, but when she ventures forth into nature again she concedes (if only temporarily) her true feelings. She will never achieve sexual peace until she comes to terms with her natural instincts (59–60). **Martin 1988a:** This is one of various stories in which Chopin investigates conflicts between strong, often sexual feelings and the conventional ethics of society. The tale is frank in its treatment of desire and its results (4). **Elfenbein 1989:** Here as elsewhere Chopin suggests that even respectable women can have strongly erotic personalities, especially since it is Mildred who takes the initiative in this story. Mildred's embarrassment keeps the story itself respectable, thus implying that Chopin herself was responsive to the same constraints, but the story still indicts the social hypocrisy that depicted white women as sexually pure. Here and in other works, in fact, Chopin describes respectable white females as erotically aggressive (124–25). White women such as the one described here tend to be more complicated characters, but less clearly victimized, than the women of color Chopin elsewhere describes (126). Mildred is just one of several white females in

Chopin's writings who flirt with eroticism but then pull back (132). **Taylor 1989**: This is one of various stories by Chopin that emphasize a female's concluding feeling of triumph (179). **Toth 1990a**: Written in Missouri in the early summer of 1891, the story presents a main male character whose name may jokingly allude to the name of Chopin's adolescent son. As in other stories she set in Missouri, Chopin here tries to emphasize local dialect (199–200). The story shows the influence of the gentility typical of much recent American writing; later Chopin would be influenced by recent European models (205–6). This was one of four of her tales published in a single month (215–16). It anticipates "Fedora," one of her later stories (289). **Guidici 1991**: This is one of various stories by Chopin in which a change of place gives a woman new options and greater power, even if only temporarily (27). **Ewell 1994**: This was one of a number of stories Chopin wrote in early 1891 that focused on the dilemmas of women and that were at first rejected by publishers (160). **Ewell 1994**: This is one of many stories by Chopin that show the dangers of ignoring the sexual or sensual aspects of human nature (168). **Koloski 1994**: For reasons not specifically explained, this work was included in a 1981 anthology of American short fiction (24). The story is included in soft-cover collections of Chopin's fiction published in 1970, 1976, and 1979 (27). **Baxter 1996**: This story lends itself to a creative writing exercise for students (240). **Beer 1997**: This is one of various stories by Chopin that resist simple responses, either by the reader or by characters within the tale. This work was repeatedly turned down by nearly ten periodicals. The story deals with the ways social pressures both enforce and undermine conformist behavior. The first third of the work emphasizes yearning; the second third emphasizes how that yearning is partly satisfied; the final third explores ambivalent responses to such satisfaction. Mildred's yearning is primarily physical, although once Fred's social status is revealed, his speech—and the way he is perceived—both seem to change. Mildred's final comment, however, makes the story truly unconventional; her words challenge gender stereotypes, making a male blush. Mildred seizes the initiative by accepting personal responsibility, thus preventing Fred from enacting a standard male routine (48–50). **McCullough 1999**: Mildred is a supercilious New Englander, proud of her economic and educational status. As an outsider in an ethnically complex environment, she resembles a local-color writer. She is motivated both by class prejudice and by lust. Although the farmhand turns out to be her social equal, she is still embarrassed at having revealed her sexual impulses. The story shows how strongly desire is affected by issues of economic status (202–6). **Toth 1999c**: This story reflects the influence of William Dean Howells (125). It was first printed in a newspaper owned by an acquaintance of Chopin (133).

"The Storm"

Written: 1898. Included in *Complete Works* (1969).

Divided into five parts, the story begins by describing the approach of a storm that causes Bobinôt and his four-year-old son, Bibi, to remain at Friedheimer's store for shelter. Bobinôt muses aloud to Bibi that perhaps his wife, Calixta, will be afraid of the storm, and he purchases a can of shrimps, "of which Calixta was very fond," to take home to her. During the storm, Bobinôt and Bibi sit on the store's porch; resting his hand on his father's knee, Bibi is not afraid.

In the story's second part, Calixta sees the storm approach while she is sewing. She begins to shut up the house and goes out on the front gallery to retrieve Bobinôt's Sunday clothes. While she is outside, Alcée Laballière, whom she has not often seen since her marriage five years ago, approaches and asks permission to wait out the storm on her gallery.

Calixta invites him in and they make small talk while Calixta tidies up. Expressing concern about Bobinôt and Bibi, Calixta goes to a window to look out in the direction of their intended approach home. Alcée joins her at the window, looking over her shoulder. While they watch the incessant lightning, a bolt strikes a nearby chinaberry tree, filling "all visible space with a blinding glare." Calixta puts her hands over her eyes, cries out, and staggers backward into Alcée's arms. He draws her "close and spasmodically to him."

Calixta, alarmed by the lightning, cries out about the possible fate of the house and Bibi. Alcée, feeling "all the old-time infatuation and desire for her flesh," assures Calixta that the house will be safe because of its location, and he asks that she be quiet. When she looks up at him, the fear in her eyes is replaced by a "drowsy gleam" that betrays her desire for him. He kisses her, which reminds him of their time together in Assumption where they had been intimate, time and time again, years ago. In a low voice, he asks Calixta if she remembers Assumption.

During the "crashing torrents" and "the roar of the elements," they make love. For both of them, the passion of their lovemaking reaches a level that neither of them has ever experienced before.

As the sun comes out, Alcée takes his leave while Calixta, on the gallery, watches him ride away. He turns and smiles at her, and Calixta lifts "her pretty chin in the air" and laughs out loud.

The third part of the story begins by describing Bobinôt and Bibi arriving at home and stopping to wash the mud off of themselves at the cistern outside. They wish to be as presentable as possible to Calixta, who is "an over-scrupulous housewife."

Calixta greets them instead with a warm, jovial welcome, kissing Bibi effusively. As Calixta feels him to see if he is dry, Bobinôt's "explanations and apologies which he had been composing all along the way, died on his lips."

He offers Calixta the can of shrimps, which she takes from him with thanks, complimenting his admirable nature. "... [W]e'll have a feas' to night! umph-umph!" she says.

When the family sits down to eat, they laugh so much and so loudly that anyone might have heard them miles away.

At the beginning of the story's fourth section, Alcée writes to his wife, Clarisse. In a "loving letter, full of tender solicitude," he tells her and the babies not to hurry back from Biloxi because their health and pleasure are his first priority. He even suggests that they remain a month longer.

In the final section of the story, Clarisse is "charmed" upon receiving her husband's letter. Devoted as she is to Alcée, the time in Biloxi, "her first free breath since her marriage," is rejuvenating to Clarisse. She is more than willing to forego their "intimate conjugal life" for a while.

"So the storm passed and every one was happy." **(EP)**

***

Seyersted 1969a: The story was composed on July 18, 1898, shortly after both her novel *The Awakening* and her third gathering of stories had been accepted for publication. Even Chopin recognized how provocative the story was; she never submitted it for publication, and even her first biographer failed to mention its existence. It is a sequel, in five parts, to the story "At the 'Cadian Ball" and is unusually explicit for American fiction of its day (164–65). Here as in her other fiction, Chopin does not treat sexual relations with humor or mockery, and in fact aspects of this tale are reminiscent of the celebratory "Song of Solomon" from the Bible. Chopin de-emphasizes suspense, offering instead a daring, direct, and non-judgmental presentation of pleasurable sex, which—like the stormy weather—is treated as a powerful natural force that is disruptive but perhaps also beneficial. The final sentence, though, may imply a more complex view by perhaps suggesting the ephemeral nature of the supposed benefits. On the whole, however, the story suggests that sexual desire is a profound, deeply rooted, and enduring human motive (166–67). Images of passivity and activity in the story imply the fundamental differences between men and women, while other image patterns—such as those of opening and closing, sewing, plowing, fountains, flowers, and trousers—all hint at sex. The phrasing, although mostly clear and direct, is sometimes a bit artificial. Nature is perhaps an even more important character than the heroine and is emphasized as a basic theme by every aspect of this utterly coherent tale, whose characters seem both realistic individuals as well as symbolic figures (167–68). The complicated mood of the narrative contributes to the success of the story, while the depiction of sex as positive makes the tale even bolder than some works by recent French authors (168). Her presentation of the relations between the sexes in this story seems less the efforts of a feminist than those of a mature, objective artist (169), and this confidence in her art may have been inspired by the recent acceptance of *The Awakening* (173). The story resembles that novel, in fact, in its amoral tone (176) and frank handling of sexual impulses (195). Both works represent the apex of her efforts to describe life truthfully, and both works should ensure her permanent importance as an American author (198–99), although Chopin herself excluded the story from her third collection, probably because she assumed that the book would not be accepted if it contained this tale (223). **Seyersted 1969b:** Perhaps Chopin felt confident enough to write this story as a result of the acceptance for publication of *The Awakening*. The tale is even more sexually frank than the writings of advanced French authors, but even more unusual is its depiction of sex as healthy and positive. Aspects of the story foreshadow the style and philosophy of D.H. Lawrence, and the work is equally interesting because it treats the sexes as equal rather than favoring one over the other. The tone is impartial and unbiased and suggests deep self-assurance (29–30). **Arner 1970:** This story has a Catholic (rather than Presbyterian) sensibility. Perhaps this work resulted from Chopin's later realization that its predecessor ("At the 'Cadian Ball") now seemed superficial, especially in its treatment of sexual desire. Chopin's willingness here to describe a sexual encounter openly is rare and praiseworthy, especially since the passion she describes is adulterous and would therefore have been avoided by most writers (3). The skill of her description of the encounter is impressive, especially her use of figures of speech to suggest mutual fulfillment. Also impressive is her use of implication and indirection and her sense of balance and tact. The story's final sentence is especially effective and is refreshingly unconventional (4). **Berthoff 1970:** This appealingly sexy tale was written not long after *The Awakening* (xi). **Leary 1970b:** This finely wrought work deserves credit for its tact, its daring, its comedy, and its objectivity (140). **Peterson 1972:** This audacious tale was composed at around the same time Chopin wrote "The Little Country Girl," a simple children's story (10). The treatment of the complexities of marriage is richer here than in some of Chopin's early writings (12). This was one of the few stories she composed during the time she was either completing or awaiting the appearance of *The Awakening* (244). Like most of the other stories she wrote during this period, this one differs from her earlier writing but does not point toward any obvious new development in her fiction (245). The work's affirmative depiction of extra-marital sex was highly unusual for Chopin's era, and the final sentence seems meant to have been shocking, comic, and objective, as well as a bit ironic because the condition it describes may not endure. Chopin's first biographer ignored this intriguing tale (250–53). This work, along with the other tales written at around the same time as the novel, suggest that Chopin was not pleased with her recent short fiction but had not yet found a satisfying new approach (256). **Rocks 1972:** This is the only story by Chopin in which a sexual encounter is presented as almost completely pleasant and without negative consequences (116). **Bender 1974:** Here as elsewhere in Chopin's fiction, defiance of custom is linked with natural events that unfold during five sections. The story shows how liberty renews all human relations. Chopin's description of the sexual encounter is mostly effective (although at one point a bit clichéd), and the story as a whole is impressive for its endorsement of erotic vitality at a time when such a theme was rarely mentioned in fiction (265–66). **Seyersted 1974:** This unconventional story was written in the aftermath of the acceptance for publication of both *The Awakening* and a third collection of Chopin's stories (16). **Arner 1975:** This story, along with *The Awakening*, is one of the high points of Chopin's literary art (21). It may be her finest work and is undoubtedly her most daring (119). Although the description of sex is perhaps a bit overdone, it is commendably honest, and its imagery of fire effectively links the encounter to an ideal of nearly sacred mutuality. Chopin shows similar candor in treating marital infidelity, and her decision to give the story a happy ending is a revolutionary development in American fiction. Chopin's use of weather imagery to suggest male and female sexual roles is reminiscent of Virgil's description of the famous encounter of Aeneas and Dido, while even the references to seafood and sweat seem symbolic. The conversations are full of complex implications (as in the references to the swollen levees), and even the characters' sentence structure often seems significant. Calixta's devotion to housework implies her sexual frustration, and the story shows how the very propriety that men often claim to prize in their wives often leads those men to seek sexual outlets elsewhere (133–38). **Bonner 1975:** This is one of Chopin's several stories on taboo topics (283). **Ladenson 1976:** In contrast to the endings of some of her other tales, where the shift in tone sometimes seems too abrupt, the conclusion here is all the more striking because the tone *doesn't* change. Chopin seems to sanction Calixta's affair, which she describes far more explicitly than was common during this time (31). **Solomon 1976:** Chopin's presentation of the lovers' union is unusually blunt and modern (xv), while the objective, ironic tone of the conclusion also seems ahead of its time (xvi). **Tompkins 1976:** This story suggests that Chopin was just achieving true artistic maturity when her career was crushed by the failure of *The Awakening* (28). **Wolff 1978:** This is one of many stories by Chopin dealing with the instability of human experience (126). **Howell 1979a:** Here as elsewhere Chopin uses an ambiguous conclusion, just as she also typically focuses not on ethics but on the emotional consequences of imposed social rules (216). **Taylor 1979:** This is now considered one of Chopin's very best stories (viii–ix). It is one of many of her tales in which a woman triumphs, if only briefly (xvi). **Wolff 1979:** Here as elsewhere, Chopin treats erotic desire as a force of nature which could both destroy and renew and which was not subject to ethical judgment despite its impact on individuals' ethical lives. Yet Chopin focused less on the moral issues sex raised than on its impact on human minds and feelings. As this story shows, the tone of her later fiction had become increasingly objective in its depiction of complex characters (218). **Lattin 1980:** Because this story shares characters with "At the 'Cadian Ball" (20), its events and persons often seem especially complex (25–27). **Dyer 1980–81:** This is one of various stories in which Chopin reveals a significant interest in the strong yearnings of males (15). **Dyer 1981a:** This is one of several stories by Chopin that use repeating male professional characters, thus adding depth and continuity to her fiction (54). **Dyer 1981d:** Here and in numerous other works, Chopin uses physical setting to imply what a character is feeling. Her frequent use of this technique is open to various explanations (451–52). **Jones 1981:** This tale may have been influenced by Chopin's recent work on *The Awakening* (139). The story optimistically suggests that a liberated view of sex liberates every major character of the work (141–43). Here as elsewhere, however, Chopin describes sex as possession (150). The story depicts a violation of one of the chief tenets of Creole culture (181) but also depicts that violation as an aspect of Calixta's maturity (354). **Davis 1982:** This tale was composed prior to the publication of reviews of *The Awakening*. The story is highly unusual for its time in its neutral moral tone and in its emphasis on the joys and attractiveness of sex. To condemn the infidelity is to miss the point of this tale (70). **Fluck 1982:** In this story Chopin splits Calixta into distinct transgressive and non-transgressive selves (164). **Lattin 1982:** This is one of several stories in which Chopin shows how change can simultaneously involve loss, maturation, and self-discovery (227). **Rogers 1983:** Like George Sand, Chopin focuses (in this tale) on a woman's complex sexuality. Chopin does not condemn the affair she describes, and the plot resembles a scene in a novel by Sand. In both cases the daring female is a lower-class Creole—perhaps because such behavior would have seemed less offensive in such a character (35). **Dyer 1984:** Storm imagery is used much more effectively here than in "The Woodchoppers," a typically undistinguished late work (189–90). **Gilbert 1984:** Here as elsewhere Chopin interrogates marriage (16). The tale was so radical that Chopin never tried to have it printed (17). **Grover 1984:** In this tale, Bobinôt seems more modest than in "At the 'Cadian Ball"; he is a moral man who has submitted to an assertive wife. The work, which is divided into five sections, seems to stress that the sexual impulse is natural; it as if the universe approves of the liaison. No one suffers, and indeed Calixta's marriage benefits. Although Chopin's contemporary readers would have been scandalized by this tale, today it seems praiseworthy for its unconventional description of uninhibited sexual feelings, especially those of women (32). **Stein 1984:** The fact that Chopin composed this story late in her career may imply that she was becoming more and more unconventional in her views of marriage (176). This is one of a number of works in which Chopin deals with the need to seek self-fulfillment, no matter what its consequences (189). This story differs from *The Awakening* by describing a situation in which there are no painful results from the attempt to achieve self-fulfillment. The wife here, unlike the one in "Her Letters," needs just a brief taste of sexual happiness to ratify her sense of self. No one seems disturbed after the affair, and Chopin describes their sexual encounter as perfectly natural. She may even imply that both marriages are now better than they would have been otherwise (205–6). **Toth 1984:** Here as elsewhere Chopin employs a kind of darkly ironic comedy that also functions as social satire. The story undercuts conventional views of what makes a woman happy (205). **Rowe 1985:** This story was so honest in acknowledging feminine sensuality that Chopin did not even try to have it printed (231–32). **Skaggs 1985:** One of the boldest stories ever composed by an American author up to that point, this tale emphasizes the same erotic power touched on in "At the 'Cadian Ball," and its conclusion leaves us expecting further encounters. Few short narratives excel this one in skill or management of plot, yet of all the aspects of the work that would have disturbed Chopin's contemporaries, the final sentence would probably have been the most disturbing by far, since it still has the power to provoke censure from some (61–62). **Gaudet 1986:** The geographical setting of this story is quite precise and implies Cajun characters (50). **Newman 1986:** The story implies the benefits of marital infidelity (152). Because of the conventional views of Chopin's contemporary editors, works like this one went unprinted (153). As in other tales, Chopin here contrasts real life with the stereotypes of fiction, particularly in the final sentence (161). **Rosenblum 1986b:** Chopin did not include this work in her final collection because she knew that its central scene and its implicit approval of infidelity would cause trouble. The story celebrates illicit passion, showing how physical happiness can lead to a more generous spirit. The story is less a rejection of marriage than an attack on its restrictions. The title implies the naturalness of the passion the story describes, and in fact imagery of nature is especially prominent in this tale. Just as the storm injures no one, the same is true of the encounter Chopin describes. Imagery implies the mutuality and equality of the united lovers (5: 2236–37). **Bonner 1988:** This story is often anthologized as an example of Chopin's broadly appealing realistic mode (100). **Toth 1988b:** If this story was rooted in Chopin's own sensual experiences and moral attitudes, that fact may help explain why she never submitted the work to a journal (64). **Elfenbein 1989:** Here as elsewhere Chopin shows how women suffer when they lack power, and she also depicts women of color who are relevant to her depiction of women in *The Awakening* (117–18). In stories such as this, which feature women of color, Chopin could deal more explicitly with topics she treated more cautiously when writing about white females. The women of color in these tales tend to be less simpler characters than the white women, but they suffer more obvious mistreatment. Stories such as this one anticipate the racial dynamics depicted in *The Awakening* (126). In this tale Chopin depicts the happiness of erotic love rather than harping on the disappointments of middle-class marriage. The open but non-censorious description of sex in this story make it a one-of-a-kind work in American writing of its era. The story is influenced by French authors and ethics, but Chopin is even more progressive in the way she focuses on an erotic *woman*. This daring subject helps us ignore her overdone description of the love-making itself (139). The conclusion of the tale undercuts conventional notions of the sanctity of marriage, while this section and others imply that sex itself can be holy in its own way by uniting humans in a natural impulse (140). During love-making, artificial social distinctions briefly dissolve. Unlike Clarisse, Calixta shows that a woman need not be coquettish about sex. The story depicts a brief breakdown of class distinctions, and a woman enjoys the physical happiness she deserves (141). Although the depiction of Calixta might seem to reinforce ethnic clichés about loose women of color, the story is more important for showing the shortcomings of middle-class marriage (141). The tale challenges both social and literary conventions (142). **Inge 1989:** Analysts generally consider this to be Chopin's best tale. All of its elements reinforce its key motif, and in this work Chopin achieved her high point as a writer. Despite its brevity the story is structurally complex: it uses alternating episodes of drama and narration, and it also effectively employs conversation to create suspense. The lovers become reinvigorated through their sexual encounter, and Chopin's unusually daring prose links their physical passion with elemental forces of vitality. Chopin never attempted to have this work printed, having learned from her experiences with *The Awakening* the limits of what would be tolerated (108). **Taylor 1989:** In this and other stories, potentially major problems are resolved fairly easily and without extreme conflict (166). This is one of various stories by Chopin that emphasize a female's concluding feeling of triumph (179). This unpublished story, composed before *The Awakening*, resembles the novel in being the almost inevitable culmination of Chopin's previous ideas about women (202). **Papke 1990:** This is one of four pivotal stories in Chopin's career in which she momentarily overcomes gloomy views of women's possibilities and instead presents resolute and confident female protagonists (60). A fascinating work, it does not handicap its two main characters by making them unthinkingly emotional, nor does it compromise their union by giving it negative results. Instead the story emphasizes sexual equality, genuine self-fulfillment, and genuine communion. In these respects the story is a startlingly optimistic vision of human possibilities achieved through unconventional behavior (175–76) **Toth 1990a:** The depiction of sewing in this work perhaps owes something to the emphasis on sewing at the convent school

Chopin attended as a girl (46). The story accurately depicts Louisiana summer weather (155) and the ways men and women could meet in such a climate (168). Alcée resembles the man with whom Chopin became involved after her husband died (169). Chopin never tried to have this story printed, perhaps because it contains the most erotic encounter she ever described (170). It was composed immediately after the American victory in Cuba, where Chopin's son served (316), and was written in one day (318). The main characters resemble persons Chopin knew from Cloutierville. She describes their romantic encounter in a way that emphasizes their equality, honesty, and clarity of conscience, and she was particularly daring, as a female author, in describing Calixta's breasts. The characters here seem more mature than they do in "At the 'Cadian Ball," and Chopin's presentation of them seems bolder. She implies that the only thing immoral about sex is sexual hypocrisy (318–22). The male characters here resemble those in the later "Ti Démon" (362), while "The Storm" itself is a more daring treatment of themes also explored by Hamlin Garland (383). **Vanlandingham 1990:** Ironically, if Chopin had had greater success with contemporary editors, and had therefore complied more with their dictates, she might never have written a story like this one (166). **Brown 1991:** Calixta achieves a momentary balance between social role and personal desires (126). She and Alcée now carry out the revolt that had been postponed in "At the 'Cadian Ball" (130). **Robinson 1992:** This revolutionary tale is at the opposite end of the spectrum from Chopin's earlier rather maudlin story "A Rude Awakening" (xii). The storm described in this highly erotic unpublished story is both literal and figurative. Calixta's behavior is surprising not only because she chooses sex freely and performs with passion but also because she has no deep feelings for Alcée. The plot events here recall those of "At the 'Cadian Ball," while Clarisse's response at the end of the story is partly dictated by her social status (xv). Here as in some of Chopin's other stories, the woman who is lower in social rank is ultimately more powerful (xx). **Thomas 1992:** This was one of the few pieces of short fiction Chopin composed in 1898 (40). **Larsson 1993:** The aftermaths of both the storm and the encounter are positive (2: 539–40). **Shurbutt 1993:** This is one of various stories in which Chopin shows an unconventional female attaining unconventional fulfillment (15–16). **Baker 1994:** Calixta's name suggests the outer covering of a flower that opens when blossoming occurs. This image, and other floral imagery in the story, helps imply her beauty as well as her sexual and psychological receptivity (225–26). **Cutter 1994:** This work is typical of the increasingly daring fiction Chopin produced in the later years of her career (18). Ironically, the assertive Calixta is saddled with the tedious Bobinôt (20). The fact that Chopin either could not or did not try to publish works such as this one or "Charlie" or "Elizabeth Stock's One Story" shows the constraints she herself faced as a woman writer (33). Ultimately, though, those constraints have been overcome and stories like this one are widely read and admired (34). **Ewell 1994:** Here as elsewhere Chopin explores how women respond to social convention—an exploration partly prompted, it seems, by her own experiences as a middle-aged female (169). **Fusco 1994:** Chopin's recent reading of Maupassant seems to have given her a clearer understanding of the implications of structures involving contrast—the kind of structure she uses here (166). **Koloski 1994:** An important 1992 anthology includes this work, but unfortunately yet typically it fails to spell out the connections between this work and "At the 'Cadian Ball" (26). The story is included in soft-cover collections of Chopin's fiction published in 1976, 1979, 1984, and 1992 (27). This work also often appears in college textbooks (28–29). **Sempreora 1994:** The emphasis here on multiple perspectives may have been partly inspired by Chopin's recent translations of some short stories by Maupassant in which such an emphasis was lacking (87–88). In this tale, unlike in its earlier companion-piece, Calixta assumes center stage; her sensuality and independent power are emphasized (88–90). Calixta is shown as active, in control, and self-aware, even though she is always seen from others' perspectives (90–91). Chopin celebrates the physical, emotional, and mental merging of Calixta and Alcée (92), and at the end of the tale Calixta's own language has become celebratory, complex, and joyful (92–93). If Calixta continues the affair, she will be the dominant partner (94). **Toth 1994:** Alcée is based on a married man with whom Chopin had an affair (10). **Fetterley and Pryse 1995:** Although other contemporary regionalist writers championed a woman's right to remain unmarried, Chopin here asserts a right to feminine sexual fulfillment (410). **Thomas 1995:** Given the self-assertiveness of this story's main female character, one might have expected Chopin to show more sympathy for other women who (like herself) dared to publish fiction (29). **Baxter 1996:** The main characters are Arcadians (7). Alcée may resemble a married man with whom the widowed Chopin had an affair (222), while Calixta may resemble the woman who superseded Chopin in that relationship (233). The story exemplifies Chopin's talent as a local color writer (239) and lends itself to a creative writing exercise for students (240). **Berkove 1996:** The story is far more critical of the adultery it depicts than many critics have assumed (184–85). Like "At the 'Cadian Ball," its morality is more traditional than it seems at first (188). The lust to which the main characters submit is not real love (190). Calixta ironically perpetuates a common anti-feminist stereotype by submitting to her passion, and she becomes a less complex human being as a result (191–92). The final sentence of the tale cannot be accepted at face value: the happiness it mentions is a delusion (192). Chopin was too intelligent and complex a writer to endorse the shallow morality the last sentence merely seems to imply (193). The references to children in the tale help support this interpretation (194). **Carr 1996:** Although the story's treatment of adultery seems radical, its treatment of class seems conservative (54). Calixta's adulterous behavior may not be progressive but simply amoral, since Chopin tends to describe Acadian women as unconcerned with ethics (56). **Johnson 1996:** Kenneth Burke's dramatistic mode of analysis can help discourage students from judging Calixta in negative moral terms. The story is explicitly divided into five separate scenes. Each scene influences the responses of the characters within it. Alcée and Calixta, in particular, respond to the weather rather than to conscious decisions of their own. Their behavior is appropriate to their environment; their conduct should be analyzed in literary rather than psychological terms. In subsequent scenes, too, the behavior of characters fits with the external traits of the scene. Although traditional means of analysis often lead readers to condemn Calixta, Burke's method makes her conduct seem appropriate to this particular work of literary art (125–27). Students often respond to this work in inappropriately negative moral terms by condemning the heroine. Burke's method of analysis, however, helps them emphasize the scene, rather than the characters, as the determining factor in the story (128). **Koloski 1996:** The central characters here are among the most vivid in the literature of Chopin's century (xiii). This is one of various tales by Chopin featuring a member of the Laballière family (21). Phrasing here recalls details from "A Night in Acadie" (52). This tale would never have been printed by a journal of Chopin's time (73). Similar in some ways to "At the 'Cadian Ball," this story also differs greatly: whereas the earlier tale ends with a clear resolution, the conclusion of this one is open-ended. Nature is more potent here than civilization, and this lucid, sensual tale became a favorite as soon as it was printed in the 1960s. The bedroom scene seems rooted in Chopin's private life and in her reading of Whitman and French authors and her familiarity with French music and with French and Creole life. This is the first outstanding tale of *modern* American literature, particularly in its presentation of its heroine. Both characters are extremely vivid and straightforward (75–77). Like some of the other late tales, this one shows that self-satisfaction is possible, if not without cost (78). **Tuttleton 1996:** Although this story has been used to support suspicions that Chopin herself had an affair, the evidence is slim (189). **Walker 1996:** This is one of many stories by Chopin in which the reading of correspondence is very significant. Such correspondence often symbolizes the power of the general written word (220). **Beer 1997:** This story raises a provocative problem: why would Chopin compose a tale she could never hope to see in print? (40–41). The story unambiguously endorses a satisfaction that involves both the body and the soul; normal standards of conduct are temporarily suspended in a moment that is both erotic and almost mystical. The story reveals how fluid the boundaries can be between extreme pleasure and everyday existence. The conclusion of the tale is open and relaxed (59–60). This narrative subverts the tidy ending that marriage seemed to have imposed on "At the 'Cadian Ball." The tale is well crafted, with effective echoes of the Biblical Song of Songs and an intriguing combination of eroticism and spiritual overtones. Chopin's tone seems less distanced here than in much of her other fiction, perhaps because she knew that this story could never be printed. Although the sexual language sometimes seems a bit hackneyed, perhaps this was inevitable given the subject matter and the Biblical precedence of the diction. In this story as in the scriptural original, the lovers go uncensured. Both the storm and the stormy encounter have purgative effects (59–62). **Ewell 1997:** Here Chopin describes sensuality in religious terms and associates it with the power of nature (114). **Bell 1998:** This tale typifies the daring nature of much of Chopin's fiction, especially in its amoral emphasis on physical satisfaction (241). **Toth and Seyersted 1998:** Perhaps this was not the only provocative erotic work Chopin wrote but could not have printed (135). **Green 1999:** This is one of several stories by Chopin that have attracted great attention from critics (14). **Koloski 1999:** This is one of Chopin's best final tales (xvi). **Toth 1999a:** An early student of Chopin rediscovered this bold, pleasing, erotic reverie and published it in 1969. Even in the 1960s the story was rejected for publication in a regional journal (2–3). It is one of many tales whose themes early critics failed to connect to Chopin's own life and views (3). Alcée in this story resembles a man with whom Chopin herself was involved, but the latter figure may have been less important to Chopin's life than Toth had earlier assumed (4). **Toth 1999b:** In the final thirty years of the twentieth century, this was one of Chopin's two most praised and widely read stories (46). **Toth 1999c:** This story is now a standard fixture of American literature (xx). Its male protagonist is modeled on the man with whom the widowed Chopin was romantically involved, and it depicts one of the kinds of circumstances in which they could possibly have met. Because of its explicitness, the tale was not printed until many decades after it was written, but its main male character resembles a male with the same name in *The Awakening* (96–98). Chopin composed this work almost precisely six years after composing "At the 'Cadian Ball." She emphasizes the shared exultation of the lovers as well as their freedom from misgivings or deceit, and she makes Alcée a better mannered character than he had been in the earlier story. Setting and diction also differ, while Calixta here is more obviously based on someone Chopin had known than she is in the previous narrative. Ironically, however, the story probably was never read in Chopin's own day by anyone except Chopin herself (205–6). This work does resemble a story by Hamlin Garland (234), but the first printing of Chopin's own story did not occur until the late 1960s—a period of renewal for American feminism (243). **Knights 2000:** Chopin probably realized that this tale would never be printed by a journal of her era (xvii). This story explores new ways of thought, feeling, and expression (xxxvi).

"The Story of an Hour"

Written: 1894. First published: 1894. Included in *A Vocation and a Voice* (1991).

The news of Mr. Mallard's sudden death must be gently broken to Mrs. Mallard due to her heart trouble. Her sister, Josephine, tells her of a train wreck and says that Mrs. Mallard's husband's name is on the list of those killed. Mrs. Mallard cries, then goes to her room to be alone. She looks out the window and sees the beauty of spring and hears the birds twittering. As she sits back in the chair with her head resting on the cushion she feels a power coming over her as she whispers, "free, free, free." She realizes that now she has to answer to no one. Her sister calls at her door, afraid that she is ill, but Mrs. Mallard tells her to go away. She opens the door and she and her sister descend the stairs together. Someone is opening the front door; it is Mr. Mallard. Josephine screams, and Mrs. Mallard collapses. The doctor later says that Mrs. Mallard died of heart disease. **(DR)**

***

Rankin 1932: Chopin's own father had died in a train accident. Chopin minutely altered the originally published version of the present story (34). **Arms 1967:** Although this relatively successful work has been called one of the best stories from Chopin's last collection, its irony seems a bit contrived (225). **Seyersted 1969a:** This genuinely noteworthy and surprising tale suggests how the success of Chopin's first published collection of stories had increased her self-confidence, artistic liberty and literary daring; she composed the tale—with its unusually blunt emphasis on feminine independence—just when the positive reviews of *Bayou Folk* had begun appearing (57–58). Ironically, the tale was rejected for publication by the first (male) editor to whom she submitted it. He probably considered it immoral (68), and it was certainly her most shocking depiction so far of a woman's desire for autonomy (111). She produced it during a year when she felt she had become more mature as a writer (123), yet serious critical interest in the story did not really begin until 1961 (189). The tale *was* translated into French by one of Chopin's contemporaries (although the translation apparently was never published [208]), and despite the fact that it was initially turned down for publication by the second journal to which she submitted it, the journal did later publish the story, seemingly unaltered, after positive reviews of *Bayou Folk* appeared (209). This tale is one of several that Chopin wrote in pairs, with one work emphasizing feminine self-assertion and the other work (in this case a journal entry) emphasizing feminine compliance (216). **Seyersted 1969b:** Chopin was prompted to write this work as a result of the favorable notoriety she had achieved with her first collection of stories; perhaps the story implies her sense of having been constrained in her own marriage. In any case, she now felt greater self-assurance. Even so, this story was rejected by an editor, probably on moral grounds (25). **Leary 1970a:** This extremely brief tale is nonetheless rich in shifts of plot and theme (xi–xii). **Leary 1970b:** This is one of Chopin's best tales (140–41). **Leary 1971:** With its rapid oscillations and brevity, this tale treats more openly than some of Chopin's local-color fiction the theme of feminine independence (168). **Peterson 1972:** Here as in some of her other best works, Chopin avoids general moralizing by keeping her focus on one specific case (123–24). The twist at the conclusion emphasizes the idea of alienation. The conclusion is a bit forced, but the need for independence is made obvious (137–39). In this work Chopin for the first time openly confronts the problems of marriage (142). The story illustrates her tendency during this period to treat unusual topics in an objective tone (161). **Rocks 1972:** Here as elsewhere Chopin shows that a loveless or oppressive marriage is unethical (119). **Bender 1974:** As in many of Chopin's tales, emotions associated with liberation are linked here with imagery of nature. The original title of the story ("The Dream of an Hour") also associated such emotions with the unconscious (264–65). **Seyersted 1974:** A month after writing this story, Chopin herself lamented her own widowhood (13). This was one of a number of the more adventurous works Chopin began to compose as her fiction began to achieve success (14). **Arner 1975:** Like Edna in *The Awakening*, Mrs. Mallard can achieve liberty only by dying (88). **Skaggs 1975:** This story shows Chopin's progress in exploring the victimhood resulting from males' sense of owning women (285). **Ladenson 1976:** Chopin builds up to the final twist with superb artfulness (27–28). **Solomon 1976:** Here as in some other tales, Chopin emphasizes conflicting human impulses. In some respects this story is reminiscent of—but also different from—"Athénaïse" (xix–xx). **Dickey 1977:** The similarities between this work and Theodore Dreiser's story "Free" (1918) suggest a direct influence, although in Dreiser's work it is the husband who desires liberty (21). **Wolff 1978:** This is one of many stories by Chopin dealing with the instability of human experience (126). **Taylor 1979:** This was one of several tales Chopin had difficulty publishing (viii). **Wolff 1979:** This is one of Chopin's most effective stories, partly because Chopin offers no judgments or explanations but instead simply and realistically describes (212–13). **Lanser 1981:** Although the teller of the tale is not explicitly identified, the teller's perspective is apparent (247). The teller seems objective and omniscient and probably resembles Chopin (250). The teller, like Josephine and Mrs. Mallard, tends to imply commentary rather than stating it explicitly, partly because the story delivers news that would be as shocking to the dominant culture as Brently's death is to Louise (251). The teller must be especially careful since she could be identified with Chopin (251). Even readers who reject the implied message of the story nevertheless agree about its radical meaning (251–52). Only the tale-teller and the reader know Louise's secret, and this fact, along with others, helps us identify with Louise (252). Chopin uses descriptions of space to enhance our closeness to Louise, especially in the shift from public to private space (252–53). Similarly, most of the *time* of the story is focused on Louise, and the relatively slow description of her psychological transition makes the change seem less sudden or selfish (253). Likewise, we move deeper and deeper into Louise's social circle until we actually enter her mind; afterwards, the movement is steadily outward (253–54). In addition, our perception of Louise when she is in her room moves from the external to the internal and then to the external again (254). It is her openly expressed and personally understood yearning for freedom (rather than any suppressed, unacknowledged longings) that threaten the dominant patriarchal culture (254). The first half of the story moves from public to private, from objective to subjective, and from social to personal, and then these movements are reversed in the second half (254–55). The phrasing similarly moves from impersonal to private and then back to impersonal (255). Louise's dismissal of Josephine is perhaps her single rejection of the outside world before she dies; this comment to Josephine is the only one Louise addresses to another person (255). One indication that the tale-teller is sympathetic toward Louise is that Louise is never criticized by anyone (256). Beginning with the very first sentence, Louise is an object of broad concern, but later aspects of the story also make her seem sympathetic (256). Thus she is linked with nature (257–58); her change of consciousness develops gradually rather than seeming impulsively *willed*; she initially resists the transition taking place within her; she acknowledges Brently's virtues; and yet she is also depicted as having suffered in her marriage (258–60). All these factors make her appealing. The story also is careful in the way it implies the general relevance of Louise's predicament (260). The fact that she dies in the end helps de-emphasize the obvious threat her awakening poses to the larger patriarchal culture (261). Nonetheless, the very subtlety of the story helps make it more persuasive in its indictment of patriarchy (261–62). Because Chopin's life resembled that of Louise in certain ways, she had even more reason to be subtle; she suffered personally for being too openly radical in *The Awakening* (262). Like other women writers, Chopin creates a protagonist who implicitly resembles herself (263–64). **Davis 1982:** In this tale Chopin skillfully controls several different levels of irony, although the ending seems a bit unconvincing (66). **Fluck 1982:** Although the tale seems to endorse feminine self-assertion, it actually shows the difficulties of achieving that goal. This approach contributes to the complexity of the work's artistry and social significance. The husband's "death" allows the wife to experience freedom without suffering blame, especially because the impulse toward freedom seems invasive and because its effects are described from a mainly external point of view. The conclusion of the tale is richly ambiguous since the story both indulges and denies transgressive temptations (154–56). Here such transgression seems more daring than in

"Wiser Than a God," even though that story might at first seem more provocative (158–59). This was one of the various unconventional, innovative stories by Chopin that were often turned down for publication (163). In this tale as in others, liberation also seems associated with regression (166), and in some respects the plot of the story resembles (but also significantly differs from) that of a popular mid-century novel (167). **Miner 1982:** An affective or phenomenological approach helps explain how the reader actually *experiences* the story, so that the tale seems to oscillate between a movement toward freedom and intimations of uncertainty (29). Chopin continually undermines our interpretive assurance, even at the level of grammatical understanding (as the first sentence demonstrates). She repeatedly refuses to provide key data and repeatedly uses ambiguous diction or syntax (29–30). Louise at first seems active but then seems passive, while the mysterious feeling that overcomes her could be beneficent or dangerous. Rarely is Louise identified by name; mostly pronouns are used to refer to her (30–31). After so much imprecision, Louise's concluding sense of certainty seems almost facile or naive, and it is soon undercut (31–32). The story routinely prompts almost immediate re-reading (32). **Bonner 1983b:** Chopin endorses Mrs. Mallard's unconventional self-assertion (147). **Dyer 1983–84:** This is one of various stories by Chopin in which characters gain insight, win resolve, and feel freer after experiencing nature (75). Mrs. Mallard's response to nature is primarily non-intellectual (77). The natural imagery here resembles Chopin's use of sea imagery in *The Awakening* (80–81). **Burchard 1984:** Theme: freedom from marriage; self-determination. The story shows that at least Chopin understands Louise's feelings (39). **Gilbert 1984:** Here as elsewhere Chopin interrogates marriage (16). **Stein 1984:** This story implies the foolishness and even danger of trying to repress the yearning for self-fulfillment. Although the final twist may be a bit unsubtle, Louise is the character Chopin seems to satirize. Her married name suggests natural liberty, but she has suppressed her natural desires and has never had the courage to pursue them. The language in which her imagined future is described seems overblown and somewhat irrational and therefore implies how much she had previously permitted herself to be a victim. If she had sought freedom earlier, before she became so physically weak, her life might have been much different. She does in a sense die from a weakness of heart, a failure of courage (184–86). **Toth 1984:** Here as elsewhere Chopin employs a kind of darkly ironic comedy that also functions as social satire. The story undercuts conventional views of what makes a woman happy (205). **McMahan 1985:** This work is superbly economical. It opens and closes by mentioning Mrs. Mallard's literal heart while using the middle portion to show how her figurative heart is transformed. Although Chopin briefly concedes that women, too, can be oppressors, her typical focus—here as elsewhere—is on women who are oppressed. The closing irony, which seems obvious now, may not have seemed so to Chopin's first readers (33–34). **Skaggs 1985:** Mrs. Mallard learns that affection and comfort are no substitutes for freedom (52–53). **Newman 1986:** Like many of Chopin's tales, this one suggests a view of marriage that seems to conflict with the views implied by some of her other stories (152). **Rosenblum 1986c:** Louise is Chopin's most potent heroine. The story ends in irony but not in tragedy, since Louise's death frees her from subservience. Brently's supposed death, which occurs in spring, ironically signals a rejuvenation for Louise. The closed-in house is contrasted with nature's expansiveness. By leaving her room, Louise reenters a kind of prison. Chopin's use of such imagery of nature is reinforced also by imagery of rising and falling (5: 2242–43). **Valentine and Palmer 1987:** Here as in other works, Chopin depicts a woman whose emancipation can only be temporary (60–61). **Bonner 1988:** This story is often anthologized as an example of Chopin's works focusing on women's issues (100). **Koloski 1988b:** Teachers reported finding the Rathborne film version of this story helpful in teaching *The Awakening* because of the works' similarities of theme and atmosphere. However, other teachers dislike the film, and one considers it a distinct work in itself. The Simpson film version was well received at festivals and by critics, and one teacher finds it more faithful to the story than the Rathborne version (17–18). **Martin 1988a:** This truly revolutionary tale may have been prompted by Chopin's recent success and may reflect a new boldness in her writing and character (5). One editor rejected the tale as immoral (6–7). **Papke 1988:** This is Chopin's most acute treatment of the theme of awakening. It explores the main character's divided selves, particularly in the main upstairs scene. Readers experience a dawning awareness that resembles Mrs. Mallard's own transformation, and their final shock is similar to hers. She does indeed die as a result of experiencing a kind of joy, and the conclusion is psychologically accurate, not melodramatic. The story shows the destruction that can result if an individual is transformed but the external world remains the same. In reacting to this story, students often raise the issue of Mrs. Mallard's childlessness (74–76). **Skaggs 1988:** In stories such as this, Chopin deals with some of the most profound and most widely shared issues of human life (80). **Toth 1988b:** The story was influenced by the early death of Chopin's father and by the girl's life with widowed relatives (61). **Elfenbein 1989:** The rejection of this story by a major magazine encouraged Chopin to alter another work to make it more acceptable (125). **Inge 1989:** After her husband's death, Mrs. Mallard enters a symbolic springtime, and her inner emancipation is clearly linked to her awareness of the natural world. The physicians at the end represent the kind of imprisoning patriarchal thinking from which both Mrs. Mallard and Edna in *The Awakening*—Chopin's two most fully alert heroines—can escape only by dying (103). **Papke 1990:** This is Chopin's best known and most concentrated presentation of a woman whose brief awakening is powerful but impermanent (60). At first only Louise's married name is mentioned, but her reliance on Josephine already suggests her potential turn toward her feminine self. As she sits in the armchair, she is passive but also receptive and is slowly resurrected in both flesh and spirit. Only now is her first name heard, but it is spoken by someone whose abrupt reentrance into the story foreshadows the ending of the tale. Chopin's final sentence is sarcastic and biting. Naturally we sympathize with Louise, since the growth in our understanding parallels her own: she is the only character in whom we are allowed to make a full investment. We are as shocked as she is when Brently appears. The ending is not merely a trick; it is a warning of what can happen to any woman who glimpses freedom only to see it denied. Chopin had earlier focused on conventional women destroyed by society; now she shows a similar fate for an unconventional woman as well. Perhaps she thus implies that mere private transformation is not enough: society must also be transformed if women are to attain true and lasting selfhood (62–64). In some respects this tale anticipates "A Pair of Silk Stockings" (65–66) and also *The Awakening* (80). **Toth 1990a:** The imagery of trees here may owe something to Chopin's fondness for tree-climbing as a young girl (43). The story reflects the same interest in freedom found in her very early tale entitled "Emancipation" (97). It also shows her later presentation of increasingly bold women (232–33). This is one of Chopin's least conventional tales, particularly in its attitude toward marriage and self-denial. The story was initially rejected, but finally accepted, by the magazine to which Chopin originally submitted it. Its original title was "The Dream of an Hour" (252–53). The story was translated into French by a translator who took various liberties in rendering it (284–85). The story was one of a number rejected by a book publishing firm (290) but was eventually accepted by another (306). It was intended to be included in *A Vocation and a Voice* (374). Here as elsewhere Chopin makes solitude seem appealing to a female character (377). This story has been filmed (405). **Toth 1991:** This story reflects events and persons from Chopin's own childhood and family, and names in the story are often significantly chosen. The story offers effectively subtle satire (viii–ix) and is one of many of Chopin's late works that were first printed in *Vogue* (xiii–xiv). Of the tales in *A Vocation and a Voice*, this is the only one that has been widely known (xxi) but is one of several that depict an intriguing female character (xxv). **Vanlandingham 1990:** This story was rejected by the editor of a major national journal (161). It was later accepted by a female editor after Chopin's first collection of short tales was well received, although the journal in which it appeared did not have a prominent literary reputation (164). **Brown 1991:** Here as in "A Lady of Bayou St. John," the heroine achieves freedom from marriage through widowhood, but Madame Delisle (unlike Mrs. Mallard) then renounces that very freedom (122). **Guidici 1991:** Here as elsewhere in Chopin's fiction, a husband's death enhances his wife's power, even if only briefly. After Brently returns, Mrs. Mallard would have died figuratively if she had not died literally (29). **Ewell 1992:** Mrs. Mallard is a less passive, more complex figure than Désirée in "Désirée's Baby" (160). **Hoder-Salmon 1992:** In this tale, Chopin's emphasis on feminine autonomy is especially forceful—a fact that may have made the story difficult to publish (21). **Mitchell 1992:** Mrs. Mallard attempts to reunite a divided self that has been shaped by biology, cultural indoctrination, and marriage (60). Her heart condition, along with social expectations and the dictates of marriage (rather than Brently in particular), keep her in check; when she begins to realize her freedom, the experience is almost sexual. Chopin uses the story to indict marriage and undercut romance (since the tale stresses the importance of individual autonomy). Mrs. Mallard's prayer that "life might be long" reflects the woman's traditional role as creator. The final tone is extremely sardonic and may be meant to suggest that true transformation cannot occur so quickly (61–64). **Toth 1992:** Here as elsewhere, widows in Chopin see possibilities in their changed circumstances (16–17). In this story as in others, the experiences of the main female may be relevant to the experiences of Chopin's married mother (21–22). The present title seems to have been imposed on the story by the scholar Per Seyersted. Filmed versions take some liberties with the tale. Here as elsewhere Chopin shows a woman whose isolation makes freedom possible, if only temporarily (23). Chopin's mother had a sister named Josephine, and other details of the story similarly suggest real counterparts (23). Here, unlike in some of her earlier fiction, Chopin seems less optimistic about the prospects for feminine independence (24). **Dyer 1993:** This story, like *The Awakening*, had been filmed twice by 1993 (29). **Larsson 1993:** This story demonstrates Chopin's interest in autonomy for women as well as her skepticism about conventional marriage (2: 537). **Moss 1993:** The story implies Louise's previous inability to speak freely of liberation (195). She discovers—and repeats and is stimulated by—a new vocabulary that strengthens her mentally and physically (196). The word "free" has a transforming (but therefore frightening) power, like other forbidden terms (196). Yet Louise's new vision is both extreme and somewhat naive: she assumes that complete liberty is possible all at once (199). **Day 1994:** Theme: how unconscious, pre-linguistic, suppressed impulses sometimes overflow into dreams (108). Originally entitled "The Dream of an Hour," this tale shows how unconscious desires can erupt into consciousness and redefine a life—even if, as here, only momentarily (113). The tale is one of several showing a woman whose self-divisions cannot be healed (113–14). **Ewell 1994:** Soon after Chopin's success as a local color writer was assured, she composed this narrative, which turns away from local color conventions. Unlike much of her local color fiction, however, this tale was not immediately accepted for publication (165). Here as elsewhere Chopin explores how women respond to social convention—an exploration partly prompted, it seems, by her own experiences as a middle-aged female (169). In this late work she both alters and rises above standard literary conventions (169). **Fusco 1994:** This is one of several later stories in which Chopin tricks her audience. Like characters in tales by Maupassant, Mrs. Mallard reveals aspects of herself she normally disguises or suppresses. Her death reveals the self-deceptive fragility of her new liberty. The story also cautions readers not to jump to conclusions, even as it shows Chopin, under the influence of Maupassant, taking greater satiric risks in her fiction (153–54). **Goodwyn 1994:** This story illustrates the ways that Chopin often uses narrative structure to subvert the conventional values the tale seems to affirm (4). The story seems to illustrate the futility of self-assertion (7). **Koloski 1994:** Included in 1975 in an early feminist anthology and then published in 1988 in one of the most important of all American fiction collections, this tale was particularly praised in the former volume for its importance to women (23–24). The story is included in softcover collections of Chopin's fiction published in 1970, 1976, 1979, 1984, and 1991 (27–28). This work also often appears in college textbooks (28–29). **Lundie 1994:** This tale has recently replaced "Désirée's Baby" as Chopin's most widely read story (129–30). **Padgett 1994:** This narrative parodies conventional tales of annunciation—an important motif in Christian culture (101). **Castillo 1995:** This tale undercuts the stereotype of the sorrowful widow, which was especially potent in Chopin's era. The ending typifies Chopin's taste for irony (86–87). **Juneja 1995:** Here as elsewhere, Chopin depicts a woman who challenges custom by seeking personal liberty (118). **Thomas 1995:** Given the self-assertiveness of this story's main female character, one might have expected Chopin to show more sympathy for other women who (like herself) dared to publish fiction (29). **Baxter 1996:** Unlike Louise, Chopin herself apparently genuinely mourned the death of her husband, although she also came to value her autonomy (222). This story lends itself to a creative writing exercise for students (240). **Bender 1996:** The story raises the uncomfortable, unconventional possibility that love may be rooted in mere sexual yearning (111). **Johnson 1996:** Kenneth Burke's method of dramatistic analysis might see this work as a series of three distinct scenes to which Louise must respond. Such analysis might discourage students from judging her negatively in moral terms. The first scene (downstairs) emphasizes elements of social convention. The second scene (upstairs) changes the tone of the story, and this change helps explain Louise's altered response. The third scene (descending the stairs) demands a significantly different response. By reading the story as a sequence of scenes, students will be less inclined to condemn either Louise as an unfaithful wife or Brently as a deliberately oppressive husband (123–25). Students often respond to this work in inappropriately negative moral terms by condemning the heroine. Burke's method of analysis, however, helps them emphasize the scene, rather than the characters, as the determining factor in the story (128). **Koloski 1996:** Here as elsewhere, the focus on a woman's potential is the theme of some of Chopin's most effective writing (xii). Mrs. Mallard's epiphany is one of the most widely studied events in the literature of Chopin's time and place, and the story itself is one of the most widely read pieces of American short fiction. The tale epitomizes Chopin's artistry, insight, progressiveness, and focus on perception and on the desire for independence. Here as elsewhere, small details produce rich complexity (3–4). Like other characters by Chopin,

Mrs. Mallard is largely impulsive (9; 83). The setting of the tale seems deliberately non-specific (54). The story both resembles and differs from "Her Letters," which was written the same year and published in the same journal (63–64). **Tuttleton 1996:** Although the sudden reversal at the end had become a formula of fiction, the ending here is effective because it is mysterious. Feminist readings of the tale simplify the ending. Louise is not oppressed in any blatant sense. Perhaps she dies because she is robbed by circumstances of the possibility of willful self-assertion. The story reveals Chopin's insights into the depths of the human soul (183–85). **Beer 1997:** The ending of this tale is subversive in quite subtle ways since the conclusion that undercuts the narrative is undercut itself (28). The story presents one of Chopin's two basic attitudes toward marriage (32). Here as in other works, she depicts the oppressiveness of a partner's presence (42). Louise tries to resist being misinterpreted and enclosed, just as Chopin offers similar resistance to neat conclusions in her fiction (45). **Bell 1998:** This surprising story anticipates *The Awakening*. The focus on theme rather than on persons or place gives the tale special force. Although Chopin accommodates social expectations by making Brently return, the wife's ironic death made the story unacceptable to one major journal (242). **Benfey 1999:** This is one of Chopin's best tales, partly because of the concluding irony, partly because of the effective visual imagery, and partly because of its psychological insight. The story may possibly allude very subtly to the Civil War (230–31). Here as elsewhere Chopin uses imagery of revival (236). **Green 1999:** This is one of several stories by Chopin that have attracted great attention from critics (14). **Koloski 1999:** This was one of a number of effective tales Chopin composed before the publication of *A Night in Acadie* but which she did not include in that collection (xv–xvi). **Toth 1999a:** An early student of Chopin denied that this story reflected Chopin's own views of marriage (2). Chopin's own father died in a railway accident (4). This story, like some of Chopin's other most currently popular works, first appeared in *Vogue* (9). **Toth 1999b:** In the final thirty years of the twentieth century, this was one of Chopin's two most praised and widely read stories (46). **Toth 1999c:** This tale is now a standard fixture in American literature (xx). Mrs. Mallard's first name and some other circumstances resemble those of Chopin's mother, whose husband *was* killed in a train accident. Yet Chopin had to alter the story of her mother's successful widowhood in order to make the story palatable to her readers. Perhaps the story reflects the benefits Chopin experienced as a result of her father's death (10). This was one of various stories by Chopin dealing with marital tensions (158). It reflects the influence of Maupassant (172) and is also one of her briefer writings (176). This is one of various tales in which Chopin uses experiences similar to those of women in her own family to explore the shortcomings of being a wife (182). The story was rejected by a progressive magazine (192), although it *was* translated by an acquaintance (198). It is one of the darker tales she had scheduled for inclusion in *A Vocation and a Voice* (208). **Knights 2000:** In technique and theme, this story epitomizes Chopin's most unconventional and skillful writing. The work subverts stereotypes, explores unstable emotions, and features ambiguous phrasing. Chopin's revisions show her careful attention to verbal detail (xxii–xxiii). This story illustrates Chopin's preference for ambiguous conclusions (xxv). Here as elsewhere Chopin implies the uncertainties of existence (xxvi).

"Suzette"

Written: 1897. First published: 1897. Included in *A Vocation and a Voice* **(1991).**

An old woman spreads the news that Michel Jardeau is dead. He apparently fell overboard from the ferry. She sees Suzette standing in the window and rushes over to tell her. Suzette is adorning her hair with a bunch of carnations; she whispers, "poor Michel," but she does not care that he is dead. A year ago she loved him, but she grew weary of his love. She could not understand why he persisted in seeing her.

Now, though, Suzette is distracted from the mirror by the distant sound of a herd of cattle. Her whole being trembles and her face flushes. She moves to the window, feeling with anticipation the glance of a handsome young cattle driver. The herd make a dash forward, however, and he is soon gone. He had not even glanced at her. It would be three long weeks before he would come back. Suzette turns from the window; her face is gray and pinched. She throws herself on the bed and weeps. The carnations fall from her hair. **(DR)**

***

Peterson 1972: Here as in some of Chopin's other late tales, life seems to lack meaning (177–78). **Skaggs 1985:** This is one of a number of tales that touch on the possibility of suicide, which Chopin may have considered the ultimate form of self-control (42). It also emphasizes the strong influence of erotic desire, which in this case reflects only superficial affection. This story seems to have influenced Theodore Dreiser's tale "The Second Choice" (46–47). **Toth 1990a:** Like other tales Chopin published in *Vogue*, this one concerns alienation (280). It was intended for inclusion in *A Vocation and a Voice* (374). **Toth 1991:** This is one of many of Chopin's late works that were first printed in *Vogue* (xiii–xiv). It is one of only a pair of stories from *A Vocation and a Voice* that emphasize local language and legends (xiv). This is one of many stories in *A Vocation and a Voice* in which love fails because of bad timing (xxiii), in which youthful females intent on autonomy are hounded by persistent men (xxiii), and in which determined single-mindedness plays a large role (xxiv). **Koloski 1994:** This tale was included in an anthology of local color fiction published in 1941 and then reprinted nearly thirty years later (23). The story is included in a soft-cover collection of Chopin's fiction published in 1991 (28). **Bender 1996:** This story reflects Chopin's dark Darwinian view that love may be less forceful than passion (112–13). **Toth 1999b:** As Bernard Koloski has demonstrated, this was one of eight stories by Chopin that were frequently republished in the twentieth century (46). **Toth 1999c:** This is one of various stories by Chopin showing young women who find attentive males tedious (172). It is one of her few late tales to be set in Louisiana (229–30).

"Tante Cat'rinette"

Written: 1894. First published: 1894. Included in *A Night in Acadie* (1897).

Tante Cat'rinette's house was given to her by her old master when he gave her her freedom, but the authorities want to take it away from her and demolish it. Tante Cat'rinette will not stand for this. She nursed her master's infant daughter back to health years ago, and, in appreciation, he named the baby Catherine after her, made her free, and gave her this house.

Tante Cat'rinette refuses to leave the house for fear the authorities will tear it down while she is gone. One morning Eusèbe comes by and tells her that Miss Kitty (Catherine) is ill and is calling for her. Eusèbe is known for being a liar, so Tante Cat'rinette is suspicious. She is afraid that he is telling her the one thing that will make her leave home. She asks one of the little girls in the neighborhood if Miss Kitty is sick. The child confirms the report.

Late that night Tante Cat'rinette locks her house up tight and goes through the woods to visit Miss Kitty. As soon as Miss Kitty hears her voice and feels the touch of her hand, she seems to get better. Before sunrise Tante Cat'rinette travels through the woods back home. She repeats this routine for three consecutive nights. On the third night she tells Miss Kitty that she is going to stay this time. She wants to lend Miss Kitty and her husband one thousand dollars and take a mortgage on her place. She says that she is going to draw a will that says everything she owns at her death goes to Miss Kitty. **(DR)**

***

Anonymous 1897 [*Post-Dispatch*]: Parts of this story demonstrate Chopin's thorough knowledge of the deep connection between blacks and nature. The work is appealing both because of its artfulness and because of its theme of altruism (47). **Rankin 1932:** Chopin was greatly pleased by the publication of this work in a prestigious magazine (136). Not even Joel Chandler Harris depicts the bond between blacks and the natural world more effectively than Chopin does in this skillfully narrated tale of self-lessness (168). **Reilly 1942:** Here as elsewhere, Chopin's talent for effectively ending a story protects the work from seeming sentimental or unconvincing (131). **Bush 1957:** Here as in other stories, Chopin depicts loyal slaves. Here as elsewhere, affection is shown to have a transforming power (244). **Seyersted 1969a:** This is one of several tales in which Chopin depicts a superstitious black (78). **Potter 1971:** As in other stories, Chopin here shows a former slave who is trapped in the past but who is nonetheless a fully-drawn character rather than a mere stereotype. Her individuality is enhanced by her distinctive religious attitudes (54–55). **Arner 1975:** This is one of the better of the less successful stories in *A Night in Acadie* (76–77). **Lattin 1980:** This is one of various stories by Chopin featuring repeating characters (28). **Dyer 1981a:** This is one of several stories by Chopin that use repeating male professional characters, thus adding depth and continuity to her fiction (54). **Bonner 1982:** This is one of various stories by Chopin that reflect the importance of selfless Christian love (119). **Skaggs 1985:** This is one of several tales by Chopin emphasizing altruistic self-denial (29–30) and featuring a black character concerned with social class (60). **Gaudet 1986:** This story shows Chopin's familiarity with the folk beliefs of Louisiana blacks (45–46). **Manders 1990:** Here as in several of her other stories featuring blacks, Chopin presents a variation of the conventional figure of the "wretched freeman"—the erstwhile slave who allegedly had benefited from subjection (37–39). She interestingly implies that the emotional attachments that blacks developed toward whites during slavery helped perpetuate their dependence after they were freed (41). Unlike some of the writings of Grace King, the present tale manages to transcend narrow stereotypes and depict blacks with a certain measure of psychological complexity (42). Although the ending of the story is predictable, the decision that leads to that ending creates real tension. Chopin treats the supernatural elements of the story without mocking the title character, whom she treats with dignity in this matter and in others (42–43). **Toth 1990a:** This was one of only several stories by Chopin published in the prominent magazine *The Atlantic*. It resembles the earlier "Beyond the Bayou" in its conventional views of race and class and may even have seemed tame to Chopin herself (235–36). This tale later appeared in *A Night in Acadie*, in which all the stories are set in Louisiana (298). One reviewer praised it for being moral without being saccharine (303). **Robinson 1992:** This is one of many stories by Chopin that depict harmony between the races—a harmony that was not entirely unknown or unrealistic following the Civil War (xix). The title character speaks a variety of dialects, thus illustrating the kind of linguistic as well as cultural mixing which could occur in Louisiana and which often involved blacks as well as whites (xix). **Toth 1992:** Like other stories Chopin published in *The Atlantic*, it shows an oppressed person submitting to oppression (19–20). **Goodwyn 1994:** This is one of various stories in which Chopin depicts the stereotype of the loyal black (10). **Koloski 1994:** The story is included in a soft-cover collection of Chopin's fiction published in 1992 (28). **Koloski 1996:** The lawyer here appears in other stories by Chopin (26), while the plot of this tale resembles that of "Beyond the Bayou." Here as elsewhere, a house is symbolically significant, and by the end of the tale the central character has overcome her isolation (40–42). This is one of several stories in which Chopin perceptively portrays African-American experience (44–45) and does so in a remarkably powerful way (47). As in other writings, Chopin gives us our first glimpse of the central character here from the perspective of the local community (50), just as she also focuses here on one of her favorite themes: voice (55). **Tuttleton 1996:** Even the title of this tale implies its regional focus (182). **Toth and Seyersted 1998:** As this story illustrates, in later life Chopin depicted maternal black women attractively (125). **Koloski 1999:** This is one of Chopin's best stories and appears in one of the best, most convincing, and most charitable collections of short fiction published in her time and place (xvi). The present work is one of Chopin's best partly because it depicts with such sympathy a black person who shows enormous resolution and self-respect. Here as elsewhere, Chopin implicitly commends one person's fidelity to another, but here as in "Tante Cat'rinette" the faithfulness of a black toward a white is especially long-lasting (xviii–xix). This work and others exemplify Chopin's complicated views of racial matters (xix). The present tale is one of various works in which Chopin shows affection that exists across color lines, and in which she presents racial issues objectively (xx). **McCullough 1999:** This is one of various stories by Chopin whose underlying attitudes seem implicitly racist (319). **Toth 1999c:** This story follows conventional patterns in depicting race relations (12). It was her first work to be accepted by one of the leading journals of the day (159). This kind of story appealed more to editors than to Chopin herself (169). The length of the work puts it in the middle range of size for Chopin's stories (176).

"Ti Démon"

Written: 1899. Included in *A Vocation and a Voice* **(1991).**

The story opens with Ti Démon telling his friend Aristides that if he goes to Symond's store with him he'll be too late to see Marianne. It is Saturday, the day they all put down their hoes and plows, dress in their Sunday best, and go to town.

Ti Démon always buys something for his Marianne and then, at half-past six, he goes to see her. She lives with her mother now, but she and Ti Démon are engaged to be married at the end of summer.

Although his real name is Plaisance, his mother has called him Ti Démon since he was a baby because he kept her awake all night with his crying. The name stuck. As he grew older, the name lost its meaning because he was gentle and kind.

On this day, Aristides joins Ti Démon in town and they walk to Symond's store. Ti Démon likes to be seen with Aristides because he is handsome, graceful, envied by men, and worshiped by women. The two go to Symond's for a friendly game of seven-up. Ti Démon plans to leave at 8:00 to go see his Marianne, but when 8:00 comes, he is too excited to leave. The game has changed to poker and he has had several drinks. He is laughing loudly when he hears the clock strike ten. He asks where Aristides is and the other men tell him that he left at 8:00. Aristides told Ti Démon that he was leaving, but Ti Démon ignored him.

Ti Démon gets up and heads towards the door, overturning chairs in his drunkenness. He hopes that Marianne is still up. He feels confident that he can hide his condition from her.

As he nears her house, he sees two people walking arm in arm towards him. When they get closer, he realizes that they are Marianne and Aristides. Ti Démon is livid, feeling betrayed and tricked. He jumps on Aristides and beats him until he is unconscious. Marianne screams and the Negroes who live nearby come running to help, but there is nothing they can do.

Marianne never sees Ti Démon after that night because she thinks he is a madman. She does not marry Aristides, for he never asks her. He has no intention of marrying her. This outburst is the only "demoniacal" one Ti Démon has ever had, but it greatly affects the community. Some one says that Aristides plans to shoot Ti Démon, so Ti Démon starts carrying a gun. The Negroes who witnessed the fight describe the incident to others in vivid detail.

Everyone is afraid of Ti Démon. The women declare that he is appropriately named.

Years later members of the younger generation, who have heard Ti Démon's story, point him out to strangers, telling them that he is so dangerous that he is called Ti Démon. **(DR)**

***

Seyersted 1969a: Chopin was invited to read this story before a ladies' club in St. Louis. Perhaps she welcomed this opportunity after the frosty reception *The Awakening* had recently received (180). The story, with its clear but relatively restrained emphasis on passion, was rejected when submitted for publication, ostensibly because its tone was too dark. Since this was the first tale Chopin had written since the failure of *The Awakening*, its rejection must have disheartened her (182). **Peterson 1972:** Here Chopin shows how alienation can result from a single unlucky incident (259). **Rocks 1972:** Here as elsewhere Chopin describes the passionate nature of courtship in Louisiana (118). **Seyersted 1974:** This story, written in the aftermath of the failure of *The Awakening*, presents a heroine who is far less independent than women in some of Chopin's earlier works (17). **Arner 1975:** In the ideas it treats, this story resembles "The Godmother" and "A Vocation and a Voice." It does not indict demon drink but shows instead how one small event can transform a person's whole existence. By the end of the story, the title character's name, which had at first seemed ironic, now seems somewhat fitting (102–3). **Wolff 1979:** The rejection of this story might have seemed to foreshadow Chopin's later difficulties in winning publication (225). **Bonner 1983b:** The unconventional theme of the story led it to be turned down (145). **Skaggs 1985:** This is one of several tales that explore the unpredictability of persons and events (45–46). It resembles in some respects the earlier work "A Gentleman of Bayou Têche" of 1893 (63). **Martin 1988a:** In this story Chopin obviously asserts her own aesthetic and personal freedom, thus responding to critics of *The Awakening*. However, one journal turned down the tale because it seemed too solemn (10). **Inge 1989:** This narrative, one of only a small number of worthwhile tales Chopin composed after *The Awakening* was badly received, deals with disastrous pride of the sort often depicted in ancient tragic drama. Here as in such plays, the protagonist suffers almost excessively for his flaws in a plot that seems highly efficient, strongly grounded in a specific locale, and almost fated to unfold. The narrative tone seems almost wry (105). **Toth 1990a:** Male characters in this story resemble some in the earlier tales "At the 'Cadian Ball" and "The Storm." The story was rejected for being too depressing (although the writing was praised), and it never saw print (362), although it was intended for publication in *A Vocation and a Voice* (374). **Toth 1991:** This is one of only a pair of stories from *A Vocation and a Voice* that emphasize local language and legends (xiv). It is one of the few stories she composed after *The Awakening* (xiv). She read

it aloud during a successful public appearance following publication of
the novel (xv). The dark tone of this story may reflect Chopin's worries
about her son, who was at war when she wrote it (xx). It is unclear
whether this story or another with a similar title is the one mentioned in a
compilation by Chopin's earliest biographer (xxi). This is one of many
stories in *A Vocation and a Voice* in which love fails because of bad timing
(xxiii). **Thomas 1992:** Chopin was paid to read either this tale or the similarly named "Horse Story" to a local club. A newspaper praised it. Her
work on this tale suggests that she had recovered from a recent illness
(46). This story of sudden loss may reflect Chopin's own worries about the
impact of negative reviews of *The Awakening* (48–49). **Koloski 1994:** The
story is included in a soft-cover collection of Chopin's fiction published in
1991 (28). **Toth 1999c:** Chopin read this story in public to a St. Louis wom-
en's club. It is one of the few stories set in Louisiana intended for publication in *A Vocation and a Voice* (228–29).

"Ti Démon (A Horse Story)"

Included in *A Vocation and a Voice* (1991). *See* **"A Horse Story."**

"Ti Frère"

Written: 1896. Included in *Private Papers* (1998).

As Ti Frère ("little brother") chops weeds along the edge of his
cotton field, he sullenly reflects on the frustrations of his life. He is
tired of laboring in the fields, tired of being poor, and even tired of
being called "Ti Frère" when his real name is Joe. Absorbed in his
brooding, he accidentally chops his own foot. When Azémia, an attractive young neighbor, rushes to help and offers her handkerchief to stop the blood, he rejects her gesture, grabs some cotton instead, and informs her that he is Joe, not her "little brother."
Azémia is shocked by his hostility; she doesn't know that he has
recently been ridiculed because of his name by a Texan at a local
gambling joint. Azémia's manner suddenly grows cold, and Ti
Frère instantly begins to regret his sharpness.

Next day he brings the young woman and her grandmother some fine peaches, telling the old lady—so that Azémia will also hear—that the accident had angered him so much that he would have spoken sharply even to his own mother. Azémia, however, ignores him, and Ti Frère is so pained by the change in her previously solicitous attitude that he even fantasizes about beating the Texan who had made him ashamed of his nickname.

When Azémia's coolness continues, Ti Frère sets off on horseback for the gambling joint in the woods. He is in a bad mood and is still pained by the injury to his foot. At first he does nothing but wander from table to table, but when the Texan, Bud Aiken, begins to mock his name once more, Ti Frère suddenly pummels him. Soon, though, his energy mysteriously deserts him, and he is led from the cabin. Mounting his horse, he becomes weaker and more disoriented and finally falls to the road. Only now is it clear that he has been stabbed by Aiken. Ti Frère's horse, meanwhile, runs off to the hills where he was born and raised.

Ti Frère is eventually discovered and taken home, but both the stab wound and his neglected foot make his condition extremely precarious. The doctors feel little hope that he will survive.

When Azémia hears of Ti Frère's condition, she instantly regrets the way she has been treating him. She now realizes how much he has always needed affection, and she sets off at once for his cabin. She vows to herself that she will never abandon him again. As she clasps his hand and sobs at his bedside, calling him "Ti Frère" again and again, he dimly begins to perceive the promise implied in her tone. **(RCE)**

***

Seyersted 1969a: This is one of several stories by Chopin in which women submit to the needs of men (112). **Toth 1990a:** Although the editors of a young persons' magazine paid Chopin for this tale, they never published the work, perhaps because they considered it too uninhibited (283). The dark atmosphere of the tale resembles that in a poem by a male writer who admired Chopin's artistry (357). **Koloski 1996:** This is one of Chopin's many stories for children (87). **Toth 1999c:** This story reflects Chopin's knowledge of the rural Louisiana countryside (96). In this work as previously, she depicts the punishment of Bud Aiken (153).

"Toot's Nurses"

Written: 1901. Destroyed or lost.

Peterson 1972: Chopin probably wrote this work with the idea of submitting it to *Youth's Companion* (265). **Thomas 1992:** This story was one of three works that may have been written over three days in 1901. Perhaps Chopin destroyed this tale (53–54). **Toth 1999c:** This was one of a trio of stories Chopin composed in several days' time (235).

"A Turkey Hunt"

Written: 1892. First published: 1892. Included in *Bayou Folk* (1894).

Not long before Christmas, three of Madame's best bronze turkeys go missing. Séverin's boy discovers the problem when he sees the brood at noon a half mile up the bayou, three turkeys short. Others report even more of them gone. So, although a cold drizzle of rain has begun, everyone is agitated enough that the household help brave the weather and set out on a turkey hunt. Alice, the housemaid, goes down the river, and the yard-boy goes up the bayou. Some go across the fields, but Artemise is just told to "go look too."

Artemise is an unusual person. She is somewhere between ten and fifteen years old, with a head that looks like a big chocolate Easter egg. She has large, round, shiny eyes that she fixes on you in a calm stare like an Egyptian sphinx. Usually she speaks only to answer a question, and she replies almost totally in monosyllables.

The household searches all afternoon, coming back from time to time in random pairings or singly, but everyone is cold, wet, and tired. No missing turkeys have been found. About an hour after she strolled out, Artemise strolls back into the hallway and stands with crossed arms, looking into the fire. She looks as if she might say something, and eventually the mystery is solved: the three missing turkeys were locked in the hen-house accidentally, and Artemise heard them gobbling as she hid there during the turkey hunt. **(CY)**

***

Peterson 1972: This is one of several rather conventional tales about unusual personalities that Chopin composed for young readers (59–60). **Arner 1975:** Brief, amusing, and full of charm, this work focuses particularly on Artemise and resemble's Chaucer's "Nun's Priest's Tale" in tone and style (62). **Bonner 1977:** This is one of only two stories in *Bayou Folk* that are narrated by a character in the tale. Such narration plays a key role here (7). In this story and others, Chopin quickly describes an event. Such brief and usually comic tales are often interspersed with longer, darker stories in *Bayou Folk* (9–10). **Lattin 1980:** This is one of various stories by Chopin featuring repeating characters (28). **Skaggs 1985:** This is one of several tales depicting unusually independent girls (12–13). **Toth 1990a:** This was one of three tales Chopin composed within forty-eight hours. All were quickly accepted (206–7). This brief work helped lend diversity to *Bayou Folk* (224). **Fusco 1994:** Sketches such as this, with their extremely simple plots and characterization, show the influence of earlier American fiction rather than that of Maupassant, whose works were usually more satirical (146–47). **Koloski 1996:** This is one of several of Chopin's children's tales focusing on an unusual person who is transformed (71; 87). **Beer 1997:** This story, like others by Chopin, uses a sophisticated narrator's point of view in a way that keeps the tale from seeming simplistic. Here as in "Juanita," Chopin focuses on a female who has attracted a certain notoriety in her community. The narrator and other characters are identified with differing degrees of specificity. The narrative has a circular structure, and the story cleverly uses differences in tense to create interest, especially about the central character. Chopin describes her in ways that provoke our curiosity; she is never pigeon-holed, and in many ways she is a provocative mystery (85–87). **Koloski 1999:** This is one of Chopin's tales that focuses on the young or were written for them (viii; xxii). **Toth 1999c:** This was one of several seemingly simple tales published in *Bayou Folk* (151).

"Two Portraits"

Written: 1895. Included in *A Vocation and a Voice* (1991).

The Wanton

Alberta is a beautiful young girl with deep brown, mysterious eyes that drink in everything they observe. She is fond of the woman she calls Mama, even though the woman beats her in between great indulgences. Alberta is praised and loved by everyone. One day her mama dies a self-inflicted death and Alberta grieves, forgetting all the beatings and remembering only the affection. She goes to live with another lady and gentleman and the beatings stop. At seventeen Alberta has a lover and she grows more beautiful. She loves when and where she chooses, and she does not know shame or reserve. Alberta now drinks wine and carries a knife.

The Nun

Alberta is a beautiful young girl with deep brown mysterious eyes that drink in everything they observe. She is loved by a holy woman who teaches her that nature is beautiful and that God is great. Alberta's existence becomes a prayer; evil turns from her. When she reaches the age when other women begin to dream of love, Alberta is instead possessed of a purely spiritual life, and she goes into a convent. There is no other woman in the convent as saintly as Alberta. She does not care that she is beautiful. It is said that Alberta's prayers help afflicted persons and that others with faith are sometimes healed by the touch of her hands. **(DR)**

***

Arms 1967: This is one of the three most successful stories in Chopin's final collection. It shows some small concern with a realistic depiction of deterministic influences, but mainly it suggests the larger complexity of human existence (226). **Seyersted 1969a:** Like other stories by Chopin, this one presents a self-assertive, passionate heroine. In its objective stance and absence of judgmentalism, it shows Chopin's growth as an artist (70). The story was rejected by all the editors to whom it was submitted (73). It typifies a common concern in contemporary fiction: the twin appeals of sensuality and religion (112). **Seyersted 1969b:** The female protagonist here exhibits Chopin's focus, after the successful reception of *Bayou Folk*, on emotional, liberated women (25). **Peterson 1972:** Chopin implies, here as elsewhere, that having a purpose can be more fulfilling than satisfying a desire (133). This is one of Chopin's more intriguing late stories. The tale focuses less on fate than on luck. Both women are linked with wine, but in each case the natural impulse to love leads in different directions. The story thus typifies the contradictions inherent in existence (180–82). **Rocks 1972:** By presenting opposite ends of the spectrum in this story, Chopin implies the need for a balanced life (115). **Arner 1975:** In this intriguing study of the human mind, an echo of the Bible helps provide the transition from the first part to the second, and other intriguing echoes of diction and symbolism help link the apparently opposite portraits. Chopin seems to suggest that strong desire will inevitably find *some* means of expression, and perhaps the ecstasies of the nun spring from the same sources as the behavior of the prostitute. Writings by Simone de Beauvoir seem relevant to this story, and Chopin's decision to exclude from this tale her originally-planned portrait of a wife suggests that she did not want to seem to sanction that socially approved woman's role. This tale demonstrates

Chopin's accurate insights into the human mind (84–87). **O'Brien 1976–77:** Even more obviously than in *The Awakening*, Chopin here rejects pious, sentimental moralism. Interestingly, the nun has a female mentor, although the work rejects the conventional view that women were naturally innocent. If anything, the tale suggests that women innately possess strong emotions, and that only circumstances affect how these emotions will be channeled (4). **Howell 1979b:** The story describes a woman who progresses from wantonness to spiritual devotion (109). **Taylor 1979:** This was one of several tales Chopin had difficulty publishing (viii). It resembles Flaubert's *Madame Bovary* in seeing resemblances between religious and sexual passion. This is one of several of her stories that subtly suggest the shortcomings of Catholicism (x). **Wolff 1979:** This brief tale is forceful, efficient, and honest. It fails to offer a conventional moral but shows instead the contrasting limitations of each woman's life (218). **Davis 1982:** As in a number of her later tales, Chopin here deals with erotic desire as a force of nature leading to many possible effects on people's lives. In this tale she links erotic and religious passion (66). **Fluck 1982:** This was one of the various unconventional, innovative stories by Chopin that were often turned down for publication. In this tale Chopin's tendency to present conflicting selves is especially clear, but the selves are now divided between two separate characters (163–64). **Rogers 1983:** This story closely resembles a novel by George Sand (38). **Newman 1986:** This tale shows how social stereotypes affect individual lives. Although the stereotypes seem to contrast, they nonetheless are both culturally prescribed roles, and (ironically) the ending of the tale about the nun almost seems erotic (161–62). **Skaggs 1985:** This is one of several stories emphasizing the significance of religion. The prostitute requires a spiritual existence as much as the nun requires a physical outlet. Each woman is incomplete (39). This is one of a number of tales that touch on the possibility of suicide, which Chopin may have considered the ultimate form of self-control (42). **Martin 1988a:** This is one of various stories in which Chopin depicts a passionate woman without censuring or penalizing her in order to court the approval of readers (6). **Taylor 1989:** This is one of Chopin's most unconventional tales (153). It was so challenging that it was turned down even by two very progressive journals and remained unprinted while Chopin lived (153). It alludes to work by continental women writers and emphasizes tensions centering on erotic yearnings (153–54). Each woman in the story is influenced by a dominant older woman. The story stresses themes of love and death, yearning and control (154) and resembles a key moment in a novel by George Sand (187). **Toth 1990a:** Chopin's best girlhood friend became a nun (98). This tale was one of Chopin's most artistically daring (306) and was intended for inclusion in *A Vocation and a Voice* (374). **Vanlandingham 1990:** Chopin sought—earnestly but unsuccessfully—to have this work published in an avant-garde journal (162). **Toth 1991:** The nun here, like Chopin herself in childhood, is most influenced by an older woman (ix). The alternatives depicted in this story reflect the contrasting impulses of Chopin and her closest childhood friend (x–xi). This story reflects Chopin's interest in the complex, often ironic links between religious and secular experience (xix–xx). This work is the earliest story included in *A Vocation and a Voice* (xxii). This is one of various stories in *A Vocation and a Voice* that defy conventional expectations about sexuality (xxiii) and in which Chopin presents complex views of religion (xxiii). **Day 1994:** Theme: how unconscious, pre-linguistic, suppressed impulses sometimes overflow into dreams (108). Here as elsewhere Chopin explores the theme of divided women, although the possibility of overcoming the division is at least implied here (114–15). **Koloski 1994:** The story is included in softcover collections of Chopin's fiction published in 1979 and 1991 (27–28). **Padgett 1994:** In its depiction of the nun, this story suggests how the physical and spiritual can ideally merge (104). **Koloski 1996:** In this tale the setting seems intentionally non-specific (54). The story is a deliberate exercise in realistic comparison-and-contrast (60–61). **Beer 1997:** Here as elsewhere, Chopin often compared the satisfactions provided by religion and sex (47). This story shows Chopin's willingness to explore taboo topics frankly. The story suggests that innate traits determine how humans respond to contrasting environments. The double subtitles foreshadow the conclusions of both narratives, and indeed the work emphasizes closure and fixity. Both narratives imply the limiting consequences of a single focus in life. Ironically, the description of the nun's existence is even more insistently physical than the description of the wanton's. Each woman lives life at an exclusively heightened pitch, with death always lurking in the background. Each chooses exclusivity, even if the kinds of exclusions differ. However, their choices are largely determined by pre-existing social constraints. Each becomes a marginal figure for whom life and death become blurred experiences (58–59). **Ewell 1997:** The real surprise of this story is the way the nun's dry, ascetic routine is enlivened by a devotion that is almost sensual in its overtones. The story implies that true religion is inseparable from a true feeling for physical nature (110–11). **Toth and Seyersted 1998:** This story is mentioned in Chopin's account books (150, 171) and letters (209) and may have been influenced by one of Chopin's childhood friendships (297–98). **Toth 1999c:** Originally entitled "The Nun and the Wanton," this highly provocative story was never accepted for publication. It proved too daring to be published in the U.S., and Chopin eventually ceased submitting it (176–77).

"Two Summers and Two Souls"

Written: 1895. First published: 1895. Included in *A Vocation and a Voice* (1991).

He is young, impetuous, and candid. She is young and naive. They have known each other for only five weeks, but during that short time his life has been transformed. There is much he wants to say, but he can only say, "I love you." She cannot respond that she loves him too. She is not sure what love is, although he begs for her love. She dismisses him, promising to think about his love and try to decide whether she can return his affection. She watches him leave and feels troubled.

She writes to him, telling him that she remembers that on the day he left she told him that she wanted to think, but since that day she has only been able to feel the loss of him. Her letters tell him that she loves him and asks him to come back.

When the letter reaches him in a batch of business correspondence, he is planning a trip with some friends. The letter leaves him in shock and feeling bewildered; it also causes him to remember the pain of her previous rejection. He feels as if someone dead and forgotten has returned. He does not ponder the situation as a problem; he does not think of telling her how she hurt him. He goes to her even though he knows there is the risk of being hurt in the end. **(DR)**

***

Seyersted 1969a: 147. **Peterson 1972:** This story is typical of Chopin's late writings for *Vogue* in its irony, its hardness, its bareness, and its lack of strong appeal. Here as in "At Chênière Caminada" and "Azélie," she examines unrequited affection. The story is full of ironies, especially in its concluding resolution in marriage (172–73). **Arner 1975:** This story shows the genesis of a frustrating marriage (90). **Toth 1990a:** This was one of the unconventional stories Chopin published in *Vogue* (280). It was intended for inclusion in *A Vocation and a Voice* (374). **Toth 1991:** This is one of many of Chopin's late works that were first printed in *Vogue* (xiii–xiv). This is one of many stories in *A Vocation and a Voice* in which love fails because of bad timing (xxiii) and which focus on determined single-mindedness (xxiv). **Koloski 1994:** The story is included in soft-cover collections of Chopin's fiction published in 1979 and 1991 (27–28). **Sempreora 1994:** The emphasis here on multiple perspectives may have been partly inspired by Chopin's recent translations of some short stories by Maupassant in which such an emphasis was lacking (87–88). **Bender 1996:** Chopin here raises the possibility that love may be ultimately sensual and therefore ephemeral (111). **Thomas 1996:** This is one of various stories in which Chopin juxtaposes contrasting women (208). **Beer 1997:** This is one of Chopin's more sexually suggestive works, and apparently she did hope that stories like this could be published (41). This is one of a number of tales in which Chopin explores the ephemeral nature of arousal. The story juxtaposes language of passion with language of business relations. As time passes, the characters ironically shift psychological places, but the social environment does not permit such change, even when it concerns one of the few choices available to a woman (51–52). **Toth and Seyersted 1998:** This story is mentioned in Chopin's account books (150, 157, 166).

"The Unexpected"

Written: 1895. First published: 1895. Included in *A Vocation and a Voice* (1991).

Randall and Dorothea are forced to part for a short time before their marriage. The parting is drawn-out, with long kisses and clinging embraces.

Passionate letters pass back and forth. Randall plans to return in a month, but he becomes ill and is forced to stay away longer. Dorothea wants to rush to his side, but her parents refuse to let her. Randall's cold grows worse, making him too weak to write.

Finally, Dorothea receives a letter saying that because of Randall's illness he must spend the season in the south, but that he will come home only for a day just to see her and hold her close to his heart. Dorothea reads his letter over and over. She stares at his portrait for hours each day, realizing that his appearance will be changed due to his long illness.

Randall arrives and, after one delirious embrace, he crumbles to the sofa, exhausted. Dorothea stares at the man sitting beside her. He is not the man who left her, the man she planned to marry. His skin is waxy and red; his eyes are sunken; and his clothes hang loosely on his wasted body. His lips are dry and parched and his breath is feverish. She shudders at the sight of him.

Randall explains that this is how his Uncle Archibald died, but he vows that he will not die if he stays south for the season. He asks Dorothea if they can be married at once. She tries to convince him that she would be a burden to him now, telling him that he will come back to her well and strong. Then they will marry. In her mind, however, she is saying, "never, never, never!"

Randall goes on to explain that he wants her to have his estate when he dies and that his wishes will be guaranteed if she is his wife.

His attendant helps him leave. Dorothea stares out the window for awhile, then changes clothes and rides her bicycle off as if she is being chased by Death. She rides for a long time until she is in the woods, totally alone with nature.

She has not spoken a single word since telling Randall good-bye. She feels as if nature is her confidant; she whispers, "Never! Not for all his thousands! Never, never! Not for millions!" **(DR)**

***

Seyersted 1969a: The woman in this story, like some in other stories by Chopin, is willing to assert her independence. She will not accept the idea of becoming a nurse by becoming a wife (111). **Peterson 1972:** The force of Dorothea's rejection of the proposal suggests that she considers the marriage an acquiescence to a kind of whoredom. She responds naturally in the midst of a natural setting. The story's title is double-edged (173–75). **Rocks 1972:** Here as elsewhere Chopin shows that erotic desire often causes suffering, not simply pleasure (116). **Arner 1975:** Symbolism of nature is used to link the woman here with life (although even this symbolism is not uncomplicated), and Chopin seems fairly sympathetic to her decision (91–92). **Dyer 1983–84:** This is one of various stories by Chopin in which characters gain insight, win resolve, and feel freer after experiencing nature (75). The male protagonist represents death, while the female protagonist's encounter with a sensuous and vital nature helps persuade her to abandon her suitor (78–79). The natural imagery here resembles Chopin's use of sea imagery in *The Awakening* (80–81). **Skaggs 1985:** This is one of several tales emphasizing the strong influence of erotic desire. The woman learns its force when she loses it (46). **Toth 1990a:** This story for *Vogue* might have had special resonance for the magazine's young unmarried female readers (281). It was intended for inclusion in *A Vocation and a Voice* (374). **Guidici 1991:** This is one of many stories by Chopin that center around rejected marriage proposals. These rejections give the women greater autonomy (28–29). **Toth 1991:** This is one of many of Chopin's late works that were first printed in *Vogue* (xiii–xiv). This is one of many stories in *A Vocation and a Voice* in which love fails because of bad timing (xxiii), in which youthful females intent on autonomy are hounded by persistent men (xxiii), and in which determined single-mindedness plays a large role (xxiv). **Cutter 1994:** Here as in some of her other later tales, Chopin presents a strong woman (27). **Koloski 1994:** The story is included in a soft-cover collection of Chopin's fiction published in 1991 (28). **Bender**

1996: Chopin here raises the possibility that love may be ultimately sensual and therefore ephemeral. The woman's passionate behavior here undermines Darwin's assumptions about feminine motives (111–12). **Garvey 1996:** This story undercuts a conventional plot of turn-of-the-century fiction: the bicycle as a means of courtship. Here the woman, using a bicycle, symbolically escapes not only from her projected marriage but also from the physical and social constraints from which women traditionally suffered. The bicycle here becomes a vehicle of social, psychological, physical, and economic freedom. Interestingly, this story was first published in a magazine which carried very few advertisements for bicycles and which therefore had little incentive to soft-pedal the potential social disruptions bicycles could cause. Chopin takes advantage of common stereotypes of bicycle advertisements but subverts those clichés (129–31). **Toth and Seyersted 1998:** This story is mentioned in Chopin's account books (140, 150, 163). **Toth 1999c:** In this story for *Vogue* magazine, Chopin chastised immature views about personal appearance (172). Like other works intended for publication in *A Vocation and a Voice*, this one is dark in tone (208). **Knights 2000:** This story, like others by Chopin, gains added interest when read in the context of the materials with which it was originally published (xix).

"Unfinished Story—Grand Isle"

Written: 1888–89. Destroyed.

Rankin 1932: Perhaps this tale was a first draft of Chopin's eventual novel *The Awakening* (114). **Seyersted 1969a:** Almost nothing is known about this lengthy piece, one of Chopin's very first works of fiction. Perhaps her new exposure to the writings of Maupassant made her dissatisfied with her own early effort (50). **Peterson 1972:** This work suggests that Chopin had originally intended to focus on writing novels (201). **Toth 1988a:** This unfinished work may have reflected Chopin's familiarity with the Creole dialect (59). **Toth 1990a:** This long work, which Chopin destroyed, was probably inspired by her own familiarity with Grand Isle (139). **Ewell 1994:** The title of this early work shows Chopin's awareness of the marketability of local color fiction (160). **Toth 1999c:** Chopin noted her work on this tale during 1888–89 (109).

"Vagabonds"

Written: 1895. Included in *Complete Works* **(1969).**

A Negro customer informs the unnamed narrator, a female shopkeeper, that Valcour is waiting to see her around the bend by the river. Never in a hurry to rendezvous with Valcour, but ready anyway for an afternoon walk, the narrator makes her way to the river. She finds Valcour, "the color of clay," looking as if he has just recovered from yet another drinking binge. In keeping with the tradition "outside the family" that Valcour is related to the narrator—a tradition the narrator strenuously denies—he addresses her as "cousin." Believing that "fine language" is wasted on Valcour, the narrator refuses to engage in small talk. She immediately asks him why he wants to see her.

Valcour explains that he has been "jobbin' roun' some, up the coas'" and is now headed to Alexandria if he can "make out to git down there." Thinking that Valcour's comments are leading up to a request for money, the narrator pleads poverty and points to the condition of her shoes, dress, and the nearby rundown cabins and fences. Valcour assures her that he does not want her money, and, with unsteady hands, he shows her the few coins he has, which the narrator suggests amount to just about enough for a quart of whiskey. Valcour denies this, claiming that whiskey "make' a man crazy." They then talk about one of Valcour's drunken exploits that involved the removal of buckshot from Valcour's backside for kissing Joe Poussin's homely wife.

At the end of half an hour, the narrator is surprised that she has spent so much time with Valcour and wishes him a good journey. Before he departs, she asks him how he manages to survive his vagabond lifestyle. He explains that he has a rifle for game—"a wonder he had never sold it for drink," thinks the narrator—and that there is always a "black wench" to prepare his food. As for sleeping in the winter, when she hears Valcour's answer, the narrator wishes she had not asked: "Grand Dieu! that was hard," she thinks. In summer a man can sleep anywhere the mosquitoes will let him, says Valcour.

Despite her attitude toward Valcour, the narrator finds herself thinking that "it must be good to prowl sometimes; to get close to the black night and lose oneself in its silence and mystery." Valcour takes his leave as the ferry approaches, walking away in ankle-deep mud. The narrator watches as Valcour heads down the muddy stream on the flat. Turning to resume her walk, she is glad that Valcour did not want money, but she realizes that she doesn't know what he wanted or why he wanted to see her. **(EP)**

***

Arms 1967: Here, as rarely elsewhere, Chopin uses a first-person narrator, yet the title implies the storyteller's connection with her visitor (226). **Seyersted 1969a:** Night is an important motif in this narrative probably based on one of Chopin's own conversations when she ran the family business in Cloutierville. She later tried to efface the two words with which she had ended the tale (70–71) and she left the work in manuscript (217). **Arner 1971:** The earthy setting implies ambiguity and complexity and thus reflects the relations between the two characters. The setting associates Valcour with primal human traits; he seems more real than the narrator and perhaps functions as her more genuine alter ego. The story shows Chopin's mastery of various kinds of dialect—a mastery which makes the story seem more convincing and honest (110). In particular, a close examination of the discussion of whiskey shows the subtlety of Chopin's mastery of diction. Repetition is a key element in this passage and helps to reinforce the story's larger point that the two characters have more in common than they realize (111). Chopin's subtlety is also shown by her mastery of two different styles for the narrator—one more formal than the other. The story emphasizes personalities more than events, and the dialogue is often thematically effective. The narrator's two distinctive voices imply her divided nature. Chopin may or may not have been fully aware of the subtleties of the story's language, but the work is one of her best (111). **Peterson 1972:** This is one of Chopin's better final tales, partly because it emphasizes character rather than incident. The irony seems more natural than in some of the other late stories (166). This work presents one of Chopin's best depictions of unacknowledged yearnings. The first-person narrator tends to make declarative assertions and then add a justification; only once does she let down her guard and unknowingly reveal her inner desires. The vagabond's character is more mysterious, although eventually he seems more polite than his interlocutor. Each of them seems to yearn for traits the other possesses. The somewhat primitive setting makes the dilemma the story presents seem more universal: all people seek both liberty *and* community. The vagabond has the first; the narrator has the second; each seeks what the other has (188–91). This story illustrates Chopin's impulse to describe life objectively (199). **Rocks 1972:** This is one of many stories in which Chopin suggests that each person must decide whether it is better to be content with one's present condition or attempt to alter one's future. The results of either choice cannot be predicted (115). **Arner 1975:** This is one of Chopin's most successful tales. The male protagonist represents important aspects of the female narrator, perhaps including her deepest desires (a possibility reinforced by the imagery with which he is associated). Chopin here demonstrates her skill at earthy dialogue—talk that lends itself to close verbal analysis even as it suggests the characters' personalities, their resemblances, and the story's larger meanings. The narrator herself uses two kinds of language (which imply her divided nature), while the tale as a whole represents an advance in Chopin's ability to depict characters symbolically as well as realistically. This was one of several works, all written at around the same time, in which she dealt with characters as sometimes contrasting pairs (128–32). **Dyer 1981b:** Although the word "night" is mentioned just once in this tale, it may be the most important term in the story since it implies the narrator's deepest yearnings, which are also symbolized by the primal mud. Eventually, however, she refuses to embrace these yearnings (224–25). Night imagery here resembles its use later, in *The Awakening* (227). This story is one of Chopin's most accomplished in its use of night imagery (228). **Dyer 1981d:** Here and in numerous other works, Chopin uses physical setting to imply what a character is feeling. Her frequent use of this technique is open to various explanations (451–52). **Dyer 1984:** Storm imagery is used much more effectively here and in "The Storm" than in some of Chopin's undistinguished late work (189–90). **Dyer 1985:** As in "Juanita" and "Cavanelle," Chopin here draws on first-hand knowledge but presents the narrator ironically in order to achieve distance from the events she describes (78). In this as in other tales, Chopin relies on readers' stereotypes about unconventional characters in order to deal with topics she might not have been able to depict otherwise (80). **Skaggs 1985:** As in other tales, Chopin here shows some yearning for the freedom enjoyed by wanderers. The fact that the story was rooted in personal experience may help explain her choice of first-person narrative. Both this tale and, later, *The Awakening* associate evening time with a selfhood that is equally profound (58–59). **Inge 1989:** To explore states of mind, Chopin in this tale uses characters who contrast in some ways but are comparable in others. The female narrator is attracted by, and vicariously participates in, the natural experiences of her male visitor (107–8). **Toth 1990a:** This early tale, based on her own experiences, was altered and toned down before Chopin submitted it for publication (164). The story reveals her personal knowledge of the countryside surrounding Cloutierville (167). **Dyer 1993:** In this wonderful tale, which has received insufficient attention from critics, mud imagery is associated with the title character, who resembles the narrator (128). **Dyer 1994:** This neglected story is one of Chopin's best tales and deserves extremely high praise (74–75). It demonstrates the necessity of heeding our individual duality (75), partly because it implies the similarities of language, conduct, appearance, and tone between the narrator and the titular character (75–77). Even the setting suggests a convergence of the conscious and the unconscious aspects of identity, as does the imagery of mud (77). The story's frog imagery may be indebted to Chopin's reading of Aristophanes and the Bible (78–79), while the vagabond may symbolize the darker, more mysterious side of the self (79–80). Chopin's method in this tale, especially in its conclusion, is artfully indirect and subtle (80–81). **Toth and Seyersted 1998:** This story is mentioned in Chopin's account books (145, 150, 161). **Toth 1999c:** This story reflects Chopin's personal experiences, although she altered some of its original phrasing (90). It shows her familiarity with the Louisiana rural landscape (96). **Knights 2000:** In this work, Chopin untypically presents a female first-person narrator who encounters an unconventional experience through mysterious contact with a male. The story was turned down by two different journals (xvii).

"A Very Fine Fiddle"

Written: 1891. First published: 1891. Included in *Bayou Folk* (1897).

Cléophas takes his fiddle from its flannel bag and plays when his children are hungry. Fifine tells her father that one day she is going to smash the fiddle into a thousand pieces.

Cléophas tells her that she must not do so, because the fiddle is older than he is and is a part of his life that he intends to live on after he is dead.

A big party is held at the plantation. Fifine carries the fiddle in its flannel bag and heads to the party. At first no one notices the barefoot little girl sitting on the steps, but when she announces that she has a fiddle for sale, people gather around her. She takes the fiddle out of its bag and three men examine it closely. They give Fifine a much prettier fiddle and a roll of money for the old fiddle.

She is ecstatic, for the roll of money is more than she can count. She envisions a new roof on the cabin, shoes for all her brothers and sisters, food, and even buying a cow and calf.

As Cléophas plays the new fiddle that night he admits that it is a fine instrument, but it is just not the same as playing his old fiddle. He tells Fifine to put it aside because he will not be playing the fiddle anymore. **(DR)**

***

Rankin 1932: The main characters resemble the kind of people Chopin would have met during her time in Cloutierville (103). This superb story, published in a magazine for youth on November 24, 1891, is brief but offers a very moving conclusion (132). Although extremely short, this tale is far better than many unnecessarily long works by other authors (138). This work is "one of the most quietly moving fragments in modern writing" (139). **Peterson 1972:** This is one of several rather conventional tales about unusual personalities that Chopin composed for young readers (59–60). **Arner 1975:** The story typifies many in *Bayou Folk*, particularly in its local color, subtly amusing yet compassionate tone, skillful characterization, and artistic subtlety. Convincing even if not particularly deep, its main concern is with the persons it describes (63). **Skaggs 1985:** This is one of several tales depicting unusually independent girls (12–13). **Papke 1990:** Most of the stories Chopin wrote during this year seem fairly predictable, perhaps because she was focusing most of her attention on calling attention to her novels. This tale, though, is one of several from this period that present unusual female protagonists, most of whom defy social rules but do so for sensible purposes and therefore seem less defiant than they may first appear (52). **Toth 1990a:** This was one of several stories from 1891 in which Chopin sought a friendly, interested readership, particularly among young persons (201). It presents the thinking of children in an amusing light (202) and was published in a national magazine for youth (204). **Ellis 1992:** The personality of Fifine here resembles that of Trézine in "After the Winter" (217). **Ellis 1994:** This is one of several stories by Chopin that uses a three-part structure perhaps influenced by, and certainly similar to, the sonata form in music (147). **Fusco 1994:** The events of this tale strongly resemble those of one by Maupassant (140). Both stories focus on characters who learn the real significance of under-valued possessions. Chopin gives her tale an added dimension that keeps it from seeming a mere imitation (148–50). **Carr 1996:** Here as elsewhere Chopin presents Cajun males in a condescending fashion (54). **Koloski 1996:** This is one of several children's stories by Chopin that depict the poor (71; 87). **Wagner-Martin 1996:** Here as elsewhere Chopin depicts an energetic, determined female (197). The passionate young woman here resembles a young man in certain ways (204). **Beer 1997:** This is one of Chopin's stories in which possessions are given unusual symbolic importance. Chopin normally does not focus on describing objects merely for the sake of description (72). Here as elsewhere, she constructs a story based on juxtaposing the past and the present. The story raises provocative questions about the practical value of art and about the symbolic value of material possessions. Cleophas does not respond in a practical way to the needs of his children; his shortcomings as a father are obvious. He shows more concern for the violin than for his offspring. By the end of the story the children are better off, but Chopin does not minimize the loss to the father. Chopin achieves an admirably poised narrative tone, and Richard Fusco perhaps misjudges her presentation of Fifine, who seems a more sympathetic character than Fusco admits. Chopin uses the story to pose—but not necessarily to resolve—the dilemma of the place of art in an impoverished society. Chopin does not use the story to pass judgments but to raise provocative questions (84–85). **Toth and Seyersted 1998:** This story is mentioned in Chopin's account books (139, 148, 174–75). **Koloski 1999:** This is one of many stories by Chopin which either feature children or were written for them (xxii). Here as elsewhere she describes children's' responses to poverty (xxiii).

"A Visit to Avoyelles"

Written: 1892. First published: 1893. Included in *Bayou Folk* **(1894).**

Doudouce has heard tales from everyone who has visited Avoyelles about how Mentine has changed, how she has about four babies, and how her husband Jules neglects her. Doudouce knows that Mentine would have married him if Jules Trodon, with his handsome smile and charming manner, had not come to Natchitoches seven years ago and turned her head. Finally, one day, he can stand it no more. His head is fairly swimming with thoughts of Mentine, and that night he dreams of her in her wedding gown holding out her arms to him in supplication. This settles it. Doudouce sets out for Avoyelles the next morning.

When he approaches Jules's run-down cottage he sees two little barefooted children standing on the porch. Next, two barking dogs rush down the steps, lunging at him. Hearing a piercing, high-pitched voice, he looks in its direction and sees a thin, misshapen woman carrying a frail baby on her hip coming out the door. Her skin is sun-browned and dry, and she has deep lines around her eyes and mouth. Instantly, she calls him "Doudouce" and says he is looking well and has not changed at all. Sick at heart, Doudouce sits down on the porch and visits with Mentine until Jules comes in for his noon meal. He looks heavier and handsomer than he looked seven years ago.

When Jules leaves to go back to his plowing, Doudouce leaves, too, riding in the opposite direction. He is surprised to realize that he loves Mentine even more than before. She has lost her beauty, and she has fallen into an impossible situation; yet he loves her now like a mother loves her stricken child. He would like to take her and her children out of there and protect them as long as he lives. When he looks back at Mentine, however, Doudouce sees her standing at the gate, still holding the baby, with her head turned lovingly to watch her husband as he rides toward the field. **(CY)**

***

Rankin 1932: Mentine is the sort of person Chopin might have met during her time in Cloutierville and illustrates her skill at characterization (103). This tale appeared with "Désirée's Baby" at the beginning of 1893 in *Vogue*, thus beginning Chopin's lengthy involvement with that magazine (133). **Reilly 1942:** This story illustrates the tendency of Chopin's heroines to remain loyal once they have made a romantic commitment (132–33). **Fletcher 1966:** As in some of her other stories about Creole women, Chopin here emphasizes a woman's fidelity (127). **Arms 1967:** This work takes an unusual approach to depicting opposed views, finding humor in the stubbornness of feelings subjected to stress (223). **Seyersted 1969a:** This was one of Chopin's first published stories for a mature Eastern audience (54). Mentine is one of a number of Chopin's women who follow custom by willingly serving men (110). Like other such works, however, this tale was written at around the same time Chopin composed a story ("Ma'ame Pélagie") depicting a more assertive woman (216). **Leary 1970a:** This is one of many works in which Chopin depicts the ambiguities and complexities of love (x). **Leary 1971:** The story manages to depict both indigence and affection without becoming maudlin (166). **Peterson 1972:** In this and other stories for *Vogue*, constraints of space dictated a standard structure consisting of an introductory discussion followed by a quick dramatization (108). This work was published as a companion piece of "Désirée's Baby." The story shows how inaccurately Doudouce perceives Mentine, who does not seem particularly unhappy and whose family life Doudouce even envies (112–14). Here as elsewhere Chopin spotlights one character whose changed perspective ends the tale (114–15). In this tale, everything is seen from Doudouce's limited perspective, and the plot is deliberately uneventful. In this latter respect the story illustrates Chopin's skill in depicting seemingly ordinary life (115). This story is one of Chopin's finest (120). **Rocks 1972:** Here as elsewhere Chopin shows the complexities but also the rewards of marriage as well as its superiority to remaining single (118). **Seyersted 1974:** The compliant heroine of this story contrasts with the more independent-minded Clarisse of "At the 'Cadian Ball," written not long before (13). **Arner 1975:** This story effectively contrasts romantic illusions with a grim reality (58–59). **Bonner 1977:** This is one of several stories from *Bayou Folk* in which travel is a key device of plot (8). The story focuses on unreciprocated affection (10). **Taylor 1979:** This is one of several tales that emphasize the power of the maternal role (xvi). **Baym 1981:** Here as in other stories, Chopin depicts rural Creoles who nonetheless possess considerable cultural and behavioral complexity (xx). **Wolff 1979:** This tale is one of Chopin's many realistic variations on the theme of marriage (213). **Stein 1984:** Here as elsewhere, Chopin presents a wife who ultimately is happy to submit to her husband (176). When the visitor in this story sees the wife's final gaze, his own perceptions (which had earlier been obscured by his affection for her) are probably clarified. Although Mentine's husband seems boorish, she nonetheless finds self-fulfillment in her marriage, contrary to the sentimental expectations of Doudouce (177–78). This emphasis on her happiness contrasts with the stress of wifely dissatisfaction in "In Sabine," but in both cases Chopin is mainly interested in whether a person feels fulfilled rather than in either satirizing or supporting marriage as an institution (189–90). **Skaggs 1985:** This is one of several tales exploring the interactions of affection and selfhood (17). It shows a woman who seems ultimately satisfied with her choice (21–22). **Gaudet 1986:** The geographical setting of this story is quite precise and implies Cajun characters (50). **Toth 1990a:** This is one of various tales in which Chopin describes infatuated men and pragmatic women (224) and is one of a number of stories describing extra-marital passion (279). **Guidici 1991:** Here as elsewhere a Chopin heroine fails to seize the opportunity for greater autonomy (31). **Shurbutt 1993:** This story offers an ironic perspective not only on marriage but also on conventional ideas about feminine beauty and males as rescuers (20). **Koloski 1994:** The story is included in soft-cover collections of Chopin's fiction published in 1970, 1979, and 1981 (27). **Koloski 1996:** This story can be valuably compared and contrasted with "At the 'Cadian Ball" (22) and also with "In Sabine," especially in its focus on travel and a savior (23). **Toth and Seyersted 1998:** This story is mentioned in Chopin's account books (139, 149, 156). **Koloski 1999:** Here as in other tales, Chopin describes a symbolic passage between places, and she also depicts the constrictions that often accompany married life (xiii). **Toth 1999c:** The woman depicted here resembled ones Chopin knew from rural Louisiana, and the story was quickly published because it confirmed readers' stereotypes about such persons (144). This is one of several tales in *Bayou Folk* showing the destructive impact of men on women and the ambiguities that sometimes bedevil affection (151). The story was first published in *Vogue* (171). **Gibbons 2000:** This story reveals progress in Chopin's movement away from local color conventions. It is less sentimental and emotional, and the design is more flexible than in many local color works. Nevertheless, both this story and "Beyond the Bayou" display many standard features of local color writing (xxxi–xxxii).

"A Vocation and a Voice"

Written: 1896. First published: 1902. Included in *A Vocation and a Voice* (1991).

An unnamed narrator tells the story of a young orphan boy who, while running an errand, gets lost. However, rather than being frightened or feeling lonely, he enjoys the freedom and the beauty of nature. He decides that no one will miss him if he never returns. As he strolls in a leisurely fashion through the unfamiliar town, enjoying his new-found freedom, he runs across a woman in a canvas-covered wagon who is trying to put out a grass fire. After he helps the woman put out the fire, she offers him a meal. The two converse as they eat, he pouring out his heart and she listening carefully. Her name is Susan, but it has been changed to Suzima to better fit her profession as a fortune teller. She is around twenty, about five years older than the boy. Her traveling companion, Gutro, sells herbs, medicines, and potions. Suzima is dark and mysterious-looking, aptly fitting the role of fortune teller. She offers to let the boy come along with them, and he accepts. As the vagabonds travel along the open road, the boy loves the freedom and the intimacy with nature, and he also loves listening to Suzima sing as they walk along with the wagon. When they stop and set up their fortune-telling and medicine-selling booth, the boy sometimes sings along with Suzima as she plays her guitar. Once the trio finds a vacant house on the outskirts of a small town and settle in for awhile, becoming almost a normal household. Having a religious background, the boy is drawn to the church; he begins to attend mass regularly and becomes friendly with the parish priest. The priest is delighted to learn that the boy is experienced in serving mass and immediately puts him to use assisting him in the services. After a short time, Suzima and Gutro become bored with a normal life and decide the time has come to go back on the road. The priest pleads with the boy to stay, but, even though he is tempted, his love of the open road wins out. One day, while watering the mules, the boy comes upon a naked Suzima bathing in the stream. He immediately looks away, but her vision is burned into his memory. That night Suzima turns to the boy, taking him with her arms and with her lips. From that moment on, his world changes. He is in love with Suzima and becomes totally enamored with her. As they are preparing to break camp one night, a drunk Gutro hits Suzima with a halter and the boy dives at him with a knife. He only scratches Gutro, but he realizes that for the first time in his life he has allowed evil to overtake him, and the feeling sickens him. Suzima calls for him to come along, but he will not go with them, choosing instead to stay in the coolness of the forest.

The narrator then tells of a Brother Ludovic who lives a peaceful life in a monastery, working hard each day until he falls into bed each night, exhausted. His only goal in life is to build a stone wall around the monastery and live peacefully within those walls of protection from the outside world. At night Brother Ludovic dreams of walking alongside a beautiful woman as she sings in the open air. One day, as Brother Ludovic lifts stones to his wall, he suddenly stops like a frightened animal. He hears a familiar tune coming through the air. As he listens, the voice comes closer and closer still, until he sees that it is Suzima. Brother Ludovic bounds across his stone wall and follows the voice away. **(DR)**

***

Seyersted 1969a: Suzima, by "turn[ing] a boy into her lover," typifies the kind of self-assertive heroines Chopin was creating at this time (70). The story was frequently rejected before eventually being printed (73), perhaps in part because it emphasizes the extreme power of erotic attraction on the young male it describes (98). As in *The Awakening* and in other stories, Chopin here implies that natural sexual desire is often confused with the ideal of love (147). The fact that Suzima is presented as somewhat exotic made her sensuality more acceptable to some editors than was true of Edna in *The Awakening* (177). **Berthoff 1970:** This exceptionally fine story was eventually published more than five years after Chopin composed it (x). It is one of her strongest works (xi). **Peterson 1972:** Chopin implies, here as elsewhere, that having a purpose can be more fulfilling than satisfying a desire (133). The story juxtaposes nature and religion and provides Chopin's fullest consideration of the latter. The story works better as an allegory than as a realistic tale; thus Suzima personifies womanhood untainted by civilization: she seems motherly and sensual. The story juxtaposes contrasting kinds of music, and the change in the boy's voice also signals the growing complication of his personality. Whereas earlier he had been untroubled, now he begins to experience desire. At first his new feelings are expressed as anger toward Gutro, but eventually he realizes, with disillusionment, that he and Gutro have traits in common. He therefore enters the monastery, determined to suppress his passions through devotion and by doing hard labor. The story shows the conflicts between religion and human nature and the tensions between conscious thought and innate instincts. The boy learns that both Suzima and Gutro reflect aspects of his own nature, but his effort to suppress his physical side in the monastery leads, ironically, only to the strengthening of his body. His final decision represents a choice to accept life in its full complexity. In various ways the characters and plot of this story are not wholly credible, but that is partly because Chopin seems less interested here in realism than in symbolism and theme (191–98). Here as in *The Awakening*, allegory takes precedence over realism (234). As in some of her other works, Chopin here offers an interesting study of the human mind (273). **Rocks 1972:** Here as elsewhere Chopin shows how people grow by being pulled in opposite directions (120). **Bender 1974:** The boy in the story is torn between custom, responsibility, and traditional religion (on the one hand) and freedom, self-fulfillment, and love of nature (on the other.) Chopin emphasizes the power of primal human instincts, which finally cannot be ignored or resisted (260–62). **Arner 1975:** This was the first story in which Chopin fully developed the symbolic links between the internal realm of mind and emotion and the external realm of nature. Symbolically the boy journeys toward true selfhood. At first he doesn't realize his own capacity for darkness, but once he confronts this aspect of himself he can achieve a more mature identity (25–26). The tale is one of the lengthiest Chopin ever composed; it reveals a growing mastery of symbolism, plotting, and theme that foreshadows the skill demonstrated in *The Awakening*. Suzima's impulsive outburst when the boy sees her naked is ironically appropriate to his subsequent passion and possession, which partly result from his first contact with his unconscious desires. Although he turns to the Madonna and the Church as alternatives to his newly discovered feelings, and although his primary job at the monastery is relevant to his attempt to tame the landscape of his own mind, even his dreams imply ejaculatory fantasies. The enclosed monastery is counterpointed to the freedom of travel, while seasonal imagery helps emphasize Chopin's theme that not even the Church can stifle the development of healthy sexual impulses. The monk cannot shut out the forces already stirring inside him. Suzima is described in archetypal terms that link her to natural rhythms, and her two names suggest her double associations with both civilization and eros (80–84). **Bonner 1975:** This is one of Chopin's several stories on taboo topics (283). **Wolff 1978:** This is one of many stories by Chopin dealing with the instability of human experience (126). **Howell 1979b:** In this tale symbolism and didactic themes eventually become more important than realistic characterization (109). **Skaggs 1979:** This story is one of many that shows Chopin's concern not merely with female identity but with the problems any human can encounter in achieving an authentic self while also pursuing inclusion and affection. Chopin emphasizes the boy's youth and representative nature and shows how he attains belonging, affection, and self-awareness after his sexual encounter with Suzima, which also introduces him to conflict. At the monastery he achieves a new but temporary identity. Like Edna in *The Awakening*, however, he discovers that sexuality cannot be suppressed. Here as elsewhere, Chopin's fiction explores the nature of all humans, not just of women (270–76). **Taylor 1979:** This was one of several tales Chopin had difficulty publishing (viii). **Wolff 1979:** This is one of many Chopin stories in which sexual attraction is an important topic (220). **Dyer 1980–81:** Here as elsewhere Chopin reverses expectations by showing how a male can be fundamentally transformed by contact with a female (11). The boy in this tale experiences many of the conflicting feelings felt by 'Polyte in "Azélie" and by Tonie in "At Chênière Caminada" (13), but he is forced to confront pain of the sort Tonie is allowed to escape (14). The boy's initial response to nature is naively positive, but his new companions initiate him into experiences of desire and violence. At first he thinks he can block out such feelings, but he becomes increasingly animalistic, as his growing contact with Gutro and the mules suggests. He also becomes increasingly drawn to external nature as he assents more and more to his own instincts (13–14). His initiation into sex also leads him to a new perception of his relation to nature, although it also helps awaken his violent impulses. By joining the monastery he tries to recover his earlier perception of nature and tries to wall himself off from its darker aspects. Eventually, though, his final encounter with Suzima stirs many of the same feelings he felt when he first glimpsed her naked. Like 'Polyte in "Azélie," he cannot suppress his instincts (15). **Dyer 1981d:** Here and in numerous other works, Chopin uses physical setting to imply what a character is feeling. Her frequent use of this technique is open to various explanations (451–52). **Bonner 1982:** This is one of several stories by Chopin in which Christianity is an important aspect (125). **Davis 1982:** As in a number of her later tales, Chopin here deals with erotic desire as a force of nature leading to many possible effects on people's lives. In this tale she links erotic and religious passion (66). **Lattin 1982:** This is one of several stories in which Chopin shows how change can simultaneously involve loss, maturation, and self-discovery (227–28). **Rogers 1983:** Here as elsewhere Chopin, like George Sand, seems to imply that physical pleasure is often a hidden motive underlying religious devotion (38). **Stein 1984:** This is one of various tales in which Chopin describes the need to be true to oneself (207). **Dyer 1985:** In this as in other tales, Chopin relies on readers' stereotypes about unconventional characters in order to deal with topics she might not have been able to depict otherwise (80). **Skaggs 1985:** In this tale exploring the power of erotic desire, the young male protagonist, in search of his selfhood, goes unnamed almost until the conclusion. His experiences therefore seem generally relevant, especially as a tale of maturation, initiation into experience, and the search for a sense of belonging. His entry into the monastery brings him both a name and a new sense of self, but eventually he discovers that his identity and desires are too complex to allow him to be happy with the limited role he has adopted. Although the protagonist is male, his feelings are relevant to anyone (49–52). **Martin 1988a:** This is one of various stories in which Chopin depicts a passionate woman without censuring or penalizing her in order to court the approval of readers (6). **Skaggs 1988:** In stories such as this, Chopin deals with some of the most profound and most widely relevant issues of human life (80). **Inge 1989:** This is one of Chopin's lengthiest and most skillfully crafted tales. It is grounded in the archetypal progress toward self-understanding, and its male protagonist achieves a better mental balance than some of Chopin's heroines. He even eventually overcomes fear of his own physical desires and sets off, at the end, on a new journey toward even fuller reconciliation of his personal needs and social impulses (104). During his initial travels with Gutro and Suzima, he becomes more fully aware of his links with nature and with his developing sexuality. Yet he also becomes more fully aware of his own potentially violent impulses.

Realizing the tensions that exist within him, he tries to control them by joining the religious brotherhood, but his decision leads to a kind of psychological repression that cannot succeed. His final decision to follow Suzima is also a decision to accept his powerful inner impulses—impulses that can be used positively and thereby lead to psychic integration. Although Chopin does not indicate clearly whether the young man will be able to unite his inner being with society's expectations, she at least allows that option. Despite language that is sometimes awkward rather than amusing, the story is nonetheless one of Chopin's best, especially because of its events, its ideas, and its use of figurative language and landscape to suggest the state of the protagonist's mind (104–5). **Toth 1990a:** The story may have been influenced by Chopin's knowledge of the St. Louis Irish ghetto (28). The young hero may resemble a later friend of Chopin (265–66; 293). The story was intended for inclusion in *A Vocation and a Voice* (374), although it was first published in a journal owned by the friend whose boyhood experiences helped inspire it (386). This was one of the last tales for which Chopin earned payment (389). **Toth 1991:** Although this story mentions Louisiana, setting is less important here than character development (xiv). The sometimes elaborate diction of the tale may reflect the tastes of the male friend of Chopin's who may have inspired the boyish hero (xvii). The tale reflects Chopin's interest in the complex, often ironic links between religious and secular experiences (xx). This was the last of Chopin's published tales for adults (xx). We can't be sure precisely how long it took Chopin to compose this work (xxii). This is one of several stories in *A Vocation and a Voice* in which Chopin presents complex views of religion (xxiii–xxiv), in which she seems to satirize contemporary class relations (xxiv), and in which she presents an intriguing female character (xxv). Although this optimistic story heads Chopin's last collection, the collection itself later becomes darker (xxv). **Davis 1992b:** By making this male-centered tale the title story of her final collection, Chopin masked the general emphasis on women in that volume (199–200). This is one of many stories from *A Vocation and a Voice* that focus on suddenly altered perceptions (200–201). **Ellis 1992:** This is one of various stories in which, as in *The Awakening*, a character is transformed partly through his or her encounter with music (216). In this case the music is associated mainly with Suzima; through his experiences with her and with Gutro, the boy discovers different parts of himself. He experiences a series of transformations, eventually breaking free of self-imposed limits. Both main words of the title carry multiple connotations, alluding to different purposes and statuses in life and also suggesting once more the idea of music. Religious imagery is important throughout the tale (224–29). **Dyer 1993:** This fine late story shows that Chopin's inspiration was not entirely crushed by the poor reception of *The Awakening* (19–20). **Ewell 1994:** This is one of many stories by Chopin that show the dangers of ignoring the sexual or sensual aspects of human nature (168). **Fusco 1994:** By not mentioning the boy's name for most of the tale, Chopin makes his experiences seem significant to a wide

audience. Although he does not lose his sanity because of the conflict between his religious and sexual impulses (as a protagonist created by Maupassant might have done), his erotic cravings do make him increasingly (if
momentarily) irrational. He loses his original sense of place as well as his
moral bearings, especially when he comes under Suzima's influence.
Chopin thus reveals the physical instincts that lie just below the surface of
social behavior. Each time the young man chooses to follow Suzima, he
renounces more and more of his commitment to conventional religion, but
he thereby comes closer and closer to achieving his full human potential
(160–63). **Koloski 1994:** The story is included in a soft-cover collection of
Chopin's fiction published in 1991 (28). **Padgett 1994:** Here as elsewhere
Chopin describes a woman who sees a male in angelic terms (103). **Bender
1996:** This is one of various stories in which Chopin's basically Darwinian
outlook leads her to examine the problems caused by an insufficiently assertive male (107). **Koloski 1996:** The protagonist here is one of the most
vivid in the literature of Chopin's era and nation (xiii). Like many of her
tales, this one features travel (23), imagery of naked feet (37–38), and allusions to opera (53). It is one of her longer stories (88–89). Here as elsewhere, voice is an important motif and runs throughout the work. The
story also stresses maturation and the conflicts between spiritual and
worldly existence. Like other works by Chopin, this one was strongly influenced by her passion for music and drama, particularly an opera by
Ferdinand Hérold (54–58). **Beer 1997:** Here as elsewhere, Chopin often
compares the satisfactions provided by sex and religion (47). **Ewell 1997:**
At first the boy can reconcile this devotion to religion with his love of nature, but tensions ultimately arise. The boy then comes to see nature and
sex as having spiritual dimensions, but his conflict with Gutro leads him
to return to conventional religion. At the monastery he tries, with a futility
like that of Sisyphus, to suppress his physical nature. Finally he returns to
the natural impulses he had tried to reject (111–12). **Toth and Seyersted
1998:** An early draft of this story was among a collection of Chopin
manuscripts uncovered in the early 1990s (135). The tale is mentioned in
Chopin's account books (135, 143, 150). The early manuscript fragment
foreshadows this work (269). **Koloski 1999:** This was one of a number of
effective tales Chopin composed before the publication of *A Night in
Acadie* but which she did not include in that collection (xv–xvi). **Toth
1999a:** An early version of this tale was rediscovered in 1992 (8). **Toth
1999b:** A newly uncovered version of this story helps demonstrate
Chopin's habits of revision (49). **Toth 1999c:** An opening setting in this
story is one Chopin herself would have known during childhood (36). A
portion of an early draft of this tale demonstrates how Chopin revised the
work (166–67). The protagonist's experiences resemble those of a male
friend of Chopin who later printed the story in his newspaper (186–87;
199).

"The White Eagle"

Written: 1900. First published: 1900. Included in *A Vocation and a Voice* **(1991).**

A cast-iron eagle stands proud on the lawn with his wings outstretched. He receives a fresh coat of white paint each year if it is available; otherwise he must settle for whitewash. He is large enough for a small child to sit in the shade of his wing, and one little girl often does this as she enjoys her childhood.

The owner of the estate dies, and although there is squabbling over the estate, only one young woman wants the eagle. As she moves from place to place, she drags the eagle with her. Finally, there is no place for the eagle except the corner of her tiny room.

When the old woman dies, none of her belongings are wanted. Nobody knows what to do with the eagle, so he is placed at the head of her grave, like a tombstone. There he gazes across the plains with that proud look that in a human would be described as wisdom. **(DR)**

***

Rankin 1932: This is the single one of Chopin's final few stories to show much innovation or invention. It implies a tone of enduring sadness (186–88). **Seyersted 1969a:** As in other works, Chopin here emphasizes a strong interplay between the masculine and the feminine—in this case the bird and the girl. The fact that the bird is iron makes it a symbol of freedom denied, just as the story implies a lack of fulfilled sexuality, even though sexual imagery is implied when the woman fantasizes about the bird attacking her and once again in the description of the children's conduct at the end (184). **Peterson 1972:** This tale is unique in Chopin's corpus. It resembles Flaubert's "A Simple Heart." Although the bird can be seen in sexual terms, it more plausibly seems a symbol of constancy in a changing world, while the central character seems locked in the past. The eagle thus represents her own static condition, and her death ultimately makes her as frozen as the statue. This was one of Chopin's few late stories to achieve publication; after writing it, she wrote little else for a year and a half (263–65). This is the only one of Chopin's final stories to display her skills to best advantage. The work is one of Chopin's better final pieces, most of which imply that her talent had begun to diminish (268–69). **Seyersted 1974:** The inert bird here may symbolize Chopin's disappointed reaction to the failure of *The Awakening* (17). The eagle in a sense represents what had become of Chopin's lofty literary aspirations (18). **Arner 1975:** After the criticism Chopin received over *The Awakening*, she generally avoided sexual themes in the few remaining stories she wrote. "The White Eagle," however, does treat such themes by using symbolism, and perhaps this is how she would have handled the topic in other works if she had lived longer. This story is one of the better of her few late tales (18). This is more than a tale of sadness. It focuses on a symbol of movement frozen, which is juxtaposed (at the start and finish) with images of mutability. The final passage uses rhythm and syntax to suggest both change and stability, and the story also effectively uses cyclical structures and images. The eagle is associated with eros, masculinity, and art, but also with an innocence that may amount to an immature rejection of a dynamic life that enters the woman's mind only in her dreams (96–99). **Inge 1989:** Chopin here demonstrates a deft and subtle use of symbol and place to suggest mental states. Her tone is strikingly and thoroughly objective. The bird symbolizes the protagonist's early hopes for fulfillment through the love of a husband and children, but these failed aspirations—which are imposed on women in her patriarchal culture—eventually torment her. The protagonist's physical, mental, and social space continually diminish, and the final sentence implies a sardonic protest against the restrictions placed on women's lives (105–6). **Dyer 1984:** This is one of the few late stories in which Chopin uses imagery and symbols as effectively as she had before. The titular symbol is richly complex; it suggests the main character's youthful past, her present inactivity, and her unrealized potential. It becomes a substitute focus for her affections, a symbol of the supernatural, a kind of alter-ego, and a herald of death (190–92). **Toth 1990a:** This was one of the stories Chopin submitted to *Vogue* and was intended for collection in *A Vocation and a Voice* (373–74). The tale, reminiscent of one by Flaubert, was the final work by Chopin published in *Vogue* (377) and was the last story she composed for more than a year (386). **Toth 1991:** This is one of many of Chopin's late works that were first printed in *Vogue* (xiii–xiv). It is one of the few stories she composed after *The Awakening* (xiv). The eagle here may have been influenced by a bird described by a Scandinavian writer, although the tale is also similar to one by Flaubert (xix). This work is the earliest story included in *A Vocation and a Voice* (xxii) and is one of several in that collection to present an intriguing female character (xxv). **Thomas 1992:** This is one of several works by Chopin written in 1900 that focus on sickness, death, or growing old. The ironically static bird may symbolize mortality (51–52). **Dyer 1993:** This fine late story shows that Chopin's inspiration was not entirely crushed by the poor reception of *The Awakening* (19–20). **Day 1994:** Theme: how unconscious, pre-linguistic, suppressed impulses sometimes overflow into dreams (108). The eagle symbolizes the girl's unconscious impulses, especially her stifled sexual longings, which can never come alive (112). The tale is one of several showing a woman whose self-divisions cannot be healed (113–14). **Koloski 1994:** The story is included in a soft-cover collection of Chopin's fiction published in 1991 (28). **Walker 1994:** This late work (and others) shows that Chopin did not abandon writing after *The Awakening* failed (17). **Toth and Seyersted 1998:** This story is mentioned in Chopin's account books (142, 147, 151). **Toth 1999c:** This was Chopin's final publication in *Vogue* (232); after finishing it she ceased composing fiction for more than a year (235).

"Wiser Than a God"

Written: 1889. First Published: 1889. Included in *Complete Works* (1969).

Paula Von Stoltz, a talented pianist, accepts an invitation to play dance music at a homecoming party for college student George Brainard. Paula's sickly mother is unhappy about the engagement. She fears that Paula is settling for a career that is beneath her abilities and giving up on the stellar musical career that Mrs. Von Stoltz and her deceased husband had always hoped for her. Paula insists that she still has her eye on a more lofty goal and puts her mother's mind at greater ease by playing "Berceuse," a piece that Mrs. Von Stoltz associates with precious memories of their family when Paula was a child. Mrs. Von Stoltz says she feels strong, but admonishes Paula not to come home too late when she sends her off to the Brainard mansion.

Paula arrives at the mansion before the guests; George is the first of the Brainard family to meet her, and he sees to it that she has sufficient light to see her music.

A few hours later, during a break from the dancing, George picks up his banjo and plays quite proficiently as his dark-eyed girlfriend dances a "Virginia breakdown." George's sister next "entertains" the group, even though an instructor has told her years earlier that she cannot sing, and in the moment of triumph that follows her performance, she condescendingly asks Paula to "play something." Paula's interpretation of a modern classic stuns her audience into silence, which is broken only by trite compliments from George's girlfriend and some of the others. When Paula discovers that she has missed the last car at the end of the evening, George offers to walk her home. Paula finds herself attracted to the athletic man at her side, and as they talk and laugh along the way, she can think of none of her male acquaintances who compares to him. At the sight of Dr. Sinn's buggy, parked in front of her home,

Paula begins to worry about her mother. Once inside, she learns that her mother has died.

For the next few months, Paula gives her undivided attention to her work, hoping to achieve the goal her parents had dreamed of for her, but two men distract her with offers of marriage: Max Kuntzler, Paula's harmony instructor and a talented composer, and George Brainard. When Paula rejects the middle-aged professor's offer, he asks to remain her friend, intending to keep a watchful eye for a more opportune time. Although Paula confesses her love for George, she expresses the fear that marrying him will distract her from achieving her life-long goal. She tells George to come back in a week to receive her final answer, but on his return, he discovers that she is gone to Leipsic. A few years later, George is settled into a domestic rut with his dark-eyed wife, but Kuntzler is in Leipsic still waiting patiently for the renowned pianist Fraulein Von Stoltz to change her mind. (JW)

***

Rankin 1932: This tale of approximately 2500 words, composed in June 1889, was the first of her early works that Chopin did not destroy (115–16). [See, however, the entry for "Emancipation" and the comment in Inge 1989 below.] **Zlotnick 1968:** This is one of many stories in which Chopin implies ambivalent, unconventional responses to marriage (2). **Seyersted 1969a:** Published in 1889 (52), this is one of Chopin's earliest surviving stories. It describes a heroine who partly fits Simone de Beauvoir's later existentialist definition of a liberated woman. Although Paula lacks arrogance, she is not afraid to stand up for her ideals, even when opposed by her strong-willed suitor (104–5). The tale's depiction of marriage seems ambivalent (107), and Paula may indeed represent an opposite view of womanhood from that of her namesake, St. Paul (115). The story offers Chopin's most explicit depiction of a liberated female. It is her one story preceded by an epigraph and her one tale with an overtly feminist heroine, and perhaps the story is hobbled somewhat by a lack of subtlety. Paula's remarks sometimes sound like speeches, and the phrasing of the story is frequently flawed by stiffness, conventionality, and slang. Chopin herself sometimes intrudes and instructs, although generally she adopts a more objective stance. The structure is solid, the opening is efficient, and the plot is coherent, and almost everything fits, but the humor sometimes seems awkward. Paula comes close to being fully drawn, but some of the other characters seem too thin (117–18). "Regret," a later story by Chopin, seems far more subtly implicit (130), while two of her very last tales describe heroines who are far more compliant than Paula (185). When assembling her third volume of stories for submission to a publisher, Chopin left out this early work, probably assuming that it would sink any chances of the book's acceptance (223). **Seyersted 1969b:** Paula typifies the kind of women Chopin often depicted—women who violated conventional contemporary views of ideal feminine behavior (27). **Leary 1970a:** In this uncollected story, Chopin treats the theme of feminine self-assertion more bluntly than in her local color tales. This was her first work to be published in a journal. Although the story's structure is a bit weak, the theme is central to Chopin's fiction (xi). **Leary 1971:** Although the story is primitive in construction, it more openly presents the theme of female freedom than is true of some of Chopin's local-color tales (168). **Peterson 1972:** The treatment of the complexities of marriage is simpler here than in later works by Chopin (11). The resolution of this tale lacks complexity; the heroine suffers no real loss (69–70). **Rocks 1972:** Here Chopin shows the possible rewards of resisting temptation (119). **Seyersted 1974:** The heroine here is a successful liberated woman (12). **Arner 1975:** In plot and theme this early story anticipates some of Chopin's mature work, especially in its focus on the ambiguities of both marriage and the single life (120–21). **Bonner 1975:** This is one of several stories that demonstrate Chopin's interest in Europe (281–83). **Ladenson 1976:** Perhaps the heroine's yearning for self-realization is merely fleeting, but at least she acts on it. The epigraph with which the tale opens suggests how hard it is for a woman in love to preserve her autonomy. Paula may have been headed for a fate as a mere decoration if she had married (28). **Solomon 1976:** This early story is important not only because it foreshadows many of Chopin's later themes but also because of its relatively happy if unconventional outcome (vii–viii). **Berggren 1977:** This is the only story by Chopin in which a woman clearly chooses her work over marriage (1). **Taylor 1979:** Here as elsewhere, Chopin depicts a female playing the conventionally masculine role of artist and ultimately enjoying some success both in romance and in art (xvii). **Wolff 1979:** This early tale is too simple in structure and characterization; it lacks vitality and force, although it does deal with some of her characteristic themes (208–9). **Dyer 1981b:** In works like this, Chopin uses night imagery in highly predictable ways to emphasize doom and/or gloom (217). Little about this story is understated; the didacticism is tedious; the characterization is shallow. The night imagery is hackneyed (217–18). **Davis 1982:** Paula's unusual views of marriage are symptoms of her unusual views of herself, and in this sense the story typifies much of Chopin's later fiction. Paula's commitment to her music seems more sympathetic since she associates it with her devotion to her deceased parents (61–62). **Fluck 1982:** In his tale the impulse toward feminine self-assertion is made tolerable by being associated with an artist who supposedly serves "higher" cultural goals that are socially beneficial. When the heroine is briefly tempted to put her personal interests first, she is punished (158–59). Yet even her limited self-assertion demands great personal strength (168). **Bonner 1983b:** Chopin endorses Paula's unconventional self-assertion (146–47). **Burchard 1984:** Here as in *The Awakening*, a woman leads a solitary life (36). **Stein 1984:** Here as elsewhere Chopin seems less inter-

ested in either endorsing or satirizing marriage *per se* than in determining
whether marriage can be reconciled with self-fulfillment. This particular
story shows marriage inhibiting self-fulfillment, but a story written not
long after described the opposite possibility. In the present case, however,
marriage would be counter-productive for Paula. George's later marriage
confirms the rightness of Paula's rejection of his proposal. The man whom
Paula may eventually wed bears a name that suggests his allegiance to art.
The story implies not only that a wisely chosen marriage may lead to self-
fulfilment but also that a marriage that restricts self-fulfillment should
wisely be avoided (166–67). **Newman 1986:** Like many of Chopin's tales,
this one suggests a view of marriage that seems to conflict with the views
implied by some of her other stories (152). **Rowe 1985:** This early story explores the ways marriage might inhibit feminine development (230).
Skaggs 1985: The title derives from an old Latin saying that implies that
the combination of love and wisdom is impossible even for divine beings.
Paula chooses wisdom over affection (55–56). **Bonner 1988:** This story is
often anthologized as an example of Chopin's works focusing on women's
issues (100). **Giorcelli 1988:** The heroine here makes a choice similar to one
faced in *The Awakening* (122). **Martin 1988a:** This story investigates the
conflicts between aesthetic ambition and societal tradition (4). **Papke 1988:**
The depiction of a female artist in this early story is relevant to the depiction of Mme. Reisz in *The Awakening* (73). **Showalter 1988:** This story reflects Chopin's early talent for (and interest in) music, especially the music
of Frederic Chopin (47). **Toth 1988b:** Chopin may have hoped that, like the
protagonist here, her own artistic career would blossom in the period following the death of her mother (64). **Inge 1989:** This is Chopin's second extant story and the second one to be printed. It deals with topics that would
become standard fare in Chopin's fiction, including liberty, conflicting affections, self-assertion, and the ways social pressures affect matrimony
(92). **Taylor 1989:** Here as elsewhere Chopin deals openly with feminist
topics (153). **Papke 1990:** Focusing on a creative woman (36), this sometimes overly emotional story examines the division between a woman's
flesh and soul but without providing a contrived optimistic conclusion.
Paula is an unusual heroine whose decisions in some ways parallel those
of Chopin herself. Her firm commitment to her ideals and her immense
understanding finally make her seem to exemplify the story's title. Chopin
depicts a wider range of both male and female attitudes and behavior than
she had in some of her earlier fiction, and although Chopin raises the possibility of real self-fulfillment for a woman lucky enough to find a man
who can be both a lover and a friend, she doesn't sentimentally show
Paula achieving that ideal within the confines of this narrative (38–39).
This is one of four pivotal stories in Chopin's career in which she momentarily overcomes gloomy views of women's possibilities and instead presents resolute and confident female protagonists (60). Paula prefigures
(although not entirely) the protagonist of "Azélie" (61) as well as Mademoiselle Reisz in *The Awakening* (75). **Seidel 1990:** This story can be

viewed against the context of contemporary writings that often depicted lesbians as artists (90). **Toth 1990a:** The story may reflect Chopin's own love of the piano (35), and perhaps the name of the character called George derives from Chopin's dead brother (66). Meanwhile, the circumstances of the female protagonist may reflect those of Chopin herself, whose career as a writer began with this story (175). In particular, the story may have been influenced by Chopin's own recent romantic involvements (180). The narrative, which first appeared in an east-coast periodical, resembles other early tales of Chopin in focusing on a professional woman (181). **Vanlandingham 1990:** This was one of Chopin's first stories accepted for publication (160). **Guidici 1991:** Paula resembles the other gifted artists Chopin often described, just as her rejection of a marriage proposal is a common event in Chopin's writings. Similarly, like other Chopin heroines, she must change locations and avoid explanations in order to escape social pressures (28). Here as in other works by Chopin, a parent's death gives a woman greater power (30). **Ellis 1992:** A piece of music mentioned here is also mentioned in *The Awakening* (217). **Dyer 1993:** Here as in *The Awakening*, Chopin depicts a talented woman willing to risk isolation to be true to her art. The final sentence of this story is merely a sop to readers desiring the possibility of a conventionally happy ending (93–94). **Larsson 1993:** This story demonstrates Chopin's interest in autonomy for women as well as her skepticism about conventional marriage (2: 537). **Cutter 1994:** Here as in other early stories, Chopin describes women whose efforts to express opposition are promptly silenced or suppressed (17). George even treats Paula as if she is crazy when she tries to explain her feelings (20–22). **Ellis 1994:** This is one of several stories by Chopin that uses a three-part structure perhaps influenced by, and certainly similar to, the sonata form in music (147). Chopin uses music as both a theme and a means of characterization in this tale (148–52). The ambiguous conclusion resembles a musical coda (152–53). **Ewell 1994:** This is one of several stories by Chopin in which she seems to ignore the marketability of local color fiction (160). **Fusco 1994:** This is one of the first of many stories in which Chopin, like Maupassant, explores how materialistic impulses conflict with aesthetic values (149). **Goodwyn 1994:** This is one of several early stories by Chopin featuring elite characters with Eurocentric values that exclude the experiences of African-Americans (1). **Koloski 1994:** The story is included in soft-cover collections of Chopin's fiction published in 1970, 1976, and 1979 (27). **Saar 1994:** Although Paula appears to turn away from marriage, marriage seems her ultimate fate (69). **Weatherford 1994:** In this early story Chopin depicts a self-assured woman whose artistic aspirations seem to reflect her own. The story treats art as a sort of mandate imposed from above. The tale focuses on Paula's crisis of decision and shows how her loyalty to her own ambition is also loyalty to her parents' wishes for her. Because Paula possesses self-understanding, she is able to resist the temptation faced by many creative females (97–98). The story ultimately suggests that Paula must (and probably will) marry a man who understands her aspirations because he has similar goals for himself. In no later work did Chopin ever depict a creative woman who is as self-assured or successful as Paula, who seems to embody Chopin's hopes for her own career. Writing the story seems to have spurred her personal creativity. Her later work, however, shows a fuller awareness of the real complexities of a woman artist's position (99–100). **Camfield 1995:** This story reflects Chopin's deep interest in the philosophy of Arthur Schopenhauer, especially in its emphasis on the importance of art. The title suggests the heroine's unusual wisdom. The last name of Paula's mother suggests her extreme self-regard. Engfelder's name is also symbolic, as are the names of Dr. Sinn and Max Kunstler; all of them have German meanings. Although the diction and plot of the story sometimes seem predictable, Chopin includes some surprises. Like Schopenhauer, Chopin seems to link art to intense feelings (9–11). **Fetterley and Pryse 1995:** This was Chopin's first story to reach print (408). **Juneja 1995:** Here as elsewhere, Chopin depicts a woman who deliberately challenges custom (118). **Beer 1997:** Here as elsewhere, Chopin focuses on members of a social upper-crust influenced by continental values and lifestyles (24). The artist in this story has none of the social responsibilities possessed by the father in "A Very Fine Fiddle." She is therefore free to make a serious commitment to her art, whereas he does not have that option (85). **Toth and Seyersted 1998:** This story, Chopin's first to be published (130), is mentioned in her account books (138, 148, 155). Like some other works by her, this one features an attractive, needy female artist (272). **Ewell 1999:** Theme: maternity. **Green 1999:** Martha Cutter uses this tale to illustrate the suppression of feminine self-expression (22). **Toth 1999c:** Perhaps the character named "George" was inspired by Chopin's dead half-brother (26). The story may also have been influenced by an early experience in New Orleans (50). The story itself contradicts its opening claim (108). This work is one of several in which Chopin depicted a "new woman" (112). **Knights 2000:** This is one of various works in which Chopin shows a woman rejecting the limits of conventional marriage (xviii). Here as elsewhere Chopin mocks audiences who fail to appreciate art properly (xxiii). Here as elsewhere Chopin implies the uncertainties of existence (xxvi). This is one of various stories by Chopin that have been (and can be) read in widely divergent ways—either as endorsing or subverting conventions (xxvii–xxviii). This story takes on an added dimension when it is read in light of efforts in Chopin's society to suppress ethnic differences (xxxii).

"With the Violin"

Written: 1889. First published: 1890. Included in *Complete Works* **(1969).**

On Christmas Eve, Papa Konrad, a watch-mender, tells three children, Sophie, Grissel, and Ernst, about the man who is featured in the painting that hangs above his fireplace. Papa Konrad calls the man with the violin an angel because he kept a despairing man from committing suicide on Christmas Eve twelve years earlier.

Papa Konrad recalls that on that bitterly cold winter night, a destitute old man stopped at a jeweler's shop to inquire about a job—his last effort to find work in a city that was unfamiliar to him. The jeweler had no openings, so the man returned to his small, cold room at the top floor of a rickety apartment building. Unable to bear his loneliness and poverty any longer, the man was on the verge of killing himself with a poisonous powder when he heard an exquisite sound of music that stirred his emotions and enabled him to recall a happier time when he sat, a child, between his father and mother at the theater. The man thought that he had heard an angelic choir at first; he threw the poison into the fire, wept, and thanked God for speaking to him. When he arose, he discovered that the music was, in fact, coming from next door. The old man knocked gently on his neighbor's door. A young man with a violin, the same man portrayed in the picture above Papa Konrad's fireplace, opened the door, welcomed the stranger, and warmed and fed him by a cozy fire. That night the old man told the younger what had transpired, how his life had been spared, and the two were friends from that night forward.

When Papa Konrad finishes his story, the children conclude that the young man must have been rich, and they wonder if he now wears wings in heaven. Papa Konrad informs them that the "angel," who was generous even though poor himself, is still alive and is coming for Christmas dinner. When Sophie corrects him and says that it is Herr Ludwig, "the great leader of the opera," who is coming to the house for a "grand" dinner, Papa Konrad claims he forgets things in his old age. (JW)

***

Rankin 1932: This tale, composed in December 1889 (116), was published slightly more than a year later as a Christmas story for children. Childish curiosity and the impact of music are two of its themes, and its well-drawn German-American characters illustrate Chopin's talent for depicting persons other than simply Cajuns and Creoles (130). **Bonner 1982:** This is one of several stories by Chopin that are centered on Christmas (124). **Skaggs 1985:** This story was aimed at a broad audience (56). **Stepenoff 1987:** This minor early tale is typical of Chopin's apprentice writing in its imprecise setting and mawkish tone (455). **Toth 1990a:** This story, Chopin's first about Christmas and her first to focus on a child, was turned down several times before being accepted (181–83). **Ellis 1992:** This is one of various stories in which, as in *The Awakening*, a character is transformed partly through his or her encounter with music (216). **Ellis 1994:** This is one of several stories by Chopin that uses a three-part structure perhaps influenced by, and certainly similar to, the sonata form in music (147). **Goodwyn 1994:** This is one of several early stories by Chopin featuring elite characters with Eurocentric values that exclude the experiences of African-Americans (1). **Beer 1997:** Here as elsewhere, Chopin focuses on members of a social upper-crust influenced by continental values and lifestyles (24). **Toth and Seyersted 1998:** This story is mentioned in Chopin's account books (148, 158). **Toth 1999c:** This affirmative early tale was quickly accepted (124).

"A Wizard from Gettysburg"

Written: 1891. First published: 1892. Included in *Bayou Folk*.

Bertrand Delmandé, a fine, lively looking young boy about fourteen years old, is riding his pony home after hunting one April afternoon. He feels surprisingly high-spirited, even though he has just been ordered back from college because of financial troubles in his family. In fact his father and grandmother have driven to town that day on business about the matter. As he turns into the path leading to the plantation, his pony shies at something just under the bordering hedge. It looks like a bundle of rags, but as he rides closer Bertrand sees that it is a tramp sitting on a stone. He is no ordinary looking tramp, either. He is an old, feeble man with a long white beard who is leaning over, trying to stop the bleeding from a wound on his foot. Bertrand puts the man on his pony and leads him to the plantation house. All the way, the tramp babbles about Gettysburg and being shot in the head. Despite warnings from everyone he meets about taking in such a vagrant and despite predictions from the servants that silver will soon be missing, Bertrand takes the man to the veranda and seats him in his father's own rocking chair. Later, though, Bertrand's father, St. Ange Del-mandé, and his grandmother return and agree that the poor man should be given shelter. That night, Bertrand ponders the stories the old soldier has told about the horrors of Gettysburg. He had described how his head wound on the battlefield had given him a sad rebirth, taking his memory and leaving him with neither friend nor kindred, nor even a name.

The next morning, however, he is back in the chair on the ve-randa. While Mr. Delmandé and his mother discuss their situation, Bertrand brings coffee and food to his unfortunate guest, who asks Bertrand what they are saying, pointing inside. The boy says that their money problems will require them to economize for awhile, and that Bertrand will have to leave college. "No, no! St. Ange must go to school," the tramp exclaims. "Come. Don't let them hear you. Get a spade." Acting as if they are conspirators, he drags the boy down the steps and out into the middle of the orchard to a huge pecan tree. There he leans against a big knot then steps ten paces forward, turns to the right and steps off five more. Pointing down, he commands Bertrand to dig. Eventually the spade uncov-ers a tin box tied around with twine. The two carry their discovery into the dining room to Madame Delmandé and St. Ange and drop it on the table, shattering the box. Gold coins spill all over the table and onto the floor. "Here's money!" the old man exclaims. Like a wizard who has only posed as a tramp, he now commands Bertrand to hitch up the horse and go bring the judge, saying, "Tell him that Bertrand Delmandé needs him." At that, Madame Del-mandé recognizes this man as her husband come back from the dead. She asks, "Do you not know me—your wife?" The former stranger makes her a courtly bow and requests that she grant an old soldier and his two little children her gracious hospitality. **(CY)**

***

Rankin 1932: Chopin spends little time here depicting setting but instead emphasizes a quick, intriguing pace and powerful, convincing feelings, even though the tale is not entirely realistic (140). **Reilly 1942:** The con-cluding line of this story rescues the story from seeming commonplace (131). **Seyersted 1969a:** Although most Creoles in Chopin's fiction are fi-nancially comfortable, St. Ange Delmandé has lost his fortune during the war (77). **Peterson 1972:** Although this story was first published in a mag-azine apparently intended for young readers, the journal's actual audience was broader than its title might suggest (61). Here as elsewhere Chopin relies on amnesia to tell her story, and she also provides a very clear moral. The self-confident, self-assertive blacks provide the greatest interest

(63). **Rocks 1972:** Here as elsewhere Chopin shows how a transformation or new experience can be destructive (116). **Arner 1975:** Like several other stories set after the Civil War, this one uses mental disturbance symbolically. This tale, however, is badly damaged by its complacent ending. It comes close to suggesting the transforming experience of the war, but ultimately it falls short of doing so (44). **Bonner 1977:** This is one of several stories from *Bayou Folk* in which travel is a key device of plot (8). Here and elsewhere in Chopin, mental illness is a major theme (10). **Skaggs 1985:** This is one of several stories featuring characters whose lives and minds have been disrupted by the Civil War (16). **Toth 1990a:** This was one of several stories by Chopin mentioning the Civil War (70). It first appeared in a young person's magazine and focuses on a veteran's delayed return to Louisiana. It is one of several takes from 1891 in which Chopin sought a friendly, interested readership (201–2). **Thomas 1992:** This story was one of three works that may have been written over three days in 1901 (53–54). **Ewell 1994:** Of the nearly ten stories Chopin wrote early in 1891, this was one of only three to be immediately accepted for publication (160). **Koloski 1996:** Here as elsewhere, Chopin focuses on vagrant recollection (71). This was one of her many stories for children (87). **Wagner-Martin 1996:** Although this story is a bit hackneyed, its appealingly altruistic young male makes it worth reading (202). Here as elsewhere Chopin also shows the important roles children often play in adult lives (204). **Toth and Seyersted 1998:** This story is mentioned in Chopin's account books (139, 148, 171). **Benfey 1999:** Here as elsewhere in her stories about the Civil War, Chopin focuses on the figures who either don't come home or come home transformed. The tale links the themes of revival and discovery, but its attitude toward the war and its aftermath is sardonic (231–33). Here as in "La Belle Zoraïde," the returning figure is misperceived (238). **Koloski 1999:** This is one of many stories by Chopin which either feature children or were written for them (xxii). Here as elsewhere she describes children's' responses to poverty (xxiii). **Toth 1999c:** This is one of various tales in which Chopin describes the melancholy consequences of the Civil War (32).

"The Wood Choppers"

Written: 1901. First published: 1902. Included in *Complete Works* (1969).

Léontine, a schoolteacher in bayou country, dismisses her four pupils early on a particularly rainy day. She sloshes through the heavy rain to her "poor little bit of a Southern house," and, upon her arrival, she finds her old mother, who is called "madame," and Mandy, a black girl, scraping together the remaining embers of a fire. Léontine, speaking French, scolds her mother for not having a fire on such an inclement day. In her defense, madame explains that there is no wood cut: "none, none, none." Léontine asks why Peter, the woodcutter, did not come today. Madame answers that Peter is working at Aaron's store, hauling freight, and his substitute, François, did not show up. Mandy further explains that François refused to come simply because his Uncle Peter told him to do so.

Upon hearing this, Léontine dons her rain gear once again and heads to the woodpile in spite of madame's questioning pleas about Léontine's sanity. True to her "spunky" nature (a term applied to her by the locals), Léontine sets to work with the "stout, sharp ax." However, her ax blows are inaccurate, and she makes little progress.

While she works, a stranger pulls up in a mule-drawn wagon and reproves her for chopping wood. He asks first whether the local men are Indians since they "let the women chop wood." He also asks whether there is a "black fellow" in the area who can chop wood for her. He tells Léontine that she ought to be ashamed of herself and to go inside. Léontine argues her situation with the "eccentric, perhaps insane" stranger, but she finally relents and goes inside. In going to her room to change out of her drenched clothing, she instructs madame to lock the door because the stranger may murder them.

Madame and Mandy, however, recognize the stranger as the young man who bought "the Slocum place and everything on it." The stranger soon has a large pile of wood cut and brings it into the gallery of the house, where he introduces himself as Willet, who recently bought the Slocum place. Professing to be neighborly, Willet offers to start a fire for the women. Because they are out of kindling, he brings some in from his buggy and makes a "glorious blaze" in the fireplace, despite Léontine's acerbic attitude toward him. Once the fire is established, Willet says good-bye and requests that Léontine not be allowed to chop any more wood: "In the first place, she doesn't know how, and in the second place— she doesn't know how." He starts his mules off at a fast trot while madame praises his gentlemanly nature and Léontine looks after him in "a blaze of indignation."

From then on, Willet leaves a gift of food—fruit or game—at Léontine's house almost every day. His courtship, supported by madame, becomes more overt, and Léontine softens when he arrives with a book and some magazines. Despite her mother's subtle references to Willet's noble character and good looks, Léontine seems to see Willet only as a troublemaker, who will one day bring a snobbish wife to live on his plantation.

On another rainy day, madame sees Willet's buggy pull up at the house and Léontine disembark. When they come into the house, Willet surprises madame—and Mandy especially—by throwing his arms around her, kissing her, and calling her mother.

Léontine and Willet marry in the following spring, and he lays claim to only one of her possessions—"the heavy old ax." He takes it away in a sort of triumph, proclaiming that it will have a place of honor in his house as long as he lives. **(EP)**

***

Seyersted 1969a: The compliant heroine of this story, one of Chopin's last, contrasts strongly with the self-assertive Paula of an early work, "Wiser Than a God" (185). **Peterson 1972:** This predictable tale for the young lacks complexity. One almost wonders whether Chopin was mocking the genre, but the story itself provides no evidence for such a reading (265–67). **Berggren 1977:** The conventional behavior of the heroine of this story for young people suggests that Chopin became less daring after writing *The Awakening* (1). **Dyer 1981a:** Gouvernail, a skeptical character present in some of Chopin's earlier work, would be inappropriate in this story (55). **Dyer 1984:** Here as in other late tales, Chopin uses imagery much less effectively than she had earlier. Storm imagery, for example, is used much more effectively in "The Storm" and in "Vagabonds" (189–90). **Toth 1990a:** This work, one of Chopin's final tales, was published in a national magazine for youth (386). **Ewell 1994:** This is one of various late works in which Chopin pulls back from the unconventional, perhaps in reaction to the poor reception of *The Awakening* (169–70). **Koloski 1996:** This is one of several children's stories by Chopin that depict the poor (71; 87). **Toth and Seyersted 1998:** This story is mentioned in Chopin's account books (142, 147, 151). **Toth 1999c:** This was one of a trio of tales for young people that Chopin composed in a three-day burst of productivity (235).

Appendix 1

"Caline"

by Kate Chopin

[1] The sun was just far enough in the west to send inviting shadows. In the center of a small field, and in the shade of a haystack which was there, a girl lay sleeping. She had slept long and soundly, when something awoke her as suddenly as if it had been a blow. She opened her eyes and stared a moment up in the cloudless sky. She yawned and stretched her long brown legs and arms, lazily. Then she arose, never minding the bits of straw that clung to her black hair, to her red bodice, and the blue cotonade skirt that did not reach her naked ankles.

[2] The log cabin in which she dwelt with her parents was just outside the enclosure in which she had been sleeping. Beyond was a small clearing that did duty as a cotton field. All else was dense wood, except the long stretch that curved round the brow of the hill, and in which glittered the steel rails of the Texas and Pacific road.

[3] When Caline emerged from the shadow she saw a long train of passenger coaches standing in view, where they must have stopped abruptly. It was that sudden stopping which had awakened her; for such a thing had not happened before within her recollection, and she looked stupid, at first, with astonishment. There seemed to be something wrong with the engine; and some of the passengers who dismounted went forward to investigate the trouble. Others came strolling along in the direction of the cabin, where Caline stood under an old gnarled mulberry tree, staring. Her father had halted his mule at the end of the cotton row, and stood staring also, leaning upon his plow.

[4] There were ladies in the party. They walked awkwardly in their high-heeled boots over the rough, uneven ground, and held up their skirts mincingly. They twirled parasols over their shoulders, and laughed immoderately at the funny things which their masculine companions were saying.

[5] They tried to talk to Caline, but could not understand the French patois with which she answered them.

[6] One of the men—a pleasant-faced youngster—drew a sketch book from his pocket and began to make a picture of the girl. She stayed motionless, her hands behind her, and her wide eyes fixed earnestly upon him.

[7] Before he had finished there was a summons from the train; and all went scampering hurriedly away. The engine screeched, it sent a few lazy puffs into the still air, and in another moment or two had vanished, bearing its human cargo with it.

[8] Caline could not feel the same after that. She looked with new and strange interest upon the trains of cars that passed so swiftly back and forth across her vision, each day; and wondered whence these people came, and whither they were going.

[9] Her mother and father could not tell her, except to say that they came from "loin là bas," and were going "Djieu sait é où."

[10] One day she walked miles down the track to talk with the old flagman, who stayed down there by the big water tank. Yes, he knew. Those people came from the great cities in the north, and were going to the city in the south. He knew all about the city; it was a grand place. He had lived there once. His sister lived there now; and she would be glad enough to have so fine a girl as Caline to help her cook and scrub, and tend the babies. And he thought Caline might earn as much as five dollars a month, in the city.

[11] So she went; in a new cotonade, and her Sunday shoes; with a sacredly guarded scrawl that the flagman sent to his sister.

[12] The woman lived in a tiny, stuccoed house, with green blinds, and three wooden steps leading down to the banquette. There seemed to be hundreds like it along the street. Over the

house tops loomed the tall masts of ships, and the hum of the French market could be heard on a still morning.

[13] Caline was at first bewildered. She had to readjust all her preconceptions to fit the reality of it. The flagman's sister was a kind and gentle task-mistress. At the end of a week or two she wanted to know how the girl liked it all. Caline liked it very well, for it was pleasant, on Sunday afternoons, to stroll with the children under the great, solemn sugar sheds; or to sit upon the compressed cotton bales, watching the stately steamers, the graceful boats, and noisy little tugs that plied the waters of the Mississippi. And it filled her with agreeable excitement to go to the French market, where the handsome Gascon butchers were eager to present their compliments and little Sunday bouquets to the pretty Acadian girl; and to throw fistfuls of *lagniappe* into her basket.

[14] When the woman asked her again after another week if she were still pleased, she was not so sure. And again when she questioned Caline the girl turned away, and went to sit behind the big, yellow cistern, to cry unobserved. For she knew now that it was not the great city and its crowds of people she had so eagerly sought; but the pleasant-faced boy, who had made her picture that day under the mulberry tree.

Appendix 2

"La Belle Zoraïde"

by Kate Chopin

[1] The summer night was hot and still; not a ripple of air swept over the *marais* [marsh]. Yonder, across Bayou St. John, lights twinkled here and there in the darkness, and in the dark sky above a few stars were blinking. A lugger that had come out of the lake was moving with slow, lazy motion down the bayou. A man in the boat was singing a song.

[2] The notes of the song came faintly to the ears of old Manna-Loulou, herself as black as the night, who had gone out upon the gallery to open the shutters wide.

[3] Something in the refrain reminded the woman of an old, half-forgotten Creole romance, and she began to sing it low to herself while she threw the shutters open:—

[4]   "Lisett' to kité la plaine,
          Mo perdi bonhair à moué;
          Ziés à moué semblé fontaine,
          Dépi mo pa miré toué."

          [Lizette, {since} you have left the plain
          I have lost my happiness;
          My eyes are like a fountain,
          Since I cannot look at you.]

[5] And then this old song, a lover's lament for the loss of his mistress, floating into her memory, brought with it the story she would tell to Madame, who lay in her sumptuous mahogany bed,

waiting to be fanned and put to sleep to the sound of one of Manna-Loulou's stories.

[6] The old negress had already bathed her mistress's pretty white feet and kissed them lovingly, one, then the other. She had brushed her mistress's beautiful hair, that was as soft and shining as satin, and was the color of Madame's wedding-ring. Now, when she reentered the room, she moved softly toward the bed, and seating herself there began gently to fan Madame Delisle.

[7] Manna-Loulou was not always ready with her story, for Madame would hear none but those that were true. But tonight the story was all there in Manna-Loulou's head—the story of la belle Zoraïde—and she told it to her mistress in the soft Creole patois whose music and charm no English words can convey.

[8] "La belle Zoraïde had eyes that were so dusky, so beautiful, that any man who gazed too long into their depths was sure to lose his head, and even his heart sometimes. Her soft, smooth skin was the color of *café-au-lait*. As for her elegant manners, her *svelte* and graceful figure, they were the envy of half the ladies who visited her mistress, Madame Delarivière.

[9] "No wonder Zoraïde was as charming and as dainty as the finest lady of la rue Royale: from a toddling thing she had been brought up at her mistress's side; her fingers had never done rougher work than sewing a fine muslin seam; and she even had her own little black servant to wait upon her. Madame, who was her godmother as well as her mistress, would often say to her:—

[10] "'Remember, Zoraïde, when you are ready to marry, it must be in a way to do honor to your bringing up.

[11] "It will be at the Cathedral. Your wedding gown, your *corbeille* [hope chest], all will be of the best; I shall see to that myself. You know, M'sieur Ambroise is ready whenever you say the word, and his master is willing to do as much for him as I shall do for you. It is a union that will please me in every way.'

[12] "Monsieur Ambroise was then the body servant of Doctor Langlé. La belle Zoraïde detested the little mulatto, with his shining whiskers like a white man's, and his small eyes, that were

cruel and false as a snake's. She would cast down her own mischievous eyes, and say:—

[13] "'Ah, nénaine [Godmother], I am so happy, so contented here at your side just as I am. I don't want to marry now; next year, perhaps, or the next.' And Madame would smile indulgently and remind Zoraïde that a woman's charms are not everlasting.

[14] "But the truth of the matter was, Zoraïde had seen le beau Mézor dance the Bamboula in Congo Square. That was a sight to hold one rooted to the ground. Mézor was as straight as a cypress tree and as proud looking as a king. His body, bare to the waist, was like a column of ebony and it glistened like oil.

[15] "Poor Zoraïde's heart grew sick in her bosom with love for le beau Mézor from the moment that she saw the fierce gleam of his eye, lighted by the inspiring strains of the Bamboula, and beheld the stately movements of his splendid body swaying and quivering through the figures of the dance.

[16] "But when she knew him later, and he came near to her to speak with her, all the fierceness was gone out of his eyes, and she saw only kindness in them and heard only gentleness in his voice, for love had taken possession of him also, and Zoraïde was more distracted than ever. When Mézor was not dancing Bamboula in Congo Square, he was hoeing sugar cane, barefooted and half-naked, in his master's field outside of the city. Doctor Langlé was his master as well as M'sieur Ambroise's.

[17] "One day, when Zoraïde kneeled before her mistress, drawing on Madame's silken stockings, that were of the finest, she said:
"'Nénaine, you have spoken to me often of marrying. Now, at last, I have chosen a husband, but it is not M'sieur Ambroise, it is le beau Mézor that I want and no other.' And Zoraïde hid her face in her hands when she said that, for she guessed, rightly enough, that her mistress would be very angry.

[18] "And indeed, Madame Delarivière was at first speechless with rage. When she finally spoke it was only to gasp out, exasperated:—

"'That negro! that negro! Bon Dieu Seigneur [Good Lord God], but this is too much!'

[19] "'Am I white, nénaine?' pleaded Zoraïde.

"'You white! *Malheureuse!* [Miserable one!] You deserve to have the lash laid upon you like any other slave; you have proven yourself no better than the worst.'

"'I am not white,' persisted Zoraïde, respectfully and gently. 'Doctor Langlé gives me his slave to marry, but he would not give me his son. Then, since I am not white, let me have from out of my own race the one whom my heart has chosen.'

[20] "However, you may well believe that Madame would not hear to that. Zoraïde was forbidden to speak to Mézor, and Mézor was cautioned against seeing Zoraïde again. But you know how the negroes are, Ma'zélle Titite," added Manna-Loulou, smiling a little sadly. "There is no mistress, no master, no king nor priest who can hinder them from loving when they will. And these two found ways and means.

[21] "When months had passed by, Zoraïde, who had grown unlike herself—sober and preoccupied—said again to her mistress:—

"'Nénaine, you would not let me have Mézor for my husband; but I have disobeyed you, I have sinned. Kill me if you wish, nénaine; forgive me if you will; but when I heard le beau Mézor say to me, "Zoraïde, mo l'aime toi [I love you]," I could have died, but I could not have helped loving him.'

[22] "This time Madame Delarivière was so actually pained, so wounded at hearing Zoraïde's confession, that there was no place left in her heart for anger. She could only utter confused reproaches. But she was a woman of action rather than of words, and she acted promptly. Her first step was to induce Doctor Langlé to sell Mézor.

[23] Doctor Langlé, who was a widower, had long wanted to marry Madame Delarivière, and he would willingly have walked on all fours at noon through the Place d'Armes if she wanted him to. Naturally he lost no time in disposing of le beau Mézor, who was sold away into Georgia, or the Carolinas, or one of those distant countries far away, where he could no longer hear his Creole

tongue spoken, nor dance Calinda, nor hold la belle Zoraïde in his arms.

[24] "The poor thing was heartbroken when Mézor was sent away from her, but she took comfort and hope in the thought of her baby that she would soon be able to clasp to her breast.

"La belle Zoraïde's sorrows had now begun in earnest. Not only sorrows but sufferings, and with the anguish of maternity came the shadow of death. But there is no agony that a mother will not forget when she holds her first-born to her heart, and presses her lips upon the baby flesh that is her own, yet far more precious than her own.

[25] "So, instinctively, when Zoraïde came out of the awful shadow she gazed questioningly about her and felt with her trembling hands upon either side of her. 'Où li, mo piti a moin? (Where is my little one?)' she asked imploringly. Madame who was there and the nurse who was there both told her in turn, 'To piti à toi, li mouri' ('Your little one is dead'), which was a wicked falsehood that must have caused the angels in heaven to weep. For the baby was living and well and strong. It had been at once removed from its mother's side, to be sent away to Madame's plantation, far up the coast. Zoraïde could only moan in reply, 'Li mouri, li mouri,' and she turned her face to the wall.

[26] "Madame had hoped, in thus depriving Zoraïde of her child, to have her young waiting-maid again at her side free, happy, and beautiful as of old. But there was a more powerful will than Madame's at work—the will of the good God, who had already designed that Zoraïde should grieve with a sorrow that was never more to be lifted in this world.

[27] "La belle Zoraïde was no more. In her stead was a sad-eyed woman who mourned night and day for her baby. 'Li mouri, li mouri,' she would sigh over and over again to those about her, and to herself when others grew weary of her complaint.

"Yet, in spite of all, M'sieur Ambroise was still in the notion to marry her. A sad wife or a merry one was all the same to him so long as that wife was Zoraïde. And she seemed to consent, or rather to submit, to the approaching marriage as though nothing mattered any longer in this world.

[28] "One day, a black servant entered a little noisily the room in which Zoraïde sat sewing. With a look of strange and vacuous happiness upon her face, Zoraïde arose hastily. 'Hush, hush,' she whispered, lifting a warning finger, 'my little one is asleep; you must not awaken her.'

"Upon the bed was a senseless bundle of rags shaped like an infant in swaddling clothes. Over this dummy the woman had drawn the mosquito bar, and she was sitting contentedly beside it. In short, from that day Zoraïde was demented. Night nor day did she lose sight of the doll that lay in her bed or in her arms.

[29] "And now was Madame stung with sorrow and remorse at seeing this terrible affliction that had befallen her dear Zoraïde. Consulting with Doctor Langlé, they decided to bring back to the mother the real baby of flesh and blood that was now toddling about, and kicking its heels in the dust yonder upon the plantation.

[30] "It was Madame herself who led the pretty, tiny little 'griffe' girl to her mother. Zoraïde was sitting on a stone bench in the courtyard, listening to the soft splashing of the fountain, and watching the fitful shadows of the palm leaves upon the broad, white flagging.

[31] "'Here,' said Madame, approaching, 'here, my poor dear Zoraïde, is your own little child. Keep her; she is yours. No one will ever take her from you again.'

"Zoraïde looked with sullen suspicion upon her mistress and the child before her. Reaching out a hand she thrust the little one mistrustfully away from her. With the other hand she clasped the rag bundle fiercely to her breast; for she suspected a plot to deprive her of it.

[32] "Nor could she ever be induced to let her own child approach her; and finally the little one was sent back to the plantation, where she was never to know the love of mother or father.

[33] "And now this is the end of Zoraïde's story. She was never known again as la belle Zoraïde, but ever after as Zoraïde la folle, whom no one ever wanted to marry—not even M'sieur Ambroise. She lived to be an old woman, whom some people pitied

and others laughed at—always clasping at her bundle of rags—her 'piti.'

[34] "Are you asleep, Ma'zélle Titite?"

"No, I am not asleep; I was thinking. Ah, the poor little one, Man Loulou, the poor little one! better had she died!"

[35] But this is the way Madame Delisle and Manna-Loulou really talked to each other:—

"Vou pré droumi, Ma'zélle Titite?"

"Non, pa pré droumi; mo yapré zongler. Ah, la pauv' piti, Man Loulou. La pauv' piti! Mieux li mouri!"

Appendix 3

The Riches of the Text:
Kate Chopin's "Caline" and "La Belle Zoraïde"
and an Experiment in Pluralist Criticism

Robert C. Evans

Any reading of any work depends on theoretical assumptions, but relatively few readers are consciously aware of the interpretive ideas they assume or take for granted. One purpose of literary study is to make those assumptions self-conscious, so that they can be carefully examined and can then be either freely embraced, ultimately rejected, or deliberately combined. By being self-consciously aware not only of one's own assumptions but also of the often contrasting and conflicting assumptions made by others, one can deeply enrich the reading of any literary work. Different interpretive approaches function, in a sense, as "equipment for readings"—equipment that gives one a huge range of questions to consider as one moves through a text. When read with such questions in mind and with close attention to their minute details, even the briefest texts yield fascinating insights into the craftsmanship and conundrums that comprise any accomplished text.

One purpose of this and the following appendices is to use Kate Chopin's short stories "Caline" and "La Belle Zoraïde" as means of testing the claims just made. "Caline" is still a relatively unknown story by Chopin, whereas "La Belle Zoraïde" is increasingly recognized as one of her best works. Nevertheless, neither story has yet received the same kind of sustained, probing attention that has been accorded to such other works as "Désirée's Baby," "Athénaïse," "The Storm," or even "The Story of an Hour." Students almost always find both stories (especially "Zoraïde") compelling and memorable, and for the past several years both have been the subject of sustained, intensive discussion in a wide variety of classes I have taught. These classes have included a broad spectrum of kinds of readers, from beginning freshmen to advanced graduate students, from business majors to English majors, from people in their late teens to people in their mid-seventies. Sometimes these students have had a sophisticated grasp of literary theories; sometimes they have been vaguely familiar with standard ways of reading; sometimes they have relied simply on good, old-fashioned "common sense."

Over the years I have solicited their written responses or recorded their in-class reactions to both stories. The results are the commentaries reproduced in the following appendices—commentaries that not only provide, perhaps, the richest, most detailed response ever offered to these particular works but that also offer (I hope) models of a kind of interactive, dialogic, pluralistic interpretive procedure that does its best to avoid the reductivism often inherent in even the best literary criticism. The numerous ideas and insights produced by the kind of on-going dialogue recorded below often conflict with one another, but that, I think, is part of their value: the chief purpose of the present experiment in criticism is not so much to provide answers as to stimulate questions. The goal is not to proscribe further thought but precisely to provoke it. By offering sometimes clashing perspectives, the commentaries reproduced in the following pages implicitly invite each reader to choose *which* interpretations, if any, make most sense—or to offer his or her own readings of a word, phrase, or passage.

At the same time, one of the most striking results of the following experiments is how often the insights of different kinds of readers, asking different kinds of questions and providing different kinds of answers, can peacefully coexist. Different responses need not inevitably *conflict*; instead, they can supplement, complement, augment, and reinforce one another. This is a comforting thought: literary criticism may not, after all, be a pointless battle of divergent, self-enclosed perspectives. Intelligent conversation may be possible; one person may actually be able to learn and profit from another's insights. The result of our dialogues need not be a meaningless cacophony of competing claims but a fuller, more detailed, more appreciative understanding of some of the most subtle, most searching, most accomplished examples of human creativity.

***

Although explicit familiarity with literary theory is not necessary to read and understand the following commentaries on "Caline" and "La Belle Zoraïde," a quick review may nonetheless help. One of the best ways of grasping any theory is still the approach outlined long ago by M.H. Abrams. In the introduction to his classic study *The Mirror and the Lamp*, Abrams argued that any literary theory that tries to be complete must account for four basic aspects of literature: the author, the text, the audience, and the universe (or "reality"). Abrams' list can be usefully supplemented by adding a fifth category: the role or function of the critic herself. Any reasonably well developed theory, in other words, will be a theory about *all* these factors and the relations among them.[1] The assumptions a theorist makes about the author, for example, will inevitably affect (and be affected by) the assumptions he makes about the text, the audience, "reality" and the purposes of criticism. Indeed, Abrams argues that each theory will tend to emphasize one of these aspects as crucial or most important.

Plato, for instance, tends to emphasize the importance of accurately understanding reality, and his entire theory of literature seems affected by this central emphasis. He thus assumes that because neither the author nor the literary text can provide such understanding, and because most members of the audience do not seek it, literature has little value. Plato's views of the critic derive directly from this conclusion: the critic functions as a kind of philosophical traffic cop, admitting certain "useful" kinds of literature to the republic but banishing the rest.

The assumptions underlying some of the most prominent theoretical approaches are summarized briefly in the following list. The key aspect of literature emphasized by each kind of criticism is italicized. These are, of course, by no means the *only* interpretive approaches worth considering; they are merely the ones that have been, either traditionally or recently, the most prominent.

---

[1]For a much more detailed explanation and defense of the ideas mentioned here and in the following paragraphs, see my "Introduction" to Robert C. Evans, Anne C. Little, and Barbara Wiedemann, *Short Fiction: A Critical Companion* (West Cornwall, CT: Locust Hill Press, 1997), xv–lxxvi. This book also contains detailed and diverse student responses to another of Chopin's fictions—"The Story of an Hour" (271–95).

PLATONIC CRITICISM: Because Plato prizes an accurate, objective understanding of *reality*, he sees "creative" writers and "literary" texts as potential distractions since they may lead the already-emotional audience to neglect proper pursuit of philosophical truth, which the critic should seek, explain, and defend by using logic and reason.

ARISTOTELIAN CRITICISM: Because Aristotle values the *text* as a highly crafted complex unity, he tends to see the author as a craftsman, the audience as capable of appreciating such craftsmanship, the text as a potentially valuable means of understanding the complexity of "reality," and the critic as a specialist conversant with all aspects of the poetic craft.

HORATIAN CRITICISM: Because Horace emphasizes the need to satisfy a diverse *audience*, he tends to see the author as attempting to please and/or teach them, the text as embodying principles of custom and moderation (so as to please the widest possible audience), "reality" as understood in traditional or conventional terms, and the critic as a fatherly advisor who tries to prevent the author from making a fool of himself.

LONGINIAN CRITICISM: Because "Longinus" (whose real identity is unknown) stresses the ideally lofty nature of the sublime (i.e., elevated) *author*, he tends to view the text as an expression of the author's power, the audience as desiring the ecstasy a great author can induce, social "reality" as rooted in a basic human nature that everywhere and always has a yearning for elevation, and the critic as (among other things) a moral and spiritual advisor who encourages the highest aspirations of readers and writers alike.

TRADITIONAL HISTORICAL CRITICISM: Because traditional historical critics tend to emphasize the ways social *realities* influence the writer, the writer's creation of a text, and audience's reactions to it, they stress the critic's obligation to study the past as thoroughly and objectively as possible to determine how the text might have been understood by its original readers.

THEMATIC CRITICISM: Because thematic critics stress the importance of ideas in shaping social and psychological *reality*, they generally look for the ways those ideas are expressed by (and affect) the texts that writers create. They assume that audiences turn to texts for enlightenment as well as entertainment and that writers either express the same basic ideas repeatedly or that the evolution of their thinking can be traced in different works.

FORMALISM: Because formalists value the *text* as a complex unity in which all the parts contribute to a rich and resonant effect, they usually offer highly detailed ("close") readings intended to show how the work achieves a powerful, compelling artistic form. Formalist critics help audiences appreciate how a work's subtle nuances contribute to its total effect.

PSYCHOANALYTIC CRITICISM: Freudian or psychoanalytic critics emphasize the key role of the human mind in perceiving and shaping *reality* and believe that the minds of writers, audiences, and critics are highly complex and often highly conflicted (especially in sexual terms, and particularly in terms of the moralistic "super-ego," the rational ego, and the irrational "id"). They contend that such complexity inevitably affects the ways texts are written and read. The critic, therefore, should analyze how psychological patterns affect the ways in which texts are created and received.

ARCHETYPAL OR "MYTH" CRITICISM: Because archetypal critics believe that humans experience *reality* in terms of certain basic fears, desires, images (symbols), and stories (myths), they assume that writers will inevitably employ such patterns; that audiences will react to them forcefully and almost automatically; and that critics should therefore study the ways such patterns affect writers, texts, and readers.

MARXIST CRITICISM: Because Marxist critics assume that conflicts between economic classes inevitably shape social *reality*, they emphasize the ways these struggles affect writers, audiences, and texts. They assume that literature will either reflect, reinforce, or undermine (or some combination of these) the dominant ideologies (i.e., standard patterns of thought) that help structure social relations. Marxist critics study the complex relations between literature and society, ideally seeking to promote social progress.

STRUCTURALIST CRITICISM: Because structuralist critics assume that humans structure (or make sense of) *reality* by imposing patterns of meaning on it, and because they assume that these structures can only be interpreted in terms of the codes the structures embody, they believe that writers will inevitably rely on such codes to create meaning, that texts will inevitably embody such codes, and that audiences will inevitably use such codes to interpret texts. To understand a text, the critic must be familiar with the systematic codes that shape it; he must master the system(s) the text implies.

FEMINIST CRITICISM: Because feminist critics assume that our experience of *reality* is inevitably affected by categories of sex and gender (such as divisions between male and female, heterosexual and homosexual, etc.), and because they assume that (heterosexual) males have long enjoyed dominant social power, they believe that writers, texts, and audience will all be affected (usually negatively) by "patriarchal" forces. The critic's job will be to study (and even attempt to counter-act) the impact of patriarchy.

DECONSTRUCTION: Because deconstructive critics assume that *"reality"* cannot be experienced except through language, and because they believe that language is inevitably full of contradictions, gaps, and dead-ends, they believe that no writer, text, audience, or critic can ever escape from the unsolvable paradoxes embedded in language. Deconstruction therefore undercuts the hierarchical assumptions of any other critical system (such as structuralism, formalism, Marxism, etc.) that claims to offer an "objective," "neutral," or "scientific" perspective on literature.

READER-RESPONSE CRITICISM: Because reader-response critics assume that literary texts are inevitably interpreted by individual members of the *audience* and that these individuals react to texts in ways that are sometimes shared, sometimes highly personal, and sometimes both at once, they believe that writers exert much less control over texts than we sometimes suppose, and that critics must never ignore the crucial role of audience response(s).

DIALOGICAL CRITICISM: Because dialogical critics assume that the (worthy) *text* almost inevitably embodies divergent points of view, they believe that elements within a text engage in a constant dialogue or give-and-take with other elements, both within and outside the text itself. The writer, too, is almost inevitably engaged in a complex dialogue, through the text, with his potential audience(s), and the sensitive critic must be alert to the multitude of voices or tones a text expresses or implies.

NEW HISTORICISM: Because new historicist critics assume that our experience of *reality* is inevitably social, and because they emphasize the way systems of power and domination both provoke and control social conflicts, they tend to see a culture not as a single coherent entity but as a site of struggle, negotiation, or the constant exchange of energy. New historicists contend that no text, audience, or critic can stand apart from contemporary (i.e., both past and present) dynamics of power.

MULTICULTURAL CRITICISM: Because multicultural critics emphasize the numerous differences that both shape and divide social *reality*, they tend to see all people (including writers, readers, and critics) as members of sometimes divergent, sometimes overlapping groups. These groups, whether relatively fluid or relatively stable, can include such categories as races, sexes, genders, ages, and classes, and the critic should explore how such differences affect how literature is both written and read.

POSTMODERNISM: Postmodernists are highly skeptical of large-scale claims to objective "truths" and thus doubt the validity of grand explanations. They see such claims as attempts to impose order on a *reality* that is, almost by definition, too shifting or fluid to be pinned down. Postmodernists assume that if writers, readers, and audiences abandoned their yearning for such order, they would more easily accept and enjoy the inevitable paradoxes and contradictions of life and art. The postmodern critic will look for (and value) any indications of a text's instabilities.

PLURALISM: Pluralism assumes that each critical approach, by asking different kinds of questions about literature, will provide different kinds of answers and that each kind of answer is at least potentially valuable in its own right. Pluralism does not attempt to harmonize competing ways of thinking, nor does it radically doubt the validity of all ways of thought. Rather, it emphasizes the potential value of a variety of approaches to literary texts.

Appendix 4

Kate Chopin's "Caline":

General Comments from Diverse Critical Perspectives

Kimberly Barron and Deborah Hill

The following comments attempt to suggest, in general terms, how particular kinds of critics *might* respond to "Caline," given the basic assumptions that different kinds of critics tend to take for granted about literature. No claim is made that these comments represent the *only* ways a given critic might react; rather, the comments merely indicate how such critics *could* plausibly respond. For fuller explanations of the critical approaches mentioned here, see the preceding appendix.[1] Numbers in brackets refer to the numbered paragraphs in the text of the story included as Appendix 1 to this volume. (RCE)

PLATONIC CRITICISM: Because a PLATONIC critic is absorbed in searching for philosophical truth and an accurate understanding of reality, he might condemn this story for its *relative* triviality, since it deceives the reader by offering frivolous descriptions and transient emotions as worthy imitations of reality. For example, Caline's body is presented in considerable detail as she is described as having "yawned and stretched her long brown legs and arms, lazily," and again as she "arose, never minding the bits of straw that clung to her black hair, to her red bodice, and the blue cotonade skirt that did not reach her naked ankles" [1]. Plato might consider this description merely an artist's impressionistic conception

---

[1]See also the "Introduction" to Robert C. Evans, Anne C. Little, and Barbara Wiedemann, *Short Fiction: A Critical Companion* (West Cornwall, CT: Locust Hill Press, 1997), xv–lxxvi.

of reality—a conception that distracts the reader from the pursuit of genuine truth. Also, a PLATONIC critic might have misgivings about this narrative since Caline's emotions, which are relatively trifling in relation to the universal truths of life, are presented as the central focus of the story. For instance, once the train leaves, taking with it her first glimpse of culture and wealth, Caline "could not feel the same after that" [8], and a PLATONIST might note that she cries in sentimental hopelessness when she finally realizes that her desire in going to the city was to meet again "the pleasant-faced boy, who had made her picture that day under the mulberry tree" [14]. Thus, because this story is merely an artistic portrayal of one young girl's emotional experience and fails to teach any universally valuable lesson regarding truth or reality, a PLATONIC critic would probably find little to commend in this tale (DH).

ARISTOTELIAN CRITICISM: Because an ARISTOTELIAN critic is interested in the artistic unity of a literary text and in how it illuminates human nature, he would commend Kate Chopin for her skill in arranging the clutter of Caline's experiences and emotions to create a vivid, unified work of art. For example, the story begins by reporting that something awakened Caline from slumber "as suddenly as if it had been a blow" [1], and it ends by noting the sudden awakening of her heart as she encounters the pleasure and pain of love. An ARISTOTELIAN critic would appreciate the artistic craft demonstrated by this kind of implied connection. However, not only is Caline awakened physically and emotionally, but she is also awakened mentally as she observes the finely-dressed, sophisticated men and women from the train and then later experiences life in the city. An ARISTOTELIAN critic would appreciate and seek to reveal to other readers the significance of Caline's awakening and the unity this theme helps give to this story (DH).

HORATIAN CRITICISM: Because a HORATIAN critic is interested in how effectively a writer satisfies the myriad tastes of a wide audience, he might possibly reproach Chopin for limiting her talent to a very slight range of interests. For instance, most young boys who are attracted to adventure and excitement might find the subject of a girl's emotions very dull. Religious men or women who value literature for its didactic qualities might disapprove because this story contains no effective moral, nor does it provide any obvious instruction. Many young women fascinated by romantic affairs might find the story disappointing in that Caline never meets the pleasant-faced boy again, and her love remains unfulfilled. A child unaware of love's misery might miss the pathos of Caline's experience, while an older man or woman whose heart has suffered countless such losses might find the tale relatively insignificant. Although a more selective audience could appreciate the story for its artistry, the wider majority might choose other stories for entertainment or instruction. Therefore, a HORATIAN critic might advise Chopin to concentrate her talent in gratifying her audience's diverse expectations (DH).

LONGINIAN CRITICISM: Because a LONGINIAN critic is interested in truly sublime (i.e., uplifting) works of art that are capable of elevating readers to heights of spiritual ecstasy and inspiring them to pursue nobler lives, such a critic might consider this story picayune, even vain. Although Chopin chooses each word with marvelous detail, her simple, straightforward style might seem to lack the lofty sublimity a LONGINIAN critic admires. Her descriptions of Caline, for example, present us with no lofty ideals or nobleness of character, only a young country girl slowly losing her naivete. Readers may admire her unaffected beauty or sympathize with her hopelessness, but her experiences do not inspire spiritual or mental exultation. Thus, a LONGINIAN critic might consider this story ineffective in achieving what should be the goal of all literature, namely to inspire the reader's desire for spiritual and ethical perfection (DH).

TRADITIONAL HISTORICAL CRITICISM: Because a TRADITIONAL HISTORICAL critic is interested in studying such matters as the writer, the writer's era, and the original audience's reaction to the text, s/he would thoroughly investigate any historical clues offered in "Caline." For instance, Chopin's mention of the Texas and Pacific railroad invites extensive research. A TRADITIONAL HISTORICAL critic might note, for instance, that the expansive Texas and Pacific Railroad, acquired in 1880 by the infamous "robber baron," Jay Gould, rendered service from El Paso in the west to New Orleans in the east. Under Gould's control it eventually operated feeder lines supplying cotton and other Southern crops for the Missouri Pacific. A TRADITIONAL HISTORICAL critic might also report that the latter 19th century produced not only the extremely wealthy railroad magnates but also class conflicts and poverty—issues obviously relevant to this story. Additionally, such a critic might show how Chopin's sympathetic depiction of Creole and Cajun life in Louisiana earned her immediate renown as a local colorist. Herself of Creole/Irish descent, Chopin painted daringly intimate portrayals of Creole culture and the feminine heart that often shocked her contemporary audience. "Caline," although seemingly simple and uncontroversial in itself, would doubtless have impressed the late-19th-century reader as a rare glimpse into the life of a poor Acadian girl. By thus delving into the past, a TRADITIONAL HISTORICAL critic would attempt to provide a better understanding of the author's intentions and of the text's significance to its original audience (DH).

THEMATIC CRITICISM: Because a THEMATIC critic is interested in the abstract ideas that a literary work emphasizes, he might focus on the central theme of Caline's innocence. For example, the story describes how, when the train stopped in its tracks, Caline looked "stupid at first with astonishment," for "such a thing had not happened before within her recollection" [3]. She stares in wonder at the travelers, and when a young man begins sketching her, she fastens "wide eyes ... earnestly upon him" [6]. Once the train leaves, taking with it her first glimpse of elegance and culture, Caline views the railroad with "new and strange interest" [8]. She wonders with almost childish curiosity "whence these people came, and whither they were going" [8]. In the city, she is bewildered and must "readjust all her preconceptions to fit the reality of it" [13]. Not only is Caline innocent of worldly behavior and mannerisms, but she is also innocent of her own subconscious desire for emotional attachment. It is her simplicity and inexperience in matters of love that prevent her from recognizing that what she had so eagerly sought was not the city or its crowds of people but, in fact, "the pleasant-faced boy, who had made her picture that day under the mulberry tree" [14]. By pointing out the recurring theme of Caline's innocence, the THEMATIC critic would seek to offer the reader a more comprehensive and satisfying understanding of the story (DH).

FORMALIST CRITICISM: Because a FORMALIST critic is interested in the ways elements of the text work together to create complex unity, s/he might focus on the overall theme of self-discovery. Thus, while the young man, confronted with Caline, finds an element of the new and unknown (or perhaps exotic) in his journey, Caline's brush with him also awakens an inner desire to explore the excitement of the unknown. In fact, imagery emphasizing awakening and enlightenment is used throughout the story, suggesting the theme of self-discovery. In this respect, the final sentence of the tale helps unify the imagery of self-discovery. Caline discovers that it was not the city, nor the journey, nor even the young man himself that she had desired; it was instead the promise of adventure or the exotic which she had sought in her journey, just as it was the exotic that the young man saw in her when he sketched her picture (KB).

PSYCHOANALYTIC CRITICISM: Because a PSYCHOANALYTIC critic is interested in the (sexual) complexity of the human mind in perceiving reality, and in how that complexity affects the ways texts are written and read, s/he might focus on the innocent yet provocative image Chopin creates of Caline in the reader's mind. For example, the reference to her "long brown legs and arms" and to the way she ignored the "bits of straw that clung to her black hair, to her red bodice, and the blue cotonade skirt that did not reach her naked ankles" [1] suggests unconscious sensuality in Caline. When a young man from the train, drawn by her natural beauty, begins to sketch her likeness, Caline stands "motionless, her hands behind her, and her wide eyes fixed earnestly upon him" [6]. Shy, yet evidently pleased by his attention, she casts an earnest gaze that could be interpreted as a voiceless appeal for his affection. Once he is gone, she becomes strangely dissatisfied. Her innate desire to be loved and desired compels her search for the first man who recognized and appreciated the beauty of her body. A PSYCHOANALYTIC critic would seek to reveal the various sexual undertones woven into Caline's behavior (DH).

ARCHETYPAL CRITICISM: Because an ARCHETYPAL critic is interested in certain basic fears, desires, and images that form the way humans perceive reality, he might focus on the first sentence of the story: "The sun was just far enough in the west to send inviting shadows" [1]. Here, the setting sun not only represents the resolution or completion of a day, but it also foreshadows the end of Caline's childhood and girlish innocence. Just as a day passes into night unobtrusively but unremittingly, so Caline's childhood passes quietly and irretrievably into a memory. The inviting aspect of the shadows may symbolize the coming pleasure of womanhood, but the shadows themselves may represent a fear of the unknown future. Thus, an ARCHETYPAL critic would seek to discover the latent symbols and images in a text and reveal their significance to other readers (DH).

Because an ARCHETYPAL critic is interested in the common stories or myths that humans use to structure experience or reality, s/he might focus on how the story reflects an overall journey or quest motif (a common ARCHETYPAL situation). Symbolism suggesting the journey motif is presented throughout the narrative, including the glittering "steel rails" of the railroad [2], the train itself [3], and the traveling passengers (who are on their own journey). Similarly, the opening sentence suggests the journey motif through its reference to a setting "sun" [1], which is often a symbol of exploration in western culture since it implies inviting shadows. Chopin's use of this opening image helps emphasize the story's many symbols of journey, thereby reinforcing the ARCHETYPAL idea that Caline is on a journey of self-discovery (KB).

MARXIST CRITICISM: Because a MARXIST critic is interested in conflicts between economic classes and the way that literature reflects, reinforces, or undermines dominant ideologies, he would definitely focus on the vast gulf between Caline's lifestyle and that of the wealthy travelers on the train. Unaccustomed to country life, the ladies in the party are described as having "walked awkwardly in their high-heeled boots ... and held up their skirts mincingly" [4], while Caline, on the other hand, barefoot and disheveled after her nap under the haystack, stares unashamedly at the newcomers. A MARXIST critic might also focus on the consequences of Caline's low position in society. All hope of her meeting the "pleasant-faced" young man [6], much less of befriending him, is utterly destroyed because of the inescapable distinction between their economic classes. However, a MARXIST critic might point out that Chopin clearly sympathizes with the poor country girl, and her story tends to produce in the reader a sense of the injustice of separate social and economic classes (DH).

FEMINIST CRITICISM: Because a FEMINIST critic is interested in the various ways that reality is structured in terms of sexual or gender differences, he or she might emphasize Chopin's demeaning description of the ladies from the train as they "laughed immoderately at the funny things which their masculine companions were saying" [4]. A FEMINIST critic would find it intolerable that these women evidently felt obliged to flatter and indulge the men they were with. Such women change their very personalities and opinions to reflect what they believe men desire. FEMINIST critics would seek to persuade readers that women should never be reduced to the degradation of gratifying men's desires in order to achieve a happy and fulfilled life (DH).

STRUCTURALIST CRITICISM: Because a STRUCTURALIST critic is interested in the codes that a text uses to structure the reality reflected in the story, s/he might focus on the repetitive use of the opposing imagery of nature versus city, light versus dark, old versus new/young, and stasis versus journey. All of these oppositions work in a parallel manner to suggest Caline's journey of self-discovery. The opposition of nature and city is a central structural device for the story. Beginning with the initial imagery of Caline sleeping long and soundly in a field, the story suggests that the element of nature is related to Caline's initially naive and innocent condition. Her "naked ankles" [1] represent the natural sensuality of a young girl's innocence and contrast with the social convention of the "Sunday shoes" [11] she wears when she finally leaves for the city. Similarly, the contrast between Caline's father toiling in the field with his "plow" while the passengers disembark from the train [3] also emphasizes the dichotomy of nature and city. Finally, when Caline arrives in the city, she must adjust to the hum of the "French market" city life [13] which she finds to be so different from the quiet of the country.

These kinds of oppositions between nature and city parallel similar oppositions between old and new (or young). While the country and Caline's initial condition are both associated with the old, her awakening is symbolized by many references to things that are new. For example, her parents are old, they speak only their foreign dialect, and they are unaware of what lies beyond their home [9]. Likewise, Caline's father employs the traditional methods of farming—man and mule [3]. Caline stands under an *"old gnarled* mulberry tree" (emphasis added; [3]) with her ankles naked, while the passengers disembark from a modern vehicle wearing stylish "boots" [3]. After the train leaves, Caline looks with *"new* and strange interest" upon the passing trains (emphasis added; [8]).

Meanwhile the opposition of light and dark images more closely parallels Caline's internal awakening. The imagery of emergence from darkness is introduced in the first paragraph. Caline sleeps "in the shade of a haystack" but awakens to a "cloudless" (that is, light) "sky" [1]. Although a dark, "dense wood" surrounds Caline's farm, it is sliced through by "glitter[ing] steel rails" [2] which suggest light and a potential journey. These images, combined with Caline's emergence from the shadow to see the train, reflect both a literal and a figurative enlightenment.

Finally, the opposition of stasis versus journey is anticipated by the previously cited contrasts. Throughout the text, a sense of stability born of stasis is juxtaposed with a sense of adventure resulting from journey. For example, Caline sleeps in the "center of a small field" [1], a fact suggesting her sense of security in her surroundings. She stands beneath an "old" tree [3] that represents stability and longevity. Her "father" is a farmer [3], an occupation which demands patience and tenacity. And, most interestingly, she seeks her information about the travelers from "the old flagman, who stayed down there by the big water tank" [10]. Since trains cannot function without a stable water supply, the flagman represents the stability of staying home and not embarking on journeys. While the previously noted imagery of newness, light, and the city present parallel journey symbols in a positive sense, the contrast between the unknown journey (on the one hand) and the security and stability of staying in one place (on the other) contributes an important element of tension to the story (KB).

READER-RESPONSE CRITICISM: Because a READER-RESPONSE critic emphasizes individual interpretations of the text, s/he might concentrate on the different responses readers might offer of Caline's home. Readers who grew up in remote, rural areas, hidden and sheltered from the world outside, may read about Caline with a twinge of nostalgia as they remember a time when they too looked upon sophisticated, cultured people with wide open eyes of wonder. More urbane readers, however, might pity Caline for growing up uneducated and with no apparent prospects of advancement in society. However, some readers who have been confined to the rush and bustle of city life, and who dream of escaping to the country someday, may in fact envy Caline for growing up on a farm in a simple, natural setting. Thus, a reader-response critic would seek to prove that every reader's impression of Caline's home might be entirely different (DH).

DIALOGICAL CRITICISM: Because a DIALOGICAL critic is interested in the exchange of voices and conflicting viewpoints within the text and between the text and such "external" entities as the audience, s/he might consider the narrator's rendition of the flagman's reply to Caline's questions: "Yes, he knew ... he knew all about the city" [10]. The narrator imbues the old flagman's words with a subtle touch of smug satisfaction, as though delicately ridiculing the old flagman's idealistic conception of himself as a vast reservoir of knowledge. Because the flagman speaks of the city as a strange, almost foreign place, his knowledge seems quite limited. However, he could be assuming an uncharacteristically simple perspective for Caline's benefit since he knows that she has never experienced city life. Through his effusive advice, the flagman conveys a pleased condescension toward Caline; he seems grateful that someone has sought out his knowledge. Both the old flagman and Caline view themselves very seriously, unlike the narrator, who describes them with a tender but half-amused tone. Thus, a DIALOGICAL critic would endeavor to analyze the continuous dialogue each text supplies within itself and the DIALOGICAL responses it incites among its readers (DH).

DECONSTRUCTIONIST CRITICISM: Because a DECONSTRUC-TIONIST critic is interested in the contradictions and insolvable paradoxes inherent in language, s/he might argue that in this story the structural codes associating age with knowledge and associating youth with innocence are by no means unequivocal or clear-cut. For example, when the rich passengers alight from the train, Caline is not the only one who stands gazing in astonishment, for her father "st[ands] staring also, leaning upon his plow" [3]. Similarly, when Caline begins wondering curiously "whence these people came, and whither they were going," "her mother and father could not tell her" [8-9]. Innocence and even ignorance, therefore, are not restricted in this narrative to the young; instead, Chopin implies that parents sometimes know less than their children. A DECONSTRUCTIONIST critic might also point out that by decisively and resolutely departing alone for an unknown city in pursuit of the "pleasant-faced boy" [14], Caline usurps the traditional assertive role of the male in romantic affairs. However, even her aggressive qualities are prone to DECONSTRUCTION, for at the end of the story, Caline dissolves into very vulnerable and stereotypically feminine tears. A DECONSTRUCTIONIST critic would thus seek to reveal the instabilities embedded even in such an apparently simple tale (DH).

NEW HISTORICIST CRITICISM: Because a NEW HISTORICIST critic is interested in power-conflicts not only within the text but also within the text's cultural setting, s/he might focus on Caline's struggle against societal restrictions and her endeavor to break loose from her family's poverty. For instance, after her initial exposure to the affluent and sophisticated travelers, particularly the young man who sketches her likeness, Caline "could not feel the same" again [8]. She seems dissatisfied with her simple impoverished life as a farmer's daughter. Therefore, with a determination and aspiration remarkable for a poor country girl in the late nineteenth century, she sets off alone for the city. By the end of the story, however, Caline seems to realize (or accept) the dismal futility of struggling against her social position and of expecting to befriend a rich young man. Her overpowering disappointment could possibly be associated not only with the consciousness that she will probably never again see the "pleasant-faced boy" [14], but also with the realization that she will probably never break away from the restrictions imposed by her social status. Thus, a NEW HISTORICIST might view the story as an illustration of the ineffectual struggles of the poor to cross the rigid, oppressive line separating them from the rich (DH).

POSTMODERNIST CRITICISM: Because a POSTMODERNIST delights in all forms of self-expression, particularly those that reveal instability or irrationality or irresolution, s/he might value the unresolved ending to Caline's emotional experience. After her seductive encounter with the young man from the train, Caline's dissatisfaction with her former life leads her on a futile search, ending in frustration. She finds no completion to her quest, no satisfaction for her desires, and no profitable denouement to her tears of disappointment. If, in fact, Caline matures from her experiences, it will be because of her perception and acceptance of life's unpredictability. The very brevity of the story, coupled with the fact that it seems to serve merely as entertainment, might attract POSTMODERNISTS, since they prefer accepting meaninglessness and irresolution rather than imposing false strictures of sense or meaning. A POSTMODERNIST would also value the story's ultimate sense of unfulfillment because such an ending presents a true reflection of reality's incoherence and lack of orderly conclusions (DH).

MULTICULTURAL CRITICISM: Because a MULTICULTURAL critic is interested in the ethnic diversity or other group identities portrayed in a text, he might focus on the unique social classification Caline embodies. For example, Caline's "French patois" [5] not only establishes her as a Creole or Cajun, but it also suggests that she is illiterate in standard English, a plight most likely irremediable due to her parents' poverty. Her simple attire, consisting of a "red bodice and ... blue cotonade skirt that did not reach her naked ankles" [1], emphasizes her position as a poor, isolated country girl and helps explains her amazement at the sight of the wealthy travelers and also her initial confusion in the city. Naturally, she is "bewildered" and must "readjust all her preconceptions to fit the reality of it" [13]. However, her naivete is principally a result of her sequestered upbringing, not of her instinctive simplicity. In fact, coming from such a secluded background, Caline is courageous indeed to brave the strange city alone. A MULTICULTURALIST critic might also suggest that Chopin's use of words distinctive to the New Orleans Creole culture, such as "banquette" [12] and *"lagniappe"* [13], reflects upon her own Irish/Creole descent, thereby validating the argument that a writer's background and experiences will inevitably affect his or her work. By thus focusing on the important distinctions between various cultures and societies, a MULTICULTURALIST critic seeks to prove that no human being can behave independently of his or her particular group identity (DH).

Appendix 5

Kate Chopin's "Caline":
Specific Comments from Diverse Critical Perspectives

CONTRIBUTORS: Jennifer Adger (JA); Jeff Alexander (JA2); Ashley Ashworth (AA); Melissa Baker (MB); Kimberly Barron (KB); Janis Blaesing (JB); Jennifer Brown (JB2); Tanya Brummett (TB); Shameka Carroll (SC); Andrea Cook (AC); John Elder (JE); Robert C. Evans (RCE); Matt Gilmore (MG); Barbara Hartin (BH); Sonjanika Henderson (SH); Deborah Hill (DH); Michael Hitch (MH); Laketa Huddleston (LH); Connie James (CJ); Steven Jones (SJ); John Kelley (JK); Barrett Lee (BL); Monica Felicia Lee (MFL); Kathy Mayfield (KM); Mike Odom (MO); Edward Pate (EP); Stephanie Reed (SR); Lorelei Jackson Sanders (LJS); Jay Sansom (JS); Debbie Seale (DS); Durand Smitherman (DS2); Patrick Steele (PS); Mark Stewart (MS); Teresa Stone (TS); Tammy Taite (TT); Eric Thomason (ET).

Caline

[1] The sun was just far enough in the west to send inviting shadows. In the center of a small field, and in the shade of a haystack which was there, a girl lay sleeping. She had slept long and soundly, when something awoke her as suddenly as if it had been a blow. She opened her eyes and stared a moment up in the cloudless sky. She yawned and stretched her long brown legs and arms, lazily. Then she arose, never minding the bits of straw that clung to her black hair, to her red bodice, and the blue cotonade skirt that did not reach her naked ankles.

Because a STRUCTURALIST critic emphasizes binary structures in literature and experience, he might argue that the references to the **"sun"** and the **"shadows"** help shape our perception of reality in the story and parallel the similar contrasts between Caline's innocence and her eventual loss of this innocence (JA; TB; BL; MH; DS). In fact, a struturalist critic might see the opposition between innocence and experience as one of the most important oppositions in the whole story (EP). An ARCHETYPAL critic might find the references to the **"sun"** and **"west"** significant because they may already suggest the idea of a beckoning frontier or horizon (MG; BH). The phrase "inviting shadows" implies some of the paradoxical flavor of the story as a whole, since Caline will later feel drawn (or almost invited) to the city but will not find real happiness there. Such paradoxical instability might be of special interest to a DECONSTRUCTIVE critic (BH). The fact that Caline has **"slept long and soundly"** and then is awakened **"suddenly,"** almost as if by a physical **"blow,"** might almost seem to epitomize the action of the entire story: in the course of this tale, Caline will experience an awakening on many different levels, including an awakening to her own physical desire (MH; DS2). This process might especially interest a PLATONIC critic, who might be troubled by the story's emphasis on physical desire instead of rational thought (DS2). An ARCHETYPAL critic might argue that all humans can relate to the desire for sleep as well as to the fear of having one's sleep suddenly or violently interrupted (TT). A LONGINIAN critic, concerned with the power of literature to elevate the soul, might be intrigued by the description of Caline as she **"open[s] her eyes and stare[s] a moment up in the cloudless sky,"** since such language can imply a sense of spiritual transcendence of the physical here-and-now (LH). A FORMALIST might note that as the story opens, Caline's mind is as free of the troubles as the sky is free of clouds; by the end of the story, however, her mind and emotions will be figuratively darkened and troubled. The **"cloudless sky"** perhaps symbolizes Caline's relative innocence and inexperience at this point in the story (JA; KM). An ARCHETYPAL critic might argue that at this point Caline is in harmony with her rural physical environment, whereas by the end of the story she will feel alienated from the city to which she travels (KM). A FORMALIST might admire Chopin's skillful use of strong color imagery in the references to **"brown," "black," "red,"** and **"blue"** in the last two sentences of this passage (LH; BL). The fact that Caline is described as having **"yawned and stretched ... lazily"** perhaps already implies a touch of boredom with her present existence—a boredom that will help explain her later adventurous behavior (SR). A PSYCHOANALYTIC critic might suggest that the description of Caline's **"long brown legs and arms"** already introduces a note of sexuality into this story (MG; SJ; DS2; ET). In fact, Chopin reverses the usual word-order (arms and legs) in a way that emphasizes Caline's sensuous **"legs"** (SJ). The fact that Caline at this point does not **"mind ... the bits of straw"** that cling to her prepares for two later contrasts: with the ladies from the train, who are quite concerned about their appearance [4], and with Caline herself after she decides to move to the big city and is concerned to dress properly [11] (TB). Note the careful patterning of this opening paragraph, especially its movement from general to specific—from the sun in the sky, then to the whole field, then to a particular haystack, then to Caline as a whole, and finally to particular details of her clothing (ET).

[2] The log cabin in which she dwelt with her parents was just outside the enclosure in which she had been sleeping. Beyond was a small clearing that did duty as a cotton field. All else was dense wood, except the long stretch that curved round the brow of the hill, and in which glittered the steel rails of the Texas and Pacific road.

Because a TRADITIONAL HISTORICAL critic believes that everything reflects the time of its occurrence, he might focus on the description of the railroads here, since such imagery implies the general period in which this story was written and therefore provides clues about the likely reactions of its original readers (BL). Indeed, nearly all the details mentioned in this section would interest a historical critic since those details help locate the story very precisely in a particular historical era (BH). Such a critic would note, for instance, how the reference to the **"log cabin"** immediately helps situate this story in a particular period and also helps locate Caline's family in a particular socio-economic status (MG). A MARXIST might find it significant that the railroad tracks, symbols of the growing capitalist economic system, run so close to the property owned (or perhaps merely rented) by Caline's family (MG). The fact that Caline still lives with her "parents" helps emphasize her youth and inexperience—important themes in a story that is largely about an initiation into psychological maturity (MH). The fact that the rails **"glitter"** helps emphasize how they stand out in—and apart from—the otherwise natural landscape; they are not only artificial but seem almost new in a setting that otherwise seems timeless (ET). At the same time, the "glitter" associated with the rails may make them seem enticing to Caline; they may symbolize new and exciting experiences (MH). The fact that the rails belong to the **"Texas and Pacific road"** helps make them seem representative of the kind of corporate, capitalist culture that was transforming the entire country during this era (RCE). Is it too fanciful to see the **"long stretch"** of the rails as they **"[curve] around the brow of the hill"** as almost suggesting a serpent gliding through a natural landscape? (MH)

[3] When Caline emerged from the shadow she saw a long train of passenger coaches standing in view, where they must have stopped abruptly. It was that sudden stopping which had awakened her; for such a thing had not happened before within her recollection, and she looked stupid, at first, with astonishment. There seemed to be something wrong with the engine; and some of the passengers who dismounted went forward to investigate the trouble. Others came strolling along in the direction of the cabin, where Caline stood under an old gnarled mulberry tree, staring. Her father had halted his mule at the end of the cotton row, and stood staring also, leaning upon his plow.

Significantly, only now does Chopin give her chief character a name—**"Caline."** Just as she **"emerge[s] from the shadow,"** so her personal name now emerges. In fact, no one else in the story is given this kind of personal identity—a fact that makes it obvious that Caline is the central focus of Chopin's attention (MH). Because a TRADITIONAL HISTORICAL critic is interested in the historical context of a work, s/he might focus on this passage as evidence of a period in which the social structure reflected a large geographic and psychological gap between the urban and rural spheres of society (KB). The description of how **"Caline emerged from the shadow"** might be seen as part of a larger theme in this story of movement from the familiar to the unknown (MO), just as it might also be seen as part of the story's use of images of light and darkness (KB). Perhaps her movement from out of "the shadow" symbolizes her transition from a private world to a social existence and thus anticipates her later move from the country to the city (MO). The responses of Caline and her father, both stopping their activities and staring at the train, further suggest that the sight of train passengers disembarking was an unfamiliar experience. Since trains pass through the field regularly, it must be the passengers themselves rather than the train that seem unfamiliar (KB).

Whereas both Caline and her father seem almost **"stupid"** with **"astonishment"** at the sudden stopping of the train, the passengers seem to regard the event with relatively untroubled curiosity. A MULTICULTURAL critic might argue that these different reactions symbolize the different larger cultures to which these different people belong (JB). A MARXIST might note how easily the passengers assume their right to walk across land presumably owned by Caline's father; they never ask his permission or even acknowledge his presence (SJ). Caline's father may be a manual laborer, but he is ignorant of the mechanics of the train engine (KB). The passengers take the sudden stop almost literally in stride—a reaction that perhaps symbolizes their greater sense of power and control over their environment (RCE). Their **"strolling"** may suggest that they feel undisturbed and relaxed (JB; DS2). In contrast, Caline **"stood ... staring"** (maybe in curiosity or maybe in fear) under the **"old gnarled mulberry tree."** Perhaps the tree represents aspects of Caline's life, implying its vitality but also its geographical rootedness and toughness (JB). Indeed, because ARCHETYPAL critics are often concerned with the natural symbols and images that frequently appear in literature, they might especially focus on the symbolic nature of the **"mulberry tree."** Just as the tree seems natural and beautiful to them, so does Caline (BL). Or perhaps the **"mulberry tree"** suggests Caline's presently sheltered life (MO). It may also symbolize her rural existence, as opposed to the upper-class urbanity of the train's passengers (KB). One can imagine many different theorists giving competing explanations of Caline's initial reticence. A MARXIST might argue that she is intimidated by the stranger's wealth. A Freudian might suggest that she is sexually repressed or inexperienced in dealing with young men. A FEMINIST might contend that she is behaving according to the "shy girl" stereotype imposed on women in her culture. An ARCHETYPAL critic might argue that she is displaying the non-aggressive posture symbolically and traditionally associated with women. A FORMALIST might suggest that her reticence here helps prepare for (and contrast with) her adventurousness later and thus contributes to the complex unity of the tale. A STRUCTURALIST might assert that her reticence fits into a larger active/passive binary pattern that helps organize the whole story. A DIALOGICAL critic might argue that at present she has no real voice of her own, but such a critic might also suggest that she literally can't speak to the stranger because her language is French while his is English. Finally, a DECONSTRUCTOR might claim that although she speaks no obvious words, she speaks volumes to the curious young man, who will soon, through his drawing, make his own interpretation of what she represents—at least to him (RCE). Meanwhile, because a MARXIST critic emphasizes socio-economic matters, he might be interested in the brief description of Caline's **"father,"** since that description indicates the social class to which she and her family belong. Caline's father is obviously a farmer and (unlike the wealthy passengers on the train) presumably must work hard, long hours of physical labor (MG; BL; MO; DS). The fact that he **"lean[s] upon his plow"** suggests the physically exhausting nature of his work (LH). The fact that Caline has been sleeping while her father works with the plow might suggest, to a FEMINIST, the ways society often links particular kinds of work with particular kinds of gender (BH). The way some members of the group **"stroll"** up the hill toward Caline suggests that she is an oddity to them, almost as if she were a roadside sight along their journey (KB). The references to the **"old gnarled mulberry tree"** and, especially, the **"mule"** and the **"plow,"** when juxtaposed with the image of the train's steam engine, imply psychological distance between the modern industrialization of the urban world and the old-fashioned, animal- and man-powered orientation of the nine-teenth-century rural world (KB; MG). Because a MARXIST critic is interested in the ways material and economic conditions affect other aspects of life, s/he might be interested in this passage as a succinct embodiment of the tensions between the poor rural working class and an affluent urban culture (KB; DS).

[4] There were ladies in the party. They walked awkwardly in their high-heeled boots over the rough, uneven ground, and held up their skirts mincingly. They twirled parasols over their shoulders, and laughed immoderately at the funny things which their masculine companions were saying.

The fact that the women are called **"ladies"** implies both their eco-nomic status and the particular gender roles they have adopted (or have been encouraged to play [JE; KM]). The word **"ladies"** also distinguishes them socially and perhaps also in age from Caline, who is more simply described as a "girl" (AA; JB2; SC; JE). The use of the word **"party,"** rather than "group," implies that the passen-gers were not on a serious journey (KB). Similarly, the image of the women walking **"awkwardly"** over the **"rough ... ground"** (be-cause of their inappropriate shoes) suggests a lack of preparation to meet the serious challenges of the real, physical world (KB)—the hard world in which Caline has grown up (JS). Of course, the women did not anticipate having to walk over **"rough, uneven ground"** when they originally dressed, but their clothing does not, in any case, seem especially suited to a long train trip. The fact that these women feel compelled to dress as they do suggests the degree to which their lives are dictated by larger cultural codes over which they have little control, especially since they *are* women (JK; TS). However, just as the **"ladies"** walk **"awkwardly"** in this rural setting, so Caline will later experience difficulty in adjusting to life in the city (JA; MO). A FEMINIST critic might note the typically passive behavior of these women, whose main purpose in a patriarchal society seems to be to act properly, look pretty, and curry favor with men (BL; KM). The **"high-heeled boots"** that symbolize their social status and power in an urban setting make them seem relatively vulnerable and powerless in a rural setting—a change that emphasizes that their social status is the product of a highly specific circumstance and an artificial code (JA). Meanwhile, the references to their **"twirl[ing] parasols"** and immoderate laughter (or giggling) reinforce an image of frivolity and vanity (KB; BH), although a PSYCHOANALYTIC critic might see these gestures as flirtatious and even playfully sexual (TS). A FEMINIST might find this passage troubling since it could be seen as reinforcing a stereotype of women as superficial and unintelligent (BH; MO). Chopin does not portray these women laughing hardily alongside the men or interjecting their own **"funny"** anecdotes. Instead, they listen politely and laugh on cue, thereby maintaining the appropriate social distance and validating the superior role of the men in their patriarchal society (TS). On the other hand, a FEMINIST might suggest that Chopin here is implicitly satirizing the behavior and values of these particular women in order to promote social change: by implicitly criticizing these women, she might be attempting to alter and improve the lives of women in general (RCE). A MARXIST might contend, however, that these women are not simply wealthy, pampered females but are symbols of the oppressive capitalist class. Ironically, they might themselves be seen as both the beneficiaries and the victims of their class status: they enjoy the privileges of wealth, but they are also treated (and even view themselves) as material objects. They have no real independent identities because they have "bought into" (or have been born into) a system that treats human beings as commodities. In contrast, although Caline is economically poorer than

these urban women, she perhaps has a much stronger sense of independent identity. Although the city women are rich in material
goods, Caline is arguably richer in autonomous spirit. The city
"ladies" walk **"mincingly"** over the ground, but Caline has not
"bought into" a system that defines dirty feet as "bad" (RCE; TS).
A FORMALIST or ARCHETYPAL critic might contrast the **"parasols"** of these ladies with the "brown," presumably sun-tanned,
"legs and arms" of Caline mentioned in section 1: Caline shows
the impact of nature, whereas the ladies are insulated from it (SJ).
MULTICULTURALIST and MARXIST critics would both find this
entire passage interesting since it symbolizes the distinctions
between urban (and upper-class) and rural (and lower-class) cultures (TS).

   **[5] They tried to talk to Caline, but could not understand the
French patois with which she answered them.**

Because a MULTICULTURAL critic emphasizes such differences as
those of age, sex, race, and gender, he might focus on how the
failure of communication here results from differences of language
and culture, which in turn help to shape the parallel differences in
character and emotion between Caline and the travelers (TB; CJ;
BL). A MULTICULTURAL critic might focus on this passage as an
example of an interaction or interface between two different cultural groups. Since the passengers cannot understand Caline, they
are obviously from a different cultural group than she (KB) and
are probably also even from a different section of the country (ET).
Because these ladies possess the social skills and self-confidence
necessary to interact with other people, including strangers, it is
they who approach Caline (CJ). Chopin's use of the word **"patois"**
might interest a DIALOGICAL critic since the story thereby includes
a bit of the very dialect it mentions (MFL). However, cultural differences go beyond even the distinction in language, as the tourists
are of a different class altogether. In addition, the tourists have
money, but Caline is poor; the tourists have experience beyond a
certain locality by virtue of travel, whereas Caline has none; the
tourists are educated, but Caline is not; the women tourists wear
nice dresses, but Caline has only her provincial clothing; one
tourist [see 6] is even artistic enough to draw her picture, while
Caline has no instruction in the arts. The tourists are urban, but
Caline is rural. Thus a wide MULTICULTURAL chasm separates
Caline and the tourists (BH).

[6] One of the men—a pleasant-faced youngster—drew a sketch book from his pocket and began to make a picture of the girl. She stayed motionless, her hands behind her, and her wide eyes fixed earnestly upon him.

A FEMINIST critic might be bothered by the fact that the male **"youngster"** never thinks to seek Caline's permission to sketch her; instead, he assumes he has a right to do so, in part because he is male and is therefore used to taking the initiative when dealing with females (AC). In light of all the differences between Caline and the travellers, the young man's response to her suggests a curiosity about the unknown. In his **"sketch,"** he is perhaps attempting to capture part of the exotic experience of his journey (JA; KB). Ironically, his attempt to capture Caline on paper, just as she is, will result in changing her in practically every way: as a result of this encounter, she will later leave her parents, move to the city, and then experience feelings she has never felt before (SH). A HORATIAN or READER-RESPONSE critic might argue that young people, in particular, would find this story of interest because it emphasizes the experiences of persons like themselves, who are learning about new aspects of the world (LH). A MULTICULTURALIST critic might find this particular moment especially interesting, not only because the young man and Caline represent two distinct cultures but also because the young man makes Caline the object of his study. The fact that the young man is privileged enough to have studied art, and that he comes equipped with the necessary materials, might also interest such a critic; certainly these facts would also be of interest to a MARXIST critic (MG). The fact that Caline has **"wide eyes"** might intrigue a FORMALIST critic, who might see such phrasing as implying her childlike innocence and curiosity (MS). Perhaps the image also implies that from this point forward, Caline will see her whole life much differently than she has seen it up till now (JS). A FEMINIST might argue that by **"mak[ing] a picture of the girl,"** the young man tries to impose a kind of control over her; he tries to make her "his" and inevitably sees her from his own limited perspective (MS). The fact that Caline is **"motionless"** and that her eyes are **"fixed"** might interest a THEMATIC critic, who might see these traits as typifying her relatively passive character throughout the story. Ironically, her later decision to take the initiative and move to the city seems to violate this pattern, but by the very end of the story she is passive and unmoving once again (JK). Her passivity here might also interest a

FEMINIST critic (AC; TT), while the contrast between his activity and her **"motionless"** state might also interest a STRUCTURALIST critic, who might argue that this kind of difference symbolizes larger differences in the typical roles of men and women in Caline's culture: the young man is the active observer, while Caline is the passive object of observation (TT). By sketching her, he imposes a kind of control over her (DS). On the other hand, the fact that Caline's eyes are **"fixed earnestly"** on the young man suggests that she is observing him at least as intently as he is observing her (JB2). Presumably Caline feels important because she is the object of this young man's attention, whereas a FEMINIST critic might argue that Caline should not need such male attention in order to feel significant (AC). A FORMALIST critic, however, might appreciate the way the single word **"motionless"** effectively epitomizes Caline's sense of the importance of this moment, especially her desire not to ruin the picture by moving (AC).

[7] Before he had finished there was a summons from the train; and all went scampering hurriedly away. The engine screeched, it sent a few lazy puffs into the still air, and in another moment or two had vanished, bearing its human cargo with it.

Perhaps the fact that the boy does not **"finish"** sketching Caline resembles the fact that Caline is not quite finished herself. She is not quite grown up, and has not had enough worldly experiences to help her along in this process. Caline really knows no other world than her own, which is isolated from all other people except her parents. The fact that the boy does not complete his sketching of Caline may also imply that he may not be finished with Caline yet. Perhaps Chopin hints—as Caline later hopes—that the two will meet again and have some sort of a relationship. Certainly this is how a more conventionally romantic story would end (AC). The fact that the passengers are described as **"scampering away"** may suggest a freedom of movement and freedom of mind that Caline will soon find very appealing (SR). Or perhaps such **"scampering"** ironically suggests the ways in which their lives are regimented and controlled by the technology originally invented to serve them (SH). The word may also imply their desire to return to the comfort of the train (JS). The **"lazy puffs"** and **"still air"** contribute to our sense of the inactiveness of Caline's environment, while the fact that the train has soon **"vanished"** shows that it disappears as quickly as it had stopped (JB). The **"puffs"** of smoke also darken the "cloudless sky" mentioned in the first paragraph of the story, just as Caline's encounter with the passengers from the train will later darken her own initially innocent and inexperienced outlook on life (JA; DS). Meanwhile, the reference to the passengers as **"human cargo"** paradoxically makes them seem inhuman and impersonal, and also separate from Caline's reality (AA; JB; MS). This phrase may imply the degree to which the industrial revolution had begun to transform human beings into mere things (JK; LJS). The words **"human cargo"** constitute a kind of oxymoron as well as a particularly concentrated bit of irony (RCE), while the fact that the passengers are described as **"scampering"** back to the train may suggest the degree to which their behavior has become conditioned (JK).

[8] **Caline could not feel the same after that. She looked with new and strange interest upon the trains of cars that passed so swiftly back and forth across her vision, each day; and wondered whence these people came, and whither they were going.**

A FORMALIST might suggest that the succinct statement that **"Caline could not feel the same after that"** is typical of Chopin's skillful economy with words. It is interesting that Chopin uses the words **"could not feel"** instead of "would not feel." Chopin's phrasing indicates that Caline is incapable of remaining the same, whereas if the author had chosen the phrase "would not feel," she would suggest that Caline makes a definite choice not to feel the same (CJ). A STRUCTURALIST critic, concerned with the ways cultural codes shape our comprehension of reality, might be interested in the contrast between the narrator's polished English diction (**"whence ... whither"**) and the "French patois" [5] spoken by Caline and her parents (SR). For a STRUCTURALIST, this contrast would be part of a larger *system* of oppositions that help organize the story—such as the opposition between rich and poor, urban and rural, etc. (RCE).

[9] **Her mother and father could not tell her, except to say that they came from "loin là bas," and were going "Djieu sait é où."**[1]

---

[1]I.e., "far over there" (or "far away") and "God knows where."

The fact that Caline's parents speak in French dialect, and that Chopin actually quotes them doing so, would immensely interest a DIALOGICAL critic, since Chopin thus includes at least two very distinct kinds of voices in her text—the standard English of the narrator and the French "patois" of these two characters. Because these differences in speech imply even larger differences in culture, they would also be of great interest to MULTICULTURAL critics (MFL).

[10] One day she walked miles down the track to talk with the old flagman, who stayed down there by the big water tank. Yes, he knew. Those people came from the great cities in the north, and were going to the city in the south. He knew all about the city; it was a grand place. He had lived there once. His sister lived there now; and she would be glad enough to have so fine a girl as Caline to help her cook and scrub, and tend the babies. And he thought Caline might earn as much as five dollars a month, in the city.

The fact that the **"flagman"** is **"old"** immediately associates him with ARCHETYPES of wisdom and experience (MS). Because a STRUCTURALIST is interested in patterns that reveal themselves in binaries, he might not only contrast the flagman's age with Caline's youth (RCE) but might also focus on the fact that the people on the trains were coming **"from the great cities in the north"** and were headed toward **"the city in the south,"** since such phrasing implies a larger structure of distinctions between two vastly different cultures (SR). It is interesting, for instance, that there are many **"*great* cities in the north"** (emphasis added) while there is only *one* **"city in the south,"** and that the size of that city is not emphasized. This single contrast implies much about the relative urbanization of the two regions (SR). Notice, too, that Chopin never mentions New Orleans by name but relies instead on the reader's historical knowledge to suggest which **"city"** she means (SR). By describing the city as a **"grand place"** before he mentions the money Caline might make, the flagman, whether deliberately or not, appeals to her romantic dreams rather than emphasizing the pragmatic facts of her life there. Perhaps he instinctively realizes that Caline is less interested in money than in more "lofty" matters—the kinds of matters that would interest a LONGINIAN critic (LJS). A FEMINIST critic would note how automatically the **"old flag*man*"** (emphasis added) assumes that he knows which traditionally female jobs will best suit this young woman: her tasks will be to **"cook and scrub, and tend the babies"** (JA; JA2; LH; SH; SR; MS). Both the flagman and Caline are influenced in their thinking by traditional stereotypes of a woman's proper role (JA). A TRADITIONAL HISTORICAL critic would obviously be greatly interested in determining precisely how much purchasing power **"five dollars a month"** would represent in today's economy (MO). Only during the period when Chopin was writing would one truly understand whether **"five dollars"** was a genuinely great or small amount (JB). A MARXIST would note that Caline's ability to move to the city and live there is determined entirely by her ability to sell her labor; she lacks the relative freedom to travel enjoyed by the wealthy people on the train (SH; MFL; KM). A MARXIST critic might also note that although the flagman himself is a member of the working class, he probably makes more money than Caline and, in this case, acts as a kind of employment broker for his sister (LJS).

    [11] So she went; in a new cotonade, and her Sunday shoes; with a sacredly guarded scrawl that the flagman sent to his sister.

An ARCHETYPAL critic might argue that the desire to seek new experiences by journeying to a new place is one of the most basic of human desires (TB; SR). Such a critic might also interpret Caline's journey to the city as part of the necessary process of individuation—of Caline becoming a distinct and mature person, even though the growth of her maturity may also involve the experience of psychological pain (JA). A READER-RESPONSE critic might suggest that different readers would react differently to Caline's decision to travel to the city: readers attracted to large cities themselves would sympathize with her choice, while those attracted to rural life might find her decision unfortunate. Readers of the latter sort might even see the old flagman as a figure representing misguided temptation (LJS). A TRADITIONAL HISTORICAL critic might see Caline's journey as typifying the more general migration that was occurring during this time from country areas to urban centers (LJS). The adornment implied by the **"new"** skirt and the **"Sunday shoes"** (worn by a poor rural girl) suggests the monumental significance of the occasion, as does the reference to the flagman's note being **"sacredly guarded"** (KB). The **"new cotonade"** is appropriate to the new experiences Caline will now undergo in her new environment (JS). A FORMALIST would note how the **"new"** skirt here contrasts with the straw-covered skirt mentioned in section 1 (RCE). A STRUCTURALIST would note that **"Sunday shoes"** derive their significance from the fact that they are part of a larger structural system in which such shoes contrast with normal or everyday shoes (JB). A FEMINIST, meanwhile, might note that Caline's change of clothes implies her need not only to make herself more conventionally attractive to men but also to dress in a way that seems culturally appropriate to other women; her change of clothes reflects her need to conform to cultural expectations (MG). Does the reference to the **"sacredly guarded scrawl"** imply that Caline herself is illiterate? If so, this fact would be of interest both to MULTICULTURALIST and MARXIST critics, since her relative lack of education would not only help determine the way she experienced life but also the ways she would be treated by others, including her need to depend on selling her manual labor (LJS).

[12] The woman lived in a tiny, stuccoed house, with green blinds, and three wooden steps leading down to the banquette. There seemed to be hundreds like it along the street. Over the house tops loomed the tall masts of ships, and the hum of the French market could be heard on a still morning.

Interestingly, the female who lives in this house is described as a **"woman,"** so that she is already distinguished from the upper-class "ladies" [4] mentioned earlier (AA). Meanwhile, the fact that she is said simply to **"[live] in"** the house may suggest that she does not own it but merely rents it (RCE). The fact that the house is **"stuccoed"** might interest a FORMALIST critic as an example of Chopin's artistic skill: she chooses a single word that immediately implies a kind of architecture associated with warm climates (TT). The fact that there are **"hundreds"** of similar houses might intrigue a THEMATIC critic since this detail can be seen as a symbol of the anonymity and lack of individuality associated with life in a big city. Just as there are hundreds of rather indistinguishable houses in the city, so Caline herself will later feel threatened with a sense of alienation and loss of individuality (MS; PS). The **"tiny"** size of the woman's house might imply, to a MARXIST critic, that the woman herself is far from wealthy and would suggest the extent to which social status is tied to income (JK). Ironically, this **"tiny ... house"** is probably not much bigger than the log cabin

Caline inhabited in the country; she has changed locales but has not really changed her status in any significant way (MH). The **"tiny"** size of the **"hundreds"** of houses might also suggest to a MARXIST that these homes were constructed both quickly and cheaply to provide housing rapidly for the suddenly expanding size of the urban lower-middle class (JA). A MARXIST might also argue, however, that although Caline's employer is by no means rich, she nonetheless is encouraged by the nature of the economic system to use the labor of someone even less wealthy than herself (JA). Meanwhile, the fact that the employer is a woman might interest FEMINIST critics, either because the woman might be seen as taking advantage of Caline, or because she might be seen as assisting another female. The fact that Caline lives in the home of a woman, moreover, would have made her situation less suspect to some readers than it might have seemed if Caline were employed by a single male (RCE). A FORMALIST might note how effectively the single verb **"loomed"** implies the size of the **"ships"** (JB). Both the **"house tops"** and the **"tall masts"** imply a physical environment that is literally "built up" and civilized, unlike the relatively flat rural landscape with which Caline is most familiar (BH). A READER-RESPONSE critic might suggest that a seasoned sailor would probably not even notice or be impressed by the **"tall masts"** that catch the inexperienced Caline's attention, just as a veteran worker in the "French market" might almost ignore the **"hum"** that makes such a strong impression on Caline (RCE). A FORMALIST would note how the word "hum" helps personify the market, making it seem almost a distinct living thing (MS) and perhaps suggesting a sense of calm purposefulness (BH). Ironically, this sense of calm will soon be disrupted in much the same way as Caline's rest was disrupted at the very beginning of the story. Thus the two halves of the work can be seen as forming a kind of symmetrical structure (RCE).

[13] **Caline was at first bewildered. She had to readjust all her preconceptions to fit the reality of it. The flagman's sister was a kind and gentle task-mistress. At the end of a week or two she wanted to know how the girl liked it all. Caline liked it very well, for it was pleasant, on Sunday afternoons, to stroll with the children under the great, solemn sugar sheds; or to sit upon the compressed cotton bales, watching the stately steamers, the graceful boats, and noisy little tugs that plied the waters of the Mississippi. And it filled her with agreeable excitement to go to**

the French market, where the handsome Gascon butchers were eager to present their compliments and little Sunday bouquets to the pretty Acadian girl; and to throw fistfuls of *lagniappe* into her basket.

Caline's need to **"readjust all her preconceptions to fit** [a new] **reality"** would seem especially interesting to a THEMATIC critic, since this need is one of the central motifs of the entire story (MS). Meanwhile, a NEW HISTORICIST critic might find the description of Caline's **"kind and gentle task-mistress"** particularly interesting since it implies that although this woman enjoys power over Caline, she exercises that power with an unusually benign thoughtfulness (LJS). A FEMINIST might suggest that the woman behaves this way because she sympathizes with a fellow female; a MARXIST might suggest that she treats her employee well either because she is a worker herself [see section 10] or because she realizes that such treatment will help her retain Caline's services (RCE). By emphasizing Caline's comfortable relationships with her employer and other urban-dwellers, Chopin prepares for her later focus on the *internal* struggle Caline experiences in the city (LJS). A FORMALIST critic, interested in every detail of the story's precise phrasing, might suggest that the word **"stroll"** implies relaxation and calm (and thus prepares, ironically, for the turmoil Caline will soon feel), while the word **"stately"** implies both the beauty and the usefulness of the steamers. A FORMALIST might also note how effectively Chopin juxtaposes the large **"steamers"** and the small **"tugs,"** just as she earlier juxtaposes the **"sugar sheds"** and the **"cotton bales."** Such diverse details quickly convey a sense of the large, complicated world Caline now inhabits. The verb **"plied,"** meanwhile, is effectively precise: it implies a regular, routine, purposeful motion (MB; RCE). Just as Caline's father had to plow his fields, so the tugs must ply the waters of the river so their operators can earn a living (MH; PS). A MARXIST critic, in fact, might note the class distinctions implied in the contrasts between the **"stately steamers"** and the **"noisy little tugs"** (SJ). Because an ARISTOTELIAN critic is interested in the text as a highly crafted complex unity and in the author's poetic skill, he might focus on the ways Chopin creates the relaxed, languorous rhythm of this sentence, thus simulating a lazy Sunday afternoon. One of the skillful techniques Chopin uses here is the alliteration of such phrases as **"solemn sugar shed," "compressed cotton,"** and **"stately steamers"** (MB; BH; SJ; SR). Chopin forces the reader to slow down and notice small details in much the same way as Ca-line does (SJ). The reference to the **"compressed cotton bales"** re-minds us that Caline's father grows cotton, but the bales represent the end-stage of the commercial process—the change of the cotton from crop to commodity (MG). Once Caline moves to the city, im-ages of journey continue in the references to the various kinds of ships and in the very strong ARCHETYPAL image of the **"Mississippi"** River, all of which suggest that Caline's personal journey has not yet been completed or fulfilled (KB). Because a MULTICULTURAL critic emphasizes differences of age, sex, race, and gender, he might focus on how the final sentence of this pas-sage is full of words implying different cultural identities: the ref-erences to the **"French market,"** the **"Gascon butchers,"** the **"Acadian girl,"** and *"lagniappe"* all suggest different cultures (BL; KM). The market (a capitalist institution) is the place where these diverse cultures come together and mix (MG). A MULTICUL-TURALIST might admire Caline's interest in (and openness to) ex-perience of other cultures (LH), while a MARXIST might note how relatively privileged she seems at this moment in the story: she is now able to **"stroll"** while others work (like the wealthy passen-gers mentioned earlier [3]), although she will soon discover just how different her life actually is from the lives lived by those privileged travelers (SH). Meanwhile, a PSYCHOANALYTIC critic might find the action of the male butchers—who **"throw fistfuls of *lagniappe*"** into her **"basket"** sexually suggestive (JA; MS). A MULTICULTURALIST might note that the actions of these males are more stereotypically masculine and assertive than those of the sen-sitive young man who had paid tribute to Caline's beauty by sketching her (RCE). A FEMINIST might point out, however, that in the cases of both the young man and the butchers, males take the initiative in making overtures to the more passive female (MB; ET). The fact that these men are not only **"handsome"** but are also **"butchers"** associates them with carnality and the flesh, while the fact that they are **"Gascon"** associates them with the unusual or exotic. Meanwhile, their physicality implicitly contrasts with the artistic qualities associated with the "pleasant-faced boy" whose attentions prompted Caline's visit to the city (RCE). On the other hand, both the **"butchers"** and the boy are presumably attracted to Caline almost entirely because of her physical beauty, not because of any deeper qualities of her character or personality (JA). Both the butchers and the artist have a special interest in the quality of flesh (RCE). Meanwhile, a HORATIAN or READER-RESPONSE critic

might appreciate this entire passage because it demonstrates
Chopin's ability to capture the essence of urban life as skillfully as
she had already sketched the countryside, so that her story would
appeal to readers interested in both kinds of locale (JK).

**[14] When the woman asked her again after another week if
she were still pleased, she was not so sure. And again when she
questioned Caline the girl turned away, and went to sit behind
the big, yellow cistern, to cry unobserved. For she knew now
that it was not the great city and its crowds of people she had so
eagerly sought; but the pleasant-faced boy, who had made her
picture that day under the mulberry tree.**

An ARCHETYPAL critic, who emphasizes the importance of basic
human desires and fears, might argue that at first the city had appealed to Caline's strong desire for novelty, but that now it awakens her instinctive fear of loneliness and the unknown. Meanwhile,
her journey to a strange place is precisely the kind of typical symbolic story on which ARCHETYPAL critics place great stress (RCE).
An ARCHETYPAL critic might also suggest that her response to
disappointment is utterly typical of the feelings most humans
would experience in a similar situation (AC; JK). A NEW HIS-
TORICIST critic, who is interested in how power affects human life,
might focus on Caline's action of **"cry[ing] unobserved."** Presumably she fears being glimpsed in her moment of pain. The fact that
she sheds tears near a water-filled **"cistern"** seems appropriate,
and perhaps the **"yellow"** color of the cistern befits the weakness
she now feels (BH; EP). Or perhaps the bright **"yellow"** coloring of
the cistern provides an ironic contrast with the melancholy that
now sweeps over Caline (RCE; EP). The mere fact that the cistern
is painted a bright color suggests that it has some aesthetic function and is not completely utilitarian (EP). The "cistern" may also
remind us (and/or Caline herself) of the big "water tank" [see section 10] not far from her home, where she began her journey to this
unfamiliar city (RCE; PS), or it may be meant to contrast, in its
metallic hardness, with the appealing rural haystack with which
the story opened (LJS). In any case, clearly Caline feels relatively
powerless at this point in the story (MO). The fact that she feels the
need to cry **"unobserved"** might suggest that she feels that a *public*
display of weakness would make her feel (and be treated) as even
weaker than she already is (RCE). A Freudian PSYCHOANALYTIC
critic might argue that although Caline tries to control her emo-

tions and even seems ashamed of expressing them publicly (since she cries **"unobserved"**), her id is too powerful for either her ego or her super-ego to dominate, and so it expresses itself in tears. These tears, a Freudian might note, are also strongly linked to her repressed (or even previously unconscious) erotic desires (RCE). In any case, a PSYCHOANALYTIC critic would certainly suggest that Caline's tears are the product, at least on one level, of sexual desire and frustration (LH). A HORATIAN or READER-RESPONSE critic might suggest that Caline's reaction here would provoke a sympathetic reaction in any reader who had ever faced a similar disappointment (MFL; MO). A PLATONIC critic, who favors objective, rational approaches to reality, might find it appropriate that Caline faces disappointment after giving in to her merely emotional impulse to move to the big city (MO). A postmodern critic, attuned to the flux and complexity of experience, might caution against any rigid, single, or specific interpretation of Caline's crying (MO). A FEMINIST critic might find Caline's tearful response unfortunately typical of the reaction of many women who have felt that relationships with men are essential to their happiness (AC; SH; MFL). A FEMINIST might lament that Caline responds to her feelings in such a stereotypically "feminine" way (SH). A FORMALIST critic, attuned to the ways artists impose shape and unity on their works, might notice how skillfully Chopin returns us, in the final words of this tale, to the **"mulberry tree"** which, in its rootedness and naturalness, had already seemed such a significant symbol of Caline's earlier life (SR). Earlier the **"mulberry tree"** had been called "old and gnarled" [3], perhaps suggesting that at that point in the story Caline was growing tired of her surroundings. Here, however, it is referred to simply as **"the mulberry tree,"** suggesting, perhaps, that Caline is remembering her old environment more fondly now that she is missing it (SR). A DECONSTRUCTOR might note that the story ends on a note of irresolution; it leaves us in a kind of limbo; it does not clearly indicate how Caline should be feeling at this moment or how she should or will respond to what she *is* feeling. In a sense, the story leaves us in the same kind of limbo as it leaves Caline (MG; EP). A DECONSTRUCTIVE critic might add that "innocence" of the sort initially associated with Caline is a privileged concept in Western culture and, thus, is given a preferred status over "experience," which is seen as the corrupter of "innocence." Caline's "lessons of experience" in the city overturn this hierarchy and put these constructs into free play. By the end of the story, Caline is no longer an "Acadian girl" but a woman of adult experience. Consequently, Caline's tears may have as much to do with her transitional feelings between the states of "innocence" and "experience" as they do with her feelings of disappointed love (EP). An ARISTOTELIAN or FORMALIST critic might be interested in the ways that the conclusion of the story relates to its opening. In the first paragraph, Caline experienced a literal, physical awakening, whereas in the concluding paragraph she comes to a different, inner sort of realization—of her yearning for the young man who drew her picture. Her first awakening was not unpleasant; her later one is far more painful (LH; LJS). A LONGINIAN critic might be interested in Caline's desire for love since it may symbolize her desire for transcendence and elevation, her yearning to be moved and transported beyond the common, mundane world that now surrounds her (JA; MFL; KM). A PSYCHOANALYTIC critic, who strongly emphasizes the importance of the unconscious, would find Caline's sudden realization extremely fascinating since it shows the degree to which human behavior can be motivated by impulses we only dimly understand. Caline, after all, has changed her entire life by moving to the city in pursuit of a dream she only now begins to consciously comprehend (JK). A THEMATIC critic might argue that Caline cries partly because she realizes not only that she is unlikely ever to meet the **"pleasant-faced boy"** again, but also because she understands now that even if they ever did meet again, the cultural and economic differences between them would make any relationship extremely improbable (BH). Ironically, this realization, although painful, may also benefit Caline in the long run (LJS). An ARCHETYPAL critic might argue that by the end of the story, Caline has undergone a process of maturation, initiation, and individuation: by suffering pain, she has become a different person than she had been when the story opens, and she now understands her relationship with the **"boy"** in a more mature (if also more painful) way than she had understood it earlier (JA).

Appendix 6

Kate Chopin's "La Belle Zoraïde":

Specific Comments from Diverse Critical Perspectives

CONTRIBUTORS: Jennifer Adger (JA); Debbie Altman (DA); Benjamin Beard (BB); Janis Blaesing (JB); Curtis Bowden (CB); Nataliya Bowden (NB); Lee Bridges (LB), Spencer Brothers (SB); Sonja Brown (SB2); Roger Burdette (RB); Melissa Crane (MC); Ree Ann Clark (RAC); Timothy D. Crowley (TDC); Shannon Dean (SD); Foster Dickson (FD); Paul Duke (PD); Kathleen Durrer (KD); Heather Edwards (HE); Robert C. Evans (RCE); Matt Gilmore (MG); Jacques Grant (JG); Shelly Green (SG); Kenneth W. Griffin (KG); Drayton Hamilton (DH); Barbara Hartin (BH); Phyllis Hedrick (PH); Charlotte Henderson (CH); Sonjanika Henderson (SH); Deborah Hill (DH2); Angelisa LaVan (AL); Barrett Lee (BL); Christy Myers (CM); Katie Magaw (KM); Kathy Mayfield (KM2); Kevin Nutt (KN); Kurt R. Niland (KRN); Pat Norman (PN); Ann O'Clair (AMO); Michael Odom (MO); Margo Paraska (MP); Edward Pate (EP); Lane Powell (LP); Neil Probst (NP); Melissa Roth (MR); Stephanie Reed (SR); Terri Richburg (TR); Denean Rivera (DR); Marie Robinson (MR2); Claire Skowronski (CS); Julie D. Sellers (JDS); Angela Soulé (AS); Frances Stewart (FS); Mark Stewart (MS); Randy C. Stone (RCS); Tammy Taite (TT); Ondra Thomas-Krouse (OT-K); Peter Walden (PW); Gwendolyn Warde (GW); Kristi Widner (KW); Claudia Wilsch (CW); Jonathan Wright (JW); Carolyn Young (CY).

La Belle Zoraïde

[1] The summer night was hot and still; not a ripple of air swept over the *marais* [marsh]. Yonder, across Bayou St. John,

**lights twinkled here and there in the darkness, and in the dark
sky above a few stars were blinking. A lugger that had come out
of the lake was moving with slow, lazy motion down the bayou.
A man in the boat was singing a song.**

The **"hot,"** **"summer"** setting already suggests a sultry, lusty, lazy,
and languorous atmosphere (JDS), and summer is also a season associated with the prime of life (FD, PD). Both points are relevant to
this story's themes and central character, especially since we will
see Zoraïde's life destroyed (FD). An ARCHETYPAL critic might
argue that the story begins by emphasizing feminine elements of
darkness, water, and heat (TR). The calm **"still[ness]"** with which
the story opens perhaps implies that something latent or hidden
might lie beneath the surface of the immediate surroundings or
one's impressions of them (PD). Certainly such stillness contrasts
with the turmoil emphasized later in the work, especially near its
end (AL). To reinforce the languid nature of the setting, Chopin
uses very simple sentences. Complex sentences might have
worked against her intention of developing a sense of the **"still,"**
oppressive evening heat (DA). The word **"*marais*,"** meanwhile,
might interest a STRUCTURALIST critic, who might see this French
word in an English text as indicative of the many significant pairings and contrasts embedded into this story: black and white, reality and fantasy, paradise and perdition, and (very shortly) a story
within a story. The linguistic duality signaled by a word such as
"*marais*" is strongly reinforced at the end of the story, where
Chopin gives us both English and French versions of the same remarks (LB). Included within her simple sentence structure are
many long, rounded vowel sounds (in words such as **"yonder,"**
"bayou," **"John,"** **"lugger,"** **"come,"** **"out,"** **"of,"** **"moving,"**
"slow," **"motion, "down,"** **"bayou,"** **"boat,"** and **"song"**) that
again help create a sense of the still air and unrelenting heat (DA).
Heavy and unhurried, the long vowel sounds almost force the
reader to pronounce each word in the phrase as slowly and deliberately as the movements of the boat itself (DH2). The sparkling
lights give the opening scene almost a fairy-tale prettiness (DR),
but this story will soon prove no fairy tale. The lights against the
darkness also presage the story's preoccupation with relations between the races (DR). Chopin uses the commonplace words
"twinkl[ing]" and **"blinking"** in a very unconventional way, perhaps to convey how uncanny even the most ordinary objects can
appear at night. For example, most people might say, "lights

blink[ed] here and there in the darkness" and "above a few stars were **twinkl[ing]**." Chopin, however, by switching the words, turns the dark night upside-down, so that the lights seem to be "**twinkl[ing]**" while the stars are "**blinking**." A FORMALIST critic might even suggest that this reversed description foreshadows Zoraïde's disoriented view of her world at the end of the story (DH2). A FORMALIST critic would take great interest in the complexity created by the description of the lights and the stars: several layers are kept separate and, at the same time, are fused through similarities in (and repetition of) sounds. Thus with "**bayou**" and "**sky**," the "y" sound is shared but is also slightly altered within each word. In addition, both depth (in the bayou) and height (in the sky) are suggested, but these contrasts are further unified by the words "**twinkled**" and "**blinking**." By describing the lights below as "**twink[ling]**" and the stars above as "**blinking**," Chopin fuses the two planes by using similar sounds while keeping them physically separate (MP). The final word ("**song**") introduces a literal note of lyricism into the story, but the lyricism will soon be submerged into an ugly brutality (RCE). A STRUCTURALIST critic might note how the story's language, even in this first paragraph, already implies various complicated codes. Words such as "*marais*," "**yonder**," "**bayou**," and "**lugger**," for instance, already suggest a definite place and time (nineteenth-century Louisiana), and properly interpreting the story will therefore depend on some familiarity with the interrelated "codes" of this complex culture (HE). The mere use of a word such as "**lugger**" helps create confidence in the author's knowledge of the remote locale she is about to describe (DA). A TRADITIONAL HISTORICAL critic might report that a "**lugger**" was a nautical term for a small boat used for fishing, sailing, or coasting and having two or three masts, each with a lugsail (DH2). The narrator's off-hand reference to a specific locality suggests the reader's familiarity with the territory described—a tactic that already lends the narrative tone a sense of intimacy and authority (LP).

[2] The notes of the song came faintly to the ears of old Manna-Loulou, herself as black as the night, who had gone out upon the gallery to open the shutters wide.

Note how efficiently yet clearly Manna-Loulou is introduced: in a few words Chopin creates a vivid picture of her age, her appearance, her circumstances, and her social role (LP). Manna-Loulou's "old" age may suggest her wisdom and depth of experience (SB). In a different kind of story, Manna-Loulou's "black[ness]" might suggest that she is an evil personality, but in Chopin's tale she in fact emerges as one of the most attractive of all the characters (PW). A THEMATIC critic might notice how the reference to Manna-Loulou's "black[ness]" enhances the motif of darkness and blackness that is so important in this tale. As will later become obvious, this theme of darkness is relevant not only to the use of colors in the story but also to its ultimate focus on injustice, despair, and insanity (DH2). Meanwhile, the word "gallery" already suggests a large, grand home (DA). By opening the shutters Manna-Loulou exposes the house to a wider world and a larger reality (KD, MC). In bayou country, however, shutters are traditionally kept closed at night to ward off dangers and troubles (especially infection); the act of opening them therefore seems ironic (FD). Perhaps the shutters are opened to help improve circulation of the air; the fact that this is necessary suggests that the night may be particularly warm and stifling (SD). The fact that Manna-Loulou hears the music only faintly is possibly relevant to the story's theme of beauty and happiness being out of reach (PN). Note how this single sentence implies three of the five senses—hearing ("notes of the song"), sight ("black as the night"), and touch ("open the shutters wide") [LP].

[3] **Something in the refrain reminded the woman of an old, half-forgotten Creole romance, and she began to sing it low to herself while she threw the shutters open:—**

The word "romance" not only foreshadows an important theme of the story (JDS) but also seems ironic in a work that deals with the actual destruction of a romance (DR). This "half-forgotten" romance seems relevant to the story that is about to be remembered and revived by Manna-Loulou (OT-K); the phrase "half-forgotten" also seems ironic in view of the story's final emphasis on memory and its loss (RCE). Within the space of only a few sentences, Chopin has moved the reader from a most general subject (the weather) to one that is quite specific (this woman's personal memory [DA]). Manna-Loulou's action of throwing "open the shutters wide" is perhaps symbolically appropriate, since she is about to unlock a storehouse of memories and allow them to escape (AMO).

[4]   "Lisett' to kité la plaine,
           Mo perdi bonhair à moué;
           Ziés à moué semblé fontaine,
           Dépi mo pa miré toué."

           [Lizette, {since} you have left the plain
           I have lost my happiness;
           My eyes are like a fountain,
           Since I cannot look at you.]

Significantly, the song deals with lost contact, with lost happiness, with weeping, and with an inability to see, just as Zoraïde will later lose her lover, her baby, her mind (JDS), and finally even her identity (JW). Significantly, too, Zoraïde will never actually see her baby after it is born (DR). A POSTMODERNIST critic might note that Chopin apparently has no qualms about including a "popular" text, this Creole ballad, within a piece of serious "literature" (KN).

[5] And then this old song, a lover's lament for the loss of his mistress, floating into her memory, brought with it the story she would tell to Madame, who lay in her sumptuous mahogany bed, waiting to be fanned and put to sleep to the sound of one of Manna-Loulou's stories.

Note the continued emphasis on age: the elderly Manna-Loulou recalls an "old, half-forgotten Creole romance," here called more simply **"an old song."** An ARCHETYPAL critic might suggest that the ancientness stressed so far implies the permanent human significance of the emotions and insights that the song (like Manna-Loulou's own later story) embodies. Even the focus on a **"lover"** and **"his mistress"** implies a concern with one of the most basic and ARCHETYPAL of all human relationships (RCE). A FORMALIST critic would admire the skillful alliteration of such a phrase as **"a lover's lament for the loss of his mistress"** (LP). However, the fact that the lover laments the loss of a **"mistress"** (rather than of a "wife" or "beloved" or "sweetheart") perhaps already suggests a note of illicit passion—a theme that is later very relevant (MC). Once again the theme of loss is emphasized here—thus foreshadowing the story's subsequent key events (JDS). The fact that the song **"floats"** into her memory is typical of the languid, unhurried motion of the whole narrative up to this point. Eventually, though, the pace will significantly quicken (JW). Chopin slowly brings the setting of the story from across the lake, onto the gallery, and then

into the Madame's room, almost in the manner of a languid unin-
terrupted tracking shot in a film, thus underscoring the smooth
unity of the opening passage (KN). Added to the setting's external
sensuality is the shift of focus to the interior of the house, specifically to a bedroom that bears a **"sumptuous ... bed"** (TR). A
MARXIST critic might note the fact that the bed is made of
"mahogany"—a detail that already implies unusual wealth (KM2).
Is the phrase **"put to sleep"** in any way foreboding or ominous?
(OT-K). Or is the gentleness suggested by the phrase ironic, since
the story will prove to be so disturbing and disquieting? Later, the
story will specifically be described as having inhibited sleep (RCE).
Madame waits to be soothed physically (by being **"fanned"**) and
psychologically (by being told a story). Yet the story she hears will
not prove entirely soothing (RCE). Ironically, it is the voice of
Manna-Loulou that her mistress wants to hear rather than the
specific content of the old woman's story. Such comparative inat-
tention suggests how relatively unimportant Manna-Loulou really
is, as a person, to the woman who "owns" her (AMO).

**[6] The old negress had already bathed her mistress's pretty
white feet and kissed them lovingly, one, then the other. She
had brushed her mistress's beautiful hair, that was as soft and
shining as satin, and was the color of Madame's wedding-ring.
Now, when she reentered the room, she moved softly toward the
bed, and seating herself there began gently to fan Madame
Delisle.**

A MULTICULTURAL critic might suggest that in some ways
Manna-Loulou fits the racial stereotype of a large black female
slave who adopts a maternal attitude toward her white owners
and their children. In this sense she can be seen as an "Aunt
Jemima" or "mammy" figure (BH). A TRADITIONAL HISTORICAL
critic might note that the term **"old negress"** alone, an expression
that would now be considered offensive and insulting, is enough
to designate the slave culture of the Old South in which this story
is immersed (DH2). An ARCHETYPAL critic might argue that the
description of Manna-Loulou as **"old"** already implies her wisdom
(RCE). Because a STRUCTURALIST critic is concerned with the binary nature of language, s/he might focus on the dualities present
in this passage (and throughout the story). These include old and
young, black and white, beauty and ugliness, and subservience
and power (MP). Indeed, note how the reference to Madame

DeLisle's **"pretty white feet"** contrasts explicitly with the earlier description of Manna-Loulou as being "black as the night." The black/white contrast, of course, is an image pattern crucial to the entire story (LB). The simple fact that so much time and detail are devoted to describing Madame Delisle's appearance, in contrast to the relatively sparse description of Manna-Loulou, already suggests the white woman's social and economic superiority (DA). Indeed, Manna-Loulou's attentions to her mistress appear almost worshipful (DH2). Chopin's use of such words as **"soft," "softly," "gently"** and **"sleep,"** combined with the alliteration of such phrases as **"soft and shining as satin,"** helps reinforce the relaxed, relaxing mood so far established—a mood the rest of the story will later disrupt (CB). Significantly (especially in light of the ensuing tale), the relationship between Manna-Loulou and the mistress seems similar to that between a mother and a child (DR, FD). Although technically the mistress enjoys greater power, in some respects she seems passive and dependent in her relationship on Manna-Loulou (DR, MC). It seems ironic that the woman who possesses the most power in this situation is also the one who seems least mature (AMO). A DECONSTRUCTIVE critic might suggest, however, that in some respects Manna-Loulou, although technically the "inferior" party in this relationship, actually enjoys a position of superiority, at least in a moral sense (CB). Despite Madame Delisle's physical attractiveness, isn't it in fact Manna-Loulou who eventually seems the more beautiful (in character) of the two? (CB). Might a MARXIST critic suggest, however, that Manna-Loulou's soft and gentle treatment of her mistress is the result of years of conditioning bred partly from fear of the mistress's domination? (CB). Alternatively, is there perhaps even a hint of eroticism in their relationship? If so, such a hint would provide still another link between this prologue and the tale Manna-Loulou is about to report (FD). Is there any allusion, in the reference to Manna-Loulou **"bath[ing]"** Madame Delisle's feet, to Jesus's washing of the disciples' feet (CB) or to Mary Magdalene washing the feet of Jesus? (PD). In either case, such a possibility would prepare for the even more explicit religious allusions later in the story (RCE). Is Manna-Loulou thereby linked with the Biblical ARCHETYPE of the Good Servant? (CB). Is there also perhaps, in the imagery of Manna-Loulou **"kiss[ing]"** the mistress's feet, a subtle allusion to Mary humbly prostrating herself before Jesus? (JW; PD). Perhaps Chopin means to imply that Madame Delisle, as a false Christ, is an unfit mistress to Manna-Loulou, as an ironic

Saint Mary Magdalene (PD). Perhaps the "kiss[ing]" indicates
Manna-Loulou's genuine gratitude for being permitted to serve as
a house slave rather than being made to work in the fields (KM2).
In any case, is the mistress living vicariously through Manna-
Loulou's tales? (OT-K). The pleasures Madame Delisle experiences
here are ones (an ARCHETYPAL critic might argue) that most readers might also find appealing (CB), but is our ability to empathize
with Madame Delisle's yearning for comfort undercut by our
recognition that her pleasure depends on her exploitation of
Manna-Loulou? (RCE). Ironically, Manna-Loulou's effort to relieve
her mistress of the oppressiveness of the evening heat symbolizes
her own social oppression (DH). In any case, the emphasis on
comfort here contrasts powerfully with the story's later emphasis
on both physical and emotional misery (RCE). Similarly, the
reference to Madame Delisle's **"wedding ring"** subtly introduces
the theme of marriage—an important motif of the later story (CB).
At the same time, a MARXIST critic might observe how the
reference to the **"wedding ring"** implies that Madame Delisle's
hair is golden and therefore further links her to wealth and
materialism (MS). A FEMINIST critic might note how casually it is
assumed that a woman will (or must) have a husband (BH). Is the
mistress's husband dead, or is he merely absent? (MC). If he is
dead (as is in fact implied in Chopin's accompanying story "A
Lady of Bayou St. John"), then the tale of lost love she is about to
hear would be particularly fitting (RCE). The suggested sensuality
of the **"sumptuous mahogany bed"** (another image implying
darkness [DH]) seems somewhat ironic, since Madame Delisle
apparently does not often (if at all) share her bed with her husband
(TR). He is obliquely alluded to only in the description of Madame
Delisle's hair as being "the color of [her] wedding ring." It also
appears that Madame Delisle is childless. Interestingly, the
absence of a husband and childlessness are two characteristics
Madame Delisle shares with Madame Delarivière, a main
character in Manna-Loulou's ensuing story (TR). These traits are
also ones later shared by Zoraïde herself (RCE).

[7] **Manna-Loulou was not always ready with her story, for
Madame would hear none but those that were true. But tonight
the story was all there in Manna-Loulou's head—the story of la
belle Zoraïde—and she told it to her mistress in the soft Creole
patois whose music and charm no English words can convey.**

A DIALOGICAL critic might suggest that Manna-Loulou's tale, like any other story told orally, changes slightly with each telling. Each storyteller invariably adds his or her own inflections and fabrications in order to emphasize what he or she deems most important (DH2). Interested in the ways each detail of a text contributes to its complex unity, a FORMALIST critic might notice the intricacy Chopin creates by telling a story within a story. A FORMALIST might also notice how Chopin's detailed descriptions encourage the reader to compare and contrast the inner story with the outer narrative. For example, Zoraïde and Manna-Loulou, both being favorite slaves, provide diversion and amusement for their mistresses—Manna-Loulou by her storytelling and Zoraïde by her happiness, beauty, and charm. However, while Zoraïde is young and "dainty as the finest lady of la rue Royale," Manna-Loulou is old and "black as the night"; while Zoraïde is expected to do nothing but sit prettily "at her mistress's side," Manna-Loulou is expected to attend to her mistress's every need; and, while Zoraïde eventually disobeys her mistress, Manna-Loulou remains submissive. The characters of Madame Delarivière and Madame Delisle also provide interesting points of comparison. For example, they are both wealthy women accustomed to the pampered, coddled lifestyle of slave owners. However, the similarities end there, for, whereas Madame Delarivière exhibits cruelty and indifference, Madame Delisle exhibits compassion and concern; whereas Madame Delarivière induces defiance and disobedience in Zoraïde, Madame Delisle induces love and tenderness in Manna-Loulou; and whereas Madame Delarivière eventually loses Zoraïde's attendance, Madame Delisle succeeds in keeping Manna-Loulou's devoted services. A FORMALIST might also point out that while the differences between these two sets of characters provide the story with a heightened degree of complexity, the similarities provide a sense of congruity and balance (DH2). Further similarities and contrasts also link the inner and outer tales. For example, in the outer story the slave woman is older than her mistress, while in the inner story the reverse is true. In both stories the slaves are favorites of their mistresses, but whereas Manna-Loulou is shown to be a hard worker, Zoraïde at first leads a life of relative privilege. Both slaves, however, are expected to please their mistresses (SR).

By mentioning Manna-Loulou's **"soft Creole patois,"** the narrator suddenly emphasizes a language barrier that further complicates a tale that had seemed to begin so simply. In fact, the nonchalant inclusion of the word **"patois"** is itself a specific instance of the linguistic complexity of the story (TDC). The reference to the **"music and charm"** of Manna-Loulou's tale seems to imply, ironically, that the tale will end happily or will be soothing; instead, of course, it ends in tragedy and is disturbing (JDS). Chopin contrasts the richly exotic and mellifluous tones of Manna-Loulou's story-telling with the indifferent brutality of the story she tells, and perhaps this contrast is also relevant to the apparently loving relationship between Manna-Loulou and her mistress and the more complicated feelings Manna-Loulou really experiences toward her mistress (JG). Note, for instance, the sense of command and assumed superiority implied by the simple phrase **"Madame would hear none but those that were true"**— words suggesting that Madame Delisle's desires are all-important (RCE). By using the device of the story-within-a-story, Chopin can play with the notion of the opposition between written and "oral" texts—an opposition likely to be of particular interest to POSTMODERN critics, who are intrigued by the mixing and transgression of conventional genres (KN).

[8] **"La belle Zoraïde had eyes that were so dusky, so beautiful, that any man who gazed too long into their depths was sure to lose his head, and even his heart sometimes. Her soft, smooth skin was the color of *café-au-lait*. As for her elegant manners, her *svelte* and graceful figure, they were the envy of half the ladies who visited her mistress, Madame Delarivière.**

A FEMINIST might note the heavy emphasis here on Zoraïde's merely physical beauty (BL). The opening sentence here suggests that although any man might first feel lust (**"lose his head"**) for Zoraïde because of the beauty of her eyes, in some cases such lust might metamorphose into a deeper kind of genuine love (**"lose ... his heart sometimes"**). Such a metamorphosis is, of course, exactly the sort that le beau Mézor experiences when he later meets Zoraïde (LP). The opening emphasis on the youthful beauty of Zoraïde's eyes prepares, ironically, for her later appearance as a **"sad-eyed"** woman (RCE). Indeed, **eye** imagery will be used significantly and repeatedly throughout the story (DH). Perhaps Manna-Loulou begins by stressing Zoraïde's beauty in order to help interest Madame Delisle (who is also beautiful) in the slave's story: by emphasizing Zoraïde's beauty, Manna-Loulou perhaps encourages Madame Delisle to view her almost as an equal rather than as just an inferior (SB; CH). The phrase **"lose his head"** is at this point merely hyperbolic; in retrospect, however, it seems ominous, not only because literally it implies death (JDS) but also because later Zoraïde herself will figuratively lose both her head and her heart (DR). Zoraïde's **"dusky"** color helps continue Chopin's emphasis on images of light and darkness (OT-K) and also gives her a quality of mystery (KD), while the reference to the **"depths"** of her eyes already suggests the complexity of her character (DR). An ARCHETYPAL critic might note, in fact, that a person's **"eyes"** are traditionally considered the windows into a person's soul (RCE). A FEMINIST critic might suggest, however, that even though Zoraïde in some ways seems an exotic figure, in other ways Chopin's description of her fits various common female stereotypes (HE). In certain respects she fits the correct, culturally prescribed image of a "proper" woman, especially in her softness, grace, and elegance (HE). The fact that **"any"** man might find her attractive suggests, significantly, that her beauty transcends artificial distinctions of race or class, although these distinctions will subsequently prove all-important (JW). The description of her skin appeals simultaneously (and synaesthetically) to the senses of sight, touch, and taste (MC), while the reference to *"café-au-lait"* already subtly symbolizes the mixing of colors and flavors that Zoraïde herself (a mulatto) embodies (JW). The fact that the dark-black Manna-Loulou so carefully describes the skin color of Zoraïde subtly suggests how important race is in her society and therefore also in her own consciousness (PP). Yet by stressing the beauty of Zoraïde's skin, Chopin implicitly challenges the artificial distinctions between "white beauty" and "black ugliness" on which the systems of slavery and racism depended (KRN). The emphasis on Zoraïde's manners, her figure, and the reaction she provokes from **"ladies"** already suggests that she occupies an unusual position for a woman of color in her society (FD). Not until the last three words of the cited passage do we discover that she is indeed a servant; only later do we discover that she is in fact a slave (RCE). Until those final three words, all the emphasis thus far has been on her own independent attractions and powers—an ironic emphasis in a story that will later stress how much she is subject to the power of others (RCE). Zoraïde arouses the **"envy"** of the **"half the ladies who visited her mistress"** not only because of her physical beauty but because such beauty reflects well on the woman who owns her: Zoraïde is a prize possession, and the other women are probably at least as envious of the good fortune of Madame Delarivière in possessing her as they are of the slave's own beauty. They perceive only her outer, physical and social attractions and care little for her inner character or personal needs. Ironically, by the end of the story, physical charms are among the few traits Zoraïde still possesses after her character and emotions have been ravaged (AMO). The fact that Manna-Loulou claims that only **"half"** the ladies envied Zoraïde not only recalls the earlier statement that **"any"** man would fall in love with her, but it also makes her latter claim seem more credible. Perhaps Manna-Loulou is also implying that the response of the men is more natural and thus more absolute than the superficial envy of the women (TDC).

[9] "No wonder Zoraïde was as charming and as dainty as the finest lady of la rue Royale: from a toddling thing she had been brought up at her mistress's side; her fingers had never done rougher work than sewing a fine muslin seam; and she even had her own little black servant to wait upon her. Madame, who was her godmother as well as her mistress, would often say to her:—

This initial description of Zoraïde makes her sound not much different from the pampered Madame Delisle, especially in the emphasis on her lack of work and in the reference to her being attended by a black servant. Later, of course, the experiences of Zoraïde and Madame Delisle will diverge dramatically. A STRUCTURALIST critic might even see Zoraïde as ultimately a reverse image of Madame Delisle—the white woman luxuriating in a serene paradise, the black woman spiraling downward into madness (LB). The reference to Zoraïde as a **"toddling"** child is perhaps a bit of ironic foreshadowing, since the same word will later be used to describe Zoraïde's own daughter (DR). Also ironic is Madame Delarivière's role as godmother, since a godparent not only has responsibilities for a child's religious and spiritual instruction (DR) but also is obliged to raise a child in the event of the parent's death (JA). Later, of course, Madame Delarivière will behave in ways that seem anything but Christian, and she will also play a very ironic role in raising Zoraïde's daughter. Is there any possibility, in fact, that Manna-Loulou is the now-grown **"little black servant"** of Zoraïde? This possibility would help to explain her intimate knowledge of Zoraïde's story (AL). Similarly, is it at all possible that Zoraïde (who is, after all, a mulatto) is herself a daughter of Madame Delarivière? (FD). This possibility might help explain not only Madame Delarivière's solicitous care for the young Zoraïde but also her later vehement reaction when Zoraïde plans to marry a black man (FD).

[10] "'Remember, Zoraïde, when you are ready to marry, it must be in a way to do honor to your bringing up.

Her opening word—"**Remember**"—implies that this is not the first time she has announced these plans (JW). The word also already implies that in Madame Delarivière's opinion, Zoraïde also needs to be carefully guided and controlled (PP, OT-K). Finally, in retrospect it seems extremely ironic that the first word we hear Madame Delarivière speak to Zoraïde is "**remember**," since by the end of the story Zoraïde's memory (and even identity) will be destroyed largely as a result of Madame Delarivière's conduct (PN). Although the word "**ready**" may simply imply being of a proper age (MR), it may also suggest freedom of choice (CM)—a suggestion immediately and ironically undercut by the next clauses, especially by the word "**must**" (RCE). Madame Delarivière's reference to "**honor**" seems extremely ironic in light of her later dishonorable conduct—although that conduct (even more ironically) is motivated by a very peculiar sense of what is *socially* honorable (JDS). The mistress speaks of Zoraïde's need to "**honor**" her obligations, thereby de-emphasizing the mistress's own obligations to the young woman who has served her so loyally (AMO).

[11] "'It will be at the Cathedral. Your wedding gown, your *corbeille* [hope chest], all will be of the best; I shall see to that myself. You know, M'sieur Ambroise is ready whenever you say the word, and his master is willing to do as much for him as I shall do for you. It is a union that will please me in every way.'

The details mentioned here reinforce our sense of Madame Delarivière's wealth and status (CH), while the reference to the "cathedral" again associates her, ironically, with Christianity. However, the fact that she mentions a cathedral rather than simply mentioning a "church" makes clear, as well, her interest in social distinctions and social display (RCE). The "**cathedral**" represents the center of both religious and political power of Madame's patriarchal faith (TR). Madame enjoys power and does not mind wielding it, and as a widow, wealthy in her own right, she appears in many respects more masculine than conventionally feminine (TR). She imagines the marriage as a public ceremony, not as an intimate union (TR), and she treats Zoraïde, in fact, as an item on display (KD), so that her kindness, paradoxically, is essentially selfish (RCE). Thus, although Madame Delarivière has showered Zoraïde with material gifts, at the same time she denies the girl any truly independent sense of hope (JW). The reference to the **"hope chest"** is therefore ironic (JW), especially since a hope chest is normally associated with the establishment of an independent home and, with it, an autonomous identity—the very possessions Zoraïde will later be denied (DR). In fact, Zoraïde's entire situation as a favored servant is fundamentally ambiguous and inherently contradictory (FD). Madame Delarivière's closing reference to her own pleasure underscores her essential self-interest (JW); and eventually, of course, she will be anything but pleased, either in her initial response to Zoraïde's plans to marry or with the final outcome of the events she sets in motion (RCE). Her promise that **"I shall see to that myself"** seems especially ironic in light of subsequent events, since her later direct intervention in Zoraïde's life will cause Zoraïde endless pain. Although Zoraïde is allowed the illusion that she has power not only over her own life but also over the life of M'sieur Ambroise (who is **"ready whenever you say the word"**), in fact it is the mistress and master of these two slaves who really control their fates, as subsequent events will show. By the end of the story, indeed, it will be M'sieur Ambroise (presumably with his master's approval) who will ultimately reject Zoraïde rather than Zoraïde who will have the power to accept Ambroise. Zoraïde will thus be denied even the small measure of control she is explicitly promised here (RCE).

[12] **"Monsieur Ambroise was then the body servant of Doctor Langlé. La belle Zoraïde detested the little mulatto, with his shining whiskers like a white man's, and his small eyes, that were cruel and false as a snake's. She would cast down her own mischievous eyes, and say:—**

The name **"Ambroise"** is extremely ironic, since "ambrosia" is the food of the gods and (by extension) anything pleasing to taste or smell (FD). Obviously Zoraïde regards the doctor as anything but appealing (FD); the word **"little"** implies weakness, pettiness, inferiority, and lack of respect (DR), while the fact that he is Doctor Langlé's **"body servant,"** although in one sense an indication of a prestigious position analogous to Zoraïde's (TR), in another sense insinuates powerlessness, servility, dependence, and perhaps even effeminacy (DR). He is a kind of living adjunct to the "body politic" of the white plantation system (TR). His **"white whiskers"** may imply that he is significantly older than Zoraïde and therefore unappealing to her partly for that reason (LB). His **"small eyes"** (which contrast with the "beautiful" eyes mentioned earlier [8] as belonging to Zoraïde and the "fierce" eyes mentioned later [15] as belonging to his rival, le beau Mézor [RCE]) make him sound almost reptilian or rodent-like (DR). An ARCHETYPAL critic might argue that Chopin here plays on a natural human fear or dislike of reptiles (MG). **"Snake[s],"** in fact, are of course conventional symbols of evil and deception (PD). Is there any irony in the fact that Zoraïde detests Ambroise in part because of his appearance? (JDS). She herself, after all, is judged largely on the basis on her own appearance, and this concern with appearances will later help determine her own fate (JDS). Does her reaction to the **"little mulatto"** reflect any confusion or essential ambivalence concerning her own identity? (DR, OT-K). Perhaps, subconsciously, she desires either one clear racial identity or another (DR); perhaps her vehement rejection of Ambroise indicates her underlying unhappiness with her own status as a mulatto (OT-K). The reference to her perception of Ambroise's moral traits—his cruelty and falseness—suggests that her rejection is based not entirely on his appearance; her assessment encourages us to pay attention to his later conduct to determine whether he deserves to be described in these ways (RCE). Ironically, whereas the whites of Zoraïde's day would regard blackness as an undesirable trait, Zoraïde is repelled by Ambroise partly because he resembles a white man (RCE). By marrying Ambroise, the servant of a master who desires to marry Zoraïde's own mistress, Zoraïde would be even more tightly tied into a position of dominance and control than is already the case. The projected relationship between these four people might even seem almost incestuously interconnected (RCE). Because a NEW HISTORICIST critic is partly concerned with the play of power between individuals within a social class, s/he might focus on the tension between Zoraïde and Ambroise. Despite the fact that they share similar social conditions, an uncomfortable exchange of energy occurs between them: Ambroise is vying for a wife over whom he might have control, while Zoraïde views him as a threat to her present position. Both are bound in servitude to their masters—a condition they cannot change—but both are also struggling to maintain or enhance what little freedom of self they possess (MP). The reference to Zoraïde's **"mischievous eyes"** is the first subtle clue that the young woman has a mind and will of her own and will not necessarily follow Madame's plans (CH). The word "**mischievous**" seems to imply, ironically, that Zoraïde is at fault for lying, whereas such deception is her only defense against further misery (AMO). Her willingness to defy her mistress slightly here through such "**mischievous**" conduct foreshadows her much more serious defiance later (RCE).

[13] "'Ah, nénaine [Godmother], I am so happy, so contented here at your side just as I am. I don't want to marry now; next year, perhaps, or the next.' And Madame would smile indulgently and remind Zoraïde that a woman's charms are not everlasting.

Chopin's skillful use of dialogue throughout this short tale helps individualize the characters; each of them has a distinctive voice and therefore each of them seems more convincingly real (HE). Zoraïde's reply shows how skillfully she can use language and play on her mistress's vanity (CM), particularly in a situation in which she has, in fact, no real choice (JW). Although she uses a term of affection ("**nénaine**"), her subservient diplomacy clearly indicates that she is not comfortable enough with Madame Delarivière simply to tell her the truth. The fact that Madame "**smile[s] indulgently**" at Zoraïde's stated reluctance to marry shows her smug assumption that she has total control over all aspects of Zoraïde's life (GW). Meanwhile, the claim that "**a woman's charms are not everlasting**" is clearly ironic in light of Zoraïde's later horrible fate (DR; PW). A FEMINIST critic might claim that Madame Delarivière's final statement here shows that, despite her apparent power and authority, she herself is subtly aware of being trapped in a patriarchal situation in which her value, like Zoraïde's, is defined by her appearance (AS). Just as Zoraïde is subjugated by a racist society, so is Madame herself subjugated by a society dominated by men (AS). Such patriarchal power affects a privileged white woman as well as a literal slave (BH). Madame Delarivière is constantly "**remind[ing]**" Zoraïde and urging her to "**remember**"—phrasing that suggests the constant indoctrination and social conditioning to which Zoraïde has already been exposed (RCE). At the same time (a FEMINIST critic might suggest), Madame Delarivière's preoccupation with her slave's prospective wedding suggests the shallowness and emptiness of her own life:

she apparently has little else to occupy her thinking or her energies (BH).

[14] **"But the truth of the matter was, Zoraïde had seen le beau Mézor dance the Bamboula in Congo Square. That was a sight to hold one rooted to the ground. Mézor was as straight as a cypress tree and as proud looking as a king. His body, bare to the waist, was like a column of ebony and it glistened like oil.**

The reference to **"Congo Square"** already associates Mézor with black Africa (FD); in this and other respects (especially physically) he is the opposite of the small, half-white Ambroise (RCE). Note that **Mézor**, unlike Ambroise, has no "M'sieur" attached to his name—a fact that suggests his relative freedom from social control (DH). The adjective that identifies him—**"le beau"**—refers to his personal appearance, not to his social standing (RCE). Even the definite article **"le"** ("the") may imply that Mézor is a unique, special individual; he is not "just another slave" (CS). Mézor has the same kind of stunning impact on Zoraïde that she was earlier said to have on men (JDS; DR): by noting that the sight of him could **"hold one rooted to the ground,"** Chopin uses language that carries connotations of earthiness, nature (FD), stability (RCE), and fecundity (TR). Zoraïde's vision of Mézor puts her in touch, in a sense, which her own ethnic and cultural roots (CS). The fact that he is **"straight"** suggests strength, sturdiness (DR), and self-assurance (PD), while his association with the cyprus and ebony trees links him with life, vitality (DR), and exotic richness (PD). (An ARCHETYPAL critic might even argue that trees are traditionally linked to the ARCHETYPE of the Great Mother, since their roots go deep into the earth [TR]). Perhaps Zoraïde's interest in Mézor also implies her interest in her black roots—an interest already suggested by her rejection of Ambroise (PH). Mézor seems to represent the natural, self-assured culture and identity for which Zoraïde longs. Her roots appear to be important to her, and Mézor epitomizes the blackness that contrasts with her half-white lifestyle (SG). When Zoraïde sees Mézor dancing, she becomes like him: she is now more aware of her position in nature. The two of them seem perfectly matched, not only in the similar adjectives attached to their names but also by the similarity of the names themselves—**"Zoraïde"** and **"Mézor"** (FS). Mézor's natural royalty (he is **"as proud looking as a king"**) belies his social status as a slave (RAC; KG), and from this point forward Zoraïde will become a social rebel as she offers allegiance to this new **"king"** (RCE). A FEMINIST critic, however, might be troubled by this depiction of Zoraïde as a creature so easily controlled by sexual desire. Is she simply sacrificing one kind of domination for another? (AS). Is her feeling for Mézor truly love or is it mere physical lust? (RB). If it *is* merely lust, perhaps this superficial attitude has been paradoxically encouraged by being raised in a society that places so much emphasis on mere physical appearance (RB). Clearly the description of Mézor's body as a **"straight ... column,"** **"glisten[ing] like oil,"** has sexual (FD), even phallic (CY) overtones, suggesting his strength and implying the potency he later demonstrates (RCE). The **"glisten[ing]"** of the **"column of ebony"** once again reinforces the story's image pattern of light counterpoised by darkness. Zoraïde sees the physicality of Mézor in sexual terms, but Mézor's master undoubtedly sees the slave's strength as an aspect of his monetary value (AMO). Although Mézor is strong, however, he is also graceful and is thus a fitting partner for the beautiful Zoraïde herself (MC). His skill at **"dance"** associates him with festivity, freedom from care, and harmony of body and soul, but his dancing is also ironically associated with a liberty he will later lose (RCE). His skill at dancing, and his devotion to it and delight in it, may reflect its status as one of his few outlets of true self-expression (AMO). Zoraïde's first glimpse of Mézor is also our first glimpse of him: he appears as unexpectedly to us as to her, and he appears in a vision that associates him with the strength and independence he will later be denied (RCE). A LONGINIAN critic might admire Chopin's use of elevated, exalted language when describing Mézor, since such language helps associate him with sublimity or elevation (CW). Does this language—which is technically the language of Manna-Loulou, the storyteller—reflect Manna-Loulou's own desire for a loving relationship with a strong black man? After all, the only relationship of hers that we know about is her relation with her young white mistress. No husband or children of Manna-Loulou are ever mentioned (RB). Perhaps Manna-Loulou, in this sense, empathizes with the loneliness and isolation later felt by Zoraïde (RCE).

[15] **"Poor Zoraïde's heart grew sick in her bosom with love for le beau Mézor from the moment that she saw the fierce gleam of his eye, lighted by the inspiring strains of the Bamboula, and beheld the stately movements of his splendid body swaying and quivering through the figures of the dance.**

Here the claim that Zoraïde's **"heart grew sick"** is partly hyper-bolic, but by the end of the story, of course, she will be plunged into a literal mental and emotional sickness from which she will never recover (SB). Her metaphorical **"sick[ness]"** here is associ-ated with a kind of pleasure; later, her true sickness will be far more literally painful (RCE). Chopin seems to play here with the standard stereotype of both male and female slaves as controlled mainly by their passions; perhaps she alludes to this stereotype in order to show later how shallow it is (BH). A FEMINIST critic might suggest that Chopin here invokes the unfortunate stereotype of women as passionate creatures who cannot control their emotions (SH). On the other hand, both a PSYCHOANALYTIC and an ARCHETYPAL critic might suggest that Zoraïde is merely manifesting the enormously powerful and primal effects of sexual longing. For both kinds of critics, such longing would be simply a part of human nature (KM2). Perhaps the reference to Zoraïde's **"bosom"** already prepares us for the story's later very heavy emphasis on motherhood (SB). Once again Chopin effectively uses imagery of light in such words as **"gleam,"** **"lighted,"** and **"splendid"** (FD), and once again Mézor combines opposites by seeming both **"fierce"** and **"stately,"** his graceful self-control making him an appropriate match for Zoraïde (MC). The **"fierce gleam"** of Mézor's eye contrasts sharply with the earlier description [12] of M'sieur Ambroise's **"small eyes, that were cruel and false as a snake's"** (DR). Mézor's eyes almost associate him with an impressive beast, such as a lion or tiger, so that he seems a natural creature rather than a product of corrupt human society (DR). Although Zoraïde seems almost possessed by the sight of Mézor, neither of them, ironically, can possess either each other or even themselves; Mézor's power is emphasized here, only to be brutally denied later (JW). This emphasis on ecstatic posses-sion, coupled with the references to **"the inspiring strains of the Bamboula"** and Mézor's **"stately movements,"** would greatly in-terest LONGINIAN critics, who tend to focus on irresistibly sublime or elevated passions (RCE).

[16] **"But when she knew him later, and he came near to her to speak with her, all the fierceness was gone out of his eyes, and she saw only kindness in them and heard only gentleness in his voice, for love had taken possession of him also, and Zoraïde was more distracted than ever. When Mézor was not dancing Bamboula in Congo Square, he was hoeing sugar cane, bare-**

footed and half-naked, in his master's field outside of the city. Doctor Langlé was his master as well as M'sieur Ambroise's.

The "kindness" of Mézor's eyes and the "gentleness" of his voice contrast effectively with the earlier description [12] of Ambroise's "small eyes, that were cruel and false as a snake's" (KD). Earlier Zoraïde had been attracted mainly by Mézor's physique; now she perceives the beauty of his character or soul (SB). He seems to embody a "kindness" which, unlike that of Madame Delarivière, is not manipulative or selfish (SB). Mézor's dignified self-respect and self-assurance are implied by his willingness to approach Zoraïde and speak to her, even though he is black and she is a mulatto and even though he is a manual laborer and she has led a life of relative privilege (RCE). Although earlier Mézor had seemed to possess Zoraïde, now their "possession" seems mutual; this relationship between equals is ironic in a story that so much emphasizes slavery, just as this relationship rooted in "love" is ironic in a story that so much stresses relationships of power (JW). The imagery of Mézor "hoeing sugar-cane, bare-footed and half-naked" is ambiguous: on the one hand it suggests poverty (KD) and primitiveness (OT-K) and thus contrasts with our earlier visions of him, when he had enjoyed freedom from labor. On the other hand, it emphasizes once more his strength and even his sensuality, his closeness to the earth (RCE). An ARCHETYPAL critic might even suggest that Mézor is linked with the feminine earth and depicted as an agent of growth and fecundity; unlike M'sieur Ambroise, Doctor Langlé's "body servant," Mézor is connected not so much with a human master as with the forces of nature (TR).

[17] One day, when Zoraïde kneeled before her mistress, drawing on Madame's silken stockings, that were of the finest, she said:
    "'Nénaine, you have spoken to me often of marrying. Now, at last, I have chosen a husband, but it is not M'sieur Ambroise, it is le beau Mézor that I want and no other.' And Zoraïde hid her face in her hands when she said that, for she guessed, rightly enough, that her mistress would be very angry.

Zoraïde's "kneel[ing]" before her mistress is functional since she is performing a service, but it also symbolically suggests submission (KD), almost as if the mistress possesses the power of a god— as indeed she does in some respects (JDS). A FORMALIST critic, interested in connections between the diverse parts of the work, might note how Zoraïde's posture and conduct recall Manna-Loulou's attention to the feet of her own mistress [6] earlier in the story (SR). Perhaps this posture is even meant to suggest a perversion of religious imagery, as if Madame Delarivière occupies a position of superiority to which she is unentitled (BB). In any case, the implied religious imagery here is part of a larger pattern in this story of religious language and allusions (BB). Ironically, the woman who wears such beautiful silk stockings will soon reveal her inner ugliness (AMO). There seems a nice contrast between Zoraïde's submissive posture and her matter-of-fact, assertive language: she does not make a request but instead announces a choice, even though she correctly anticipates the response (MC). A DIALOGICAL critic, concerned with the negotiation of different voices within a work, might focus on the subtle changes in tone and control of Zoraïde's speech. Zoraïde begins by addressing her mistress as **"Nénaine,"** a soft, placating word, so that her voice at first seems childlike and unthreatening. However, she soon mentions how she has been **"spoken to"** (not "spoken with"), so that the subtle use of a single preposition implies her mistress's superiority or condescension rather than any conversational equality between the two women. In her next sentence, however, Zoraïde undermines her previously subservient tone by stating, **"I have chosen"**—phrasing that implies a certain strength and power of will, although even here the suggestion is somewhat muted (MP). Zoraïde's claim to have **"chosen"** is ironic, because the only "choice" her mistress will permit is the "choice" of when to acknowledge the mistress's choice *for* her of Ambroise. Zoraïde's use of the verb **"want"** when referring to Mézor also reminds us that her choice is simultaneously an expression of will (PP), possessiveness (MC), and sexual desire (O-TK). The word **"want"** also reminds us that although all of Zoraïde's material needs have been taken care of, she is the only person in a position to know what she truly desires (PN). The contrast between the fine beauty of the mistress's clothing (**"silken stockings, that were of the finest"**) and the ugly anger of her reply will soon be apparent (JDS). Does the fact that Zoraïde hides her face imply that she anticipates a potentially violent reaction, or does it suggest that witnessing the mistress's anger would be too psychologically painful? (SG, RCE). Might it even suggest an element of shame? (SG).

[18] And indeed, Madame Delarivière was at first speechless with rage. When she finally spoke it was only to gasp out, exasperated:

"'That negro! that negro! Bon Dieu Seigneur [Good Lord God], but this is too much!'

Ironically, the religious Madame Delarivière, who serves as Zoraïde's godmother and looks forward to a wedding at the cathedral, instinctively takes God's name in vain: a small but effective symbol of her larger hypocrisy (CH). She not only indicates her frustration that her own long-held plans have been threatened (FD) but also suggests, perhaps, a condescending assumption that this threat will pose no final problem: she seems **"exasperated"** in the way one might be with a misbehaving child, yet still seems confident of eventually exerting her authority (KD). As with any idealized object, Zoraïde is quickly plunged from pedestal to pit in her mistress's eyes (PP). It seems both ironic and appropriate that Madame Delarivière invokes **"God"** when expressing her racism—ironic because from a modern point of view her attitude seems to contradict her religion and her role as Zoraïde's godmother, but appropriate because from Madame Delarivière's point of view Zoraïde seeks to violate the God-given, natural order of things. By invoking God, especially in the exact terms that she uses, Madame Delarivière indicates her acceptance of a hierarchical power structure, which Zoraïde seems about to violate (RCE). Later Manna-Loulou herself will mention the phrase "good God" in a way that may communicate a subtle irony (PW).

[19] "'Am I white, nénaine?' pleaded Zoraïde.

"'You white! *Malheureuse!* [Miserable one!] You deserve to have the lash laid upon you like any other slave; you have proven yourself no better than the worst.'

"'I am not white,' persisted Zoraïde, respectfully and gently. 'Doctor Langlé gives me his slave to marry, but he would not give me his son. Then, since I am not white, let me have from out of my own race the one whom my heart has chosen.'

The fact that Zoraïde addresses Madame Delarivière as **"nénaine"** ("godmother") makes the mistress's brutal anger seem all the more ironic, and perhaps Zoraïde's use of the term is even slyly calculated (RCE). By asking whether she is white, Zoraïde not only tries to make her mistress acknowledge reality (PP) but also subtly uses the mistress's own logic against her; Zoraïde thus demonstrates her mental agility and resourcefulness (MC; RB). At this point Zoraïde is described as **"plead[ing],"** but, with typical balance, Chopin will later describe her as **"persist[ing]."** Once again, then, Chopin suggests the complexity of Zoraïde's character (MC)—a complexity neatly underlined by the shift from the question **"Am I white"** to the statement **"I am not white"** (HE). When Madame Delarivière exclaims, **"You white!"**, is she expressing stinging sarcasm (KD) or is she indicating that to her it seems absurd to link the two words? (MC). Her exclamation here recalls her earlier reference [18] to Mézor as "That Negro!" (RCE). It seems ironic that the mistress calls Zoraïde **"miserable,"** not only because it is the mistress who is responsible for the slave's misery but also because Zoraïde's true misery is only just beginning, and Madame Delarivière will also be responsible for it, as well (AMO). It seems ironic that the mistress claims Zoraïde has **"proven"** herself so awful, because as yet Zoraïde has done nothing more than merely announce her choice (PP). Ironically, too, it will soon be Madame Delarivière who will actually prove herself **"no better than the worst"** (RCE). Since Zoraïde's identity has been clouded by her upbringing, it seems significant that she speaks of choosing **"from out of [her] own race"**; is she here attempting to claim or regain her identity as well as naming a lover? (KD). A READER-RESPONSE critic might argue that nearly all readers could empathize with Zoraïde's desire to choose her own mate (SG). An ARCHETYPAL critic might even argue that such desire for self-determination is deeply rooted in human nature (KM2).

[20] **"However, you may well believe that Madame would not hear to that. Zoraïde was forbidden to speak to Mézor, and Mézor was cautioned against seeing Zoraïde again. But you know how the negroes are, Ma'zélle Titite,"** added Manna-Loulou, smiling a little sadly. **"There is no mistress, no master, no king nor priest who can hinder them from loving when they will. And these two found ways and means.**

Is there, perhaps, any touch of irony in the phrase **"you may well believe,"** especially since these words are addressed by Manna-Loulou to her own mistress? Does she perhaps (unconsciously?) suggest that the woman who dominates her own life will naturally be able to understand the perspective of the woman who owns Zoraïde? (SB). A FEMINIST critic might note that whereas Zoraïde is **"forbidden"** to speak to Mézor, the latter is only **"cautioned"** against seeing Zoraïde again. Perhaps such phrasing implies the extent to which female slaves were regarded as weaker than their male counterparts (SR). Although Manna-Loulou claims that erotic self-assertion is a behavior specific to blacks, it is actually universal (PH, FD) and partly involves the attraction of anything that is forbidden (MC). Manna-Loulou tells the story in the way she expects her mistress will want to hear it, which partly explains why she speaks of blacks as if she were not one herself (FD). Yet this odd expression of apparently racist sentiment is also counter-balanced by a tone of admiration at the determination and will of Zoraïde and Mézor (MC). What might have seemed a statement reflecting racial self-hatred can thus be seen as reflecting a sense of strength—an assertion that although blacks may have been physically enslaved, no one could subjugate their hearts (SG). Manna-Loulou seems almost defiant but is sly enough to appear to agree with her mistress's point of view about the behavior of blacks (FS). The old woman is described as **"smiling a little sadly,"** partly because she knows the unfortunate outcome of their meetings—the defeat that will result from this apparent success (KD). Perhaps this phrase also suggests that Manna-Loulou can identify and sympathize with the kind of emotion she now describes (TDC). Does Manna-Loulou's final statement here reflect at all on her own relations with her own mistress? (FD). Does she here imply the limits of her own loyalty? (RCE). Does her list of authority figures—**mistress, master, king, and priest**—subconsciously reflect the patriarchal hierarchy that controls her culture, with religion as the chief instrument of patriarchal control? (AS). Perhaps the list also helps mitigate any suggestion that Manna-Loulou is specifically challenging the system of slavery in particular; perhaps she instead implies that literally no power could thwart the intentions of determined black lovers (DH).

[21] **"When months had passed by, Zoraïde, who had grown unlike herself—sober and preoccupied—said again to her mistress:—**

"'Nénaine, you would not let me have Mézor for my husband; but I have disobeyed you, I have sinned. Kill me if you wish, nénaine; forgive me if you will; but when I heard le beau Mézor say to me, "Zoraïde, mo l'aime toi [I love you]," I could have died, but I could not have helped loving him.'

Ironically, Zoraïde addresses her mistress almost as if the latter were a deity: **"I have disobeyed you, I have sinned"** (PH). In fact, the phrase **"I have sinned"** is used by Catholics in making confession (KD). This confession puts Madame Delarivière in the godlike position of being able to choose to respond either with mercy or with punishment (SG). Surely Zoraïde does not truly believe that she has "sinned" by loving Mézor, but she knows her actions and beliefs are morally reprehensible to her mistress. Zoraïde's own moral code seems to involve doing what is right according to her own heart and soul (KG). If, on the other hand, Zoraïde *does* genuinely believe that she has in some sense **"sinned,"** then her phrasing suggests how much she has indeed internalized the values of the larger culture (RCE). Alternatively, in confessing to her mistress, is Zoraïde perhaps motivated by knowledge that she is already pregnant? (PH). Would she confess otherwise? Or is she motivated to confess by her fundamental honesty? (FD). Her two references here to potential death are examples of ironic foreshadowing, since in a very real sense she does die as a result of her love (JS). Emotionally and mentally (if not quite literally), Madame Delarivière does indeed help **"kill"** Zoraïde: by the end of the story the young woman is alive but lifeless (SB). Paradoxically, although Zoraïde can (at least temporarily) accept the love of le beau Mézor, she will never have the opportunity to show any love to the child that will be born of this union (AL). Perhaps part of the reason that Zoraïde finds Mézor's appeal so irresistible is that she has never (because of her status) really felt truly loved and has never, perhaps, been told before that she was loved (MC). Indeed, an ARCHETYPAL critic might argue that **"loving"** and being loved are two of the most primal of all human emotions (TT; MS). A LONGINIAN critic might find her final statement here an excellent example of a sublime emotion—the overpowering force of **love** (SB2).

[22] **"This time Madame Delarivière was so actually pained, so wounded at hearing Zoraïde's confession, that there was no place left in her heart for anger. She could only utter confused reproaches. But she was a woman of action rather than of words, and she acted promptly. Her first step was to induce Doctor Langlé to sell Mézor.**

Madame's feelings of being **"pained"** and **"wounded"** seem obviously ironic in light of the much deeper pain and suffering she later inflicts on Zoraïde (SB). Does Madame Delarivière's lack of anger paradoxically reflect her lack of fundamental love for Zoraïde? (MC). Or does the mistress understand Zoraïde's feelings but act as she feels she must? (AL). Or, alternatively, does she express her anger through her swift actions rather than through words? (PP). The fact that she is described as **"hearing Zoraïde's confession"** contributes to the pattern of ironic religious imagery that runs throughout the story. A priest who heard a confession would be obliged not only to show some compassion to the sinner but also to keep the confession private. A priest would also seek to reconcile the sinner to God and the community by imposing an appropriate penance. In contrast to all these ideal responses, Madame Delarivière is full of rage, immediately reveals her knowledge to her accomplice, Dr. Langlé, and imposes a punishment that seems to exceed by far the "sin" committed (PD). The word **"promptly"** implies the mistress' succinct efficiency (FD); she is calculating and methodical in her vindictiveness (MR). She doesn't take time to sulk; she simply acts (PP). The mistress here cannot speak clearly but does have complete control of her will; in contrast, by the end of the story Zoraïde will still be able to speak but will lack true self-control because of her radical emotional disturbance and deterioration of intellect (PD). Although at first Chopin might seem to suggest that the mistress had decided to relent (she lacks anger; she seems confused), this momentary possibility only emphasizes the suddenness of her cruelty (KD). Although the word **"induce"** might suggest that she had to convince or persuade the doctor to sell Mézor, we soon discover that he was only too eager to act (RCE). The fact that he is a doctor, and thus professionally committed to the alleviation of pain and suffering, makes his callousness seem all the more ironic (RCE).

[23] Doctor Langlé, who was a widower, had long wanted to marry Madame Delarivière, and he would willingly have walked on all fours at noon through the Place d'Armes if she wanted him to. Naturally he lost no time in disposing of le beau Mézor, who was sold away into Georgia, or the Carolinas, or one of those distant countries far away, where he could no longer hear his Creole tongue spoken, nor dance Calinda, nor hold la belle Zoraïde in his arms.

Paradoxically, Madame Delarivière exploits Doctor Langlé's affection in order to destroy Zoraïde's own chances for love (JA). A

FEMINIST critic might note the irony of a strong woman using her social power to destroy another woman (SB2). A FEMINIST might also note how Madame Delarivière takes advantage of the power she enjoys as a single woman and potential wife (SR). Although Langlé acts on his own desires, he thereby prevents Zoraïde from acting on hers (MR). Although slaves were theoretically inferior to their masters and were often considered subhuman, Manna-Loulou describes Langlé as if he were a ridiculous animal; his professional degree apparently does not enhance his wisdom (RCE). The black narrator is obviously contemptuous of her white "superior" (MC), and Madame Delarivière treats the doctor with the same kind of condescension (as if he were a child) she had earlier displayed toward Zoraïde (PN). Ironically, however, although the reference to Doctor Langlé **"walking] on all fours"** is merely a bit of sarcastic hyperbole in the case of a white professional, such demeaning behavior could actually have been commanded of a slave such as Mézor or Manna-Loulou (MR2). The idea that he might behave like an animal is simply a joke, but in reality he treats other human beings as if they were truly animals (SR). Contrast Doctor Langlé's presumed willingness here to make a public fool of himself with the dignified, manly public display Mézor had made of *him*self when earlier dancing the Bamboula (RCE). Langlé is presumably willing to debase himself to win the woman he desires, whereas Mézor treats Zoraïde as a worthy equal (SB). The word **"[n]aturally"** is powerfully ironic, since Langlé's behavior is so completely unnatural and inhuman (FD), while the word **"disposing"** suggests a quick, efficient, emotionless (FD) use of power (PP). The word implies that inconvenient people can literally be thrown away (PP). Manna-Loulou's contempt for Doctor Langlé is perhaps one of many subtle reflections of the pervasive feminine point-of-view of this entire story: the tale is told by a woman, to a woman, and about a woman, and Chopin's own audience would presumably consist mostly of women (FD). Note how the description of Mézor's fate directly echoes details mentioned earlier, such as his dancing, his speech, and his physical contact with Zoraïde (BB). Does Mézor's banishment to a land where his Creole tongue will not be understood recall, in any respect, the confusion of tongues that resulted from the Biblical Tower of Babel? (OT-K). The indefiniteness of Mézor's new location (**"one of those distant countries far away"**) implies how impossible it would be for Zoraïde ever to find him, even if she were somehow able to try (FD). The very word **"countries"** emphasizes the cultural gulf and sense of geographical distance between Louisiana and other states (TDC). From this point forward, Mézor effectively vanishes not only from Zoraïde's experience but from ours as readers (RCE). Certainly Mézor is in some sense a victim (DR), particularly since he was originally Zoraïde's choice. The final three phrases of this passage emphasize his complete isolation—his alienation from his familiar tongue, from his favorite activity, and also (most important) from the person he loves—the mother of his child. Ironically, not even Mézor's **"Creole tongue"** is even really **"his"**: instead, it is the language he has learned from his owners and is the language of their culture. Yet it is also the only language he knows (RCE). Although Mézor may bitterly lament his separation from Zoraïde, at least his sale removes him to a new location in which he may build a new life, while his opportunity for mobility may help him cope psychologically. Zoraïde, in contrast, remains forever rooted to the locale where she first found love and then lost it (GW). For her there is neither geographical nor mental escape (RCE).

[24] **"The poor thing was heartbroken when Mézor was sent away from her, but she took comfort and hope in the thought of her baby that she would soon be able to clasp to her breast.**

"La belle Zoraïde's sorrows had now begun in earnest. Not only sorrows but sufferings, and with the anguish of maternity came the shadow of death. But there is no agony that a mother will not forget when she holds her first-born to her heart, and presses her lips upon the baby flesh that is her own, yet far more precious than her own.

Zoraïde is aptly described as a **"poor thing"** not only because Manna-Loulou (unlike others) pities her (AMO) but also because it is partly her literal poverty that allows her to be treated as a **"thing"** rather than as a full human being (SB; NB). If the word **"heartbroken"** seems a cliché, it is nonetheless exactly the kind of language one might expect from an unpretentious narrator such as Manna-Loulou (RCE). The word also echoes the earlier claim that when Zoraïde first saw Mézor, "her heart grew sick in her bosom" [15]; now her heart is not merely sick but shattered (SB). Typically, the innocuous passive voice is used in the description of how Mézor **"was sent away"** (NB, AO). Note Zoraïde's desire to clasp **"her baby"** to **"her breast"**: the alliteration and repetition of the personal pronoun "her" (TR) imply her intense yearning to feel that she owns at least one thing that belongs personally to her (NB), while the verb **"clasp"** is much more forceful than another word (such as "hold") might have been (LP). The word **"clasp"** suggests that Zoraïde feels a need to cling to her baby, whereas usually it is a baby who clings to its mother (AMO). Calling Zoraïde **"la belle"** at this point simply highlights the ugly circumstances in which her daughter is taken from her (KW). Note how this whole passage oscillates between positives and negatives: from negative (**"heart-broken"**) to positive (**"comfort and hope"**) in the first sentence, then from negative (psychological **"sorrows"**) to even more negative (physical **"sufferings"**) at the beginning of the second, then to even more intense pain (**"anguish"**) followed immediately by the prospect of at once forgetting such anguish in anticipation of the pleasure of physical and emotional contact with one's newborn (RCE). This kind of oscillation is typical of Chopin's style and helps her stories achieve a great deal of moment-by-moment complexity and suspense (RCE). Even the last clause of this passage is typical of this oscillating pattern: Chopin first makes what seems to be a definitive statement (**"flesh that is her own"**) and then immediately modifies and complicates it (**"yet far more precious than her own"**) (RCE). The reference to the **"shadow of death"** not only explicitly recalls the famous language of Psalm 23 [22 in the Catholic Bible] (SD) but also contributes to the story's larger focus on imagery of darkness (MC). However, while the psalm traditionally lends comfort and support to those facing death or any other great obstacle, here the allusion starkly emphasizes the fact that Zoraïde can find no comfort and can never regain her former self (NP). Although the word **"shadow"** seems to imply an agony that is merely temporary and passing, Zoraïde in a sense will never emerge from the mental anguish she now suffers, even though her physical pain will cease (KM). Paradoxically, Zoraïde is literally close to death as she brings new life into the world (OT-K). A LONGINIAN critic might regard Zoraïde's powerful motherly instincts as sublime yearnings that supposedly lie deep within human nature—a point of view with which an ARCHETYPAL critic might well agree (TT). FEMINIST critics, on the other hand, might object to any claim that all women feel such maternal yearnings (RCE). The reference to a mother's **"first-born"** seems ironic not only because Zoraïde, so far as we know, will never have another child (RCE) but also because she is deprived of her first and only child in the same way that she was deprived of her first and only love (KM). The phrase suggests a hope for the future that seems especially ironic since Zoraïde's future will hold such little hope (NB). Although a mother may indeed forget all agony when she holds her first child, Zoraïde will never have even this opportunity for happiness (KW). The anticipated baby seems **"precious"** to Zoraïde because it will be one of the few things in life that will seem truly her **"own,"** yet it seems **"far more precious than her own"** partly because it is also the product of her union with the now-banished Mézor (SB). Ironically, of course, because Zoraïde is a slave even her child does not truly belong to her or its father (KM): it immediately becomes the property of Madam Delarivière (SB). The **"flesh"** of Zoraïde's flesh—her baby—is not her own any more than Zoraïde's body is her own, except perhaps during the passionate encounters when she gave herself to Mézor (CS).

[25] "So, instinctively, when Zoraïde came out of the awful shadow she gazed questioningly about her and felt with her trembling hands upon either side of her. 'Où li, mo piti a moin? (Where is my little one?)' she asked imploringly. Madame who was there and the nurse who was there both told her in turn, 'To piti à toi, li mouri' ('Your little one is dead'), which was a wicked falsehood that must have caused the angels in heaven to weep. For the baby was living and well and strong. It had been at once removed from its mother's side, to be sent away to Madame's plantation, far up the coast. Zoraïde could only moan in reply, 'Li mouri, li mouri,' and she turned her face to the wall.

The word **"instinctively"** not only implies natural conduct that contrasts with the unnatural behavior of Madame Delarivière and Doctor Langlé (KW), but it also suggests that Zoraïde, unlike so many other characters in this story, innately tends to care about others: her immediate impulse is to reach out in love, which makes the treatment she herself suffers seem all the more ironic (SB). **"Instinctively"** also immediately suggests that Zoraïde intuitively senses that something dreadful has happened (KM), and it additionally seems an appropriate word since Zoraïde, from this point forward, will largely be a creature of instincts who will lose her ability to reason (AMO). The word **"trembling,"** meanwhile, suggests physical frailty and sickness that bitterly foreshadow the mental breakdown Zoraïde will shortly suffer (KM). She comes out of the temporary or physical **"shadow"** of childbirth, but she is never able to overcome the permanent or psychological shadow of being a slave and being deprived of her child (BH). The reiteration

("Madame who was there and the nurse who was there") per-haps makes the lies of the attending women seem all the more brazen and heartless: both had seen Zoraïde give birth, both had seen her anguish, both had seen her **"imploring"** quest for her child, but both denied Zoraïde her joy, and the repetition stresses the deliberate nature of their crime (KW). Such conduct seems ironic enough for two women but especially ironic in a **"nurse"** (TR). Of course, a MARXIST might argue that the nurse merely ac-quiesces to Madame Delarivière's greater economic power (RCE). Once more Madame Delarivière shows her perversion of her role as Zoraïde's godmother (TR). Being apparently childless herself, she shows no understanding or concern for the psychological bond that Zoraïde had already established with the baby as she carried it (TR). The cold-hearted way in which Madame disposes of both Mézor and the baby raises the matter of another missing person in the story. Where is Zoraïde's mother? It certainly appears that at some point the absent mother must have shared a close bond with Madame in order for Madame to serve as godmother to her child. Yet she is never mentioned. Did she die within a year or so of Zo-raïde's birth? Or is her absence more ominous? Did it foreshadow the later "disappearances" from which Zoraïde suffers? Did Madame covet Zoraïde enough to wrest her from her mother's arms? (TR).

The adjective **"wicked"** greatly intensifies the noun **"false-hood"** (AMO); although some falsehoods can be motivated by good intentions, Manna-Loulou wants there to be no doubt that this one is evil (MC). The weeping **"angels"** seem strangely pas-sive and ineffective (BB)—an ironic touch since **"angels"** are usu-ally depicted not only as constantly rejoicing (BH) but as agents who intervene to promote human good (CH). Here, however, they seem impotent (CH), just as later God will be described as almost sanctioning Zoraïde's earthly suffering (BB). The speculation that the angels **"must"** have wept accentuates the ironic reality that on earth no one sympathizes with Zoraïde except for Mézor, whom she now has also lost (NB).

The baby's life and strength emphasize, by contrast, Zoraïde's mental and physical weakness (JDS). Note the progressive strengthening of the adjectives: **"living ... well ... strong"** (RCE). Of course, in spite of these positive terms, the baby is nonetheless still condemned to slavery (AMO). Note the antiseptic, passive verb **"was removed,"** which de-emphasizes any sense of personal responsibility or blame (AO; NB). Although Zoraïde accepts the

explanation that her baby is dead, that acceptance marks the beginning, in a sense, of her *own* demise—her own mental death
(MC). By turning her face to the presumably blank and empty
"wall" (SB), Zoraïde in a sense turns her back on life (AL), hope,
and the future (NB); this is just the first stage in a slow process of
withdrawal (RCE). An ARCHETYPAL critic might argue that
Chopin here plays on two of the most powerful and basic of all
human instincts: the desire to have children and the fear of losing
them (JB).

[26] **"Madame had hoped, in thus depriving Zoraïde of her
child, to have her young waiting-maid again at her side free,
happy, and beautiful as of old. But there was a more powerful
will than Madame's at work—the will of the good God, who had
already designed that Zoraïde should grieve with a sorrow that
was never more to be lifted in this world.**

A TRADITIONAL HISTORICAL critic might note that Madame Delarivière acts in accordance with the accepted norms of her culture
and that the reaction of her contemporaries to her behavior would
have been far less outraged than our own is likely to be (JB). How
ironic that Madame Delarivière wishes Zoraïde to be **"free"** as before: not only will Zoraïde from this point *never* be free, but even in
the past she was never truly free (FD; NP; KM). Ironically, there is
a sense in which Madame Delarivière, by denying Zoraïde access
to (and knowledge of) the child, is trying to get back her *own*
child—Zoraïde (PP). Is there any resemblance between Zoraïde
and the Virgin Mary, both of whom had children taken away from
them and thus became famously grieving mothers? (PN). Fittingly,
Madame Delarivière's attempt to deny Zoraïde what the young
woman herself desires will result in the mistress being denied her
own desires as well (MC; NB). Is Zoraïde, from one perspective,
rightly punished for her sin of illicit sex? (MO; SB; NB; AS). Or is
there a sense in which Zoraïde exemplifies the Jansenist idea that
those chosen by God must suffer in this world? (FD). Chopin's
phrasing seems to imply that only the **"will"** of **"God"** can undermine the determined and forceful will of Madame Delarivière—as if the latter were herself a kind of deity (KM). Earlier, it
was Madame Delarivière herself who had invoked the name of the
"good God" (PW). Note, however, the powerfully ironic syntax of
the final cited sentence here: at first Chopin seems to suggest that
the evil of Madame Delarivière will be thwarted by **"the will of**

the good God," but then the apparent direction of the sentence seems thrown into reverse when it is revealed **"that Zoraïde should grieve with a sorrow that was never more to be lifted."** Such reversals are typical of Chopin's style, even at the level of individual sentences (RCE). The crucial phrase in the final sentence, of course, is **"in this world"**: it implies that Zoraïde will no longer suffer in the next world, and it may imply that she will be compensated there for her sufferings here (PH; NP; MO). Does the phrase perhaps also suggest a less comforting eternal fate for Madame Delarivière? (RCE)

[27] **"La belle Zoraïde was no more. In her stead was a sad-eyed woman who mourned night and day for her baby. 'Li mouri, li mouri,' she would sigh over and over again to those about her, and to herself when others grew weary of her complaint.**

"Yet, in spite of all, M'sieur Ambroise was still in the notion to marry her. A sad wife or a merry one was all the same to him so long as that wife was Zoraïde. And she seemed to consent, or rather to submit, to the approaching marriage as though nothing mattered any longer in this world.

An important theme of Chopin's story may be the importance of freedom: the story may be designed to show what human beings would be like if they exercised no choice or control in their daily lives (MO). Significantly, from this point forward Zoraïde is never again called **"la belle"** by Manna-Loulou, the narrator (KW). She continues to exist physically, as the same body, but she is now no longer the same person. The young girl whose eyes had earlier been one of her greatest charms is now merely a **"sad-eyed woman"** constantly mourning for the loss of her baby—mourning that probably also reflects a continued mourning for the loss of Mézor (RCE). This woman who has already been shown so little pity is now shown even less: **"others grew weary of her complaint"** (SB)—with perhaps the word "complaint" even suggesting that they regard her as a weak, self-indulgent whiner (AMO). M'sieur Ambroise, however, continues to regard her (at least for the time being) as a kind of trophy who is still worth acquiring (TR), perhaps as a means of cementing his link with the powerful Madame Delarivière (and thus winning the regard of his own master, Doctor Langlé) or perhaps as a desirable physical object whom he can sexually exploit and whose mindlessness is therefore, in some sense, advantageous. A FEMINIST critic might argue that his attitude epitomizes the ways in which women are so often objectified—that is, regarded as mere objects or possessions (SH; MS). It seems doubtful that the **"approaching marriage"** would still have been the once-anticipated grand celebration planned for the cathedral (RCE).

[28] "One day, a black servant entered a little noisily the room in which Zoraïde sat sewing. With a look of strange and vacuous happiness upon her face, Zoraïde arose hastily. 'Hush, hush,' she whispered, lifting a warning finger, 'my little one is asleep; you must not awaken her.'

"Upon the bed was a senseless bundle of rags shaped like an infant in swaddling clothes. Over this dummy the woman had drawn the mosquito bar, and she was sitting contentedly beside it. In short, from that day Zoraïde was demented. Night nor day did she lose sight of the doll that lay in her bed or in her arms.

Despite her loss of mental power and psychological self-command, Zoraïde, as a mulatto owned by Madame Delarivière, still apparently enjoys greater power than the **"black servant"** who now enters to attend to her needs (RCE). The fact that Zoraïde is described as sitting and **"sewing"** suggests both her physical passivity and her lack of mental engagement: her movements are mechanical and repetitive, and her focus seems at first entirely on her work. As it happens, however, her focus is less on the cloth she sews than on the rag baby she now considers the center of her universe (RCE). Although her **"happiness"** is described as **"vacuous,"** this is an external judgment: Zoraïde herself knows why she is happy (AMO). And, typically, her happiness seems rooted mainly in love: once more her instinctive reaction is concern for another's comfort, even if the object of her attention can never return that affection (SB). Ironically, the **"black servant"** to whom Zoraïde lifts a "warning finger" is one of the few other humans over whom she now exercises any control: even a mindless Zoraïde is still higher in the racial hierarchy than the pure black maid (RCE). Despite her mental breakdown, however, Zoraïde still has command over her language: she speaks in coherent sentences and in ways that would make perfect sense in a different context (PD). Part of the poignancy of her condition, in fact, is that she seems so rational in her irrationality (PD; RCE).

Contrast the plain **"bed"** on which Zoraïde and her "baby" lie with the "sumptuous mahogany bed" [5] in which Madame Delisle now listens to this tale (DR). The word **"rags"** suggests the tattered, discarded ruins of Zoraïde's former life and hopes (RCE). Ironically, Zoraïde, who was herself raised almost as if she were a precious doll on display, now herself mothers a considerably less attractive doll of her own (DR). While earlier the real baby had been referred to as "it," Zoraïde now imagines the rag-baby as **"her,"** once again reinforcing the feminine emphasis of the entire story (FD). By attributing her own sex to the baby, perhaps Zoraïde subconsciously treats it as an alter-ego, giving it the nurturing and genuine love she herself never received (MR). As always, though, her instinct is to love and protect another (AO; SB). Because the rag baby is "senseless," it ironically resembles Zoraïde, its now-demented "mother" (DR). Perhaps, by using the word "shaped," Chopin implies Zoraïde's active attempt to shape, construct, or resurrect her substitute child. Ironically, though, she lacks any real power to shape her own life except by removing herself from the world (DR). Clearly the reference to **"swaddling clothes"** alludes to the story of the infant Jesus, but this rag-baby (unlike the infant savior) has no power to redeem or undo or even share in Zoraïde's suffering (BB). Paradoxically, Zoraïde both loses (RCE) and gains (DR) freedom through her madness. Perhaps Chopin refers to Zoraïde as **"the woman"** to suggest the universality of her maternal instincts (DR), but perhaps the phrase also suggests that she is no longer the seemingly happy, carefree girl on whom the story at first focused (RCE). The phrase **"in short"** seems somewhat ironic, since the evolution of the demented Zoraïde was anything but short. It required years to confuse Zoraïde about her place in society, yet only a few short and thoughtless decisions by Madame were required to trigger Zoraïde's madness (DR). Chopin mentions **"night"** and **"day"** as if there were no difference between them, and for Zoraïde there *is* no difference. Since she no longer allows the outside world into her mind, light and dark are largely irrelevant (DR). Having lost sight of her lover, her living child, and her earlier dreams, Zoraïde will now not allow herself to lose sight of the rag doll, which has become her world (DR). From the perspective of the outside world, she seems unfocused; from her own perspective, however, she is now totally focused on the only thing that matters (RCE).

[29] "And now was Madame stung with sorrow and remorse
at seeing this terrible affliction that had befallen her dear Zoraïde. Consulting with Doctor Langlé, they decided to bring
back to the mother the real baby of flesh and blood that was now
toddling about, and kicking its heels in the dust yonder upon
the plantation.

Does the word **"stung"** suggest, perhaps, merely a small prick of
pain? (AMO). Certainly Madame's **"sorrow and remorse"** are
nothing compared to Zoraïde's suffering (RCE). Ironically,
Madame Delarivière feels that she has lost Zoraïde in much the
same way that Zoraïde feels she has lost her own daughter (BB).
Note again the passive phrasing **"affliction that had befallen"**:
once more Madame accepts no obvious personal responsibility
(MR2), and perhaps the passive voice is even somewhat appropriate, since it is largely the social system that gives people like
Madame power that is responsible for the **"affliction"** of people
like Zoraïde (AMO). Even Madame's decision to reverse course
does not express an impulsive or instinctive concern for another
(of the sort that Zoraïde so often demonstrates [SB]). Instead, she
reaches the decision only after first **"consulting"** with Doctor Langlé (NB).

Ironically, the word **"toddling"** had earlier been used to describe Zoraïde herself as an infant (FD). When the baby was born it
had been described as an **"it,"** as a mere thing or abstraction [25];
now, suddenly, it is a **"real baby of flesh and blood"** (KD). Nevertheless, it is still never referred to by name—a fact that indicates its
relative unimportance to the people who control it (MO). The fact
that the baby possesses much of the liveliness once associated with
its mother makes their separation, and Zoraïde's present condition, seem all the more pathetic (OT-K). Does the reference to the
infant **"kicking its heels"** also remind us of its father's passion for
dancing? (RCE). Because it has been born a slave, however, the
child's freedom and joy can only be temporary and ephemeral
(SB).

[30] "It was Madame herself who led the pretty, tiny little
'griffe' girl to her mother. Zoraïde was sitting on a stone bench
in the courtyard, listening to the soft splashing of the fountain,
and watching the fitful shadows of the palm leaves upon the
broad, white flagging.

The sentence beginning **"[i]t was Madame herself"** may at first seem to imply that her act is honorable (RCS), but it may also suggest an attitude of pride and self-important condescension (BH): she engages in a typically grand gesture (MR2). Even her decision to return the child manifests her power (SR). Nevertheless, we don't easily forget that **"it was Madame herself,"** after all, who first removed the girl from Zoraïde (RCS). A TRADITIONAL HISTORICAL critic would note that a **"griffe"** was the child of a black and a mulatto (SG). The fact that such a word even existed in Zoraïde's culture suggests again that culture's obsession with minutely detailed racial classification, and because the infant girl is a **"griffe"** rather than a mulatto, she will enjoy even less freedom and even fewer opportunities than her mother (RCE). On the other hand, it is (ironically) precisely because Zoraïde's position was once so favored that she is now so afflicted: perhaps if she had been born a mere black slave and had attracted no special attention, she would have been free to choose her own mate and raise her own child (RCE).

Ironically, when Madame finally shows compassion, it is too late: Zoraïde, like the lifeless **"stone"** she passively sits on (NB), has already lost all feeling and sense (NP); like the stone, she now seems cold, hard, stiff, and inert (SH). Sadly, there is no indication of thought, no indication that Zoraïde is *contemplating* her surroundings or her circumstances. She seems nearly catatonic, perceiving the world merely through the senses of sound and sight, perhaps choosing the comfort of these senses over the pain of remembrance and contemplation (RCS). Also, Chopin's description of the **"shadows ... upon the broad, white flagging"** seems to symbolize the state of affairs between the black slaves and the white slave owners. Such phrasing seems to suggest that the slaves are in a way not real, not tangible, but are mere silhouettes against a broad white world (RCS). Interestingly, the only other **"fountain"** previously mentioned in this story [4] had been mentioned as part of the song of sorrow with which the story opened (RCE). Even the water seems lifeless and controlled in this artificial, man-made environment (TR). Perhaps as a final irony, the tree that towers over Zoraïde is a **"palm,"** the tree sacred to the Roman Catholic Church, the tree of Christian triumph (TR). Yet such a tree is also, of course, appropriate to the setting in Louisiana (RCE).

[31] "'Here,' said Madame, approaching, 'here, my poor dear Zoraïde, is your own little child. Keep her; she is yours. No one will ever take her from you again.'

"Zoraïde looked with sullen suspicion upon her mistress and the child before her. Reaching out a hand she thrust the little one mistrustfully away from her. With the other hand she clasped the rag bundle fiercely to her breast; for she suspected a plot to deprive her of it.

Here again Madame presumes to present herself as a source of wise and beneficent power. By claiming that **"no one"** will take the child again, perhaps she subsconsciously tries to relieve herself of responsibility for her own part in the initial taking of the child: she speaks as if someone else had been responsible. The phrase **"keep her; she is yours"** diminishes the very act it describes: Madame still disposes of people as if they were her personal property (RCS), and in the very act of granting Zoraïde possession of her own child, Madame shows who is still in control (SR). Ironically, no one *will* **"ever take"** the child from Zoraïde again, but only because Zoraïde herself will refuse to accept the infant (RCE).

It hardly seems surprising that Zoraïde is suspicious. After all, she has been led to believe that her child was dead, and it would be perfectly in keeping with Madame Delarivière's manipulative personality to try to deceive Zoraïde into accepting a false substitute (RCS; RCE). The very suspiciousness that thus seems to confirm Zoraïde's insanity is also, paradoxically, in some ways perfectly rational (RCE). Even so, the following sentence has an amazing effect. For an instant, we see Zoraïde **"reaching out a hand,"** and we hope that she will accept her child into her arms. Just as instantly, however, she **"thrust[s] the little one away from her."** We now know that there is no hope for a reunion. We also know from Zoraïde's behavior that she has now truly lost her mind (RCS). Ironically, this is one of the few moments in the story when the usually passive Zoraïde is both angry and active, but the target of her hostility is her own child (TR).

[32] "Nor could she ever be induced to let her own child approach her; and finally the little one was sent back to the plantation, where she was never to know the love of mother or father.

Here the irony is stinging. For once, Zoraïde is given the opportunity to take what is rightfully hers. We know, however, that she is fated for unhappiness, so we are not surprised that she doesn't accept her child. We are saddened, further, knowing that her inability to reason was, in the first place, caused by the pain of losing her child, and that it is this very inability to reason that now prevents her from realizing that her child is being offered back to her (RCS). Paradoxically, Zoraïde's real child will know her place in the world much more clearly than her mother did. She will be raised as a slave and will have no expectations that can be trampled on by white masters (DR). It seems ironic that it is now said that the little girl is **"never to know the love of mother or father,"** since this, after all, had been Madame Delarivière's original plan for her (AMO).

[33] **"And now this is the end of Zoraïde's story. She was never known again as la belle Zoraïde, but ever after as Zoraïde la folle, whom no one ever wanted to marry—not even M'sieur Ambroise. She lived to be an old woman, whom some people pitied and others laughed at—always clasping at her bundle of rags—her 'piti.'**

The opening sentence here serves two very important purposes. First, it literally announces the conclusion of Manna-Loulou's telling of Zoraïde's story; secondly, it implies, figuratively, the end of Zoraïde's life as a beautiful, intelligent, passionate woman—la belle Zoraïde (RCS). Yet the statement that **"this is the end of Zoraïde's story"** is also powerfully ironic, since this is not really the "end" of her story but merely the end of our knowledge of it (CH). Zoraïde's life will continue for a long while (SB): she is not allowed even the relief of death (FS), and she has even lost one of her chief values to society—her value as a potential wife (AMO). She is no longer attractive even to M'sieur Ambroise, who had earlier seemed easy to satisfy (RCE). Is there perhaps a note of increased empathy on Manna-Loulou's part toward Zoraïde, who is now described as an "old woman" (thus resembling Manna-Loulou herself [RCE])? As before in her life, Zoraïde now receives little real sympathy, and perhaps she is **"laughed at"** (ironically) even by some of her fellow slaves (MO). Whereas earlier Zoraïde had longed to "clasp" her own child, now she is left merely **"clasping at her bundle of rags,"** and perhaps the words **"clasping at"** even suggest a sense of fear, desperation, and anticipated loss (RCE). Ironically, her real, true child will never receive this kind of attentive concern (NP)—concern which contrasts sharply with the kind of meanness Zoraïde herself is shown by others (SB). Might a

POSTMODERNIST critic, however, find Zoraïde's transformation too abrupt and the tragic ending too neat—too much a concession to the audience's desire for a tidy, pat conclusion? (CY).

[34] "Are you asleep, Ma'zélle Titite?"
"No, I am not asleep; I was thinking. Ah, the poor little one, Man Loulou, the poor little one! better had she died!"

A FORMALIST critic might admire the fact that Chopin's story ends where it began: with Manna-Loulou and Madame Delisle in the latter's bedroom (KN). The story moves from the present to the past and then back to the present (KN), and it begins and ends on the same note of languor (DH). Paradoxically, a story that was presumably intended to promote sleep has apparently inhibited it (RCE). Note the intimacy apparently implied by the diminutive phrase **"Ma'zélle Titite."** On the other hand, Manna-Loulou may be employing a childhood term in order to appease or placate her mistress in the event that the latter's silence indicates not intimacy but instead anger at a slave who may be perceived as attempting to manipulate her mistress's emotions by telling a tale that reflects so poorly on the behavior of whites (EP). A NEW HISTORICIST critic, interested in the complexities of power relations, might suggest that it would be cognitively difficult for Manna-Loulou to be outraged by what happens to Zoraïde without also being outraged by her own oppression. Since emotional rebellion would cost her too much, she acquiesces (DH). Does the phrase **"I was thinking"** raise the hope that Madame Delisle has learned a profitable lesson by hearing the story? (RCE). Ironically, however, Madame Delisle's final statement, if it refers to the baby, seems to suggest that *she* would have responded not much differently than Zoraïde's mistress in the same situation (RCS). Given the moral complexity of "La Belle Zoraïde," the realization that nobody in Manna-Loulou's tale except the child seems to have stirred Madame Delisle's sympathy even strikes the reader as horrific (CS). Ironically, Madame Delisle seems to miss the whole point of Manna-Loulou's story, perhaps deliberately failing to realize that Zoraïde's problems are caused by the system and by those, such as Madame Delarivière, Doctor Langlé, and even Madame Delisle herself, who unthinkingly represent that system (FS; BH).

Even for an avowed storyteller, Manna-Loulou's knowledge of the details of Zoraïde's life, from infancy through old age, seems surprising. Manna-Loulou seems most affected after she recounts

Madame Delarivière's derision of Mézor as "'That Negro! that Negro!'" [18]. It is then that she looks sad. Unlike Zoraïde, the *"café-au-lait"* mulatress [8], Manna-Loulou is "herself as black as the night" [2]. Similarly, Mézor's skin was "ebony" [14]. Zoraïde's child is described as "'a pretty, tiny little 'griffe' girl" [30]. A griffe is the offspring of a Negro and a mulatto. Presumably, then, Zoraïde's child was dark-skinned. Could Manna-Loulou in fact be Zoraïde's lost daughter? If so, such a relationship with Zoraïde would add ironic significance to the last exchange in the story (TR).

Madame Delisle shows compassion, but she misses the point by thinking that Zoraïde's child would be better off dead. This view disregards the value of the child's individual life and the ultimate value of maternity, both of which appear to be important themes in the story. Manna-Loulou nurtures Madame Delisle. In this she represents the story's strongest abiding feminine principle. In this respect she may be the story's literal "manna," that which feeds and promotes life (TR).

[35] But this is the way Madame Delisle and Manna-Loulou really talked to each other:—
"Vou pré droumi, Ma'zélle Titite?"
"Non, pa pré droumi; mo yapré zongler. Ah, la pauv' piti, Man Loulou. La pauv' piti! Mieux li mouri!"

The resounding **"But"** with which this passage begins, along with the abrupt lapse into Creole dialect, seems purposely designed to remove the average American reader from sharing Manna-Loulou's and Madame Delisle's conversation and sentiments, yet this very strategy paradoxically engages the reader's attention even more intensely (TDC). In one sense this final re-emphasis on linguistic differences seems to imply that what the reader has just read would really be incomprehensible to the common English-speaking American. However, the tactic may also be intended to convey just the opposite implication: that we have just been given a true glimpse into the life of Louisiana Creole culture (TDC). Manna-Loulou's tale ends simultaneously with the ending of Chopin's story (CS). An ARISTOTELIAN critic or a FORMALIST might argue that this over-all structure, which is that of a story-within-a-story, contributes to the complex unity of the piece: for an ARISTOTELIAN or FORMALIST, not only does mentioning Manna-Loulou and Madame Delisle before and after the story of Zoraïde unify Chopin's work, but this structural device also emphasizes how the tale functions as a moral parable from which its readers can learn a lesson (CW). The inter-related stories of the two mistresses and two servants might definitely provoke a STRUCTURALIST critic, meanwhile, to explore the similarities and differences between the two codes (or sign-systems) embodied in the two stories. For instance, might analogies be drawn between Zoraïde and Manna-Loulou? A LONGINIAN critic, meanwhile, might argue that Madame Delisle's sympathetic reaction implies that Zoraïde's fate arouses a response that transcends artificial divisions of race and class (CW). The repetition of the ending in two different languages arguably makes its meaning all the more emphatically heart-breaking. Metaphorically, the two women (slave and mistress) in each story do not really speak each other's language. This lack of true communication is ironically underscored by the repetition of the final dialogue between Madame Delisle and Manna-Loulou. A rigidly hierarchical society separates the two sets of women, and no "common" spoken word can bridge the gap between them (CS; JG).

An Archetypal Analysis
of Kate Chopin's "La Belle Zoraïde"

Kimberly Barron

In studying a literary text, the archetypal critic is interested in symbols and "patterns of imagery or of theme" that reflect universally shared thoughts and feelings, especially those that reflect general human "psychological responses." These patterns imbue the text with a "deeper unity or coherence" which "can help explain the underlying psychological traits or patterns of behavior common to all human beings."[1] An archetypal approach proves especially fruitful when analyzing the themes and imagery in Kate Chopin's story "La Belle Zoraïde."[2]

One archetypal image that is especially prominent in Chopin's story is the "shadow"—a symbol which, for archetypal critics, commonly stands for the unknown, the individual's fear of the unknown, and/or the individual's unconscious. The extensive shadow imagery in "La Belle Zoraïde" suggests all of these meanings and operates within a general pattern of archetypal imagery and themes that symbolize the psychological tensions and journeys of the story's characters. This pattern is especially significant not only when one examines Zoraïde and Madame Delarivière but

---

[1]Robert C. Evans, "Introduction: Literary Theory and Literary Criticism: What's the Use?" in *Short Fiction: A Critical Companion*, ed. Robert C. Evans, Anne C. Little, and Barbara Wiedemann (West Cornwall, CT: Locust Hill Press, 1997), xv–lxxvi, esp. xlv–xlvi.

[2]For the text of the story cited here, see Kate Chopin, *Bayou Folk and A Night in Acadie*, ed. Bernard Koloski (New York: Penguin, 1999), 152–57. All subsequent references to this edition will be cited parenthetically.

also when one explores the effects of Madame Delarivière's persona upon Madame Delisle and the reader.

Theorists of Jungian psychology argue that the shadow archetype embodies (in the words of Anthony Storr) the "sum of all ... psychic elements which ... are denied expression in life and therefore coalesce into a relatively autonomous 'splinter personality' with contrary tendencies in the unconscious."[3] This unconscious "shadow" personality manifests itself through a variety of conscious responses or impulses, either positive or negative, depending on the psychological needs of the individual. "Whether the unconscious comes up at first in a helpful or a negative form," the Jungian psychologist M.-L. von Franz explains, "the need usually arises to readapt the conscious attitude in a better way to the unconscious factors."[4] In recognizing and responding to pressure exerted by the unconscious onto the conscious self, the individual experiences what Jung himself called "'the realization of the shadow'" (qtd. in *Man and His Symbols*, 168). Through this realization, s/he can integrate the repressed elements of his/her personality and progress toward psychological wholeness, or "individuation." The shadow imagery in Chopin's story supports the Jungian concept of individuation and is supplemented by related archetypal imagery involving rites of initiation and symbols of transcendence.

In Zoraïde's character, for example, the shadow involves the repression of her instinctive nature and the resulting obstruction of her progress toward individuation. Chopin skillfully weaves archetypal imagery into a unified structure that illustrates this oppression. Moreover, Zoraïde's psychological journey illustrates von Franz's Jungian contentions that the shadow figure contains "valuable, vital forces" which should be assimilated into the individual's experiences and that, when ignored, misunderstood, or repressed, the shadow exerts a hostile influence on the individual's psyche (see Jung, *Man*, 173-75).

Conversely, as Madame Delarivière illustrates, the shadow also may embody what the Jungian writer Joseph L. Henderson calls "unfavorable (or nefarious) aspects of the personality" (see Jung, *Man*, 118) which emerge in the guise of what von Franz

---

[3]C.G. Jung, *The Essential Jung*, ed. Anthony Storr (Princeton, NJ: Princeton University Press, 1983), 422.

[4]See C.G. Jung, et al., *Man and His Symbols* (New York: Doubleday, 1964), 168. This valuable book contains essays not only by Jung but by M.-L. von Franz, Joseph L. Henderson, Aniela Jaffé, and Jolande Jacobi.

terms "impulsive or inadvertent act[s]," often leading to "results that were never intended or consciously wanted" (see Jung, *Man*, 169). Within the shadow of one's unconscious, von Franz asserts, there "is such a passionate drive ... that reason may not prevail against it" (see Jung, *Man*, 173). Madame Delarivière's shadow manifests itself in her irrational and cruel efforts to control Zoraïde's life until, producing effects unwanted and unintended by Madame Delarivière, her actions drive Zoraïde mad. Despite the apparent hopelessness of Madame Delarivière's psychological blindness, however, von Franz suggests that for such an individual, "a bitter experience ... may occasionally help to put a stop to shadow drives and impulses" (see Jung, *Man*, 173). Indeed, the story's ending does support this hopeful suggestion when Madame Delarivière, "stung with sorrow and remorse" at Zoraïde's condition, demonstrates her newfound awareness by attempting to reverse the effect of her actions by reuniting Zoraïde with her real child.

Finally, von Franz asserts that the shadow makes the individual especially susceptible to negative social movements, because the shadow "is exposed to collective infections to a much greater extent than is the conscious personality" (see Jung, *Man*, 169). These collective infections can have a profound impact upon a person's attitudes and behavior. Von Franz, following Jung, illustrates the dangerous potential of a "collective infection" by citing the Ku Klux Klan as an example of the collective infection of racial intolerance, which can weld "people into an irrational mob" (*Man*, 168). The institution of slavery and its inherent racial prejudices embody similar collective infections to which Madame Delarivière, Madame Delisle, and in fact all of society are vulnerable.

The process of individuation requires acknowledging and integrating one's repressed unconscious. Von Franz, following Jung, calls this integration of the unconscious "the realization of the shadow." Von Franz also notes, however, that often this realization requires the individual to become acquainted with painful aspects of her/his personality that s/he has previously preferred to avoid. Therefore, the individual's initial step in the "realization of the shadow" may involve "projection," whereby s/he observes her/his own unconscious tendencies in other people. "When an individual makes an attempt to see his shadow," Jung explains, "he becomes aware of (and often ashamed of) those qualities and impulses he denies in himself but can plainly see in other people—such as ... schemes and plots; carelessness and cowardice; inordi-

nate love of money and possession" (see Jung, *Man*, 168). By re-
counting the story of la belle Zoraïde to Madame Delisle, then,
Manna-Loulou acts as a medium through which Madame Delisle
may experience psychic growth by projecting the negative poten-
tialities of her own shadow onto Madame Delarivière. Moreover,
Chopin performs a similar service by creating the literary work itself: she provides all readers with the opportunity for psychic
growth by illustrating the negative consequences of the "collective
infections" of racism and slavery.

"La Belle Zoraïde" is thus a story rich in archetypal theme and
imagery. The shadow imagery is especially applicable to the psychological journeys of Zoraïde and Madame Delarivière, and it has
important implications for the psychological growth of Madame
Delisle and the readers. Chopin interlaces this shadow imagery
with a variety of supporting archetypal images, including images
related to rites of initiation and symbols of transcendence. All of
these elements become apparent during a close reading of the text.

* * *

The concentration of shadow imagery in the story's opening
paragraph suggests the dual archetypal themes of discovery and
of the dark side of human nature. It is significant that Manna-
Loulou opens the shutters to a summer night; in the cycle of life,
summer represents a time when the individual enters the initial
stages of adulthood. Moreover, Jungian analysis considers summer to represent a time when the ego, protected in childhood by
the parent, must separate and free itself from the parent figure in
the first step toward differentiation of the psyche and, ultimately,
individuation (see von Franz in Jung, *Man*, 160–67). Thus the
summer night foreshadows Zoraïde's emergence from childhood
and her ego's effort to assert itself through a psychological break
from her godmother.

The image of a "hot and still" night during which "not a ripple
of air swept over the *marais*" (Chopin 152) perhaps symbolizes the
mounting psychological pressure exerted by the shadow, or the
unconscious self, within Zoraïde, Madame Delarivière, Madame
Delisle, and the reader. While the conscious self rests unaware in
still darkness, the boggy unconscious simmers below, ready to
seep into the individual's consciousness. The twinkling lights and
blinking stars reinforce this imagery, signifying the shadow's
struggle to break through the darkness and enlighten the individ-

ual by raising into consciousness the repressed elements of his/her personality. Alternately, a related interpretation of the still darkness of the night is that it foreshadows Zoraïde's eventual permanent immersion into a boggy subconscious (the *marais*), when "not a ripple" of reality can return her to sanity.

The image of the lugger that "had come out of the lake" and "was moving ... down the bayou" (152) parallels a notion of the journey into the unconscious. Jungian theorists such as von Franz interpret a "passage" as "a symbol of the unconscious with its unknown possibilities" (see Jung, *Man*, 170); the movement of the boat down the bayou thus represents such a passage from the individual's conscious self, which is represented by the lake. Complementing the passage symbol is the traveler archetype embodied in the image of the man in the boat; this traveler perhaps symbolizes Zoraïde, Madame Delarivière, Madame Delisle, and Chopin's readers, all of whom are about to embark on their own journeys toward psychic growth. The song sung by the man in the boat, a song which "came faintly to the ears of old Manna-Loulou" (152), perhaps represents the message of the unconscious shadow, which is struggling to be heard by the individual's consciousness. From this perspective, therefore, Manna-Loulou's ears may represent the self's conscious awareness, her blackness may represent the darkness in which the individual's consciousness rests in advance of this communication from its shadow, and her action of opening "the shutters wide" may signify the removal of obstacles preventing communication by the shadow.

The bedtime rituals performed by Manna-Loulou and Madame Delisle further imply the archetypal motif of a psychological journey. Sleep is the condition under which dreams surface, and dream imagery is commonly associated with manifestations of the unconscious. The performance of bedtime rituals rouses mental associations of sleep and dreams, thereby implying a ritualistic summoning forth of the unconscious self, or shadow. Similarly, Manna-Loulou's loving attention to her mistress's feet, the appendages that physically transport the body, provides an overt physical symbol of a ritual in preparation for the journey. Even Manna-Loulou's act of fanning her mistress conjures up a mental image of Manna-Loulou waving good-bye as Madame Delisle slips into a dreamy journey bound for the underworld of her unconscious shadow.

At this point the internal narrative begins. Manna-Loulou commences by saying of La Belle Zoraïde's "dusky" eyes that "any man who gazed too long into their depths was sure to lose his head, and even his heart" (Chopin 153). Perhaps these eyes symbolize the shadow that lurks deep in her unconscious, behind her conscious awareness. The repressed elements of Zoraïde's personality, which are reflected in her shadow, include her need for psychological separation from her godmother and her need to integrate her conscious mind with her instinctual nature.

Jung argues that the individual must navigate a series of psychological events in order to move successfully from childhood into the ego-emergence of adulthood. Separation from the parent figure(s) is the critical event in this process, and this separation is often represented by archetypal imagery of initiation, heroism, and sacrifice. Thus the marriage ceremony commonly symbolizes initiation, or an individual's passage from a singularly dependent parent-child relationship into a mutually dependent husband-wife relationship. If elements of the child's personality are repressed by the parent figure, however, the child's shadow may seize the opportunity to assert itself through the initiation event. This, in fact, is precisely the psychological conflict that emerges when Zoraïde seeks to integrate her repressed physical nature by choosing her own marital partner.

As a child under the tutelage of Madame Delarivière, Zoraïde was taught to embrace white social values and to reject attitudes or behaviors that might reinforce her status as a black slave. "Brought up at her mistress's side," she developed "elegant manners" and a "*svelte* and graceful figure"; she "was as charming and as dainty as the finest lady"; and "her fingers had never done rough(er) work" (Chopin 153). Moreover, the "collective infection" of slavery that dominates the social system in which Zoraïde was raised correlated with a collective infection of racism that viewed black individuals as sub-human. Therefore, Madame Delarivière's efforts to "civilize" Zoraïde by infusing white social values into her consciousness effectively associated her black heritage with her instinctual nature. Thus the repression of her black heritage also involved the repression of her instincts.

According to Jungian psychology, however, "instinct" is the foundation of all human nature, and this foundation is embodied in the "animal soul." The individual cannot achieve individuation (or psychological wholeness) without first integrating her/his basic animal nature into his/her total personality. In fact, Jungians warn (in the words of Aniela Jaffé) that "in man, the 'animal being' (which lives in him as his instinctual psyche) may become dangerous if it is not recognized and integrated" (see Jung, *Man*, 239). The collective significance of man's animal nature is evidenced by what Jaffé calls the "boundless profusion of animal symbolism," historically prominent in human art and ritual, which "shows how vital it is for men to integrate into their lives the symbol's psychic content—instinct" (see Jung, *Man*, 238-39). In reflecting the shadow's struggle to free Zoraïde's repressed instincts and to assert her psychological separation from Madame Delarivière, Chopin employs an array of archetypal animal and nature images.

For example, the emergence of Zoraïde's unconscious shadow is symbolically represented in the extensive archetypal imagery surrounding her initial observation of le beau Mézor dancing the Bamboula. The act of dancing itself is an archetypal symbol of man's attempt to connect with his "animal" nature. Dancing, known to have been included in ritualistic ceremonies as far back as the Ice Age, "was originally nothing more than a completion of the animal disguise by appropriate movements and gestures, supplementary to the initiation or other rites" (Jaffé in Jung, *Man*, 236). Chopin's description of the dance's power to mesmerize, "to hold one rooted to the ground," suggests a spiritually profound rite-induced trance-like state. Le beau Mézor's primitive dance thus represents a ritualistic symbol celebrating the emergence of Zoraïde's shadow and the integration of her instinctual nature, and perhaps also foreshadowing the eventual sacrifice and death of her psyche.

Zoraïde's impression that Mézor's bare body resembles a column of ebony, straight as a tree, similarly suggests the emergence of her unconscious. A common archetypal symbol for psychological wholeness is the circle, and the column is therefore a symbol of the path to individuation. Several Jungian interpretations of tree symbolism are applicable to Zoraïde's psychological journey as well: for Jung, trees can represent evolution, growth, or psychological maturation; emotional conflict and intervention of the unconscious; and sacrifice or death (see Jung, *Man*, 90).

The positive nature of the imagery associated with Zoraïde's strong emotional response to Mézor's dance suggests that her psychic awakening correspondingly affirms her instinctual nature and her racial heritage. The image of Mézor "as proud as a king," "like a column of ebony" that glistens like oil (Chopin 153) evokes images of royalty, such as glistening palace columns composed of rare and precious materials. More overtly, the image of Mézor looking "proud as a king" while performing a primitive dance with his half-naked black body implies that his racial heritage is indeed something of which to be proud, something worthy of a king. Likewise, the description of "the stately movements of his splendid body" (154) reinforces the imagery of nobility and pride, as does the mention of "the fierce gleam of his eye, lighted by the inspiring strains of the Bamboula" (154). The suggestion that this ethnic dance, a symbol of Mézor's racial heritage, possesses the power to inspire and sustain its dancers, aligns the Bamboula with a sacred ritual that inspires and prepares tribal warriors for battle. Thus, by witnessing Mézor's dance, Zoraïde realizes the beauty and nobility of her instinctual nature, which is also linked to her racial heritage. She therefore embraces and integrates this nature, partly by conceiving and bearing Mézor's child.

Mézor thus personifies Zoraïde's subconscious need for separation from Madame Delarivière. The Jungian scholar M.-L. von Franz argues that "often the urge toward individuation appears in a veiled form, hidden in the overwhelming passion one may feel for another person" (see Jung, *Man*, 206). The intensity of Zoraïde's love for Mézor, while no doubt based on strong physical and emotional attractions, suggests that her passion is indeed magnified by unconscious pressures to achieve psychological separation from her parent figure. Zoraïde is controlled by her passion for Mézor to such a degree that she disobeys Madame, knowing that the consequence could even be her own or Mézor's death. "Passion that goes beyond the natural measure of love ultimately aims at the mystery of becoming whole," von Franz explains, "and this is why one feels, when one has fallen passionately in love, that becoming one with the other person is the only worthwhile goal of one's life" (see Jung, *Man*, 206). Because of her drive for psychological wholeness, Zoraïde becomes, first, emotionally obsessed with Mézor and, later, psychologically obsessed with her imaginary child.

Despite Zoraïde's psychological awakening and her embrace of her instinctual nature, however, Madame Delarivière has experienced no such awakening. She lashes out at Zoraïde, articulating the "collective infection" of racism that lurks in her own shadow. First Madame Delarivière attempts to shame Zoraïde by accusing her of being "'no better than the worst'" slave. Madame Delarivière expects this accusation to humiliate Zoraïde, who has been "civilized" according to white social values and should, therefore, abhor lowly slaves. Madame Delarivière further exposes her perception that blacks are subhuman when she threatens that Zoraïde, like any other slave, deserves "'to have the lash laid'" upon her.

This threat suggests that whites have the right to treat blacks just as they treat their livestock. However, Zoraïde has already embraced her instinctual nature, and her godmother's actions, paradoxically, only strengthen Zoraïde's drive for psychological separation. Ironically, Madame Delarivière's harsh and irrational response to Zoraïde's needs contrasts with Zoraïde's sincere, nonthreatening, and rational conduct. This contrast highlights the cruelty inherent in Madame Delarivière's character, in the institution of slavery, and in the prejudice of racism. Madame's response therefore provides an opportunity for Madame Delisle and the reader to project and uncover similar negative qualities that may lurk in their own shadows.

Madame Delarivière's attempts to control Zoraïde and stunt the emergence of her ego present Zoraïde with a psychological dilemma. When the ego is confined, as in Zoraïde's situation, "its battle for deliverance" may be symbolized by a heroic effort, a sacrifice, or a death which leads to rebirth (see Henderson in Jung, *Man*, 120). All three of these archetypal actions are apparent in Zoraïde's battle for separation from Madame Delarivière. Zoraïde demonstrates heroic efforts to fight for autonomy in her pleas to her godmother to be free to marry Mézor and in her rebellious act of engaging in a relationship with Mézor. By declaring her love for Mézor, she experiences sacrifice through Mézor's subsequent banishment. Most significantly, however, Zoraïde's impregnation with Mézor's child represents a parallel psychological impregnation with "a message of deliverance and healing" (see Henderson in Jung, *Man*, 156). In addition, ultimately the pregnancy will lead to her own psychological death and rebirth.

This psychological emphasis on "deliverance and healing" is at the core of Zoraïde's battle for separation, and it is symbolized by her breast, or bosom. At the moment of her initial psychological awakening, when she falls in love with Mézor and embraces her instinctual nature, Zoraïde's "heart grew sick in her bosom with love for le beau Mézor" (Chopin 153-54). Later, after Mézor is banished, she takes "comfort and hope in the thought of her baby that she would soon be able to clasp to her breast" (155). Tragically, at the end of the story, she "clasped the rag bundle fiercely to her breast." These parallel images involving Zoraïde's breast suggest that she gradually transfers the "message of deliverance and healing" away from her passion for Mézor and, initially, onto her hope for her baby and then, finally, onto her obsession with the rag doll.

The extensive use of shadow imagery in the latter part of the story is especially interesting in its application to an archetypal interpretation of the story. Manna-Loulou notes that "with the anguish of maternity came the shadow of death," and that to the mother "the baby's flesh" was "far more precious than her own" (155). These comments reinforce the archetypal imagery of death and rebirth. Associating maternity with the shadow of death implies that through birth comes death, or perhaps its shadow in the form of a spiritless or languid life. Similarly, the assertion that the mother considers her baby's flesh to be more precious than her own suggests the possibility of maternal sacrifice. Although the symbolism is unclear, there are definite allusions to death and rebirth in these comments.

Zoraïde does not physically die during childbirth; instead she is told that her child has died. This sequence of events provides the symbolic parallel to Zoraïde's death and rebirth: the result of her child's death is that Zoraïde's conscious self dies and her psyche is reborn in the dark recesses of her unconscious, as a "shadow of reality," just as her child is reborn in the form of a doll, a "shadow of humanity." Imagery that evokes the Christian concept of spiritual rebirth also supports this archetypal interpretation.

Zoraïde's immersion into insanity represents, ironically, her attainment of a sense of "transcendence" over her psychological condition. Transcendence involves the individual's release from any confining pattern of existence. In myths, the lonely journey or pilgrimage often symbolizes liberation through transcendence. On such mythical journeys, says Henderson, "the initiate becomes acquainted with the nature of death ... not death as a last judgment or trial of strength" but as a "release, renunciation, and atonement" (see Jung, *Man*, 152). Symbols of transcendence often involve elements of nature, especially bird flight and the wilderness, as well as depictions of the individual in reflective or trance-like conditions. The image of Zoraïde sitting in the courtyard, then, provides multiple symbols of transcendence.

Zoraïde sits "upon a stone bench in the courtyard, listening to the soft splashing of the fountain, and watching the fitful shadows of the palm leaves upon the broad, white flagging" (Chopin 156). The natural imagery associated with the courtyard reinforces the archetypal concept of Zoraïde's connection with her basic, instinctive nature, thus suggesting that she has achieved transcendence (see von Franz in Jung, *Man*, 207). Zoraïde appears mesmerized by the shadows of the palm leaves, and this image connects with the previous image of her standing "rooted to the ground" while watching Mézor dance the Bamboula. In both cases the imagery suggests that Zoraïde is in a trance-like state that symbolizes transcendence. Significantly, Zoraïde watches the *shadows* of the palm leaves rather than the actual palm leaves themselves, and this focus symbolizes the shadow of reality in which her psyche now operates.

The stone bench on which Zoraïde sits may also symbolize transcendence. In medieval symbolism, a preeminent symbol of man's wholeness is the philosopher's stone (see von Franz in Jung 205-06). In fact, stones are common archetypal symbols of the psychologically whole self because they are unchanging and lasting, representing a permanent base (see von Franz in Jung, *Man*, 209-210). Stones are also lifeless matter, however. Paradoxically, these conflicting associations, inherent to the stone bench, symbolize Zoraïde's psychological condition. In her subterranean, demented world, Zoraïde has found a permanent base from which she will never depart. It is a world that, within itself, has enabled her ego to emerge and break free from its dependence on Madame Delarivière. Her condition is unchanging and lasting. However, it is also a world that reduces her to a child-like condition, in which her self is not and never can be fully integrated. Thus Zoraïde has been "reborn," but her rebirth is a dark and sterile emergence into the recesses of her unconscious.

Jungian psychology notes that the opposite extreme from individuation or psychological wholeness is complete psychological dissociation or madness (see von Franz in Jung, *Man*, 221), and this is the condition in which Zoraïde is ultimately trapped. By repressing Zoraïde's natural drive for psychological growth, Madame Delarivière has stunted the healthy emergence of her god-child's ego and has instead summoned forth the dark side of her shadow. As the Jungian scholar M.-L. von Franz notes,

> Every personification of the unconscious ... has both a light and a dark aspect. The dark side ... is the most dangerous thing of all ... (because) it can cause people to "spin" megalomaniac or other delusory fantasies that catch them up and possess them. A person in this state ... loses all touch with human reality. (see Jung, *Man*, 216)

This is the tragedy of Zoraïde, the result of the collision between her own shadow and the "collective infection" of racism and control that is buried in Madame Delarivière's shadow. By exposing both the positive and negative qualities of the shadow archetype in

"La Belle Zoraïde," Manna-Loulou and Kate Chopin provide a medium for Madame Delisle and the reader to become aware of the dangers of such collective infections and also of universally shared psychological responses of the individual. The archetypal manifestations of these shared psychological responses (about which Chopin's story is especially illuminating) include the realization of the shadow, the integration of the instinctual nature, and the drive for individuation. By exploring these widely shared archetypal impulses, Chopin has created a story of universal relevance and deep psychological impact.